The Law and Regulation of Solicitors

Serious Breaches and Practising Certificate Conditions

The Law and Regulation of Solicitors

Serious Breaches and Practising Certificate Conditions

Katie Jackson
LLB, MSc

Bloomsbury Professional

LONDON • DUBLIN • EDINBURGH • NEW YORK • NEW DELHI • SYDNEY

BLOOMSBURY PROFESSIONAL
Bloomsbury Publishing Plc
50 Bedford Square, London, WC1B 3DP, UK
1385 Broadway, New York, NY 10018, USA
29 Earlsfort Terrace, Dublin 2, Ireland

British Library Cataloguing-in-Publication Data

A catalogue record for this book is available from the British Library.

ISBN: PB 978 1 52652 068 5
Epdf 978 1 52652 070 8
Epub 978 1 52652 069 2

Typeset by Evolution Design and Digital (Kent)

Acknowledgements

Thank you to all the following who have helped with this book in some way:

Darren, who has been supportive while I wrote it.

Bloomsbury Professional, the publishers and in particular Andy Hill, Jane Bradford, Jenny Lank and Peter Warren, who I am absolutely delighted to work with.

All the staff at MBL Seminars, and the staff at the venues; with particular thanks to Angela, Alison, Catherine, Claire, and Carole.

All the staff at Datalaw; with particular thanks to Charles, Sean, Abi, Tom, and before she moved to MBL, Catherine.

The delegates on all of my courses, who participate, or consider the position quietly, thank you.

The Law Society, the Solicitors Regulation Authority, and the Council for Licensed Conveyancers, who have given me such a firm grounding in professional conduct and regulatory discipline.

The Legal Services Commission, who back in 2004, taught me about legal aid solicitor accounts, how to investigate them and how to conduct a reconciliation.

My company, Honne Limited.

Legal Eye and The Cashroom; Paul Saunders and Alex Holt, particularly, who helped me continue during a difficult time.

Pete Bott, who advised me on this book.

All my colleagues and clients, who have been anonymised here to protect their contractual confidentiality, but who know who they are, thank you.

For Finley
and for my family

Preface

This book has been developed from a course I delivered through MBL Seminars originally entitled 'SRA Renewal: Material Breaches and Practising Certificate Conditions'. The course has evolved over time, most notably with the SRA's move to serious breach and even expanded to include accountant and COFA views, in a version of the course called 'Qualified Reports and Material Breach'. However, it has remained the same in one important aspect; we debate, analyse and discuss whether solicitor breaches of their code of conduct or handbooks in force are 'material' or 'serious', what to do next, and consider viewpoints from all angles.

The course has run for eight years; always in person (except during the Covid-19 pandemic), in conference venues across the country. The debates involve solicitors, COLPs, COFAs, and their staff, and in the 'Qualified reports' version, Reporting Accountants. The course has been very successful, and I have run mini versions with Datalaw. However, I am in the position now where there is so much to say; there have been so many debates, that I have written this book to accompany the course and capture the detail and debates we don't always have time to cover.

As you will see as you read the book, we cover a great deal more than just these subjects from the last ten years. I have included material from many more of my other courses delivered through a variety of different organisations; excerpts from my own research and publications; and presentations I have delivered across the country to solicitors, their staff, and associated businesses.

The book is set out in Parts. Each Part covers first the relevant legislation, for example underpinning practising certificates and relationship to the roll, the renewal, reporting breaches, and the relevant regulatory obligations. The second part of each chapter covers the debates we have on the course; from management debates to reoccurring themes.

This second part is also designed to provide ideas for debate within your own firm, highlight common regulatory issues, and provide practical ideas of how to reflect your management style within compliance. As part of this, I include exercises, scenarios, and team talk ideas for you to bring the material to life and use as CPD. These are hopefully of use for solicitors and accountants working with law firms at all stages of their careers, and are intended as CPD. Other legal professionals may also find them helpful.

Do take care with the use of these group exercises; professional ethics is a complex and personal subject. As I explain during the book, I undertook this work for many years, I am trained in facilitation, and have more generally been trained by psychologists. I run my training courses as safe sessions, and my design and delivery is copyrighted. You may want to give your staff quiet time for reflection if they wish.

When we discuss serious breach, it is a debate and discussion about professionalism, and the constitutional role of solicitors. The course came from my many years of employment at the Legal Services Commission, and Solicitors Regulation Authority (and latterly, the Council for Licensed Conveyancers), and the experience of handling decisions on behalf of the regulators, but also in spending many hours with and on the telephone to, solicitors and their representatives in these situations.

I also have something of a background in education and 2013 I was working as a Consultant for Ofqual. I had finished working for the Solicitors Regulation Authority some months before. I had completed my master's, and I was keen to return to the law in some way. I had the idea of delivering compliance as management consultancy for law firms following my master's degree, and also delivering some training as well.

First in writing, and then over the telephone in 2013, I pitched the idea of a course on the new SRA Handbook 2011 and approach under Outcomes Focused Regulation to Angela Watson at MBL Seminars. She asked about Anti Money Laundering: 'always popular, always needed', she said. I said we could do something about 'material breach', the new requirement for self-reporting. I was also keen on practising certificates and renewal as there was no course out there, but it was an annual requirement. She agreed, saying: 'we'll see how you get on' and the course was born. Six months later, Catherine Jordan asked me to do a version for Datalaw, and thus began a commitment to CPD and a discursive approach which has not changed.

My seven years at the SRA were marked by a continuous ethical debate and discussion of issues for regulatory reporting and decision making. Setting boundaries and developing and applying regulation is a complex task; not solely for the regulator, but for the regulated community as well. I have spoken to people distraught by having to make decisions to report, even in cases where solicitors have committed very serious criminal offences. Their perspective is one I can well understand. Any form of reporting can be very upsetting.

Importantly, I have also often and regularly been in the position where regulatory action or intervention is the right action for the wider interests of consumers; for the solicitors and their families; their staff; and their clients. Sometimes solicitors have been incapacitated, or are seriously unwell, and the business cannot continue. For them, the support of the regulator in closure was essential. Those experiences and decisions will stay with me for life.

Self-reporting is controversial, as is expecting higher standards from solicitors when other members of society are not in the same position. I wanted to make the course a safe space for discussion and debate, an opportunity for delegates from the regulated community to voice their opinion, or to attempt to argue a different viewpoint to see where it takes us. When we started the position was far from clear. In a sense I am asking: *Can we clarify the rules for self-reporting?* The provision of clear, neutral, and accessible regulatory information is important for all of us, and also goes to the heart of procedural fairness. On the course I signpost people to sources of assistance, both pastoral and legal, and my very sincere thanks goes to those who provide their time and support to those organisations.

I am often reminded on the courses that assessment can take many forms; we do not necessarily need an exam to tell us we are competent. We take for granted that COLPs and COFAs are competent to make very complex ethical decisions, and put together processes of what to do next in difficult situations; at the risk of prosecution if they are incorrect. Recognising the complexity of regulatory debate and getting involved in our own way is what I aim for the delegates to achieve, hopefully also aiming for more confident regulatory interaction. This means an understanding of regulatory expectation, practice at making decisions and planning with the management team, and the ability to make representations to the regulator. I hope during the years the course has run, we have developed ideas, clarified expectations, and provided practical examples of what staff can do within firms to address regulatory requirements.

The scenarios within the book are all anonymised and are all fictional; any resemblance to real life situations is coincidental. In some cases original fictional scenarios have had additional fictional elements added to them (making them doubly fictional). It is important to remember I have seen and dealt with a vast number of cases, and all matters are 'within my experience', being of the type of report the regulator would receive or investigate.

The book is aimed at solicitors, their staff, and management within law firms. Part 6 of the book is also aimed at Reporting Accountants, but they may find all of it helpful. However, anyone in the legal or associated legal sector may also find much of use: for example, you might be managing a solicitor in one of the new unregulated businesses. Any legal business, or individual who needs a good understanding of the ethical and management requirements of current legal sector reporting, and would also like to complete CPD or some additional learning, is very welcome. I sincerely hope it is useful.

Katie Jackson
December 2021

Contents

Preface	*vii*
Table of Cases	*xiii*
Table of Statutes	*xv*
Table of Statutory Instruments	*xvii*
Table of SRA Rules and Regulations	*xix*
Introduction	*xxi*
Part 1 Professional practice	**1**
Section 1: Technical content	1
Section 2: Discursive content	26
Part 2 Practising arrangements	**59**
Section 1: Technical content	60
Section 2: Discursive content	89
Part 3 Practising Certificate Conditions	**123**
Section 1: Technical content	124
Section 2: Discursive content	154
Part 4 Firm Conditions	**179**
Section 1: Technical content	179
Section 2: Discursive content	187
Part 5 Serious Breach	**225**
Section 1: Technical content	226
Section 2: Discursive content	259
Part 6 Reporting Requirements for Accountants	**289**
Section 1: Technical content	290
Section 2: Discursive content	312
Part 7 Conclusions and Future Developments	**345**
Part 8 Previous Problems	**379**
Appendix Bibliography and References	427
Index	*441*

Table of Cases

[All references are to page numbers.]

B

Bawa-Garba v General Medical Council [2018] EWCA Civ 1879, [2019] 1 WLR 1929, [2019] 1 All ER 500, [2018] 8 WLUK 117, [2018] Med LR 561, (2018) 163 BMLR 43 50
Beckwith v Solicitors Regulation Authority [2020] EWHC 3231 (Admin), [2020] 11 WLUK 421, [2021] IRLR 119 .... 28, 247

D

De Vita, Platt & Scott, Solicitors Disciplinary Tribunal, 20 February 2017 . 279
Dreamvar (UK) Ltd v Mishcon De Reya (a firm) [2016] EWHC 3316 (Ch), [2016] 12 WLUK 523 280

H

Harcus Sinclair LLP v Your Lawyers Ltd [2021] UKSC 32, [2021] 3 WLR 598, [2021] 7 WLUK 387, [2021] PNLR 26 185

M

Morgenbesser v Consiglio dell'Ordine degli Avvocati di Genova (Case C-313/01) [2003] ECR I-13467, [2003] 11 WLUK 316, [2004] 1 CMLR 24 47

R

R v Ghosh [1982] QB 1053, [1982] 3 WLR 110, [1982] 2 All ER 689, [1982] 4 WLUK 44, (1982) 75 Cr App R 154, [1982] Crim LR 608 263
Razeen, Re a Solicitor No 15 of 2008 [2008] EWCA Civ 1220 .... 132, 138, 154, 155

S

Solicitors Regulation Authority v Malins [2018] EWCA Civ 366, [2018] 1 WLR 3969, [2018] 3 WLUK 141, [2018] PNLR 22 263

T

Twinsectra Ltd v Yardley [2002] UKHL 12, [2002] 2 AC 164, [2002] 2 WLR 802, [2002] 2 All ER 377, [2002] 3 WLUK 573, [2002] PNLR 30 .... 262, 280

W

Wingate v Solicitors Regulation Authority [2018] EWCA Civ 366, [2018] 1 WLR 3969, [2018] 3 WLUK 141, [2018] PNLR 22 263

Table of Statutes

[*All references are to page numbers.*]

Administration of Justice Act 1985 .... 4, 5, 60, 61, 183
Pt I (ss 1–10A) 21
s 9 .... 21, 130, 132, 181, 183
(2F)–(2I) 182
(2I) 130
16 154
Sch 2 .... 21, 22
Bribery Act 2010 .... 122, 211
Companies Act 2006 313
Courts and Legal Services Act 1990 .... 4, 5, 22, 30, 60, 61, 70
s 66 21
Pt IV (ss 85–98) 21
s 89 77
Sch 8 154
14 .... 21, 22
Deregulation Act 2015 346
Employment Rights Act 1996 278
s 43 277
Enterprise and Regulatory Reform Act 2013 .... 277, 278
Equality Act 2010 392
European Communities Withdrawal Act 2018 77
Financial Services and Markets Act 2000
Pt XX (ss 325–333) 85
Insolvency Act 1986
s 283 142
Internal Markets Act 2021 97
Legal Services Act 2007 .... 2, 4, 5, 12, 13, 15, 20, 24, 25, 41, 60, 61, 62, 63, 65, 69, 75, 76, 78, 82, 84, 95, 105, 107, 120, 126, 127, 128, 129, 130, 154, 155, 183, 186, 208, 209, 210, 211, 212, 213, 215, 223, 231, 253, 254, 257, 282, 292, 305, 362–364, 366
Pt 1 (s 1) 64
s 1 .... 13, 23
Legal Services Act 2007 – *contd*
Pt 2 (ss 2–11) 11, 213
s 12 .... 6, 9, 64, 85, 122
18 .... 181, 182
Pt 4 (ss 27–70) 213
Pt 5 (ss 71–111) 21, 82
s 72 182
85 .... 182, 186
91 .... 29, 231, 232
92 .... 29, 231, 232, 312
ss 105–107 364
Pt 6 (ss 112–161) 12, 213
s 157(5)(c) 13
Sch 4 21
5 21
13 187
Pt 5 (paras 41–51) 187
Sch 14 22
Proceeds of Crime Act 2002 .... 38, 83, 242, 300, 301, 382
Pt 7 (ss 327–340) 291
s 333 291
Public Interest Disclosure Act 1998 278
s 1 277
Solicitors Act 1974 .... 4, 5, 23, 60, 61, 67, 70, 75, 121, 126, 127, 128, 183, 187, 254, 257, 301
Pt I (ss 1–30) 21
s 9 76
10 .... 128, 130, 132, 144, 145
12 .... 126, 127, 128, 130, 135, 143, 144, 145, 154, 169
13A 128, 144
13B 250
15 .... 137, 250
28 .... 6, 24, 128
Pt II (ss 31–55) 21
s 34 .... 290, 295, 300
43 .... 41, 83, 99, 195, 232, 249, 267–268
44B 257
Sch 1 .... 21, 250

Table of Statutes

Table of Statutory Instruments

[*All references are to page numbers.*]

European Communities (Lawyer's Practice) Regulations 2000, SI 2000/1119 .... 22, 61, 69, 70
reg 17 76
19 7
General Data Protection Regulation 2016 (EU 2016/679) 55
Money Laundering, Terrorist Financing and Transfer of Funds (Information on the Payer) Regulations 2017, SI 2017/692 .... 37, 83, 102, 143, 313, 423

Table of Solicitors Regulation Authority Rules and Regulations

[*All references are to page numbers.*]

Handbook 1999 86
Handbook 2007 .... 87, 388
Handbook 2011 .... 88, 126, 127, 136, 144, 152, 182, 183, 232, 238, 292, 346, 381, 383
  Accounts Rules 2011 .... 279, 290, 292–296, 299, 300, 302, 305, 307, 309, 334, 337
  Authorisation Rules 2011 ... 185, 295, 296, 298, 300
    r 7 182
      8.5 .... 233, 245
      8.7(a) 233, 245
      8 guidance note (xi) 233, 245
      9 182
  Practising Regulations 2011 ... 126
    reg 3 .... 129, 135–137, 144, 145, 148, 151, 152, 169, 182, 308, 396
      3.1 143
      7 .... 132, 182
Standards and Regulations 2019 .... 6, 15, 24–26, 65, 69, 86–89, 104, 112–121, 126, 127, 146,151, 152, 182, 186, 188, 231, 232, 233, 238, 246, 247, 251, 300, 302, 305, 309, 332, 333, 346, 360, 362, 364
  Accounts Rules 2019 ..... 86, 88, 290, 292–294, 299, 300, 302, 303, 309–312, 331–334, 360
  Authorisation of Firms Rules 2019 .... 182, 185, 295

Standards and Regulations 2019 – *contd*
  Authorisation of Firms Rules 2019 – *contd*
    r 3 .... 182, 183
      3.1 144
      3.2 144
      11 77
  Authorisation of Individuals Regulations 2019 ...... 6, 183, 246
    reg 7 .... 77, 129, 132, 144, 182
    reg 7.1 144
        (b) 144
      7.2 144
      7.3 .... 129, 130, 144
      8 77
      8.4 78
        (b) 77
      10 122
      10.2 .... 63, 69, 100, 121
        (b) 122
  Code of Conduct for Firms 2019 .... 240, 247, 262, 263, 310
    Pt 3 (paras 3.1–3.12) 230
    Pt 9 (paras 9.1–9.2) 231
  Code of Conduct for Individuals (Solicitors, RELs and RFLs) 2019 ..... 240, 247, 262, 263
    paras 1.2, 1.4 262
    Pt 2 (paras 2.1–2.7) 262
    Pt 5 (paras 5.1–5.3) 263
    Pt 7 (paras 7.1–7.12) 230
  Regulatory and Disciplinary Procedure Rules 2019
    r 3.1(e) 144
  Transparency Rules 2019 322

Introduction

This book concerns the operation of two key components of the solicitor regulatory system as it stands; the requirement to report to the regulator, and the use of restrictions on practice (conditions) to manage any perceived or actual problems posed by the individual or practice. The book considers these two regulatory forces in the context of solicitor professionalism, the atmosphere of change in legal services, and the various modes of practice as a solicitor.

The writer's experience at the SRA, and since, has shaped this book. Firstly, the requirement for solicitors to report drives many of the credible and prosecutable concerns to the regulator. The SRA receive thousands of reports of misconduct every year from a wide variety of different sources, including consumers, third parties, and individuals on the other side of cases. Although we see some of those matters prosecuted before the Solicitors Disciplinary Tribunal, many do not reach this stage. The reports made by other solicitors, self-reports, law firm reports, and accountant reports are often have the clearest understanding of the rules and operation of professional conduct, and are often the matters which are pursued. The reports they make allow the regulator to act in the public interest, to uphold solicitor practice in the interests of justice, and to protect consumers from unscrupulous individuals or dangerous situations. They also in some cases allow the regulator to support the regulated community by taking action when a solicitor is unable to continue.

However, solicitor self-reporting causes a problem; we require solicitors to report themselves in situations where they could lose their careers or financial stability. We require 'higher standards' from a group of professionals who are only human beings and can be subject to the same pressures as any other group.

The regulator has at its disposal a wide range of investigatory capabilities and regulatory tools or sanctions (including prosecution before the Solicitors Disciplinary Tribunal) for those who have broken the rules, and who have or may have put consumers, clients, and others at unacceptable risk, or in positions of loss. Solicitors are prosecuted for a wide range of different reasons, including inappropriate use of client monies; involvement in scams and frauds; and using their position to take unfair advantage. The regulatory rules are set up to counteract this, including rules relating to consumer and client information, complaints, and use of client monies. Compliance with these rules is a complex political issue in the sector, but it is fair to say that the vast majority of solicitors agree with most of the requirements, and many work very hard at compliance and delivering an excellent service for their clients.

Concerns about a solicitor or practice are sometimes apparent at an early stage and could develop into a real problem. Or in other cases, a problem has occurred and a prosecution has taken place, but the solicitor requires additional support to manage their practice. In these situations, a practising certificate condition, restricting practice or otherwise placing conditions on it, can prevent harm to those around the individual solicitor.

A condition, and the ability to impose them, is a regulatory decision rather than a prosecution decision, it is in a way, a practice management decision on the part of the regulator. It is a means to manage a situation to ensure it does not develop in a particular direction, or alternatively, to set the course in a way the regulator would be happy with. Of course, individual professionals are free to run their own businesses in ways which suit them, but there are lines beyond which the regulator would take prosecution or intervention action. The imposition of the condition allows the regulator to protect the resources dedicated to those serious matters and that later prosecution step, at an earlier stage, as well as acting in the broader public interest, by attempting to resolve the matter through conditions.

Solicitors reading this book will realise that much of the press reporting around solicitor conduct concerns the operation of the Solicitors Disciplinary Tribunal and their prosecution decisions. It is perhaps because of the existence of the specialist Tribunal that so much of the work of the SRA concerns breaches and their prosecution. We see comparatively little in comparison in respect of imposition of conditions or the management decisions taken by the regulator. This is quite different in comparison to some regulatory bodies where there is not a specialist Tribunal; where restrictions on the business or proactive management of an individual situation is their main power or operational tool.

Conditions and the more extensive use of them, could provide a useful tool in the management of many of the situations which are reported to the regulator; cutting off the prosecution decision and protecting the public at an earlier stage. As we see during the book, the system of conditions currently focuses on the individual and that may also assist the management of employees working in unregulated practices or freelance solicitors as well.

If we envisage a situation where solicitors are more extensively managed by conditions, along with a list of reportable situations; perhaps with specified outcomes, we might see the re-imagining of the professional regulator towards a more proactive, interventionist body. Regulatory rules can of course accompany this outcome, but the use, operation, and decision making that surrounds them takes a different form or slant away from prosecution and towards proactive management. This means earlier intervention into problems by using a wider range of regulatory powers, including conditions on both firm and individuals.

This book covers the current situation of serious breach (and its predecessor, material breach), practising certificate and firm conditions, in the context of legal services regulation and solicitor professionalism. When discussing serious breach, we also discuss the position for obtaining an accountants' report, for Reporting Accountants, and for sending the report to the regulator, as a form of serious breach or self-reporting. The book, although the writer's view, is a reference work, but also provides many opportunities for continuous professional development and learning throughout.

If we can discuss the regulatory tools in operation around us, and learn from them, we can design a system of reporting, management, and professionalism that reflects modern solicitor practice and the ways in which solicitors would like to work. The writer would like the work to design this system to be solidly grounded within the regulated community so it reflects their voice, engages them, and happens in a way which is not imposed upon the regulated community, but comes from them too.

We have to remember that this book is written at a time of intended change for solicitors, and now is the time to try to influence and shape that change. The legal system as it stands in England and Wales has been the same for many generations and solicitor practices have operated in the same ways for hundreds of years. We are in the position where solicitors are being given the option of change, with new ways of working, including in unregulated businesses. The aim is to reduce prices for consumers and make legal services more accessible. These intended changes come alongside Brexit, and a need to boost the economy, and make our goods and services even better.

The changes have been in intended operation since 2007, and even before, with the introduction of the Legal Services Act, which brought in Alternative Business Structures. There was not the 'big bang' many were anticipating, and law firms have been left asking whether or not there will be much change to the way solicitors operate. Less than ten years after implementation of that Act, and in the most recent twist, we have seen the introduction of freelance solicitors, and the ability for solicitors to work in unregulated practices, providing external advice to members of the public. This will be an attractive option for some solicitors and the combination of all of these new options is likely to result in some change, particularly as the country recovers following the coronavirus pandemic.

We will then need a regulatory response to this change, and the details and focus of the requirements in this book could provide that option.

In Parts One and Two, we introduce the background to the later concepts. We look at technical requirements of practice that underlie some of the main ideas and themes of the book, to ensure the reader has a broader backdrop of the different forms of practice and constancy of change or attempted change in the sector.

Part One covers the idea of the solicitor as a professional and the development of solicitor practices; this is with particular reference to the annual Practising Certificate and the rules of professional conduct.

In Part Two, we consider the current regulatory situation, looking at the approved regulators and their operation, alongside the current practising arrangements available to solicitors. This part covers the different types of practice solicitors can run, and how they are distinguished from each other.

In Part Three, we cover Practising Certificate conditions, and the various requirements for imposing those conditions. We look at common conditions, and how the regulations for imposing conditions have developed over many years.

In Part Four, we cover firm conditions, and the requirements for imposing conditions on regulated entities. We look at the reasons why this is so rare, and discuss options for the future. This section also covers some material on law firm management, alternative business structures, and change in the sector.

In Part Five, we consider serious breach, and the requirement to self-report. This section primarily focuses on the requirement to make a self-report to the regulator. The section also looks at the consequences of reporting, regulatory investigations and conducting your own investigation.

In Part Six, we cover the position of the accountants' report as a form of self-reporting to the regulator, and the various different iterations of the accountants' report and guidance in recent times.

In each Part we cover the current position related to the regulatory rules, and any applicable changes in recent times, allowing the reader to keep up to date with the latest regulatory positions. In particular, we reflect the changes brought in by the Standards and Regulations 2019, and their consultations. The writer worked alongside the SRA during 2017 during the consultations for the Standards and Regulations and is confident about the approach outlined in this book. Some of the writer's material from that time is also included and readers will also appreciate that the writer worked on some aspects of policy related to the earlier Handbooks as well.

Part Seven of the book contains the conclusions from the content of the book, and also a look at possible future regulatory developments.

Part Eight is the final part of the book and is a learning and development section of the book. In this section we cover many of the exercises and discussion points the writer has posed over the years as part of her work on the Serious/Material Breach courses. The section also includes wider compliance problems drawn from the writer's other CPD courses that have been in use since 2012, including some accounts and reconciliation problems to solve, and exercises from the optional elements of the Practice Skills Course for solicitors taught by the writer. Readers can use these exercises to help them understand their own ethical perspective, develop their contingency planning, and gain a broader insight into reportable types of matters. The scenarios cover issues which are relevant for COLPs, COFAs, and Reporting Accountants. However anyone working in a solicitors' firm, or with a Reporting Accountant, can find the scenarios helpful and useful.

Throughout the book there are also suggestions for activities for you and your team to complete either personally or individually. The book is intended to be used for personal reflection as well, and there is no obligation to use it with your team if you don't want to. Our own ethical perspective and the development of the same can be very personal and you may not want to share it.

At the moment, we use a system of CPD which allows the individual solicitor and their staff member to sign off their own learning and development through a system of self-reflection, supported by the firm. If you are using the exercises and materials for CPD (which they are designed to be used for), then do make sure you reflect on your learning as you go along and keep a record of your activity in your learning and development plan. Of course, even reading the book counts as CPD! There is a reflective exercise in Part 7 to help you reflect on your learning from the book, overall.

You might ask whether you can use this book if you are a licensed conveyancer or other legal professional. The writer often produces material for both solicitors and licensed conveyancers. The book is aimed at solicitors and those associated with solicitor practices, however, many licensed conveyancers and other types of lawyer also work in solicitor practices and find it helpful to understand a solicitor perspective, and there are comparative sections specifically referring the Council for Licensed Conveyancers, who have some similar regulatory requirements (as do other legal regulators). Licensed conveyancers and other lawyers may find parts of Part One and Part Two helpful for the discussion of the current system of regulation, types of practice, and future analysis of trends in the market. Licensed conveyancers may also find the learning and development exercises in each section helpful. There are several different ways to apply the ethical scenarios at the end of the book, including to licensed conveyancer or other lawyer practices. No sets of rules are specifically mentioned, in relation to any of the CPD scenarios, so they can be applied to many different types of legal and even accountancy practice.

At this point it should also be mentioned that COLPs and COFAs are referenced extensively within the book; readers can take this to also mean HOLPs and HOFAs in most cases. Also, Part 6, which refers to Reporting Accountants can also be used by COFAs, COLPs, any accounts staff, or any accountant that may be assisting a law firm.

Regardless of how you decide to use this book, do consider when reading, the types of regulatory tools available to your regulator, and how they are being used. *Could we get by with just serious breach and practising certificate conditions?*

Part 1

Professional practice

Contents

Section 1: Technical content
- Historical development of professional practice for solicitors
- The annual practising year and the embodiment of professionalism in a Practising Certificate
- Introduction to Legal Services Regulation
- The impact of the regulator
- Historical development of regulation
- Entry and exit: the professional hurdle
- Current regulatory position
  - Intervention
  - Regulatory objectives
  - SRA Standards and Regulations

Section 2: Discursive content
- Individual expression and professionalism as a form of practice
- Ethics and reporting
- Complaint handling, customer service, and reporting
- The reasonable man in regulation
- Governance and decision making
- Freelance solicitors and unregulated practices
- Checks and balances in legal regulation
- Solicitor Continuous Professional Development (CPD)
- Comparative standards of regulation and professional practice:
  - qualification and CPD
  - Regulation by Code
- Comparative professional practice: management consultants
- The human touch

Section 1: Technical content

This book is about solicitors, their forms of practice, and the regulatory requirements placed upon them. In the context of that discussion we are also covering the legal services market, and intended changes to the ways in which solicitors practise; moving from solicitor led high street firms into either larger unregulated structures or working more fluidly in different contractual spheres.

We can see that historically solicitors have worked in high street practices, based around centres of population, and individuals or families have turned to them in times when access to justice or even access to other state functions has been required. The world has changed around solicitors over the last 70 years, and we now see very large organisations operate in society; multinational organisations who require access to state functions and to justice in the same ways individuals would. Delivering services is much more difficult now – the expectations of consumers and businesses alike have changed – and it is difficult for a profession built around historical structures to move with those changes.

In this first part of the book, we cover the professional status of solicitors and how they are regulated as a background and basis for discussion of some of the ethical issues we discuss later in the book. All of the issues we cover are set against a backdrop of change. Professional structures that have developed to provide security for solicitors over many decades are changing, and we have to ask whether the ethics of society are also changing, or just their expectations.

In all cases, we are dealing with matters related to England and Wales, unless otherwise specified. This includes references to the law, professional practice, legal professionals, and legal regulation.

Professional practice encompasses:

- the entry to a profession, usually by meeting educational or attainment standards;
- the acceptance by the group and individual of the profession and its common standards; and
- for the individual, abiding by the standards of behaviour expected.

Those standards of behaviour can set a higher standard than might be expected by other businesses or tradespeople. There may also be a route of recourse for those who have a complaint, or a professional body who can consider concerns that conduct does not meet the standard required.

The legal services regulators in England and Wales regulate distinct professions practising law and providing rules and regulations of professional conduct. They set educational requirements for entry into the professions and develop bodies of work, encompassing their rules, regulations, guidance, and policy making that cover the standards expected. They also, along with the Legal Ombudsman, and other schemes, provide different forms of 'recourse' if the client or a third party has a concern; with the Legal Ombudsman looking at client service complaints, and the legal regulators considering issues of misconduct from any source.

The Solicitors Regulation Authority (SRA) is the current regulator for solicitors operating in England and Wales, and is an arm of The Law Society. The Law Society is referred to within the legislation as the regulator, but the Legal Services Act 2007 separated the previously combined representative and regulatory functions of The Law Society into separate organisations. At this point, the SRA was created and took over the regulatory powers and operations of The Law Society. The SRA now operates as an independent organisation, although it remains part of The Law Society Group.

There are other types of lawyer, for example barristers, licensed conveyancers, notaries, and costs lawyers, and their regulatory bodies can seem quite similar to the SRA; often there are similar requirements and standards. More information about legal regulation is provided in later in this Part of the book, including a discussion of the different regulators and the shape of regulation in the sector.

The solicitor qualification is broad compared to that of a barrister, for example, with high street solicitors expected to have a wide-ranging understanding of general legal practice related to the application of law to the general public. The intention being that solicitors are the first port of call for legal advice for members of public and small businesses. Of course, solicitors also work in a variety of other settings including in government and in the city. Although there are other legal professionals, solicitors are the largest group and arguably the most well-known.

For solicitors, there are a significant number of regulations and professionally-expected behaviours in relation to dealing with members of the general public, including in client care, client information, complaints, pricing information and acting for both sides.

If they do not meet the standards expected, or there is a serious breach of the rules of professional conduct, solicitors can be prosecuted by the regulator. Where very large fines or serious sanctions will be imposed, cases may be prosecuted before the Solicitors Disciplinary Tribunal, a specialist Tribunal. In very serious cases, these sanctions can be removal from the profession via striking off or suspension from practice.

The constitutional role of the solicitor, as part of the checks and balances within the separation of the powers, mean the solicitor plays an important part in:

1 interpreting and upholding the rule of law;

2 the operation of the court and the administration of justice; and

3. the defence of individual human rights

The representative and regulatory bodies within law, including those of solicitors, also provide an important collective voice in challenging the legislative and executive branches of the state, beyond their voice within the administration of justice. More than that however, the regulators uphold the constitutional position of the solicitor, and society's confidence in the judicial system, through their own rules of professional conduct, associated guidance, and disciplinary system.

Historical development of professional practice for solicitors

There is a whole body of work comprising the rules of solicitor conduct. With rules of professional conduct in various forms, stretching back for generations, the rules demonstrate society's changing expectations of solicitors, expectations of their behaviour, and how they are expected to uphold their constitutional role. We can also see evidence of learning through history; how in performing their role solicitors and others in the legal profession have written a set of rules which are workable and provide the expected outcomes. These rules and associated guidance go beyond guiding professionalism; they reflect solicitor practice at that point in history and offer a sociological insight into the operation of the rule of law within communities across the country. The traditions of private practice in high street communities are communicated so clearly in some of the guidance, the reader can imagine themselves there.

In modern day formats there have been ten editions of the Code of Conduct (previously called the Guide to the Professional Conduct of Solicitors), with, in some editions, extensive comment on the position of the solicitor, their practice, and how to behave in certain situations. Common regulations for solicitors include prevention of conflicts of interest; restrictions on running outside businesses; and until the Legal Services Act 2007, a prohibition on non-solicitors owning solicitor businesses.

If we cast our eyes much further back to the 1800s, the Attorneys and Solicitors Bill, debated in 1843, gives us indications of the training requirements, or preferred training arrangements in place at the time, including an emphasis on time spent in academic study and in what we would now call work-based learning. There are also examples of prohibited conduct, such as practice whilst in prison! This prohibition also made it into the Solicitors Act 1974.

By the time of the Second World War, we can see in a proposed Solicitors Bill that the annual accounts inspection was put forward for the first time, along with regulations for holding monies in client account, as a result of frauds by solicitors. We also see, in 1939, The Law Society requesting the power to impose conditions on Practising Certificates.

Moving forward again to the debates in respect of the Solicitors Act 1974, a number of issues are raised which reveal society's attitudes at the time to solicitors and their moral standing. It was said they expected The Law Society to consider whether a person was a fit and proper person to become a solicitor, but not consider all aspects of their private lives; for example affairs, some drugs, and political views might all have been acceptable, and a person might be able to carry on as a solicitor.

Following entry to the European Union (EU), a new form of lawyer was allowed to practise in England and Wales. Registered European Lawyers (RELs) are lawyers from within the European Union who practise under their home title in England and Wales, under rights derived from the EU. They are however, also registered with the SRA, as well as being registered under their home title. The REL status is disappearing as a result of Brexit.

We also have Registered Foreign Lawyers (RFLs). These are lawyers who come from other countries, are registered under their home title, and with a regulator here in England and Wales, but they are not from within the EU. In the case of both RELs and RFLs, and certainly in the case of RELs, the default legal regulator is and has been the SRA.

As a result of the EU treaties, Registered European Lawyers have practised in England and Wales with the same rights as solicitors for some time. Registered Foreign Lawyers have fewer rights than solicitors and RELs, and brief discussion of a discussion of regulatory powers and references to relevant legislation is provided later in this part, and also in Part 2 of the book.

The statutory basis for much of SRA powers is set out in the Solicitors Act 1974 and the Legal Services Act 2007. The Acts reference The Law Society, but in recent years and as a result of the Legal Services Act 2007, the power has been devolved to the SRA. Further powers are derived from the Courts and Legal Services Act 1990, and the Administration of Justice Act 1985. The other approved legal regulators have the Legal Services Act 2007 as a basis. Broadly speaking, the Council for Licensed

Conveyancers, Master of the Faculties (regulator for notaries), and Bar Standards Board also have some overlap into these four Acts.

The reason for four Acts (as opposed to one) is the variety of circumstances and situations in which the SRA can regulate solicitors' or lawyers' practices and individual solicitors or lawyers. Each of the Acts contains (broadly speaking) the same or similar powers, but they each apply to different sets of eligible persons (including companies). The Solicitors Act 1974 covers traditional solicitor practices and individual solicitor practising arrangements. Next in chronological order, the Administration of Justice Act 1985, provides powers to the SRA to deal with corporate structures. The Courts and Legal Services Act 1990 provides powers in respect of RFLs, and the Legal Services Act 2007 provides powers in respect of Alternative Business Structures. Each of the Acts also has, or did have at the time of implementation, additional impacts on the legal services markets, and on the regulator. For example, the CLC (which introduced competition into conveyancing) derives much of their powers from the Administration of Justice Act 1985, and the Legal Services Act 2007 made changes to the structure of The Law Society, as explained earlier.

Previous Solicitors Acts before 1974 provided The Law Society with the ability to issue Practising Certificates, set rules, and discipline solicitors. The current Acts provide some specific powers, and also give the SRA the right to develop its own set of rules and regulations, which form the Codes of Conduct and associated rules. Some of these associated rules can be quite important, for example the Solicitors Accounts Rules, which control the holding of client monies.

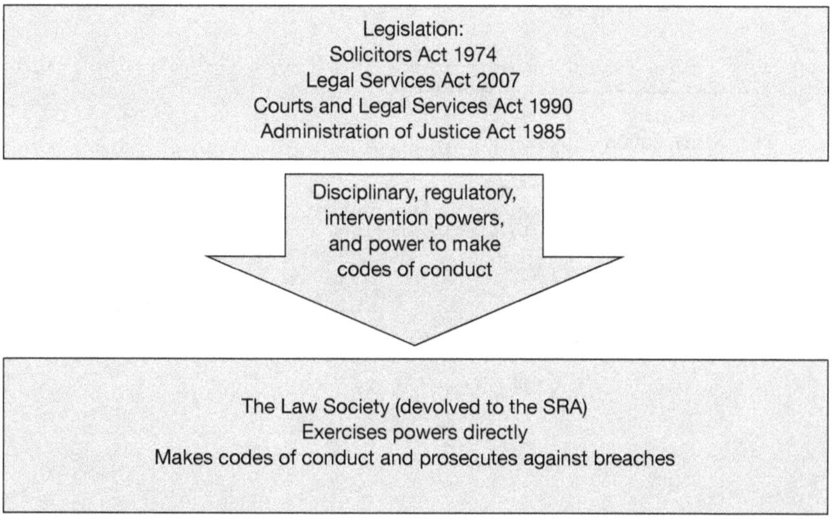

We can see the legislative development and intention towards creating a legal regulator with a broad basis to regulate different types of solicitor practice structure, with specific disciplinary and regulatory powers, but who has a focus on setting and maintaining standards. The SRA has teeth; with rebukes, fines, and powers to close a practice all at its disposal, and access to a specialist Tribunal for prosecutions or powers it does not have itself. This book provides a particular focus on Practising Certificate conditions; another power derived from statute.

There are further provisions within both Acts which comprise the full breadth of the powers of The Law Society, including disciplinary powers. Some of these feature in later chapters of this book particularly discussions of the requirements for Practising Certificate and firm conditions. We also have some comparisons with other approved regulators, such as the Council for Licensed Conveyancers.

The annual practising year and the embodiment of professionalism in a Practising Certificate

To be called a solicitor and to practise, is usually to have qualified as a solicitor, been admitted to the roll of solicitors, and to have a Practising Certificate. A Practising Certificate is the certificate provided by The Law Society (devolved to the SRA), which demonstrates your qualification and rights to undertake the practice of law. These rights including undertaking work which is 'reserved' to solicitors, barristers, and other approved categories of lawyer. Those reserved activities are defined in the Legal Services Act 2007, s 12.

The annual practising year is governed by sets of regulations made by the regulator under the Solicitors Act 1974, s 28. These regulations prescribe the annual renewal, how it is run, and what information needs to be provided to gain a Practising Certificate. They also prescribe the situations in which conditions can be imposed on the Practising Certificate, which is covered in Part 3 of this book. At the time of writing, the set of regulations which govern Practising Certificates are the Authorisation of Individuals Regulations 2019, which form part of the Standards and Regulations 2019.

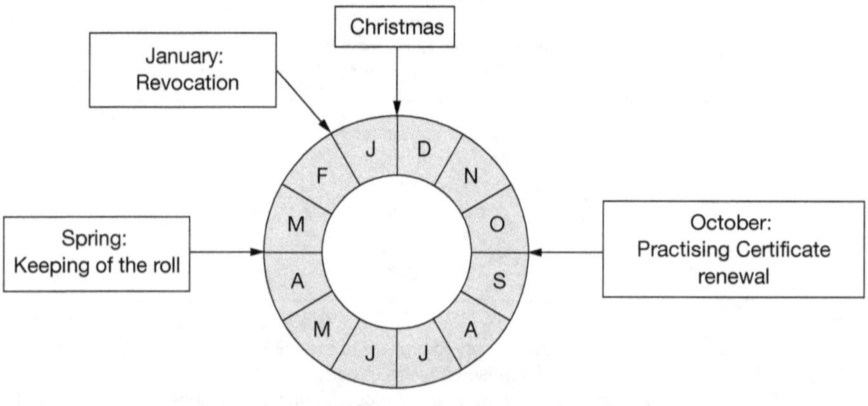

The practice of law means the representation of clients, the interpretation of the law, and advice to clients. There may be a degree of formality to this relationship. If you are practising in an area which is reserved you should be authorised (approved and registered with an approved regulator, such as the SRA), and have a Practising Certificate in force. Reserved and non-reserved work is discussed further in Part 2.

A Practising Certificate can start at any time during the practising year, and is renewed in October each year. It entitles you to exercise solicitor's rights of audience, and practise law including reserved work. Without a Practising Certificate you cannot undertake reserved work.

Often solicitors who are on the roll of solicitors, but not practising, and do not have Practising Certificates, call themselves non-practising solicitors. At one time this distinction was required by the regulations, but has since been removed, and the greater focus now is on reserved and non-reserved work. However, solicitors may still want to make a distinction between their time spent in practice and time in other careers, so the title non-practising solicitor is still in use. Generally speaking solicitors who work within legal services are expected to have a Practising Certificate. This can cause problems, and often does, as businesses and business models change, and traditional definitions of work in legal services increasingly face demands to change to meet the needs of consumers, and others. Often solicitors contact the SRA asking whether a Practising Certificate is needed for a new and innovative project, and wonder how their compliance requirements will impact this project.

Registered European Lawyers and Registered Foreign Lawyers also obtain Practising Certificates each year in the same way. Their 'roll' is not the 'roll' of solicitors, it is a register of lawyers. At the time of writing, the REL register was being withdrawn as a result of Brexit. The only lawyers continuing on the REL register were Swiss lawyers, however this was expected to change.

Accordingly, the practising year runs from October to October each year and each October requires the solicitor/REL or RFL to renew their Practising Certificate during the October window. This requires making a return to the Solicitors Regulation Authority to confirm they have met the requirements for ongoing competence, and where necessary, making a return for their solicitor practice as well. The regularity of the point afforded by the annual year provides the opportunity for the solicitor to reflect on the maintenance of their skills, whether they have or want to develop new skills, and their own areas of specialism.

This annual renewal window is also the time when the SRA traditionally consider imposing conditions on a Practising Certificate. We cover Practising Certificate conditions in Part 5 of this book, but the annual return and change of Practising Certificate is an opportunity to consider the regulatory position of the solicitor and whether their practice poses a risk to the public. There are a large number of solicitor Practising Certificate conditions considered each year; each situation is considered individually at the SRA by an individual caseworker. Consequently the decision making can run into the following calendar year. However there has been a six month limit on decision making for the regulators as a result of Regulation 19 of the European Communities Practice Regulations 2000, meaning the regulators only have six months from receipt to make a decision if they are to comply with the regulation. We wait to see whether this changes after Brexit.

Those that do not renew their Practising Certificate in October are likely to have their Practising Certificate revoked in the new year, following warnings from the SRA. If an application is received which is under consideration for conditions, the Practising Certificate from the previous year is 'held over' until a decision is made on the new certificate. Practising Certificates can in theory be held over indefinitely, and for a variety of reasons, but practitioners are asked to renew on an annual basis. More information relating to Practising Certificates is provided in Part 3 of this book.

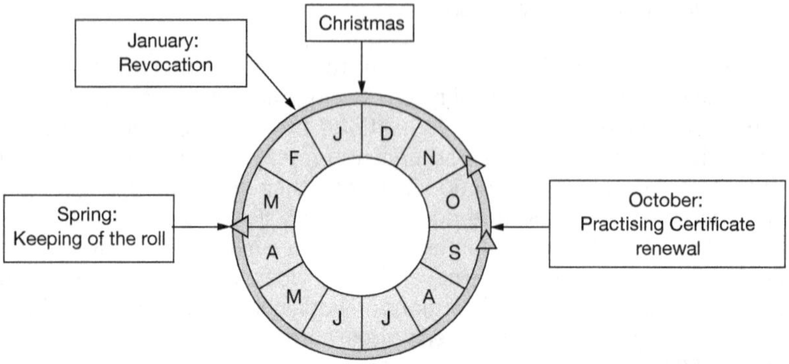

The outer circle here demonstrates the ongoing consideration of Practising Certificate conditions throughout the year. The arrows represent the particular volumes of applications which could be subject to conditions received in October, and the volume of conditions decisions reached in March/ April due to the EU deadline.

The annual renewal also includes an annual return for regulated law firms. This covers the activities of firms during the previous year, and how they meet the terms of the current version of the SRA's rules and regulations. Example questions include types of work undertaken, complaints received, and referral arrangements.

The annual return, particularly for the authorised body, is a major annual event. It is the largest information gathering exercise from the regulator, covers all recognised bodies and their staff, and allows the regulator to assess the risk of each body using the information provided. This information then informs any regulatory or monitoring activities.

For some solicitor practices not under the regulatory microscope, this will be the only interaction with the regulator during their existence, albeit an annual one.

Again, the annual pause and reflection point could provide the opportunity for authorised bodies to consider their goals, strategic paths, and skillsets. However very few firms align their strategic planning activities with the annual renewal; perhaps instead seeing regulation and compliance as a part of annual company life rather than the driver.

Freelance solicitors, examined further below, along with in house solicitors, and other solicitors who do not work in regulated law firms, only need to complete a Practising Certificate return. They, and any business they work with, do not need to complete the law firm annual renewal. This may leave freelancers, in house solicitors, and others not working in regulated law firms, in an enviable position. Their annual return is much smaller than others, and the SRA uses the information it gathers to make decisions about the risk posed by different types of practices. This means some individual solicitors may escape the regulator's attention by being so small.

We examine the responsibilities and statutory objectives of the legal regulators later in this in this book, providing us with a deeper understanding of their purposes for gathering information and the risk-based monitoring of practices.

Introduction to Legal Services Regulation

Legal services regulation is a large subject. Solicitors may be the most famous of all the legal services professionals, but there are many more. Currently, the Legal Services Board oversees a number of 'approved regulators' who regulate professionals to provide 'reserved' legal services. Reserved legal services are defined by the Legal Services Act 2007, s 12 and include conveyancing, litigation, and the grant of probate.

Of the regulators regulated by the Legal Services Board, several are also authorised to regulate 'Alternative Business Structures'; these are law firms where non-lawyers have an interest in the partnership or corporate structure. Further information about law firm structure and Alternative Business Structures is provided in Part 2 of this book.

At the time of writing, the list of approved regulators is (with the regulator's name first, followed by the title of the regulated community):

- Solicitors Regulation Authority – Solicitors
- Bar Standards Board – Barristers
- CILEX Regulation –Legal Executives
- Intellectual Property Regulation Board – Patent Attorneys and Trade Mark Attorneys
- Council for Licensed Conveyancers – Licensed Conveyancers
- Costs Lawyer Standards Board – Costs Lawyers
- Master of the Faculties – Notaries
- ACCA – Chartered Accountants
- ICAEW – Chartered Accountants
- Institute for Chartered Accountants for Scotland – Chartered Accountants

It should be remembered that this list is a list of approved (within the meaning of the Legal Services Act) regulatory bodies that operate in England and Wales, and the Legal Services Board also operates within this boundary. Scotland and Northern Ireland have separate legal systems and regulators (as do the Isle of Man, Jersey, and Guernsey). The inclusion of ICAS (Institute for Chartered Accountants for Scotland), indicates they are regulating cross border work from Scotland and into England and Wales. Some of the approved regulators do regulate cross border practices that are based, for example in Scotland, but provide services in England and Wales and subject to the law of England and Wales.

Some (but not all) of the approved regulators also have a representative arm, referred to in the legislation. For example, the SRA is part of The Law Society, and the Bar Standards Board is part of the Bar Council. Historically both were self-regulatory organisations, who also had a representative function. The same is true for some of the other regulators on the list. However, some regulators are independently established, with a completely separate representative arm. The Council for Licensed Conveyancers is an example of this approach, with the Society of Licensed Conveyancers operating as an entirely separate entity. The writer's experience is that the approach is markedly different between those organisations that are completely separate and those that are not. There are much closer ties and communications between regulatory and representative organisations where they used to work as one body.

Not all approved regulators are approved to regulate all reserved activity. The Council for Licensed Conveyancers for example is approved to regulate probate and conveyancing, but is not currently approved to regulate litigation, despite the Acts underpinning it allowing it to do so. The accountancy regulators are commonly authorised to provide probate services.

Non-reserved activity is a different subject. Theoretically there is no need to be regulated at all within legal services if you do not carry out reserved legal work. There can be other regulatory duties to other regulators such as HMRC, OISC or the FCA, but these may not exist at all.

Some approved regulators commonly allow their regulated community to undertake a full range of non-reserved work under their regulatory umbrella (for example, the SRA regulates solicitors to do a whole range of legal work falling outside the bounds of reserved work), but other regulators do not. The Council for Licensed Conveyancers, by contrast, regulates purely for the work it is authorised to regulate (probate and conveyancing), and nothing else, arguably placing the licensed conveyancer community at competitive disadvantage as they do not receive cross referrals into their conveyancing teams from other community work. However, the licensed conveyancer qualification does not have the same breadth as the solicitor qualification and this is often cited as the reason for the difference.

All of the work undertaken by the approved regulators is overseen by the Legal Services Board. In a way, you could argue that the Legal Services Board is a secondary line of regulation (or defence) for each regulated community.

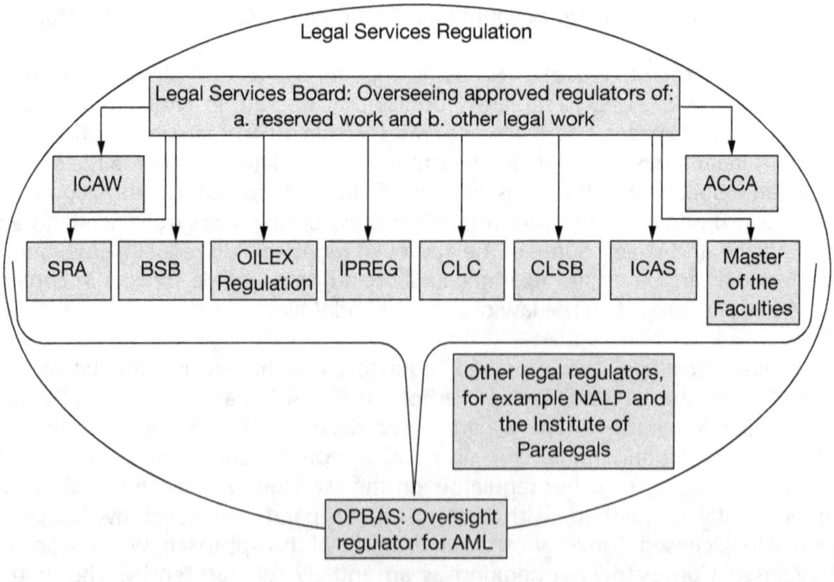

The Legal Services Board, the oversight regulator for the approved regulators, derives its statutory powers from the Act which established it, the Legal Services Act 2007, and in particular, Part 2 of that Act. Prior to the Legal Services Act 2007, there was not oversight of the legal regulators in the same way. The legal regulators were not approved, there was no oversight of their management; they were in some senses, and because of the constitutional position, self-regulating regulators.

Certain classes of complainants previously had the right to ask for a regulatory decision of The Law Society to be independently reviewed. This right arose as a check and balance on the misconduct investigations of The Law Society due to the conflict of interest position The Law Society was in as a representative and regulatory body.

This right was removed when the Legal Services Board (LSB) was introduced, with its much wider powers of management oversight. The previous power considered one regulatory decision at a time. The LSB reviews the work of the regulators, maintains annual reports on their practices, and monitors their compliance with the statutory framework. The LSB also approves their rules and considers applications for extensions to their authority or changes to their arrangements.

The political context of the situation has then changed with the introduction of this Act. It had previously been perceived that The Law Society could act in the interest of their members in determining legal complaints or investigations of misconduct and making regulatory decisions. The separation of the Law Society's functions and creation of the SRA, alongside the introduction of the Legal Services Board has provided a different dimension to this picture. The LSB is sponsored by the Ministry of Justice but is not formally part of the civil service.

OPBAS, the Office for Professional Body AML Supervision, also oversees the approved regulators, but only for Anti Money Laundering purposes. OPBAS' remit is wider, and they oversee a range of bodies beyond legal services and into financial services professional regulation as well.

The approved regulators are known in European legislative terms as the 'competent authorities', a term currently reflected in some of our Acts and Regulations, which relates to the ability of the regulator to make decisions about practising statuses.

Beyond the approved regulators, there are also other non-approved regulators operating within legal services regulation offering qualifications and regulation to legal services professionals. Sometimes these qualifications are regulated by the Office of Qualifications and Examinations Regulation (Ofqual) as vocational qualifications. These bodies are not approved regulators and are not subject to Legal Services Board or OPBAS oversight. These include the National Association of Licensed Paralegals, and the Institute of Paralegals. Many employed individuals within legal services are paralegals but there is no requirement for them to have specific qualifications or join a representative body.

Some individuals working within law firms or in legal services can be very highly qualified, but without a professional status. These individuals are regulated through firm they work in (for example, through the SRA's regulation of regulated solicitor firms). Alternatively, individuals without a recognised professional status can do non reserved legal work without primary[1] regulation (that being, without regulation for legal work).

The approved legal regulators do not however handle consumer complaints which require redress. The approved regulators only deal with issues of misconduct, which in practice means a breach of the rules of professional conduct. The majority of consumer complaints are not serious enough to fall into this category, for example if:

- a transaction had been slightly delayed,
- there was a failure to return telephone calls, or
- a fee earner had changed, and the consumer would prefer someone different

None of these scenarios would be sufficiently serious to amount to misconduct on the part of the solicitor, but could result in a complaint.

Part 6 of the Legal Services Act 2007 sets out the provision for an Ombudsman scheme for consumer complaints. This is known in the legislation as the Office for Legal Complaints, but has been branded and marketed as the Legal Ombudsman, or 'LeO', for short. LeO investigates complaints against legal services providers according to their Scheme Rules, and the terms of the Legal Services Act 2007. Before LeO undertakes an investigation, the consumer must exhaust the internal complaints system of the legal provider.

LeO make referrals to the approved regulator if they perceive there is an issue of professional misconduct. The SRA do not make referrals direct to LeO. If the SRA mistakenly receives correspondence intended for the firm or LeO (or if the problem is diagnosed as one for LeO), the consumer is asked to approach the Ombudsman scheme directly.

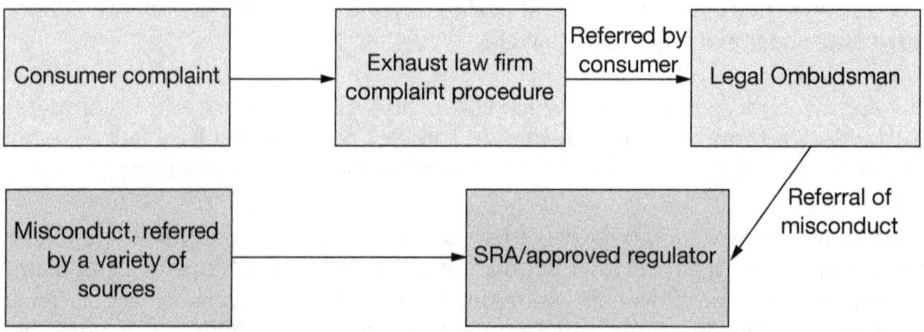

The terms of the LeO scheme correspond closely with the approved regulators, in that LeO deals with complaints about these types of lawyers, but does not deal with complaints about those who exist beyond the scope of the schemes of regulation, such as paralegals or unregulated providers of non-reserved work.

1 Some form of regulation may be required in some circumstances, for example by HMRC, the FCA or Claims Management regulators

Practitioners may remember The Law Society used to handle consumer complaints about their members directly under their previous regulatory set up; The Office for Supervision of Solicitors. The Legal Services Act 2007 and the separation of The Law Society's regulatory function into the SRA resulted in the abolition of this function and the establishment of LeO.

The Legal Services Act 2007, s 157(5)(c) prevents any of the approved regulators from making provision about offering redress; preventing competition between complaint handling schemes. In practice all approved regulators require their regulated communities to have a complaint handling system in place, and advise clients of their rights to approach LeO.

Issues of misconduct can be investigated by the approved regulator alongside consumer complaints, and the two bodies can communicate over cases simultaneously under investigation. The approved regulators receive reports of misconduct from several sources including:

- third parties
- other law firms
- outside bodies
- Members of Parliament
- law firms themselves

The types of matters referred to the regulator by law firms themselves (and others) are considered in Part 5 of this book as a discussion of serious breach.

The impact of the regulator

We might measure the operation of the SRA and their impact using a model such as the one below, which the writer drew in approximately 2016. The SRA is intending to deliver their regulation for the regulated community, who are their primary audience. They however also work to serve the interests of consumers, in the broader public interest, and to benefit the market overall. The Legal Services Act at s 1 contains the Regulatory Objectives for the Legal Services Board and approved regulators which capture this broader public interest activity.

As well as these points, the SRA have an organisational impact. With a staff of over 600, the regulator has weight; as do its staff members. The two final pulls we can see are the influence of the oversight regulator, the LSB, and the Ministry of Justice, both of whom may shape regulation and regulatory policy.

The current system is complex. There is a variety of professional statuses, regulatory bodies, and two oversight regulators in the Legal Services Board and OPBAS. Not all regulatory bodies in the sector are overseen. Some work (reserved work) can only be done by certain professionals, but those same professionals can sometimes do other non-reserved work as well. Certain groups of professionals conducting reserved work are excluded from conducting non reserved work. Complaint handling is commonly excluded from professional regulation.

The system is full of anomalies, complexities, and in some cases, a complete lack of parity. We are looking at the result of history; lawyers as a constitutional force, with modern day organisations and developments built around very old ways of working.

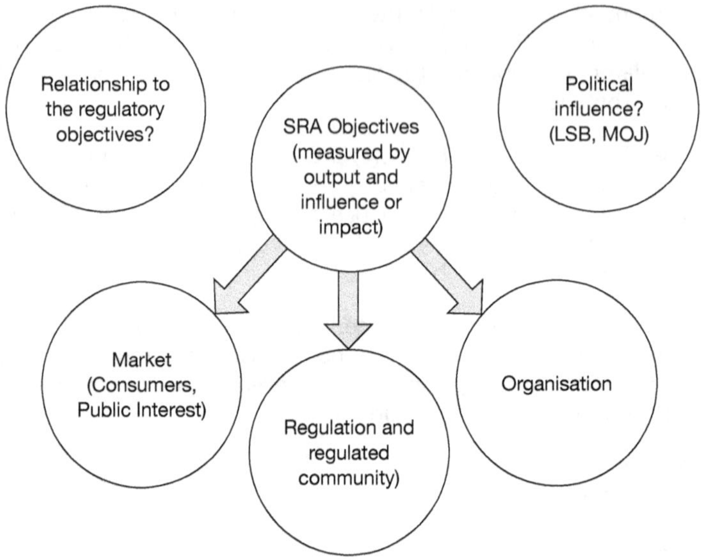

Historical development of regulation

Examining Hansard from the early to the mid-20th century provides an insight into the working life of solicitors and their trainees. Matters related to solicitor discipline and conduct concerned ensuring that staff within solicitor practices had the opportunity to train themselves, and to provide for their pay and conditions. In keeping with the politics and social mobility concerns of the time, including the birth of the modern Labour Party, these were matters for debate in parliament.

What we now see as modern life started after the Second World War, and individual home ownership became more common across society. However there were a series of scandals in the 1980s concerning solicitor charges and questions were asked about why certain work was reserved to solicitors, and why solicitors could not work in partnership with others.

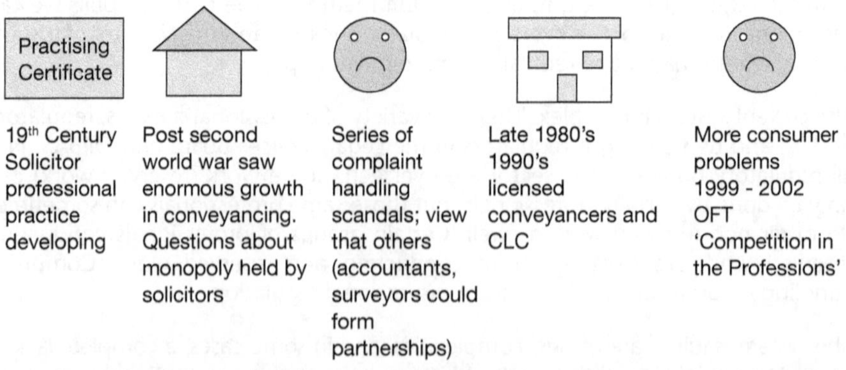

At around this time we see the establishment of the Council for Licensed Conveyancers. The Council was established to offer competition within the sector for the benefit of ordinary consumers.

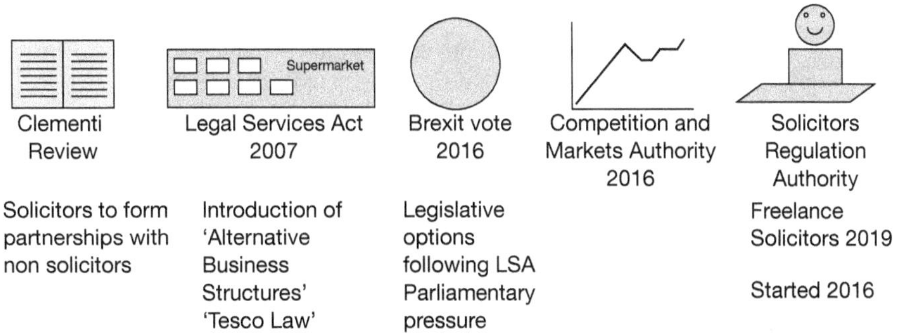

Following further investigation into the legal services professions and their hold on reserved work by the Office of Fair Trading and Sir David Clementi, the oversight regulator, The Legal Services Board, was established by the Legal Services Act 2007. The Act also started the process of separating the representative and regulatory functions of the legal regulators, and established Alternative Business Structures (ABS). ABS was known as 'Tesco Law', as it was perceived that the supermarkets would enter the legal services sector.

The latest occurrences in the regulatory market are reviews by parliament into the Legal Services Act 2007, following its failure to make an impact. The paper 'Legislative Options following the Legal Services Act' considered a range of options including a single legal regulator. Most recently, Professor Stephen Mayson's report 'An Independent Review of Legal Regulation' recommended the establishment of one legal regulator for all legal services providers, to be known as the Legal Services Regulatory Authority. At the same time, the SRA introduced a new handbook, now known as the Standards and Regulations, which aims to open up the solicitor market further by allowing solicitors to work with unregulated businesses and as freelancers. The new models of practice are covered in Part 2 of this book.

Whether the latest attempts to bring more competition into legal services will work, remains to be seen. However there have now been some very strong attempts at unwinding statutory and regulatory positions in legal services, with the intent of opening the very traditional legal market up to innovation and development. Legal services is perceived as a potential growth area and could be used to stimulate other markets post-Brexit. So far, there has been limited success in introducing competition; the latest Codes of Conduct from the SRA may be the eighth or ninth attempt.

The following is an excerpt of a presentation written by the writer in July 2013. The presentation covered the introduction of Alternative Business Structures, the benefits and drawbacks of entering the legal market, and what the future held for legal services in the advent of ABS.

> 'In 2001, the OFT reported on competition in the professions and started the move towards ABS we see today. We have been here before; change has come – and gone. What will happen next is an interesting question.
>
> Behind the government intention [introducing ABS] is a need to better serve consumer demand.
>
> ABS take up has however been slow so far. Around 120 exist now, who will employ a fraction of the approximately 248,000 employed in legal services at the moment.
>
> Pros and Cons of entering the legal services market for ABS:
>
> **Pros**:
>
> - Established market
> - Established consumer base
> - Clear horizontal integration
> - Perceived professionalism
> - Ease of service for consumer
> - Innovation
> - Your needs protected through regulation
>
> **Cons**:
>
> - Uncertainty in the market
> - Uncertainty in future regulation
> - Lack of independence in the market
> - Conveyancing downturn in recession
> - Globalisation
> - Commoditisation
> - Indemnity costs
> - Structural changes required in law firms
>
> The benefits of expanding into legal services for are clear. This is an established market, with clear demand, where you have an established customer base requiring these services. The legal profession retains a certain amount of professional status and this may be marketable. If you added other business models, a one stop service could be easy for you and your clients – you may even be able to offer legal services cheaper than elsewhere.

However, there is a great deal of uncertainty in the market. Conveyancing is in a downturn in the recession, other parts of legal services have been affected by structural reform (such as personal injury and legal aid). Many firms are simply looking to survive and those that will are having to implement dramatic efficiency savings. Indeed, legal services are increasingly commoditised – and referred overseas, to India or South East Asia. It may be that in 10 years more of our legal work is outsourced overseas and it becomes a more cut price competitive service.

Integrating your services with legal services could require a significant cultural and structural change on your part; and the end result – with lower fees, high indemnity costs and uncertainty over how legal services will be regulated in the future may mean it is not worthwhile.

The economy is likely to be a driving factor behind changes in legal services. The current economic climate is not conducive to change and if the recession continues change is likely to take a long time.

Consumer demand has driven changes in the legal services sector since the 1950s and 1960s and continues to be the reason behind the changes. Anything that meets their needs is likely to survive, ABS or not.

IT will change the way we deliver services, from virtual law firms to allowing us to find cheaper means to do the same work overseas.'

ABS are likely to increase vertical and horizontal integration:

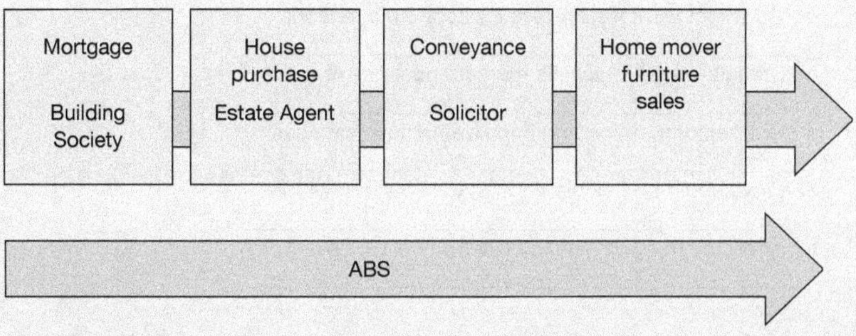

'However ABS are likely to change the shape of some law firms.

An example of integration is above. You may see firms offering the whole process from mortgage to showing you round a house, completing the conveyance and moving you in. In vertical integration, groups of solicitors, barristers, search firms, marketing organisations, may band together.

We will also see some innovative shapes of new firms.

The risks of ABS come down to knowing who you're doing business with. There are always concerns that criminals seek to take over law firms and I'm sure many of you have seen some very odd transactions in your time – ones that bear all the hallmarks of mortgage fraud. In those cases, the SRA and CLC investigates the firms, but ABS just made it easier for criminals to take over law firms, providing them with an enormous amount of power in the conveyancing process.

As it stands, the ABS application processes are rigorous in an attempt to keep out criminals, but the SRA still gets it wrong sometimes. Could the regulator deal with the fall out if a large ABS went wrong?

There is an issue about how far regulation can go here – the regulators cannot cover all aspects of the ABS business, but they do cover some. So what if the legal part of the business failed – who would step in – the regulator or the business? What happens if something goes wrong in another part of the business that affects legal services? Is there a regulator remedy? If not, could the insurer cope? To a large extent these questions are still to be determined.

Outside shareholders could give rise to new conflicts of interest. If your client fails to get independent advice this could also jeopardise your interests; it brings a little uncertainty into a transaction – who knows what advisor with other interests might do?'

The following conclusions were drawn from a presentation the writer gave to the Big Voice conference in London in November 2020

New modes of practice
New business models
We might want freelancers for economic reasons
Stimulate slow business markets post-Brexit
Create competition and improvements in services
Law should be flexible enough to allow innovation
Attempts to open legal services since 1970s
...in legitimate attempt to stimulate UK economy

'There is a clear economic rationale for change in the legal services sector, and the feeling that barriers to economic access to the professions are restricting growth and development in the country as a whole. The freelance market and using unregulated businesses appears risky for the constitutional requirements of the country, but equally, failing to change could have negative implications for other sectors and consumers as individuals fail to achieve justice and fail to make an impact on the decision making within the country through the Court system.

The consequences are not only economic, they are constitutional; the position goes full circle. As consumers and small businesses fail to use the Court system because representation is unaffordable, they fail to hold parliament to account, meaning both parliament and lawyers control the country in an unintended manner. The system of the separation of the powers, if left unchecked, will dramatically fail.

The separation of the powers assumes perfect competition, but no such state exists. Economic intervention is required to balance the power of law firms and individuals, along with parliament, in order to safeguard democracy and the role of the state.'

Entry and exit: the professional hurdle

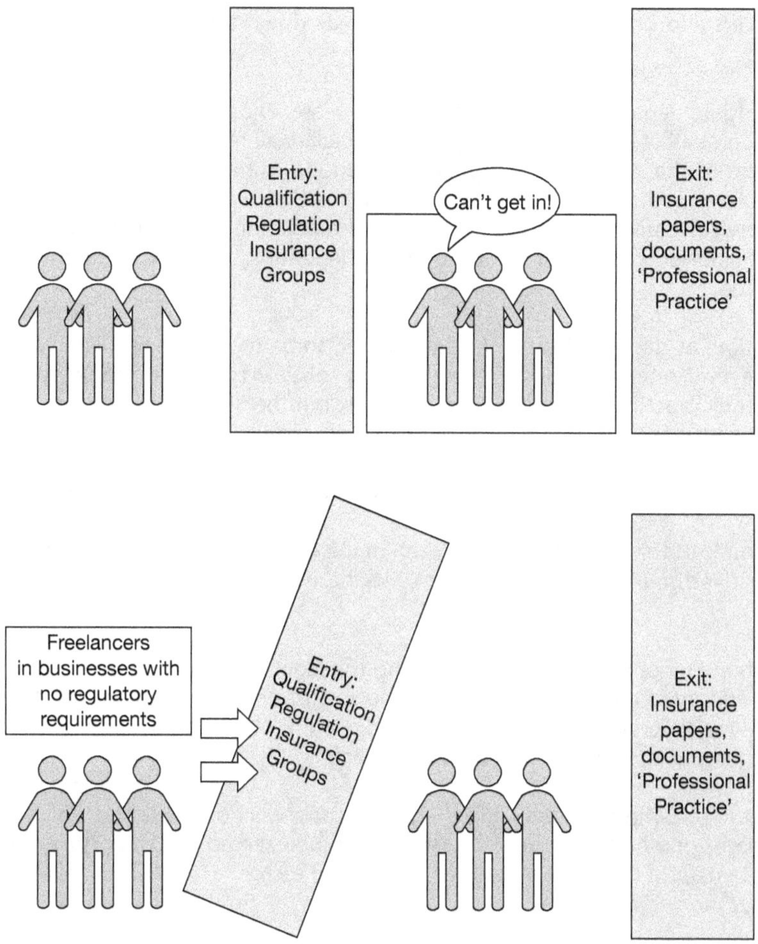

As well as overseeing the legal services regulators, the Legal Services Board can also admit new regulators to the delivery of reserved work. This, and the delivery of freelance solicitors under the new SRA Standards and Regulations may result in the opening up of the solicitor market further, by removing some of the barriers to entry and exit from the market.

We can see the entry requirements to the profession quite clearly. There are costs for qualification, regulation and insurance, and particular groups may have sway within the process. There are also barriers to exit from the profession, including insurance costs for run off cover (which can be substantial), holding and dealing with ongoing client papers, documents and monies, and other professional requirements to be fulfilled when practitioners exit.

Freelancers in particular may challenge accepted ways of thinking in the market; taking on less agile businesses which have compliance overheads and more regulatory rules to comply with, and challenging some of the accepted methods of contracting or delivering services. Solicitor qualifications and regulation will still remain in place, but we wait to see whether or not there is sufficient challenge by freelancers and unregulated businesses to break down the barriers to entry in the market.

Returning to legal services regulation, there are anomalies in the overarching system. Not all of the approved regulators regulate all reserved work, the previous examples of the accountancy regulators are good examples of limited regulation (for probate), within legal services. This means that a lot of work undertaken in legal services could fall between the gaps of regulation. The perceived entry and exit requirements may not be there at all, depending on how the business was structured.

In addition, as described earlier in the chapter, some regulators regulate work that goes beyond reserved work. For example, a solicitor might do employment law within their practice, that is not reserved work, but the SRA would regulate them in the same way as they do other forms of solicitor work. The historical development of The Law Society means that all forms of solicitor practice are covered by their regulation, rather than the narrower development of the other regulators.

An example of this is the regulatory reach of the Council for Licensed Conveyancers whose advertised regulation and regulatory basis only extends to certain reserved work.[2]

The patchwork of legislation underpinning the legal regulatory system means that not all approved regulators have the same sets of powers. The consolidating Act was the Legal Services Act 2007, but this did not remove the previous powers for each legal regulator granted under the old Acts.

We wait to see whether a new single legal regulator will be established which will fill these gaps, or whether some work will remain unreserved to certain professionals for the benefit of competition and growth in the sector.

---

2 The activity of conducting probate is not itself reserved work, it is the grant of probate which is reserved.

Current regulatory position

The SRA, in common with the other approved regulators, and perhaps regulators in general, have a range of roles:

- *Entry and exit requirements* – The SRA set standards for solicitor qualification; issue of Practising Certificates; recognise and authorise different types of practice; and handle the closure or exit of practice (this part refers to the exit of practice not as a result of enforcement action, which is covered separately below). The SRA derives its powers from the Solicitors Act 1974, Pts 1 and 2, the Legal Services Act 2007, Pt 5 (in respect of ABS), and the Courts and Legal Services Act 1990, s 66, Pt 4, and Sch 14. They also have powers set out in the Administration of Justice Act 1985, Pt 1, and Sch 2.
- *Setting standards* – this includes the development of rules for the profession, and of rules which govern the use of their own powers. The SRA's powers in this respect are derived from the Solicitors Act 1974, Pt 2, including the power to make rules as to professional conduct. Other relevant provisions include the Administration of Justice Act 1985, s 9, and Sch 2, the Courts and Legal Services Act 1990, Pt 4 and the Legal Services Act 2007, Pt 5, and Schs 4 and 5.
- *Taking enforcement action* – this in the SRA's case includes:
  - prosecution before the Solicitors Disciplinary Tribunal which can result in outcomes such as strike off or fine;
  - internal sanctions such as rebukes and fines; and
  - closure of any form of practice or body recognised by the SRA, this is known as 'intervention'. The SRA's powers in this respect are also drawn from the same Acts, with some of the Tribunal's powers and some internal SRA disciplinary powers being drawn from the Solicitors Acts, Pts 1 and 2, the Legal Services Act 2007, Pt 5, the Administration of Justice Act 1985, Sch 2, and the Courts and Legal Services Act, Sch 14.

Intervention

The Solicitors Act 1974 also provides the basis for intervention into some types of practice in Sch 1. This schedule is a good reference for anyone who would like a simple overview of when the regulator may intervene (close the practice). Although the list in the Act applies to solicitors (with the other three Acts covering other circumstances), it can also be used as a quick shorthand for intervention into any form of practice if you are not looking formally and are short on time. The kinds of circumstances it covers include, but are not limited to, the following:

1 reason to suspect dishonesty;

2 breaches of the Accounts Rules;

3 incapacity; and

4 abandonment of practice

In practice, the first two in the (writer's short, non-comprehensive) list above cover most circumstances related to the Accounts Rules. If for example, a solicitor was dishonest in relation to their dealings with the accounts and evidence of this was conveyed to the regulator, the regulator could likely make a decision to intervene in respect of either point one or two.

It should be mentioned at this point that intervention grounds are exactly that; grounds. There is a requirement upon the regulator to consider the position carefully before exercising that right. The consequences of intervention can be devastating for the solicitor. It can lead to the destruction of their income, and practice, and may also result in them being responsible for costs. In serious cases (for example in relation to serious dishonesty outlined previously), could also lead to simultaneous disciplinary action, for example leading to a strike off from the roll.

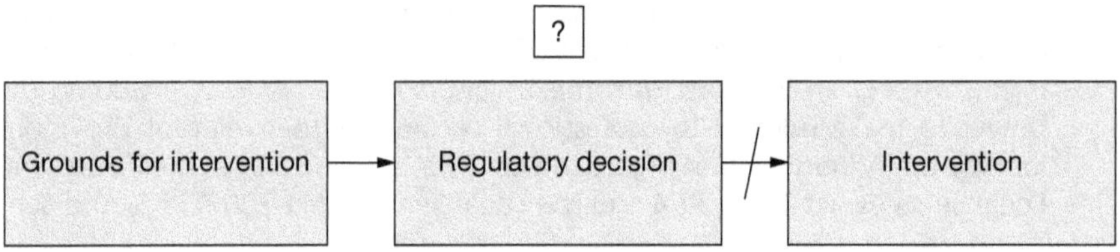

The regulator must consider the consumer perspective, the risk posed by the continuation of the practice, the ongoing delivery of legal services by that practice, and the likely overall outcome. The regulators have acted very decisively before if the practice is putting at clients or wider society at risk. There is a great deal more that could be said about intervention, including the legal basis for the decision making, but this is not a book about intervention, and we do not cover the full legal basis for intervention or the decision making here.

Suffice to say, the closure of a practice is a strong part of the regulatory armour of the SRA, and forms an underlying counterbalance to unprofessional practice, criminal activity by law firms, and the potential of those types of action to cause significant damage to clients and society, particularly given the standing and constitutional significance of the legal professions.

Intervention means the closure of the solicitor practice. This is usually done by a decision on the part of the SRA, and then effected either by SRA staff or intervention agents. Sometimes, if the practice has live matters, the intervention agents are solicitors, who take on the matters or disperse them to a panel of other solicitors.

Separate but very similar (almost identical) grounds for intervention to those in the Solicitors Act 1974 are contained in the other Acts related to different forms of legal practice recognised by the regulator, including in the Administration of Justice Act 1985, Sch 2, the Courts and Legal Services Act 1990, Sch 14 and the Legal Services Act 2007, Sch 14.

Registered Foreign Lawyers (RFLs) are covered in the provisions above (particularly in the Courts and Legal Services Act 1990). Registered European Lawyers (RELs) have been covered in respect of the above by The European Communities (Lawyer's Practice) Regulations 2000 (as amended), and therefore by virtue of the same Acts as solicitors, but these provisions will likely be amended as a result of Brexit.

Regulatory objectives

No discussion of the role of the SRA and current regulatory position is complete without considering the overall regulatory objectives of the regulator. The regulatory objectives apply to all of the approved regulators, and the Legal Services Board and are contained within section 1 of the Legal Services Act. They include objectives in areas such as acting in the public interest, promoting the rule of law, and protecting the consumer interest. This is not the full list of regulatory objectives, but they are wide reaching, and even encompass a citizen's legal duties and rights, which is a major change to the previous basis of regulation. No such objectives were contained within the Solicitors Act 1974; in fact that Act is a comparatively flat list of powers and restrictions, which in comparison seem designed to contain the solicitors' profession and protect the public. It appears, if we look back through time to the 1980s and 1990s, that the public interest was felt to need further protection, and we are seeing the emphasis placed differently for the regulator.

At this moment in time, the citizen's legal rights and duties do not seem to feature in the activities of the regulators. There are no public legal education programmes, for example, and limited public information about legal rights. The regulatory objectives are not prominently placed within the approved regulator's work, and anyone reviewing the websites or other output of the regulator might find more information about anti money laundering, for example. We might question whether some regulatory objectives have been given more prominence than other objectives.

None of the approved regulators has an economic objective. This means they do not regulate the market as a whole, and cannot for example set prices, or look at consumer monetary issues. There is no capacity for the SRA to look at the economic operation of the solicitor market or to intervene in that in any way. The approved regulators are professional services regulators only, meaning their role is to look at professional services, misconduct, and breaches of the law, in line with their identified statutory duties. There is currently no body able to regulate the economics of the legal services market.

Solicitors, who are the professionals being regulated, must also to some degree, share these identified goals, possibly including the regulatory objectives, to avoid a complete mismatch in expectation with the regulator. However, they are also in business as legal advisors and are naturally concerned with their income, promotion and marketing, and ensuring profitability of the business as a whole. Professionally, and as Officers of the Court, they must ensure that the administration of justice is part of their balanced role in delivering services to the client and others.

The administration of justice is used in the widest possible terms here, to include matters such as:

- the proper functioning of the court and the overall legal system
- the upholding of the law
- the effective and actual delivery of justice
- judicial or legal issues
- outcomes through solicitor (or other legal professional)
- any form of advice and representation.

Of course, the solicitor role must also consider their own ongoing professional status and competence, as well as the ethical considerations of the operation of the legal system. All of these parts combine to underpin the current system of regulation.

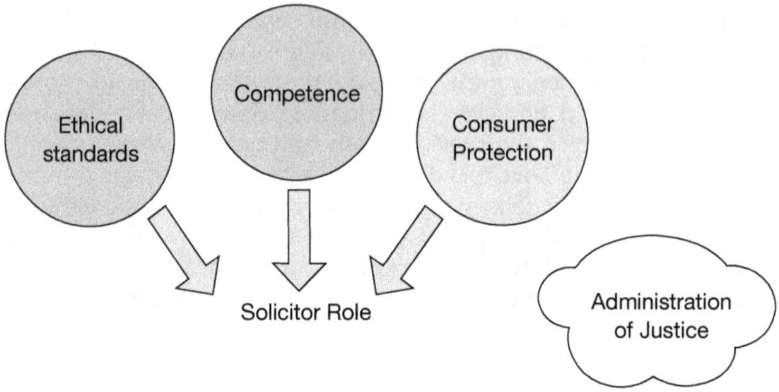

SRA Standards and Regulations

The SRA in 2019, published their Standards and Regulations, which are the latest sets of regulations from the body. The SRA, in common with the other approved regulators, have the right to make their own rules under the Solicitors Act 1974, s 28. These rules then must be approved by the Legal Services Board also under the Legal Services Act 2007.

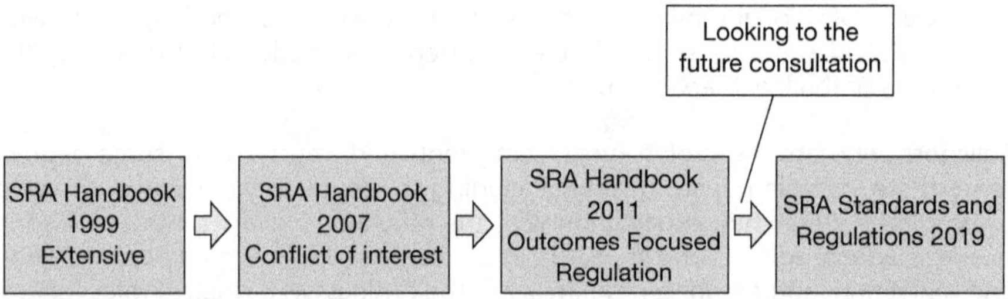

The SRA's new rules are a departure from the previous SRA Handbooks and Guides, including in name. Intended as much shorter versions of the rules, the SRA have stripped away many of the lengthy requirements which characterised the previous rule books. There are a number of previous Handbooks and Guides, with rules, descriptions of appropriate behaviour, and suggestions of outcomes in certain situations. By 1999, the Handbook was very large, and full of information to guide the solicitor's behaviour. Back then, the Handbooks were known as 'Guides' for example 'The Guide to the Professional Conduct of Solicitors'.

In each Guide, Handbook, or Standards and Regulations, there is usually a Code of Conduct, along with other rules and different guidance that in totality comprise the set of rules.

In 2007, the Guide was first shortened, with less behavioural and discursive content and a sea change in attitude towards conflict of interest. One major change at this point, was that the Code allowed acting on both sides for the first time, subject to some controls and exemptions. The Legal Services Act 2007 brought in Alternative Business Structures (ABS) and the 2011 Code reflected that implementation, with wider and more open sets of rules based on the theory that the new investment into legal services would need room and space to grow into new business models. The new rules were accompanied by outcome-focused regulation, a regulatory style that focuses on the end goal rather than prescribing how that will be delivered – again allowing the freedom for new structures to develop.

By 2016, there was another new handbook being proposed as ABS had not delivered the change in the market that was expected. 'Looking to the Future' proposed even further radical change to strip away what was perceived as unnecessary regulation. We now have the Standards and Regulations 2019; much shorter, and with two new modes of practice – as individuals employed in unregulated organisations (including delivering advice to the public, which was not previously permitted), and as freelance solicitors.

There is still guidance to support the Standards and Regulations 2019, but the rules themselves are not as extensive as they once were. The intention is that the rules are a condensed set of regulations, in some cases summarising what has gone before. A great deal of time is spent on compliance and regulation, for some practitioners this has gone far beyond what seems reasonable. The new approach is intended to make compliance easier.

The SRA's new Standards and Regulations have been developed in consultation with the profession, and the SRA also sought the input of the public in their view of what they expect from a solicitor during their Question of Trust exercise. However, the brevity of the new regulations has caused some concern about their interpretation, misinterpretation, and difficulties in prosecution.

The corollary is that the SRA may find it may be difficult to prosecute against such a short set of rules, without the explanation, clarity, and direction that the extensive handbook and previous guides provided. Building a body of work that reflected the expectations of the regulator and the understanding of the professions had been accomplished over many years, and had been, in the face of modern business developments, discarded. The writer advises the firms she works with and those on her training courses to continue to use the old rule books (all of them), if necessary.

Solicitors have a constitutional role, and there is a need for them to be able to challenge the country's institutions, represent their clients, and deliver justice, all within the rule of law. There has to be a check on the role of the lawyer; ensuring their honesty and integrity, and that they represent clients effectively. However, the importance of the role of the lawyer within the constitution means power is concentrated in the hands of the regulators and the lawyers themselves. The legal regulators have to balance *their* regulatory powers in overseeing lawyers, and their policy making, with the need to uphold the constitutional rule of law. In some respects, the removal of the long lists of regulatory requirements not only gave the businesses freedom to move, it also gave the regulator far more freedom in the interpretation of those rules and the manner in which they exercised those powers.

As much as the regulator exercises their authority, solicitors and other lawyers also have to also be able to understand their regulator, and make effective challenge in areas where the supervisory system may overstep its power. Sometimes, the writer has seen situations where the solicitor or firm under investigation does not understand the position, their regulator, or the consequences of their actions, and this was even in a position where the rules were set out in a detailed manner. Given the level of interpretation available now, there is an even greater need for an involved regulated community; the views of the public; and the effective challenge to the regulator. The counterbalance of the representative body also begins to again appear attractive as a means to pull against the weight of the regulator, and we can see why The Law Society was both the regulator and representative body for so long; the inbuilt counterweight prevented the legal regulator holding too much power.

There is a regulatory system of sometimes complex regulatory checks and balances in place underlying the idea of professional regulation for solicitors. None of these systems is perfect or complete, but each provides the opportunity for challenge in their own way. There is the need for further checks and balances on the power within the system to provide a balance to the authority of any one group or body.

Section 2: Discursive content

In discussing concepts of professional practice, the writer is struck by the different feelings that are apparent and expressed in the courses. When teaching on the PSC, there were people who were becoming solicitors because they wanted a sense of belonging, a desire for a recognisable and respected job and ongoing employment; for others it was a sense of duty that drew them to practise as a lawyer.

Individual expression and professionalism as a form of practice

For the solicitors on the serious breach course, there is a difference in their physicality when discussing serious breaches, and their current practices. This is apparent in their body language, which varies according to their feelings. You can often observe the pride in discussing a Practising Certificate with the smiles, acknowledgements, attentiveness, and quiet nods. There can be a difference in the serious breach discussion which can require a lot of contemplation, quiet time away for some people, or even bustle in their workspace. The concern for other practitioners when we discuss serious breach is apparent in their expressions.

Being a lawyer is sometimes a lifetime's work, and often lawyers practise alone, even with other practitioners. The writer has often seen practices of two or more partners where one partner's individual practice is very different from the other's. This individual work rests on the professionalism of the person.

Complying with the codes of conduct can be challenging, particularly when the individual practitioner practising in some senses 'alone' has to generate an income and has many things to attend to. Whilst working for the SRA, the writer was often told that solicitors relied on each other for expectations of professional behaviour, and that they would support each other in delivering services to meet those expectations. We can see now the development of the practice around the solicitor with the expectations of COLPs, COFAs, and other governance arrangements.

When discussing serious breaches, solicitors on the courses often say if they were to report something it would be because they felt they had no other choice. Solicitors express a collective sense of belonging, with a baseline of acceptable behaviour. They often discuss reporting matters which they felt might invoke a sense of outrage, distrust, or inappropriateness in another professional. Often the solicitors on the course work in small groups and the group will discuss a perspective they have come to, with a spokesperson possibly expressing a viewpoint of the type just discussed.

There may be a collective 'we' which might be expressed by, for example, high street practitioners collectively, conveyancers collectively, or city solicitors collectively. For example, if a problem is discussed or posed, a group with knowledge of that situation might step forward and offer their particular, and authoritative perspective. This might be in the sense that 'we' would take these steps, or this would be what 'we' within this group would expect. There may be a sense in some cases that the group the practitioner identifies with would have their own means of dealing with the situation or there may be some other form of response within that group to take ownership of the situation and act appropriately.

In that sense there is a collective sense of belonging, which might be to the profession overall, and to groups within that. This baseline might sit underneath layers of individual expression within an area of law; so a practitioner might practice in their own way, giving what they see as the correct interpretation of the law within their knowledge and specialism, and that practice might vary even between practitioners in the same field, dependent on their background learning.

Sometimes practice is done with flair, and we can see the individual's personal expression in their client base and form of practice; through their writing or other outward facing work; through their social media or their marketing. Historically, some expression has been frowned upon; even today the SRA issues guidance on social media use for example, and solicitors have in the past been banned from advertising. Our communication channels allow us to express personality and that includes our professional communication channels.

Otherwise, practice is expressed in advice and responses, and the support provided to clients in different ways. This can be a particular solution to a problem, or way of dealing with a situation which is novel or innovative. Sometimes the knowledge of the professional and their practising style is only known to those who work directly with the practitioner or work in their area of law and therefore know or have seen something of their work. This might be why we see practitioners band together and support each other across areas of law.

At a meeting of a local Sole Practitioner's Group, the writer was once told that sole practice was a choice which allowed the individual to practice and express themselves freely. This may not be an available choice in a larger firm, where individual expression is part of a larger sum or package which the firm has chosen as their strategic marketing direction.

With solicitors, we can see individualism and personal expertise as a cornerstone of professional practice. The benefit of partnerships or corporate structures is the assistance with all aspects of management of practice, including the support structures, the check and balance partnership provides, and the security of placing the practice within defined boundaries. Additional expertise in the form of other partners can also bring in new clients and provide a new angle to your business.

Individualism within practice could bring the related concern that personal expression forms the basis of private practice. The most recent edition of the SRA Rules contains the phrase 'You do not allow your personal views…' drawing the line between views held personally (but perhaps not expressed), and views held professionally. The same set of regulations also notes that the rules apply to solicitors in their private lives as well as in their professional lives. There has been a recent challenge in the Courts to the overlap[3] of the rules into the personal and professional, but the SRA continues to intervene and have statutory powers on a number of matters which cross the line between the personal and private, including individuals committing criminal offences in their personal time; solicitor incapacity and mental health issues; and solicitor personal insolvency.

In some cases, the personal representatives of a deceased solicitor would be required to take over a practice and close it down. The writer has dealt with more than one family member of a deceased solicitor attempting to close down their relative's practice. In some cases, the Law Society can step in and intervene, but it is another example of where the solicitor does have duties extending into their personal lives. In some cases they touch the lives of others around them as well.

Options and ideas for discussion in your firm.

You can:

1. Discuss the questions below with your staff (qualified and unqualified – we may all have a professional practice). You may choose one or two questions you think are suitable for discussion.

   You can frame this in a discussion either of the concept of professionalism and the content of the current set of regulations, or the need for a regulator who draws lines, sets rules, and intervenes into certain situations.

   Or

2. Reflect on this in your own time.

QUESTIONS TO CONSIDER:

What is your professional practice? Where does it begin and end? What does it encompass? Do you find individual expression in your work?

Is a handbook or set of regulations essential for professional practice? Does our personal knowledge, competence, or training address these points without a set of regulations?

3 *Beckwith v Solicitors Regulation Authority* [2020] EWHC 323 (Admin).

What about our ethical standpoint, does this address the issue of professionalism or is the ethical standpoint individual or personal?

Which parts of the current Code of Conduct do you think best reflect professionalism? What about previous Codes of Conduct?

Does your professionalism impact your personal life? What about the requirements to act with independence, or not to act with a conflict of interest?

Has being a solicitor (or working in a solicitor firm) impacted you or your family personally? How and what is the impact?

Ethics and reporting

Part of the SRA regulatory requirements cover the need to report yourself to the regulator in certain circumstances. Self-reporting is, for most, a regulatory requirement, rather than a statutory one. HOLPs and HOFAs (in ABS) have a statutory requirement to make a report under the Legal Services Act 2007, ss 91 and 92. Serious breach is covered in detail later in this book, and practitioners are reminded that regulators have a statutory right to make regulatory rules.

However, the SRA receives hundreds of thousands of reports about solicitors annually. These can be from consumers of legal services, through to third parties, MPs, other solicitors' firms, state institutions such as the police, other regulators, and the court. The SRA is set up to receive, process and understand these reports, and to act on potential issues of misconduct and this is part of their operating framework and reason for being.

Common issues reported include:

- taking unfair advantage, particularly in litigation
- overcharging
- inappropriate withdrawals from client account
- incompetence – this can occasionally be a referral from the Court
- breach of undertaking
- failure to pay debts
- failure to keep beneficiaries updated in probate, or incorrectly conducting probate

It is fair to say that the majority of reports of misconduct are received from third party lay persons. Consumers of legal services, if complaining about their own solicitor, must go through the Legal Ombudsman first. They decide whether the issue was one of poor service or not, and whether it also amounted to an issue of misconduct before making a referral.

This system is quite complex for a lay person, but there have been controversies in alleged overcharging by solicitors. We saw earlier in this Part of the book, the development and timeline of some of the major pieces of legislation in legal services. There were overcharging scandals in the 1980s which led to the introduction of the Council for Licensed Conveyancers and, in the Courts and Legal Services Act 1990, complaint handling and costs provisions for legal services. Some complaint and misconduct matters have been so serious in legal services, the response has been direct legislation.

We have to bear in mind the potential power of a legal adviser and the checks and balances that may be required on their influence, when we discuss the reporting of misconduct. The SRA takes reports from a range of sources, and practitioners may be surprised by who gets in touch with the regulator.

Less commonly than consumers, but still fairly regularly, the SRA may be contacted by other state institutions, such as the police and other regulators, to report issues of misconduct. This might be about the solicitor's behaviour, such as behaviour in court, at the police station, or with another professional. The SRA spends a great deal of time and money in responding to and investigating all of the reports received.

Unfortunately, and from time to time, the police contact the SRA to highlight serious issues, and allegations of crimes concerning solicitors. These can include issues of fake claims, money laundering, fake law firms, scams, and fraud. In these instances, law firms responsible are often investigated by the SRA.

The question of whether to report another professional can be a complex one. Solicitors are expected to uphold the rule of law and protect the reputation of legal services for the benefit of society.

The question becomes more complex when solicitors and other legal professionals are asked about reporting other solicitors, perhaps from other firms, or even in relation to matters outside their practice. Maintaining professional standards and the reputation of the profession is paramount for some solicitors. The SRA regularly receives letters from solicitors advising that they have a policy of not reporting their fellow professional, but in this case they must because the action taken has either seriously adversely affected their client, in a way which also amounts to a breach of the rules, or is in another way a fundamental breach of the rules of professional conduct.

Serious breach and self-reporting is discussed further in Part 5 of this book.

Complaint handling, customer service, and reporting

Complaint handling

Do we think good complaint handling or even having a complaints procedure is part of professionalism? Professional bodies usually provide some form of redress, or there is often another redress body available for those with a complaint.

As an extension to the question above, we might also ask whether being cheerful with customers is also part of professionalism. The writer has had this debate with a number of people after meeting solicitors who were extremely direct with their clients, but the clients loved the straightforward advice. Traditional meanings of 'good customer service' might translate differently when dealing with serious advice-giving professions, when understanding the weight of the subject matter. We have said elsewhere in the book that individuals often approach solicitors when they are at difficult times in their lives. Demonstrating gravitas in advice and approach can also be important, alongside showing your individual personality, and we have covered individualism in professional practice earlier in this Part of the book.

Below are some pointers the writer produced for new solicitors on the Practice Skills Course in 2017 about complaint handling:

> 'It is important to be open and accountable when dealing with a complaint.
>
> If you are dealing with a complaint on the telephone, start by acknowledging the situation, and considering immediately what you can do to put it right. Sometimes, simply listening and acknowledging can calm or diffuse a situation.
>
> When dealing with a complaint in writing, make sure you have conducted your investigation first, unless there are immediate steps you need to take, or can take. You may need to acknowledge the complaint and say you will revert to the complainant after you have completed your investigation, but if there are immediate actions you can take, this can be the time to take them, and say that is what you are doing. If you intend to revert to the complainant, after your investigation give a timescale, for example 14 days.
>
> Start by acknowledging their correspondence and concerns, explaining your understanding of each concern in detail. Next, address each point of concern in writing, explaining what happened and your investigation. Say sorry if you need to. Otherwise, frame your response; you might say "I am sorry you feel this way, but...", or "I have reviewed the situation and on this occasion I feel we have acted appropriately because."
>
> If you do need to compensate the customer, consider them within the compensation. Sometimes our compensation is monetary when it should be a different solution or a thoughtful gift. What solution can you find that would please them in some way? Also, how can you resolve the situation with the customer so they are happy going forward? Can you find a long term solution; for example if the customer would like to be kept up to date, will you agree a reasonable schedule to do so?
>
> However, you should be fair and proportionate, we can all overcompensate clients, or commit to doing too much for them because they complain. It is important to be pragmatic in your overall solution and consider what is reasonable for you and the firm overall. For example, agreeing to an update schedule with a client that you cannot keep to is not reasonable for the firm, and in the end will not please the client if you cannot achieve it. Ensure you have a strong and grounded sense of what you can achieve and what would be fair to the client as well.
>
> Many practices record complaint outcomes and look for continuous improvement. See a complaint as a chance to learn and you might find something that takes you in a new direction.'

EXERCISES FOR DISCUSSION IN YOUR FIRM:

Conduct these exercises with your team:

Exercise 1

Discussion: Look at the list of common reported matters under 'Ethics and Reporting'. Which of these would you report a fellow solicitor for?

Problem solving: Can you think of alternative solutions to the above issues, rather than the SRA receiving hundreds of reports? What action would you take if there was no Solicitors Regulation Authority?

This problem-solving exercise is not designed to prevent or discourage reporting to the regulator, it is however designed to inspire you to think about different forms of redress, which regulatory, consumer, or other bodies might be appropriate to approach in different situations, and what other solutions you can find. This all helps us knit together a picture of the different solutions available to clients and society, of the institutional responses to different problems, and how our rights can be expressed in a variety of different ways.

Exercise 2

The following issues are common reports to the SRA. Review the reports and debate the following solutions within your team:

Common Report: A person receives a debt collection letter from a solicitor. They complain to the SRA that the solicitor has taken unfair advantage.

Proposed solution: All persons receiving a solicitor letter regarding their debt should be given standard information from the state concerning sources of help and advice available and explaining the limitations of the assistance the solicitor acting for the other side can give.

Common Report: A person instructs a solicitor, but the solicitor fees are too expensive.

Proposed solution: Solicitor charges – these should be fixed at a set % of the amount the transaction is worth or what is recovered.

Even if you do not agree with this idea – run the idea through – what would that do to charges in different areas of law and/or the profitability of your firm?

Exercise 3

This exercise follows on from Exercises 1 and 2 and is also to debate with your team.

The question for debate is:

Do you think we need a Code of Conduct or other set of rules?

Refer your team to the scenarios in Exercise 2. Explain that this is just an exercise and not reality. You are ten years in the future and instead of using rules and regulations the regulators have introduced set ways of working, and standard information for all clients.

For example, the client care requirements in the Standards and Regulations have been abolished, and all law firms are instead required to charge at fixed percentages, providing standard information to clients approved by the state. The standard information outlines each stage of their matter.

Do your team think this idea would work? What would be the outcomes? Can your team think of any other requirements in the Standards and Regulations that could be removed in a similar way?

'The reasonable man' in professional regulation

Professional regulation may have the same basis as other areas of law for considering how 'the reasonable man' or 'the average man' would act. For this section, we must put to one side questions of specific conduct. The reasonable man is often invoked in different areas of law with specific issues in mind such as dishonesty, negligence and criminal behaviour. However there is a broader role for the reasonable man than just those concepts and the same is true of bounds of regulation.

We can see the legislation and concept of professional behaviour has built parameters of regulation, including:

- requirements for admission and maintaining businesses
- detailed regulatory standards governing general and specific circumstances
- disciplinary requirements
- requirements for closure or exiting the profession, including closure by an authority

Of course, these are all areas that operate in the public interest. If we asked the public what they expected, not from the solicitor, *but from the regulator*, we might hypothesise they would say:

- action when needed
- preventing harm
- looking after consumer interests

We can see all of these points embodied in the regulatory standards provided by the regulators. We can also see consideration of the issues of dishonesty, negligence, and criminal behaviour, which form backdrops to the regulatory system; each with its own solution. For example, dishonesty might result in a prosecution before the Solicitors Disciplinary Tribunal, and possibly intervention into a practice. Negligence might result in advice from a caseworker at the SRA to take legal advice, or may result in a sanction against the practitioner or firm (which could even go before the Tribunal), dependent on the seriousness. Criminal behaviour has consequences for a practitioner's Practising Certificate, as we will see in later Parts of the book, and again, can result in internal sanctions or prosecution.

The reasonable man then has an influence in taking society's (non-political) expectations and placing them at the heart of the regulatory system. The regulatory system as designed has a great deal of consumer fairness; there has been a clear attempt to balance the status, influence, and power of the solicitor and The Law Society as a whole, with a system designed to monitor and ensure the behaviour of the solicitor.

We can see many of SRA Standards and Regulations are formulated around consumer protection. From client care regulations to taking unfair advantage, in a sense they protect the average man or consumer from the additional knowledge and ability of the professional lawyer.

Additionally, the concept extends into professional negligence. How would the reasonable solicitor have behaved in the circumstances, given their training and knowledge? Sometimes we can see that poor service or negligence is so bad as to amount to misconduct and warrant regulatory action alongside what might be a negligence claim or decision for poor service by the Ombudsman. In these cases we are saying the position has gone beyond the decision making of a reasonable solicitor, in one or more areas covered by the Code of Conduct or other rules in force. For this reason all of the rules, or Standards, are important.

There are sometimes regulatory prosecutions of solicitors or other professionals working within legal services which relate to the concept of the reasonable man. We can see cases in which professionals exercising their professional legal skill or managerial or business skills (in which they may be highly trained), may also relate to the reasonableness of their actions in exercising that skill or judgement. We see increasing numbers of non-lawyers working in law firms and as partners, or otherwise occupying senior positions in law firms, as a result of Alternative Business Structures. These partners and others may need their professionalism and reasonableness to be considered during any investigation and intended prosecution; judging them by the standard or expectation of a solicitor may not be correct. They may need to be considered with reference to the behaviour of the reasonable professional within their field. We should also note that 'professionalism' has been extended to certain types of job role, but not to others. This distinction may not be fair, given the expectations of qualification levels for some job roles, and the bodies of empirical work, research, and skill that can be taught and learned in these areas. There are reasonable approaches within a number of areas of business, which do not have representative bodies or a professional status at this point in time.

We must remember now that ABS have been introduced, and we are looking at solicitors working with outside businesses, that solicitors and other legal professionals have a very different educational qualification to other professionals. Many other professionals may be trained in business or specific roles within that context. The reasonable man on the Clapham omnibus might even perceive the difference between the two roles, their respective professional training and knowledge, and their consequent ability, or decision making.

However, those within these new non lawyer roles within law firms, or working alongside freelance solicitors, do not necessarily have the same training in solicitor professional conduct as their solicitor counterparts. Do the new members of a law firm team who occupy these positions, *need* a similar level of professional training and knowledge of the rules of professional conduct as trainee solicitors?

If we take the rules of professional conduct themselves; we could ask whether they are based on either the voice of:

- the reasonable solicitor
- the reasonable man as a solicitor
- the reasonable man

We may find different regulatory expectations within the rules that reflect all of those different voices, and we have seen earlier in this Part of the book that there are many different pushes and pulls on the SRA, including the professional regulated community, the broader public interest and the consumers. Some of those different interests are reflected neatly in the different voices of the Regulatory Objectives and The Law Society. If we based the rules on the voice of the reasonable man, the professional knowledge and experience of the solicitor would be lost. The reasonable man as the solicitor may place more emphasis on the personal and private distinction in the rules and there may be more scope for non-lawyers. What we have seen through time might have been the reasonable solicitor, and certainly it is sometimes easier for solicitors and those in the legal services market to find their ethical perspective and compass through that voice, which is a voice the regulated community understands and accepts. We discuss culture further in Part 2 of this book.

The SRA consults with solicitors about the rules; their history is based on development by The Law Society over many decades. The Law Society of course exercising the role of representing and being the voice of the profession. The SRA does not take that role, but the two organisations are still connected and the rules come from this historical development, even in their current form. You might say the rules then reflect the solicitor community and their view of the requirements for the profession, along with a reflection of consumer need.

In the writer's view, the rules have not yet fully considered the new or potentially new persons in the Alternative Business Structures or unregulated businesses, who work within legal services. From the courses run, it is clear sometimes the surprise of such persons at the strictness of the requirements and potential consequences of a breach. There are limited examples of similar requirements and serious consequences in other business sectors, but there are also limited examples of holding client monies, providing access to the state's functions, and holding constitutional roles in other sectors.

The serious breach courses discuss how we feel about certain scenarios, within a safe environment. The writer uses her professional training from her master's degree (as a management consultant) to deliver those courses, and readers are asked not to attempt the same themselves. This is for two reasons, firstly describing the delivery of the courses themselves is beyond the scope of this book and copyright belongs with the writer. Secondly, the writer has been specifically trained, and within that has completed her own independent work to design and deliver the courses.

The scenarios on the course are intended to help us judge both:

1. *How we feel about a scenario* – this is helpful from a personal and a CPD perspective. Personally it allows us to both ethically judge the scenario and explore how we feel about it, what would change if we changed small parts of the scenario, and how we would feel if it happened to us. From a CPD perspective, completing a number of scenarios allows us practice in making such decisions and to explore the rules relating to those scenarios and their application.
2. *How others feel about a scenario* – this is the reasonable man part of the scenario. We might be the reasonable man, others around us might be, or we might all be. Those on the course work in small groups and discuss the scenarios. It should be remembered that persons are put into groups randomly and do not know the others in the group. They are sometimes encouraged not only to make decisions on an ethical basis, but *also* to take different perspectives or challenge assumptions to see if they can change anyone's mind! Some groups make quick decisions, others work through the scenarios slowly considering all perspectives and whether there are arguments for and against. In each case, we examine the scenarios both at face value and, on occasion, add additional facts in to see if helps us make a decision.

We must always appreciate that any description of events could be incorrect, but in the case of the scenarios, it is given to be correct as stated.

Some of the scenarios the writer has used in the courses are in Part 8 of this book. Try to consider them from your own perspective and the perspective of the reasonable man.

Governance and decision-making

Maintaining professionalism within your firm and meeting the various legal, regulatory and insurance obligations you are required to meet, requires firms to have the capability to investigate matters themselves.

The roles of COLP and COFA within law firms, and MLRO or MLCO within many professional services firms, are roles of statutory responsibility, with the requirement or implicit requirement of specific knowledge and skills. In all these cases there is the underlying regulatory or law enforcement interest and requirements which raise the awareness of the seriousness of decision making in some circumstances and put the onus on the firm to make the correct decision and record it appropriately.

These roles are not simply decision-making in isolation, the required seniority of the roles implies a leadership element to the position, and that decision-making will be taken which will influence the implementation of standards within the firm. Indeed, the roles of COLP and COFA are required to be senior members of staff with oversight of the whole business and the ability to themselves assure the regulator of the implementation of regulatory requirements.

On the other hand, decisions within law firms can be subject to the overarching interests of the firm. For example, under company law the Directors have obligations to the business. Governance structures, partnership interests, and the roles of those involved in investigations and decision making can all play a part in how we consider potential breaches and how to solve them.

We might ask whether there is an inherent conflict of interest between implementing the compliance requirements and regulatory standards implemented by the regulator, and serving the overarching commercial interests of the law firm. The roles of COLP and COFA were introduced alongside Outcomes Focused Regulation in 2011 which was meant to allow a greater freedom in practice and perhaps go some way to defining the scope of the role of COLP and COFA (for example, in that implementation are we still compliant?). However the role is increasingly a governance and directional issue; we have to ask to what extent are the rules and regulations setting and defining the direction of the business – from marketing (for example in the Transparency Rules), through to decision making around new areas of work (as defined by the terms of regulation and the scope of work permitted under a firm's authorisation).

MLROs and MCLOs may also find themselves in a similar position to COLP and COFA. Imagining the firm structure now includes *four individuals* who have senior management responsibility for compliance and directing the business in a compliant fashion is evidence of the incredible regulatory burden placed on law firms and the restriction on their practice. Taking an alternative point of view to the regulator or law enforcement could be a prosecutable offence under the Money Laundering Regulations 2017.

As law firms have grown so has the need for knowledge in areas which are not traditionally within a lawyer's knowledge. Individuals within information technology, learning and development, human resources, finance and accounting and other areas which sit alongside the business of law. This is in common with many other businesses; for example a car manufacturer would also have HR functions, IT professionals, expertise in learning and development, and finance and accounting, as well as other departmental functions.

Traditionally known as 'support functions', there are specific skill sets, learning, knowledge, and professionalism in these areas in their own right. Discussion about the role of these external forces is important in their professional development. For example, discussions about the role of human resources can mirror that of the compliance department – to what extent does compliance or HR direct the business? We can see the rise of 'HR Business Partners'; the terminology intended to indicate that the HR professional work, alongside the business to achieve the results the business wants. We have to make a similar, but ultimately different case for compliance. Compliance cannot direct the strategy of the business; that must sit with the appropriate governance structure, but regulatory requirements and professional standards must be adhered to in guiding the business, and in some cases determining business structure and model.

The professionalism of solicitors and their constitutional role means this is a highly regulated space. However the influence from external forces and the growth of law firms as businesses means these external experts come with their own training, which may not have included the standards set by the Solicitors Regulation Authority or The Law Society. Accordingly, decisions can be made and stances taken that may not reflect regulatory requirements, but this might be completely unintentional and might reflect the standards of their own training or professional qualifications.

Similarly, the business must look after itself, and put itself forward. Some of the parts of the business may be employed to defend the business or safeguard it from external threats. This can include some of the support functions above. The current SRA rules require the business to report serious breaches, and it can be prosecuted for failure to do so. Similarly, businesses can be caught by the wide wording in the Proceeds of Crime Act 2002, requiring firms and individuals to report their concerns if they suspect money laundering.

Ensuring and possibly assuring effective decision making becomes essential for meeting the regulatory expectation of professional, balanced decision making, and avoiding the consequences of failing to do so. It may be essential to consider your governance requirements within a firm. Some are prescribed for Alternative Business Structures by the Legal Services Act 2007, but all may need to look carefully at the requirements, and decision making may need to be cascaded within the business. It may also be important to take independent legal advice and decide the formality of the structure and authorisation level within the business for doing so.

Producing a governance plan and decision making structure is not only part of day to day management it can also be a form of contingency planning for reporting.

We consider serious breach and reporting in Part 5 of the book.

EXERCISE FOR DISCUSSION AND IMPLEMENTATION IN YOUR FIRM:

Exercise 1 – Decision making review

Consider how decisions are made in your firm.

Do you have a central committee (for a small firm) or series of committees (for a large firm)?

Are your committees assured in any way?

Is there any other means by which decisions are taken outside of this structure, for example by your COLP, COFA, or MLRO?

There may also be individual job descriptions that allow for specific decision making, for example by:

1. Partners
2. Different departments
3. HR, IT
4. Compliance.

The below exercise will help you consider how these decisions might work in an investigation context. Try to run the exercise a few times with different scenarios and with different teams.

What can you learn, are decisions going to the right place, and do you need to make any changes?

None of us are infallible; try to remember when running the exercises below. Can your firm offer a sympathetic ear to those who have made a mistake? (Ensure this is within permitted bounds; some individuals in some situations may need legal advice.)

Exercise 2 – Investigation Review

If you had a breach:

- Who would investigate?
- Does the investigator need a deputy, perhaps in another part of the organisation?
- What would they look for?
- Do you have a formal investigatory HR or management procedure to follow that might be suitable to use?
- When would the COLP and COFA be notified?
- Will the investigation be formal, and would it be notified to the persons involved?
- What decisions need to be made and who would make them?
- Who would take charge of communications with the subject?
- Would the firm need external legal advice and support and who would provide that advice?
- Would the individual need external legal advice and support and who would provide that advice? Does the firm offer insurance or legal advice and support for individuals?
- Do other external parties need to be notified, such as the SRA?
- Who needs to sign off on the decision-making process and take account of the perspective of the individual, the firm, and the management?
- Are there conflicts of interest within the decision making and can these be resolved through independent advice?

You might need the input of HR if there are personnel decisions, the COLP or COFA if matters may need reporting, and the partners or governance structure of the firm.

Using the above exercise and working backwards, who needs to make the decisions, what support do they need, and how can you achieve that balance in investigation and decision making?

We discuss the requirements for reporting in Part 5 which you will find helpful in exploring the SRA requirements. Do not forget the requirements for the NCA and that other regulators (such as accountancy regulators) may have different requirements.

Exercise 3 – Mock Investigation

Conduct your own mock investigation. Produce find a fake a scenario from this book, examples in Part 8, and investigate or discuss how you would investigate within your firm. Implement the results in your procedures if you learn lessons.

For example:

Exercise scenario: There is an allegation that a junior fee earner in your Personal Injury team has misled a client.

The allegation here could go a number of different ways; it may not be true, may be true, or there may be an alternative explanation. Test your decision making processes to ensure you have the skill sets and procedures you need to investigate and make decisions.

Exercise 4 – Decision Making Review Part 2

Consider the questions and scenario above. Who drives the investigation and where should that responsibility be placed? What is or would be the role of the management structure and governance in decision making, direction, and oversight?

Freelance Solicitors and Unregulated Practices

We can contrast the position and governance of the regulated firm with that of a freelance solicitor. The freelance solicitor may work alongside different businesses in different ways and has the freedom to practise alongside different commercial interests. This agility may allow the freelancer the opportunity to take on work not open to, or more difficult for, a corporate regulated firm.

Similarly, solicitors can now work within unregulated practices as solicitors, providing services to members of the public, as long as they are not conducting reserved work, and we explore the position related to forms of professional practice available, in Part 2 of this book.

In both of these cases, businesses could work with or employ a solicitor, but without the business itself being regulated. This means those decision-making structures discussed above do not exist in the same way, and the governance of the delivery of legal services and the compliance issues are left solely to the individual solicitor and his or her judgement. This position is mirrored in the gathering of information for the annual renewal of the Practising Certificate and annual return; at the time of writing the unregulated practice did not have to provide information to the SRA on the annual return. This is a dramatic difference in the level of information provided to the SRA by regulated practices; the information available about a regulated practice and the record keeping will become far more. This could provide an important distinction in the ability to prosecute, and in the decision making in doing so. Our decisions can all be influenced in different ways. The provision of additional information in a situation could make the difference in the human decision making to take investigations forward; we often may look for additional information to confirm if we are not sure. Regulated practices could find themselves more often under investigation and more likely to be prosecuted if they are, as a result of the additional information they have provided. The annual return is covered in more detail in Part 2 of this book.

Unregulated practices will owe some duties to the delivery of legal services, and the SRA could for example pursue unadmitted persons 'working' for the solicitor under the Solicitors Act 1974, s 43. The unregulated practice could also owe some duties to the regulator, and would need to support the solicitor in their compliance. Some of the regulator's powers, such as the imposition of conditions, or the objection to individual involvement in legal business, could be used to restrict conducting business with unregulated practices. Unregulated practices may still need to be aware of their own compliance in this respect.

Checks and balances in legal regulation

The Legal Services Board is set up to provide oversight and structure to the legal regulators. As we have seen earlier in this Part of the book, the Legal Services Act 2007 provides the regulatory objectives for the Board and the legal regulators. The Board was established following a review of the legal services market by Sir David Clementi, and earlier reviews over a number of years by a number of different bodies.

The legal regulators have extraordinary levels of power. The Law Society (and associated structures, such as the SRA) arguably controls access to the courts and judicial system, along with the Bar Council (and its associated structures). These are functions of the state, and while responsible for the regulation of solicitors, the structures also speak for, represent, and provide guidance to society in a variety of ways.

Important checks and balances in the regulatory functions include:

1. The division of the representative and regulatory structures put in place by the Legal Services Act 2007
2. The court structure. Solicitors are officers of the court and the court can direct their behaviour.
3. The Legal Services Board reviews the rules and regulations provided by the legal services regulators and sets an agenda for the legal services sector as a whole.

The importance of the smaller or alternative regulator also cannot be understated. They provide both an alternative form of regulation facilitating competition, and an alternative perspective and representation for distinct communities with different qualification pathways, as a form of democratic participation in legal services.

Solicitors should welcome these many and varied checks and balances as an expression of a democratic society and value the participation of those within legal services, as well as those using legal services.

EXERCISE FOR USE IN YOUR FIRM: DYSTOPIAN FUTURE

Discuss the following scenario in your firm:

Dystopian Future

British history remains as it always was, including today's current situation.

It is now 2055, and there has been a coup based on a political ideology.

Legal services are now delivered as follows:

1. Consumers now pay a fixed price for 'property transfer' rather than conveyancing.
2. Certain low level criminal offences are charged and convicted by police without representation or involvement of the Court.
3. Personal injury is now payable on a fixed fee without representation, for all matters including death.
4. There are no employment rights; jobs are allocated on the basis of grades from school and workable for life.

Legal representation is very rare and must be paid for; there is no help from the state. The cost of becoming a lawyer is beyond the means of the average person and it is regarded as a dangerous job.

The government decides that property will no longer be held in the same way and all those occupying property will need to pay part of their wages in a ground tax. Persons occupying any property can also be moved at will.

You are an elderly solicitor with a team working with you (your team sat around you). What do you do? Discuss your course of action with your team. How do you all feel?

Reflect with your team after your discussion:

How do you and your whole team (currently, outside the above scenario) protect the rights of your clients, the wider public, the country's institutions?

Discussion points:

- The constitutional role of solicitors and other institutions in legal services
- Protections of rights and individual freedoms, and the role of solicitors in delivering those rights and freedoms
- Your personal responsibilities (possibly for life)
- Your role as a business within law
- The exercise of regulatory power in legal services, and who exercises it?

- Conditions imposed on the practice of law (for example in legal services)
- Criminal offences being a bar to practising law
- The rights to practice of those who have been disciplined or struck off
- The cost of legal services – should the market be regulated to ensure access?
- The importance of the role of parts of the business regarded as 'support functions' or the role of unadmitted persons in a solicitor firm.

Importantly how do you feel about reporting serious breaches within your firm to the regulator?

What can or should you do in your firm to reflect the above?

- Do we need to see more marketing of solicitors on the basis of protecting rights? Is that justified?
- Are consumers of legal services really consumers or are they clients exercising their rights?

Solicitor Continuous Professional Development (CPD)

Professionalism and professional standards have to be maintained, and so far in this book we have focused largely on examining the rulebook and reporting to provide that solution. The other means of delivering those ongoing standards is the continuous education and professional development of members of the profession. CPD is not prescribed for solicitors in that it does not require the completion of further qualifications after set periods of time.

Through the prism of CPD, we can see the development of professional standards through experience of the individuals, and their self-reflection on expected standards, norms, and client service or interaction. The CPD system is currently based on the personal view of the solicitor, requiring them to consider their own requirements for personal learning and development and their own view of how that should be implemented. This happens continuously and solicitors are expected to maintain their own personal learning and development plans.

Previously solicitors were required to complete 16 hours of CPD per year, some of which was required to be in their area of law so as to update and maintain their skills and knowledge. The position changed during 2015 to a personal reflection system. As we will see in Part 7, the system has not been effective in all firms as some solicitors have not kept up to date with the CPD requirements without minimum hours. As a result there may be a requirement for ten-yearly revalidation.

Going back to the current position, at the annual Practising Certificate renewal, the solicitor is required to sign off that they have considered this learning and development and taken appropriate steps to maintain their competence during the year. The requirements which set out competence are known as the Competence Statement. Partners and senior staff may have gone beyond the Competence

Statement dependent on their experience and qualifications; this position is known as mastery. In which case they are asked to consider how they can develop their own knowledge and skill set even further.

This system is designed so all solicitors are encouraged to take responsibility for their own learning and development - indeed this is a requirement under the Competence Statement. The system has benefits in that staff can be more motivated when they are in control of their own competence, and have a say in how they can contribute to organisational goals.

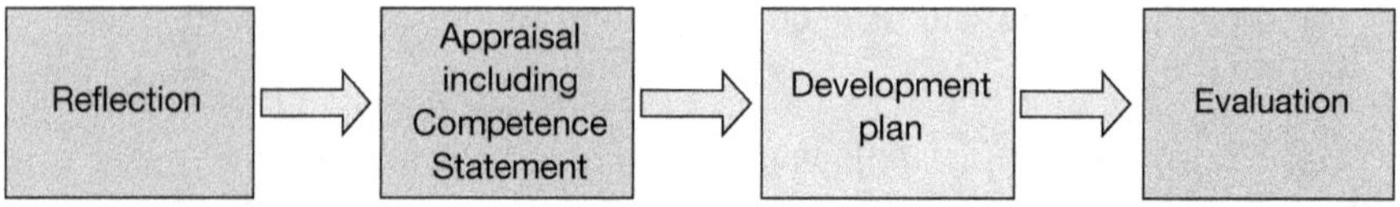

All solicitors should reflect on, and demonstrate their competence in:

- ethics, professionalism and judgement;
- technical legal practice;
- managing themselves and their own work;
- working with other people

> The writer's consultancy has worked with firms on their responses to the Competence Statement since it was introduced in 2015 and has provided the following advice:
>
> > 'We often suggest solicitors should run their own learning and development plans, with oversight from senior staff. Individual plans for solicitors can contribute to a wider learning and development plan for the firm, which covers the training the whole firm will undertake. Of course, individuals may select to undertake their own individual training as well, sponsored by the firm.
> >
> > We suggested firms and individual solicitors review their learning and development plans in May, August and November. This was done by asking them to evaluate both their progress against their learning outcomes, and the training they have undertaken to date. If training has not met the learning outcomes, learners were asked to consider re-planning their next steps.
> >
> > Firms were encouraged to plan yearly updates to:
> >
> > - review the progress made in learning objectives for the firm and individuals;
> > - ensure all plans are up to date;
> > - make recommendations for next year

This was expected to take place usually in August before SRA PC renewal so the firm can confidently sign off learning and development obligations as part of the renewal.'

BELOW IS SOME ADVICE AND GUIDANCE THE WRITER PRODUCED IN 2015 CONCERNING THE NEW APPROACH TO CPD

New SRA approach to CPD

What is it?

The SRA have altered CPD.

Previously a solicitor needed 16 hours accredited CPD per year.

Now they must demonstrate their competence against a 'Competence Statement'. The number of hours to achieve this is not specified.

Why alter it?

There was no evidence the system produced ongoing competence in lawyers. The 16 hours was a tick box system. 'Accredited' CPD was provided by commercial training providers but was not policed.

When is it implemented?

The SRA removed accredited CPD in November 2014, meaning any training now counts toward CPD.

The new system of demonstrating competence is available to firms voluntarily from 1 April 2015, and becomes mandatory from November 2016.

Firms and lawyers not wishing to demonstrate competence yet can continue with doing 16 hours until it becomes mandatory.

Anything else?

Yes. The SRA expect it to be employer led, so firms should make decisions about implementation for employees.

The SRA say solicitors should reflect on their own competence, plan their actions to plug gaps, and reflect on how well the training has gone. Firms may be doing this through appraisal and other HR mechanisms.

Full records need to be kept, and firms will be asked to make an annual declaration of compliance.

If there is a regulatory problem which suggests an issue with competence, the SRA will be looking to see how the firm has complied. Non-compliance in this scenario would be an aggravating factor and likely to lead to enforcement action.

At the time of writing there were plans for ten-year revalidation of qualifications for solicitors. The qualification and CPD scheme is a key part of the solicitor professional status and practising status. Ensure you take the time to complete your CPD and reflect on your learning and development to date. If you are subject to conditions, complete the same, but also take account of why you became subject to the condition and how.

EXERCISE: REFLECTION AND PLANNING – THE TEA TASTING

This exercise is designed to help you reflect on your own learning and development needs and plan them.

You can use this exercise yourself or ask your staff to complete to complete their own learning and development.

Firstly:

Reflect on your job role and your performance:

How are you performing?

What have you learned recently?

What would you do differently next year?

Identify your development needs:

How do I do this better next time?

Consider a scenario where you could have performed better. How would you do this better next time?

Now we need to plan the requirements for our CPD this year. Don't forget to take account of feedback from others and be creative in how you obtain your CPD.

This example below is from a person who would like to learn more about tea. They have identified their goal, their activity and learning method, and the outcome they would like to reach. They have also identified the timescale by which the outcome should be met. Once they have met their outcome they can add more information to the plan, concluding that action, and considering the next steps.

See whether you can use the table on the next page to plan your CPD and learning and development needs.

Goal	Steps	How will I acquire this knowledge?	What will I gain?	Complete by	Completed? Y/N Date	Evaluation. Did I learn what I wanted?
Learn about tea	Step 1: Expand knowledge of different teas	Tea tasting / training course	Knowledge of more types of tea and their tastes	May 2021		
	Step 2: Understand tea cultivation	Internet research/ reading	Basic understanding of tea cultivation, plus ability to plan step 3	April 2021	Y End April 2021	Basic understanding of tea cultivation. Understand hot + humid climate. There is a tea garden in Cornwall. More research needed. Visit tea garden.
	Step 3: Understand tea cultivation	Visit tea garden/hands on experience	Understand tea cultivation in UK and method used in garden	June 2021		
Review timetable. Outcomes will be reviewed in May, August, and September.	**Review Outcomes:** Review completed in May. Step 2 complete and Step 3 added.					

Comparative Standards of Regulation and Professional Practice:

Qualification and CPD

Requirements in Scotland, Northern Ireland and other bailiwicks reflect a similar approach to England and Wales, with a two tier approach; using solicitors for general legal advice and barristers (or Advocates in Scotland) for representation before the higher courts.

Regulation of lawyers across the EU is similar to the regulation of solicitors and barrister in England and Wales. In some EU countries there are separate systems of lawyer for transactional work, and others for court work or representation, in other countries there is one type of lawyer (or one main type of lawyer). Many of the EU countries allow qualification through University degrees, and the case of *Morgenbesser* allowed a person with a three-year law degree, plus work experience in France to complete a legal thesis in Italy to finish her qualification as an Italian

Avvocato. Other regulatory requirements for entry to the legal services market include:

- master's degrees
- extended university study
- PhD study
- work experience in the legal departments of the civil service or equivalent (sometimes extensive)

Comparative standards were expected to be set for the exercise of legal professionalism across the EU, prior to Brexit, and Britain was no exception. Law Societies, or equivalents, set standards, including entry and exit to the market, and Codes of Conduct across the continent. The societies have taken on the role 'Competent Authorities' within the EU, becoming responsible for admission and regulation standards. Similar structures exist in the USA, Australia and Canada.

The EU provided for the freedom of movement across the bloc, along with the freedom to establish businesses on the basis of equivalent qualifications. In response, The Law Society (as it was then) introduced a new form of practice lawyer called 'Registered European Lawyer', which we discussed earlier in this Part of the book, and we discuss further in Part 2. This position is now changing because of Britain's departure from the EU.

Similarly, solicitors from the UK were allowed to practice in the European Union as solicitors of England and Wales; including by establishing their own businesses. Persons in this position were (and may still be) subject to dual deontology; the position of being regulated by more than one regulator, including overseas.

If we contrast the position of the European Union's solicitors with those from elsewhere, the SRA also has another status known as 'Registered Foreign Lawyer' which allows those registered as lawyers in other countries to practice law in England and Wales while retaining their home title. However in this case RFLs have restricted practising rights in England and Wales; they cannot practice alone and their work should be supervised. Again, further discussion is available in Part 2 of this book.

EXERCISE: QUALIFICATIONS

The qualifications system in England and Wales is complex and varied. We have school qualifications, NVQs, university qualifications, and professional qualifications. There are in fact even more than this!

What qualifications do you and your colleagues have? What level are you qualified to? Don't forget that experience counts. For example, NVQs are based on experience, and take you to degree level and beyond.

Do you have anybody with the following qualifications or statuses?

- NVQs in Law?
- More than three- five years' experience in law?

- University degrees in law? What level?
- Post graduate qualifications in law?
- Barristers, solicitors, CILEx, licensed conveyancers, notaries, or other legally qualified professionals?
- Qualified paralegals?
- Accountants?
- Business managers?
- Degrees in other subjects?
- Tax advisers?
- Financial advisers?
- Pensions qualifications?
- Overseas qualifications or experience?

Allow your team the opportunity to show off their qualifications and experience. What does their qualification entail and include? Praise your staff and congratulate them on their qualifications and experience.

Discuss with your staff – how do they feel about their professionalism? Are they subject to more than one system of regulation, and what is the difference?

We often overlook the skills and experience of those around us in law because some legal work is reserved. Consider the qualifications of those in your team on a qualification levels chart from the government. Consider whether others have equivalent qualifications and how they can be best used.

Discussion or reflection point:

You can discuss this with your solicitor colleagues or reflect personally.

Should solicitor or legal CPD lead to further formal qualifications?

Regulation by Code

The SRA is a regulator that, as we have seen, relies on regulation by Code or standards, which has historically relied on reports into the regulator. It is a professional regulator providing a professional route that encompasses a specific title, educational standards, and disciplinary measures. This operates in common with other professional forms of regulation including doctors and other medical professionals and chartered accountants. Other regulators by code include specific industry regulators, such as in financial services. In some cases there are voluntary schemes of regulation by code; examples of this include management consultants and drinks licensing.

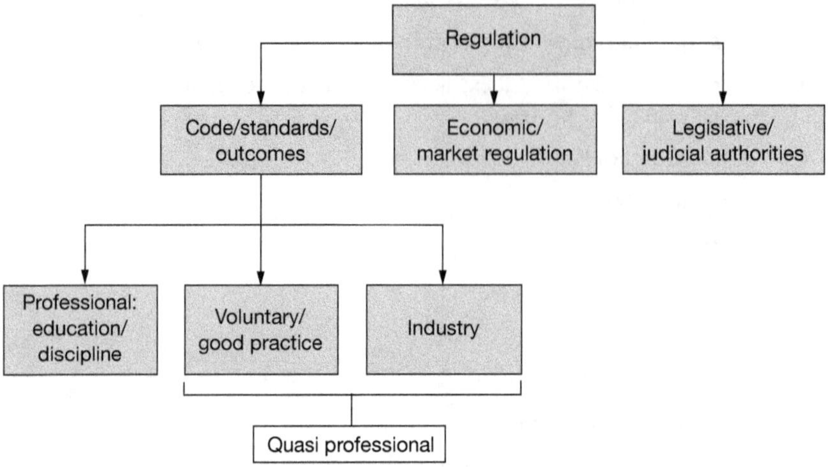

Of course, there can be other types of regulator. These include economic or market regulators, who regulate by considering prices for consumers, financial investments needed in infrastructure, and insurance or capital (monetary) requirements. Other legislative and judicial authorities include regulators which are established and operate primarily through statutory powers, but without their own Code of standards to govern those they regulate. Examples of this include the education regulators, such as Ofqual and Ofsted. HMRC may also fall into this category, along with local authority regulators and some NHS regulatory bodies that are not regulators of the professions. The writer uses the word 'judicial' as the courts system as a decider of disputes may also perform a regulatory role of sorts. The Employment Tribunal may operate in this way, as an overseer of industrial relations for workplaces in England and Wales. Of course, we may say their remit is far wider than a professional regulator and would be too unwieldy for such a body, but the reader is asked to consider the similarities of the judicial function to regulatory decision making and internal sanctions imposed by regulators.

Of course, amongst all of this, it is possible to see some industries as professional in different ways. Management standards for example have developed and grown since the development of modern companies, post 1950, and it is possible to obtain well respected management and business degrees at master's level and beyond, which focus on the proper operation of business, and the implementation of management knowledge and techniques.

The solicitor's profession, in common with other professions, has a specialist tribunal,[4] which operates to oversee the professional discipline of the members and their operation in accordance with the standards or Code in force. Breaches of the Code can if serious enough, lead to removal from the profession. As a specialist Tribunal, the Solicitors Disciplinary Tribunal, has more knowledge and understanding of the legislation, relevant rules and regulations from the SRA which are in force, and a working knowledge of their implementation, than other judicial bodies.

[4] *Bawa-Garba v General Medical Council* [2019] EWCA Civ 1879.

Some regulators also undertake project work alongside standard setting, and this includes projects to improve conditions in their sector; support their sector in its development, or improved experiences for consumers. The regulators do not have an economic remit, so they have no capacity to regulate prices themselves or adopt interventionist strategies which would shape the long term future of the market. Even the introduction of Alternative Business Structures did not cause the market to dramatically alter. The lack of economic intervention for the professional regulators could also be an additional check and balance on the power of both the regulator and the regulated professional community.

Comparative professional practice: management consultants

If we contrast solicitors with management consultants, there is a historical difference. Individuals and businesses have always had interactions with courts and the state and therefore have needed representation and advice. By contrast, modern companies started to develop post-war in the 1950s along with a body of management work and empirical management literature. Management consultants started to develop their own standards of behaviour and expectations in client interaction starting in the 1970s and 1980s and continuing in the present day.

The writer's masters' degree covered the professionalism of consultancy. The types of matters discussed and that the writer learned about during her masters' degree included:

- the composition of a business, the main tasks and goals of each department in a business, and the main challenges in running each department
- challenges with change management and cultural or human behaviour within businesses
- learning, and specifically learning within workplaces; the challenges of professional reflection
- the complexity of businesses (size, departments, authority, and management)
- management prerogative within the business and how this restricts the consultants' freedom and operation
- the client intention, whether the assignment is offered in good faith, or what the true intentions of an assignment might be
- client instructions, the complexity of receiving instructions to start work in a business environment, and the complexity of solving management problems
- consultant ethics in the context of sales, expertise, and the management prerogative; with a particular focus on the consultant relationship with the governance of the business and the limitations of the assignment
- understanding the consultants' own motivation for taking on the work, and declaring conflicts of interest
- consultant qualifications and competence to complete this or related assignments
- managing client expectations before and during an engagement

- establishing authority within an engagement, and how to agree contractual outcomes
- appropriate closure of an assignment once completed

The notable difference is consultants operate without the regulatory rules. There are no client care letters because the consultant can operate in a number of different ways to suit the business. Indeed, consultants are encouraged to develop their own personal style to allow them to help the client in the way that suits the business the best overall. This has the following effects:

- allows the consultant to concentrate on the client business and what is best for the business overall; and
- encourages the client to do the same.

This means in some instances the personal style of the consultant is a consideration for some businesses and will suit some engagements more than others. Most consultants will accept that is the case.

The initial engagement phase is important for the consultant as the main goals of the project should be agreed and discussed. This phase can be very open ended and it is important for the consultant to establish parameters and an initial idea of their approach. This can blur the line from consultancy work if the consultant provides advice. The client should at this stage understand the consultants' scope, intended work, and provide the authority for the consultant to deliver what is needed. The list of factors set out just previously should also be considered, and issues from that list should be raised by the consultant as needed (or even in order!).

Once the above factors have been established *on both sides* (sometimes the consultant takes the lead in managing this discussion), the consultant should agree terms with the client. The discussion and the terms usually establish a clear ethical basis for the engagement and allows a clear debate of the issues.

This initial engagement phase, and the self-awareness of the consultant, are very important. Engagements might fail at this stage, because, for example:

- the consultant feels unable to assist;
- the business might decide that the particular consultants' approach is not the right fit for their business; or
- the business feels that consultancy cannot provide the solution they are looking for.

It is here that we see some of the clearest expressions of consultant ethics. The consultant must clearly be able to add value to a business environment before accepting the engagement and have confidence they can solve the problem posed. A business may have framed a problem in a particular way and be looking for a certain solution. The consultant may not always be aware of or be told about that proposed outcome. In these situations, consultants sometime have to step away if they cannot provide what the business is looking for overall. Similarly, a consultant should also not accept an engagement if the business does not know and take ownership of its own business; the consultant has to work with and alongside the business, rather than taking over.

This can differ to solicitors as the solicitor usually has set transactional outcomes based on legal advice, or on the court system, whereas a consultant operates *within* a range of different businesses, and might offer a range of different solutions. The solicitor would produce a client care letter which specifies the steps of a matter and go through those steps to meet the client outcomes, whereas the consultant would not. For the consultant, the initial engagement, ethical discussion, and meeting allows the client and consultant to understand each other and the full terms of the engagement. The client remains in charge of their business but can specify outcomes. The consultant will specify the solution to reach the outcome.

Some of the writer's clients have limited experience of working with consultants, and often solicitors expect the same service from a consultant that they would from a fellow solicitor. The writer is often asked for a client care letter, and has to explain that the flexible nature of consultancy means we are expected to agree outcomes, boundaries of the assignment, and terms, together at the beginning.

There are also limited forms of informal redress, but consultants usually provide solutions within their contractual terms to provide for concerns to be raised and even suggested outcomes for those concerns. Insurance requirements are also up to the consultant, but again consultants expect each other to be reputable.

There are no consequences from the regulators. Consultants can challenge businesses in unconventional ways, and many do. There is no client care letter, and no third party to complain to; the consultant's reputation rests on their ability to develop a solution to meet the client's needs, and agree that with the client. So far, the main concerns about consultants are questions as to their constitutional position. The question is whether consultant's decision making or recommendations could have such a significant effect on the decision making of businesses, and even countries, that they should be restricted or regulated in their activities.

Management consultants practise as well; their professional practice and style is developed differently from that of solicitors. There is at the moment no handbook, but there might be in the future. Literature on the subject includes discussions of different management interventions, consultant ethics in engagements, and charging for problem solving. There is also a particular problem with the implementation of a suggested solution. Once a consultant has worked with a business to develop a model solution for them, the consultant does not always implement that solution; sometimes that is for the client to take on, unless specifically agreed otherwise and in very clear terms.

An example an engagement might be as follows: consultants attend a meeting with a management team to hear about their issue. There may be a standard response, drawn from empirical management research, or there might be an individual solution. Terms are often agreed at that point, to include charging. Charges would be made for creating and bespoke solution, the creative element of charging is removed if a standard solution is used. The consultant then works within the business to observe, understand, and create the solution. Once the solution is created, the consultant engagement might come to a close.

Management consultants do not then have client care letters, complaints processes, or even minimum terms of insurance. There is very often not a conflict issue to consider. Reputable consultants would consider competence an issue and their practice may concern primarily empirical and peer reviewed management literature. Individuals may have particular expertise in particular areas.

The comparison across to solicitors is quite stark. Solicitors have to provide a lot of information upfront to their client, adhere to minimum terms and conditions of insurance, and adhere to fairly strict rules about their business relationships. However the benefit of being a solicitor is membership of a professional body, regulation and redress for clients, and access to reserved work and to the courts, which gives solicitor practice its specific nature and professional requirements.

EXERCISE: CLIENT CARE

This exercise is suitable for discussion in your firm or for individual reflection.

Consider the discussions of management consultant client care in your firm.

- Do you have commercial clients – do you offer standard solutions to them? Would you benefit from a more creative approach?
- How could you develop your client care for individual clients to be more flexible and creative? Are there any areas where you do not offer standard solutions or where you could develop your approach differently and still be both fair and clear with the client?

If you can, think about how you could expand your client care offering to be more flexible or wider, but within the scope of the rules. Could you deliver a client care 'experience' instead?

The Human Touch

Do we see the professional as a human being?

When the writer first started on her consultancy journey, she was fortunate to meet some solicitors who were starting to develop will writing through automated technology. It is not easy, apparently! The writer was at the time writing and developing her approach to the serious breach courses and the bigger question at that meeting was apparent. It was a question of humanity and human solutions. Can individual solicitors perform to the standard expected of them, and do we see mistakes as a far greater problem in today's society than we ought to?

We have spoken about the reasonable man, and do at other times in this book, but society's expectations can sometimes become flawed in their expectations of solicitors. Expecting 'higher standards' can be too much for some people to bear. Solicitors are no different from other members of society.

People often do want the human touch and experience. It can be incredibly frustrating to deal with a computer system. The writer recently paid for a car parking space next to a hotel for a conference, but later received an automatic fine for not paying. The writer had paid, there was a witness, and a receipt. To complain you had to use a computerised system to select options about what had happened and why, but there was no option to say you had paid. Eventually, after dealing with three or four automated complaint systems and getting nowhere, the writer received a response from a human being stating the fine was wiped.

Sometimes systems can be very sophisticated in their responses, but at other times they can be very difficult to deal with. It is often said in legal policy circles that we approach lawyers at difficult times in our lives, and sympathy might be expected. The experience of the solicitor and their professionalism can be reassuring that we can approach someone who has an answer to the problem.

However, we do see solicitors being penalised for making mistakes, when they are also human. This is also true of the rise in cybercrime or the responsibilities of firms under GDPR. It only takes one mistake in a firm; a click on a link unexpectedly, and a criminal can steal all the data you have.

Human experiences and human professionalism will not go out of fashion, but the professional world and humans giving advice is under threat from automation.

The following excerpts are from a presentation the writer contributed to on digital legal services in 2019

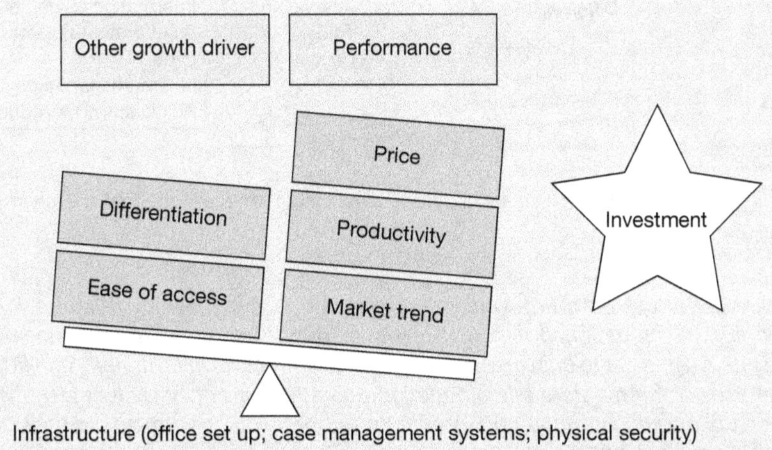

Digital legal services provide important new opportunities for growth and improving existing performance.

Whether it is infrastructure improvements, such as artificial intelligence on case files, facilitating remote working around the world, or differentiating yourself from your competitor by offering clients access to online portals which store their data, many firms are taking the opportunity to digitise their offering.

We are seeing an increased online offering from many large firms. Clients, staff and third parties can keep up to date with information from a transaction as it happens. Using technology means we should see improvements in client satisfaction, competition in the market, and in profits, as firms can charge more for such a service, or strengthen their brand. Productivity can be improved through automation, meaning again profits increase and/or prices are driven down. Artificial intelligence and artificial decision making is replacing advice in some cases.

There remains concern about the lack of consumer information in the market, and whether consumers are told how their sensitive information is being stored, what level of protection is being offered, and how advice is provided (whether via AI or otherwise).

Consumers may start to expect their legal services to be provided in this way. A minimum level of investment is needed to ensure firms are adequately protecting client data, but the details of how to protect yourself and what would be considered adequate, have not been publicised by regulators. This is an area of self-regulation.

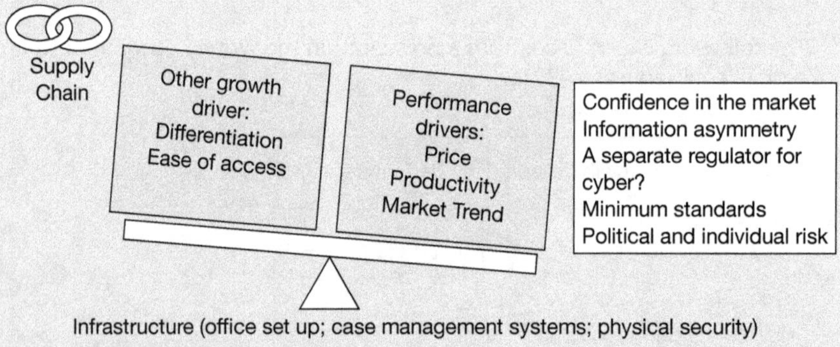

A cyber-attack on a firm could completely knock out the infrastructure within a firm, or be designed to target a specific area, such as a case management system – in order to gain access to client data or financial information. Significant numbers of firms store full information about their clients including identifying and financial information on website portals or upload documents to their case management systems.

A single successful cyber-attack could have implications for a firm in terms of their growth, confidence in the brand, as well as whether the firm continue to utilise the system they have set up.

If there are a series of cyber-attacks, on large supply chains, this could destabilise legal services as a market overall. Consumers could start to lose confidence in legal services; in the solicitor brand, and in the provision of digital legal services.

There could be supply chain consequences – everyone in a chain may be impacted by a data breach, even if the data breach has not implicated your firm. For example, in a conveyancing transaction, information is exchanged about all parties to a transaction. It may not be your firm's data which is stolen, but if a firm in the chain is impacted, your clients' data may be at risk as well if the firm is holding it as part of a transaction. Cybercriminals may target weak points in a chain in order to obtain information.

To prevent this, you may choose to share information with those around you about cybersecurity. If links in the chain do not meet your requirements, they may be restricted accordingly, or have extra security measures put in place.

We have seen attempts to address information asymmetry in the legal services market with extra information for consumers about the price and type of service being offered.

Will we next see information about the standard of security provided or solicitors start to differentiate themselves with additional security provision and add-ons? For example solicitors' firms offering anti-virus or firewalls in the same way as some banks? This could be done in groups of firms to counteract the problems discussed.

There may be a requirement for a separate regulator for cyber security in the same way as there is for data. If significant amounts of client data and monies continue to be lost, without expertise about the level of security required, we perhaps need a separate regulator for cyber security, or a minimum standard to be set for holding client data digitally. The same may apply to transacting with clients. Perhaps firms would need to insist on a minimum level of security before interacting digitally with their clients. At the moment there is a complete lack of guidance in this area.

One final point is the risk assessment of the clients of the firm. Are you handling controversial client data? Is anyone you are representing particularly contentious? What about the work you do – anything which might cause disagreement between groups could be a target for cybercrime and cyber hackers. The exposure of non-controversial client data might be a by-product or initial warning. Consider what the firm does, who it represents, and whether it could become a target. Firms may also consider vetting staff to establish their political motivations.

Part 2

Practising arrangements

Contents

Section 1: Technical content
- Available practising arrangements
  - Practice as a solicitor
  - Practising arrangements
  - Practising statements
- Alternative Business Structures
- Foreign lawyers
- In house solicitors
- Consumer protections
- Practising options – a summary
- The practising year
  - Annual declaration – CPD
  - Practice events
  - Individual practice
  - Practising Certificate events (First issue, Suspension, Revocation, Holding Over)
  - Firm recognition
  - Management and non-solicitors
  - Reserved work and the relationship to other forms of regulation
  - Non reserved work
  - Standards and Regulations 2019

Section 2: Discursive content
- The practising year and timelines for management
  - Diversity data
  - Practising Certificate conditions
  - Accountants' report
  - Annual compliance timetable
- What does the practising year mean to you?
- Options outside regulation, or with alternative regulators
- National and international implications of practising arrangements
- Differences in regulatory outcomes for different forms of practice
- Organisational structure – freelancers, non-reserved work, and unregulated practices
- Separate business rule
- Law firm strategic direction and qualifications
- Management metrics and investigation tools
- Organisational lifetime events and closure
- Standards and Regulations 2019: development, history and change
- Will freelancers be self employed?

Section 1: Technical content

This part of the book concerns the available practising arrangements of solicitors and others regulated by the Solicitors Regulation Authority (SRA), how these are organised by the SRA, and the management implications for firms.

We do not cover company or partnership law, and nor does this book cover in any detail the corporate legal or associated personal implications of practice. We are purely concerned with the regulatory arrangements and structures available within legal services and their specific management and market based implications.

Specifically, we look how different practising structures for solicitors can be authorised by the SRA and how these arise as a result of the Solicitors Act 1974, the Legal Services Act 2007, the Courts and Legal Services Act 1990, and the Administration of Justice Act 1985. We also consider associated legislation along with the regulatory rules arising from the legislation.

Available practising arrangements

Practice as a solicitor

As we have seen in Part 1 of this book, to be a solicitor, you must:

- qualify as a solicitor
- have your name entered on the Roll of solicitors

Being a solicitor is different from practising as a solicitor. If you also wish to practise, as well as being a solicitor, you require a Practising Certificate. A Practising Certificate is sometimes shortened to the title 'PC'. This is obtained from the SRA and renewed annually, as needed. We have covered the process of annual renewal briefly as an issue of professionalism in Part 1 of this book, and we also cover it in more detail in this Part of the book.

At the moment, the qualifications to be a solicitor are usually:

- an LLB (law degree); and
- the SQE (Solicitors Qualification Exam), which has been introduced in 2021.

When you have these (or equivalent qualifications, with equivalence defined by the SRA), you can apply to be on the Roll of solicitors, which is administered by the SRA. After that you can apply for an annual Practising Certificate, which allows you to practise law.

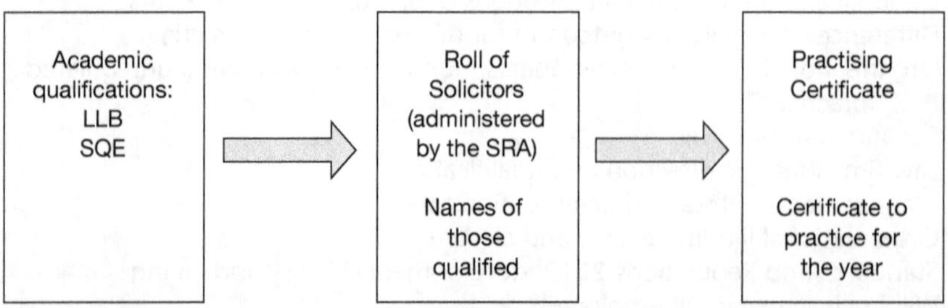

Appearing on the Roll of solicitors is not the same as holding a Practising Certificate. The SRA administers the Roll, and it contains the names of those who are qualified to practise and could ask for a Practising Certificate. There is no obligation to practise, and a PC can be requested at any point during the practising year.

If you do not have a Practising Certificate your name stays on the Roll indefinitely, or until such time as you ask for it to be removed. However, many solicitors who are not practising choose to stay on the Roll and to maintain their status of solicitor.

Practising arrangements

Practising arrangements for solicitors are many and varied, and there are a number of different terms for different types of arrangements. The 'four acts' (Solicitors Act 1974; Administration of Justice Act 1985; Courts and Legal Services Act 1990; and Legal Services Act 2007) provide for, on the face of it, six different ways to practise:

- Individually – the relevant act is the Solicitors Act 1974. This mode of practice covers both Sole Practitioners who do not practise through a corporate entity, and the new 'freelance solicitors'.
- In a corporate structure (non ABS) – the relevant Act is the Courts and Legal Services Act 1990.
- In partnership (non ABS) – the relevant Act is the Solicitors Act 1974.
- Through other tracks (European or foreign qualification), also allowing, often mutually, for solicitors to work abroad – the relevant provisions are contained within the European Communities (Lawyers Practice) Regulations 2000 and for foreign lawyers in the Courts and Legal Services Act 1990.
- In an Alternative Business Structure (ABS) – the relevant Act is the Legal Services Act 2007.
- In house (primarily giving advice to your employer) – the relevant Acts are the Solicitors Act 1974, but also the Legal Services Act 2007.

However, we must also take into account that some legal work is reserved to solicitors and some is not. Solicitors have been a dominant force in legal services for many years and the reservation of large swathes of work to them means they dominate private practice.

Imagine the position with four separate Acts, and six broad ways of practising. To describe the position of the various practising arrangements, we have to take account of the reserved and non-reserved work, the different types of lawyers involved (and their permissions), and the regulatory arrangements that apply to each situation. If you take the six broad tracks of practice above and then say practices can combine them in many different ways, and with unregulated businesses, and that there are different rules which apply to each, we start to see the complexity of the different arrangements. Attempting to explain the different ways in which solicitors practise can be a nightmare!

The explanation below is divided into four broad statements, which are *the writer's* way of conveying this information. Each statement impacts on firm and individual regulation, or the expression of the same, in different ways. This means if you are considering how to practise, note that some people might consider which form of practice gives them the *personal expression they are looking for.* In other words, you might find a combination of forms of practice that suits you best, which the writer has expressed in a different way, or not at all.

Practising statements

There are four statements. A further, more detailed explanation follows the statements:

1. Solicitors can practise on their own or in firms.
2. Regulation varies and permissions change dependent on whether work is reserved or non-reserved.
3. Firm regulation differs from individual regulation.
4. There are different terms for the regulation of firms and individuals, depending on the type of structure you are in.

The practising arrangements for RELs and RFLs are dealt with separately below.

STATEMENT 1: SOLICITORS CAN PRACTISE ON THEIR OWN OR IN FIRMS

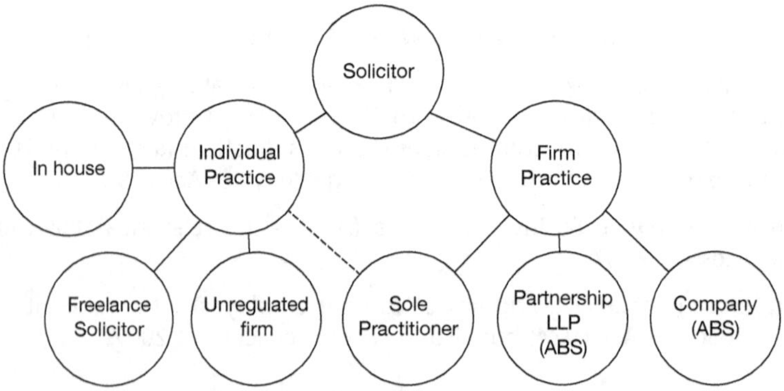

The current practising arrangements allow for solicitors to practise either as individual solicitors or through firms.

In firms, solicitors will commonly practise with other solicitors, often in partnerships, be that limited liability or otherwise. They may also practise through (other) corporate structures; some of these structures may be straightforward limited companies; others may be complex company structures. Both partnerships and companies can be Alternative Business Structures, which allow for the investment or management of law firms by persons who are non-lawyers (as defined by the Legal Services Act 2007).

In both situations (company or partnership practice), the SRA has to recognise or authorise the body itself. The SRA continues to regulate the solicitor (and staff) individually, but also regulates the practice as well.

Solicitors may also be Sole Practitioners. The SRA now recognises sole practices as regulated practices. For many years, the SRA recognised this form of practice as the practice of an individual solicitor, and to a certain extent that may still be true (hence the dotted line in the diagram), but the practice itself is now also recognised in its own right.

Solicitors may also practise as individuals. The most recent form of practice to be permitted is that of a freelance solicitor. The SRA has allowed this form of practice in some situations, but there are conditions attached (such as no staff, and no corporate or other structure).

Freelance solicitors are a new form of practice that allows a solicitor, subject to some conditions, to work freelance, without the structure of a regulated body around them. The SRA has re-interpreted the Legal Services Act 2007, to allow this new form of practice. Freelancers rely on their Practising Certificate instead of a recognised body status, in order to practise.

The difference between the freelance solicitor and a Sole Practitioner is that the SRA is not recognising the surrounding 'practice', and the SRA is limited in the influence it can have on any business the freelancer may work with. The freelancer does not need to confirm any engagement to undertake freelance work with the SRA, although they do need to inform the SRA before they commence freelancing. The freelancer also does not need to, at the time of writing, complete the extensive questions on the SRA annual renewal (known as the annual information return, and covered below). They simply need to confirm that they have maintained their competence when renewing their Practising Certificate.

The end result is likely to be dramatic disparity between established law firms and freelance solicitors. Not only do freelancers not have to complete the information return on the annual renewal, the organisation they work for or with is also limited in the compliance steps they need to take. Competing with this will be difficult for the average established, regulated firm, which does have to comply. Additionally, the SRA will begin to hold significantly more information on established law firms than they do on freelancers, resulting in an investigatory disadvantage to established law firms.

Aspiring freelancers, and the SRA, may however note the attention paid to freelance working by HMRC.

The requirements for becoming a freelancer are set out at Regulation 10.2 of the Authorisation of Individuals Regulations 2019, and notably restrict the practising style of the freelancer (for example, this includes not practising through a company structure, not employing anyone, and taking fees directly from clients). The restrictions are onerous and mean that the freelancer will need to be clear about their set up and the work they take on. However, if this new form of practice succeeds it could change how solicitors practise in the long term.

Another form of individual practice is in unregulated firms; the SRA has historically permitted this for in house solicitors, who work in house for their employer and provide advice only to them. Along with the introduction of freelance solicitors, another form of practice has also been introduced; that of solicitors working (employed) in unregulated firms, providing advice to members of the public. This latter form of practice allows the solicitor to serve members of the public without running a business themselves, and is restricted to non-reserved work only.

For now, traditional partnerships still exist, and solicitors still practise most commonly in some form of partnership, albeit with a rise in the numbers of LLPs. Firms have traditionally been established on high streets across the country offering wills, probate and conveyancing to the clients of the local towns. Local knowledge has been developed and nurtured, and firms have been brought up by the next generation. However, the cost of practising; from insurance, to IT, to compliance and training and maintaining new staff, all adds to the burden upon quite small businesses. These small high street firms increasingly compete with large corporate practices who offer services direct to local consumers through the internet or over the telephone. Digital communication and the information age is slowly changing the face of the solicitor firm, and we may wonder whether there will still be an in-person solicitor presence in our towns in another 100 years' time.

STATEMENT 2: REGULATION VARIES AND PERMISSIONS CHANGE DEPENDENT ON WHETHER WORK IS RESERVED OR NON-RESERVED.

We have already seen above, that solicitors employed in some unregulated firms, are restricted in the work they do; they must not undertake reserved work.

Reserved work is defined in the Legal Services Act 2007, s 12 and is covered later in this Part of the book.

If undertaking reserved legal work, firms and individuals are required to be regulated by the SRA. We have already seen above that solicitors practising as such need to meet certain criteria and have a Practising Certificate in order to offer reserved work on a freelance basis. The position with firms is similar, in that a firm must be regulated by the SRA to offer reserved work.

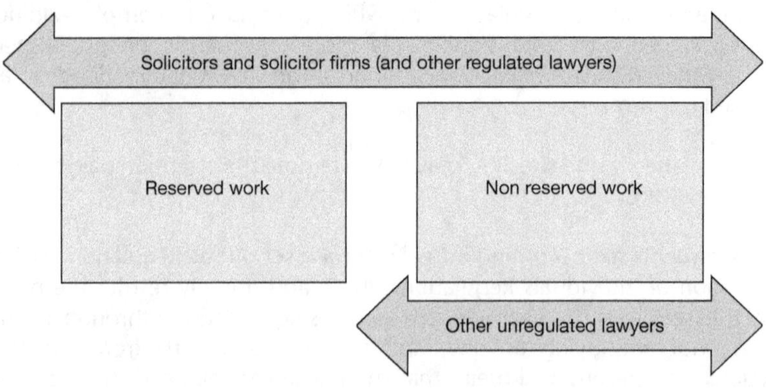

Lawyers of course exist outside of SRA regulation; their firms may or may not be regulated in different ways, and we have covered the various forms of legal practice and professional titles which are approved under the Legal Services Act 2007 to deliver reserved legal work, in Part 1. There are other unregulated lawyers, but unless they are regulated by an approved regulator, they can only conduct non reserved legal work. Some are individuals with qualifications in law or related subjects which have not led them to the title of solicitor (or another approved regulated title), and who practise law in different ways outside of the approved regulator system.

STATEMENT 3: FIRM REGULATION DIFFERS FROM INDIVIDUAL REGULATION.

If a firm of solicitors is setting up to practise law, then authorisation (regulation by the SRA), should be obtained by that firm. Firm authorisation is for the life of the firm. The authorisation is not renewed on annual Practising Certificate renewal, but the structure must answer additional questions on the renewal. These questions are known as the 'annual information return' for firms.

As we will see later in the book, conditions can be imposed on firm or individual regulation. The SRA also has differing powers according to the position of the firm or individual, but could choose to prosecute either in the case of misconduct.

Alternative Business Structure firms are authorised on the same basis as traditional firms, albeit with more consideration of the risks of the ABS, and a process to ensure the firm meets the requirements of authorisation imposed upon it.

The basis for firm regulation is and has been the practice of the individual solicitors within it. Firms of solicitors have been regulated for many years, and despite the new forms of practice available, most firms are traditionally regulated.

Under the Standards and Regulations 2019, the SRA gave permission for unregulated firms to employ solicitors doing non-reserved work in public facing roles. In this situation, the individual solicitor is regulated rather than the firm. Like ABS, this may or may not take hold. Some firms of solicitors have existed for hundreds of years, and the profession is proud of its history. However, economic opportunity and encouragement may see solicitors branch out into other sectors in the future. We wait to see whether this new approach to the Legal Services Act 2007 transforms the legal market in the way the regulators intend it to.

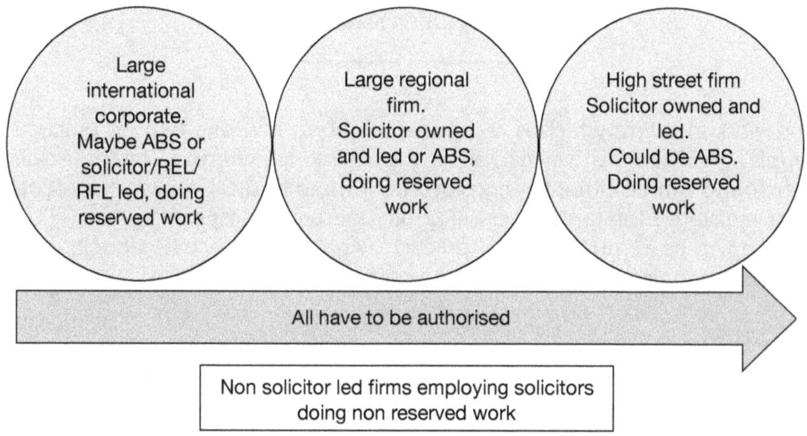

STATEMENT 4: THERE ARE DIFFERENT TERMS FOR THE REGULATION OF FIRMS AND INDIVIDUALS, DEPENDING ON THE TYPE OF STRUCTURE YOU ARE IN.

This is a particularly complex statement to explain.

All non ABS firms, including recognised Sole Practitioners, are known as 'recognised bodies'. Individual solicitors (who are on the Roll) are known as 'recognised individuals'. Freelancers are not operating in recognised bodies because the SRA does not regulate the firm around the freelancer or recognise them as having a legal business (they do recognise the individual solicitor as having a 'practice' as a freelancer, and this is explained later in this section).

As a result of the legislation, and for some references, Alternative Business Structures are known as 'licensed bodies'. Licensed bodies and recognised bodies are known collectively as 'authorised bodies'. The diagram demonstrates the position.

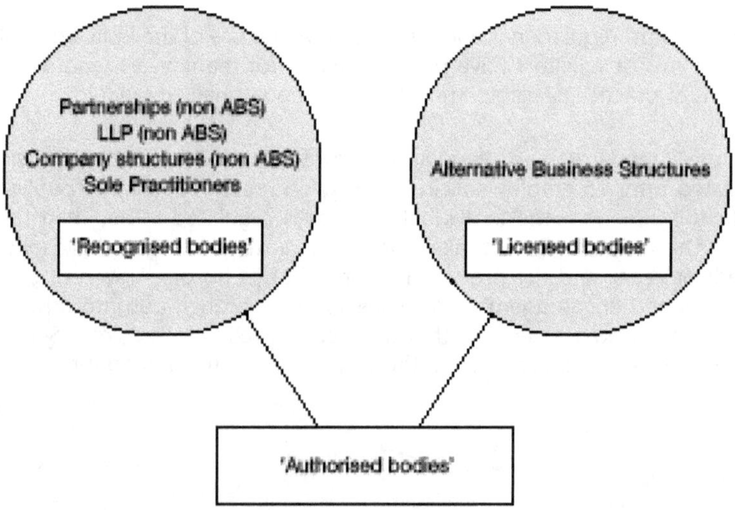

If you work in a firm which is comprised of more than one type of practice (for example, a solicitor with a barrister), this is *also* known as a 'multi-disciplinary practice' and can be either a recognised or licensed body. If you work in a practice with a registered foreign lawyer (RFL) or registered European lawyer (REL), this is *also* known as a 'multi-national practice'. Again, either multi-national or multi-disciplinary practices can be recognised bodies or licensed bodies.

'PRACTICES'

'Practice' is a conceptual term relating to the practising of law and is different from formal recognition (of a partnership, for example), or formal authorisation.

The Solicitors Regulation Authority recognises and regulates the 'practice' of:

- a body; and
- an individual.

Those two points can be separate, and it is also noted that solicitors sometimes practise in their personal lives.

The 'practice' can include the business arrangements, premises, contractual agreements, assets, and anything else that may be encompassed within it. Equally it does not have to include these things; it may simply be advice given or actions undertaken by a lawyer, which can exist outside of the entity itself. The SRA recognises a practice as a conceptual entity which exists beyond any corporate, company, or other recognised structure at law. We have to imagine it in our heads. The practice of a Sole Practitioner is now recognised as a 'recognised body' by the SRA as a result of this anomaly, when the Sole Practitioner used to have an endorsement on their Practising Certificate. This is why the practice of a freelancer is also an issue. The practice of the freelancer exists, in the same way as the practice of a Sole Practitioner or firm might, but the concept might be a bit freer in that it does not have premises, branding, payroll, or perhaps commitment in the same way as a Sole Practitioner might. We might regard these factors as being concrete lines which establish the boundaries of a traditional practice, or business. However the conceptual 'practice' must also exist beyond these lines because the clients, courts, and regulators, have expectations of fulfilment of duties, confidentiality, professional advice, insurance, and legal interpretation. The results of these expectations might be individual to the solicitor, and may bind them personally, beyond their recognised business. The practice attaches to the solicitor personally, and their professionalism (discussed in Part 1), in a way, both regardless of their surrounding environment, and because of it.

The first diagram (p 68) demonstrates the position relative to the established forms of practice (recognised bodies and licensed bodies). We can see the overlap as the 'practice' extends to into the personal life of the solicitor. Arguably, the Solicitors Act 1974 covers this point (covering the personal 'practice' of the solicitor). The other Acts, discussed earlier in the book, cover the other forms of 'corporate' or entity based practice.[1] This position is accepted.

The second diagram (p 68) demonstrates the position with regard to the new forms of practice, and how they must also be seen because the solicitor is still practising. After all, they have a Practising Certificate, give confidential advice, and some of their advice might not be disclosable to the business they are working with. Sole Practitioners are shown separately within the diagram to acknowledge their recognition as a result of this concept, however they are also within the category of 'recognised body' (sometimes referred to as 'recognised sole practice').

We may also find that lawyers have copyrighted information and other assets, which is a particularly important point for the new 'freelance solicitors'. New forms of practice will need to consider carefully who owns the papers and proprietary information.

The second diagram represents the conceptual position, showing that a solicitor's 'practice' can exist separately from any business. The professional status of the solicitor and their professional duties could cause problems in any unregulated business if they left. The unregulated business might not be able to have access to the papers, documents, or confidential information and the consumer would have expectations of confidentiality. The position is particularly sensitive in respect of privileged information.

---

1 The position with Registered European Lawyers and Registered Foreign Lawyers is similar, in that they also have a practice. The legislation is derived and applied in a similar way.

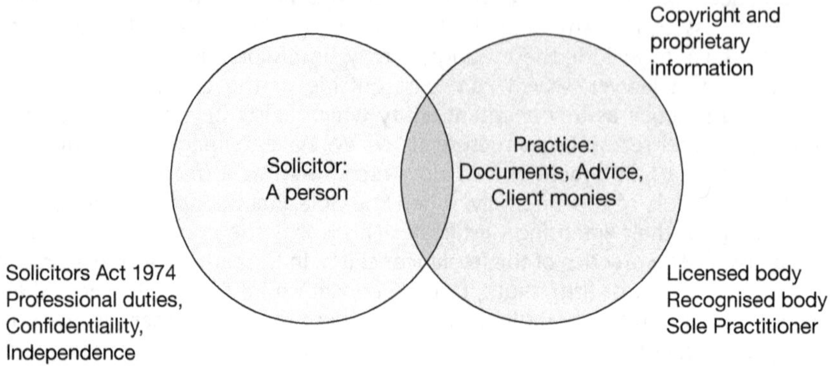

The concept of solicitor intervention is based on the idea of this 'practice', wherein the regulator can close down the practice and take possession of all papers, documents and client monies. The regulator is not restricted to looking at the authorised body in this respect. If closing down the individual practice of the solicitor, this extends to any matter in which they have given legal advice in any capacity, and therefore recognises the status of the solicitor, their professional purpose, and their ability to carry that status in to their personal life or beyond their formal business interests.

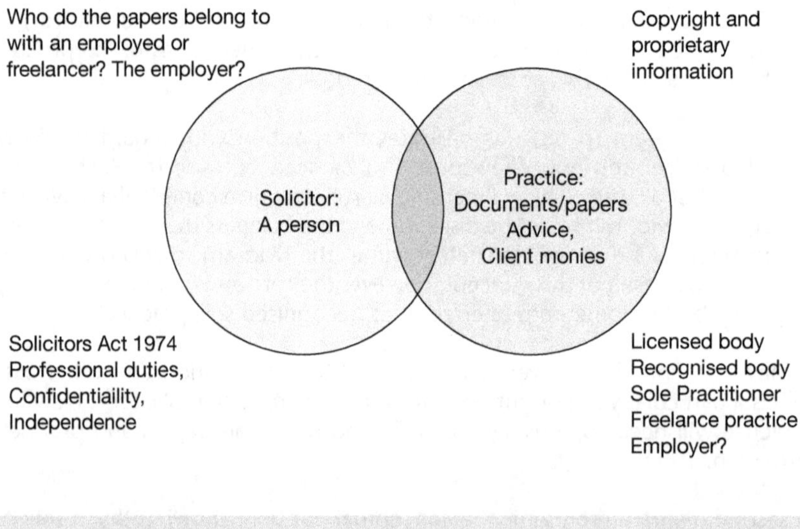

Below is an excerpt from training written by the writer in 2019, just after the new forms of practice involving freelance solicitors and unregulated businesses were confirmed.

> '...In working in these new arrangements, solicitors could design an arrangement they felt was appropriate with those they had chosen to do business with [in compliance with the rules]. Solicitors should consider the level of consumer protection required; also noting that they should discuss this with the client, as well as any referral arrangement to

> separate businesses. Freelance and employed solicitors should note their obligations to comply with the handbook [Standards and Regulations] and how they will comply, alongside any unregulated business, in the event of unforeseen emergencies.
>
> The relevant rule is 10.2 of Authorisation of Individuals Regulations. Written in the negative, the regulation allows for a 'practice' to exist that is not a sole practice, but exists as a solicitor's practice for the purposes of regulation and the Solicitors Act. It means the SRA can intervene into a practice and take possession of papers and client monies, and a distinction arises in the professional life for that purpose, but it also allows the individual solicitor to practice in different situations which suit the individual and their clients. The flexibility of practice, and achieving a variety of results in favour of the client is arguably an important part of being a solicitor.'

Consumer protections, referral arrangements, and separate businesses are discussed later in this Part of the book.

Alternative Business Structures

Alternative Business Structures are law firm structures where a manager or owner (or a percentage of management or ownership), is a non-lawyer. There are stringent requirements for non-lawyer ownership set out in the Legal Services Act 2007. The requirements for ownership are not conditions on the firm in the same sense as the conditions we cover in Part 4 of this book, however they do restrict the license of the firm. Further information about ABS is contained in Part 4.

Foreign lawyers

Those coming from overseas have different opportunities to practise in England and Wales. Notwithstanding any immigration requirements, which are not covered within this book, the SRA, has offered the following statuses:

1. Registered Foreign Lawyers (RFL) – this is for lawyers qualified elsewhere than within the EU wishing to practise in England and Wales
2. Registered European Lawyers (REL) – this is for lawyers qualified in European Union Countries, who would take advantage of the provisions within the European Community Treaties and work in England and Wales.

The second status has been impacted by Brexit, and many RELs have now transferred to being solicitors; the exception at the time of writing being Swiss lawyers, who retain the title REL.

Both the system for RFLs and the system for RELs runs parallel to the system for solicitors.

As a result of the European Communities (Lawyers Practice) Regulations 2000, in the main, the statutes applying to solicitors apply to RELs as well.

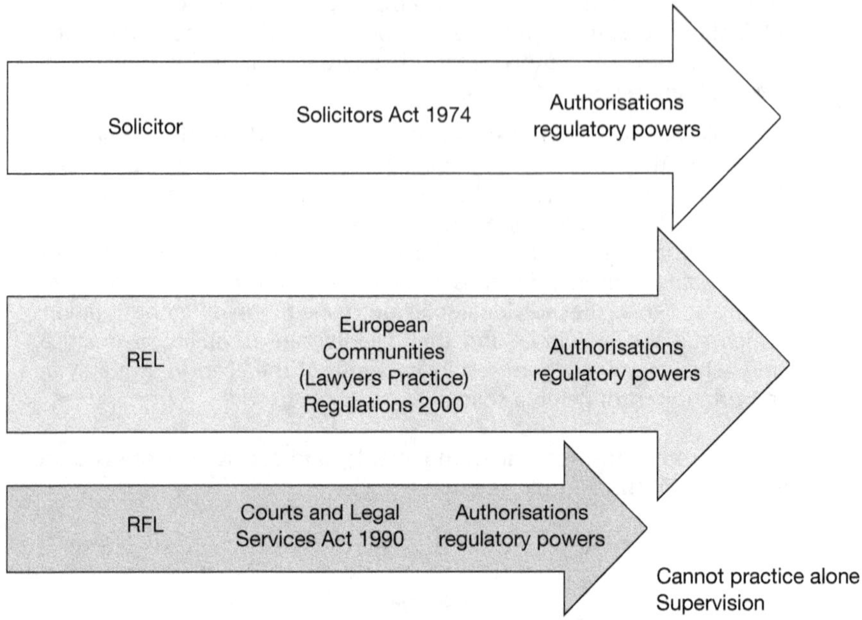

The SRA has broadly the same powers for RELs and RFLs as they do for solicitors, but arising in different ways. There are a few small variations, but for example, the SRA could intervene into a practice which involved RFLs and RELs, could discipline them, and could take regulatory action against them. This action would have consequences in this country, and may have consequences for the registration abroad.

An RFL or an REL is also granted a Practising Certificate, must renew on an annual basis, and can have conditions imposed on that certificate. In effect, the system works the same way as it does for solicitors, with the same practising year, and in the main, the same powers.

There are more restrictions on how RFLs practise. An RFL must practise with lawyers qualified in England and Wales, and their work should be supervised. It is not possible to run a sole practice if you are an RFL. RFLs are able to continue using their home title, provided they are still registered as such, and clients understand their status.

These restrictions have not applied to RELs. RELs have been given the same practising rights as solicitors, meaning RELs have been able to set up and operate sole practices in England and Wales. At the time of Brexit, there were approximately 700 RELs in England and Wales. The only disadvantage to being an REL was that the lawyer did not carry the title 'solicitor', which is a recognised brand name. However they were able to keep using their home title.

Lawyers registered abroad then have two regulatory systems to adhere to and can theoretically be disciplined twice. This 'dual deontology' means the SRA also must consider what can be reported and disciplined abroad.

Those taking on RFLs may also consider whether the RFL has ongoing files, matters and considerations of practice abroad, and whether the firm could become involved in their ongoing practice abroad. This can cause complications for the firm. As above, the SRA has rights of intervention and this includes into all papers, files and client monies, which can impact practices held here and abroad, including where the lawyer holds the matters personally.

As a result of Brexit, the REL status looks set to disappear. European Lawyers will no longer have the same practising rights in England and Wales as they did previously. However, the SRA, during 2020, offered to transfer RELs to solicitor regulation. In effect, RELs had been recognised as at the same level, status and qualification as solicitors. They had simply been recognised as being the same in a parallel legislative system, so the lawyers have been given the opportunity to acquire the same practising status.

The SRA have said that remaining RELs will become RFLs, meaning they will no longer be able to practice alone, unless they move to the status of solicitor.

With the removal of the REL status, we may see changes to the RFL status, as the country seeks alternative relationships worldwide. The SRA have already said there will be particular qualification recognition requirements for those qualified in the other parts of the European Union, and in Ireland. The harmonisation of requirements across the European Union, particularly in the commonality of law or legal requirements, may also provide some basis for the recognition of qualification going forward. However, at the time of writing that had yet to be determined.

The SRA is now simultaneously moving to the Solicitors Qualification Exam as the primary mode of qualification as a solicitor in England and Wales, and of course qualification as a solicitor is open to those holding qualifications or practising statuses from overseas.

In-house solicitors

Solicitors can also be employed to work directly for their employer as an in-house lawyer. This means giving advice internally and supporting the decisions of the business. Solicitors employed in house do not give external legal advice unless they are also part of a recognised body; have registered as a freelancer to do so; or have another form of practice which is approved by the SRA. Solicitors wishing to take this route should contact the SRA for advice.

In previous handbooks, the SRA has issued detailed rules for in house solicitors, which have been removed in the latest iterations. The SRA rarely receives complaints about solicitors practising in house, and conditions are rarely imposed. The position is largely the same as that for freelancers and others employing solicitors; in that the business should respect and adhere to the guidance and regulations for the solicitor.

In house solicitors must renew their Practising Certificate on an annual basis, but the business or organisation employing them does not need to make an annual return. However the organisation is listed as the employer of the individual by the SRA, and the SRA can in exceptional circumstances, contact that organisation directly.

This contrasts with the status of freelancer, where the organisation using the freelancer is not registered with the SRA.

The SRA retains the same power over in-house solicitors as it does over other solicitors; it can intervene, discipline, and also restrict the practice of individual solicitors through Practising Certificate conditions. At times, the SRA may remind the employing organisation that a solicitor must comply with the rules of professional conduct, but the SRA has no formal powers over the external organisation. Theoretically, the SRA could intervene into the practice of an in-house solicitor, as the practice is considered to be held personally, however in fact this rarely happens. Those organisations large enough to employ an in-house solicitor rarely have the financial difficulties seen by smaller private practices, and generally the position of the solicitor has been respected. Also, the client papers are held by the client themselves (the organisation), so if a solicitor becomes unwell or cannot practise anymore, they are not usually being placed at risk. In house solicitors also often work in public sector organisations which are consistently funded, with arguably strong governance in place. The departure of a solicitor from such an organisation does not cause the same difficulties as the closure of a Sole Practitioner.

Consumer protections

Consumer protections required and in place do differ according to the style of practise you choose. Traditional law firms are protected by minimum terms and conditions of insurance imposed by the regulator, and if the worst should happen and the regulator intervenes, then consumers are compensated by the Compensation Fund. The Compensation Fund is administered by the SRA and pays compensation to those impacted by events such as intervention.

Solicitors going to work in unregulated firms as employees conducting non-reserved work will not have Compensation Fund protections, and there is no minimum insurance requirement. However, unregulated businesses are asked to note the current standard of insurance in the market. Solicitors working as freelance solicitors conducting non-reserved work do have compensation fund protections, but there is also no minimum standard of insurance, although they have been warned about the standard of insurance usually expected, and the personal consequences of not obtaining it. Freelance solicitors conducting reserved work also have Compensation Fund access and whilst there are no minimum terms of insurance, a note to the standard of insurance expected is contained within the regulations; whether this will be enforced and to what extent remains to be seen.

There have been questions as to whether the protections offered to consumers by traditional firms constitute a gold standard of regulation and whether the disparity between the different types of practice is clear to those purchasing legal services. At the moment, firms (and solicitors) are asked to provide information on their website or in writing to consumers outlining the protections available and where they can find further information. This includes information about complaints, complaints bodies available and forms of redress or regulation, insurance, and the Compensation Fund. Whether consumers understand the regulation available, or Compensation Fund access is, in the writer's experience, questionable after dealing with many consumers confused about both. However, consumers often understand the protections available when purchasing a holiday. Sufficient consumer information and publicity concerning the Compensation Fund and other regulatory benefits may, if understood, be a popular safeguard for consumers.

Practising options – A summary

The diagram below represents the broad requirements and current position discussed above, also noting that solicitors can also work in unregulated practices as solicitors providing services both to their employer and directly to the public.

Styles of practice – Regulated by SRA

Recognised body	Partnerships, LLPs, Ltd Companies	The business needs to be authorised
Licensed body	As above, but Alternative Business Structures (non lawyer partners)	
(Recognised) sole practice	Sole practitioner, but within 'body' structure	
In house lawyer	Providing services to their employer (business doesn't need licence)	

Coming soon! Freelance solicitors!	Businesses that don't need to be authorised

The practising year

The practising year runs from October to October. We have already covered some information regarding professional practice and the broad issues of the renewal in Part 1 of this book. This small section covers the practical aspects of the renewal.

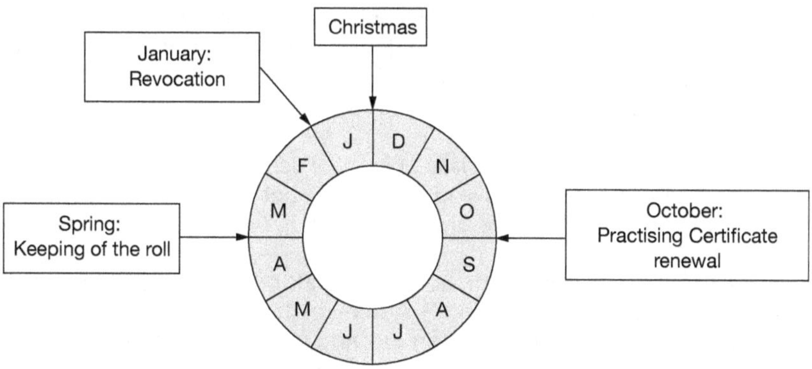

The year provides the opportunity for solicitors to demonstrate their ongoing competence. Some solicitors display their Practising Certificate in their offices, demonstrating their continuing license to practice.

ANNUAL DECLARATION – CPD

In 2016, the SRA introduced the annual declaration on the annual renewal, meaning individual solicitors (and possibly their firms) have to certify their ongoing competence during the annual renewal. This requires a signature and confirmation from the firm and individual. The annual declaration is made with reference to the Competence Statement.

This paragraph was included in the writer's 2016 Renewal Training:

> 'Competence Statement – The use of the Competence Statement becomes mandatory for all solicitors after 1 November 2016. This means no more CPD hours, but instead solicitors and their employers should certify that they have considered their competence on the annual renewal. Competence is assessed against the Competence Statement and [its] supporting documents. The SRA suggest solicitors should ensure their competence by planning for development, reflecting on their individual learning needs and ensuring their development activities meet those needs.'

Solicitors require a Practising Certificate to undertake reserved work, which commonly forms part of a solicitor practice in England and Wales (and in fact across the United Kingdom). A failure to obtain or renew a Practising Certificate can ultimately result in disciplinary and enforcement action against the solicitor and firm involved, and even in intervention (intervention is the forced closure of a practice by the SRA, which can often bankrupt a solicitor). The consequences of not renewing are very serious for a solicitor and this section should be read in that context.

From the SRA's perspective the practising year can be divided into different parts. If we start from October, this is the point of renewal and the SRA has a list of all currently licensed firms and individuals. From this list, the requests for renewal are received. Some requests will be removed for further consideration, such as conditions, and we examine that further later in this part of the book. The rest will be automatically renewed. The renewal is conducted digitally. All information about a solicitor (and authorised firms or some firms employing solicitors) is held online on MySRA, and the renewal is conducted through this online portal, allowing the automation of the process. MySRA was introduced in approximately 2011 or 2012.

The renewal window is usually officially open between 1 October and 31 October. Individuals can renew their Practising Certificate, but firms often undertake this exercise for their staff, and pay the annual fee. This is known as the bulk renewal.

The renewal applies to many hundreds of thousands of solicitors, and there can be difficulties. This can be with the SRA's IT system, as 196,000 solicitors try to renew at the same time. Sometimes, solicitors do not renew. The SRA or the solicitor may then follow up on the situation. Sometimes, solicitors are unwell, a life event has occurred, or they are unable to obtain insurance. On other occasion, they may be closing and don't require a Practising Certificate to attend to the business arrangements left, or for some other reason they have not been able to complete the renewal.

Often the SRA leaves the window for renewal open until just into the following calendar year (at some point during January). This is done unofficially, and solicitors should make every effort to renew on time, noting that if they do not renew before 31 October they could be subject to regulatory action, including intervention.

Any Practising Certificate applications which have not been made by the end of October are then chased by the SRA. This can be the start of regulatory and enforcement action. The letters or contact from the SRA will usually request an explanation as to why the PC has not been renewed and what the requirement is for renewal. Sometimes a number of these chaser letters are sent. Failure to respond may result ultimately in intervention into that practice if necessary. The SRA would make every effort to contact the practitioner, including via their listed firm, before taking such a step. Obviously, the position is serious for the Sole Practitioner, who may not have anyone else at their firm. In some cases, the SRA will attend the solicitor's home address, contact other practitioners in the area, and seek to attend their premises.

Solicitors waiting for a Practising Certificate hold over on their previous Practising Certificate. This means the Practising Certificate from the previous year continues to operate until it is revoked or renewed. All Practising Certificates continue to run until either of those two events occur. However, as above, the SRA does not tolerate non-renewal, unless a solicitor has stopped practising. At some point in the spring, the SRA revokes the Practising Certificates of those who have not renewed; this may be in late spring and after consultation with those involved. This could result in intervention for those who do not renew on time.

During approximately the same time frame (between October and March), Practising Certificate conditions are being considered for those who need them. Under European Community legislation, these decisions should be made within six months of application. The SRA only accepts the application once it has received all of the information it needs, so some decisions will go beyond the March deadline, because the SRA has asked for additional documents or explanations from the practitioner or firm. We wait to see the impact of Brexit on the decision-making timescales of the SRA, and whether they retain the six-month window. We examine Practising Certificate conditions themselves in Part 3 of the book.

Practising Certificates are in a way, annual individual practising licences. Firm licenses are issued for the lifetime of the firm recognition.

Below is a selection of information drawn from the writer's Serious/Material Breach courses from the years 2014–2020, covering the annual renewal:

> **[2014]** 'The renewals process is an extremely powerful regulatory event. Every year solicitors have to submit information about themselves and their businesses to the SRA. The SRA re-authorises those solicitors and their organisations, reviews their status and imposes conditions if necessary.
>
> Since the introduction of the Legal Services Act 2007 (and the repeal of certain sections of the Solicitors Act 1974) SRA has begun creating new systems and procedures to modernise regulation and handle the challenges of Alternative Business Structures.
>
> …

Practitioners should increasingly expect the SRA to understand their businesses; good and bad. Part of the emphasis of Outcomes Focused Regulation was on good governance, and regardless of the policy shift for the future, practices can expect this to continue. The legal services sector has not been known for its strong management and financial awareness, but the Legal Services Act changed the situation. Increasingly it is necessary for legal businesses to understand their markets, client needs, and financial position, and practices who do not consider these elements of their business could find themselves more heavily investigated by an SRA who do.

Until relatively recently, the SRA made limited use of the information it gathered at initial authorisation and renewal. The information sent in on the paper form was looked over by the person dealing with the application, and may occasionally have come to light if an investigation was launched, but there was no systematic analysis. Times are changing; the SRA is building a system capable of analysing the information it gathers and hopes to use this to monitor regulated firms and individuals more effectively.'

[2016] 'Following the introduction of the Legal Services Act 2007, the SRA began creating new systems and procedures under OFR to modernise regulation and handle the challenges of Alternative Business Structures. However, the intended further regulatory reform in this parliament could spell the end of the SRA entirely. There now appears to be a policy shift away from the OFR approach as the SRA seeks to open up the legal marketplace further and de-regulate the profession entirely. We may yet see the end of the SRA.

The most dramatic shift has been in the Looking to the Future Consultation which opens the prospect of solicitors working in unregulated businesses, providing (unreserved) legal advice to the general public. With this prospect comes the question of whether ABS are necessary, and whether firms will hive off sections of their business along reserved and unreserved lines. Given the distinctions of reserved and unreserved work are arbitrary, could we see the abolition of this work altogether in future?'

[2020] 'The renewal is an extremely powerful regulatory event. Under OFR, the SRA started to build a more sophisticated risk management system capable of systemic analysis, including analysis of the information provided on the renewal. Law firms should be aware of the information they are providing and how to calculate their own risk profile and score.

…

The 2020 renewals process runs between 1 October and 31 October. It applies to:

- Solicitors applying for replacement Practising Certificates under section 9 of the Solicitors Act 1974 (as amended by Legal Services Act 2007). Registered European Lawyers applying for renewal of registration in the register of European Lawyers under regulation 17 of the European Communities (Lawyer's Practice) Regulations 2000*.

- Applications for renewal of registration in the register of foreign lawyers under section 89 of the Courts and Legal Services Act 1990.
- All of the above in completing the applications for individual renewal under Regulations 7 and 8 of the Authorisation of Individuals Regulations 2019.
- Licensed Bodies (Alternative Business Structures - ABS) and Recognised Bodies (non ABS solicitor firms, including Sole Practitioners) completing the information return under Rule 11 of the Authorisation of Firms Rules 2019.

Authorised non lawyer managers ((a) partner in a partnership, (b) member of an LLP, or (c) director of a company) and those holding important posts in a firm also need to provide information as part of the information return.

Authorised (non-Sole Practitioner) firms do not need to apply to renew their recognition as they now have lifetime recognition, unless it is revoked or suspended by the SRA.

* This remains in force as a result of the European Communities Withdrawal Act 2018, but is subject to the negotiated exit from the European Union. The transition period comes to a close in December 2020.

Sole Practitioners are now recognised bodies and no longer have an endorsement on their Practising Certificate.

There is a new mode of practice – freelance solicitors, and to become a freelance solicitor, you must inform the SRA of your intention to do so. Your business may need to be regulated (by the SRA or another regulator) if it provides reserved legal services or immigration advice; if it provides services subject to the financial services regime or if it provides services subject to AML regulation under the money laundering regulations.

....

If you do not renew your Practising Certificate, regulation 8.4(b) of the Authorisation of Individuals Rules allows for your Practising Certificate or registration to be revoked. This is a major process for the SRA as every year there are hundreds, even thousands, of individuals that do not renew. Many of these people do not wish to continue practising, however some forget, have other emergencies in their lives, or they choose to delay their renewal because they cannot yet pay for their insurance. The 2013 renewal stayed open (unofficially) until 4 February 2014.

During this time period, a Practising Certificate is held over from the previous year. The same situation occurs when you are awaiting a decision.

The SRA must give notice of revocation before it takes place. They are often reluctant to revoke, particularly if there are a lot of Sole Practitioner applications outstanding. The implications of revocation are significant for Sole Practitioners; revocation means they would be practising uncertificated which in a Sole Practitioner firm could lead to intervention. This is also the same position for practices.

If you fail to renew on time this will be noted by the SRA and fed into your risk profile. If you do it every year, this could become a significant issue. It should also be noted that leaving the renewal until later poses a risk of practising uncertificated for everyone who does it, which will ultimately lead to disciplinary action and intervention.

Under the Standards and Regulations, and the SRA Authorisation of Individuals Regulations, your Practising Certificate can be revoked under Regulation 8.4 in a variety of other circumstances as well.

The revocation process also means that freelancers or individual solicitors working in unregulated practices who have not renewed could also be subject to intervention of their individual practices. Be aware of the consequences of non-continuation, and involve your associated businesses, and the SRA, in planned decision making in the event of an emergency or orderly closure.

[2014] 'The SRA use the renewals to gather information for their risk profiling. Ultimately this informs their supervision and enforcement activity. Historically the SRA has not been very good at using the information sent during renewals, but we should expect this to improve.

This means that this year and in coming years, the SRA will be looking at your data submitted more carefully. They will be comparing it to other firms of similar sizes – looking for differences and similarities to determine who the riskiest firms are; a lot like your insurer does.'

The majority of applications are made via bulk renewal, with the firm completing the renewal online for their staff. This is often for Human Resources or compliance to organise, with a partner signing off the renewal on behalf of the firm. Some of the information required can be complex such as turnover, starters and leavers, complaints, and referrals.

Applications for Practising Certificates which require further consideration for conditions are removed from consideration within the bulk renewal, and a decision in respect of those is issued later.

Practice events

During the lifetime of any organisation, different events occur. No organisations last forever, but some solicitors' firms have been running for hundreds of years, with the names of the founding partners above the door! Doubtless much has changed in those hundreds of years; from the style of practice, to the work offered, and the staff available to see clients. The regulator needs to be appraised both of those changes within individual firms, but also of the changing market place as a whole. As a result, the regulator operates an annual renewal for individuals, and annual information return for firms.

The regulatory objectives within the Legal Services Act 2007 also mean the regulator must assess the risk of the practices and make decisions about the best regulatory mechanisms available to take action.

The practice, as we have already seen, does not need to renew its recognition on an annual basis. The same is now also true for Sole Practitioners, who until recently did have to renew their Sole Practitioner status on an annual basis.

The information return on the annual renewal collects a large amount of information about the practice and the SRA uses this to profile the practice, analyse the regulatory landscape, and ultimately to take action to manage risks.

Other practice events include starting up, changing individual approval for certain roles, and closing down. All of these events require the submission of specific applications to the SRA, outside of the annual renewal. For example, some individuals working in firms need approval, such as the COLP, COFA, MLRO and MLCO. Non-solicitor managers need approval in Alternative Business Structures, as do beneficial owners. Approvals should not be taken for granted, and authorisation structures within the regulator do have the right to decline approval for a range of concerns including regarding individuals, proposed organisational structures, and external investments.

We can also see potential practice events which are notified to the SRA in different ways, in the following circumstances:

- Reporting serious breaches (covered in Part 5 of this book).
- Grounds for suspension of a Practising Certificate – insolvency and criminal offences (covered in Part 3 and Part 5 of this book).
- Action being taken abroad against a dual qualified individual solicitor, manager, REL or RFL.
- Temporary approval for the manager posts discussed just previously, perhaps while a full application is being considered or prepared.
- Change or departure of an individual (for example a solicitor or partner) outside of the annual renewal window.
- Notification of maternity leave.
- Obtaining and sending an accountant's report to the SRA, which is discussed at Part 6 of this book.
- The diversity data collection return, which happens most summers, and involves firms confirming their diversity statistics against set criteria. This data is collected anonymously and voluntarily.
- The keeping of the Roll, which occurs every spring, and covers whether solicitors who are not currently practising, would like to retain their name on the Roll of solicitors.
- Exemption requests, which cover exemptions from certain parts of the Standards and Regulations. Linked to this are approaches to the SRA under the banner of 'innovation', whereby the SRA have allowed exemptions to parts of the rules for innovative practice.
- Closure or merger of a practice.
- Responding to SRA investigation.

Individual practice

Part of SRA regulation is based on the idea that a solicitor practice is an individual practice, and we have covered this earlier in this chapter. The SRA recognises that a solicitor's 'practice' may encompass work product, papers, and client monies, held outside of a recognised body.

This is not common, and should not usually be undertaken without recognition, but it is theoretically possible. Accordingly, when intervening into a practice for example, the SRA would intervene into the authorised body, *and also* the individual practices of the solicitors concerned. This means *all* papers, monies, and work undertaken vests in the SRA.

It is not common for solicitors to use these 'personal practices', as to do so would require insurance and technically some form of recognition. However, in cases of intervention, we may be dealing with firms who have fundamentally disregarded the rules of professional conduct and the regulations and law of practice, and the SRA has to consider the possibility that matters may have been undertaken personally by the solicitor. This has happened in the past; sometimes practices which are intervened can be complex and confusing spaces, without clear organisational boundaries.

Readers might realise that practices where the SRA has had to consider that an individual solicitor has a personal practice are firms where much has gone wrong, and the firm may be in a real mess.

Accordingly, there is the potential for solicitors to have an individual or personal practice, although practices should be authorised appropriately.

Practising Certificate events (first issue, suspension, revocation, holding over)

We have seen 'practice events' discussed above. A Practising Certificate itself can also have 'events'; aside from its annual renewal.

It is important to remember when discussing 'events' that the practitioner must maintain their Practising Certificate if they wish to continue working as a solicitor (or at least conducting reserved work). Without a Practising Certificate, a solicitor cannot practise. If a regulated law firm did not have a solicitor with a Practising Certificate, they could not continue to operate. For example, if a small one partner firm failed to maintain their Practising Certificate, the firm would have to close or be closed down (intervened) by the regulator. Any solicitor who continued to practise without their Practising Certificate may not be covered by their insurance and could face disciplinary action. These are extreme examples, but the Practising Certificate is very important.

The first event which needs examination is the first issue of the Practising Certificate. This is a joyous time for the soon to be practising solicitor, as they have just qualified, but can, in some circumstances, be tempered by conditions. The regulator can examine the new solicitor's qualification record when considering their first Practising Certificate. They may consider any references, or any reported incidents related to the individual who has just qualified. The regulator may impose conditions if there is a concern about the potential practice of that individual solicitor.

A Practising Certificate can also be suspended at any time during the calendar year, if certain situations arise. These include bankruptcy or insolvency generally or committing certain criminal offences. This position is discussed further in Parts 3 and 5 of this book which cover Practising Certificate conditions and serious breaches.

We cover the annual renewal in this Part of the book, but what happens if you do not renew in October? The solicitor's Practising Certificate is 'held over' until such time as the SRA either revokes it, in spring the following year, or it is renewed. This means you continue to hold the previous Practising Certificate and it continues to be in force. Many people do not realise that a Practising Certificate does not automatically expire; it continues until such time as it is revoked, or it is renewed.

Holding over and awaiting revocation is not recommended as this can lead to the loss of the Practising Certificate, which can be disastrous, as set out earlier in this section. If a solicitor continues to practise without renewing, as well as revocation, the solicitor could face disciplinary action, loss of insurance, and even intervention if they work alone.

If the solicitor is waiting for a decision from the SRA on their Practising Certificate, for example if conditions will be imposed, it is held over at that point, and continues to be held over until the SRA makes a decision. This can take up to one year, or even longer. We discuss the timescales for decision making in respect of conditions in Part 3 of this book.

Revocation is the removal of the Practising Certificate, as if it never existed. The Practising Certificate is replaced with a new, up to date Certificate, and the individual continues their practice. Any conditions imposed on a Practising Certificate are therefore automatically time limited.

If a solicitor decides to stop practising, but would like to remain on the Roll, the correct procedure is to inform the SRA of the intention to stop practising, with a future date in mind. Once that date is reached, the solicitor then confirms their intention to stop practising. Following this date, the solicitor does not renew their PC in the annual renewal but confirms during that annual renewal process that they are no longer practising. The difference between this process and the previous example is the very deliberate decision not to continue, and communication of the same, versus a non-renewal which may or may not be intentional.

There is further coverage of closure of solicitors' practices later in this Part of the book.

Firm recognition

As we have seen, one of the ways solicitors can practise is through firms. These firms are authorised as entities. This means the SRA considers their functions on a parallel with individual solicitors; considering their functioning, operations, management of different situations, and decision making. Firms can be held responsible for their actions as a matter of professional conduct, alongside or instead of the individual solicitor, and the regulator will look at where responsibility properly lies and who should be prosecuted. As well as prosecution, the SRA also has several other opportunities to regulate the firm in the public interest, and the full range of its powers can be used against the firm or individuals.

Potential firms must apply to the SRA for recognition. The first application is usually quite extensive and covers the policies and procedures of the firm, the approved individuals, qualifications, insurance, and intended areas of practice. In some cases, the SRA will ask to see a business plan demonstrating the intended investment, spending, work to be undertaken by the firm, and projected income. This business plan may be required to cover several years to satisfy the SRA as to the intentions of the firm. The SRA may also require extensive information regarding the firms' policies and procedures, including in relation to AML, also including the firm's initial risk assessment.

Information provided at first application stage by firms is extensive and can be quite a daunting task to complete. However, most firm applications for recognition are approved.

Some firm recognitions can be complex. Corporate structures can be set up in a number of different ways and the introduction of Alternative Business Structures by the Legal Services Act 2007 was an attempt to bring more extensive competition into law through different types of firm recognition. The idea was that investment in law, possibly through these different types of structures, would grow. We have seen a move towards remote, standardised advice, and away from an exclusively high street model of practice. The opportunities for scalable profits are certainly available in both the demand for advice from consumers and businesses, and the value in the existing book of business held by local high street firms, which has yet to be fully released.

Ten years on from the Act, ABS have not changed the face of firm recognition, and we have not seen the growth in different business structures some expected.

The potential complexity of firm recognition, outside investment, and the consequences for independent advice, have not been lost on either the SRA or Parliament. The Legal Services Act 2007 at Part 5 provides an insight into the restrictions placed on outside investment, including the limited percentages available to outside owners.

As we have seen, firm recognition is for the life of the firm, and continues until it is revoked, or until the firm closes. Firms do not need to renew their recognition annually, but they do need to ensure they make an annual information return to the SRA at the time of the renewal. This includes ensuring all practice details are up to date, all management and approved office details are up to date, and all questions are answered on the renewal. Questions posed for the firm include:

- Insurance
- Client monies held during the last accounting period
- Complaints received
- Work undertaken
- Turnover

This is by no means the full list and the questions are extensive and designed to provide a full picture of the firm. To the experienced regulator or business assessor, the information provided on renewal can provide a clear outline of the type of business practice and the likely risks and issues poses within the practice during that practice year or thereabouts. Dramatic changes and shifts in answers year on year can also provide the regulator with additional insights about a firm's working pattern, clients, and likely risks, which could be acted upon.

For most firms, this information return and annual renewal is the only contact they have with the regulator throughout the year. Many firms complete the annual renewal without giving a second thought to the information they are providing to the SRA. Firms should have an understanding of their own risk profile. This can help firms manage risks and explain the same to the regulator. Developing your own understanding of the management metrics a regulator might use to assess your risk in comparison to other firm both in the market, and of the same type, can help you to understand your local position, sub-sector profiles, sub-sector risks, and your own individual risks as a firm.

Risk management is not simply a something the regulator does. Although you might see intervention, regulation, and PC conditions as something of a safety net for solicitors, the majority of practitioners do not want their firm to be shut down, or to be subject to regulatory action. Managing risk may be part of wider good business practice alongside similar business objectives such as ensuring security, profitability and liquidity.

Management and non-solicitors

Those holding managerial positions within firms should note not only that their decisions, but also the direction, and the positioning of the firm, can all be subject to regulation and regulatory consequences, even if they as individuals are unadmitted. In serious circumstances, featuring serious breaches of the rules of professional conduct, the unadmitted individual can also be subject to regulatory action under the Solicitors Act 1974, s 43. This power prevents non solicitors working in a solicitors firm. Further discussion of s 43 can be found in Part 5 of this book.

Management within firms also have a role to play in the renewal. An individual may not fall within the categories required for approval, for example within Alternative Business Structures, but might still be listed as a manager within the firm by the SRA. Their details should remain up to date. Those with managerial responsibility within firms can be held jointly and severally liable for breaches of the SRA rules, and authorised firms have to make the extensive annual information return discussed earlier.

Non solicitors working in solicitor firms should also note the implications of the Money Laundering Regulations 2017 and the Proceeds of Crime Act 2002, and their associated offences. Sometimes the provisions of these requirements are keenly felt in legal services due to the nature of the work, and non-lawyers should be aware of the serious nature of some of the potential issues and consequences.

Reserved work and the relationship to other forms of regulation

Reserved work is legal work which can only be conducted by certain professional people, including solicitors, barristers, CILEx, some accountants, notaries, and licensed conveyancers. Those professional persons must be registered with their regulator and have a valid, suitable Practising Certificate in force to conduct reserved work. The Practising Certificate should be from a regulator able to supervise reserved legal work. If the Practising Certificate has conditions placed on it regarding that reserved work, those conditions should be observed.

Undertaking reserved work when not authorised to do so is a prosecutable offence, and is prosecuted in the case of solicitors, before the Solicitors Disciplinary Tribunal.

Reserved work includes conveyancing, advocacy, and the grant of probate, and the full requirements are set out in the Legal Services Act 2007. In particular, the term 'reserved instrument activity' provides the basis for some areas of law to be reserved, including conveyancing. This means that the practice of that area of law is not itself reserved, but the preparation of some particular legal documents within the area of law. This can lead to some confusion, and in practice can mean that entire area of law can be treated as being reserved work.

The exception to this situation may be probate, where it is the grant of probate itself which is reserved. Once the grant has been obtained by a person authorised to do so, probate itself can be conducted by anyone, including for example, the executors of the estate. Outside of the structure of approved regulators there are paralegals authorised and regulated to conduct probate work in their own businesses by regulatory organisations. They do not obtain the grant of probate, but they do conduct the probate itself. Some of these paralegals are very highly qualified and there is a regulator empowered to award qualifications, consider complaints, and take regulatory action against the paralegal should there be any concerns. Some of the qualifications are also regulated by Ofqual. However these regulators and qualifications are not 'approved' by the Legal Services Board for the purposes of conducting reserved work.

Reserved work might be seen as the cornerstone of the solicitor profession. Certainly, it underpins the need for a professional qualification in law if you wish to work in certain areas of law. It also provides a key strength of the organisational structures around solicitors and other regulated legal professionals, who are authorised to conduct reserved work. Reserved work is the basis for seeking regulation from the SRA in the form of professional qualification, firm recognition and a Practising Certificate. None of these things are theoretically needed if you do not conduct reserved legal work. The SRA however, regulates all different areas of law conducted by the registered practitioner, not just the reserved legal work.

Immigration does not fall under the category of reserved work. However different rules apply to immigration practitioners which are not covered by the definitions of reserved and unreserved work, and immigration practitioners must be authorised and regulated. The SRA regulates solicitors for immigration work. Those not regulated by the SRA but delivering immigration work, must be regulated by the Office for the Immigration Services Commissioner (OISC).

The SRA also regulates for anti-money laundering, in accordance with the Money Laundering Regulations. The SRA's regulation also provides some exemptions from the Financial Conduct Authority regime for those firms who would otherwise be regulated by the FCA. Neither of these categories of work are reserved in themselves, but they do require careful consideration of whether a firm is or should be subject to regulation. In some cases, a law firm also requires regulation by the FCA, dependent on the type and amount of work it conducts. The position with other regulators can change, and different regulatory permissions can alter. One example is the situation regarding consumer credit work, which is examined briefly below.

Until 2013, the Office of Fair Trading exclusively regulated the market for consumer credit work, and a licence was given to The Law Society on a renewable basis to regulate this form of work for solicitors.

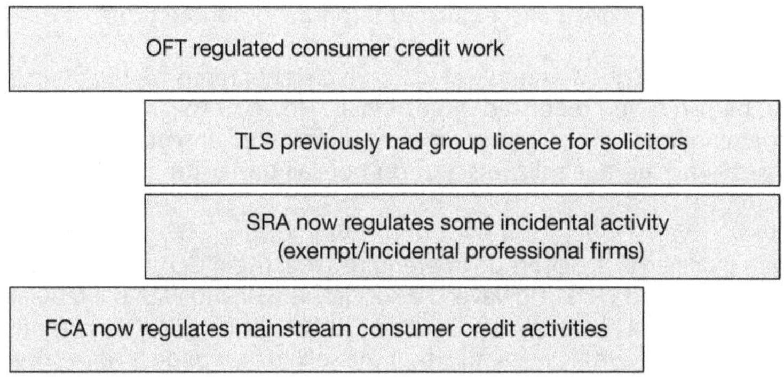

Regulation was passed to the Financial Conduct Authority during 2013/2014, but subject to a transitional period of a number of years.

Firms currently undertaking consumer credit activity such as (but not limited to) credit brokerage, debt counselling, and debt adjusting are asked to consider periodically whether they are exempt professional firms under the Financial Services and Markets Act 2000, Pt 20 or whether they are required to also register with the FCA.

If a law firm is undertaking the work incidentally to its main services they may be exempt from FCA regulation. The FCA has in recent years conducted further work reviewing the consumer credit regime which has altered the form and style of regulation from the OFT regime.

Further discussion of alternative regulators is contained later in this Part of the book in the section entitled 'Options Outside Regulation or With Alternative Regulators'.

Non Reserved Work

Non reserved legal work is any legal work which does not fall into the categories set out in the Legal Services Act 2007, s 12. As discussed above it is not theoretically necessary to be a solicitor, barrister, or hold any particular qualification or status to conduct non reserved legal work. In practice, however it is necessary to have qualifications and insurance to set up and operate effectively.

The position relating to non-reserved work is not widely known as the majority of those practising law are solicitors and barristers; two statuses which have successfully built a brand. Qualifications within law, such as degrees, are tailored to meeting the track to become a solicitor or barrister.

Many individuals, companies and organisations may be practising law to some extent. Any interpretation of legislation, reference to case law or research into a legal position could be counted as practising. Providing advice within an organisation may also be the same. This is, if within the boundaries, the same as conducting non reserved work. There are however specialists in some areas of law that are not reserved, and it is not necessary to be a solicitor, or hold approved qualifications or professional status to conduct them. As we have covered earlier in this Part of the book, non-reserved work is also regulated through authorised firms.

Employment law is a good example of work which is not reserved, but often involves solicitors, barristers and regulated professionals. However theoretically anyone can conduct employment work, and there are a number of unregulated employment law advisers who are not solicitors and do not fall under the regulatory scope of the SRA.

Individuals qualified as solicitors do not require a Practising Certificate if they are not undertaking reserved work. However if a solicitor is working within a regulated law firm or doing work which may be construed as 'solicitor work', it is commonplace to have a Practising Certificate. Similarly, if the solicitor is conducting work where it might be construed that they are doing so as a solicitor, they are often expected to hold a Practising Certificate; this may be particularly true if they are working with consumers.

This is a point of contention, as there are many other types of lawyer within legal services, with different qualifications in law, who cannot conduct work reserved to solicitors, and do not have a Practising Certificate, placing them at a competitive disadvantage. Solicitors feel differently; complaining that extent of the regulatory burden within legal services, means solicitors themselves, are at a competitive disadvantage to other lawyers.

Standards and Regulations 2019

The Standards and Regulations were launched in 2019, following three years of consultation under the banner 'Looking to the Future'. The changes are extensive. They introduce the introduction of solicitors working in a variety of different ways; new Accounts Rules; and broad changes and reductions in the regulations intended to allow for as much flexibility in practice as possible.

As well as or perhaps because of the legislative and political context, the Standards and Regulations come with a backdrop of condensing of the rules of professional conduct, which has been occurring for many years. If we look back to the SRA Handbook 1999, the rules were extensive and the Handbook was very large. The

2007 Handbook made a number of changes, included most notably in conflict of interest. We then saw major changes in 2011 as a result of the introduction of outcomes focused regulation and ABS. The Standards and Regulations 2019 were introduced in November of that year, following the Looking to the Future Consultation. The Standards and Regulations introduce the further new forms of practice of solicitors working in unregulated practices and freelance solicitors.

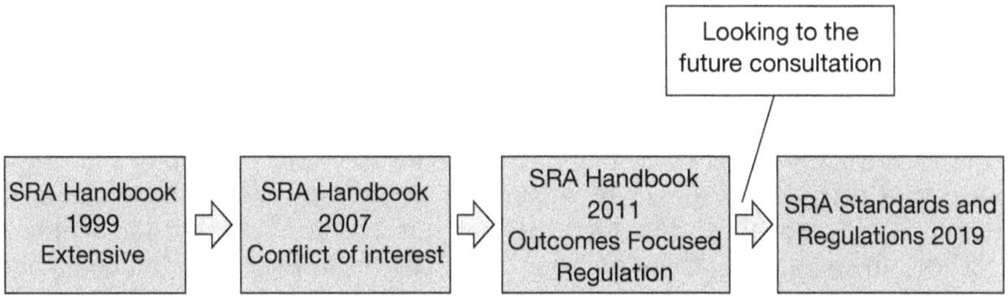

The Standards and Regulations have been known as the 'STARs', or even 'StaRs', or StARs', and some have already attempted to make a distinction between Standards on one hand, and Regulations on another. This implying that the name suggests there are some non-compulsory elements of the Codes and associated rules (known as the Standards), and while other aspects are compulsory (Regulations). This is not a supported argument; neither the regulator, nor any associated body has taken this approach, and the regulations should be applied in full. There is not a distinction between any of the sets of regulations, making some 'standards' and some 'regulations'. The writer believes the name has been chosen to make a distinction between the lengthy approach of the previous handbook and the intended brevity of these requirements, as well as describing the overarching nature of the requirements despite their concise style. We can see the expectation of the professionalism of the solicitor reflected in the title with reference to the 'standards', such as the 'higher standards' expected of solicitors, which we discuss elsewhere in this book.

Reviewing the Standards and Regulations, we can see a separation of two Codes of Conduct; one for firms and one for individuals. With the new regulations providing new forms of practice, including freelance solicitors, the SRA is clarifying that its regulation applies both individually, as well as to firms. We have seen this mirrored in the legislative provisions in the 'four Acts' discussed in the first part of this book and earlier in this Part of the book.

The content of the Codes themselves however is very broadly similar across firm and individual Codes, providing the same duties for both firms and individuals, but also separately, underlying their separate importance and application. We have to wonder whether the intention is to add to these Codes in future or perhaps take firms and individuals in different directions. We said in Part 1 of this book that this is the 11th version of the Solicitors Code (which has had various names), and the changes in the last two Codes have been very dramatic. We have gone from large books of information in and before 1999, to a much-reduced set of information in 2019.

In the previous Codes of Conduct, and under OFR, the SRA had published lists of 'indicative behaviours'. The idea was to say to the sector; set your business up with policies and procedures as you wish, but keep within these behaviours, as a means of allowing greater freedom in practice. Under their Standards and Regulations 2019, much of the detail has been removed; practitioners will find a much shorter Code of Conduct. The indicative behaviours have gone, but the rules should not be read flatly or without interpretation (overarching or otherwise); they are meant to continue to apply to a variety of situations and importantly *guide* practitioners' behaviour as an anchor. The practitioner (and their firm, COLP, or COFA) might ask: 'in taking this action have I also met this requirement?' The Codes as written are meant to be overarching and are intended to be applied widely to all circumstances.

In many cases, there are other statutory and regulatory provisions in place which affect solicitors. The Code of Conduct relies on these in some cases, without seeking to replace them with its own solution. There are statutory provisions and duties owed to a range of persons, where breaches of the same would likely also be a matter of professional conduct, because that person or firm is a solicitor or firm of solicitors. In some cases, there are short requirements in the Code that could also be breached if the underlying duties were not met.

The new overarching principles sit above all the other requirements in the Code. These are often the points where the SRA prosecute before the Solicitors Disciplinary Tribunal. The regulatory requirements that sit underneath should be seen as falling from the overarching principles, and each regulatory requirement should be able to be traced back to one or more of the relevant principles. In the Standards and Regulations, the SRA has distinguished between the two previously linked principles of honesty and integrity and posed them separately, as separate principles. They can be separate points and possibly should be written separately, although the separation of the two may raise eyebrows, as if it is an acknowledgement that solicitors may act without honesty but with integrity, and only be prosecuted for that! To consider the behaviour together as 'honesty and integrity' might be a different set of required conduct, to when taking the two together. We have examined honesty and integrity more closely in Part 5 of this book.

The SRA has removed several Principles from the 2011 Handbook, including those related to client services and client monies; duties to the regulator; and financial management. We examine the position of the Accounts Rules in Part 6 of this book and the how changes there might fundamentally challenge some of the duties owed to clients. The SRA said, including in conferences organised by the writer, that the changes were not to downgrade the effect of the remaining Principles on these areas. Certainly it is true from the writer's experience that breaches of the Accounts Rules are often prosecuted as issues of dishonesty or integrity, and that financial or practice management could be prosecuted as an issue of proper standard of work, acknowledging that solicitor work is not simply client facing and is also an issue of business management.

The Codes of Conduct cover the main aspects of the STARs, but there are also other sets of rules that comprise the totality of the STARs, including the Accounts Rules and Transparency Rules. We should also of course mention the various sets of authorisation regulations which contain the requirements relating to Practising Certificate and firm conditions. There are often long forgotten parts of regulatory approaches that sit within the SRA's sets of rules, and reviewing the full sets of rules allows us to take a fresh view of their regulation, beyond the Codes. Practitioners looking for innovation and new approaches are encouraged to view the Standards and Regulations as comprising many sets of rules, not just the Codes of Conduct, which could provide vast inspiration for new ways of working.

The main headline arising from the STARs is the option of practising in different ways. The new forms of practice provide the opportunity for firms to restructure their business as well as inform business decisions about interactions with third parties.

The new ways of practising mean people could set up businesses in new forms. Do be careful if conducting reserved work to obtain the correct authorisation as it is a criminal offence to conduct reserved work when not qualified.

Section 2: Discursive content

This next section contains more discursive content based on some of the key themes we can pull from the current set up of practising arrangements for solicitors. There are ideas and exercises for discussion or implementation in your own firms. Take the time to reflect on the exercises as part of your CPD and use them with your teams.

The practising year and timelines for management

As we have seen, there could be a number of reportable issues throughout any year, with the practising year running from October to October each year.

Renewal

As we have seen earlier in this Part of the book, the renewal is the largest information gathering event from the SRA in the calendar, taking place every October. It can take some time to plan, and some firms start over the summer, alongside the diversity data collection. Starting early also helps to notify all staff of the need to confirm that they have reflected on their learning and development needs and that they have been addressed during the year.

The renewal data can be a useful source of management information. We can ask some important questions, and use this data as an administration tool within law firms:

- What does the data tell you about the firm?
- How can you analyse the data both within this year and over the course of many years? What patterns and trends can you find in respect of both?
- Can you see any risk management issues? These might be one off events or particularly high numbers in one area, or continuing issues where you might notice the firm has a particular profile that puts it out of step with other similar firms.
- Can you see any issues that the SRA might be interested in that need to be addressed? How should these be explored?
- Can you compare yourself to another firm of a similar size and profile?

Anything that you are reporting to the SRA may be of interest to them, so it may be worthwhile considering whether this is standard within the area of law you are working in, and whether there is a pattern or trend specific to your firm. Seeking to understand the underlying cause of any patterns, or outlying issues can help manage the firm and its risks.

There is an opportunity to reflect on the renewal data which occurs while you are collecting it, and considering what you are submitting to the regulator, but also after the renewal. Considering the data afterwards may give more time for reflection on areas for compliance development for the forthcoming year.

There are some ideas of how to use the data collected in the renewal in the later section of this Part of the book entitled 'Management Metrics and Investigation Tools'. That section has a particular focus on using the data for counteracting fraud and other serious breaches within your law firm. You may be able to come up with alternative measures for the data and analyses for both within and across years.

The rest of this section considers some key events in the annual timetable.

Diversity data

The diversity data collection usually occurs every summer, and practices can ask their staff to submit data in the run up to the collection.

This is often also the time when practices start preparing for the annual renewal, and notify staff of the need to ensure their training plans are up to date to answer the question for reflection on learning and development needs.

It can be helpful to ask staff to update their data before or at the time of diversity data collection to ensure your records are correct (or close to being) for the renewal. Staff taking charge of their data in the diversity collection can also be helpful as they then own the 'equality and diversity' aspect of the data collection which can be quite personal.

Practising Certificate conditions

We will explore Practising Certificate conditions in the next Part of the book, but the SRA has the right to impose conditions both on renewal and at any time during the year. During the renewal is most common so we can see a delay sometimes in obtaining a new Practising Certificate in the autumn.

Decisions from the regulator can take some time, as the regulator gathers all the information it needs, and it is not unheard of for Practising Certificate condition decisions from the renewal to be outstanding until the following summer. Conditions can also be imposed during or following an investigation. You will usually have some form of notice from the regulator, before they are imposed, and the process for imposing conditions is covered in Part 3 of this book.

You can simply wait for the SRA to decide, but it is helpful to make representations, particularly as a firm, and explain how you will manage the perceived risk. Explaining that you intend to take steps to manage the risk, what those steps are, and when or how they will be implemented, can go a long way to reassuring the

SRA and could result in a decision not to impose conditions. If the decision from the SRA will take some time, it can be helpful to show that you have already taken steps to manage the risk.

Accountants' Report

An Accountants' Report is due six months after the end of an accounting period for solicitors. Many solicitors run their financial year to coincide with the established financial year, meaning the report is often due just after the renewal.

There are clearly other events within the financial year that need to be acknowledged; these may well fall to the COFA, or they might form a part of the work of another member of the finance team.

The Accountants' Report now only needs to be sent to the SRA if it is 'qualified'. That means the accounts demonstrate a substantial defect or issue in the accountants' opinion. However the planning, discussion and preparation of the report can all take time. If the report is being sent to the SRA it is because there is some form of risk. The SRA may be receiving that report just after the renewal information. This allows them to form an up to date picture of risks occurring within a firm, and whether they need to take regulatory action.

This complete information gathering occurs in October and may result in investigatory or regulatory steps within the following six months (into the spring the following year), or even beyond. Practices may perceive October as being an annual springboard for the rest of the year in risk management terms. Of course, the annual renewal and Accountants' Report are not the only causes of regulatory action and we discuss regulatory reporting by various sources in other Parts of this book.

Further discussion of the Accountants' Report is contained in Part 6 of this book.

The timing of these events (renewal, Practising Certificate conditions, Accountants' Report), may lend itself to a review of the practice's compliance and overall risk position before, around, or following the annual renewal in October.

ANNUAL COMPLIANCE TIMETABLE

Could your compliance department adopt an annual timetable? Would it help to have set dates for compliance activity throughout the year to ensure effective management of compliance within the firm?

Have a look at the two timetables below and consider whether they would work in your firm. Could you use these ideas to help provide structure to the COLP and COFA role, or could you develop your own timetable?

The timetables below also include events for other qualified lawyers. Do use what is relevant for you, add in whatever is necessary in your practice, and change the timings to suit your firm.

Sample Standard Annual Timetable

April	Begin Accountants' Report
April	Barrister PC renewal
April – June	End accountants' report
June	Licensed Conveyancer PC renewal
June – July	Reminder to staff to reflect on learning and development needs and begin renewal data collection
June - July	Diversity data collection
July – September	Insurance renewal (including planning and quotes)
July – August	Receive accountants' report and discuss any issues
September	Finalise renewal data
October	Complete renewal
October – December	Send accountants report (if needed to, if not before)
November	Notify staff that CPD year begins again.
November	Annual practice procedures update.
	Reflect on any compliance issues arising from the accountants' report, renewal, and any other practice events. Also consider any legislative or regulatory developments current or forthcoming.
	Do we need to make any changes and can we implement them now?
November – June	Plan any compliance associated tasks such as Lexcel or SQM renewal.
November – March	Manage any regulatory contact with SRA arising from renewal or accountants' report.

Sample Thematic Annual Timetable

When planning the annual renewal, what information do you need to gather? We can link the themes of the annual renewal questions to the activities of the year, helping COLPs and COFAs better understand both the risk profile of the firm and have an ongoing grasp of the different issues measured by the SRA.

The issues the SRA considers are:

- Organisational details, including individual details of solicitors and management. This includes their ongoing competence and diversity data. They also look at offices, organisational structure, and the type of work you complete.
- Financial matters, including turnover, client money held, and stability.
- Satisfaction and resolution, including PII, claims and complaints.
- Other relationships including introductions and referrals, separate businesses and outside influence.

As there are four broad groups, why not try attaching one group to a quarter of the year each, and run your own 'thematic' reviews on each subject. This might include themed file reviews, activities to raise awareness, and work with staff.

January – March	Firm Thematic Review – Financial Focus – client monies, turnover, and stability. Work on:
	Financial policies and procedures
	Client money file reviews
	Accounts rules training
April	Begin accountants' report
April	Barrister PC renewal
April – June	Firm Thematic Review – 'Satisfaction and resolution' – Review matters such as:
	Complaint and claim file reviews
	Client care procedures
	Customer satisfaction surveys
	Complaint handling training
	Client identification
	Transparency Rules
June	End accountants' report
June	Licensed Conveyancer PC renewal
July – September	Firm Thematic Review – Organisational details – Work on:
	Data integrity for the firm, offices, individuals, work profile of the firm (see Diversity below)
	Ensuring learning and development needs have been met for all staff
	Competence based file reviews
July	Diversity data collection
July – September	Insurance renewal liaison
July – August	Receive accountants' report and discuss any issues
September	Finalise renewal data
October – December	Firm Thematic Review –'Other relationships'
	Work on:
	Introductions and referrals policies
	File reviews looking at external relationships and client relations
	Payment and contractual terms
	Separate businesses
	Advertising and marketing
	Conflict of interest
October	Complete renewal
October	Send accountants report (if not before)
November	Notify staff that CPD year begins again.

Using this to understand the risks the SRA measures can help you understand your risk profile in more detail.

You don't have to run the thematic reviews all during one year; you could spread them over a number of years and include other topics as well including:

- Anti-money laundering
- Cybercrime
- Client conflict of interest
- Duties to the Court
- Equality and Diversity

You could also focus your thematic reviews on areas of particular risk for you, such as overseas instructions or remote clients, or particular areas of law.

What does the practising year mean to you?

Many people come into practice as a solicitor without considering the symbolism of the annual renewal. The renewal occurs at the same time as an annual harvest festival in the UK, and the timing might be considered to have cultural, historic, or even for some, religious significance.

The pattern of life in the UK also follows this familiar pattern, with the months of June to August being traditional summer holidays, and September the return to work and school for children.

Does your year look different and do you have a different expression? If so, how, and can you express that?

The renewal asks the question whether individuals have reflected on their individual learning and development needs and have addressed any issues. The renewal is also asking many questions about turnover, relationships, and business constructs. There is the opportunity to at this time of year pause and consider your practice over the past year, and what your practice as a firm has achieved, how it operates, and in some cases, how it reflects you and your staff as individuals.

Sometimes practice can be busy and stressful for the practitioner. Consider what is good about what you are achieving and allow yourself positive breathing space. Try to do this without considering what comes next; just take a moment to understand and acknowledge what you have achieved, and the efforts of the year just gone.

REFLECTIVE EXERCISES

There are two exercises below.

Complete exercise 1 alone and take up to a week to reflect on the answers.

Complete exercise 2 alone and take up to a week to reflect on the answers.

Do not complete exercise 1 and exercise 2 at the same time.

Exercise 1 – Personal reflection

Why did you become a solicitor?

How does your practice as a solicitor or your work within your firm reflect you as an individual?

How do you express yourself in your practice as a solicitor?

What have you achieved over the past year?

Exercise 2

What has your firm or organisation achieved over the past year?

Where have there been real efforts?

How has your firm or organisation interacted with your community or work contacts in the last year and provided benefit?

What do you and those around you deserve positive acknowledgement for?

Options outside the scope of regulation, or with alternative regulators

The distinction between reserved and non-reserved work means it is possible to operate a legal practice either outside the scope of legal services regulation, or with another regulator.

Obviously, reserved work can only be undertaken if you are qualified and regulated to do so, by an approved regulator. Additionally, regardless of whether regulated by an approved regulator, any business may fall within the scope of the Money Laundering Regulations, requiring regulation by an approved regulator or HMRC. Or a business may fall under the umbrella of a different regulator, such as the Financial Conduct Authority. Businesses considering whether they need to be regulated should consider the full implications of their proposed business model, including any associated businesses.

Alternatively, legal businesses may consider whether one of the other legal regulators covers their area of law and choose that form of regulation. One aspect of the Legal Services Act 2007 was to facilitate competition between legal regulators. Consequently, we see some accountancy regulators now offering to regulate probate practices, and the CLC competing with the SRA for conveyancing and probate.

The CLC were also the first regulator to regulate Alternative Business Structures in 2011. A move which caused shock amongst many; that the SRA, as the dominant regulator, were not the first! The CLC now regulate some of the largest conveyancing practices in the country, and openly competes with the SRA for the regulated community. Many solicitors have moved their practices or parts of their practices over to CLC regulation. For conveyancing (and probate) solicitors it is a viable option, but a large move with a lot of planning required, and firms should note that the regulatory requirements and standards are comparable, but different.

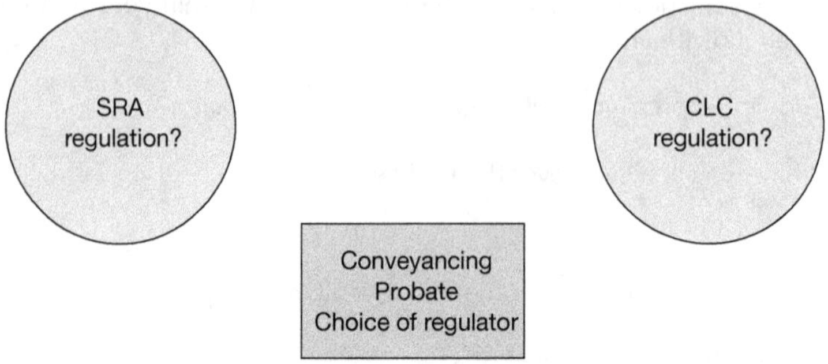

The same may also be true of the Bar Standards Board regulating advocacy providers. They offer recognised body recognition for those practising law with a substantial emphasis on advocacy. However the SRA also recognise bodies for rights of audience, and the CLC have within legislation the right to recognise bodies for rights of audience, albeit the CLC are not approved to offer those rights at the moment.

To make a decision about which form or forms of regulation is right for the business, we can look at the difference between the various regulatory protections and standards offered by the different regulators. We can also compare this to those without regulation. We can ask – what are the benefits of regulation and membership of the various associations, alongside the perceived drawbacks and economic impacts of compliance?

There may be an issue of consumer perception. The brand 'solicitor' is well known, as is the brand of barrister, and is trusted as a source authority and the preferred point of resolution for disputes. Perhaps this is at least in part due to the availability of legal aid, which although has since been dramatically restricted, was for many years widely available as a point of redress for consumers. A generation have grown up with relatively straightforward access to solicitors through the legal aid scheme, and although that scheme is now curtailed in comparison to what it was, the reputation of solicitors and barristers remains.

THE BENEFITS OF REGULATION – THE MICHELIN EFFECT?

An exercise to conduct in your own firm.

The Michelin Guide rates restaurants across the world and awards stars for excellence. It is a luxury brand, but is famous for identifying up and coming restaurants and eateries with exceptional standards of food.

The effect of a Michelin star can be dramatic. It can benefit the local area, including local house prices, local businesses, and suppliers, and inspire new business opportunities.

Discuss with your team:

How can we learn from the Michelin experience?

Does the qualification and title of solicitor signify a gold standard of:

a. Legal education?

b. Ongoing work?

As the following questions:

How can you and your team work to achieve high standards of everyday practice?

Can you assess and manage quality; can you work collaboratively or provide a bespoke service? How can we ensure excellence in practice even at a low level?

Are there local or bespoke suppliers we can work with to provide a personal service?

Remember that excellence is available even to the smallest suppliers.

National and International implications of practising arrangements

Solicitors are usually qualified as Solicitors of England and Wales; alternative qualifications and statuses are available in other parts of the United Kingdom. The recent Internal Markets Act may be the beginning of change in this area, but at the moment, the separate parts of the United Kingdom have their own Law Societies and Bar Associations, with their own criteria for qualification and practice. Outside observers will also note the corresponding differences in legislation in the separate parts of the UK, and the devolved powers in some areas.

Similarly, the treaties of the European Union allowed practising lawyers qualified in one European Union jurisdiction to exercise those rights and practice in another state on the same basis without completing further qualifications. Those from outside the European Union could also practice alongside solicitors (and previously alongside European Lawyers), or in some instances, complete further qualifications to become solicitors themselves.

To be a qualified lawyer might suggest that you have:

- knowledge of the law in *a particular jurisdiction;*
- the skills and experience to research the law in any particular area;
- knowledge of practice of the law in particular areas.

Obviously there are specialisms in different areas of law, but generally speaking the qualifications that exist in law cover a broad base of the law making capacity of England and Wales (and the United Kingdom), the position of the European Union, and core knowledge of the law in common areas of practice such as land law, wills and trusts, contractual obligations, and criminal law.

European Union qualified lawyers had been allowed to practise in England and Wales because of the overarching nature of community law. Jurisdictional knowledge or speciality is important, particularly if the individual practising solicitor intends to practice the law of that particular jurisdiction. However it is also possible for lawyers to work overseas and specialise in an area of law in another jurisdiction and practice that exclusively. For example working in England and Wales but your practice being primarily based overseas.

The writer has dealt with a number of cross-jurisdictional problems as well during her career. It is never easy to find solutions as the mesh of different legal systems and their separate jurisdictional requirements cause headaches for everyone involved. You often end up with two different systems of law, representation in both countries, and if there are complaints or issues of misconduct, different solutions reached on each side due to the different systems of regulation and complaint handling. Occasionally, there can be a positive arising from this which is the different perspective we see in legal solution and the viewpoint in regulation and regulatory standards. The perspective of the consumer might be different! We can only wonder how the consumer from Britain will fare, post Brexit, particularly as many have taken the opportunity to move to the EU or spend part of their time there.

EXERCISE: CROSS BORDER REGULATION

Have a look at some regulatory standards in another jurisdiction. What can you find that is similar to the standards you use? What is different? Does any of it give you a new perspective on the standards you see day to day?

Examples might be the Codes for Advocats in Paris, which require 'fairness' on the part of the Advocat in dealing with the opposing side, or standards of conflict of interest in Scotland where there is specific guidance on different scenarios that could cause a conflict of interest.

Choose a jurisdiction that interests you and have a look.

Differences in regulatory outcomes for different forms of practice

We have, earlier in this chapter, discussed the various practising arrangements for solicitors; whether individually or in firms. We have also discussed the options for those conducting non reserved work. One key difference in the arrangements for different forms of practice is the responsibility for breaches of the rules of professional conduct, and requirements to comply with different types of regulation.

COLPs and COFAs

COLPs and COFAs were quite controversial when they were first introduced and many within the sector felt they could be held responsible for the breaches of other members of staff, or the firm. We discuss the position of the COLP and COFA later in the book, but they have in some ways been singled out. Many firms put in place insurance arrangements, payable by the firm, to secure the position of the COLP or COFA, particularly considering the potential fines payable.

Alternative Business Structures

Alternative Business Structures, as we have seen, have their own practising arrangements. This is a complex technical area. However, a common discussion point is the fining position of Alternative Business Structures (ABS) in comparative terms to ordinary recognised bodies. ABS, which allow external investment, have the highest liability for fines in the sector; with fines available to the SRA of a maximum of £250 million. If we compare that position to the position of the recognised body, the difference is clear, with fines available to the SRA of £2,000, beyond which the SRA will refer the matter to the Solicitors Disciplinary Tribunal.

In practice, and due to the size of the fines, all potential fines of any reasonable level are referred to the SDT.

The large fining limit was set by the Legal Services Board when ABS were first introduced. COLPs and COFAs within ABS are known as HOLPs and HOFAs. The individual HOLP and HOFA within these structures can also be fined up to £50 million.

The reason for the extreme fining powers is the threat from external investment. The financial position of some organisations could pose such a threat to the independent practice of solicitors and other lawyers or could be seen to jeopardise the practice of law and operations of England and Wales. The extent of the fining powers reflects the gravity of the situation and the potential for very significant investment in the sector.

As we will see in the next Part of the book, Practising Certificate conditions can be imposed on both individuals and firms, and the SRA also has the power to restrict non lawyer ownership or management.

Unregulated firms

Anyone working in or supervised by a solicitor in an unregulated firm could have action taken against them if they seriously breach the rules of professional conduct.

It is questionable to what extent the SRA will seek to regulate businesses and individuals who are not registered with them. However, the SRA has the power to ban a non-solicitor from working for a solicitor or in a solicitor practice under the Solicitors Act 1974, s 43.

The SRA's approach in this area could leave the door open to unregulated firms and individuals being subject to the exercise of their powers. This is a subject unregulated firms will want to be aware of and fully brief any member of staff working with a solicitor.

EXERCISE: VIEWPOINT

An exercise for self-reflection and discussion. You can discuss these viewpoints with your team or management team.

Consider the following statements. What are your views? Do you agree or disagree?

- It is less attractive to become an ABS than a partnership because of the fining powers.
- Fining powers need to be high for ABS as a deterrent to exercising undue influence.
- Unregulated firms should be fully subject to the rules of professional conduct for solicitors if they employ a solicitor.
- We should revert to a system of regulation without COLPs and COFAs (or HOLPs and HOFAs), as COLPs and COFAs cannot be held responsible for breaches caused by other members of staff.

Organisational structure – freelancers, non-reserved work, and unregulated practices

The new rules under the Standards and Regulations provide the opportunity for firms to structure themselves in new ways. We must start by reviewing Rule 10.2 of the Authorisation of Individuals Regulations 2019. This rule provides that:

1. Individual solicitors can work freelance, conducting reserved work, subject to some restrictions.
2. Individual solicitors can work in unregulated practices providing non reserved work. The relevant rule describes this in the negative, describing that in some circumstances where a practice would ordinarily be a regulated sole practice, and would require regulation, it will not be taken as such.

Point 2 is more difficult to grasp if you are unfamiliar with regulation and regulatory law relating to solicitors. Firstly, remember that individual solicitors were regulated as Sole Practitioners through their Practising Certificate for many years. Then remember that solicitors have 'practices' in conceptual senses. Finally, remember that those same Sole Practitioners (discussed a minute ago) were regulated as recognised bodies in more recent years (rather than through their Practising Certificate) due to the existence of the conceptual practice (which the SRA was formally recognising). Once you have that point, the regulation makes more sense; you can start to see that the SRA taking away the formal recognition of the conceptual practice for the freelance or unregulated solicitor, allowing them to take their conceptual practice into freelance work or unregulated organisations, without it being formally regulated.

Both freelancing and working in unregulated firms provides the opportunity for far greater freedom in practice and practice structures. There are many different ways in which businesses might work together. Businesses can come together to:

- tender for contracts;

- work on research and development together to create new products or even stimulate growth in the market through new ideas;
- use each other's resources or key assets for the benefit of both parties;
- commission joint projects,
- increase buying power, for example buying in training or IT solutions together;
- work to help each other, for example through consulting or outsourcing within the same market;
- develop referral arrangements for excess work;
- move into new areas of work using each other's supporting frameworks;
- develop joint marketing or communication messages;
- see if there are areas of commonality;
- develop and deepen working relationships; and
- exchange ideas and information with the aim of raising standards.

The diagram shows how businesses might work with a range of other businesses in different areas all around them to develop their services and add value to the company or product offering. This does not have to be in your direct supply chain but could be with any other company where you share similar requirements or common goals.

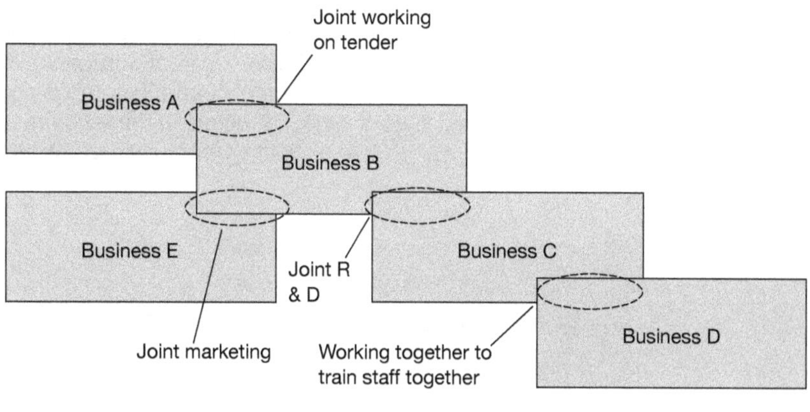

The opportunity to provide services to clients outside of the formal regulation of authorised bodies (and their recognition process, which takes many months), provides the opportunity for legal businesses to be structured in new ways. Perhaps some of these businesses will go on to seek authorisation from the SRA, or perhaps some will simply require the presence of a solicitor for a few months or on a trial basis while they consider a new idea or test the market.

However, there are challenges in implementation such as:

- Confidentiality, and how this will be maintained by an unregulated practice, particularly after a solicitor leaves. Should a solicitor take those files with them?

- Undertakings, and whether the individual solicitor should give these when in freelance practice or working for an unregulated provider, given the firm may not be able to assist when they leave.
- Insurance arrangements, and how these should or would be arranged. Usually, a firm pays for the insurance, so how will individual solicitors meet the costs and arrangements of appropriate levels of insurance? The SRA have said insurance is not always required to the minimum terms and conditions, and may be accepted at a lower level.
- Client protections: individual solicitors will not always have access to the same level of client protection and the compensation fund, there are also some restrictions on handling client monies.

For firms who have established themselves already, there are routes they can consider to ensure they take advantage of the new rules. The new rules provide the opportunity to hive off reserved and non-reserved work. As a result, it could be worth asking, what needs to be regulated?

There are specified areas of law within the Money Laundering Regulations that require regulation if you are an 'independent legal professional'. Reserved work still requires regulation, and individual solicitors can be regulated whether they are conducting reserved work or not. Other regulators may also have an interest in your work and you may still need to be regulated by the FCA, OISC, or HMRC for example, if you leave SRA regulation. You may still wish to be regulated by the SRA to ensure you meet these regulatory requirements, and offer suitable client protection, and this might have an implication on your marketing and branding.

In Diagram 1 is a potential scenario for firms who are considering how to organise their new structure under the new rules. You could have a parent company which is not regulated and separate out the various departments into different corporate arms along reserved and non-reserved lines of work. By following the reservation of the work, we can separate out the firm into two distinct corporate structures under the line of the parent company.

Diagram 1

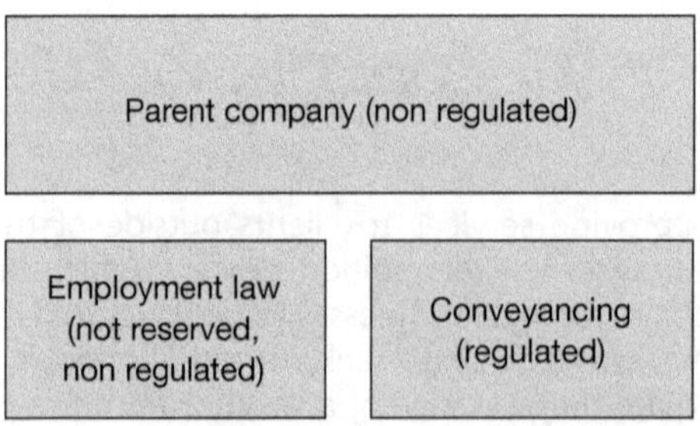

However, referring to Diagram 1 there are a number of considerations:

- Individuals could be regulated within the employment law structure, as you may have individual solicitors who wish to retain their PC and remain on the roll. In this scenario there would be no COLP, leaving the organisation to manage the support and obligations for the individual solicitors, or for the individual solicitors to manage this themselves. This might be a shock for individual solicitors who have been used to the support of a COLP structure.

- Whether the employment law firm would require regulation in any event if they were holding client monies (or whether they could use a TPMA).
- The conveyancing firm would be regulated as a separate business, meaning the business would need to be managed as such, limiting the crossover into the conveyancing firm and parent company.
- If the employment law firm suffered as a result of moving outside the regulated structure would it later be regulated to attempt to resolve those problems? We sometimes forget the supporting arrangements a regulator provides and the basis for management and decision making that is provided for legal services firms. Regulation can be useful for a firm and anyone considering a division should think about future strategic moves, including whether any part of the firm would wish to return to the regulatory fold in the future.
- How risks and potential conflicts in appointments would be managed across the structures.

Ultimately, although part of the firm would be 'hived off', individual solicitors in the unregulated part could still be regulated, and in fact, the entire business may be better off under regulation.

In the scenario described, we can also see there can be ethical stumbling blocks which we might want to take account of in the way we develop policies and procedures. This might include:

- considering ethical obligations across companies and whether they would have a different approach, or how they would be overseen from a central structure;
- how to manage client confidentiality (when the company does not have the same obligation);
- ensuring independence of advice to clients;
- ensuring staff who are regulated without a COLP have access to advice and support;
- ensuring clients understand who is offering the service and why; the separate business rule. This separate business rule is discussed further in the next section.

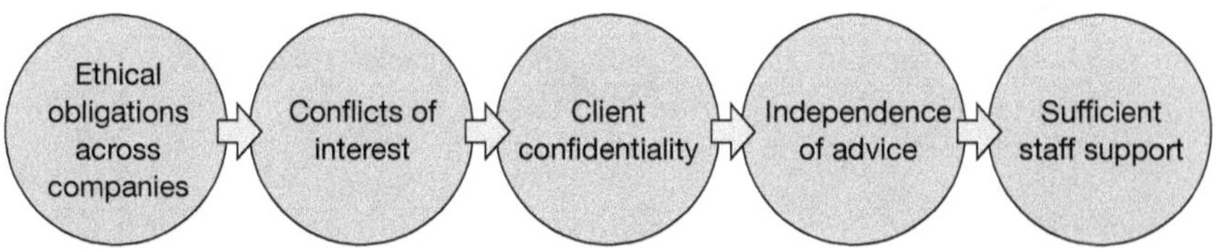

An alternative to the model shown at Diagram 1 might be a model with the administrative staff hived off and regulated legal staff in another business. This is theoretically possible, but very difficult due to the complexity of legal business. Again, firms would find themselves falling into a trap of confidentiality issues and legal professional privilege. Arguably of course, this final option was already open to firms prior to the new rules being introduced. There might be clear reasons why it is not often adopted.

The diagram labelled 'Diagram 2' is from a presentation the writer produced in 2017 and demonstrates the considerations a firm should cover when thinking about hiving off their work or part of their firm into an unregulated structure. We can see that some firms delivering reserved work must be regulated, but there can be a choice of regulator. Reserved, regulated work also has the benefit of support systems such as COLPs and COFAs, quality marks and membership schemes. Holding client money directly is another benefit of regulation. Given the extent of change in the new Standards and Regulations 2019, the firm can also consider how to approach compliance in their own way.

At the moment, the market is also still feeling its way with the new ways of delivering these forms of practice; it remains unclear to many whether there are restrictions on publicity for the new structures in respect of how they can describe solicitors and the firms. There is the possibility however that a new entrant into the unregulated space will be able to communicate this position effectively and build a brand which consumers will understand and trust. Of course, given the change in the market, testing entry by using freelancers becomes much easier, meaning firms could use this approach to try out new areas of law and marketing messages, if they needed to.

Firms considering the unregulated route may still require strong contractual positions to cover the traditional solicitor compliance requirements of complaint handling, conflict, confidentiality, insurance, and client care, alongside other matters. This may result in the 'unregulated' firm still being regulated to some extent.

Diagram 2

Reserved work	Non reserved work
Must be regulated	Require alternative regulation? FCA, ICO
Choice of regulator	Cost of organisational re-structure
COLP & COFA	Individual solicitors carry burden
Other regimes – Lexcel, CQS, Panel membership	No publicity guidance
Account Rules	Other contractual requirements
Start again with handbook? Question whole firm – do I need to do it this way? Revisit	May require 'systems'
Stick with current?	
Could simplify – Accounts, Breaches Register, Client Care, Conflict, Referral Fees, Supervision	

The question may be whether to change your structure or not. The Legal Services Act 2007 was intended to revolutionise legal services and the delivery of law, through the introduction of ABS. That change has not happened. We have seen further attempts at stimulating growth in the market since; this being the latest attempt. As we explore in Part 7 of this book, there is likely to be more change in the future, with indications of a single legal regulator for all law firms.

When considering your strategic direction therefore it is important to consider where you see the long-term developments in the market. There are, and remain, clear indications that the state is unhappy with the legal services market in its current disparate format, and there may be further change ahead.

Separate business rule

Law firms considering any association with other firms will also need to consider the SRA's separate business rule. This regulates different types of marketing. It also regulates the types of information the regulated individual or firm would need to provide to their clients concerning their regulation and how their services are being provided. The separate business rule has been in place for many years and previously prevented a solicitor from running or having any involvement in, another non-solicitor legal business.

The SRA started developing their approach to this area in 2015, alongside other changes to the Handbook at the time.

We have said a lot about the structures available for solicitors to practise in, earlier in this Part of the book, but we have failed to address the difficulty that is the separate business rule. The SRA have changed the way this rule is presented under the Standards and Regulations to previous handbooks, but the general meaning remains the same, that being that solicitors have to be careful when working with separate businesses to ensure those businesses providing 'solicitor-like' services are not confused with solicitors, and the protections offered to clients are explained carefully. The concern for a long time has been solicitors working with different businesses in different capacities, and this being used to attract clients, when in fact the client was not in receipt of solicitor advice. The worry being particularly for consumers who may be confused about the provision of legal services.

Solicitors must be clear about the protections offered to clients and when they are providing solicitor services.

Previously solicitors were restricted in the businesses they could become involved in. Generally, the restrictions applied to businesses that provided lawyer-like services, such as unregulated wills providers. Changes during 2015 saw such restrictions removed, provided firms were clear with clients about whether they are acting as a solicitor, and when certain protections such as the Legal Ombudsman and Compensation Fund, were available.

The current – 2019 – rule has become more complex, with attempts to clarify the relationship with unregulated practices.

One major change from 2015, which remains consistent, is that informed consent is necessary if you intend to refer, recommend, or introduce a client to a separate business, or divide a matter between the businesses. Informed consent means to clearly explain the position to the client, obtain their consent to that position, and even give them time to consider the situation if they wish. Some firms may wish to reiterate that clients are free to instruct another provider. In all cases, the client should be made aware of the links the firm has with the separate business, and any interest (particularly financial) in making the referral.

None of the above takes away the additional duties required by the remainder of the SRA Standards and Regulations, such as the prohibitions on own interest conflict, or acting with independence, honesty, and integrity.

BELOW IS AN EXTRACT OF TRAINING THE WRITER DELIVERED IN 2015, CONCERNING THE 'SEPARATE BUSINESS RULE'

> 'Changes to the separate business rule from 1 November 2015 have the potential for significant change in the legal services market. Previously solicitors were restricted in the businesses they could become involved in. Generally the restrictions applied to businesses that provided lawyer-like services, such as unregulated wills providers. Changes during 2015 have seen such restrictions removed, provided firms are clear with clients about whether they are acting as a solicitor, and when certain protections such as the Legal Ombudsman and Compensation Fund, are available.
>
> …
>
> The changes offer the potential for firms to place large parts of their firm beyond the reach of the SRA. We could see many firms hiving off their unreserved work into separate businesses, which if done in sufficient numbers could change the makeup of the legal services market in its entirety.
>
> *Client safeguards*
>
> Clients will need to be provided with clear information about when they are in receipt of regulated services and when they are not. …'

In 2015, the SRA introduced a requirement for informed consent to referral outside of a regulated business. There is not a definition of informed consent.

The writer defines informed consent as the clear knowledge of the individual concerning the situation in full, and their express consent to the action proposed. This means in practice that the firm (or individual) should be discussing their status and the level of their regulatory protection with the client and the consequences of any referral including:

- who they are being referred to, including whether that business or individual is a solicitor or solicitor firm (it is important to be clear when they are not);
- the extent of the regulatory protections or otherwise;
- the difference in the level of regulation, qualifications and regulatory protections available from the separate business (vis-a vis the solicitor business);
- the extent of the service provided by either business and whether referrals will be made back to the solicitor business and if so, when;

- any interest in making the referral, and the impact on the relationship (noting of course that firms cannot act in conflict of interest positions so financial interests may be quite small).

This information should be provided as simply as possible and ideally in writing for the client to sign. However also providing video information, considering your marketing and branding, or thinking about the different ways you can communicate with consumers effectively can also be helpful.

Regulated law firms may also find making these distinctions helpful in their own promotion, as they provide clear benefits when compared against unregulated firms.

Law firm strategic direction and qualifications

Alternative Business Structures were permitted by the Legal Services Act 2007 and first came into the legal services market in 2011.

We have seen outside forces such as accountants and estate agents entering the legal services market. Alternative Business Structures have not resulted in the major change or investment that some expected.

LAW FIRM DIRECTION AND QUALIFICATIONS

Exercise for your team

This exercise is designed for teams to complete together.

Step 1

Write down the traditional career path you would expect for a qualified solicitor from the point of qualification to retirement.

Does that change dependent on the size of the firm? Map out a few different options as a team.

Step 2

Write down all the businesses you can think of that your firm interacts with. Try to map out your supply chains.

Step 3

Imagine the integration of the businesses you have mapped out with law firms. What services would merged businesses offer and how would they be delivered to clients?

Step 4

What qualifications would you need to integrate your businesses with those around you? What qualifications would they need to integrate with your business?

Step 5

This integration (and more) is theoretically possible. Consider the career path at step 1. Can you see that changing and how might careers look in the future?

Final thought

ABS has so far not resulted in major change in the sector, although the roots of change may be there. Discuss whether you think change will come about during your career.

Management metrics and investigation tools

The renewal is not only useful for the SRA, firms can also use the data, alongside the diversity data, to develop your own management metrics. We explored some ideas for this earlier in this Part of the book.

Reviewing and analysing the data on an annual basis may provide you with the tools to paint a picture of your firm over the course of several years. You can also use the data to help you investigate possible issues of fraud and breaches of the rules.

Some of the renewal measures are the beginnings of useful management metrics in their own right. Below are a few ideas for analysis. See if you can develop your own.

MANAGEMENT METRICS AND INVESTIGATIONS FROM THE RENEWAL

Renewal theme	Analysis
Client monies held	Review your client account sums held over years; is there a consistent average? (Review mean, median, and mode averages).
	Do the sums you hold accord with what you expect, and reflect any changing work profile?
	Pay particular attention to the mode average if there is any concern about client account fraud or misreporting. You may see similar numbers come up repeatedly.
Complaints data	Review the number of complaints received, settled, and referred to LeO. It can be useful to review this by type of work undertaken, fee earner and department. Compare this data to customer satisfaction scores.
	Complaints data often presents itself in a normal distribution curve. Develop a graph showing on the side of the graph (y axis) the number of complaints received and across the bottom (x axis), the amounts paid out. This may demonstrate a clear average for your complaint handling, represented in a curve.
	Variations in your normal distribution curve can indicate issues of possible negligence (larger numbers of complaints, possibly settled for larger sums), or fraud (larger numbers of complaints settled for smaller amounts).
	The latter case may be attempts to find out about you or your firm for future use.

Referrals data	Review your referral contracts and consider how much you have received in from your referrals over the last year. What percentage of your turnover is received from referrals overall? Do not just consider the firm as whole; consider each department or even individual fee earners. If referrals or one source of work accounts for their work profile, would this impact their independence? Does it pose a risk to the business overall?
	Have a look at the statistical variation in the work generated between different referrers. This again may be a normal distribution curve. Plotting the income you receive and the amount of referrals, on a regular basis. Will help you find your average curve. This can help you find anomalies that, without alternative explanation, may be a cause for investigation.
	Referral fees can be a useful starting point for considering your business model. How much would you spend on marketing and maintaining a marketing database as an alternative? Have a think about where your most profitable work is, how else you receive work, and how much of your profit is paid out in referrals.
Organisational data	Check the data integrity of your firm.
	Organisational data can be useful for considering staff turnover and qualification mix.
	It can be useful to see who has a MySRA profile and who hasn't; an exercise in reviewing who makes decisions and whether staff intend to have a career as a solicitor.
Risk mapping	Use the data from the renewal to inform your risk mapping.
	There is a calculation of risk on the SRA website which looks at how the SRA calculates risk from the reports received.
	Why not use your data to discover what the calculation can tell you about your firm and how risky the SRA might perceive you to be?

Organisational lifetime events and closure

Does an organisation have a lifetime? We might see the legal organisation develop through its life from inception, authorisation, and then development. Development stages might include new areas of law, new partners, and outside investment. The organisation might be sold, or it may merge. Similarly, individuals may leave, departments may be closed, and an existing book of business may be sold before the final stages of closure are apparent. After closure, if there is no successor practice, the remnants of the firm must maintain run off cover.

There are a number of reasons to involve the SRA in the closure of the practice, but some of these reasons are limited to notification:

- Informing the SRA that you intend to close the practice.
- Informing the SRA of the sale or merger of the practice.
- Informing the SRA that they have authorised your practice in error.

We have seen that in some cases the SRA can intervene in the practice, but these are limited to serious risks to the public and clients. The SRA can revoke a firm's authorisation, but this is an anomaly in that it suggests the practice should never have existed – the SRA can use this power, and threatens to sometimes, but their preference is for orderly closure. The SRA can recognise an orderly closure of a firm and that it has been wound up or has ceased to exist.

The closure of a firm might cover attending to:

- Live client files and monies, or matters where items remain outstanding. Monies and papers usually belong to the client and should remain with them, so seeking their view on the choice of firm is important.
- Closed client files and their storage and maintenance.
- Insurance and run off cover.
- Premises and staff requirements.
- How enquiries will be dealt with – this can be a telephone number to contact if another firm is taking on old matters for you or another practice who might be able to help with future with different types of work. The writer has known former solicitors who continue with their practices long after they have ceased working within them, and it can be helpful to consider your own retirement.

Although a difficult subject, it can be helpful for practitioners and their families to consider what happens to their practices in the event of their death. Making a will is essential for partners in one or two partner firms, and involving family in these decisions is important. Don't forget that intervention is a consequence of the death of a Sole Practitioner, or in some cases a family member might be expected to assist with the closure of the firm, even by the regulator.

You might consider this as part of your contingency planning and which local or other firms could assist you.

Freelancers and solicitors working in unregulated firms should take particular care when considering the arrangements for their departure. How will the unregulated practice you have been working with or employed by work in the future, and how will they work alongside the professional requirements of conflict and confidentiality? It is unlikely they would be able to open your papers and files after you had left, so arrangements would need to be made for storage and enquiries. The position may also need to be made clear to the unregulated provider that they were unable to take such steps.

Clients are still likely to require confidentiality and just because you are no longer at the business does not mean the SRA cannot intervene in the parts of the practice you have left behind. This can be an intervention (or part intervention) in your name, causing a regulatory issue, and reputational damage to you. The SRA also often impose costs where an intervention could have been avoided. Do ensure you make plans for your departure and how matters will be attended to.

If we discuss the position of ongoing firms, some firms have been maintained for hundreds of years with successive partnerships taking over from each other. However we see more corporate structures being established in recent years. With the move away from personal responsibility and liability do we think that more or less firms will be closed by way of intervention in future years? What will the closure of corporate solicitor structures look like in 100 years' time?

EXERCISE FOR DISCUSSION WITH YOUR MANAGEMENT TEAM

Adams Gregory are a (fictitious) local law firm established in 1830 by the then partners John Adams and Phillip Gregory. They are based in the South of England and currently have a number of offices, but started from just one office. The firm has been sold a number of times. At one point in 1980s it was known as Adams, Gregory and Young, but reverted to its original historic name in the 1990s for marketing reasons; the firm is very well known in the local area and amongst lawyers. Over the years, the firm has operated in various areas of law including commercial law, conveyancing, crime, agriculture, construction, wills and probate, litigation (including personal injury).

You are the current partners of Adams Gregory. Due to the rise in consumers giving instructions remotely and the availability of lawyers over the internet, there has been a steady decline in business for the last twenty years. There is still a large local demand for conveyancing, wills, and probate, but price matching, information available on the internet and the new rules in price transparency have all made the prospect of investment in the firm more questionable. The firm still relies heavily on its local presence and reputation.

Two of the partners are due to retire shortly and would like to sell their parts of the business, however there are no obvious candidates who would buy amongst the staff. The remaining three partners cannot buy the retiring partners out of the business for financial reasons. The two who are retiring conduct conveyancing and personal injury litigation. The remaining three partners conduct wills and probate, agriculture, and crime. Both partners who are retiring are willing to semi-retire and work flexibly, for example, as consultants, or in different ways.

Consider:

With reference to historical events:

(a) Which of the historical events described would have been notified to the regulator (The Law Society as it was)?

Currently:

(b) The work profile and position of the firm and the attractiveness of retaining certain departments;

(c) The options for the firm;

(d) The options available for the individuals;

(e) Discuss what practical steps need to be taken to affect any transfer of work;

(f) Discuss what needs to be notified to the SRA;

(g) What power does the SRA have if there is a disorderly closure?

For the future:

(h) What changes (if any) do you think Adams Gregory will need to make to continue in the future? (We are assuming it would continue, it might not, and feel free to take a different view.)

(i) Should the remaining partners prepare now for their futures, and if so, how?

You may wish to consider the position with reference to the structural options available to the firm.

Standards and Regulations 2019: development, history and change

With the announcement of new forms of practice open to solicitors, and the prospect of unregulated firms entering the market with none of the regulatory burden of solicitor firms, there has been a question mark over the fairness of the new system to existing firms.

As a result, debates have begun about whether to 'hive off' the parts of law firms that do not conduct reserved work, or parts which can be done without regulation, and we have covered some of those debates earlier in this Part of the book. We saw in Part 1, that there are barriers to entry in joining the legal services market, particularly from an individual perspective.

Conversely, there can also be barriers to exiting the market. Law firms and individuals have invested significantly in set ways of working, in jobs, and in the infrastructure needed to run and maintain a business in this sector. All of this has been done under the cover of regulation and within the bounds of regulatory rules which have been in place for many years. The majority of law firms the writer knows and works with have been set up to adhere to the regulatory rules in place pre-ABS, and whilst those changes have not had the impact expected, the freedom of the new changes, puts some firms in the position of potential closure due to the flexibility of the competition in comparison.

We might use the analogy of turning around a large ship to describe the ability of a large law firm to move against the unregulated business in competition. Some firms simply will not be in a position to make such a move. We might think about:

- the investment needed;
- the firm's physical positioning (for example office infrastructure) and storage;
- existing contractual agreements and sources of work;
- staff contracts and training commitments;
- ongoing work and existing client bases; and
- insurance commitments.

It could be a major change to re-structure to compete with new forms of practice. Most businesses might run on a five to ten-year strategic planning life cycle, but this change has been introduced within the space of three years, with consultations starting in 2016, and the relevant rules being introduced in 2019. Firms simply have not had the time to consider the consequences or prepare. Firms could be taken by surprise by the ability of new forms of practices to work in innovative ways or capture their market base.

The writer's master's degree covered business related subjects and the winter has been struck by the relative comfort of solicitor practices from the challenges of competition which other sectors and individual businesses face. This is clearly due to reserved work. This work has been shielded and has provided a basis for the establishment of a business. There is an ongoing need amongst local communities for legal services, and solicitor firm have been protected from other forms of business which otherwise would have taken a share of their market.

The agility of freelance solicitors and unregulated businesses, as well as the potential opportunities available to them might cause major long term effects. The legal services market could well look very different in ten to fifteen years than it does now.

There is one sticking point which may challenge this vision of the future. The unexpected impacts of the coronavirus pandemic, coupled with the impact of Brexit might cause major downturns in the legal services market, making investment in this area much less attractive. The coronavirus has taken us all by surprise and the shock may be felt economically. It also may be felt emotionally and psychologically by citizens, which could result in a delay to the impact of the changes as people seek comfort in the familiar.

Below are excerpts from courses the writer has produced over the last six years covering the:

- Looking to the Future consultations
- Standards and Regulations
- Developments of freelance solicitors
- Possibility of solicitors working in unregulated businesses

We can see from the materials how the regulations have developed over the last six years. Some of the presentations and materials were delivered in conjunction with the SRA.

2016 Material Breach and Practising Certificate Conditions

> 'The most dramatic shift has been in the Looking to the Future Consultation which opens the prospect of solicitors working in unregulated businesses, providing (unreserved) legal advice to the general public. With this prospect comes the question of whether ABS are necessary, and whether firms will hive off sections of their business along reserved and unreserved lines. Given the distinctions of reserved and unreserved work are arbitrary, could we see the abolition of this work altogether in future?

2016 Discussion with the SRA – Presentation

This presentation was delivered by the writer with the SRA to a group of law firms and solicitors in London, in September 2016, at the beginning of the consultation of Looking to the Future. The material below is the writer's slides from the presentation. There was a separate presentation from the SRA.

Compare this presentation to the presentation from 2017, which is featured later.

'Solicitor regulation separated from firm regulation

- Solicitors free to deliver non-reserved legal services in unregulated firms (no LPP?, two tier system, conflict / confidentiality)
- Separate Code of Conduct for firms and individuals
- Brings SRA into line with ICAEW, CLC and CILEx (single regulator?)
- Competence Statement remains
- Sole solicitors providing reserved legal services must be regulated as entities
- Special bodies
- PII & Comp Fund
- In-house'

'Revised Principles & Handbook

- Reduced
- 6 Principles
- Material Breach / Serious Breach
- Indic Behaviours removed
- Compliance officers retained (but up for discussion)
- Managers and employees responsible & liable in firms
- Some overlaps between codes
- Qualified to supervise?'

'Sep Consultation

- Simplified rules
- Solicitors in unreg firm not permitted to hold client money
- Changes to definition of client money to inc disbursements for which firm is liable (not client)
- Escrow provisions'

2016 – Looking to the Future – Discussion note on dividing a firm into regulated and non-regulated work

In 2016, the writer produced this discussion note on hiving off part of a law firm into regulated and non-regulated lines, following concerns over competition from unregulated businesses. At the time, the Standards and Regulations 2019 was expected to be launched in 2018.

'Following the SRA Consultation "Looking to the future", it appears in 2018 it will be possible to run an unregulated business offering non-reserved legal work, delivered by solicitors. It was already possible to hive off non-reserved work, but a business could not employ solicitors practicing as such unless they were regulated by the SRA. The consultation proposes to change that rule.

The changes are arguably more radical than the introduction of ABS, yet they have had very little discussion in comparison – either in legislative terms or between law firms.

Here are our points to note if you're thinking of hiving off part of your business:

1. This is not a done deal – The Law Society have reacted very strongly against it calling for substantially re-worked and re-presented thoughts, with more guidance. The Legal Services Board have also recently backed the idea of a single legal regulator who focused on individual subject areas. If you are strategic planning, be sure to factor in this uncertainty – any solicitor you employ may be subject to changing rules and regulations for some time.
2. There may be considerable advantages in hiving off part of or a whole firm. A lack of SRA regulation provides a greater degree of freedom in almost all areas of practice. Client referrals, confidentiality, billing, and even money laundering obligations lessen significantly when you are not regulated. The cost of insurance substantially reduces under the proposals, which say there should be no minimum terms and conditions for unregulated firms employing solicitors.
3. The insurance position is a little unclear; solicitors would need to satisfy themselves that the insurance of an unregulated firm was sufficient. This lacks some clarity – what constitutes sufficient?
4. LPP arguably disappears if a retainer is with an unregulated entity – but consider whether you are likely to need it or whether clients expect it.
5. Can you be sure you will not cross into reserved work? If you are likely to need to issue proceedings the time to call in a law firm will need to be carefully thought through. Carefully consider all types of work you might take on to ensure you do not accidentally cross the line.
6. Consider how you will manage the potential conflict between a solicitor's professional obligations and those of the company. The SRA have issued limited guidance on this and it could have a substantial impact. Would a solicitor be obliged to operate an individual complaints procedure? How would they behave if the company wanted to disclose confidential information? We believe to a degree this could be navigated with clear explanations to the client, well-crafted terms and well thought out policies, though it could take time and compromise on the part of the company. Over time this will be become clearer.
7. You may consider not employing solicitors at all. After all, you can offer unreserved work to clients without them. It may be simpler to

run separate but associated businesses, with the law firm providing legal advice as necessary.

8. Consider client information and how this will be crafted. What client safeguards are you willing to adopt as a result of a solicitor employee's regulatory obligations? Don't forget there are also consumer protection laws to adhere to.
9. Consider how solicitors in a new organisation would be supervised and managed. How will they be supported to ensure their ongoing competence and professional development, as well as ensuring the correct interpretation of the Handbook.
10. Ensure you have considered how you will manage the practicalities of such a move – including conflict with past clients, confidentiality of information you are holding, and other points such as IT, HR (TUPE) and infrastructure. A full change management programme, looking at all of the pinch points, may be needed.'

The SRA's Looking to the Future: A Song of Fire and Ice

Published 2017 and 2018 in Legal Futures

2018 – 2021 Material Breach and Practising Certificate Conditions

The following article was written by the writer in 2017, and has previously been published in a number of locations.

> 'Much like Game of Thrones, the latest handbook plans from the SRA have plenty of strategic intrigue, a long political backstory, and ancient traditions at stake. Will winter come for the average high street firm, or will the barriers to entry of the legal services market (let's call it 'The Wall') keep them out?
>
> Opening up of the legal services market has been on the agenda for longer than any of us have been alive, but it hasn't been achieved yet. It started with barristers granting rights to solicitors in in the 1800s. In latter day terms, control of legal services came under review from the Benson Commission in the 1970s, saw the introduction of Licensed Conveyancers in the 1980s, and the in more recent years the suggestions of the OFT and Clementi led to the introduction of Alternative Business Structures.
>
> Outside investment has transformed some individual firms and legal services groups, but has not been the 'big bang' many anticipated. Six years on from the last major handbook review, the SRA have recently confirmed their intent for a further relaxation of the rules, aiming to promote business flexibility.
>
> Looking to the Future means solicitors will be able to practice in non-regulated businesses, while still carrying the title solicitor, provided they are not conducting reserved work. Two new draft codes (one for the individual, and one for firms), will sit alongside reformed (and individually focused) principles, and – of course – the new Competence Statement, which underpins the professional ability of the individual.
>
> While the detail of the new Handbook and potential structural changes isn't confirmed yet, there are some thoughts worth considering now, whether your firm intends to stick or twist:

Stick

For those busy working in firms, the changes to the new Handbook are unlikely to impact much on the day to day operation of the firm. Although the draft handbook is smaller, most of the overarching themes of the current handbook are still there. The SRA have indicated an intention to publish guidance, and firms will undoubtedly need to take that into account. Approaches to conflict will be interesting as the new wording appears to be a slight relaxation of the current position (although the SRA do not present it that way).

Firms who do not wish to change their structure or way of working should be aware of the potential for increased competition and that there may yet be further changes aimed at opening the market.

Consumers informed the SRA that they would value being told about the protections afforded by the compensation fund and compulsory levels of PII. Regulated firms should note the consumer campaigns run by the SRA and consider whether to take advantage of this promotional point.

Twist – Working in an unregulated firm

Should a firm decide to adopt a different strategy, they could consider hiving off part of their firm which does unreserved work.

New entrants to the market could also set up providing solicitor-led non-reserved legal services in unregulated firms.

However, there are a number of considerations for those taking an unregulated route, including:

1. Compliance – this is here to stay. The SRA has specified that unregulated firms will need 'systems' to help solicitors manage conflict. Unregulated firms will likely still have to assist the individual solicitor(s) in in complying with the obligations in the individual handbook, as well as the SRA's guidance. If a number of solicitors worked for a business, the compliance obligations would be broadly similar to current arrangements, but without the overarching management and structure requirements.
2. PII cover – Although this would not be a regulatory requirement it is probably sensible to have some in place. Solicitors will still have to be clear with clients about when they make a mistake.
3. A position on the issue of Legal Professional Privilege, and how this would work (or not) in their individual business. The SRA say this is a matter of law. The similar issue of 'privileged circumstances' in reporting AML matters also arises, although the SRA have not addressed this. The question arises – will it be attractive to firms or clients to operate without privilege if necessary?
4. A position on intervention – the SRA will still have the right to intervene into the practice of a solicitor based in an unregulated firm. Where does that leave work product, papers, and monies belonging to an unregulated provider? The unregulated business may look for additional insurance against this eventuality.

5. Branding and marketing - hiving off part of a firm may also mean it needs a new identity. To what extent will an existing firm require different branding to differentiate it from a regulated SRA firm? The detail of the new Handbook should hopefully provide answers.
6. Other regulatory concerns – if you move to an unregulated provider do your activities fall under the scope of another regulator? Firms using the exemptions in consumer credit work may need to be regulated by the FCA, for example.

Twist – New entrants to the market

'Do the changed regulatory requirements make it easier to enter the market? Possibly not; "The Wall" is still quite high. New entrants to the market will need to consider all of the above, and more.

There will be barriers to exit – it's not easy to "test" entry to legal services on a trial basis. The rate of growth and profitability varies between unregulated areas so we should not make the mistake of assuming new entrants will see each opportunity as attractive. There is, importantly, also the extent to which new unregulated businesses can build a brand. Consumers have thus far proven fairly loyal to the current legal services model. They understand and trust the solicitor name. Joint ventures or integration between solicitors and other current players in the market seem more likely than brand new ventures.

Those in watching these developments see other movements on the horizon, from the possibility of the single legal regulator, to the question of reserved and unreserved work. If the new handbook doesn't stimulate competition in the market, further attempts may be made.'

2017 / 2018 New SRA Handbook – Strategic and Compliance Implications of Looking to the Future– Presentation

This presentation was delivered exactly one year after the 2016 presentation. Again, the presentation was delivered alongside the SRA, with the SRA delivering a separate presentation. In particular this presentation focused on the compliance aspects of the new rules, and the content of the proposed Standards and Regulations.

Compliance Implications:

Conflict/confidentiality

Privilege/privileged circumstances

PII cover/Comp Fund

Consumer branding

Intervention

LeO jurisdiction – unauthorised LS providers?

Consumer protections – LSCP – logo?

Undertakings

Extent of compliance systems – little change?

Reduction in size of SRA? Higher fees to SRA? Single legal regulator?

Firms	Both	Individuals
Compliance and business systems	Maintain trust and act fairly Service and competence Client money and assets Referrals and introductions Conflict and confidentiality Co-operation and accountability Client care	Competence statement 'Systems' in unregulated firms

Firms

[Increased emphasis]

Wider wording on accountability

Able to justify your decisions

Do not abuse your position

Changes to COLP/COFA?

Firms

[Less emphasis]

Governance

Supervision

Outsourcing

Publicity

Indicative behaviours

Considerations: Hiving off your firm

Consider whether work is reserved or not reserved

Consider movement around you:

'The Wall' – Qualification, Regulation, Ownership, IMF, barriers to entry/exit

Rate of growth/profitability in your area

Extent to which new entrants will build a brand

Joint ventures – vertical or horizontal integration?

Will distinction between reserved/non reserved last?

Single legal regulator

Reputation of regulated sector – will consumers care?

Considerations: Hiving off part of your firm

Reserved Work

Must be regulated

Choice of regulator

COLP & COFA

Other regimes – Lexcel, CQS, Panel membership

Accounts Rules

Start again with handbook?

Question whole firm set up – do I need to do it this way?

Revisit

Stick with current?

Could simplify – Accounts, Breaches Register, Client Care, Conflict, Referral Fees, Supervision

Non Reserved Work

Require alternative regulation? FCA, ICO

Cost of organisational re-structure

Individual solicitors carry burden

No publicity guidance

Other contractual requirements

May require 'systems'

2019 – Material Breach and Practising Certificate Conditions

"Following the introduction of the Legal Services Act 2007, SRA began creating new systems and procedures under OFR to modernise regulation and handle the challenges of Alternative Business Structures. However this has failed to introduce the 'big bang' many hoped for in the market. As a result, the SRA is attempting further opening up of the market by introducing two new forms of professional practice:

- Freelance solicitors
- Solicitors working in unregulated practice, carrying on unreserved activities

These are being introduced in November 2019 with the introduction of the new SRA Standards and Regulations. The potential contractual opportunities are vast; businesses could set themselves up in different ways as a result of the changes.

…

Competition may increase with different business models within the legal services market. There are however some caveats; reserved work cannot be conducted by those in unregulated practices, and different arrangements might need different forms of regulation. Not all activities will attract the coverage of the compensation fund, and the insurance requirements are different.

These latest developments have not been before parliament; the SRA have reinterpreted the provisions of the Legal Services Act to provide greater flexibility. These new business opportunities come alongside Brexit; with the timing seemingly intended to stimulate competition in the market.'

Will freelancers be self employed?

WILL FREELANCE SOLICITORS BE SELF-EMPLOYED?

This question was posed to the writer during the Big Voice Conference 2019, and the answer provided is set out below.

'This is an excellent question, with quite a technical answer. We do not know the final answer for sure yet, as it appears the market will decide (we cannot foresee every business outcome or opportunity).

The Solicitor's Regulation Authority, in their rules, has arguably allowed for both self-employment and worker status [under Regulation 10.2 of the Authorisation of Individuals Regulations 2019].

In the course of practice there will undoubtedly be issues with the creation of expertise, advice and proprietary information, as well as the solicitor's duty to act independently and keep client documents confidential. This is the diagram outlined in your presentation and is conceptually contained in the Solicitor's Act 1974 (albeit not in the context of self-employment or tax).'

[The diagram referred to is the diagram produced earlier in this book (p 68) discussing solicitor 'practices']

'The existence of 'the practice' means there is likely to be a difficulty with finding a solicitor to be a worker or not genuinely self-employed. The only way round it might be some very cleverly worded contractual documents, and a limitation on the work undertaken for external clients.

For example, a freelance solicitor gets a gig at a supermarket advising clients on wills. If the solicitor left after 6 weeks, because it was a short term gig, the supermarket would have a difficulty accessing the papers and documents because they are client confidential. It might mean the supermarket couldn't open them! The solicitor may also have an ownership argument for the ideas contained within them. In this situation the solicitor and supermarket need to find an agreeable solution.

Solicitors practising on their own have been required to have 'recognised sole practices'. This is the regulator's way of recognising 'the practice' and protecting ownership and confidentiality of client documents and papers. It also maintains independence. This is the concept outlined within the presentation. It also means that certain aspects of some legislation (such as the Bribery Act), arguably apply to those bodies at a corporate level.

Under rule 10 of the Authorisation of Individuals rules it says solicitors are required to have a sole practice, unless certain conditions apply.

The first condition is that the solicitor conducts only non-reserved work*. If this is the case, the solicitor does not need to meet any further conditions.

The second scenario is that the solicitor does do reserved work*, in which case the conditions in 10.2(b) apply, which state that a solicitor must be self-employed. The guidance supporting this confirms it must be genuine self-employment. We spoke about the need for a solicitor to be independent; this particularly applies to reserved work as it is a criminal offence to conduct reserved work when not entitled.

You will note that one of the conditions in 10.2(b) is the need to have 'adequate and appropriate' insurance. This is different to the requirements imposed on the recognised sole practice and arguably at a lower level, so an attempt at removing some of the barriers to entry and exit from the market.

There is no obligation on a solicitor to become a freelancer, and the SRA will still be recognising sole practices, if the solicitor wishes.

*Reserved work is defined within section 12 of the Legal Services Act 2007, and is the work which is defined to certain classes of lawyer. It includes advocacy, conveyancing and the grant of probate (although not will-writing).'

Part 3

Practising Certificate Conditions

Contents

Section 1: Technical content
- Historical development and use in other areas of professional practice
- Imposition of conditions
  - Public interest
- Process for imposing conditions
- Regulation 3 (The List)
- Suspension of a Solicitor's Practising Certificate
  - Criminal charges and dishonesty
- Risk management
  - Risk management: mathematical or lateral decisions?
- Common Conditions
  - Sample Set A and B
  - Sample Set C
  - Sample Set D
  - Notes from the samples
  - Further Analysis

Section 2: Discursive content
- Conditions as a regulatory outcome – the CLC example
- Regulatory decision making
- Achieving a balance in risk management
- Conditions, unregulated firms, and freelance solicitors
- Representations for conditions and risk management
- SDT outcomes and SRA outcomes
- Restriction or more practice?
- Managing others with conditions: COLP, COFA or HR?
- Do conditions work?
- Addressing personal development needs
- Confidentiality, public confidence, and publication in an age of digital information
- Alternative employment
- Imposing stricter sets of rules as conditions
- Annual renewal and information for decision making
- Legal advice and conditions

Section 1: Technical content

The first two parts of this book outline the different forms of regulation and how solicitors can practise – both in firms and individually. This next part of the book explains a powerful regulatory tool within the SRA's armour; the ability to impose Practising Certificate conditions.

The imposition of conditions on a Practising Certificate is intended to restrict the practice of the individual solicitor. This power is used by the regulator in the public interest. This restriction 'in the public interest' means for example that the solicitor's practice poses a risk to the public and should therefore be curtailed until such time that risk has been resolved. This risk may be resolved to the regulator's satisfaction through additional training, support within or outside the firm, or prevention of the operation of such roles that have caused or may cause a difficulty for the solicitor or their clients.

Conditions can be imposed on individual solicitors through their Practising Certificate. As we have seen, a Practising Certificate allows the solicitor to 'practise' law. Maintaining a Practising Certificate is both convention within the industry and required for certain types of work (which are covered in Part 2 of this book).

Conditions *cannot* be imposed directly individually on non-solicitors, managers or other unadmitted persons working in legal services or for solicitors. The same is also true of unregulated firms; conditions *cannot* be *directly* imposed. Conditions can only be imposed directly on solicitors and regulated firms; the firm position being explored further in Part 4 of this book.

Unadmitted persons working for solicitors with conditions or within firms with conditions may be impacted by the condition, although they are theoretically not subject to it themselves. The same is true of managers working in firms. Similarly, unregulated firms could also be impacted by a condition on an individual working in their firm.

It is *theoretically* possible to use the direct imposition of conditions on individual solicitors and regulated firms to:

a. prevent, restrict or otherwise manage the actions of unadmitted persons; and

b. prevent, restrict or otherwise the operation of an unregulated firm within legal services.

However the writer has not seen these actions taken previously; conditions have been to address a concern related to the individual solicitor or their overall position.

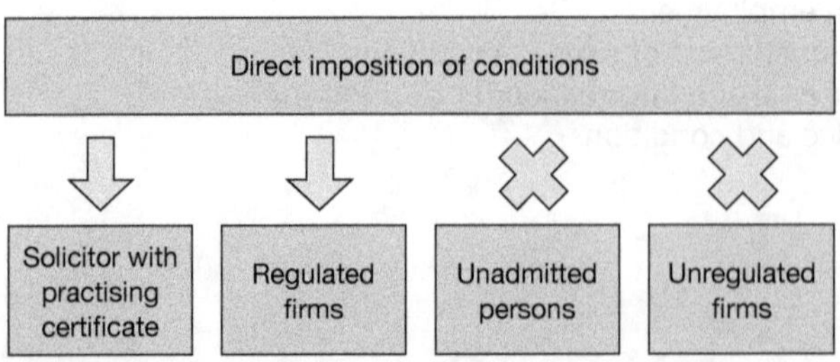

In order to impose a condition, the SRA must be able to articulate their concern, and draft a suitable condition to express the potential resolution. We cover the technical detail of the SRA's rules on this subject in this Part of the book. There are also a number of serious situations in which conditions would be imposed which are provided for in the legislation.

The imposition of conditions is just one of the regulator's statutory powers; there are many more, and they must of course take care as to which power they choose to exercise dependent on the situation. The usefulness of conditions is two-fold; first they restrict just one section of the solicitor's practice, allowing the solicitor to continue to practise as previously, otherwise; and secondly, they are resolvable on an annual basis with the issue of a Practising Certificate. The risk might be resolved in a specific timeframe, and the condition can be removed promptly. The condition allows the regulator to demonstrate proportionate, risk-based decision making, and allows targeted action which also allows the solicitor to continue practising.

The diagram shows how we might see the practice of a wills and probate solicitor. The regulator, if perceiving a risk, can impose a restriction on part of the solicitor's practice. In this example, the solicitor has made some mistakes in their handling of client money. Accordingly, they may be restricted in holding client money. In this example the solicitor is allowed to handle client money under supervision, as it is a key part of probate practice, but there is someone who can supervise them, so a restriction is imposed to handle client money under supervision.

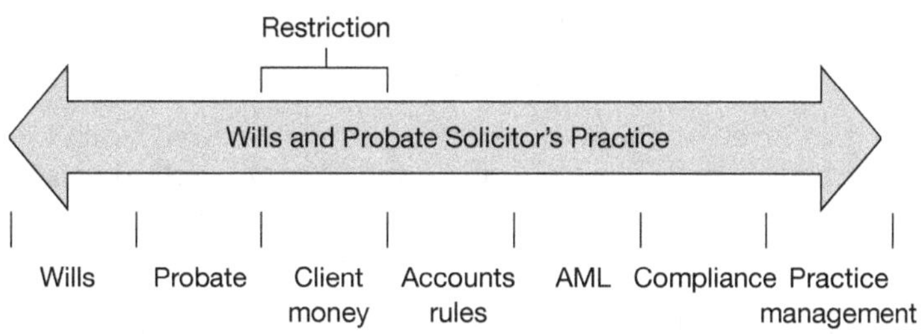

Broadly speaking, the SRA can exercise the same powers across firms, as they can to individuals, meaning conditions can also be imposed on a firm. As might be evident, the consequences are different as the firm potentially covers several different solicitors and their individual 'practices'. We cover this subject more in Part 4, along with an analysis of the seriousness of the position for firms. There is a question; if conditions need to be imposed on a firm, is that is already such a serious situation that the firm requires additional regulatory sanction, even closure? It is worth remembering that we are speaking about firms of solicitors rather than firms of other legal services professionals, and that firms can operate across a wide range of legal services. Solicitors receive a broad general legal education, and many serve the public directly; they also are expected to maintain their broad professional standard to a degree. Imposing conditions on a firm could impact the breadth of practice of a number of solicitors.

Returning to this Part of the book, over the coming pages we will look at Practising Certificate conditions, their historical development, imposition and justification.

We will also examine debates about whether conditions work, alternatives to conditions, and how to address personal or development needs when you are faced with conditions. Turning across to Part 4, we will contrast the position with firm conditions and some of the debates about restricting the practice of a legitimately operating business, and also have a look at the context of placing conditions on changing business models.

Historical development and use in other areas of professional practice

The Solicitors Act 1974 is the main tool for the imposition of Practising Certificate conditions. Conditions have historically been used as a tool for the management of risk. Section 12 of this Act (before it was repealed by the Legal Services Act 2007) provided this solid basis and a list of circumstances in which conditions would likely be imposed. The writer has referred to the list of circumstances as 'The List', hereafter.

The List included (but was not limited to) the following types of circumstances:

1. Where a solicitor was insolvent.
2. Where a solicitor had previous practising conditions.
3. Where a solicitor was restored to the roll.
4. When a solicitor had been suspended/struck off from the roll.
5. Where a solicitor had failed to deliver an accountants report on time.
6. Vesting a discretion (this is where the regulator had asked for an explanation but one had not been provided), and at the point of investigation a 'discretion was vested' in the next Practising Certificate. This meant the solicitor had been warned of likely conditions at the next renewal.

Although it was repealed, the SRA kept The List in their new 'outcomes focused' Handbook of 2011, in a section of more formal regulatory powers, known as the Practising Regulations. These regulations worked with the corresponding regulations for authorised bodies (known as the Authorisation Regulations), providing the framework of practice. These sets of regulations provided more prescription than other areas; perhaps needed as the SRA had to provide concrete rules around professional practice, particularly for the new and more controversial 'Alternative Business Structures'.

In more recent times the SRA have removed The List from their regulations. They are now replaced under the Standards and Regulations by less concrete circumstances in which conditions will be imposed.

Was The List right for all those years? The Legal Services Act 2007 introduced new forms of practice and going forward the SRA needs to adapt to potentially new ways of working; the new rules in the Standards and Regulations do provide the flexibility which is potentially required.

The List of circumstances in which conditions will be imposed have provided a backdrop to The Law Society's and latterly the SRA's regulatory action, and a risk-based check on the actions of solicitors. Many hundreds of thousands of conditions were imposed while The List was in force from 1974–2019. It is tempting as a regulator to rely on this established word and practice. It has clarity, historical justification, and allows the individual regulatory staff member (who is after all a person), a clear basis for their decision. For the solicitor, they have the benefit of concrete regulations specifying those red lines which are consistently in place and consistently applied over many years.

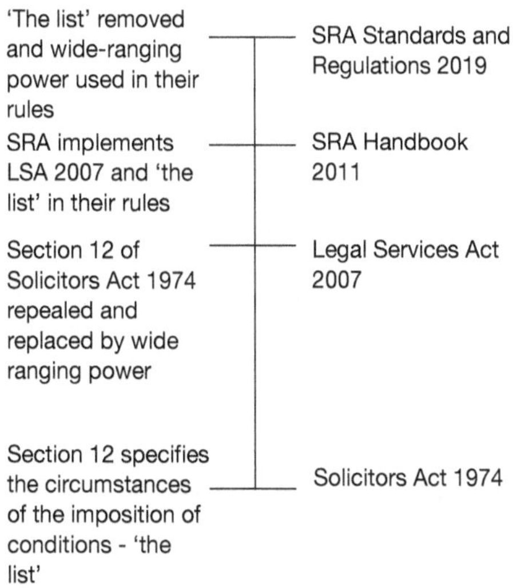

The red lines that made up The List were established in the 1970s. Businesses change, societal pressures change, and expectations of solicitors and their staff, as well as expectations of the risks they face may be very different now than they were when The List was established. The List does not for example, tackle the common complaints raised before the SRA now, or the most common causes of non-compliance at the moment.

We have discussed the 'Four Acts' in Part 1 and Part 2 of this book as fairly stable pieces of legislation which have provided the regulator's powers. These are not new pieces of legislation, and none of them reflect particularly new ideas. We can say however that (although the power derives from the Solicitors Act to impose conditions), the 'Four Acts' which are identified earlier in this book, have provided a steady basis for the imposition of conditions as a regulatory tool. The Law Society and SRA have experienced consistency in a range of regulatory powers, and seen their rules applicable to a wide range of circumstances. It is the writer's experience that Practising Certificate conditions have been imposed on a steady basis for some years now.

The idea, expressed neatly by the original versions of the Solicitors Acts, is to express the circumstances in which a solicitors' practice might pose a risk to the public and therefore allowing the regulator to restrict the solicitor practising in that area.

The powers to impose conditions on Practising Certificates are still held in the Solicitors Act 1974, as amended by the Legal Services Act 2007. These are basic powers, which allow the SRA to develop rules for the imposition of conditions in certain circumstances.

The List was historically expressed within the statute as individual and very specific risks to be managed. Accordingly, not all common breaches, or matters that need referring to the SRA are included in this list. We can instead perhaps see cornerstones of regulatory power, designed to pinpoint areas of investigation; decision making; and behavioural red lines, on which the professionalism of the solicitor turns.

If we look at the actual idea of imposing conditions, unless power is restrained it could be a disproportionate measure. Restricting the practice and business activities of an individual or organisation is an extremely serious step. As well as providing direction to the regulator about the imposition of conditions, The List may have been a necessary check and balance on their power, perhaps providing an implicit direction that these are the circumstances in which conditions should be imposed, and these are the matters conditions should be about.

For a regulator with such significant power, powers could be expressed in statute in a way which may also be intended to limit their operation. It is of interest that The List was removed from the statute books in 2007, along with the introduction of Alternative Business Structures. It is certainly true that the perceived risks of ABS are dramatically greater. We only need to look at the possible fines for non-compliance by ABS – up to £50 million for individuals and £250 million for firms – to realise the perceived threat legal services market could face from their existence.

Imposition of conditions

The power to impose conditions is still derived from the Solicitors Act 1974, which was amended by the Legal Services Act 2007. The powers are contained within ss 10 and 13A. They specify that the SRA may impose Practising Certificate conditions, under regulations it prescribes under s 28, and these conditions may be imposed either on the issue of a new Practising Certificate or while the Practising Certificate is in force. As we have seen in Parts 1 and 2 of this book, a Practising Certificate can be held over and does not expire until it is renewed. The movement through the annual year and the annual renewal means those who may need a Practising Certificate condition will have one imposed on a new certificate while the existing certificate from the previous year is still in force.

This is a powerful mechanism for imposition as the solicitor needs a new certificate. They may have their certificates on the wall, or the insurance company may ask where the certificate is. The regulator imposes the condition at the point the practitioner has to apply for a new certificate, to avoid the practitioner taking a different turn or seeking to avoid the imposition.

We have also already seen that the regulator revokes previous certificates at the beginning of the following year (provided conditions are not under consideration), placing the solicitor facing a condition in a position where a condition will be imposed. The alternative is revocation of their certificate.

For the first eight years of the implementation of the Legal Services Act 2007, The List was transposed from the Solicitors Act 1974, s 12 to the SRA Practising

Regulations 2011, reg 3 which formed part of the SRA Handbook 2011. It was known as 'Regulation 3' or 'Reg 3'. We could debate whether the legislation intended the regulator to reproduce what it said so faithfully within their rules, but following the introduction of the Legal Services Act 2007, the regulator was required to undergo major organisational change to introduce Alternative Business Structures and separate from the representative arm of the organisation.

We have to look at the change happening to and around the SRA at the time to understand why the regulator chose to maintain The List. The annual renewal is a major undertaking for the SRA, with many staff devoted to its smooth running. It is a driver of information gathering, a chance to take regulatory action, and examine the circumstances of practises and individuals. It is also an excellent example of the unity and uniformity in solicitor's practice; all solicitors renew at the same time. Changing processes completely as a result of the Legal Services Act 2007 and moving 'The List' to the discretion of the regulator was not undertaken. There was a lot of change already as a result of the Legal Services Act, and the introduction of outcomes-focused regulation. Maintaining stability through a transition period is essential for the ongoing delivery of major events, such as the renewal, particularly ones with a regulatory implication.

The latest set of rules from the SRA, under the Standards and Regulations, is a good example of the wide breadth of powers it now has. The rules now specify a broad set of situations in which they must consider imposing conditions, and goes on to discuss what those conditions must be to do. The power to impose is open and wide ranging. The List was specific, but also a form of restraint; this set of circumstances provides the regulator with the freedom to impose conditions for almost any reason. As we explore below, the restraint in these new forms of condition comes in what the SRA can ask the individual solicitor to do for their condition.

The SRA can now, under the Standards and Regulations, impose Practising Certificate conditions under the Authorisation of Individuals Regulations 2019, reg 7 (part of the Standards and Regulations 2019). Regulation 7 provides significantly wider circumstances than previously, including where the SRA is satisfied that the individual:

1. Is not going to comply with the regulations.
2. Poses a risk to clients and others.
3. Is unsuitable for certain activities in practice.

These are very widely worded provisions in comparison to The List, and while we can see how the previous lists fit into these situations (for example concerns about compliance with a previous or current condition might fall into situation 1, and insolvency might fall into situation 2), they can be used far more widely than The List. We will see further in this Part of the book that conditions can be extremely restrictive, so the breadth of this power causes some alarm.

There is a slight restriction to the regulator's power, and that is a restriction on the type of condition that can be imposed under the Authorisation of Individuals Regulations 2019, reg 7.3. It might be true to say the SRA have not been very creative with their conditions previously, and have largely stuck to the same types of condition (common conditions are explored later in this Part of the book). However, this is also some evidence of reasonableness, consistency, and proportionality in regulation. Regulation 7.3 allows the imposition of conditions to:

- Take particular steps.
- Prevent certain steps being taken without SRA approval.
- Restrict access to certain roles.

The wording for these requirements for conditions is taken from the Solicitors Act 1974, s 10 (as amended by the Legal Services Act 2007) and the Administration of Justice 1985, s 9 which applies to conditions on recognised bodies. The wording is very wide.

Arguably, it was not intended for the SRA to use this wording directly. If we look at the wording in the Solicitors Act 1974, this wording is used in s 10 which applies to the imposition of Practising Certificate conditions on the issue of a Practising Certificate; there are further provisions for the imposition of conditions on a Practising Certificate in force, which do not address the same circumstances. The legislation provides wide powers to impose conditions on the issue of the Practising Certificate; driving annual consideration of the risks of individual practice.

The extent of the powers operating on an annual basis causes a problem of logistics related to the volume of applications. If we can see that the issue of the Practising Certificate occurs annually and there are hundreds of thousands of applicants, we can also see that the issue of the Practising Certificate becomes delayed, meaning the solicitor has started their next practising year (and may be some way into it), when conditions are finally imposed. For the recipient of conditions, this may be technically the issue of the new Practising Certificate, but the old certificate simply held over, meaning there is an argument that the new certificate is in force due to the length of time in considering the position.

The legislation was written some time ago, perhaps when numbers of solicitors were lower, and the annual renewal could be conducted promptly. Situations which may have been discussions between regulator and renewer about what they would do to ensure their practice was suitable to continue for another year, could have been conducted quickly. Now we are in a position of almost blind renewal from the practitioner who may be unaware that the regulator perceives a risk in respect of their practice, and who may not receive a decision on conditions for another six months.

In reading the Administration of Justice Act 1985, s 9(2I) it is clear the regulator were expected to make their own lists about the circumstances in which conditions would be imposed. We can also see that the regulator has previously adopted the wording from the repealed Solicitors Act 1974, s 12, which provided those lists of circumstances. The List did provide clarity about when conditions might be imposed for a following year. Solicitors with this clarity can of course make decisions about whether they wish to continue or not in the face of likely conditions, but are having that option taken away from them by the volume of solicitors who renew, the delay in the process, and the openness in the wording of the regulations which places a great deal of power in the hands of the regulator.

If we look again at the requirements for imposing conditions, the types of condition the SRA can impose include ones to:

- Take particular steps.
- Prevent certain steps being taken without SRA approval.
- Restrict access to certain roles.

There could be wide variations in the conditions. They allow the SRA to say, 'do this, or don't do this unless we say', both the positive and negative sides of a wide restriction. They can also restrict access to certain functions within a firm. The SRA may have missed a point with this final type of restriction as they are also promoting innovation and new types of business model. These new models may move away from traditional law firm structures and into designing job roles which have been thought about in new ways with far greater flexibility, or which they are not used to dealing with. This may be a point to remember for the regulator when considering conditions which restrict access to functions; whether in the new styles of practice a job role will be the same as it is now. There could be a question about whether an unscrupulous individual could get round a condition by altering the function the regulator was concerned about.

Traditionally, conditions were imposed at the commencement of the practising year, and practitioners may remember sending their Practising Certificate application to Redditch for approval. This process occurred until approximately 2010. The Law Society and later the SRA needed six weeks' notice in advance if you were subject to conditions, or any of that list of circumstances had arisen. This could be further evidence of the need for decisions to be made 'on issue' of the certificate and that practitioners should understand in advance that they could be subject to conditions.

Today the system of annual renewal is online and applications for annual renewal are removed for further consideration if the solicitor's position warrants consideration of conditions. This is all done in October and there is no need for six weeks' notice. Although The List has been removed, practitioners may still find this is the basis for the SRA's consideration of the imposition of conditions, as institutional memory persists.

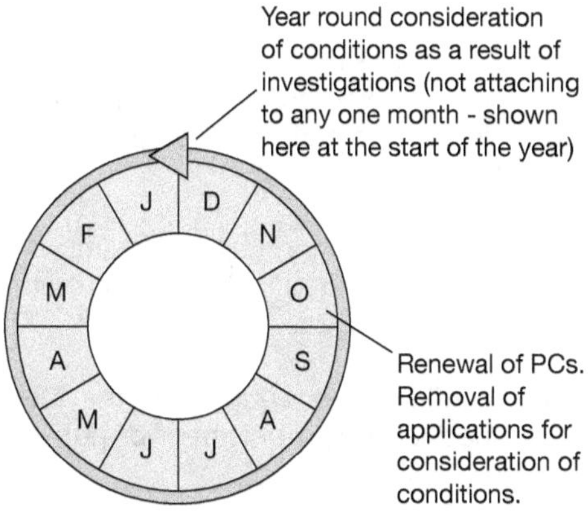

Otherwise, conditions can be imposed at any time, and it is not uncommon for solicitors to have conditions imposed:

- During a regulatory investigation.

- When a regulatory sanction is being imposed, or a regulatory outcome is being reached.
- By the Solicitors Disciplinary Tribunal.

The Solicitors Disciplinary Tribunal has powers to impose conditions in respect of the practitioner before them.

Public Interest

The imposition of conditions is subject to a public interest test.

We will consider the 'public interest' to be the wider public good, or what is in the best interests of everyone in wider society. There is both a general intent to this statement and an element of protecting individual members of the public.

The wording of the new regulations under the Standards and Regulations also changed the wording of the public interest test.

Under the Authorisation of Individuals Regulations 2019, reg 7, if the SRA considers it in the public interest to do so, it must impose conditions. This wording results in a change, or it might in some situations.

Again, it appears the switch in wording has come from the Solicitors Act 1974, s 10, and Administration of Justice Act 1985, s 9, which divides the imposition of conditions from the type of conditions, and imposes the public interest test on the imposition of conditions rather than on the condition itself.

The previous wording was that the condition itself should be in the public interest; this was contained within the Handbook 2011 at Regulation 7 of the Practising Regulations 2011. The SRA also used this wording in their decision letters for conditions very commonly for many years.

The current wording is that the imposition of conditions must be in the public interest. This wording is wider than the first wording, and does not mean the condition itself has to be in the public interest, only that the imposition of the condition must be.

As we have seen, the types of condition that can be imposed are prescribed, however circumstances have changed including the method and mode of issue of the new Practising Certificate.

The case of *Razeen*[1] confirmed in 2008, that the SRA should impose conditions to meet a specified risk, an element of public interest was also required.

If we take this to an ultimate conclusion, the SRA could under the Standards and Regulations, consider it was in the public interest *to* impose a condition,

1 *Razeen* [2008] EWCA Civ 1220.

but impose a condition which may not be wholly in the public interest. To use a nonsensical example, the SRA could decide it was in the public interest to impose a condition on an insolvent solicitor, but impose a condition that the insolvent solicitor remove their name from the firm branding. This would not be in the public interest as it would not address the risk, and it would arguably prevent persons from knowing who they were dealing with.

Therefore, it appears the SRA have attempted to challenge the public interest test in respect of the imposition of conditions itself.

Often primary conditions can be imposed with a secondary condition that the person concerned must notify their employer of the condition. This secondary condition is imposed for example when there might be an impact on the employer, where the person concerned may move employment, or where the person may need additional supervision. Sometimes this secondary condition is worded in such a way as to encompass informing any employer as to the reasons for the condition. Common primary conditions are explained later in this Part of the book.

Some solicitors choose not to continue holding a Practising Certificate if conditions are imposed. This is a dramatic reaction, and conditions are not imposed forever. There have been cases of repeated conditions, year on year, but if the circumstances have changed such to minimise the risk of the scenario being repeated, the condition should theoretically be removed.

Practitioners who return to the profession when they last held a Practising Certificate subject to conditions can be subject to the imposition of conditions again, sometime later. This was a specific risk identified in The List of circumstances but remains a red flag due to the risk of 'phoenix firms'. These are firms or individuals who seek to hide their regulatory history either by the passage of time or by operating under a new name, and remain a regulatory issue for the SRA.

When imposing conditions, these should be proportionate, necessary, and (in the writer's view), in the public interest. This means that the condition should consider the risk of the situation and how best the firm and individual can manage that position in the context of their firm and situation. Imposing unmanageable conditions is unfair, and a burden on that practitioner and their business. Further discussion of actual conditions is set out below.

In practice the issue of conditions has been fairly predictable based on the circumstances. For example, practitioners breaching the Accounts Rules in rectifiable ways would be required to attend a course on the Accounts Rules in order to improve their knowledge, whereas those with more fundamental failings may be prevented from working with accounts altogether. The range of conditions imposed is in practice very small, but the potential range of conditions that could be imposed is potentially limitless.

Conditions have in the past been imposed year on year, with the same condition being imposed each time. However, with some creativity, the SRA could theoretically impose more targeted and variable conditions over a longer time period as part of a regulatory package solution. The difficulty with this is the ownership of the external business; the extent of the regulatory intervention and the other potential impacts on the business as a whole. Intrusive and sustained intervention into a business requires strong justification from the regulator.

Process for imposing conditions

The process for imposing conditions is for information to come to the SRA's attention which they feel would warrant the imposition of a condition. In the past this has been information which fell into the categories outlined in The List. This part of the process often takes place at renewal, and it is anticipated this will continue due the statutory requirements to impose conditions on issue of the Practising Certificate, and due to processes and procedures already in place.

The individual solicitor may be told that their Practising Certificate could be subject to conditions. The solicitor concerned might already know they could have conditions imposed, either because they had been informed during an ongoing investigation or because they were in a situation where conditions would usually be imposed, which are discussed later in this Part of the book.

The next stage is for a decision maker, such as a caseworker, at the SRA to consider the situation and whether they need to impose any conditions to manage any specific situation. We consider some situations later in this part of the book where conditions would often be imposed immediately, such as bankruptcy. The decision maker at the SRA would decide whether any further information was required from the individual solicitor, and may request it at this point.

After this point, the possible condition would be sent to the individual solicitor for representations from themselves or their representative. They usually have 14 days to make representations.

At the close of the representations period, a decision is made based on the information available to the decision maker and the representations received. The decision can sometimes be made by the caseworker, but will in more serious situations or where there are resourcing issues, be sent to a more senior decision maker or Adjudicator.

Once the decision has been made, the caseworker will send details of the outcome to the solicitor. The solicitor then has the opportunity to appeal. The appeal is usually heard by the Appeal Panel, but in some instances an Adjudicator may decide an appeal.

Following any appeal the decision is usually final. The SDT can vary conditions on a Practising Certificate, but this is not an appeal, and such an application is rare.

Practitioners subject to conditions are reminded that the Practising Certificate is usually renewed within a matter of months of a decision being made. The time taken for the process outlined here is so long, and there is such a volume of decisions to be made, we end up with decisions being made in March after applications are made in October. The Practising Certificate is due for renewal again within a few months.

There is an annex to this Part of the book showing the process for the imposition of conditions (p 177).

In some cases, the solicitor could have conditions imposed immediately, such as where they have failed to co-operate with the regulator, or where a matter has been raised during an investigation, but the decision might wait until the renewal of the Practising Certificate. This is particularly true where the Practising Certificate renewal will shortly be upon the regulator. However, in making this statement, resources may also be considered, as may any ongoing investigations, and the nature of the risk posed by the situation. When considering conditions, we are not departing too far from outcomes for breaches, and they can also take some time to investigate and decide. Conditions are no different in that respect, and sometimes a condition may accompany a decision made during or as a result of an investigation.

The decision to impose a condition is reflective of a situation that has arisen or is likely to arise. Evidence of that situation has come to the regulator's attention. Therefore, it can be acted upon if that risk or situation continues or the regulator believes it will continue.

Regulation 3 (The List)

We have seen earlier in this Part of the book, the move away from 'The List' in Regulation 3 and the old Solicitors Act, s 12 and to a more open set of circumstances in which conditions can be imposed. The use of regulation persisted beyond its repeal in legislation and in circumstances in which the SRA was having to re-design its regulatory mechanisms to cope with ABS and their possible risk factors.

There has not been as many ABS or as extensive investment as was envisaged; there are still a number of barriers to entry into the market including those to ownership of law firms, qualification as a solicitor, and the regulatory requirements for the delivery of legal services. However, the new models of individual regulation (working in unregulated firms) and working as freelance solicitors may present greater risks that need to be managed in the long term. The loss of The List now somehow seems too great not to discuss; it was a set of clearly expressed circumstances which were deemed to require regulation or a regulatory response, the majority of which seemed very reasonable and well considered. The List is likely to affect regulatory decision making in those that used it, and may still be in the institutional memory of the SRA. Practitioners are encouraged to understand it as a reference point for when regulatory action can be taken. It may be possible to reproduce The List in some way to counteract the risks of freelance solicitors and unregulated practices.

It is arguable that regulatory policy has overtaken The List in some way; some matters on The List would be picked up automatically anyway – for example, a sanction or finding against the individual practitioner may result in conditions regardless of The List, particularly if the matter was serious (for example before the Solicitors Disciplinary Tribunal). Once conditions have been imposed the matter would be referred for consideration the following year on the renewal (even if the conditions were to be removed), again regardless of The List, and the position remains the same under the new regulations.

Similarly, conditions may automatically be considered or imposed as a result of insolvency and convictions (see below), and that position has not changed.

One area of change is the failure to respond to the SRA. This was a reason for the imposition of conditions under The List; however it is not now specifically mentioned. There is justification within the new regulations for imposition of conditions if the practitioner does not respond, and you might say they were unlikely to comply with the regulations. There was previously a facility for the SRA to 'vest a discretion' in respect of a Practising Certificate application, meaning the SRA could make a decision at some point during the year and then wait until the solicitor submitted their Practising Certificate application in order to consider imposing the condition at that point.

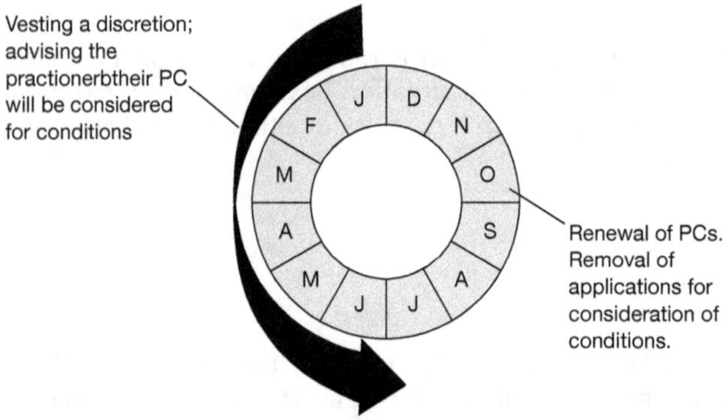

This power to vest disappeared with the introduction of the Handbook 2011 and the argument has been that if the risk is great enough to impose conditions on the practitioner, this should be done at the point the risk has occurred and has been drawn to the regulator's attention. If the risk has for example, occurred during the months January to June, when the SRA is not renewing Practising Certificates or preparing to, the practitioner may have some wait to have a condition imposed. The 'unacceptable' risk can continue in the meantime. If the risk was identified in the summer, and even right the way through to the point of renewal, the SRA had the chance of catching it at the renewal and imposing the condition. Otherwise again, the risk continues, and readers will see later in this Part of the book that conditions can be imposed late, even during the summer after renewal as there has been a delay in considering the renewal application. Some renewal applications are still sometimes being considered in the summer after renewal, a full nine months later.

The Handbook 2011 and regulation 3 removed the power to vest and instead suggested the condition *could be* imposed at any time. In practice, many conditions continue to be imposed on renewal, or their imposition is triggered by renewal, although some are imposed during the year (outside the renewal process at all).

There is a hangover from 'vesting a discretion' that we can see in the decision making of the regulator today. The regulator may wait until the Practising Certificate is issued next before imposing the condition. This does also reflect the statute in that conditions should be imposed on the issue of the Practising Certificate, but the idea was that the practitioner would be informed at the time the circumstances arose, and would know to expect a condition in the autumn. This may still take place in a way, but without the formal 'vesting', as practitioners can be informed of the likely imposition of conditions on the next issue of their Practising Certificate, following a regulatory investigation or other action. We revert at this point to whether the condition should be imposed or considered immediately, as an issue of procedural fairness, given the concept of 'vesting' has gone, and therefore the formal authority to delay the imposition of conditions is no longer with the regulator.

Whilst there are arguments against a delay in imposing conditions, these are not sufficiently robust to prevent the imposition of the condition in itself. The regulator cannot simply leave a risk unabated because they did not act on it sooner. In the regulator's favour the argument might be that they should be proportionate, so perhaps allowing time for the risk to abate or a situation to develop so perhaps conditions are unnecessary. Another argument in favour of imposing conditions regardless of the delay is that a risk may be continuing, so should be actioned when the procedures allow it to be; and any regulator has finite resources, so they may not physically be able to consider it immediately. Also, the regulator may point out that procedurally it is complex (and possibly unfair) to conduct an investigation and impose conditions simultaneously, again another reason for possible delay.

Sometimes it can also assist both the regulator and the solicitor to have a second pair of eyes on the situation and proposed imposition of conditions if any investigation has been delayed, to ensure procedural fairness. In this situation the practitioner may want to consider legal advice, and of course this is an option always open to those who may be in receipt of a condition.

Suspension of a solicitor's Practising Certificate

Under the Solicitors' Act 1974, s 15 a solicitor's Practising Certificate is *automatically* suspended by an insolvency event. This is not a decision of the SRA or SDT to suspend the Practising Certificate of the solicitor, it is an automatic suspension. It does not matter whether the SRA have been informed or not; the Practising Certificate is suspended by statute. The solicitor may therefore be unable to continue practising.

All insolvency events must be reported to the SRA. The SRA likes to have sufficient advance notice of any potential insolvency to ensure the situation is managed effectively. Practising uncertificated may invalidate a solicitor's insurance and lead to prosecution of the individual solicitor and the firm. Therefore, matters should be reported to the SRA and arrangements made at the earliest opportunity.

Insolvency events include not only the insolvency of the individual solicitor personally, but also the insolvency of the regulated firm and any associated businesses the solicitor is involved in.

Failure to report such an event could result in practising uncertificated. Both practising uncertificated and insolvency of a regulated law firm is a firm ground for intervention by the SRA. Intervention is the closure of a practice by the regulator; provided for in statute. Solicitors and their firms who are facing intervention may require legal advice. It is rare that insolvency or bankruptcy would result in intervention, even though it is a ground for the same.

Of course the circumstances of an insolvency event would be taken into account by the regulator when making a decision, but the decision of the regulator is expected to be a *regulatory* one, which does not have to double down on restrictions already imposed.

Sometimes Practising Certificates which have been suspended can be reinstated by the SRA. At this point they often become subject to conditions. Any reinstatement of a Practising Certificate following automatic suspension for insolvency is usually subject to conditions as there is a perceived risk to the public of a practitioner who cannot manage his or her financial affairs. If a solicitor was personally insolvent but the firm around him or her was unaffected and able to continue and offer the appropriate support to him or her, the conditions could theoretically be imposed which would reflect that risk; for example, to prevent control of:

- the firm's finances
- the client account
- the strategic direction of the firm
- the compliance functions

However, whether conditions would be imposed and the continuation of the individual solicitor's practice would depend on all the circumstances.

Further discussion of this position is provided later in the book under the heading 'risk management'.

Criminal Charges and Dishonesty

Suspension of a Practising Certificate also occurs in the case of criminal charges against a solicitor for an indictable offence or an offence involving dishonesty. This occurs on the application by the SRA to the Tribunal, which is done automatically and incredibly promptly (the same day) in such circumstances.

In this situation, the Practising Certificate often remains suspended until the police investigation and any criminal justice process is concluded in respect of that matter. If the solicitor is convicted the Practising Certificate remains suspended and there will be a separate regulatory investigation and prosecution.

The SRA consider it a particular risk to authorise practitioners who are subject to criminal charges, and cases are considered on an individual basis, including whether to take additional regulatory action. It is unlikely, if a solicitor has been convicted, that their Practising Certificate would simply be reinstated and subject to conditions, unless the offence was considered incredibly minor and there was mitigation.

As we discuss in Part 5 of this book, the solicitor is an officer of the court, an important part of local justice in his or her community, and an integral part of both the criminal and civil justice systems. Solicitors also have a constitutional role collectively and individually, meaning their role is to uphold the system of law and justice. Convictions are taken very seriously indeed.

Risk management

Conditions must be imposed in order to address a specific risk (*Razeen*) and conditions are often matched to the perceived risk to the public in order to eliminate that risk, or manage it going forward.

Conditions have been preferred in as a regulatory power, to for example, undertakings, limited licences to practise (for example authorisations issued for certain categories of law), or instead of a regulatory process which directly intervenes into the management of the practice. For example, Solicitor A has a lot of complaints against them, and fails to respond to the regulator. Solicitor A could be subject to a condition on their practice. The SRA uses the power of conditions because it has the statutory powers to do so. But what would the alternative be if there was no power to impose conditions?

Alternative options for the regulator might be to:

1. Seek an undertaking from Solicitor A to improve their professional practice;
2. Seek the support of another practitioner to support the professional practice of Solicitor A;
3. Work with the Solicitor A to improve client care information and standard template letters, including complaint letters, in order to inform the clients;
4. Consider whether this problem also affects other clients in other firms; does the regulator need to take steps to improve information provision about using law firms in wider society?
5. Consider the type of clients Solicitor A is serving; would there be any additional reason for challenge to the practitioner?

The SRA in practice might attempt points 3-5 in some circumstances, but it has a limited amount of resource and it may be more proportionate to impose a condition, for example to attend a course on client care. Conditions themselves sometimes take account of point 2, for example the regulator may discuss the position of the firm and whether they can support Solicitor A and in which ways. Firms with individuals facing conditions can also make representations about the support they can offer those members of staff to help resolve or manage the perceived risk. There is a danger in using point 1; that Solicitor A is already perceived to be non-compliant and asking for an undertaking may further place them into non-compliance. Points 1 and 2 may also in reality be conditions, just expressed in a different way.

> In the writer's view, the *risk management* in imposing the condition is:
>
> a. an analysis of the specific problem facing that practitioner which has resulted in that practitioner being subject to a regulatory outcome, and
>
> b. the identification of a suitable regulatory response to either:
>
>   i. cut off or curtail the potential risk, or
>
>   ii. improve the practitioner's ability to deal with their situation, or
>
>   iii. both (i) and (ii)

In imposing the condition, we may see serious matters dealt with by cutting off or curtailing the risk (for example in the case of the personally insolvent solicitor, who has their access to the financial functions of the firm restricted), and less serious matters dealt with by improvement mechanisms such as educational conditions. We may see restrictive conditions operate alongside educational conditions or become educational conditions over the passage of time.

Lateral consideration of the risk posed by the *situation* and how to prevent the situation occurring is important, and the SRA often considers the entire situation as described, including the management of the firm and the position of the practitioner when the risk arose.

In all of this, the SRA has to ensure their intervention is proportionate, cost effective, and timely. With several hundred thousand applications to consider annually, and with a view to:

- the individual risk posed by each solicitor,
- the risk posed by each firm,
- the investigations currently underway,
- the risks present within the legal services market, and
- the new risks emerging as a result of the new ways to practise in legal services.

The approach adopted could be applauded for its effectiveness at delivering short term, easy to implement, regulatory action which focuses on the risk posed in each situation, even if there can be delays in imposing conditions.

We have however seen that conditions are commonly imposed on individuals, and we see in Part 4 that conditions are not often imposed on firms. This may be placing the regulatory outcome at the door of the individual. We should always be mindful that the position could be a firm problem overall, but for some reason the outcome has resulted in a risk being posed by that individual or the perception of the same. A more holistic approach to conditions might result in the firm being held responsible for the risk and conditions imposed there. We examine firm based conditions in the next part of the book.

RISK MANAGEMENT: MATHEMATICAL OR LATERAL DECISIONS?

Conditions should meet a risk, but what do we mean by risk and do we think that is the right phrase for describing the circumstances of the imposition of conditions?

The following is an excerpt from the writer's Material/ Serious Breach and Practising Certificate conditions course notes, first used in 2014:

Risk management is a form of decision mathematics. It helps you make transparent decisions about what could cause your law firm harm, and what will probably not.

However it is not an exact science; it might sometimes be wrong. In using this technique, you are relying on the best information you have at the moment you make the decision - sometimes that information is not complete.

Nonetheless, when making decisions, we go through a similar 'weighing up' in our heads. Using risk management is a technique to organise those thoughts, write them down so we can demonstrate them to someone else, and feel more in control.

This worksheet does not explain the full risk management process, and should not be taken as advice, because decisions about what is right for your firm depend on individual circumstances. However it does explain the basic principles and could help you think about whether this way of working might be right for your firm.

Risk management is not a licence not to comply with certain areas of the handbook and should not be used as such. Rather you can use it to help prioritise and identify areas for improvement.

[We can define risk as impact x probability]

Impact is the effect of an event if it happened. Probability is the likelihood of an event occurring in the first place.

An example would be computer hacking. Let's say you have 5,000 past and present client matters listed on your computer system. The system is linked to the internet and a successful hacker could see all of those matters. That is high impact for you as it would affect all of your clients. Let's also say it has happened before and you have not taken any extra security measures – that makes the probability also high. Therefore it falls into red, and you should immediately act on that risk and put in places measures to protect your client information.

However let's say you only go online on one computer, not linked to the network, with nothing of any interest on, and it has a quite good firewall. In that case the impact would be low if it was hacked, and the probability medium (as the firewall is only quite good), most likely putting you in the green area. This means you do not need to act unless the situation changes.

Another example of a low impact, low probability outcome might be a client account that is barely used by a well-run firm. The SRA often grant waivers for accountant's reports for client accounts in these situations. If you have a very small amount (relative to your business) going through your client account it will be low impact, and if you have the right procedures in place, low probability. This is why sometimes the SRA considers the risk to be low and issues a waiver.

Having read this analysis do we think impact x probability is the correct formula to use before imposing a condition? We might be defining risk more loosely in our heads, or simply considering the possibility of harm. However if we take the personal bankruptcy of a solicitor as an example, we could argue that the personal bankruptcy is in pure mathematic risk terms not likely to impact the client account. Personal bankruptcy might be evidence of poor financial management skills in relation to, for example, levels of debt. However, it is not necessarily evidence of an intent to misappropriate client monies, and with suitable assurances from another partner that the bankrupt solicitor would not be hiding monies within the client account or firm, this might be a mitigatable risk.

We might then argue from this point that the *risk* is to the financial stability of the firm rather than the client account. However, conditions are often imposed on:

- the financial functions of the firm,
- the management of the firm,
- access to client account,

and in deciding the conditions, reference is made to the individual circumstances of the bankrupt and the restrictions on their bankruptcy; the views of the trustee in bankruptcy and of the Court; and the corporate (or otherwise) status of the firms concerned.

Regard may be had to the due to the position of any ongoing bankruptcy, and perceived resultant difficulties with holding the client monies on trust or as a fiduciary, rather than the position of the *risk*. Noting of course that the bankrupts' estate does not include assets held on trust for another person (section 283 of the Insolvency Act 1986).

This is an example of where a condition is commonly imposed that does not meet the definition of *risk,* but where there is an overarching or perceived need for an additional regulatory solution. However, there may be in this situation also a risk to the reputation of legal services.

The writer's earlier definition of risk management is preferred in this situation.

In the writer's view, the risk management in imposing the condition is:

a. *an analysis of the specific problem facing that practitioner which has resulted in that practitioner being subject to a regulatory outcome, and*

b. *the identification of a suitable regulatory response to either:*

  i. *cut off or curtail the potential risk, or*

  ii. *improve the practitioner's ability to deal with their situation, or*

  iii. *both (i) and (ii)*

In the scenario of personal bankruptcy we can see in imposing restrictions on access to the financial functions of the firm, the management of the firm, *and* the client account, a *full* analysis of the problem facing the bankrupt solicitor is considered, and there is a regulatory response to deal with that risk. The regulatory response is the response which deals with the bankruptcy rather than the risk, in that although there may not be a *risk* to client funds, any option is cut off completely due to the situation and perceived wider risk, which perhaps goes beyond the consideration of the regulator.

The question we might ask in imposing a full set of conditions on a personally bankrupt solicitor is whether this meets the public interest test, given the position of the bankruptcy already addresses some aspects of public interest. That decision might be for the regulator to take on case by case basis.

Whether or not we need an additional form of regulatory conditions beyond the restrictions imposed on the bankrupt solicitor by the bankruptcy is debatable. In this sense, the solicitor is being subjected to two regimes (one for bankruptcy, and another regulatory), which would not happen to any other person.

Of course, the regulator would need to know and be aware of the situation, and formulate a general regulatory response, including whether the affected solicitor could continue with their practice, and whether they were separately subject to any conditions on their professional or personal life that may impact their practice. We have covered some of these points previously. However that decision making is entirely separate from the decision making to impose conditions on a Practising Certificate.

We encompass both (a) and (b) in the decision making. Lateral decision making about the full circumstances of the situation is formulating not simply a risk-based solution, but a full risk management solution to take account of all the circumstances of the situation, including wider risks.

Risk management is also a feature within money laundering, and firms are required to undertake their own risk assessments to assess their risk of being subject to money laundering or terrorist financing. This can include a consideration of the risks inherent in their delivery mechanisms; the risks posed by the transactions; and the risks posed by their services. The current guidance from the Legal Sector Affinity Group supporting the implementation of the regulations also requires firms to ensure management or board level oversight of AML.

The requirements for AML have generated a lot of focus from the regulators in the last few years (particularly following the introduction of the oversight regulator, OPBAS). It will be interesting to see whether the recent attention from the regulators in risk management will focus practice's minds on risk within their firm, and what type of representations could be made concerning conditions. Theoretically the greater attention on risk could allow firms to demonstrate proactive management of risk, which might result in less conditions, or more effective representations from firms about managing individual risk, which may alter, downgrade, or result in the prompt removal of, conditions going forward.

It is of course interesting that the Money Laundering Regulations apply to so many other regulated communities. Not all regulators have the power to impose conditions or operate in the way the SRA does. If the SRA imposes conditions on a Practising Certificate as a (perhaps indirect) result of a breach related to money laundering, is that a consistent approach with other AML regulators? There is perhaps an argument that both the public interest and regulatory proportionality requires a consistent approach to AML breaches in regulated organisations.

The following is excerpt is drawn from the writer's Serious Breach and Practising Certificate course for 2021.

> 'As we have seen, the previous Regulation 3.1 of the Practising Regulations 2011 (which provided a list of special circumstances in which the SRA may impose conditions, and replaced the old Section 12 of the Solicitors Act 1974), has been removed.

As explained above, there is now, no known list of circumstances in which the SRA will consider an application for a Practising Certificate worthy of additional attention, and the publication of guidance in this area from the SRA would be welcome as a point of balance between the applicant and the decision maker. Whether the SRA have removed the list in order to further examine the public interest test at the point of deciding to further consider the applicant for the imposition of conditions, will be of interest to see (see further discussion of public interest test below).

Conditions can be imposed upon Practising Certificates in force as a result of s13A of the Solicitors Act 1974, and on the issue of a Practising Certificate as a result of s10. Within the Standards and Regulations, this is set out at Regulation 7 of the Authorisation of Individuals Regulations 2019.

Regulation 7.1 provides the SRA the ability to impose conditions at any time during the practising year. Regulations 7.2 and 7.3 set out the circumstances in which conditions can be imposed (although in a much less specific way than previously), and how the condition must be designed. Further regulations specify the timescales. In addition, Regulation 3.1(e) of the SRA Regulatory and Disciplinary Procedure Rules specifies that conditions can be imposed by a decision maker at the SRA

The provisions for imposing conditions on firms and individuals mirror each other; this has been the case since 2011.

If conditions are imposed, the decision and reasons will usually be notified to the subject with 14 days to appeal. If no appeal is made the decision is final. A decision can usually be appealed internally (to an adjudicator if the first instance decision maker was not one, or an adjudication panel if they were). All SRA decisions can be contested before the High Court.

Regulation 3 is also known as Reg 3 or REG3. It in effect replaced the old Section 12 of the Solicitors Act 1974 when that was repealed.

Under the Standards and Regulations, the following regulations are in effect for conditions:

Regulation 7.1 (b) of the SRA Authorisation of Individuals Regulations (must impose conditions if in the public interest to do so). Followed by 7.2 which specifies the circumstances, and 7.3 which specifies what the conditions might look like. Similar requirements on firms are imposed under Regulation 3.1 and 3.2 of SRA Authorisation of Firms rules.

Public Interest Test

The statutory basis for the imposition of conditions … [is]… Part 1, s10 of Solicitors Act 1974, as amended.

The previous regulations under the 2011 Handbook required the SRA to demonstrate the condition was in the public interest. The current rules and regulations require the SRA to impose the condition where it is in the public interest.

The distinction being when the public interest test is considered; whether at the point of deciding to impose a condition or at the point of deciding which condition should be imposed. If the SRA have done away with a Regulation 3/Section 12 style list it may have a major impact on the decision making, both in terms of transparency and the type of condition that is imposed.

Case law also supports the position that conditions themselves should be in the public interest. Conditions should manage a risk and should be necessary, reasonable and proportionate in the public interest

The text of the decisions published on the SRA website has also be updated to reflect the public interest test as well as the statutory basis for the decision and test.

Common conditions

We will have to wait and see whether, as a result of the introduction of the Standards and Regulation, the type, frequency and nature of conditions change, and whether the SRA alter the way in which they are imposed.

The SRA are obliged to ensure conditions are imposed according to the description of that type of applicant, according to the statutory provisions which provide the basis of the conditions (see Part 1, s10 of the Solicitors Act 1974, as amended). Conditions can be generally allocated according to the risk posed by the solicitor (or in other words, that type of applicant), whilst also being tailored to meet the circumstances the solicitor finds themselves in. For example, solicitors who are personally subject to bankruptcy, may expect to have their financial management and managerial functions restricted (this being the response to the circumstances of this type of applicant). They may also be subject to additional accountant reports. However, these conditions could be adjusted according to individual circumstances of the applicant

At the moment, if a solicitor's competence has been called into question in any area (from management to practice) they may be restricted from performing duties in that area, may have to attend additional training, or may even be subjected to approved employment or be restricted in their ownership and running of a firm.

If bankrupt, a solicitor could expect the following types of restrictions:

- not being a Sole Practitioner, or a manager or owner of a firm;
- not having access to client monies;
- acting as an employed solicitor only;
- informing their current or prospective employer of the conditions and the reasons for them.'

Common conditions

While the type and nature of conditions are theoretically never ending, with a myriad of possibilities dependent on the individual situation of each solicitor, in reality, conditions are often imposed which follow fairly set patterns.

These conditions are useful because they have:

- worked in the past;
- are well established as reasonable interventions on the part of the regulator;
- ranged from restriction to educational interventions dependent on the situation and seriousness; and
- are suitable for publication and general discussion without revealing too much information about the situation.

The last point may be more important than is often realised. We increasingly see problems with fake law firms, particularly in an age of digital information and marketing, and those committing this type of fraud will also target legitimate law firms. A condition could, on publication, reveal a possible weakness of that solicitor or the firm. Ironically, if the condition has been imposed it may be the opposite, revealing the ability of the firm to (hopefully) manage the risk effectively. Nonetheless, the regulator has to take care to ensure the situation is manageable for the firm and the individual. Further discussion about publication of regulatory information is contained later within this Part of the book.

There are a number of common conditions imposed on practice including:

1. Not to be a COLP or COFA
2. Not to operate a client account
3. Not to be a freelance solicitor
4. Must seek approved employment
5. Not to be a manager in the firm
6. Not to operate in certain areas of law

The SRA's recent changes to the rules on Practising Certificate conditions under the Standards and Regulations 2019 provides a much wider basis for the imposition of conditions and the justification for the same. However, we will see whether it results in different decisions being made.

During the practising years 2012/2013, 2013/2014, 2018/2019, and 2019/2020, the writer sampled and recorded conditions imposed from the decisions available on the SRA website for the purposes of demonstrating common conditions to the delegates on the training courses. The decisions considered were conditions imposed by internal decision at the SRA and not by the SDT. Although the SRA publishes the majority of conditions, not all are published, so the samples may exclude certain types of sensitive conditions. The writer undertook the samples over different time periods, and the total number of decisions sampled varies (in that the writer looked at all decisions published by the SRA during a set time period, but only recorded the ones involving conditions) so there is an element of difference between each sample. In some cases, conditions were imposed as part of a wider decision, for example, to rebuke a solicitor or refer a matter to the SDT.

The data is published and analysed below in the same format as on the training courses. As you will see from the 2018/2019 sample, in this year, the writer also considered the month in which the decision was made. The SRA makes decisions in large amounts at different times of the year and this is clear from the data; this appears due to the EU requirement to make a decision within six months. However the date at which the decision is published can vary, and some decisions are not published until some time after the decision is made.

The following pages also contain analysis of the different conditions imposed by the SRA.

Sample Set A and B

This shows the very first sample of decisions undertaken by the writer, first used in 2014.

The graph and data set below covers the period from 22 July 2013 to 27 August 2013 inclusive and 1 July 2014 – 12 September 2014 inclusive. It shows the decisions to impose conditions between these two dates. The graph is an analysis of the summer periods of two years, showing the different conditions imposed over these two periods. In these years we can see a number of restrictions on management and ownership, and conditions to attend courses on the Accounts Rules.

Between 22 July 2013 and 27 August 2013, the SRA made 17 decisions to impose conditions. Between 1 July 2014 and 12 September 2014, the SRA made 28 decisions to impose conditions. The following graph shows these conditions and how frequently they were imposed. The SRA made proportionately more decisions in 2014 to restrict client account access, attend courses in Accounts Rules or the Handbook, and act in approved employment, than previously. However the date range of the sample is longer in 2014, and it encompassed more decisions to impose conditions. We could draw a basic inference from the data and graph that the SRA would impose more conditions in these areas if we sampled over a longer period. However, as you will see from the data sets in 2018, a longer sample date did not reflect a larger imposition of conditions. We might be able to conclude from the data in total that the SRA are driven in the timing of the imposition of conditions, and this impacts the sample. Factors which might impact the timing of the decisions include:

- Other or general workload
- Regulatory requirements to make decisions within a set time period.
- Traditional receipt and planning of work within certain times of the year.

All of the samples show the following to be the most frequently imposed conditions:

- Not Sole Practitioner, or manager or owner of a firm – this is the most common condition in every sample, aside from 2019 to 2020.
- Shall inform actual or prospective employer of the condition– a secondary condition commonly imposed alongside other primary conditions.
- Not to be a COLP or COFA – this is less frequently imposed in the earlier samples, but more frequently imposed in the later ones.
- Other restriction on client money – the 'other restriction' is a catch all term which covers a range of conditions, which are conditions to restrict access to the client monies function of the firm, but are not conditions to fully restrict access to the client account (this is entered as a separate condition in the sample in its own right). An example of 'other restriction' includes not being the sole signatory to the client account.

Returning to 2013 and 2014, the writer has recorded at the time of the sample that the majority of the conditions imposed in both years were as the result of being subject to Regulation 3 of the Practising Regulations 2011. This means these Practising Certificates were being issued the following summer despite applications the previous autumn; a significant delay on the part of the SRA.

It should also be noted that more than one condition can be imposed at a time. The writer has recorded each condition separately. For example, decisions to inform an employer of the reason for a condition are frequently imposed alongside other conditions.

In the datasets below, SP stands for Sole Practitioner.

Condition	**Number of times imposed 22 July 2013 – 27 August 2013**	**Number of times imposed 1 July 2014 – 12 September 2014**
Not SP/ Manager/Owner	10	16
Shall inform actual or prospective employer	8	17
Act as solicitor in employment only	5	13
Not sole manager/sole owner/SP	5	0
Approved employment	4	3
Client /office account access restricted	4	11
Attends unspecified course within six months	2	0
Not manager with others less than 3 years' experience	2	1
Not COLP/COFA	2	3
Half yearly accountants' reports	1	1
May act as locum supervised	1	0
Attends course on Handbook and Accounts Rules	1	9
No conveyancing or supervise anyone doing conveyancing	0	1
Course on mortgage fraud	0	1
Application to be manager or owner	0	2

Sample Set C

This shows a second sample from 2018 to 2019. This sample was not by date, but was from the first 70 *decisions* published on the SRA website between September 2018 and September 2019. There were not 70 conditions imposed during this time, the sample was of the first 70 decisions, including all other internal decisions.

The total number of individuals who had conditions was 30. Individuals could have more than one condition imposed.

The data below reflects the number of conditions imposed during that sample. The sample was extended by date to see whether the variation in the two samples above was consistent. The conclusion is, it might be, in that if we see approximately 30 decisions to impose conditions, we are likely to see similar conditions imposed (not to be a manager or owner, and restrictions on client monies access).

The sample could not be extended beyond 70 decisions overall, as otherwise individual data could be identified from the sample.

In this sample, we can see again, similar to the 2014 sample that there are a number of conditions imposed not to be managers or owners of law firms, and not to be COLPs or COFAs. Again, similar to the 2014 sample, there are a number of conditions imposed not to hold client monies.

The number of repeat conditions imposed in this sample was 13. These are conditions imposed for more than one year running.

Condition	**Number**
Not manager /owner	33
Not COLP/COFA	21
Not sole manager	3
Approval of employment	13
Not hold client money	13
Other restriction client money	18
Subject specific	3
Not training supervision	2
Inform employer	11

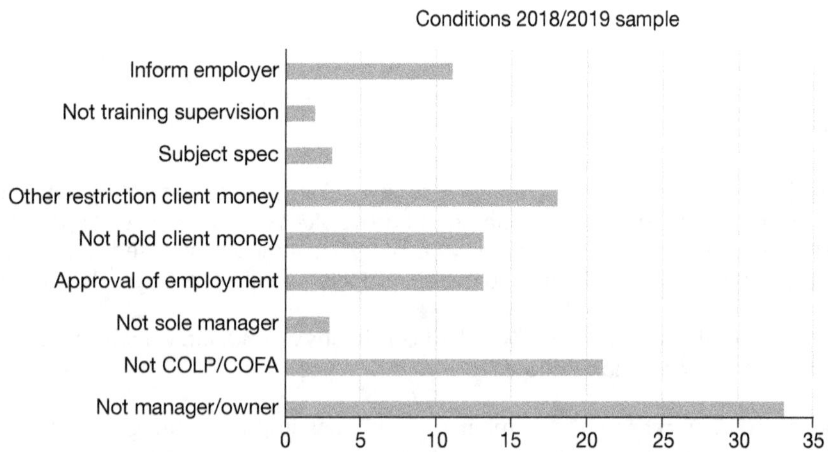

Sample Set C Graph 3

With the data collected for sample C, a secondary analysis was possible. This shows the date at which the majority of conditions were imposed. Under EU derived legislation, the SRA has six months to make a decision in respect of a Practising Certificate. If it receives the application in October, it should make the decision by April. We can see a number of decisions made during March, close to the deadline for completing the decisions. We can also see a number of decisions made during January, a relatively quiet period for the SRA. It will be interesting to see whether the spread of decision making continues after Brexit and the reconsideration of EU derived legislation.

Month	Number imposed
October	4
November	2
December	3
January	5
February	1
March	10
April	4
July	1

When condition imposed – 2018/2019 sample

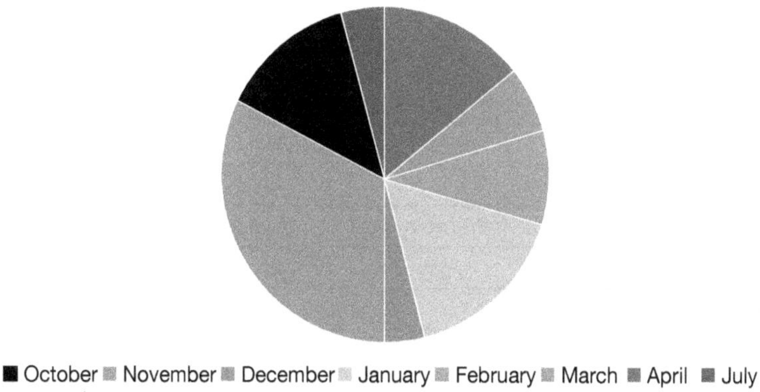

Sample Set D

This final sample shows the imposition of conditions on Practising Certificates during the practising year 2019 – 2020. This data was drawn from the first 50 decisions on the SRA website during the same time period as the 2018/ 2019 sample. This sample size was slightly smaller, stopping at the first fifty decisions published to ensure anonymity was preserved.

Again, the majority of the conditions imposed are restrictions on handling client monies and not to be a COLP or COFA. The number of restrictions not to be a manager or owner are also in place.

For the first time, we have seen restrictions not to be a freelancer, reflecting the new Standards and Regulations in force from 2019.

In this sample, 20 individuals had conditions imposed and 15 were repeat conditions or repeat sets of conditions (conditions imposed year on year).

All conditions imposed in this year were conditions arising as a result of Regulation 3 of the Practising Regulations 2011. There are two points to make in respect of this:

1. The condition arose (along with the initial application for the Practising Certificate) under the Handbook 2011, and not under the Standards and Regulations 2019. The Standards and Regulations 2019 were not introduced until November 2019.
2. The SRA has done away with Regulation 3 under the Standards and Regulations 2019, but it was still being used as a basis for the imposition of:
   a. strong conditions on individuals; and
   b. fairly consistent conditions.

   We will need to continue this analysis to see whether the position changes as time passes, and how conditions under the new regulations are being imposed.

Condition	Number
Not manager or owner (or variant)	5
Not COLP or COFA	9
Not to hold or receive client money	8
Other restriction client money	15
Not sole owner	6
Prior approval for manager or owner/employee	7
Not freelancer	8
Inform employer	5

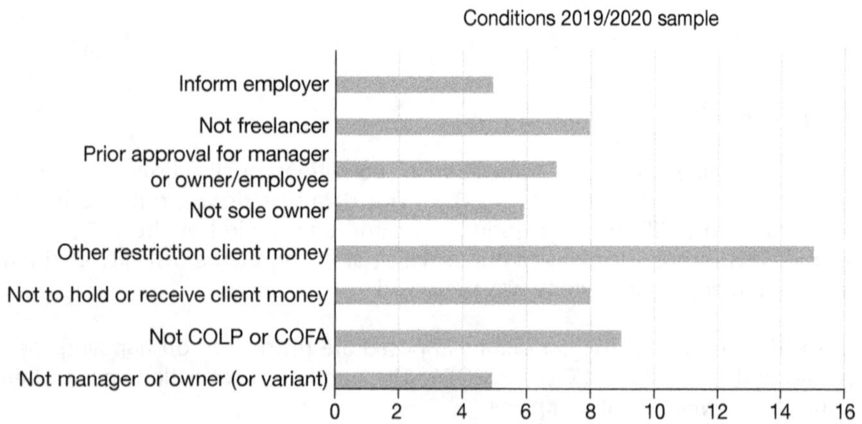

Notes from the samples

The first two samples were drawn from decisions to impose conditions within the time periods stated. The second two samples were drawn from set numbers of decisions published, over a longer date period. To compile the first two samples, a greater number of decisions would need to have been sampled, in order to identify and record the conditions amongst them. We might therefore compare the data from 2012/2013 and 2013/2014 to the two later sets of data and record the data from 2014 as being the more reliable data sampling method for conditions, given the difference between the two original samples (sample A and sample B).

There is variation between the samples, but they do show consistently certain types of condition being imposed, particularly samples B, C and D, with samples B and C perhaps being the closest proportionately.

We could factor in whether or not the SRA have delayed in publishing the decisions to impose conditions, but this has not been noticed by the writer.

We may therefore conclude that the SRA is driven in the imposition of Practising Certificate conditions by the factors identified above, namely time of year, other workload, regulatory requirements, and traditional timings for these types of work during the year. Practitioners with a long history with the regulator may remember having to send Practising Certificates early to the The Law Society for consideration if they were subject to section 12 of the Solicitors Act. Consideration of the PC in late summer is not unusual, and the work may still be planned for that time frame, even despite the regulatory deadlines. Those who have been on the course will know that the regulator can extend the deadline for a PC application by asking for more information, and that the application is not made until it receives everything it needs.

Further analysis

There is a continuing trend to impose conditions on firms which are fairly restrictive; conditions not to run or manage law firms, not to be in positions of compliance responsibility, and not to hold client monies can be some of the most stringent conditions available.

Conditions to inform an employer are fairly common and arise because the individual is being told they must inform an actual or prospective employer of a different condition. In some circumstances failure to inform the employer is not dishonesty or counted as such by the SRA, such as where the circumstances are personal to the individual. However the condition provides the opportunity for the individual and the supervisor to have a discussion, or at least for the supervisor to make a decision about their work and how they will be managed.

The number of conditions to go on courses or considering the type of work that can be conducted has reduced since the original small samples of 2013 and 2014. There has long been a debate about whether these conditions work, and we explore this subject later in this section of the book.

Some of the conditions can be restrictive. Imagine a two-partner firm where one partner can no longer operate the client account or has to do so under supervision, or where one can no longer be the Compliance Officer for Legal Practice (COLP). The management implications of that situation are dramatic, and the SRA has to take care in such a situation to ensure the situation is manageable for a firm or consider what other conditions can be imposed. In that situation the firm would need to accommodate both the partner who has been subject to the condition, and the additional needs of the partner who has to take over. This places additional strain on the remaining partner and the rest of the firm, which is not reflected in the decision making that is published by the SRA. What if the firm attracted additional risk as a result of the additional work taken on by the partner with the full Practising Certificate? Let's imagine the partner with the full Practising Certificate becomes unwell due to overwork with having to take on the additional work as a result of the condition.

The implications for management of those with conditions are an important risk based factor to consider, and an important point for firms when considering how you will discuss management of any regulatory issue with the SRA. We discuss representations later in this Part of the book.

Section 2: Discursive content

The following topics are issues which often arise in the context of discussing Practising Certificate conditions. Have a look at the ideas for issues to discuss or implement in your firm.

Conditions as a regulatory outcome – the Council for Licensed Conveyancers example

If we review the Administration of Justice Act 1985 at s 16, and the Courts and Legal Services Act 1990 at Sch 8, the Council for Licensed Conveyancers (CLC) has the power to impose conditions in the same (or similar ways) as the SRA (The Law Society) previously had under the Solicitors Act 1974, s 12. There is a very similar list to the SRA's 'List' discussed earlier in this Part of the book, which the SRA have recently removed in their latest set of regulations.

The CLC therefore has a very specific set of powers to impose conditions, in a very wide range of circumstances. However the circumstances are specific enough to require the CLC to consider whether they have grounds to impose the condition, and if so, how. In essence, nothing has changed at the CLC and they still have their same statutory powers; meanwhile at the SRA they have taken their decision making in house, dramatically widened their powers, and removed (or attempted to remove) an element of their check and balance (the public interest test).

If we compare the enforcement approach, the CLC has been much less likely to impose conditions on members of their regulated community than the SRA. Whilst the CLC has the regulatory power to impose conditions, this is a power very rarely used. The CLC also has a specialist regulatory remit and supports this through regular face to face inspections with the whole of its regulated community. The difference in the CLC approach is to look for a balance between regulator and regulated community with a more informally interventionist style.

This means the CLC takes a more direct approach to working with the regulated community, and the outcome is the development of management processes, technical ability, and client facing documentation at the firms. In the CLC's view, this interventionist style can avoid the need for regulatory sanction or risk management, because the risk management is built into the regulatory process.

The decision in *Razeen* is also worth examining from a comparative perspective in that the decision and case took place in 2008, after the repeal of the old s 12 of the Solicitors Act 1974, by the Legal Services Act 2007. It acts as a check and balance on the power of the SRA. The CLC however were unaffected by the Legal Services Act 2007 in respect of conditions, and their powers remain the same. Does the decision in *Razeen* then apply to the CLC situation? It may have some sway, and of course decisions to impose conditions may be imposed to address a risk in any event. However, the CLC finds itself in a very different situation to the SRA and the writer may be more comfortable with their powers, their list, and the statutory (parliamentary) reflection on the need for that position. Solicitors, as we have seen, do work in CLC regulated firms, and they may be authorised directly by the CLC, with a Practising Certificate directly from them. Solicitors working in the CLC regime may therefore want to be aware of the difference in potential approach to conditions between the regulators.

Accountants and others working with CLC firms may also find it helpful to reflect on the imposition of conditions and the circumstances in which they could be imposed. The SRA's approach to conditions (which can include regular accountants reports), provides ample opportunity for discussion of risk and approaches to the same (including in financial procedures). Accountants will of course note that the changes introduced by the SRA in respect of their accountants' report and Accounts Rules are not mirrored by the CLC.

When we discuss conditions, the CLC approach offers a different perspective in risk management. The SRA impose their condition as a redirection of the practitioner away from a previous risk, and this assists in managing the situation. The CLC are taking a different approach to risk management, but also from a different perspective. By attending the office of the practitioner, considering their set up and practice, and requiring actions to be taken, the CLC are taking a similar action – redirecting and refocusing the practitioner's attention on a particular problem area, and seeking to resolve the issue. But they are doing so by looking at the situation in significant detail which may result in a more nuanced response. By contrast, the SRA cannot visit all of the firms it regulates; there are too many.

We might ask the question – which regulatory style would you prefer? Some find support in regular visits from the regulator. Others may question whether the regulator would understand their line of work, and do not appreciate the interference. In some cases, the CLC cannot regulate some solicitors firms due to their risk profile; the CLC is a small regulator and must manage its own risk profile to work it knows well, however it does authorise some of the largest conveyancers in the country.

Undertake the exercise below and consider your preference in regulatory style.

REGULATOR STYLE

Consider the advantages and disadvantages of the different regulatory styles described. Consider:

- What might you get from a direct relationship with a regulator?
- If the regulator visited you what powers might you find yourself subject to? Do you think the regulator would use them?
- Have you seen any conditions imposed? Would earlier or a different type of intervention have prevented them?

- Have you seen any other regulatory styles from any other regulators other than those mentioned above?
- How can large regulators with large regulatory communities best use their resources to deliver regulation in the public interest?

Regulatory decision making

Regulatory decision making is a practised skill. For the solicitors and legal practitioners reading this book, it is a different skill set from that of giving legal advice or finding the correct legal solution.

On one hand, you have the risk of an action occurring, with the associated risk to clients, the public, the reputation of legal services and wider society. On the other hand, you have the rights of the practitioner and their business, along with their clients, and associated businesses. Somewhere else, you have the role of the state, different legislative requirements which might pull you in different directions, and an underlying need to serve the overall public interest.

As a regulator with power, it is always tempting to use it, but there is of course the requirement to operate within the bounds of reasonableness, with proportionality, and in the public interest. Regulatory decision making is sometimes about balancing the public interest and business interest with the exercise of power; often it is better not to exercise power or make any regulatory intervention (with a small i) unless necessary. Often the most desirable regulatory action is an effective light touch redirection, although this can be very difficult to achieve.

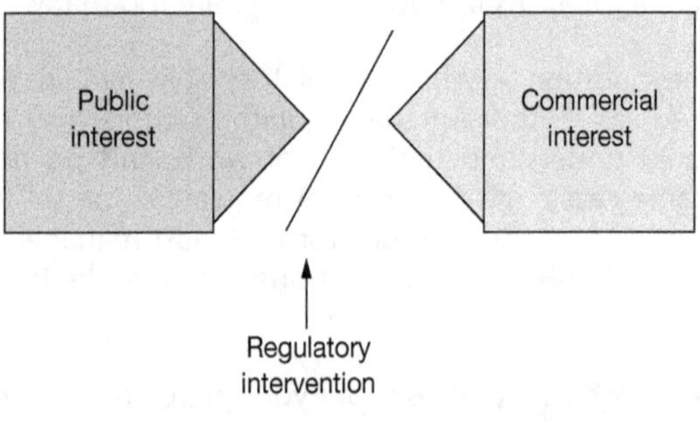

Weighing up the scales as a regulator is an interesting choice of career if we compare it to that of a solicitor. There can be a law enforcement angle to the work; it is often closely related. There are also policy considerations, often on a national basis. The costs consequences for regulators are not often litigation based, but the challenge of appropriately directing resources to manage the position in a market.

There are red lines, but ethical, publicly focused, risk-based decision making is at the core of the job. The motivation of those undertaking the work is often to protect the public, and there is little commercial interest.

Understanding the motivation of the regulator and employees can help with responding to and liaising with their staff. You may be able to take account of their perspective and concerns in grounding representations, making submissions, and framing your arguments. It also helps understand why conditions are being proposed, and to recognise even if they are imposed, they are intended as a short or medium term measures and that they are likely to be lifted.

The writer's own experience in running courses in this area for the last ten years is that when presented with a regulatory problem, solicitors often attempt to solve the legal issue rather than the public interest or regulatory issue. The answer to the problem below is often given as a legal answer, with the solicitor being given legal advice about their options.

Conversely, the same might also be true. If regulators were faced with giving the solicitor in the scenario below legal advice, how would they respond? Is it possible to see the position without the public interest question and risk management clouding the response? There may need to be substantial re-education or even significant work experience on both sides to re-position the two perspectives.

Should a decision making structure such as a regulator reflect the regulated community to ensure decisions are not made which are based on perceptions? Given the regulator is there to serve a public interest, should the staff also reflect the wider public interest remit and be there to reflect society as a whole? The answer may be attempting to achieve a balance of both.

Consider the following scenario:

YOU ARE THE REGULATOR

Read the scenario below. Consider the position yourself from the perspective of the regulator. There is further analysis of the situation below. Ensure you complete your consideration before reading any further.

Gary is a solicitor and COFA who has made a few bad financial decisions in his personal life. He invests heavily in a separate company that produces peppermint flavoured confectioner's sugar. He finds, to his financial ruin, that it is not a big seller. Most people are used to adding peppermint to confectioner's sugar if they want to make peppermint creams.

Gary has a number of creditors and has been personally threatened with insolvency. Fortunately, his law firm is not affected. The firm has strong management procedures in place.

Gary is not yet in a position of insolvency.

Gary reports the matter to the regulator.

What should the regulator do next?

When solving the above problem, most solicitors look to Gary's options for insolvency, and what he could do next. The regulator would of course want to know what was likely to happen, but this is not their primary concern. The most pressing concern for the regulator is whether Gary's position and decision making in his separate company poses a risk to the law firm, the clients, or the wider public, and if so the impact of that. However, there is the possibly Gary's Practising Certificate could be suspended if there was an insolvency event, and the regulator needs to consider the seriousness of the position. It is highly likely the regulator would perceive Gary to be a risk, particularly given he is a COFA, and may curtail his Practising Certificate with conditions restricting him from working with the financial functions of the firm, particularly if it is likely to be suspended shortly.

The regulator would seek information from the firm or Gary about what he was doing next, relying on the firm or Gary being appropriately advised and passing information on to the regulator about the intended next steps. The regulator would use this information to make a decision.

As above, the regulator also has to consider the position of the firm. In this case we do not know the details of Gary's practice, whether they are set up to support him and take over the COFA role. If Gary was a Sole Practitioner, this could be a difficult position because the suspension or restriction of the Practising Certificate could seriously negatively impact the practice. However, we will assume he is not, as he is not also the COLP.

What is the difference between regulatory decision making and client-facing legal decision making or advice? The client-facing legal advice would target Gary as the client with the legal problem and provide advice as to his resolution in his best interests. The firm may need separate advice dependent on the situation and how it was constituted.

Regulatory decision making focuses differently. It considers the position of the firm and professional in the context of societal and client needs, and the potential risk posed by the situation. It also considers the reputation of legal services. To take account of the whole situation it must take account of the advice given in the legal decision making, and the regulator may also form their own view of that advice. The regulator has regulatory objectives. The context of the decision making is informed by that approach, as is the range of powers available to the regulator. We could say the regulatory decision making is informed by the position of the solicitor and firm, as well as the context of the legal services market.

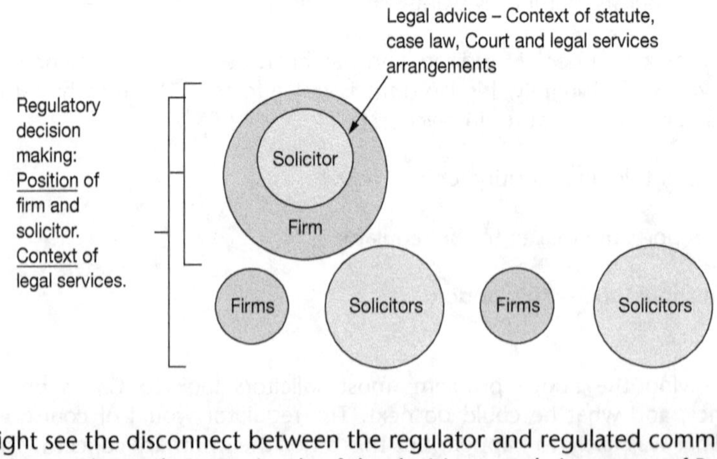

You might see the disconnect between the regulator and regulated community in micro-chasm. The analysis previously of the decisions made in respect of Practising

Certificate conditions reflects the consideration of the regulator in respect of many of its decisions. The discussion of the different types of decision making here demonstrates the differences in day-to-day work undertaken by the solicitor in private practice and the regulatory staff at the SRA.

Of course, the regulator cannot get too close to the regulated community. It must be independent to avoid issues of regulatory capture; achieving the balance between the public interest; independent prosecution; and the knowledge of the solicitor's profession.

There is a distinction between this description of regulatory decision making and that of Ethics Guidance, which helps practitioners solve problems and provides ethical decision-making advice. Ethics Guidance may be closer to the position of the practitioner in private practice than the regulatory decision making described above, and there is a debate as to whether this function appropriately sits with a regulator. However, a regulator may, within the limits of their powers or roles, take different steps to solve problems, and this could include different functions.

EXERCISE: JOB ROLES

This exercise is one for managerial staff. It considers the skill set of staff members and what might be required for any particular job role.

Task 1

The first task is write an imaginary job advert or job description for a law firm member of staff. They should be in a role which practises law and the job description should specify the qualifications and skills needed.

When completing this job advertisement have regard to the requirements for:

a. reserved and non-reserved work

b. the skills you consider valuable for this role

c. the potential for partnership in the long term

d. your ability to offer additional training and qualifications

e. the commercial perspective required for the role

Task 2

The second task is to imagine yourself working in a regulatory role at the SRA. Write an imaginary job description for a regulatory member of staff; perhaps one who corresponds with law firms and makes regulatory decisions. Your job description should specify the skills and qualifications necessary for the role.

Have a re-read of the first two parts of this book if needed.

When completing this job advertisement consider:

a. the wider public interest

b. the requirements for independence and the SRA

c. the statutory requirements for The Law Society and SRA to be separate and the requirement for independence

d. where a future career path may take a regulator

e. the ability to undertake additional training and qualifications

Conclusion

You may find the job descriptions look quite different.

The perspective of the regulator may feel quite different from yours if you work in a law firm. This exercise may develop your understanding of the perspective of the regulator and their obligations. Making representations of your perspective to the regulator is important; whether that is in consultations; providing feedback; or during a proposal for Practising Certificate conditions. Making your ideas viable and your voice heard is essential for balanced decision-making.

Achieving a balance in risk management

The term 'risk management' is used widely within the regulators to denote a style of decision making based on the likelihood of one individual set of circumstances, or wider group of circumstances, occurring, and allows for the allocation resources accordingly. All of the legal services regulators, under the Legal Services Board, have adopted this approach in common.

Advocates of the approach discuss its ability to demonstrate decision making in action, and provide justifications for different causes of action. We can see the approach being taken in the consideration, measure, and imposition of Practising Certificate conditions.

The premise of risk management is to tackle the most pressing concerns and manage the situation in the overall public interest. Different risks, such as the risk to clients, or the risks to third parties, may be taken into account in decision making. Broadly speaking the SRA have adopted the equation *impact x probability = risk*, but the reality is the situation is more nuanced than that. For example, if we take situations which are potentially very high impact, but the probability is very low, the average law firm may not be equipped to deal with them as they may have to deal with other matters first. Consequently we often need a baseline in law or minimum standard from the regulator to adhere to.

In the case of a Practising Certificate condition, some degree of probability has already occurred so the imposition of the condition manages the impact of any future events (for example through supervision or re-training) and if the situation is serious enough may remove the probability altogether by the restriction on part of a practice.

However risk management is not a perfect form of decision making. Common sense, the backdrop of the legislative remit, and expected standards within the regulator all form a body of work that is remembered and referenceable. There are other forms of decision making that could be applied within the regulatory remit.

Consider the exercise below and the many and varied forms of decision making that could be applied to regulatory work. In the context of Practising Certificate conditions some of the techniques may be used as part of investigatory work and to inform decision making if for example, the circumstances are unclear.

RESEARCH QUESTION

What other forms of decision making can you find out about?

Have a look at the question below and conduct your own independent research to find:

- Common formulas
- Management tools, techniques and exercises
- Professional research tools and techniques
- Investigative tools and techniques (these might be any investigations from be law enforcement investigations to medical investigations)

Your research may take you into different forms of logical reasoning.

Question for research:

How can decisions be made?

- Mathematically?
- Iteratively?
- Discursively?
- By deduction?
- To take account of unknown future events?
- Within different areas of our businesses?

Try to find one example of each of the above bullet points.

Are these decision-making techniques suitable for public bodies? What about for private businesses?

Conditions, unregulated firms, and freelance solicitors

Conditions could in the future be an important part of regulating the practising arrangements of a freelance solicitor. We have already started to see conditions being imposed which mean solicitors cannot work freelance. It may be that becoming freelance implies a certain standard and responsibility for maintaining compliance that the SRA seeks to impose in the future. The expectation of a certain standard and introduction of the same may be a solution to the apparent problem of restricting the practice of a freelance solicitor who is already freelance. At the time of writing freelancers were a comparatively new form of practice so we wait to see whether this issue or outcome materialises.

As we have explored earlier in this Part of the book, it is also theoretically possible to prevent solicitors working with one or many unregulated firms in various arrangements by restricting the practice of the solicitor. The restriction does not need to be on the unregulated firm, the restriction could be placed on the solicitor. For example, this could be a restriction which names the unregulated firm(s) or one which targets an area of law specifically. Of course, if the unregulated firm was a significant concern there are various other bodies that may deal with the issue. Those working with unregulated firms, should be aware of the legal position of the unregulated business as a whole, including the relationship to those in the regulated sector and the importance of compliance. In some cases, there are offences for failing to comply with broader regulatory standards.

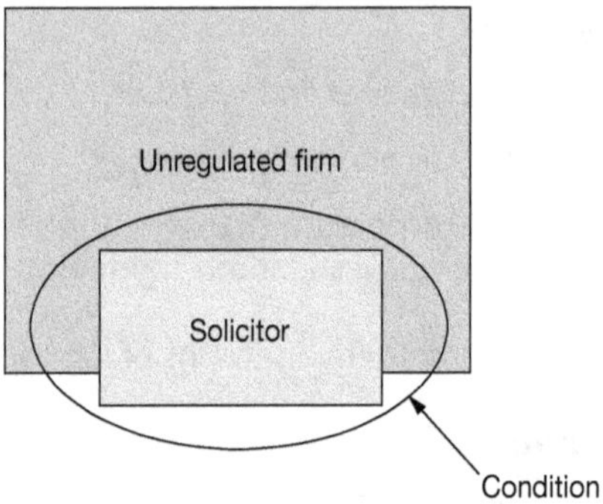

The imposition of conditions on a solicitor to impact an unregulated firm is an untested area, but we can see how it could operate. If a solicitor was prevented from acting in a certain area of law, but was a freelancer offering that area of law and working with an unregulated business, it would impact them as well.

As we have seen earlier in this Part of the book, a condition involving doing or not doing something can impact those around you, including the management of the law firm you are operating in. The position of the freelancer could be particularly jeopardised by the imposition of conditions as they are reliant on the Practising Certificate in order to practise freelance in the first place, they do not have the support system or the 'cushion' of the law firm to protect them.

We can see from many of the common conditions that they are fairly serious. They restrict access to the financial and management functions of the firm. We can assume that in an equivalent situation the freelancer would be prevented from working freelance. Even the ones which are less serious could have an impact on the freelancer, for example the 'subject specific' conditions (the ones which prevent a solicitor working in certain areas of law), could negatively impact a freelance practice based in that area of law. The imposition of conditions could spell the end of a freelance career, which, if we work backwards, *could* give us an indication of the risk taken on by working solo without the support of a steady firm.

We wait to see how freelancers will be impacted by conditions going forwards.

Representations for conditions and risk management

What should you do if the regulator decides to impose a condition on your Practising Certificate?

If you disagree, you can make representations to the regulator. Consider what you would do to manage the risk in your own firm and to your own 'practice'. That might include how you would manage the risk yourself, how you would manage the risk as a firm (and a firm might make separate representations), and what steps you could take to prevent any perceived risk to the clients of the firm. You may also consider any mitigations and how to prevent future occurrences.

You may have an alternative course of action to propose to the regulator, other than their suggestion. Making commitments to specified improvements is helpful and can assist.

There is of course the option to do nothing if you agree with the condition, or to write and say you agree so the later sanction is not worse.

The flow chart at Annex 1 to this Part of the book, and the process earlier in this Part of the book demonstrates the procedure for imposing conditions. There are a number of touch points or potential touch points between the practitioner and the regulator. The main point at which representations would be made is when the regulator writes to you with a proposed condition, and provides 14 days to respond. However, as described in earlier in the book, you may be spoken to about a possible condition before that, if for example there is an ongoing SRA investigation and a condition appears appropriate.

'Representations' in the correct use of the term are made formally in writing to the regulator in response to allegations raised during an investigation, or in this context, proposed conditions. They occur with the 14-day time period allotted, and are placed before the decision maker (who might be an Adjudicator or Adjudication panel) alongside the caseworker's report. However, any points that you wish to raise with the regulator at any stage might be informal representations, and can be helpful. You can also re-iterate these points in your written representations if you still feel they are valid. Representations are useful, even to caseworkers, who want to make the right decision or recommendation. Do make them.

You can make representations by letter, including by email. You may also find it helpful to speak to your allocated caseworker by telephone if you have a particularly sensitive point to make (noting of course you may also wish to put it in writing).

You do not have to have legal advice or a legal representative to make representations, you can do it yourself. However, do take the time to consider your approach. Also, different parties with different interests may need separate representation.

REPRESENTATIONS AND CONTINGENCY PLANNING

Exercise

Consider how you would represent yourself in the event of an SRA investigation. This can form part of your firm's contingency planning, but equally applies to individual solicitors as to firms. Remember you (firms and individuals) may need separate representation.

There are different organisations that exist to support solicitors and their staff, along with law firms who represent solicitors. Have a look at the terms of your insurance; do they require representation by any particular law firm or will the insurer organise it? Consider your membership of different groups – do they have favourable terms or recommended firms?

Taking a few minutes to plan representation for the firm and the staff can really assist you in clear and timely decision making if this event ever occurs (remember it may not, but it can help to know what to do). Put this in your contingency plan and your policies and procedures if appropriate. Alternatively, leave a copy with your COLP and COFA and management structure, and refer the staff to them.

SDT outcomes and SRA outcomes

The writer sampled the decisions to impose Practising Certificate conditions on the SDT website in the same way as the decisions on the SRA website. The time period of the sample is not provided here so the data remains anonymous. Of the first hundred decisions available, a small number (anonymised) related to applications to vary conditions imposed and in force on a Practising Certificate.

A further 20 decisions were sampled at random to obtain data related to the Practising Certificate conditions in detail. The following conditions were imposed (conditions can be imposed more than once):

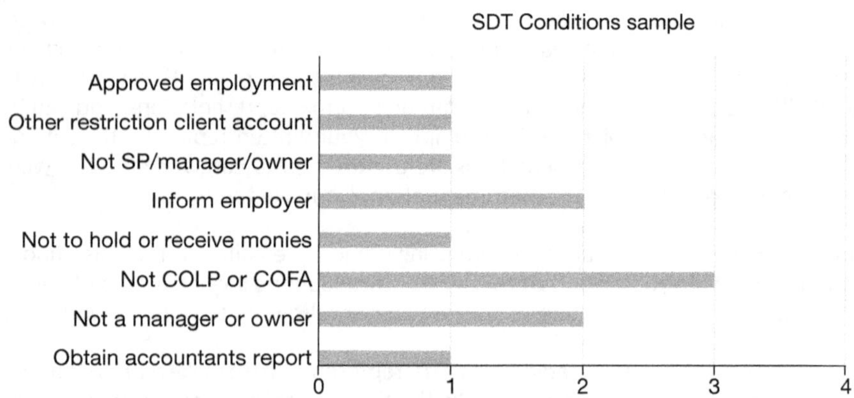

Conditions	Number of times imposed
Obtain accountants report	1
Not a manager or owner	2
Not COLP or COFA	3
Not to hold or receive monies	1
Inform employer	2
Not SP/manager/owner	1
Other restriction client account	1
Approved employment	1

The data shows a similarity to the SRA internal decision data in that:

1. Similar types of condition are imposed.
2. The most common condition is not to be a COLP or COFA (Compliance Officer for Legal Practice or Compliance Officer for Finance and Administration).
3. Conditions are often imposed together, and the condition to inform a prospective employer is a common condition to utilise along with other conditions.

We can also see the general work of the Tribunal from the conditions imposed and varied. Conditions do form part of their regular work, but there are also often other circumstances which are so serious that the practitioner would be struck off or suspended rather than a condition being imposed. This means that there was a large sample size (encompassing a large amount of decisions), but a small number of conditions actually imposed. We may need to take data from the SDT year on year to see trends emerge, but we may also note that the matters in front of the SDT are:

- intended to be more serious than internal decisions at the SRA; and
- usually linked to issues of misconduct rather than standalone issues (for example it would be rare for the SDT to deal with insolvency).

As a result, we can make comparisons with SRA decision making, but we should also make a distinction between the two.

The appeal from the regulator in respect of the Practising Certificate is to the High Court, rather than the SDT. The first paragraph in this small section refers to applications to vary conditions. An application to vary a condition can be made at any time a condition is in force, including some time after the original decision was made, and when conditions have continued to be imposed. Applications to vary conditions are comparatively rare.

Restriction or more practice?

Conditions can be imposed for a variety of reasons, but it might be because there is a risk to the public in respect of a certain aspect of a practice. The question is whether a restriction needs to be imposed, or whether the practitioner actually needs more experience, or support, in this area.

Should we restrict the practice of those who pose a risk, or should we enable their improvement through more intensive practice and support? Conditions are sometimes imposed which require the practitioner not to work in a certain area, but these can also be supplemented with a condition that the practitioner attend a course, or that their work should be signed off.

The imposition of the condition not to conduct certain work seems counterintuitive. Solicitors have a broad practice basis and are automatically authorised to conduct all types of legal work. They must then certify their own competence on an ongoing basis through the renewal. Reports to the SRA or other regulatory bodies; or other types of investigations, can bring them to the regulator's attention and result in conditions. Restricting their practice in some areas is designed to remove the risk to the public, but would re-education be a longer term resolution to the problem?

COMPETENCE – A DEBATE WITH YOUR TEAM

This debate below is designed to debate the issue of competence; how and when we feel truly competent in a task and where we draw our knowledge from. You can use examples from the workplace (perhaps focusing on a narrow task within a process), or from outside of the workplace. Using examples from outside the workplace may help you make this less challenging for staff and illustrate more neatly the importance of a full range of points of view in competence.

The writer uses 'making a cup of tea' as her example of competence. This is a great leveller for all staff and is not challenging. In using the exercise below you can ask people to describe why they are truly competent in making tea and how that helps them understand competence. If your staff do not drink tea or do not make tea, try ask them for any other activity they do at home where the outcome has to be 'just right'.

This exercise is not recommended if any members of staff are tackling work place competence issues.

Achieving competence

Ask the members of your team to think about something they feel truly competent in. This does not have to be legal work, it could be answering the telephone in a professional manner, making a cup of tea, or cooking breakfast. It could be one aspect of the legal process, such as the signing of wills, or the exchange of contracts in conveyancing. We are all involved in the legal process in some way so involve everyone, from partners to administration staff.

Then facilitate the discussion:

Ask different people to discuss why they feel truly competent in that specific part of the process; whether there are any debates about how to do this properly; and what they bring to the task. Importantly ask them; when did they feel truly competent and why? Is there anything they would like to learn in the future and how will they do that?

From this debate you may come to a position of discussing a full range of viewpoints on competence, from specialist knowledge and focus, through to research, and understanding or knowledge of other views on the subject. Encourage your staff to take this debate into their personal learning and development plans (PDP), to start to develop their legal subject knowledge over the next year. If they have used non workplace examples, encourage them to conduct the same process again but with one or more aspects of their legal work to develop a part of their PDP.

There will obviously need to be feedback into the PDP and ongoing staff competence, but it is a useful exercise in self-reflection.

For the facilitator or the management team:

Ask yourself the following questions:

What is your reflection on competence?

Would you like to see staff with certificates and qualifications?

How do you ensure ongoing competence as a matter of management practice?

Do you think staff can be supervised to competence in legal work?

You may take the time to consider your own workplace development as well.

Managing others with conditions: COLP, COFA or HR?

As said elsewhere in this Part of the book, being subject to a condition on your Practising Certificate is not the end of a career. Career development, opportunity and support are still required in the same way for those with a condition rather than those without. Arguably, as we have seen above, those with conditions may end up with more career development through additional attention on their learning and development, than those without!

The responsibility for assessing the condition and the circumstances might in the first instance fall to the COLP or COFA. This may include:

- consideration of the condition;
- the circumstances of imposition;
- representations and assurances provided to the regulator;
- circumstances of employment within the firm; or
- proposals for how the condition will be met or managed within or by the firm

This final point is particularly pertinent in the context of the rules related to COLP and COFA. We have seen the example of Gary, and his peppermint problems earlier in the book. It is likely the SRA would restrict Gary's access to the financial and management functions of the firm, and prevent him being a COFA. The steps to tackle this situation might fall as follows:

- consideration by the COLP of the situation;
- referral to the management team of the position;
- selection by the management structure of a new COFA; or
- work by the COLP, COFA, and management structure to implement the condition according to both the wording of its terms and overall meaning.

Given the situation, the impact of the condition may be keenly felt by the firm, and the COLP, management team, and new COFA will want to review the situation when the condition is reviewed, possibly the following year. The firm will also want to be aware of Gary's potential insolvency, but this is a separate consideration we will not cover here. It is noted that such separate considerations can place additional pressure on the individual and the firm.

Firms should also be aware of conditions which involve attending courses or similar. We have seen the debate concerning competence earlier in this Part of the book, and also in Part 1. Do the courses you are arranging meet the objectives of the condition? Again, consider the terms of the condition and its overall meaning; to do this you may need to consider the context of the imposition. Sometimes, trainers and those leading courses are unaware of the attendance of those with conditions, and that people are attending because they have conditions. Consider whether you would like specific courses for your firm to ensure the condition is addressed, rather than using standard courses which might not quite meet the wording of the condition.

The COLP or COFA does not necessarily need to be involved in day-to-day management of the individual, but they would need to be aware of a condition. Day to day supervision may still be able to be undertaken elsewhere, with a line back to the COLP or COFA and a regular monitoring of the position related to the condition.

Assessing the overall position will assist with developing an action plan to address the condition, deal with day-to-day supervision, and ensuring effective management. It may be implicit by the imposition of the condition, that the regulator expects the firm to take steps to manage the situation, the risk, and the person concerned. Elsewhere in this Part of the book we have covered making representations to the regulator in respect of conditions and firms can consider making those representations in respect of how they might manage and mitigate a situation if they think it would be helpful.

Dependent on the nature of the condition, systems to manage the situation within a firm could include:

- Regular 1-2-1s
- Mini appraisals at different stages of the year
- Training needs analysis, and additional training
- Additional support with other staff
- Team support through regular meetings
- Regular file or accounts reviews (dependent on the condition)
- Third party support
- Considering and supporting the career development of the individual

Conditions should result in a balanced approach to the situation, with the acknowledgement that sometimes situations arise where regulatory intervention is necessary, but also firms can support that person appropriately.

SYSTEMS TO MANAGE CONDITIONS

The writer proposed another system as part of the courses to clarify the risk of a condition. The system was to:

1. Identify the risk to your firm, by asking two questions:
    a. what would the impact be if the situation were repeated?
    b. measure the probability. How likely is it to be repeated? The background of the person and the circumstances are relevant.

2. Take steps to mitigate the risk if one is identified.

It was to be noted that if you are weak in the area of impact, the risk is increased, but firms should be proportionate because the individual can still have a great deal to offer. Risk management can be supportive as it can identify the risk and manage it effectively.

If the condition is not imposed with, for example, additional training and learning requirements, these may still be helpful to the person subject to the condition and may also go some way to meeting the COLP and COFA requirement to ensure the firm is compliant. The COLP and COFA will note that their requirement is to comply with the SRA's regulatory arrangements, and that could be interpreted to include a condition.

Human resources may therefore also have a part to play in the support of the situation. HR may be involved if that person moves firms or if you recruit a new person with conditions on the Practising Certificate. A condition in itself should not be a barrier to recruitment, and if the condition specifies the employer should be informed, this may be HR, COLP or COFA, or even a recruiting manager.

Vetting processes prior to recruitment may also turn up persons with conditions or in situations where conditions may be imposed. In some cases, a condition may not be published by the SRA, because it is not in the public interest to do so. Recruitment processes may need to take account of the fact that some conditions (and indeed other regulatory outcomes) are sometimes kept confidential and asking the question of future employees may sometimes be appropriate. You may also find conditions are about to be imposed on future employees if they are holding over on their Practising Certificates from the previous year.

RECRUITMENT, HR, AND VETTING PROCEDURES

Consider your recruitment, vetting and renewal procedures with your COLP, COFA and HR team. Do your policies and procedures cover the following?

- Current or previous Practising Certificate conditions?
- Circumstances which may give rise to a condition?
- Conditions which are about to be imposed?
- Practising certificates which have been held over?

Also consider how you can work with these situations and what you as a firm can offer. Small firms might find this more complex than large firms.

Do conditions work?

Year on year the SRA imposes conditions on Practising Certificates, and can impose a large number. The work the writer previously did saw the SRA impose many conditions on practitioners subject to the old s 12 and later, reg 3.

The condition may be said to work in that it prevents a potential harm. The legislation, and the SRA's regulatory approach in this area has remained largely the same for many years, and the SRA continues to use the tool. While we cannot examine specific decisions in this book, anecdotally it is true that many practitioners return to the SRA with an update on their condition the following year, often in a position to demonstrate improvement and progress.

Conditions are not primarily intended to be a regulatory penalty, but are a situation management decision. The regulator has other powers which are intended to act as a deterrent, such as fining powers, rebukes, and referrals to the Solicitors Disciplinary Tribunal. However the threat of having a practice curtailed, and the reputational impact of the same, may be sufficient to ensure the practitioner does not take the position lightly, and avoids the same situation again.

We do not have statistics on the number of individuals with conditions who go on to receive further regulatory penalties for similar matters (which are unrelated to the original incident). The writer's experience is that the number of solicitors investigated for misconduct or potential misconduct is correlated with (but not drawn from) the number with conditions or with previous conditions. The two issues (misconduct and conditions), are often treated as separate processes. That position could change if the SRA imposed more conditions as a result of regulatory investigations into potential misconduct.

Sometimes the condition imposed can be as simple as to go on a course. In this situation, you might imagine the practitioner attends the course, but what proof is there that the course has made the difference to the practitioner? We might also ask the following questions:

- To what extent was the course intended to meet the requirements of the SRA?
- To what extent was the trainer or other individual facilitating the course aware of that and prepared to take that responsibility?
- To what extent has the individual person with the condition taken responsibility for their own learning and development needs and addressed those during the year or in relation to the overall learning intended either on the course or by the condition?

Often CPD trainers design specific courses, and it is up to the individual solicitor to judge whether those courses meet their learning and development needs and if so to what extent. The trainer may not be able to know or agree that the course content is suitable for the solicitor with a condition in that situation.

The recipient of any condition, and the firm, should view the condition holistically. A condition to attend a course may be in reality be a condition which also has a learning and development objective that should be taken in good faith and adhered to in that way. If the solicitor attends a course which does not quite meet those learning and development objectives (if it is designed for example to meet 50% of the learning and development objectives), then the solicitor with the condition should attend another course which covers the remaining of the required content, as well as considering whether or not they believe they have fully met the overall learning and development requirement for the condition.

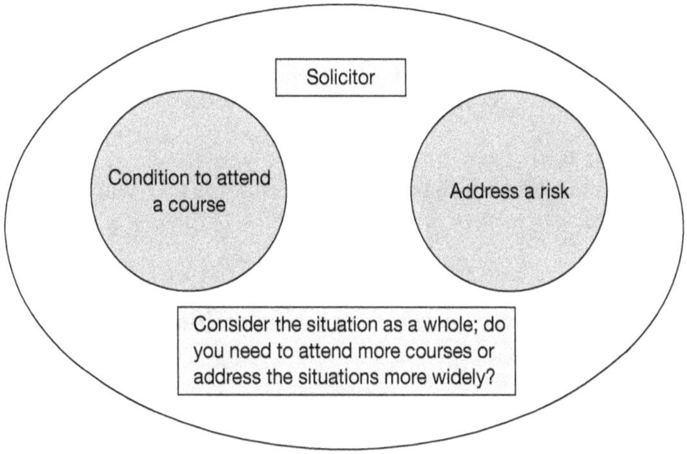

A firm could implement this by looking for courses which meet the objectives of the learner; deal with situations like the ones that arose; and discuss with the trainer the needs for and reasons behind the use of the course.

Do ensure that when dealing with conditions your firm is able to view the conditions holistically. Considering all perspectives of a condition will allow your firm to take different angles to the risk posed and ensure that the condition does work, and the situation does not occur again.

Addressing personal development needs

To what extent does your firm address personal development needs of the staff and others? Do you conduct learning and training needs analyses or measure employee growth and development in some way?

Sometimes conditions are borne of the need to focus on training and learning for yourself or in your firm. There are many different management tools and techniques out there for self-analysis and to develop learning goals, but the exercise below is simple and easy to implement:

EXERCISE – CAREER GEOGRAPHY

You can do this exercise yourself or ask your staff members to complete it. This exercise might be quite personal and staff members might want to keep it to themselves.

Reflect on your career. Draw a 'career geography' showing the landscape of your career. This should be a physical map. It might include your qualifications (show where you obtained them), all the different organisations you have worked for (show where they are located), your valued connections and clients (show where they are located), and a physical representation of your current career position.

Be as creative as you like. You can draw pictures to represent all of the above and place them on a map.

The point is to reflect on where you are now and how you got there.

What can you learn from this about where you are now? Are there any learning and development needs you can identify to take you on to the next place?

Confidentiality, public confidence, and publication in an age of digital information

As we have seen in during this section, and as explored further below, the SRA publishes decisions in the public interest. Decisions are now far more likely to be published than they were 15 years ago. Decisions sometimes may not be published due to the health of the practitioner or because there is another factor that goes against publication.

However the decision to publish was brought about in a time when data was not commonly used for marketing, data mining, and data analysis, in the way it might be today. It is possible to extract data from websites and publish that data elsewhere. The blanket justification for the publication of conditions 'in the public interest' may not be such. The public interest test for a regulator must be weighed carefully against the potential harm to the individual practitioner and firm, such that the condition itself does more harm than good. This can be in the reputation of legal services, for example.

When considering the public interest we should also consider how this data could be used. For example, individuals who are subject to conditions could be targeted by others with ulterior motives because it is perceived they have shown particular weakness in one or more areas. This may be indicated by the presence of conditions and the publication of the same.

It is possible to restrict the use of the SRA data tightly, or impose conditions upon its use. It would be possible for the regulator to impose conditions on the use of regulatory information from its website to ensure it was not used and published inappropriately. They could also consider providing access only to registered users, however this may disrupt the public interest.

We might legitimately ask whether the public understand the condition imposed and whether they need to be informed of the detail or not. Whether in fact a solution to this problem could be simply to say the practitioner had conditions imposed, and whether that would be sufficient to inform the public and address the public interest. The writer doubts that the public are using information about conditions to make informed decisions about which practitioners they use; some conditions, as we have seen, need to be explained to practitioners! Explaining a condition not to be a COLP or COFA to a member of the public is unheard of, and the writer doubts most members of the public have any idea what a COLP or COFA is.

So, if publishing is only really for professionals, should the data be restricted to those who can login to make a search? If we see such a system in future, it might be possible for search companies to make such searches, or instruct neutral parties to make searches for you in order to preserve the confidentiality of *your searches*, as you may not wish to be identified in searching for the individual in question.

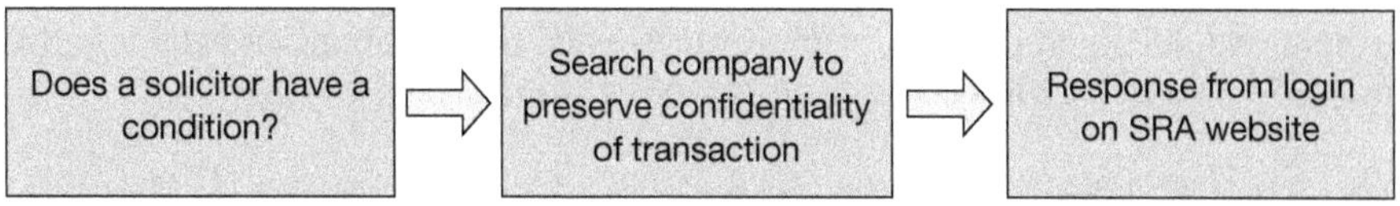

The rise of social media and new media such as Twitter, LinkedIn, YouTube and blogging has democratised information and provides insight in to the day to day lives of others. We are more used to insight into other's lives on a more direct level than before and the decisions available on regulator websites might be used in ways that are unintended.

If we take the example of Twitter, their terms of service restrict data mining and re-distribution to nominated research agencies (Twitter Rules of the Road). A substantial fee is required to gain access. Otherwise individuals can build computer programs to crawl data. The SRA might wish to consider how data could be mined and re-purposed or re-published, and the potential impact on the subjects.

Alternative employment

Obtaining alternative employment and ceasing to be a solicitor is a common situation. Every year thousands of individuals decide they will not continue to practise law any longer. Sometimes solicitors come off the roll, sometimes they simply stop holding a Practising Certificate. Often this is completely legitimate and due to a change in career, new ambitions, or a particular professional focus of that individual which is not expressed in private practice.

However on occasion this happens because conditions have been imposed, or there is another type of investigation underway against the individual. This situation can have overlaps with firms who close down to avoid regulatory investigation, and then restart under a different name, known a 'phoenix firm'. The point of a phoenix firm is to re-start in a way that clears the regulatory history attached to the previous firm. The same can be true of the individual, with starts and stops in their regulatory career. The regulators are aware of phoenix firms and monitor accounts for such activity.

Returning to practise after a period in alternative employment is a reason for conditions in some cases; particularly if the period away is substantial. The SRA seek to tackle competence in such situations, as well as ensuring the individual is more broadly up to date with modern aspects of law practice.

Imposing stricter sets of rules as conditions

One theoretical way to impose conditions is to have a separate, stricter set of conduct rules to impose as conditions. We see this already in respect of accountants' reports being issued on a more frequent basis. Whether in some cases, referring a practitioner away from the current outcomes focused rules and into a more prescribed way of working would assist.

We have seen above that the SRA can impose conditions where they are not confident that the subject will adhere to the current set of regulations. The question is here, would the imposition of more rules assist the situation, and manage the risk, or would those rules also not be complied with?

We have seen already that some solicitors have switched over to CLC regulation. The writer has some experience in dealing with firms that have moved over. In some cases the reason was unhappiness with some regulatory requirements and outcomes. There can come a point with some situations where the level of unhappiness cannot be solved by a move to outcomes focused regulation. Sometimes a complete change of regulatory approach is required and new approach can revitalise a practitioner and provide space for new thoughts and a different way of delivering services amongst persons who themselves take a different view.

Annual renewal and information for decision making

The annual renewal is a major event for solicitors every year. Firms renew their Practising Certificates for solicitors, or individual solicitors complete their own Practising Certificate renewal.

Solicitors are asked for information such as whether they have completed their CPD and addressed their learning and development needs. Recognised firms have to make an information return to the regulator providing information about matters such as:

- Referrals
- Turnover
- Client money held
- Roles within the practice
- Complaints and negligence claims
- Insurance details
- Work undertaken

The list above is not complete, but it provides a picture for the regulator about the firm and allows them to pinpoint possible risks to manage. It is possible from the data provided every year to map trends and spot outlying firms from within the data. When imposing Practising Certificate conditions, or considering other risk based solutions, the regulator may take into account the information provided on the annual renewal in order to assess the overall risk of the practice and the risk to the public.

The writer's experience is this risk assessment is a skill. The writer started learning about the risks of law firms when working for the Legal Services Commission (now the Legal Aid Agency), and has continued in work at The Law Society/SRA; at the CLC; and as a Compliance Consultant. Continually considering the position of different law firms, visiting them, speaking to them, and understanding in detail the risks and problems they face provides a vast array of situational experience, particularly as you often see what happens next.

The annual renewal then provides this background information to the regulator, allowing them to compare the picture one year to the next, consider the overall position of the economy, the capacity and ability of the individual, and then take representations if they intend to impose conditions.

The renewal itself can be a complex process for those that manage it; firms often have:

- a large number of applications to consider;
- maternity leave and other leaves of absence to consider;
- to ensure fee earners have completed their CPD;
- to obtain the information required from throughout the firm;
- to input all this information into MySRA within the renewal window (October each year).

There is limited training available on the MySRA computer system, and there are every year, difficulties with the system due to the volume of applications they process.

We have seen in other parts of the book that unregulated firms will not need to make the annual return to the SRA each year, meaning that solicitors can work freelance with unregulated firms or as an employee within the unregulated firm each year, and the unregulated firm does not need to make the annual information return. This would then lead the solicitor to simply making a CPD declaration each year, and providing other basic information.

The long term implication of this is that the SRA will gather increasingly more data on the regulated firm and less on the unregulated firm, possibly making it more likely that they would make a regulatory decision against a solicitor in a regulated firm than an unregulated firm, simply because they have information about a situation, but they don't have the same information about the unregulated firm.

This position shows the importance of information, and sometimes the importance of a lack of it. Sometimes, seeking more information is a delaying tactic, but increases the certainty of our decision making. On other occasions, we may not have sufficient information at all; information may be a luxury. The scenarios we use on the course demonstrate the need for information when making our decisions, and perhaps we need more to determine with certainty what happened, however often management and others in decision making positions require short reports of circumstances or make decisions on an ethical basis.

EXERCISE: DECISION MAKING AND INFORMATION

Exercise 1:

Consider some of the scenarios in Part 8 of this book. Consider the scenarios for Serious Breach and the ones for the Practising Certificate Conditions.

Try to:

a. Firstly, make a decision without further information. How confident are you without that information?

b. Secondly, consider what further information would help you be certain about your decision?

c. Finally, imagine if the information in b. was not available or you could not ask for it. How do you feel about your decision now?

Exercise 2:

Consider the following statement:

What difference do you think it makes to know or understand the regulatory history of a solicitor or firm?

Exercise 3:

This exercise is about information asymmetry.

Information asymmetry is a term used in economics usually where one party uses the data or knowledge they have to take unfair advantage of another in a deal. We saw a reference to information asymmetry in Part 1 of the book when looking at digital services. We discussed the use of personal data and how this can be passed between parties.

Sometimes it is said that consumers do not fully understand legal services and as a result do not fully understand the transactions they enter into. Perhaps you can see this in complaints data or discussions with the client about their transaction.

What steps can you take to counter information asymmetry by making your services as clear and well explained as possible?

Don't forget that we have spent many years studying law and working in legal services. We might make assumptions about what the client knows or understands about legal services.

Legal advice and conditions

It can be a good idea to obtain specific legal advice if needed concerning the imposition of conditions on a Practising Certificate. The imposition of conditions should not be taken lightly. Information is provided at Part 4 of this book concerning the imposition of conditions on the firm and the differences with the individual, which may also be helpful to read if you are facing conditions. At times, firms and individuals will need separate legal advice due to a conflict of interest, or diverging interests between the two, and that they may wish to make separate representations to the regulator. Sometimes however, interests of the firm and individual can be aligned.

As well as covering some of the issues in Part 4 where advice would be required, for example on the condition itself, and on arguments which can be made to the regulator concerning the condition, the legal advisor can also contact the regulator on your behalf and discuss practicalities of imposition. This discussion or representations in this regard can assist if you feel a condition is impractical or unworkable.

Not only will you obtain advice about the imposition of a condition on your Practising Certificate, you can also obtain advice about the implications for your employment (for example how you should comply with the condition and what steps to take), additionally it may be useful to discuss how the condition could be managed in future.

We have also seen that there can be a delay in imposing conditions, that the regulator's powers are now very wide, they can impose conditions in almost any circumstances, and that there are questions over the public interest test. Taking legal advice can help you ensure procedural fairness, that the outcome is in line with what should be expected, and that you have explained your position to the regulator effectively.

Annex 1: Process for imposing Practising Certificate conditions

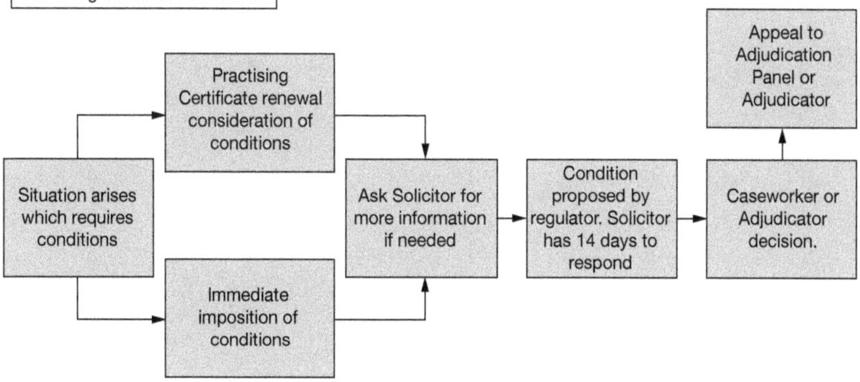

Conditions take effect at the point of final decision (Casework, Adjudication, or Adjudication Panel).

Part 4

Firm Conditions

Contents

Section 1: Technical content
- Imposition of conditions
- Current imposition of conditions
- Standard conditions of recognition
- Alternative Business Structures
- Imposition of conditions by the SRA and at the SDT

Section 2: Discursive content
- Firm vs Practising Certificate
- Achieving a balance in risk management
- Corporate requirements: additional standard conditions
- Firm compliance: a focus on learning, development and competence
- Unregulated firms and freelance solicitors
- Do conditions work?
- Representations for conditions and risk management
- Responsibility within firms
- Conditions and the relationship to intervention
- Regulators and regulatory decision making
- Compliance leadership
- Improving compliance through management
- Annex 1: Alternative Business Structures – macro culture post Clementi
- Annex 2: Alternative Business Structures – ABS and their development

Section 1: Technical content

Imposition of conditions

The following excerpt appeared in the writer's 2020 Practising Certificate/Material Breach course, when discussing Firm Conditions:

> 'The SRA has the power to impose conditions on regulated firms and individuals. This is a strong mechanism for regulation, but can be extremely restrictive for those affected. Conditions are usually imposed on an annual basis, according during the annual renewal. This process has been running since the 1970s and has formed the basis for regulatory action and enforcement for the SRA and predecessors ever since.

> …
>
> When outcomes-focused regulation was introduced in 2011, there was an intended focus on the firm. However, conditions on the firm remain comparatively rare.'

The SRA has powers to impose conditions on a firm's overall recognition or licence. As we have seen in Part 2 of this book, this means this applies to both recognised bodies (partnerships, LLPs, limited companies, recognised sole practices) and licensed bodies (ABS), who are collectively known as authorised bodies.

The imposition of firm conditions does not apply to freelancers and unregulated firms as they do not have a 'recognised' practice around them. The freelancer would have conditions imposed on their Practising Certificate. The unregulated body is not subject to regulation and therefore there cannot be any condition upon it. However, in reality it may be impacted by a condition on the freelancer, or employed solicitor and their Practising Certificate. Practising Certificate conditions are covered in Part 3 of this book.

Sole Practitioners used to have conditions imposed on their Practising Certificate, but their wider 'practice' (as discussed in Part 2) was formally recognised by the SRA in approximately 2014. As a result, conditions can now be imposed either on their Practising Certificate or on their recognised body.

The authorised body (the business subject to authorisation) is the subject of this Part of the book. For the purposes of this book, and for ease and clarity, the writer refers to 'authorised bodies' as 'firms'.

The regulator has powers to:

- impose conditions at the point of initial firm authorisation; and
- impose conditions at any time during the lifetime of firm recognition, including during the annual Practising Certificate renewal and firm information return.

Firms do not renew their ongoing recognition, but they do make an annual information return to the SRA during the annual Practising Certificate renewal. Further detail of the renewal process is contained in the first three Parts of this book.

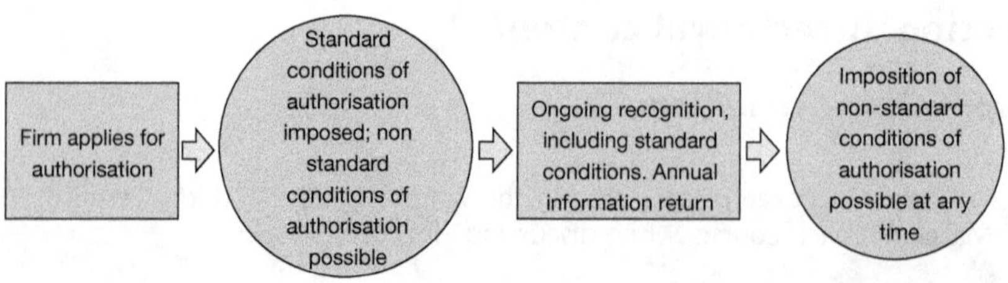

The SRA automatically imposes standard conditions on all firms' recognition at the point of first authorisation. Non-standard conditions of authorisation are also possible at first authorisation. This means the firm is always subject to some conditions; all firms are. The SRA also has the power to impose suitable additional conditions on the firm. However, in practice this is very rare.

Authorisation of the firm continues for the lifetime of the firm. This is until the SRA is formally notified that the firm has closed; for example, in the case of a limited company, notified that it has been wound up. Firms can also stop doing legal services work, but in the writer's experience this is extremely rare and we have discussed barriers to exit from the market in Parts 1 and 2 of this book.

The firm makes an annual information return to the SRA every year and this contains the risk-based information the SRA needs to continue to regulate the firm. As part of that return and as a result of that person's connection to the firm, the SRA also regulates non-solicitors (such as non-lawyer managers – which are briefly discussed in the section of this Part of the book entitled Alternative Business Structures). The annual information return to the SRA may also contain some information regarding those solicitors working in the firm (who of course renew their PC at the same time).

The SRA has the power to impose conditions at any time during the year. We have seen in Part 3 that the conditions for individuals are usually imposed at renewal, and the process has been historically linked to the annual renewal. However, the SRA does not review the authorisation of the firm at annual renewal; the authorisation continues.

Therefore the conditions can be imposed on authorisation, or at any time. The renewal is not the driver.

Standard conditions, which are imposed on first authorisation, are contained within the set of rules and regulations in force at the time. They can change when new rules and regulations come into force, meaning all firms have the same standard conditions on their practice. Standard conditions do not vary according to when the firm was first authorised. This would create the effect of firms from hundreds of years ago having conditions from then imposed! Each time new rules and regulations are implemented, it is a good idea to consider the new standard conditions of authorisation that apply to your firm.

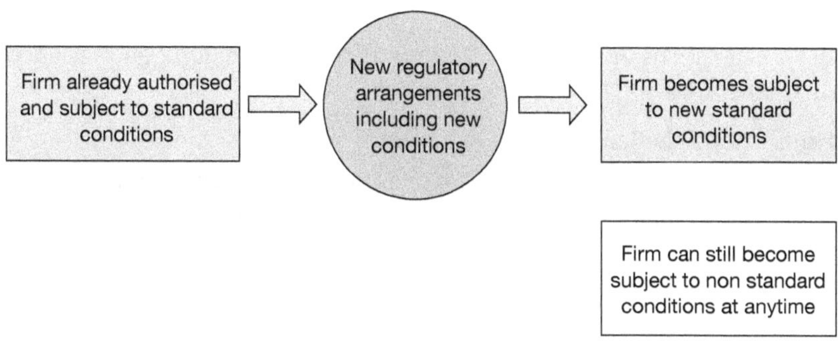

Again, when considering the basis for the imposition of conditions, we must revert to the 'four Acts' we have seen in the previous Parts of this book.

The statutory basis for imposing conditions is:

Firstly:

- that partnerships, LLPs, limited companies and sole practices can be authorised by the SRA (Administration of Justice Act 1985, s 9 and Legal Services Act 2007, s 18); and

- that Alternative Business Structures can be authorised by the SRA (Legal Services Act 2007, s 18 and Legal Services Act 2007, s 72).

Secondly:

- that conditions can be imposed on partnerships, LLPs, limited companies and sole practices (Administration of Justice Act 1985, s 9(2F)–(2I)); and
- that conditions can be imposed on Alternative Business Structures (Legal Services Act 2007, s 85).

In each of these cases, the regulator has the right to make rules specifying its regulatory arrangements, including the imposition of conditions. These rules are currently contained within the Authorisation of Firms Rules 2019, and specify when conditions can be imposed, including the type and nature of the conditions. The relevant rule is Rule 3.

The writer is very aware of the confusion that can be caused with the numbering of rules and regulations in comparison to the imposition of conditions on Practising Certificates, which is covered in the box.

HANG ON – WASN'T THAT REGULATION 3?

The SRA, in writing the new Standards and Regulations 2019, has switched around the regulation numbers for the imposition of conditions, which make the regulation numbers for imposing firm conditions similar to the *previous* regulation numbers for imposing Practising Certificate conditions. This unwelcome move may cause confusion.

In the *Handbook 2011*, the references for imposing conditions are:

Individuals – Practising Regulations 2011

1. Regulation 3, specifying the circumstances when conditions would be imposed
2. Regulations 7, which specified the types of conditions, and included the public interest test

Firms – Authorisation Rules 2011

1. Rule 7, specifying when a condition can be imposed (and that they can be imposed)
2. Rule 9, which specified the types of conditions, and included the public interest test

In the *Standards and Regulations 2019*, the references for imposing conditions are:

Individuals – Authorisation of Individuals Regulations 2019

1. Regulation 7, specifying all aspects of conditions

Firms – Authorisation of Firms Rules 2019

1. Rule 3, specifying all aspects of conditions

Do be aware of the switch when discussing conditions and the potential confusion.

It is common for the SRA to make the same rules for the imposition of conditions on individuals as they do for the imposition on firms. This was the same in the 2011 Handbook.

Current imposition of conditions

The SRA's current Rule 3 of the Authorisation of Firms Rules 2019 provides the regulator will impose conditions on firms, including in circumstances where:

- the SRA are not satisfied that the authorised body (or person within an authorised body, such as a manager, owner or compliance officer) will comply with the regulatory arrangements; or
- the firm will otherwise pose a risk; or
- the firm are unsuitable for certain tasks.

The rules further specify the types of condition that will be imposed, and this is mirrored across from the Authorisation of Individuals Regulations 2019.

These types of conditions include:

- taking particular steps;
- preventing certain steps being taken without SRA approval; and
- restricting access to certain roles.

Readers will recognise the similarity between the individual position (outlined in Part 3 of this book) and the firm position. The positions are so similar, there could be a question whether to impose the condition on the firm or individual, in that, if the situation and condition meets the criteria for individual imposition, does it also meet the criteria for firm imposition? As we will see later in this Part, individual imposition of conditions has historically been preferred and that continues to be the case.

The SRA has taken the wording from the Administration of Justice Act 1985 (section 9) for the circumstances in which it will impose conditions. An explanation of the use of the wording and the basis in the Administration of Justice Act and Solicitors Act is contained in Part 3 of this book.

In the case of Alternative Business Structures, the SRA has additional powers. It also has the right to object to individual or other involvement in the ABS, and ABS must comply with the ownership requirements set out in the Legal Services Act 2007. ABS-specific issues are addressed later in this Part of the book. It is questionable whether the ownership requirements specified by ABS are conditions, because they are the basis of the existence of a structure, but they might be similar to conditions.

The imposition of conditions on a firm's authorisation, beyond the standard conditions of recognition, is rare. The SRA regulates individual solicitors as well as firms and has commonly used the powers it has to impose conditions on Practising Certificates rather than firm recognition. Alternative Business Structures have not overtaken the partnership (including LLP) model, and even with the ABS presence, in many cases the practice is still in the majority ownership of solicitors or other qualified legal professionals. The partnership (or LLP) model has also endured, and it can be complex for those who have invested in a firm to leave or for new partners to join. All of this means attaching conditions to an individual has also in some way been a means to regulate a firm through the long-standing nature of the relationship between the firm and the individual. As a consequence, individual practising conditions have been preferred and there has been no impetus to change this way of working.

Where firm conditions have been imposed, these have been imposed as standard conditions on authorisation.

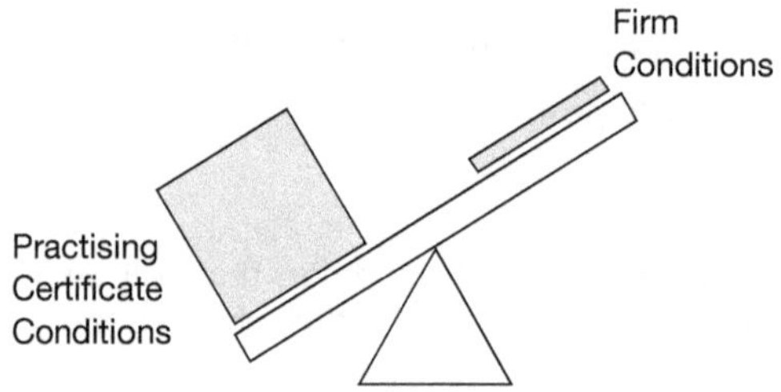

If conditions are imposed, they must be imposed on the authorisation of the firm. In other words, to continue to be recognised by the SRA as authorised to carry out the work they conduct, they must comply with the condition. Failure to do so could result in prosecution of the firm or individuals. Theoretically, a firm could also be intervened as a result of failure to comply with a condition.

Freelancers are in a similar position to the former position of Sole Practitioners in terms of their recognition. Any condition would automatically be imposed upon the individual and not the (possibly unregulated) firm. The SRA may not recognise all of the firms that a freelancer works for, so it is important for the individual to note their own personal responsibility.

There are several other reasons why conditions may be imposed on the individual rather than the firm:

- Management working within law firms are held jointly and severally liable for compliance within a firm. If the SRA took the step of imposing conditions on a law firm practice, this may be part of a wider prosecution or regulatory action in which all management or the firm needed to take specific steps. The regulator may be addressing the management individually.
- The SRA may argue that it is able to pinpoint the risk and responsibility and that this falls to the individual. Therefore, imposing conditions on the whole firm is not necessary as there is and has been sufficient will within the firm to comply, and it is the individual causing the problem.
- Even if there are groups of individuals within a firm who bear responsibility for the problem or potential problem, these could be dealt with by way of individual conditions, rather than a firm condition.
- Firm recognition is also not renewed on an annual basis, so the condition would not fall away automatically. A firm would need to be kept under review

by the regulator for the condition to be managed effectively. If we contrast this with the position of the individual, the individual Practising Certificate is renewed on an annual basis, providing the prompt for review of the condition. Given the number of conditions imposed or considered each year, this is a complex annual process, and many hundreds of Practising Certificates can be considered for conditions. Adding firm conditions increases the workload, but manages the same risk.

- Alternative Business Structures, where there are associated risks of outside investment into legal services, are being covered by in-depth examination of their proposed structure and potential risks, and the imposition of standard conditions on entry. As discussed, the SRA also has the power to object to an individual or investor. These powers may negate the need for conditions.
- If a firm poses a risk to the public, it is arguably more of a risk (or a greater risk) than one, two, or a few individuals. In many circumstances, the risk may be so great that the firm is intervened rather than conditions being imposed.

We can make parallels with the position of corporate responsibility, and it seems the regulator has been reluctant to take this step. The development of corporate responsibility has taken hold in other forms, for example in the Bribery Act and in more recent debates surrounding anti-money laundering; whether the SRA will follow suit in its imposition of conditions is a question for the longer term.

Recently, there has been a challenge to the position of the rules of professional conduct as applying to a body authorised by the SRA in *Harcus Sinclair v Your Lawyers*, but this matter continued at the time of writing and may or may not result in an outcome of note.

Standard conditions of recognition

The SRA imposes standard and automatic conditions of authorisation on all firms it recognises under the Authorisation of Firms Rules 2019. There were similar provisions in the Authorisation Rules 2011.

These requirements include (but are not limited to):

- appointing a COLP and COFA, and for the COLP and COFA to be notified to the SRA*;
- complying with the rules of professional conduct;
- approving management or certain role holders; and
- making an information return.

*including a HOLP (Head of Legal Practice) and HOFA (Head of Finance and Administration) for Alternative Business Structures.

The standard conditions of recognition are *not* regulatory 'decisions' and would not of themselves appear on either:

- the recent decisions list on the regulators' website; or
- the individual firm's authorisation description on the regulator's website.

However, firms should remember that these are conditions of their ongoing recognition to carry on work under SRA regulation and failure to do so could have enforcement consequences. Also, the standard conditions are published for anyone to read, within the Standards and Regulations 2019 on the SRA website.

Recognition is required for the firm or the individuals within it to carry on reserved legal work. There may also be difficulty with calling yourself a firm of solicitors without the recognition required.

Alternative Business Structures

Alternative Business Structures are firms which are partly owned or managed by at least one person who is a non-lawyer or entity which is an unregulated entity. A non-lawyer is an individual who is not authorised to undertake reserved work, as defined by the Legal Services Act 2007. The definition of non-lawyer is controversial and we have discussed the concepts of reserved and non-reserved work in Parts 1 and 2 of this book, as well as the range of regulatory bodies.

There were very serious concerns when Alternative Business Structures were introduced that non-lawyers would introduce commercial interests into the legal services market which would jeopardise the independence of justice within England and Wales. The regulators were also concerned that the introduction of outside investment could lead to unregulated criminal involvement in the sector, and that our constitution could be at threat.

Consequently, Alternative Business Structures are subject to additional requirements within the legislation, beyond those imposed on other authorised structures.

The requirements are intended to restrict:

- **Their operation** – only certain approved regulators offer Alternative Business Structure licences. This means an ABS cannot set up to work within any area of law or with any type of lawyer; they can only approach certain regulators, including the SRA. To offer this work, the approved regulator must have an additional approval in the form of the licence to regulate ABS from the Legal Services Board.

  The licence of the Alternative Business Structure must specify the reserved work they intend to offer, under the Legal Services Act 2007, s 85.

  Alternative Business Structures must have a HOLP and HOFA as a statutory requirement, whereas other authorised bodies have the equivalent COLP and COFA as a requirement in the regulations.

  All persons providing investment or management under the Alternative Business Structure are regulated by the relevant regulatory body by virtue of their involvement in the regulated entity. This means the non-lawyer (individual or entity) is also a regulated person and must comply with the regulatory requirements, and make an annual return on the renewal.

  ABS have also been required to maintain registers of their non-reportable breaches in the past. This is still a statutory requirement, but the SRA has not enforced it due to the volume of work it creates. The writer's Material Breaches courses record in 2013 and 2014 that the SRA intended to provide advice and guidance concerning how this would be monitored on the annual renewal, but that advice and guidance was not forthcoming. ABS may still want to maintain such a register and an example breaches register is provided in Annex 1 to Part 6 of this book.

- **The outside investment they can attract** – The conditions for the outside investment available and percentage shares the firm can offer are set out in the Legal Services Act 2007, Sch 13.
- **The persons who can work as management within the firm** – the SRA approves non-lawyer managers within law firms, as well as those holding positions such as HOLPs and HOFAs. Matters checked can include credit referencing, criminal convictions, and criminal connections.

The broad restrictions are set out in the Legal Services Act 2007, Pt 5, Sch 13.

The approved legal regulators that license Alternative Business Structures are required to ensure these restrictions are adhered to, and the bodies themselves are required to comply with the restrictions.

These are not conditions of recognition, but separate statutory requirements for operation. They can seem quite similar to conditions. Those with a further interest in this area can refer to the Legal Services Act 2007, Pt 5, Sch 13.

Imposition of conditions by the SRA and at the SDT

As discussed earlier in this section, imposition of conditions on a firm is extremely rare. In Part 3 of this book, the writer has demonstrated samples taken from decisions published on the SRA website over the course of several years.

During the sample selections discussed in Part 3, the writer has never found a condition imposed against a firm. No firm conditions have been recorded in any of the writer's Practising Certificate and Material/Serious Breach courses, beyond standard conditions.

The writer has also sampled decisions from the SDT website, and the results are available in Part 3 of this book. These decisions were sampled over a much smaller time frame. Again, there was the same outcome. The writer has never found a decision made to impose conditions against a firm, or any evidence of the same.

The writer does have some evidence of intent by the regulator to impose conditions against firms, and on their recognition. This includes some training she wrote in approximately 2010 when working for the regulator. However, we have not seen firm conditions imposed, and they do not appear to be imposed on a regular basis.

Section 2: Discursive content

Firm vs Practising Certificate

The position we have seen so far is one which strongly prefers the implementation of conditions on the individual rather than the firm. This position has arisen from history: through the Solicitors Act 1974, which had very strong powers relating to conditions, and from the previous SRA Handbooks.

The Standards and Regulations make a clearer delineation between firm responsibilities and individual responsibilities. This may mean that in the future the firm takes a greater responsibility for the regulatory failings than the individual. We have explored this position further in Part 2 of the book.

Arguably of course, the 'four Acts' already created the regulatory powers to take regulatory action against firms, and that is why we have four Acts in the first place (to reflect the variety of means of practising and different types of structure). However, the regulator, rather than Parliament, has preferred the individual focus in the use of its powers for conditions.

The latest position, from the Standards and Regulations 2019, may bring in a new focus on law firms as a whole. However, equally it may be a position of regulatory policy in seeking to achieve firm-wide compliance, rather than being an indicator of enforcement intent towards firms. There has not been any recent indication from the SRA that it will seek to impose conditions on firms.

Thus far, the argument that some firms have a corporate status and should provide protection to their members from regulatory action (and therefore conditions or other regulatory penalty) has not borne fruit with the SRA. Individuals are prosecuted, as are firms, with no current difference due to corporate status. Firms *are* held responsible for the actions of individuals within them, as well as actions the firm has taken itself. Simply because conditions are not imposed does not mean other regulatory action is not taken against firms. There is evidence of firm prosecution and regulatory penalties against firms overall. However, conditions have not been amongst the solutions chosen.

The SRA appears to be advancing the argument (at least with or through conditions) that, where it is possible to pinpoint an issue, it can and should take action against the individual. Moreover, the individual is also regulated as a professional by the regulator and, arguably, the recognition of the firm rests on the regulatory status and qualifications of the individuals employed by it. Alternative Business Structures remain a minority in the regulated field, as do the interests of the non-lawyers who manage or invest in them.

While the firm may have a corporate status, the regulator also regulates the individuals for their conduct, behaviour, and risk posed to the wider public and professionals. These are statutory powers which sit alongside and with the other rights of the firm. Nothing within the corporate status prevents the regulator from taking action against the individual, who is regulated separately, and with whom the problem has arisen.

Of course, firms have the option to structure their businesses differently should they wish not to be regulated as firms. The reminder is the new options for practice available under the Standards and Regulations. However, equally, we have to ask whether adopting the new forms of practice (such as freelancing) is viable for established firms, particularly given the level of organisational change required. The investment needed, and the ability to start again with a new structure, is going to be too much for some firms. That may be particularly true given the change predicted as a result of ABS (and not yet achieved), and given this is just a new set of rules (that may be revised in a few years' time). Freelancing also becomes a further issue when discussing HMRC's view of the position, and in fact whether working freelance is a viable option for solicitors.

At the moment, regulated firms have more to comply with than unregulated structures. If individuals decide to take up freelance work in any large numbers, this position may become even more apparent, and possibly unjustifiable from a regulatory position.

A reflection of the change position in respect of ABS is contained in Annex 1 to this Part of the book, with a view to revisiting ABS and understanding whether or not we need to see firm risks in a different way. Certainly at the time of ABS introduction, many thought there would be large-scale change and that we needed to manage risks. There is not large-scale change; much seems the same.

Do we need to ask questions about whether change has passed us by unnoticed, and if so, were there firm-based risks we did not manage?

Achieving a balance in risk management

We have discussed whether to impose conditions on a firm structure as a whole, or on individual professionals.

To envisage the problem in a different way, we need to imagine the firm as a bridge.

EXERCISE: BRIDGE CONSTRUCTION

Build a bridge from whatever materials you have*.

Once you have built it, imagine your firm as that bridge. You are seeking to assist people, companies, organisations to cross a gap in their knowledge by supporting them to solve a problem.

Now imagine a small crack begins to develop in one place in your bridge.

Look carefully at your bridge and answer the following questions:

- Do you need to replace the entire bridge?
- What would be the risk be to anyone crossing that bridge?
- Can you fix that small part of the bridge?

If you can, try damaging a small part of your bridge, perhaps where you imagined the crack. Can you fix it? You should be able to without replacing the entire bridge.

What can we learn from the exercise above?

Just like your bridge, an entire law firm does not need to be remodelled if one small issue appears. We might think the bridge needed to have significant work and remodelling if many cracks appeared.

The same with a law firm; conditions may not need to be imposed on the entire firm unless there was a significant firm-wide problem. Conditions on a firm might result in the remodelling of the entire firm, and avoiding that might be part of proportionate regulation. You might also say it was avoiding the risk of additional and unforeseen consequences.

You can push this idea further by mapping your law firm as a bridge:

- What roles are the pillars or supporting structures?
- Which parts directly interact with the clients and provide the paths they need?

It may take you some time to identify all of your departments and/or roles.

Can you update your contingency planning, training and development, or key people lists as a result of this exercise?

Are some departments and figures more key than others?

What if we imposed conditions on those key people? Would this be equivalent to imposing conditions on the firm?

*The caveat here is, for the purposes of this exercise, you should be able to make a crack in the bridge or a small hole.

Corporate requirements: additional standard conditions

Could we impose more standard conditions on firms? The question is whether there are some key areas of policy that firms consistently fail to deal with which would be met appropriately by standard conditions on all firms.

There is a list of different areas below which the writer has chosen at random. Which of these would undermine any firm to such an extent they could use reinforcement? Would further standard conditions enhance regulatory protections or would they cause too much of a regulatory burden?

For example:

- risk of disorderly closure;
- lack of contingency and succession planning;
- consumer information;
- advice competence;
- financial stability and capital adequacy; or
- cybercrime.

However, these may simply be areas for additional regulatory requirements or protections within the existing rules. We may be looking at grey areas that have not been sufficiently tackled by the Codes of Conduct in force to date; and, if we instead implemented even small changes in favour of these points within the Codes, we might see them addressed with more clarity by firms.

A good example is the risk of disorderly closure, a common problem which can result in intervention for firms. Providing rules in this area, or avenues of support for closure and exit, would assist the issue. At the moment, there are a number of regulations concerning:

- the entry to the market of firms,
- their authorisation,
- their ongoing recognition or licence, and
- the conditions that are imposed.

There is also a very full regulatory requirement relating to renewal.

There are much less statutory and regulatory requirements on the exit of practice. The only powers the SRA has in this area are revocation of authorisation (which has the effect of the authorisation not existing), or intervention. Creating a process for the closure of a firm, with support and stages, would greatly assist not only existing practitioners, but also potential investors in the market, giving them the confidence in protecting their investment should the worst happen.

At the moment, standard conditions are not imposed to solve regulatory problems, but they can be imposed to solve structural issues or capabilities (the example being the COLP and COFA). We could see standard conditions imposed to solve the issue of disorderly closure (for example, having an exit plan or putting in place succession planning as a condition). We could also see the rise in cybercrime being tackled in the appointment of IT officers. Capital adequacy speaks for itself and may suit a condition of authorisation as well. These are the writer's ideas for structural conditions to solve some of the common regulatory problems the SRA is tasked with solving, which go beyond allegations of misconduct.

EXERCISE: ABS, INDEPENDENCE OF ADVICE, AND THE STATE

This exercise is designed to examine a part of the legal services market in the context of supervisory protections. It gives you the opportunity to consider the importance of the sector and the need for regulation.

The regulators have been given extensive powers to fine and penalise ABS in the event of a breach of the rules. When ABS were first introduced, the regulators and others were worried about the constitutional implications of outside investment in the legal services market. Some forces, such as legal services, might be viewed by the public as part of the fabric of the state. We could draw a parallel to health care services.

Have a think about the following questions:

How do you feel about ABS? Are some services best left without external outside investment, and the accompanying commercial interests, or do you feel legal services will miss out on key skills, growth, and modernisation without them?

Should the legal services market be opened further, for example:

- Should ABS be further publicised to attract more outside investment into the sector?

- Should further investment be permitted in law firms beyond the limits imposed on ABS?
- Would you or anyone you know consider becoming a freelance solicitor?

Now let's consider the supervisory arrangements of ABS. They have historically been restricted by statute. If we decide to further publicise ABS to attract more outside investment, should additional restrictions also be introduced on ABS, for example:

- Should consumers be informed about the external investment the firm has received as a balance to commercial interests and independence?
- Should ABS be restricted in providing services?
- Should further standard conditions also be introduced to restrict the provision of services by ABS? If so, what should they be?

In opening up any market, there has to be a balance to the overall public interest. Have a read of the information from the time in Annex 1 to this Part of the book and see how you feel now about ABS. What can you say now that would change your mind about ABS?

FIRM COMPLIANCE: A FOCUS ON LEARNING, DEVELOPMENT AND COMPETENCE

We have seen that law firms can be held responsible for their compliance, and that there are specific regulatory and statutory provisions that apply to them.

A similar position can also be seen in other areas of regulation and of law, as we see fines for firms in Data Protection, and entities and companies being held corporately liable for actions. Firms also defend actions in a variety of courts.

The renewal applies to the regulated firm, in that they have to make the return for the individual solicitor, and provide an information return to the regulator. Even though the individual solicitor has to make the annual declaration, the firm is the one completing the form and signing it off, through their appointed representatives. These are known as the ORC, which is the 'Organisation Contact', and the AUS, which is the 'Authorised Signatory'.

In reality, the firm often takes some responsibility for the competence of individuals working for it, rather than this being the responsibility of the individual alone. The firm often has and owns a learning and development plan or strategy, and reviews the implementation of that plan with the staff. Firm preferences may differ as to who delivers training, and when it is delivered. The firm may have a particular focus on learning, staff development, and in some cases, broader or outside learning and development, as a benefit of working for the firm.

When individual solicitors leave a firm, they do not take with them their learning and development plan, just as they do not always take their caseholding. The individual solicitor has not booked on to the training the firm is offering after they have left, so they have to organise their own learning and development.

There is a firm ownership and direction to the learning and development of the individual solicitors and other legal professionals within it.

Offering training and staff development is a key staff attraction and retention strategy for some businesses. To be able to develop your staff and take them to meet their career goals is an aspiration for many firms, and a planned career path is a benefit offered by some in order to attract the best talent within their area. This attraction and retention allows the firm to plan for their long-term strategic goals.

How can we use this position to plan to meet those strategic goals of the firm, but also how can we use learning and development to implement conditions on a firm which will have direct benefits to staff and the firms themselves? If we stop seeing conditions on firms as a negative or restrictive standpoint, and proactively recognise their development potential, can we turn them around to meet future goals of individuals, firms, and compliance?

For example, if a firm had a fee earner who could not be a COLP or COFA, due to concerns about their previous regulatory history, could we turn around this individual with investment in their learning and development? Certainly, the individual may feel their career aspirations are limited at that time, but a commitment from them to make improvements, and reduce the number of investigations, could also be matched with a development program focused on management and compliance knowledge. This may open up the career door for the individual in the long term. In all likelihood, the firm would need to drive this programme, although some individuals may be motivated to take the steps themselves.

Firms can be impacted by the consequences of conditions on key members of staff, but also on those members of staff who are possibly earmarked for future management of the firm. Ensuring staff stay motivated in circumstances where conditions are imposed, and that firms can continue to see those persons as potential leaders for the future, is important and should not be forgotten.

If we take the idea of utilising conditions to meet firm strategic goals, could we, instead of restricting firms from taking on certain types of work, require them to focus on other areas in which they have shown particular competence? There is an argument that framing the condition in a positive fashion will motivate the career goal and compliance of the individual more fully in future.

When discussing all of these options, we must of course not forget that we could see a position in the future where a firm could be held responsible for the learning and development of the individual. We have seen in Part 3 of this book the imposition of conditions to attend courses on the individual; we could see a learning and development objective imposed upon a firm.

Unregulated firms and freelance solicitors

The introduction of freelance solicitors brings new commercial opportunities. Solicitors will now be able to work freelance in a variety of contractual forms. The SRA, with the introduction of first ABS and now freelancing, is offering the solicitor the freedom to work in the way that best suits them and the economic or business need or situation.

The structures the SRA has in place regulate for the provision of legal services by recognised bodies, Alternative Business Structures, and solicitors. The new freelance model may challenge some of the ways the SRA currently regulates and bring new types of prosecution, along with new guidance, and new challenges for those who are regulated.

Unregulated firms cannot have conditions imposed, but freelancers may. The SRA may need to consider the impact on any relationship with other businesses around them should the freelancer be subject to conditions unexpectedly. Does the unregulated business need to consider additional legal provision in the event of the freelancer's restriction in some way? It may need to for the purposes of ill health anyway, and the freelancer should be aware of the precarious nature of their contractual status with other businesses.

Freelancers sometimes obtain insurance for ill health, and there may need to be additional cover for both the freelancer and the unregulated business if the freelancer is restricted. The freelancer may also consider using another person to step in should their provision be restricted; other local providers of the same services may be able to assist.

Considering practicalities before becoming a freelancer can also ensure you do not end up in a position of conditions. Consider where your income will come from, how much your insurance costs, and how you will pay for your training. There are many benefits to working freelance, but there can also be many personal risks.

The following excerpt appeared in the writer's Serious Breach and Practising Certificate course in 2021 to discuss the position of freelance solicitors and ideas of how to manage their situation:

> 'Below are some thoughts for achieving compliance whether you are a freelance consultant or an established law firm.
>
> It can be a complex task to put systems in place if you are a freelancer. However do not forget that the Authorisation Rules suggest freelancers are in fact self-employed. Therefore having effective policies, controls and procedures in place for all manner of scenarios might well be essential.
>
> There might be two main options:
>
> a. Consider your own policies, procedures, and compliance. This may be essential when considering the 'nuts and bolts' of practice; for example ensuring you can undertake certain work; maintaining your own insurance; and considering your interactions with your

clients. You may also need to consider AML and reporting. However it can go further and encompass all elements of the Standards and Regulations and cover matters such as equality and diversity and full client care. Always ensure you consider file management, conflict and confidentiality, and how your commitments will continue if you are unwell.

b. Consider how you will be working, and who you will be working with. If you intend to take on a series of short term outsourced assignments, do the companies you are working for have policies and procedures in place that you would be able to adopt? This might be an agreed way of working, and in order to demonstrate your compliance this could also form part of your contract with those businesses. At times, it can be difficult to ensure unregulated third party organisations adopt the required standard, but contractual arrangements are a solid means to ensure all sides understand and adhere to what's expected. Also consider what would occur if there was a breakdown in this relationship – do you have your own systems to fall back on?

In both situations it is important to consider at the outset what will happen to files, clients, and enquiries when you leave any connected business. There could be restrictions preventing any connected business accessing the information or files without appropriate authorisation, and you may need to discuss this with them, along with an exit strategy.

Additionally unregulated firms may need advice about those working for or with a solicitor, and in particular the powers of the SRA under s43 of the Solicitors Act 1974.

With either option there can be investment up front in creating systems to meet requirements, and ongoing investment in those policies and procedures. However if you are caught in a position without an adequate procedure due to a breakdown in a relationship with a connected business, then take steps to correct the position. It is possible to create your own at any time and this can be evidence of compliance or an intent to comply, even when the regulator are involved.'

EXERCISE – FREELANCE SOLICITOR CONDITION

This exercise is designed to help unregulated firms plan for different eventualities.

Pen is a freelance solicitor and agrees to work with a local unregulated business on providing will writing for a few weeks connected to their funeral service. Pen has made some mistakes on previous projects that have resulted in severe consequences for clients, and that have come to the attention of the regulator. Pen cannot demonstrate that he can manage the risk of the situation. The regulator is concerned about his competence and that he poses a risk to the public. Pen becomes subject to a condition that prevents him delivering wills and probate part way through the agreed term with the unregulated business.

What are the options for Pen?

What are the options for the unregulated firm?

How could the unregulated firm forward-plan for this type of situation?

Do conditions work?

We have already asked this question in the Practising Certificate section. The answer there is that conditions are imposed and removed after the improvements needed are implemented, and that conditions do get removed after periods of time, and after solicitors have demonstrated they have taken the steps needed.

The condition does serve a function in:

- delivering improvements;
- managing risk;
- allowing the regulator a proportionate response to a problem; and
- managing a problem between a regulator and solicitor.

Conditions might be appropriate as targeted, problem-solving pieces of regulatory apparatus, but the manner in which they are implemented might impact whether they solve the problem or not.

Applying them incorrectly could cause a problem, and this may be the distinction between the firm and individual implementation in the eyes of the regulator.

We have to ask whether conditions would work if they were imposed on the firm rather than the individual. By imposing them on the firm, we are shifting the balance of responsibility away from the individual solicitor and on to the firm. We have seen, and do see in the course of this book, that individual conditions target the individual but often need the support and involvement of the firm to make them work. Of course, the individual can part company with the firm if the support does not work or the individual does not take responsibility.

If we impose conditions on the firm, the management team or governance structure becomes responsible for the compliance with the condition and the resolution of the same. We have all seen evidence of organisations where individuals attempt to avoid taking responsibility. Strong compliance leadership would be required; or, as proposed by the writer, a greater sense of normality in everyday conditions would avoid panic, blaming, and a negative association with the condition for the department involved. To impose conditions on a firm effectively, it may be necessary to either:

- specify who within a firm would be responsible for compliance, whilst perhaps expressing at the same time that they were not personally responsible for the cause of the condition, or
- explain and publish the reason why the condition was imposed, including a positive framing or forward-looking explanation of the condition where possible.

This may avoid individual blame. As we have seen, conditions are pieces of structural apparatus which allow curtailing of activities to manage an overall risk. We are not attaching blame in this situation to an individual, but we could see that the regulator may wish to restrict a firm in delivering certain activities. It might, in that situation, be inappropriate to place compliance at one person's door in case they were unfairly believed to be responsible; after all, a condition is not a regulatory misconduct outcome in the same way a fine is; it is an attempt to manage risk.

Anecdotally, the writer has seen a large number of conditions imposed. Some do last year on year, but the vast majority are removed when the risk is addressed. This might be improvements in the firms' bookkeeping, or a return to sending accountants' reports to the SRA (when they had not been sent before); whatever the original condition was designed to address.

We can see from the data analysis in Part 3 of this book that, from the data sample in 2018/19, 30 conditions were imposed on individuals and, of those, 43% were repeat conditions (conditions imposed for a second year running). In 2019/20, the data sample found 20 individuals with conditions imposed and, of those, 75% were repeat conditions. The data samples were small and this may have impacted the result. The repeat condition could be the result of individuals and firms being content with the condition imposed and considering it to be fair, reasonable, or supportive. Additionally, a reason to impose a condition could be a fairly substantial potential issue, which may not be resolved within a year, necessitating the need for an ongoing restriction. Nonetheless, the repeat condition numbers are high. We do not have any data for the removal of conditions after two years, but the writer's experience is that, in many cases, conditions are removed after what may seem to be a relatively short period of time (within 1 to 3 years).

We could theorise that we would see a similar repeat effect with firm conditions; possibly even higher numbers of ongoing conditions, for a number of reasons:

- The breadth of responsibility of the firm and their 'footprint' causes a wider area of potential problems or risk.
- Making changes in an organisation which are sufficiently embedded can be a complex and messy process; change is far more difficult than many project managers would have you believe! Staff often have accepted ways of working and informal processes which exist alongside formal documented office manuals. Introducing day-to-day change requires staff acceptance, belief, and willingness to make change. We discuss 'Compliance Leadership' below.
- Rates of staff attrition, management decision making and strategic direction can all change year on year, meaning a condition which does not impact these areas could be left to one side while the firm continues to push forward as a commercial entity.
- Instead of making changes, staff and management may find 'work-arounds' to deal with the condition.
- If the publicity or reputational impact of the condition is negligible, and the operations of the firm are able to deal with the condition, there may be little impetus to change.

It might be important to make a distinction in these points, about compliance strategy. Firms do not have to go beyond the requirements within the regulations in force at the time. Often the regulations have a wording which sets out an acceptable level of compliance. The regulations do not necessarily require a very positive and proactive management of compliance; they simply require the set standard. If we saw conditions imposed more regularly on firms, or they were accepted as a regulatory response to a situation which was not always or usually misconduct, there might be less stigma attached to conditions. This might mean firms (and individuals) were more content to accept conditions and may be able to live within their bounds (as an issue of compliance strategy) for a number of years.

Some firms choose to take a more positive approach to compliance than required by the regulations, because they have made the strategic decision to, or because they feel that is right for them. This explanation is not a veiled justification for non-compliance; it is, however, an explanation of the levels of compliance and compliance decision making we may see within firms. A more positive approach to compliance could see the resolution of the condition straightaway.

Ironically, we might say the approach to conditions lends itself to a year-long compliance strategy, or even longer, because of the expected time a condition is in force. There may be no drive to comply any sooner if a condition will not be removed.

Of course, we still might want to consider whether firm or individual imposition of conditions is correct. Have a look at the bridge exercise again below.

EXERCISE: THE BRIDGE PART 2

Revisit the bridge you built in the exercise earlier in this Part of the book. This time you will need to:

- enlist the help of a colleague (it says when, below); and
- make a very small cavity in the bridge, but say nothing about it to your colleague.

We are going to replay the scenario, but slightly differently this time.

Your cavity in the bridge has drawn attention from people crossing the bridge. However, this time a surveyor has been to inspect the whole bridge. The surveyor's report says:

> 'Any and all problems must be repaired across the whole bridge.'

The surveyor has not commented on your specific cavity in his report.

Ask your colleague to repair the bridge in accordance with the surveyor's recommendation. This means you have to ask your colleague to:

> 'Repair any and all problems with the whole bridge.'

Do not mention or draw any attention to the very small cavity you created.

Leave your colleague to it.

When your colleague returns, have a look at their response:

- Have they made a lot of repairs or improvements? The changes or reinforcements as the result of a surveyor's report such as this might be extensive.

Is there a chance that, if you instructed for repairs of the bridge in line with the surveyor's instruction, your cavity could be missed?

Now imagine the position in relation to a firm. Imagine an individual issue has been identified, and can be fixed, but instead the regulator imposes a condition that the firm should fix all such issues. The firm may have to complete additional work beyond the individual issue, and the individual issue itself could be missed if not specifically mentioned.

Targeted regulatory action can sometimes be the most proportionate response.

Representations for conditions and risk management

You may wish to take legal advice when dealing with proposed conditions. The SRA may investigate a report or situation and decide to impose conditions. We have covered some circumstances in Part 3 of this book detailing when a Practising Certificate would be subject to conditions.

As firm conditions are not often imposed, you might ask, why would we need legal advice? If conditions would be imposed on the individual, the firm may also need advice as well. Advice and representations might cover:

1. Whether the condition needs to be imposed, and arguments may be made to the regulator to the contrary.
2. Whether the firm can support the individual so the condition does not need to be imposed, or how they can support during the lifetime of any condition.
3. The proportionality of any condition and the impact on the firm.
4. The responsibilities of the management team, the firm itself, and COLP and COFA when dealing with the condition.
5. Associated consequences such as publicity, the renewal, and answering questions about the condition.

If the firm and individual have a conflict of interest, the advisors dealing with each may be different.

Obtaining the correct advice can bring an independent perspective into the firm, hopefully allowing a proportionate and measured response by the firm itself.

Some firms also have external advice when applying for authorisation and, again, it can be helpful to understand standard conditions as appropriate.

Responsibility within firms

The COLP is often the person assumed to be responsible for communication with the regulator. While the communication may naturally sit there due to their compliance role, and general responsibility for risk management, the contact with the regulator can be given to another person within the firm if required.

You may also appoint another person or persons to organise any:

- investigation;
- report of the situation;
- consideration of the possible remedies for the firm;
- management of the ongoing situation; or
- response to the condition.

These responsibilities are separate to the COLP role. The COLP role is already sufficiently large; and day-to-day compliance will also need attending to. However, the COLP will need to be mindful of any condition and take overall responsibility for the compliance of the firm.

Much of the weight of compliance falls on the shoulders of the COLP and COFA. The COLP or COFA does not, however, have to take responsibility for the individual condition or even a firm condition; they only must consider the position as far as it relates to the operation of compliance within the firm. Indeed, the condition may well relate to the professional conduct of an individual, even outside of the firm, and full responsibility may not be fairly ascribed to the COLP. The compliance with a condition may be for the firm to ensure overall, such as with the appointment of a COLP.

The COLP is there to ensure compliance, provide leadership and prevent breaches of the rules, but there will evidently be actions within firms which go beyond their control. It should be recognised that, while a COLP may lead part of a response to conditions (and any regulatory breach), compliance is not their responsibility alone. In circumstances where there are conditions, you may need more than just the COLP to take responsibility.

The following excerpt appeared in the writer's Material/Serious Breach and Practising Certificate course between 2014 and 2020 and discusses managing conditions within your firm. The excerpt demonstrates the implications of applying a condition to a firm and the implications for both management and the running of the firm as a whole:

> 'We might ask: by applying conditions to a Practising Certificate, are we applying conditions to a firm overall?
>
> **Managing conditions within your firm**
>
> If an individual within your firm, or an applicant for employment, is subject to conditions, you will likely need to put in place controls to manage the risk yourself. We can see that the SRA often requires actual or prospective employers to be notified, and this is because they believe this person represents a current risk to firms.

To manage the risk, the steps to take are:

Identify the risk to your firm:

- You could decide how serious the conduct is and what it would mean for your firm and clients if it was repeated.
- You could to look at the background of the individual. This could include seeking explanations for the conduct, and reading any available documents (such as SDT judgements). Look at the circumstances in your firm. Are you weak in the area where conditions have been imposed? If so, managing a person with these conditions and the risk they posed, may be too much without outside help. If you are strong in that area, you may be able to support that person.
- Take steps to mitigate the risk if one is identified.

However it is also important to be proportionate. Many people practice with conditions on their Practising Certificates. You may assess that the individual has a significant amount to offer your firm and the risk management can be supportive. It can also be important to identify whether there are underlying concerns which led to the circumstances. Your HR department may be able to support if there are personal circumstances involved.

For example a senior solicitor with an excellent track record applies for a job with your firm. She was a salaried partner in a firm who were intervened for putting clients at risk due to poor financial management. All client money was in order at the time of the intervention. You decide this would be disastrous if the conduct occurred again.

You interview her, she explains she did not know what was happening at the firm. This is consistent with the explanations in the investigation and the judgement of the SDT. The SRA noted the explanations, but imposed conditions restricting her access to client and office account. You have strong financial management in place with an excellent and very strict COFA, an office manual that is well adhered to, and astute equity partners. Your accountants' reports show no problems and the company is in good financial health.

Accordingly you could propose:

- Another named solicitor from the firm help her with client account transactions and she have no access to office account, save through the COLP or COFA.
- A named accounts assistant is available to assist with any accounting issues.
- A quarterly review of the accounts associated with her files; this is done jointly with her to discuss things together and to ensure all is well.
- A review at the end of the practising year to see how the firm can support her next year.

Taking on or managing a large number of individuals with conditions theoretically requires a very strong managerial approach.'

Conditions and the relationship to intervention

Conditions should be a proportionate response. Some of the legal regulators, including the SRA, have a separate power called 'intervention' which provides the regulator with the power to close the firm in some circumstances. Intervention is a formal, statutory, power. Conditions are a lesser regulatory power and must remain proportionate to the circumstances. A condition must not have the effect of closing the firm. The regulator already has the power to intervene if necessary; a power which is only applicable in some circumstances. Conditions must not be used in place of intervention or as if they were intervention.

We might, however, draw a distinction between intervention or closure of a business and the imposition of conditions to prevent an individual being an owner, manager, or Sole Practitioner of a firm. In most situations where this type of condition is imposed, the individual is not in that position, so it is not the closure or otherwise of a firm, but rather suggesting that the individual is not suitable to work in that position for the time being, and needs additional support.

The SRA has the right to impose conditions on the legal professionals within, and to intervene into, an Alternative Business Structure, which can disrupt the outside investment. Non-regulated persons and businesses should be carefully advised prior to taking shares in law firms due to the extensive powers of the SRA, the potential that they could be heavily regulated and be subject to conditions and, in some circumstances, lose their investment in the event of intervention.

It should also be said at this point that conditions do not, in the writer's experience, have a strong correlation to intervention. By imposing conditions, the regulator is not saying they are about to intervene or close the firm. Intervention may be more likely if there is a range of decisions against a firm. We might also say that regulatory action correlates closely with more regulatory action. However, a condition is intended to be proactively managerial, with the intention of the firm or individual continuing in practice.

Regulators and regulatory decision making

When thinking about the position of the firm overall, it may be important to emphasise that the regulator is not there to run your business for you. Sometimes in regulation the regulator sets the rules for professional conduct, and considers whether, in the circumstances, the correct managerial approach or corporate decision making has been implemented.

This is quite a complex decision-making process to undertake. The question as to whether the individual acted within the rules of professional conduct is one decision. However, the question as to whether the firm, management structure or corporate body acted appropriately may be less clear cut.

There are evidently cases of corporate liability, and the SRA and SDT do take regulatory action against the management of firms for their failings. However, we do not have the same body of work published by the regulator (or their previous organisational structures), covering their expectations in management, governance and assurance.

In a sense, asking a decision maker at the SRA to impose conditions on the firm is a strange decision. What skills does the SRA decision maker have in managing businesses that would result in effective conditions to manage risks to a firm? Can we say with any confidence that the decision maker would be able to identify those risks and effectively manage them? Individual regulatory staff faced with decisions at firm level are faced with a difficult choice, and are choosing to impose conditions on the individual in the face of a business or corporate body that cannot come under the ongoing control of the regulator. It is not the regulator who can manage the business.

To manage risk themselves, firms may be well served by considering the wealth of academic and management literature, including empirically based management literature, covering subjects such as:

- human resources;
- finance and accountancy;
- strategy;
- people and management development;
- professional practice; and
- governance and audit;

for ideas to implement in their firm. There are also outside professionals in these areas who can help deliver such services. This, however, is the writer's suggestion and is not an SRA suggestion.

We wait to see whether the SRA will take steps in this area. Given the regulator's reticence to impose conditions at a firm level, despite the legislative and regulatory options to do so, the question is whether this needs further policy development to cover the extent of the regulator's remit, their ability to manage such situations, and how they might use management, governance, and finance to their overall advantage, without overstepping the mark into corporate management.

Of course, other regulators manage this task, and the writer has herself undertaken some work with very large firms whilst working for regulators. This has included in respect of management and finance. It is possible to conduct this work as assurance, by undertaking:

- financial analysis and meetings to discuss corporate financial positions;
- management reviews and meetings, to discuss management practice on a day-to-day and strategic level;
- governance reviews, to consider the impact of different governance arrangements as they have been reported to the regulator (perhaps through the annual return); and
- discussions of strategic developments and the implications for short-, medium- and long-term moves in the marketplace.

The SRA introduced relationship management for large firms in 2011. We have not, as a result of this, seen conditions imposed on firms, when it could have been seen as a natural consequence.

Compliance leadership

We discuss leadership as a force for cultural change below, but it is very difficult to change organisational culture, and some attempts to do so can backfire. Culture is a force around us which is unspoken.

Leadership, however, can instil confidence and promote compliance throughout your firm. You may therefore wish to consider how to deliver compliance leadership, whether across the firm or in your unit. Compliance leadership is not reserved to COLPs and COFAs or HOLPs and HOFAs, it is something we can all use and demonstrate.

What can we see as Compliance Leadership?

- **Decision making in compliance situations** – From making decisions about reporting (for the COLP or COFA or HOLP or HOFA), to making the decision to refer the matter to the COLP / COFA / HOLP / HOFA in the first place. Making decisions and using effective judgement is a good part of compliance.
- **Finding compliance solutions** – Being able to manage both day-to-day decisions as well as firm goals through compliance and utilising the regulations demonstrates your understanding and competence in this area.
- **Exercising good judgement** – Very experienced managers are often patient, solid and proactive. Sometimes, solid experience in compliance decision making is evident, with clear systems and procedures in place, and a grounded sense of the right outcome, drawn from many years' experience. Practising your decision making can help.
- **A thorough understanding of the rules, or a knowledge of where to find them** – Sometimes, we can see individuals with a detailed knowledge of the rules; at times, those rules were learned many years ago, and the understanding of those basic principles has not changed for the professional. Compliance leadership can be about understanding the range of tools available to you in the rules and how you can flex your advice to meet the requirements of your firm.
- **Measuring your approach to risk** – Understanding risk is essential for a law firm, given the compliance consequences of different decisions and actions. We are also in a time of flux, with the intent to change the legal services market. You might be asking where your firm will go next. Whether it is a stable and solid performance you aim for, measured growth, or movement into a new area, understanding your risk is important. Some leaders will seek that solid approach, while others will risk it all. Arguably, both types of leadership are required.
- **Balancing the needs of the commercial business with the rules** – Not all of a business can be focused around compliance. We need to consider turnover, profitability, and liquidity, as well as reputation and practicality of implementation of some solutions. A business purely focused on compliance could forgo those. As is often said throughout this book, that is not an argument not to comply, but is an argument to embed compliance in wider decision making so that strategic goals can be met with a compliant outcome.

Improving compliance through management

The writer has written about cultures of compliance within law firms and currently runs a regular course in this area based on the writer's masters' thesis and 20 years' experience in legal services. This book is not intended to replace that course, but we include some of the ideas here.

The purpose of the inclusion of these ideas is to start to build a dialogue around management practice in law firms, and compliance practice, to professionalise the management of the law firm (an ABS from within, perhaps), and also to start the serious debate about whether firm-wide management or conditions can solve the ongoing compliance problems we all struggle with.

In a sense, the writer does not advocate attempting to develop a culture of compliance at your law firm. Compliance is a support function to the wider business. Just as we have seen, earlier in this section, that professional regulation struggles to direct the business, compliance has the same difficulties.

Promoting compliance internally and promoting a culture of compliance are two concepts that COLPs and COFAs often struggle with. The COLP and COFA are charged with overseeing compliance but, as we have seen, the practice of the professional can be an individual matter. Can we create an inclusive firm culture that goes beyond the collegiate style of traditional law firms?

Culture can be the things we talk about, what we promote, the social rules and norms of a law firm. Some firms might be quite friendly, others quite competitive. Some may be dominated by one person, others may be more collegiate. Your culture is unique to your firm, and probably strongly influenced by the management and those in charge.

Instead of recommending a culture of compliance, the writer recommends developing one which reflects your firm – whether that be creative, commercially minded, or customer focused, these are all excellent aspirations. Compliance should work in conjunction with the other aspects of the business. If we put regulation and compliance centre stage, where does that leave the other aspects of business?

In this sense, delivering a compliance agenda can be extremely tricky. Balancing compliance requirements with commercial needs is an essential skill, but the key is to look for ways in which both can win. Can you offer a less burdensome alternative? If you cannot help on this occasion, can you assist on something else?

Some analysts say only uniting leadership can change culture. If you are not within the senior leadership team, but want to improve the influence of compliance throughout the organisation, you can still exercise leadership in your role.

Other methods for getting your message across include:

1. attending other teams' regular meetings to answer questions and promote your service;
2. being creative about getting your message across – film videos for staff, or communicate your ideas through posters and creative wall coverings;
3. inviting key members of other teams to your team meetings or lunches to discuss their priorities and how you can assist;

4. getting other staff members to talk about the benefits of what you are doing;
5. running a competition to promote what you are doing (make the prize really worthwhile, like a lunch out or a day off); and
6. taking staff out of their usual environment – for a coffee, run an event, on a visit elsewhere. Taking staff out of their usual environment inspires their creativity and openness to new ideas.

Don't forget that the conditions we have discussed in this Part and Part 3 are actually about management and leadership in a sense. If the regulator can see you are making efforts with management and leadership, this can be noted, and can affect the decisions about whether to impose conditions or not. What steps have you taken to manage risks to the business alongside that and how can you get staff to join in?

There can be very serious problems with attempting to change culture or implement new cultures within businesses. Culture provides us with a sense of belonging and value. Culture can go to the heart of who we are as people, and attempting to say this culture is not valid, and therefore we should change it, is a difficult message to give. People have often chosen a job or a firm because of the culture within the firm and made a place for themselves there. They may gain an enormous amount from their place within a business, and the person attempting to change the culture may have no right to. Individual behaviour may not in some senses be an issue for a business to accept or otherwise, particularly when that behaviour is driven by individual values.

We must remember therefore to be extremely cautious when dealing with issues of culture and potential culture change. Even exploring culture can be a sensitive subject and one which arguably you should conduct alone, to understand your own viewpoint. There can also be issues relating to social dignity and mutual trust and confidence in dealing with issues of organisational culture, so do take care.

The example, and the Honne approach to culture, is the following:

- A human positive or centric approach to organisational culture.
- A focus on communication as the driving force for culture – some cultural analysts have pointed towards leadership as a means to change or address culture, but communication has an effect on a range of levels within an organisation, and may help us address how we are feeling.
- A recognition of culture and communication methods as a form of democratic expression within organisations (particularly where there is a mismatch between the two) – do we, for example, want the same communication internally as we do externally?
- An understanding and recognition of the political standpoint of regulation and compliance. Traditional ideas of right- and left-wing political expression are relevant here, with right-wing ideas being the expression of commercially focused ideologies, demonstrating a lack of involvement by the state, but with left-wing ideas being the greater state intervention and management or control of business. We might then see, on a basic analysis, a pro-regulatory approach as being left wing in its basis, and those ideas which are against regulation being right wing. We cannot say that expressing a negative idea concerning regulation or compliance is a breach of the rules because it might well be a legitimate political expression or viewpoint.

EXCERPT FROM AML: HOW TO DEVELOP A CULTURE OF COMPLIANCE FOR LAW FIRMS

(Training course 2019–2021 – Honne Ltd/Katie Jackson)

> 'As a compliance consultancy, we consider culture with a regulatory and political dimension; to acknowledge the common thoughts and feelings about regulatory burden and the arguments against over regulation. We also seek to explore the ways in which we communicate, both internally and externally, and how that shapes views or otherwise. The extent to which the organisation has a disconnect between it's published (internal and external) perspective, and the actions on the ground, can be an important point of exploration for compliance practitioners, and a source of organisational culture. How do staff know what to do or find their way? We value the human perspective and gaps in processes and procedures or mismatches can be important if they allow for staff to have a democratic participation, and a genuine voice in their organisation.
>
> The organisation and individuals are subject to a great many external influences and internal influences and these can shape the way we feel and how we develop our culture within the organisation. We might, as individuals, be subject to different social or group norms through our interactions outside the organisation. The organisation might behave differently because it is international, or small firm, for example.'

Provided is an example of a cultural assessment you can undertake in your own firm. It is for compliance officers and covers AML, but you might be able to tailor the questions to general compliance. You may want to do this personally, for reflection and learning purposes, but you can also share the outcomes with others, again if you do so very carefully and judge the reaction. Also take care with trying to implement cultural change, you might instead attempt to go slowly (but positively and proactively) with your leadership, communication and compliance agenda.

Honne AML Culture Table

External politics and influence	**Internal politics and influence**	**Matching**
What external stakeholders* does your organisation interact with? What influence do they have? What is the legal structure and impact?	What does your organisation do and seek to achieve? What internal stakeholders can you find?	To what extent do the internal and external communications match? Are there areas of mismatch? **Is that mismatch valuable (for example, as a form of freedom or democracy)? Do we want them to match?**
What political stance does your organisation take?	What does your organisation say internally about its political stance?	How do staff feel about this approach?

External politics and influence	Internal politics and influence	Matching
Who interacts with external stakeholders?	How do you know what to do at work? Formally and informally?	What is the relationship between management and staff?
What does the organisation publish and why?	What does the organisation publish internally? What is popular and unpopular?	Is the organisation communicating in a way which has not been published? Do the actions match the words? Does something different happen?
Is external influence accepted? Do external forces drive change?	Is internal change accepted? Who drives change and why?	Does change cause problems? What are the impacts?
Does external influence impact your job role?	How do you measure organisational productivity?	What measures would you give to the relative success of the organisation? What has been a success? What improvements could be made?
How are people presented externally? As experts, as friendly, etc?	How are people perceived internally? Are people happy?	What determines how people are perceived? What can we do to change that?

Annex 1: Alternative Business Structures – macro culture post Clementi

The writer's master's degree thesis (*Macro Culture Post Clementi*) considered the position of the Legal Services Act 2007 and whether or not organisational culture would have an impact on the implementation and intended change behind the Act. The writer theorised, firstly, the existence of a macro culture in legal services and, secondly, that such a culture would prevent the Act from being fully implemented, or at least impact the intended change.

The writer conducted this research in 2011, and excerpts are included here as a discussion of the change intended by the Act, and the forces acting against change.

When we consider this in the prism of firm conditions, we can see the Act was intended to bring dramatic change to the sector, and the potential risk was considered to be severe. The writer worked for the regulator at the time and the position was clear; the new structures could pose a significant risk. The idea of non-lawyers running legal services businesses alongside lawyers was so alien to solicitors that the bodies were considered a major potential problem. We did think, back then, that conditions would need to be imposed, might be imposed regularly, and might be quite restrictive. We have not seen those conditions imposed to date.

We often say now that the change has not been as great as we thought it would be back then. But perhaps the change has occurred, that there has been change in ownership, but we have not noticed because the legal staff have stayed the same.

When we consider the position from that perspective, imposing conditions on the individual rather than the firm may make some sense. The professional regulator is considering the professional status of the individual, their ability to practise as a solicitor, and their resultant conditions, rather than imposing conditions on a non-lawyer-owned business employing solicitors. We now know that unregulated businesses can employ solicitors without being subject to the control of the regulator, so it may have been the correct decision not to impose firm conditions on non-legal businesses, and concentrate on the individual professional.

We can, however, take the analysis from 2011, and compare the position to that of freelance solicitors. What can we learn about the anticipated change or potential change in the market as a result of freelancers, and how can we adapt a future regulatory strategy (including conditions), going forward?

If we analyse the position now, we might see views from the sector, firstly, that change from ABS has not been as dramatic as expected, but also, secondly, that ongoing change (including that from freelancers) is also not expected to be that significant.

In order to effect change, we perhaps should have been considering how to change the existing law firms in place, but that is not possible – individuals and entities have invested large sums into their businesses and have rights. Perhaps making change through outside investment more attractive through regulatory certainty or guaranteed regulatory outcomes for a set period would be helpful. This could include stated intentions around firm conditions and the types of conditions that could be imposed and when. A very concrete structure, agreed across a number of regulatory agencies, might be very attractive.

AIM – THE AIM OF THE ORIGINAL RESEARCH PROPOSAL WAS:

'The aim of this proposal is to evaluate and explain the extent of organisational change arising in legal services and other impacted sectors as a result of the Legal Services Act 2007.

Within this evaluation, the winter aims to consider whether sector specific cultural values exist within the legal services sector, and if so, their potential impact on the intended or operational change initiatives.

The research is therefore explanatory, in considering the extent of change caused by the Legal Services Act 2007 (LSA), and exploratory, in considering the possibility of the existence of a sector specific macro culture. The winter considers the proposal sits within the critical realist theme, seeking to explore change at organisational level within the context of:

- the intent of the LSA;
- legal services sectors in the UK and abroad;
- regulatory sectors in the UK and abroad;
- associated sectors;
- other factors which may drive change, such as organisational self-determination, economic or technological developments, etc.

The outcomes of this research may have wider interest and uses. Research considering the sector specific implications of the LSA will be of interest to firms operating in and agencies associated with this market, both in the UK and abroad.'

In fact, as with many research projects, the scope of the project evolved and changed over time. The project examined the impact of culture on legislation – in essence, can we overcome culture through legislation – by the will of Parliament and parliamentary sovereignty?

The final project comprised the following:

- A literature review of the relevant legislation related to ABS, the related legislation, and the historical and policy development of that legislation which led to the current position of regulation and delivery of legal services through a variety of qualifications and statuses.
- The writer also conducted a limited literature review of legal services culture, limited by the lack of studies available in this area.
- A literature review of theories of organisational and group culture, and empirically based research on the impact of organisational culture within businesses on attempts at large-scale change.
- A data review of twitter and, in particular, tweets from the legal services sector covering the real-time reaction to the implementation of ABS (in 2011/12), with the aim of understanding:
  - whether the sector believed there would be change as a result of the Legal Services Act 2007; and
  - whether there was an identifiable culture or macro culture being expressed.

  In order to do this, the writer conducted two samples of twitter to gather data. The first sample considered the impact of ABS, and the second sample considered whether there was an identifiable macro culture and, if so, what that macro culture's impact might be on the legislation.

  The data from the first sample and some of the corresponding analysis is included here, where possible. Some redactions have been made to the data and analysis provided. The data and analysis that is provided is not a complete record of all of the data gathered and analysis conducted or submitted with the thesis. This is to preserve the anonymity of the subjects and to ensure the work printed here makes sense.

  Only very limited data from the second sample is included here. The secondary sample drew a surprising effect; the writer is uncertain whether this effect would be repeated, and does not wish it to be. The writer would ask others not to undertake the same experiment, and the writer wishes to prevent secondary analysis. Also, due to the small sample size comparative to the subject matter, and the medium of the data, it is not included.
- A consideration of the theories above and the data gathered:
  - to establish the potential impact of the Act;
  - to establish the impact of legal services culture; and
  - to theorise that there was both a legal services culture and that there was more than one legal services culture, stratified by group qualification or expressed status (and this dual concept was termed 'macro culture').

The writer has excluded the legal literature reviews and final conclusions from these excerpts. The final conclusions from the thesis are also not included.

The data and description of the project is provided to demonstrate the analysis undertaken at the time, when ABS were first introduced. The conclusions we can draw now are that change was widely anticipated in the sector, to the extent it was anticipated to be momentous. We can also see that solicitors are still working in a variety of geographical locations, in the same firms, spread according to population. We might also see now, as the thesis theorised, that there is a cultural force at work within legal services which has disrupted the implementation of Legal Services Act 2007. The results from the thesis are not. The writer might go on to theorise that the same forces could disrupt the implementation of freelance solicitors over the coming few years.

The use of the term 'macro culture' was intended to ensure the legal services culture as defined encompassed more than simply the professional culture of solicitors. Solicitors are the dominant force, being the largest population in the sector. Solicitor culture might be distinct in itself within legal services, but do we also have an umbrella which covers all others within the sector, or are we organised culturally along stratified qualification (and non-qualification) lines, within legal services, but also joined together through shared qualifications, experiences and values? If so, what is the impact of that? The research covered other non-solicitors within the sector, such as paralegals. We saw during the time of the thesis, for the first time, non-lawyers joining the market in an overt and publicised manner. The key here was that they would be regulated, when now the 'unregulated' businesses would not be. The question back then was to ask, what was the extent of intended change; would the solicitor brand continue to dominate the professions, and how could others within the sector make themselves heard? The same questions may be asked now, but in a different way. Can the solicitor brand survive the outside impacts from unregulated businesses, which would be felt by freelance solicitors?

We can reflect on the intended impact of ABS and say now with hindsight they have not had the effect we expected, or perhaps they have changed the outlook and background to the sector without removing or destabilising the individual professional, who remains the focus of much of the regulation and regulatory action.

Do we need to look again at the ownership, overall risks, and picture of the *future of the sector* to plan for and understand potential conditions against firms in the future? Perhaps what we needed at the time was a view of regulatory capacity for future change and future business which could have delivered more proactive solutions going forward. We could draw those same conclusions now, and ask, how will the regulator have the capacity to make decisions about law firm management, ABS, freelancing, and other market moves, in five or ten years' time? Will the regulator be equipped to make those decisions going forward and to work with a range of businesses and professionals in different commercial and non-commercial situations, and to understand their management concerns?

It may be too much for a single decision maker at the SRA to either understand or develop suitable outcomes for firms in order to manage the potential risks. In order to make such an assessment, the person concerned would need to be very qualified in management, and possibly across a range of organisational disciplines, in order to identify and pinpoint where different issues might lie and how these could be resolved through conditions. As we have explored elsewhere, such conditions can take away the managerial prerogative of the firm, and we have to question who would be responsible if the condition was not appropriate from a management perspective.

Additionally, the regulator (which has historically been a professional services regulator) has been required to make decisions about a position of finance and business, when the sands were shifting below their feet. The shock of ABS and the potential sector change to the regulator may have produced this position of a stalemate. The regulator has been watching the sector to see how it moves, perhaps always expecting change, but with a very similar set of tools available as it had before. However, no change is occurring on the surface (the writer believes due to the existence of a culture in legal services), and the position of firm conditions consequently remains the same. In adopting this approach, if ownership is changing, is the regulator making the individual professionals responsible for matters which should belong to the firm management?

There can be an issue with assuming that, as an individual solicitor has qualified in legal work, and has done some work on law firm management as part of their qualification, they are qualified in business or management overall. Business and management are vast areas of specialism with specific job roles and theories behind them, empirical research, theories of management and business departmental operations, and theories of change. Even managers qualified in these areas have consultants, specialists, and advisors to assist them. The individual solicitor is unlikely to be equipped to deal with all these business management approaches themselves, but appears to be the anchor for the regulatory action and decision making of the regulator – even when that regulatory action may be an issue of management. Some of that responsibility should stay with the firm.

We have not covered here some of those business theories or management perspectives in themselves; that is another book. Included here are the aspects of the thesis which are relevant to change in the sector.

The writer asks, as a further question, whether it is time to consider the changing nature of professional management in the sector, and how best to regulate that in the future.

EXCERPTS FROM MACRO CULTURE IN LEGAL SERVICES POST CLEMENTI (2012)

The writer's dissertation concerned ABS and was written during 2012, when ABS was first introduced. The dissertation set out to discuss the potential change from ABS in the context of the Legal Services Act 2007, the previous legislation, and the policy intent for change within the sector post Clementi. The dissertation considered whether or not there would be change and the extent to which culture impacts on change, and legislative change in particular. The idea was that legal services culture (seen as a macro culture, explained above) would prevent the implementation of the Act.

Firstly, there are some very short excerpts (minus the content which is focused on legislation or policy, historical development, or academic / empirical research) and, secondly, there are some tables of data. The data shows information from an analysis of twitter which demonstrates the feeling on social media that there was likely to be structural change in the sector as a result of the Legal Services Act 2007:

> 'The Legal Services Act 2007 (the Act) set out to transform legal services. It strikes at professional status by allowing, for the first time, non lawyer ownership of law firms. Fully in force from 2011, the Act is the biggest ever overhaul of the UK's legal market.'
>
> 'The Act represents the most significant attempt at reforming legal services in England and Wales to date. On 6 October 2011 for the first time ever, non-lawyers were able to take majority ownership in law firms – these are called "Alternative Business Structures" (ABS). This opens up the previously closed market to competition.'
>
> 'The name "Alternative" demonstrates how different these structures are. They will bring innovation, as well as stimulating competition.'
>
> 'At the time of writing the Solicitors Regulation Authority (SRA) and Council for Licensed Conveyancers (CLC) regulated fifteen and three ABS respectively (SRA, 2012 and CLC, 2012).
>
> Aside from creating ABS, the Act had three other effects:
>
> - Creating a Legal Ombudsman to deal with consumer complaints about legal services (Part 6);
> - Creating a Legal Services Board to oversee legal regulators (Part 2);
> - Dividing the representative and regulatory functions of legal regulators (Part 4).
>
> These provisions demonstrate a lack of confidence in legal regulation and complaints handling, which prior to the Act was handled by the professions' representative bodies.'
>
> 'With hindsight, the opening up of legal services was inevitable. Closed professions mean restrictions on trade which is difficult to justify in a country seeking economic growth.'
>
> 'The Act passed in 2007, with ABS permitted from 6 October 2011 allowing outside investment, new structures and different perspectives. ABS may even overcome reserved activities; owners will simply hire a professional into their firm.'
>
> 'So what will change? Of all the pre-legislative policy papers mentioned, only the impact assessment of the Legal Services Bill addresses the question, suggesting an unspecified number of smaller firms would fold. No assessment is given of the impact upon medium or large firms or upon the regulators. The omission may be a deliberate tactic – why risk a backlash by estimating a large potential change? Better to keep quiet and emphasise the future economic growth.'
>
> 'There are few academic studies predicting the impact of the Act and no empirical data to date. What is available can be divided in to three camps:
>
> - The economy will stimulate change (The Economists)
> - Consumers will stimulate change (The Consumerists)
> - It is complex; there are too many factors (The Uncertaintists)

> The Economists
>
> This analysis promotes one factor; the economy, suggesting that existing firms are struggling in the current economic climate and cannot consider ABS.
>
> ...
>
> The Consumerists
>
> This analysis suggests consumer preference will force change, a persuasive analysis given the history of the Act.
>
> ...
>
> The Uncertaintists
>
> This analysis favours complexity; there are so many factors, one or two cannot be distinguished. It is not a convincing argument, given the clear reasoning behind the Act.'
>
> 'The economic and consumer pressures which led to the introduction of the Act will be the same pressures which determine the extent of the change. Those who are best able to exploit the market, whether they are existing firms, outside investors or large brand names, will be the ones who shape the future.'
>
> 'The Act is the most recent addition to a growing body of legislation aimed at reforming legal services. It questions the relevance of a long standing professional system. However the Act itself will not bring change. The growing pressure on legal services came from rising use by consumers. The OFT argued competition was in their interests; the principle of a free market embodies individual choice. However the economy is an important factor and may resist the number of firms able to take advantage of the new system.'

During the course of the research, the writer sampled twitter feeds to obtain the views of those in the legal services sector about the proposed changes to ABS. Results from the data were sorted into solicitor and paralegal tweets, where it was known or identified that a paralegal was tweeting.

MACRO CULTURE POST CLEMENTI – DATA ANALYSIS OF TWEETS CONCERNING CHANGE

THE FOLLOWING EXCERPTS EXPLAIN HOW THE DATA WAS OBTAINED AND ANALYSED:

> 'I used content analysis as it is unobtrusive and suitable for a large volume of data.'
>
> 'I developed some codes from the literature review and by reading the tweets first. The remainder as I developed as I coded."
>
> "I coded most of the data twice and used Nvivo10's word search and correlation tools to remove inconsistencies and improve reliability. I

used Nvivo10 for relational analysis; conducting word frequency and association analyses.'

'I found conceptual analysis easier in examining the ABS data, which was relatively similar. Relational analysis was more useful in examining the culture data, where the concepts were dissimilar, and less obvious associations were stronger.'

'Twitter data

"I searched Tweepz [to find twitter data]"

"I searched Tweepz using the terms 'solicitor', 'law firm' 'lawyer' to identify solicitors using Twitter. I sampled the first 384, selecting the most recent work related tweet posted between July 2011 and July 2012. Ninety of the 384 accounts belonged to solicitors' practices; I sampled those who identified their primary tweeter as a solicitor. ..."

"My results are not truly representative; not everyone tweets and I did not reach the required sample size for ABS data. Also, they are not random. I sampled every tweet regarding Alternative Business Structures (amounting to 175) and the tweets of the first 384 solicitors listed by Tweepz."

....'

'The results are my interpretation. I am the only coder, but the steps taken to counteract this are described above.'

'Online data may not be truly representative; 'reputation management' is a concern, however the data will be at least as reliable as published research, news and industry publications, all of which may similarly have been edited.'

'Finally, my own values may limit the research. I have worked in legal services for almost ten years. I am not a solicitor. I will choose unknown groups for future studies.'

'TWITTER DATA: THE IMPACT OF THE LEGAL SERVICES ACT 2007

"Data characteristics

I found 122 tweets by solicitors and 53 by paralegals containing the words 'ABS' or 'Alternative Business Structures' (hereafter both are referred to as 'ABS'). I found no tweets using the keywords 'Technology' 'Economy' 'Recession', 'Globalisation' or 'LPO' (legal process outsourcing). The keywords were combined with 'Law Firm' or 'Law' to narrow the results. The recession is national news so the absence of tweets is surprising."

"The results are indicative rather than representative, as there were only 175 tweets."

"The number of tweets rose according to news stories; March and April's levels coincided with the first licensed ABS and October 2011 with the legal licensing date. A short spike for solicitors in July coincided with the SRA announcing it would delay receiving applications."'

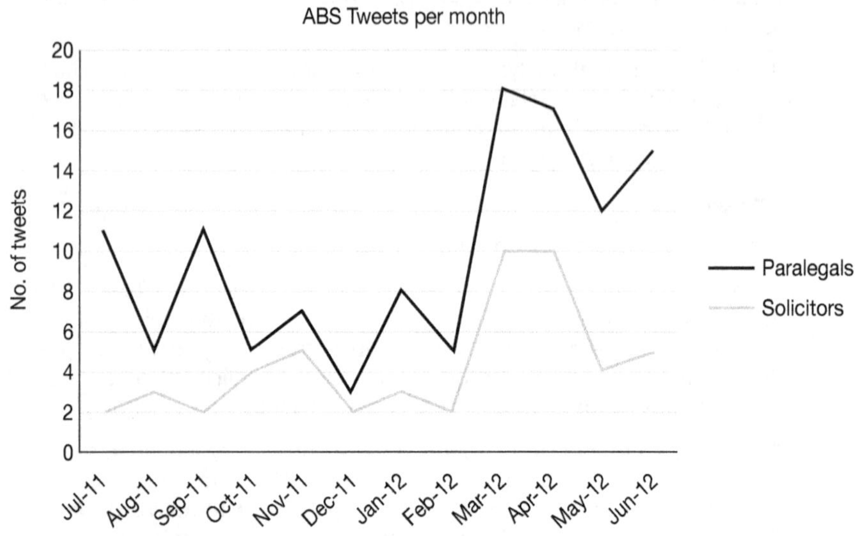

Tweets about Change – Conceptual analysis

> 'I coded the tweets for common concepts and conducted horizontal and vertical analysis to identify trends. This analysis is set out in the two tables below; the first covers all ABS tweets and the second is a sub-analysis of the tweets that predicted or reported change.'

The rules the writer followed to categorise the data into the subsets below can be found at pages 220 to 222.

In the tables below, the left-aligned text shows an overall group for the data; right-aligned groups show a sub-category.

Tweet Categorisation	Total References		Solicitors			Paralegals		
	Number	Vertical analysis	Number	Vertical analysis	Horizontal analysis	Number	Vertical analysis	Horizontal analysis
Total tweets about ABS	**175**	175	122	122		53	53	
Expressing a view on change	**151**	86%	113	92%	75%	38	71%	25%
Predicting or Reporting Change	127	84%	93	82%	73%	34	89%	28%
No change	10	7%	8	1%	80%	2	5%	20%
Not sure	10	7%	3	1%	30%	7	18%	70%
Not the real issue	6	4%	3	1%	50%	3	16%	50%
Focusing on one or more groups	**163**	93%	116	95%	71%	47	88%	29%
Agencies	27	16%	17	15%	62%	10	21%	38%
Consumers	5	3%	2	1%	40%	3	6%	60%
Law firms	125	77%	93	80%	74%	32	68%	26%

Tweet Categorisation	Total References		Solicitors			Paralegals		
Politicians	6	4%	4	3%	66%	2	5%	34%
Expressing feelings	**45**	25%	29	24%	66%	16	30%	34%
Negative	33	73%	22	75%	66%	11	68%	34%
Positive	12	26%	7	24%	58%	5	31%	42%

Tweet Categorisation	Total References		Solicitors			Paralegals		
Number	**Vertical analysis**		**Number**	**Vertical analysis**	**Horizontal analysis**	**Number**	**Vertical analysis**	**Horizontal analysis**
Total tweets about ABS	**175**	N/A	**122**	**122**	69%	**53**	**53**	31%
Total predicting or reporting change	**127**	73%	**93**	76%	73%	**32**	60%	25%
Predicting type of change	85	67%	62	66%	72%	23	71%	28%
Large-scale	42	49%	26	41%	61%	16	70%	39%
Quick event	22	26%	11	17%	50%	11	47%	50%
Slow event	38	44%	25	40%	65%	8	34%	35%
Predicting or reporting size of firm impacted	50	39%	35	56%	70%	15	47%	30%
In-house	1	0%	1	3%	100%	0	0%	0%
Large	22	44%	16	45%	73%	6	40%	27%
Medium	21	44%	13	37%	62%	8	53%	38%
Small	6	12%	5	14%	83%	1	6%	17%
Reporting organisational structure impact	63	50%	38	32%	60%	25	47%	40%
Law firm closure	7	11%	3	8%	42%	4	16%	58%
Law firm merger & acquisition (non-ABS)	6	10%	3	8%	50%	3	12%	50%
More staff at SRA	1	2%	1	3%	100%	0	0%	0%
New firms	49	78%	31	82%	63%	18	72%	37%
(Of new firms) ABS of existing firm	18	37%	12	39%	66%	6	33%	34%
(Of new firms) New firm ABS	12	24%	7	22%	58%	5	27%	42%
Unsure	11	22%	4	10%	27%	7	44%	73%
New firm	8	16%	8	7%	100%	0	0%	0%
Other impact	16	13%	11	9%	69%	5	16%	31%
New rules	7	43%	6	55%	85%	1	20%	15%
New Strategy	8	50%	5	45%	62%	3	60%	38%
Public opinion	1	6%	0	0%	0%	1	20%	100%

TWEETS ABOUT CHANGE – CONCEPTUAL ANALYSIS – CHANGE

'87% of the total tweets were about change. Of those, 84% predicted or reported change, phrases included "game changer", "I think this is big", and "you don't have to be a solicitor".'

'Impact was evenly spread between large and medium sized firms, with solicitors arguing for the larger firms and paralegals medium sized. Both paralegals and solicitors thought the change would be large scale, but paralegals thought it would be quicker. Overall, the tweets for large scale and slow event were more closely correlated than those for large scale and quick event, suggesting the change will occur across the market, but over time.'

'A small minority of tweets (13% of the total commenting on change) concentrated on other impacts such as new regulatory rules, developing a new strategy or a change in public opinion.'

TWEETS ABOUT CHANGE – CONCEPTUAL ANALYSIS – FEELINGS

'Across both groups, strong fighting metaphors like "revolution" "battle" and "last stand" contrasted with calmer nature metaphors like "wind" "temperature" and "new dawn", demonstrating the complexity of feelings about the change. ....'

'Solicitors also used transport metaphors like "green light" and "launch", suggesting being carried forward by motion – perhaps beyond their control.'

'I categorised just 25% of the total tweets with an identifiable positive or negative feeling. This is because the winter only included tweets which expressed explicit negativity or positivity. Implicit negativity (such as the fighting metaphors referred to above) was therefore excluded. This measure is therefore indicative rather than representative. The majority (73%) were negative. Solicitors expressed concern ABS were here "whether you like it or not!" One who was positive said the "future is bright".'

'A word frequency analysis ... showed solicitors made more personal and legal references in their data than paralegals. I have explored this further in the section on culture. The main trends in the data for both solicitors and paralegals reflect the subject matter; structures, rules, ABS and business. Both mention change, with the word appearing at 10th and 13th in word frequency for paralegals and solicitors respectively. Paralegals also frequently used the word "big"; the similar words "titanic" "monumental" and "great" reflect the scale of the change, discussed above.'

'Whilst there is a limited number of ABS to date, Tweeters overwhelmingly expect the Act to result in change across the sector. This cannot be said of the economy, technology, globalisation or other forces mentioned by academics in the literature review.'

'Change has already occurred beyond the creation of ABS; more than 50% of the organisational changes reported were other structural changes such as closure and mergers.'

'Solicitors are not concerned about the Act on a day to day basis, and the majority of tweeters suggested it would be a slow event ...'

Tweets sampled for solicitor culture

Only very limited data for the solicitor culture sample is included here, for the reasons set out above.

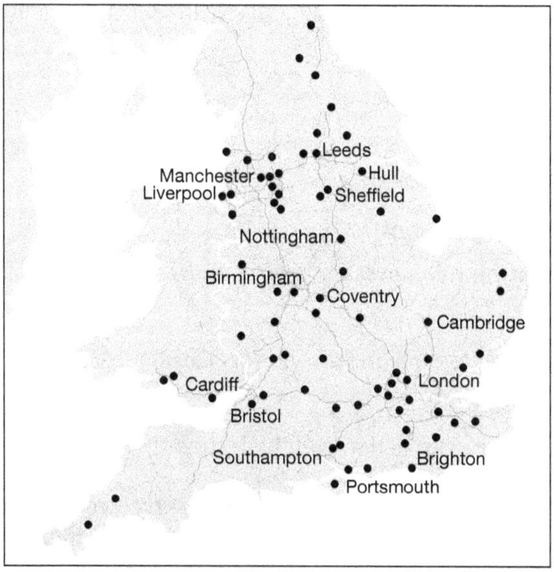

SOLICITOR CULTURE RESULT: GEOGRAPHICAL DISTRIBUTION

'I sampled 384 tweets work related tweets from solicitors.'

'The map … shows the geographical distribution, with concentrations in the northwest, south east and along the major motorway, broadly mirroring the spread of the population (right).'

'Solicitors follow the rest of the population who need them for representation in life time events.'

SOLICITOR CULTURE RESULT: CONCLUSIONS

While the writer has not included the results of the tweets or other analysis gathered for culture; some of the conclusions are summarised below.

The writer found that there was an identifiable culture within legal services, which was evidenced in the collective behaviours of the group. The writer also found this could be stratified or collected into sub-cultures dependent on qualification.

Evidence of culture in legal services was observable. The following evidence was clear through explicit or implicit discussion or observable categorisation:

- Names of law firms (literally and figuratively) – honouring local individuals and maintained through many years.

- Underlying statuses (partnership; equity partnership / PQE)
- Qualifications – Solicitors/Licensed Conveyancers/Paralegals and unqualified persons
- Respect of peers
- Principles of professional conduct and role in society/administration of justice
- Keeper of confidences
- Solicitors Disciplinary Tribunal
- Legal Professional Privilege
- Architecture/historical locations
- Serving society (locations)
- Restriction of information (case law; libraries)
- Pay
- Reporting (Gazette, Roll on Friday, Legal Cheek)
- Legal language
- City firms and the distinction with high street firms

The writer's analysis went further than this; discussing management and business structures within legal services as evidence of culture. All of these points, and more were apparent, and being re-enforced by the communications of those within legal services.

When observing these traits of the legal services market, it was clear that outside investment and intended change would struggle to alter the position and accepted institutions in the sector.

APPENDIX – RULES FOR CONCEPTUAL ANALYSES

> 'All categories are mutually exclusive. Some categories have sub-categories which make up the total category score. Main categories are left aligned and sub-categories are right aligned below their corresponding main category.'
>
> The rules are shown below. Tweets could be categorised into more than one category.

Conceptual analysis 1 – ABS data – The Rules Tweet Categorisation	**Rule**
Expressing a view on change	Whether an impact of the Act is mentioned or evaluated. Covers the following categories (more than one categorisation not allowed):
Predicting or Reporting Change	If evidence of change is presented or if a positive view is given change will occur
No change	If no evidence of change is presented or if a view is given the impact of the Act will be limited

Conceptual analysis 1 – ABS data – The Rules Tweet Categorisation	**Rule**
Not sure	A view the impact of the Act is unknown, including asking others about the impact and expressing there are a lot of factors
Not the real issue	A view mentions the impact of the Act but disregards it as something else is more important
Focusing on one or more groups	Identifiable groups (including organisations) are mentioned within the tweet. More than one categorisation required in the subgroups when more than one name mentioned, regardless of the sentence clause. Covers the following categories (more than one categorisation allowed if separate evidence of each):
Agencies	Mentions government departments or quangos or their names, excluding consumer quangos
Consumers	Mentions consumers or consumer agencies / quangos
Law firms	Mentions law firms or names of law firms
Politicians	Mentions politicians or names of politicians
Expressing feelings	Includes tweets which express explicit negativity or positivity, e.g. 'good' or 'bad'. Implicit negativity and positivity, including metaphors for the impact of the change is excluded. Covers the following categories (more than one categorisation not allowed):
Negative	As above, for negative
Positive	As above, for positive

Conceptual analysis 2 – ABS Data (sub-analysis) – The rules Categorisation	**Rule**
Total predicting or reporting change	**Tweets which fall into this category above.**
Predicting type of change	Tweets which implicitly or explicitly refer to change, including the impression given by metaphors. Covers the following categories (more than one categorisation allowed, except between slow and quick):
Large-scale	Implicit or explicit references to a large event, e.g. 'revolution' 'big bang'
Quick event	Implicit or explicit references to a quick event, e.g. 'big bang'
Slow event	Implicit or explicit references to slow event e.g. 'tide', 'changing landscape'
Predicting or reporting change in size of firm	Categorisation of all law firms, new ABS and in house departments mentioned in the change tweets. Used with reference to Legal 500 (2011). Covers the following categories (more than one categorisation not allowed unless more than one firm mentioned):

Conceptual analysis 2 – ABS Data (sub-analysis) – The rules Categorisation	**Rule**
In-house	Mentions in-house department or uses the term 'in-house'
Large	Mentions London magic circle firm, law firm with national presence (in more than one region) or ABS with national and/or international presence
Medium	Law firm or ABS classified by Legal 500 (2011) as 'regional heavyweight' or has more than 5 partners
Small	Has less than 5 partners or is Sole Practitioner (commonly self-employed)
Organisational structure impact	Evidence of organisational impact which has already occurred in one of the following areas (more than one categorisation allowed if separate evidence of each):
Law firm closure	A law firm has closed
Law firm merger & acquisition (non-ABS)	Law firms have merged with each other or one has acquired the other, but neither is an ABS
More staff at SRA	The SRA is employing more staff
New firms	A new firm has been created (non-M&A), or an existing firm has become an ABS. Covers the following categories (more than one categorisation allowed if more than one firm mentioned):
ABS of existing firm	An existing law firm has become an ABS
New firm	A brand new firm has been created (including ABS of existing commercial practices)
Unsure	The tweet provides insufficient information to clarify in detail which firm or what has happened other than there is a new firm or new structure
Other impact	Mentions other organisational impact. Covers the following categories (more than one categorisation allowed if separate evidence of each):
New rules	Mentions new regulatory or legislative rules
New Strategy	Mentions new strategies for commercial enterprises, excluding structures
Public opinion	Mentions public opinion

Annex 2: Alternative Business Structures – ABS and their development

This second Annex is a presentation from 2013 concerning Alternative Business Structures.

This final piece is provided as another analysis of the intention of ABS at the time and the future it was thought to hold. Again, the writer asks whether businesses can remain stable at a time of such uncertainty, and whether in turbulent times we need to provide and offer long-term clarity in business regulation and outcomes in order to provide a stable basis for change. Readers may also wish to reflect on your feelings about change in the sector and whether ABS, coronavirus, or any other event has impacted you and your business. Would greater certainty about regulatory development and outcome be helpful in these times and, if so, could this be facilitated in terms of both structures and regulatory outcomes (including conditions) by the regulator?

In 2013, the writer wrote and delivered a presentation to a group of legal professionals about Alternative Business Structures. This group will remain anonymous, as will the full content of the presentation so as to preserve their anonymity. The group were very concerned about the impact of ABS, what the future held for them, and whether they needed to make strategic decisions as a result of the changes under the Legal Services Act 2007. For a group of established legal professionals, ABS was a major shock and the writer was invited to deliver her thoughts, having worked at the SRA during the development of the Handbook 2011 and as ABS policy was being considered.

The result was a presentation which covered the up-to-date position at the time of writing, and thoughts for the future. The writer has made notes on her copy of the presentation to speak to and hasn't touched this presentation since 2013. The writer's notes say (redacted to be anonymised):

> 'Intro you. Happy to be here, etc.'
>
> 'Not advice – just thoughts on the current position.'
>
> 'Before start – picture of current regulatory turmoil. What we have seen just the beginning. Message: Be careful permitted now may not be in future.'

The presentation covered the definitions of Alternative Business Structures, their uses, the benefits and risks of ABS and some thoughts for the future.

The first slide covered ABS and its definitions, but broadly speaking it was defined as where a non-lawyer was a manager of a firm or had an interest in the body. There are a number of ways to operate an ABS and set one up, including a straightforward ABS where a non-lawyer joins the partnership. It can also mean another body having an interest, provided that body has a non-lawyer interest of a minimum percentage. We discussed the meaning of the term 'non-lawyer' and how it was applied.

The following slide discusses the slow revolution occurring. By this point, we had seen 74 licences issued and there were 454 applications in process. The writer's handwritten (redacted) notes say:

> 'This is just the beginning. If doesn't change the market, there will be further legislation to do so and there appears political will to address the position. The 74 licences is low, but is increasing due to political pressure.'

We looked at a range of firms who had converted, or entered the market. We also considered large brands, and small firms, and noted the wide range of types of firm who were choosing this route.

The following slides address the possibility of an ABS using an overarching body system or complexity in business structure, and whether this was worth pursuing.

This, the writer has noted on the slide, was 'something of a regulatory grey area'. The writer's handwritten notes on the point were:

> 'ABS more into space of outside influence, so if outside influence can be regulated what legitimate place do umbrellas have? Policy agenda may not see this addressed immediately, but they will be.'

The writer used the examples of legal process outsourcing, marketing companies, and claims management companies as areas which raise questions of outside influence and regulatory space (specifically whether or not the regulator has regulatory jurisdiction). The slides also discuss using overarching companies to support managerial skills, soft skills, branding, and integrity, but questioned where the governance sat with such organisations.

The slides record a feeling of fluidity in the situation, and the handwritten notes say 'we don't know what is coming next. The regulations were set up to cover a traditional law firm …'.

The slides cover the benefits and risks of setting up an ABS, and these are shown below as they appear on the slides:

ABS	
Benefits	**Risks**
Clear, regulated structure	Responsibility
Control over integrity	Loss of control over your own firm
External investment	Change in culture
Reward other professionals	Not popular overseas
Join other parts of the value chain	Greater risks?
	Size may be unwieldy

The final slide is a 'Thoughts for the future' slide. It says:

> 'Ensure your independence, safeguard your reputation, and ensure good governance and management – Handbook principles 3, 6, & 8.'
>
> 'Decide on your intended outcomes … and choose which suits you.'
>
> 'Regulation is likely to change again to keep pace with the market – SRA Strategy 2013 – 2015.'
>
> 'Ensure you understand your risk appetite and the risk appetites of your associates.'
>
> 'Ensure good decision making and governance in all associations. Draw sensible lines between outside associations and your business.'

Part 5

Serious Breach

Contents

Section 1: Technical content
- Reporting requirements
- Definitions of 'serious'
- Example serious breaches
  - The impact argument
  - Practical application
- Other reporting and regulatory requirements
- COLP and COFA
- Reporting Relationships to other roles
- Seeking advice
- Serious breach and material breach
  - Material breach
- Serious breach
- Freelance solicitors
- Statutory events
- SDT and the standard of proof
- Evidential requirements for reporting
- Regulatory investigations
  - Regulatory reporting
- Disclosure considerations
- Regulatory outcomes
- Other firm and individual implications

Section 2: Discursive content
- Standards of behaviour for solicitors
- The Reasonable Man
  - Turning a blind eye/dishonesty
- Integrity and dishonesty
  - Dishonesty
  - Ethical considerations
- Dishonesty and reporting
- Section 43
- Prosecution for failure to report
- Managing investigations
  - Investigation response
- Pastoral support; thoughts and feelings
- Improving compliance following a breach – the importance of leadership
- Whistleblowing

Fiduciary duties
COLP and COFA
Management and compliance
COLP and COFA: balanced scorecard
Annex 1 – SRA Regulatory Investigations Process

Section 1: Technical content

Serious breach is a complex and controversial subject in solicitor regulation. Tied to the role of the solicitor in a constitutional and reputational sense, it is a requirement to self-report (or possibly report another solicitor) in respect of any serious breaches of the rules of professional conduct. It applies to regulated firms and individuals and can impact the individual rights and freedoms of those solicitors and those working in those law firms.

The effect of the regulation is to prefer to see the solicitor not as an individual person with a job, but as a professional whose position within the state goes some way to defining their behaviour. This chapter explores the roles of the solicitor, the firm, and the COLPs and COFAs within those firms.

A solicitor has a constitutional role; they work as an officer of the court, and the rules of professional conduct are intended to safeguard the rights of individuals within the state to:

- independent, competent advice centred on the individual (or entity);
- independent representation before the courts; and
- advice which provides a check and balance to the powers of the state.

The rules of professional conduct also importantly uphold the administration of justice, providing a clear path of behaviour of the solicitor, who has a leadership and decision-making role within state functions.

Parliament is the sovereign body but, adopting the theory of the separation of the powers, the judiciary (including the solicitor) provide the check and balance against the power of the state and in the representation of the individual.

In order to provide their advice, the solicitor must maintain their independence, their integrity, and their competence. The reputation of legal services as an independent point of advice must also be upheld.

Other functions of the state have separate checks and balances. Parliament as a law maker must provide the function, with elections and an opposition to keep it in check. The judiciary also makes law, through case law, and this is kept in check by Parliament. The lawyers that represent individuals in the courts also have a role to play.

But with lawyers themselves controlling access to functions of the state, there must be a check and balance to their power. The legal services regulators therefore perform an important role themselves in overseeing the lawyers and ensuring services are provided correctly, independently, in the interests of justice, and effectively. The court also provides a quasi-regulatory function, in that the solicitor is an officer of the court and has duties to the court. The courts do contact the regulator when they are concerned about the conduct of a solicitor.

The Legal Services Board also provides oversight of the approved regulators, with approvals of their rules, regulatory powers, and functions. The LSB also reviews the operation of the approved regulators.

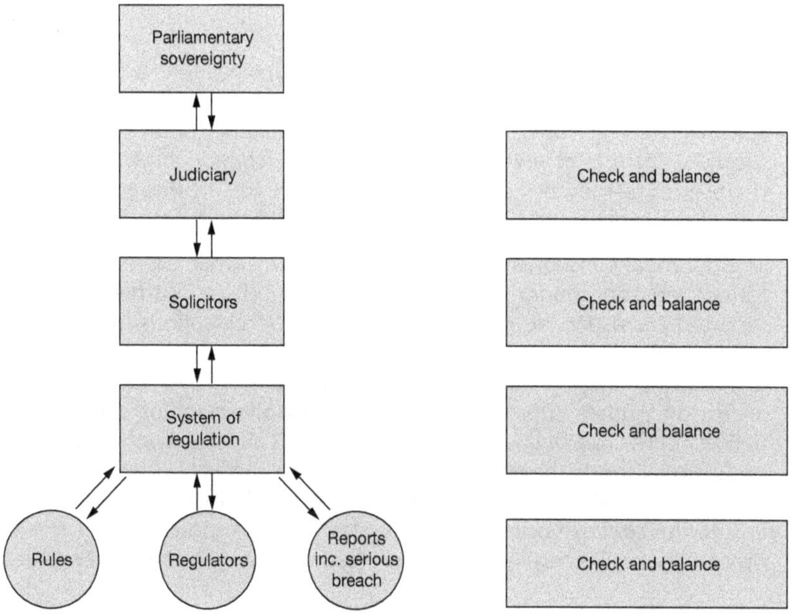

This all provides the background to the concept of self-reporting and what is currently termed 'serious breach'. The solicitor is required to self-report any breach of the rules that may be sufficiently serious to warrant the regulator's attention. This is justified on the basis that: the regulator must have a check and balance on the solicitor; the solicitor should behave in the interests of the reputation of legal services; and those solicitors have an important function in the operation and administration of the justice system. It would not, for example, be appropriate for a solicitor to continue to operate if they had been charged with a criminal offence. The solicitor's role in society means they must be seen to behave in the interests of the client, with honesty, and with leadership and purpose in the discharge of their legal and justice-based functions.

Another example is that the solicitor also commonly holds monies for the client. The oversight of this function is, again, comparatively limited to that of, for example, a bank's internal system. The bank is a large organisation with a number of internal checks and balances in place. The solicitor's firm, by contrast, may be a small local firm with limited scope to provide internal checks and balances on the use of client monies. The solicitor is subject to oversight from the regulator in this respect and must obtain an annual accountants' report. The solicitor must then be trustworthy and compliant with the law (and rules of professional conduct) in the handling of monies from the client. Breaches of the duties, in the handling of client monies, are taken extremely seriously, and serious breaches of the Accounts

Rules with the intent of depriving clients of their monies inevitably result in the responsible solicitor being struck off.

There are other justifications for self-reporting serious breaches, including:

- Legal Professional Privilege – the right of an individual to obtain confidential advice from their solicitor, which is not always disclosable, even in court (noting that privilege does not apply, when the retainer is in furtherance of a crime). This means the solicitor cannot disclose the situation to a third party, meaning a self-report is necessary.
- The number of regulatory bodies potentially involved in the process – there are a number of different qualifications available in law and potential professional statuses which are open to lawyers. Whilst regulatory bodies do their best to promote the rule of law and, within that, to exchange information between themselves, sometimes those situations can be lost or misreported, and the role of the lawyer is to address the professional issue themselves.
- The potential consequences for the rule of law – while there can be reasons for not reporting minor breaches to the regulator, serious breaches must be reported to ensure the rule of law is upheld. Some serious breaches can be criminal offences. The trust placed in the solicitor and their access to all parts of the justice system means they could deliberately override or circumvent justice and other court procedures. The involvement of solicitors in the delivery of the rule of law in this role of trust has consequences not just for the professionalism of the solicitor, but impacts all aspects of criminal and civil justice and public law. The solicitor is held to higher standards as a means to ensure the effective operation of the state in the supply chain of the justice process that relies heavily on their professionalism, honesty, and probity.

The solicitor must be able to give independent advice, beyond the reach of the state, in some cases. Without these independent advice functions, beyond the oversight of the state, the individual may not be able to have independent legal advice, and the exercise of power in the state could be absolute. It is a natural consequence of asking persons to give this advice in these circumstances that we then say they must comply with rules of professional conduct or professional behaviour, which provide guidelines for what is or is not acceptable, and how this should be delivered.

Serious breach and self-reporting sits within this context; that the professional status of the solicitor is what is at stake, if those rules are not adhered to, but also that the standards are expected so the system can function with public confidence.

Requiring the regulator or other investigating or prosecuting authority to investigate the solicitor, with their role in the justice process, is complex. The solicitor has to be able to give independent, confidential advice to the public, and should not be disrupted by the state in that delivery. Any investigation can require access to client files, office premises and confidential information. Making a self-report is a solution; the solicitor or the firm has to consider their position in light of, for example, a criminal charge against a solicitor, or the dishonest removal of client monies from the client account; then they should make a self-report and discuss their investigation. This enables the regulator to form a view of the situation and confidence in the firm continuing. Self-reporting is therefore a natural consequence of the situation; the regulator expects the firm and the individual to make a report to them. In either of the situations outlined above, the regulator may also receive information, but it is helpful for the regulator to receive this detail as soon as possible to enable them to take regulatory action.

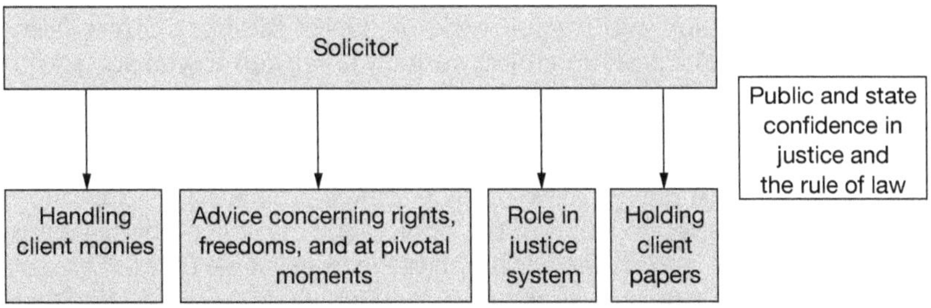

Accordingly, a heavy weight rests on the solicitor to behave appropriately, uphold professional standards and make ethical decisions. In a sense, solicitors drive the respect and trust the public places in the sector. Solicitors are, however, just human beings; they make mistakes, and some find the pressure of the professional conduct rules quite intense.

Solicitors also run businesses and have commercial interests. This latter point attracts a lot of regulatory attention. The amounts solicitors can and should charge for legal services are a matter of debate. As, of course, is expecting solicitors to behave more ethically than other members of society. The regulator's reach sometimes extends into the personal life of the solicitor, and the duties on them, their families and employees can be onerous. Positions that might be taken by an ordinary member of the public might be unacceptable for a solicitor and their family.

Self-reporting serious breaches is another example of that extended duty which requires the solicitor to behave more ethically than other members of society. In very few other circumstances are people required to self-report their own mistakes, particularly in situations that could be career ending, threaten their livelihood, and jeopardise their workplaces. However, without the requirement to self-report, the solicitor or their firm may be able to continue in circumstances that could cause difficulty for others, or undermine the justice system.

Of course, solicitors can be reported by many others, including the judiciary, third parties, the other side and other solicitors, other lawyers, and there is an independent system of legal complaint handling for clients to raise concerns. However, without the internal check and balance that self-reporting requires, many matters may be overlooked; the system creates a requirement in internal professionalism and review for both the individual and firms.

Solicitors have a separate Tribunal in the Solicitors Disciplinary Tribunal, who, along with the regulator, decide on the disciplinary matters of solicitors who have broken the rules, once the potential breaches have been investigated.

This book focuses on the requirement to self-report serious breaches of the rules of professional conduct to the regulator by solicitors, their firms and their staff. Part 6 of the book looks at the relationship between the requirement to self-report and the annual accountants' report, covering the aspects of self-reporting that accountants and financial staff should be aware of. We do not cover the requirements for reporting for legal consumer complaints, third party misconduct allegations, or any other types of referral to the regulator. We do have a section later in this Part of the book covering what happens next, once a report is made.

The focus of this section and the following section of the book comes from the requirement to self-reflect on an ethical position in relation to yourself and those around you. This can be as an issue of continuous professional development or wider self-development in ethical awareness. The writer's course, which this book accompanies, has a basis in personal development and psychological theory. As part of the courses, we discuss some of the potential positions a solicitor and their firm may find themselves in. Part 8 of this book provides some of the scenarios the writer has used in the courses she has run over the years. Some of those are serious breach scenarios and you can use them to consider what you would do in such a position.

This book seeks to build on some of the activities and discussions within the course, without describing how the course is run. This is a deliberate decision on the part of the writer as to describe how the course is run takes us into those bases in personal development and psychological theory, which in themselves are not part of reporting serious breach. The intent is to place the focus on the solicitor or person with the obligation to report and their own reflection. Positioning the reporting of serious breach alongside the renewal and the annual information return gives us the opportunity to reflect on the year just past, and considering any Practising Certificate conditions, firm conditions, or near misses of these. It also allows us to reflect on where the firm or individual is or might be in terms of risk posed and issues to manage.

Serious breach and personal reflection are complex, weighty subjects of self and state responsibility. Discussing the position further and reflecting on the requirement to self-report means consideration of this issue must be managed with a degree of safety. All solicitors, their staff, and firms, are advised strongly to take independent legal advice prior to reporting if they feel they need to report an issue to the regulator. At the time of writing, legal advice was available from the Solicitors Assistance Scheme and a number of specialist firms who offer professional conduct representation.

Reporting requirements

The duty to self-report applies to:

- the individual solicitor;
- the firm; and
- the COLP and COFA, who are often required to actually make the report.

The duty to self-report can also, in some circumstances, extend to unadmitted individuals working for the solicitor.

The SRA's requirement to self-report is contained in Regulation 7 of the Code of Conduct for Individuals and Regulation 3 of the Code of Conduct for Firms, both in the Standards and Regulations 2019. Specific requirements to report also exist for the COLP and COFA, and these are contained within the Code of Conduct for Firms 2019 at Regulation 9.

Regulatory action can be taken by the regulator against:

- the individual solicitor;
- the firm;
- non-lawyers working within a firm (including but not limited to trainees, paralegals, managers, and non-lawyer managers); and
- overseas lawyers registered and regulated in England and Wales.

Regulatory action can also be taken against an individual holding a position in a firm (such as a COLP or COFA, in respect of the discharge of that function).

Overseas lawyers registered and regulated in England and Wales (or who are required to be) can be subject to regulatory action for breaches of the rules. They can also be prosecuted by their own regulator. Individual solicitors of England and Wales working overseas may also be subject to separate regulations from the regulatory body overseas. This dual system can cause problems for those subject to two sets of rules and requirements and different obligations to behave in different ways according to the various rules. Reporting may differ, as may expectations, and even disciplinary outcomes.

The duties to self-report in England and Wales are set out in the regulations. The separate obligations on individuals, firms, unadmitted, and overseas staff have been provided for in the rules for some time, but have been made explicit by the Standards and Regulations 2019, which in particular set out the separate reporting duties of firms and individuals.

Any breach, which may be classed as serious, should be reported to the regulator. There is a definition of serious, formed of extensive examples, and the regulator requires firms to consider the position carefully. There is also a requirement to notify the SRA if the firm believes they should be involved in an investigation.

The COLP (Compliance Officer for Legal Practice) or COFA (Compliance Officer for Finance and Administration) is the person responsible for compliance with the standards of professional conduct within the regulated firm and is tasked with not only ensuring compliance with the rules but also ensuring any report to the regulator. The COLP and COFA is a product of the SRA's regulatory rules, and is a position that was introduced in 2011 alongside the authorisation of ABS and the introduction of the Legal Services Act 2007. The position is known as the HOLP (Head of Legal Practice) or HOFA (Head of Finance and Administration) within the Legal Services Act 2007 (under sections 91 and 92 of the Act). Under the Legal Services Act 2007, the role only applies to ABS. However, the SRA was introducing outcomes-focused principles-based regulation at the same time as bringing in ABS, and considered there was a risk to firms if they reduced the amount of information and guidance to firms in the new rules of conduct, so introduced firm based roles for oversight.

The move to outcomes-focused regulation was also intended to promote 'freedom in practice' in that it intended to allow firms to adopt their own procedures and policies more autonomously and with the firm in mind. This new freedom, alongside

ABS, with its capacity for firms and individuals to make greater decisions themselves without prescriptive rules, required, the SRA felt, a consideration of compliance within firms. This was intended as a leadership role with the compliance decisions of the business at its heart. They therefore renamed HOLP and HOFA as COLP and COFA, and introduced the COLP and COFA requirement for all authorised firms, not just the ABS.

COLP and COFA have, since the introduction of the Handbook 2011, become one of the defining features of compliance in law firms, and have been adopted well by the sector. Practices may draw a comparison to the previous 'Rule 15 Complaints Partner' which may have provided a blueprint for this role. We discuss further the role of COLP and COFA later in this Part of the book and in Part 6, in the context of the accountants' report.

In the newly available structures (freelance and working in unregulated firms), there is no COLP or COFA as the firm is not regulated. Whether this will hinder individuals working in these structures who are used to the presence of that level of support, or whether those individuals will be subject to more regulatory scrutiny without the COLP or COFA there, is a question for future analysis.

The current set of rules from the SRA under the Standards and Regulations 2019 provides a fairly close comparison between COLP and COFA and HOLP and HOFA. The main differences between the two roles as drawn is the width and breadth of the roles, with the regulations seemingly providing a wider role for the COLP and COFA. There is no difference in the regulations for Alternative Business Structures; the roles of COLP and COFA apply to them as well.

Both the regulations and the legislation (respectively) require the COLP and COFA and the HOLP and HOFA to make a report to the regulator. Here the wording differs slightly again, with the legislative duty (defined in the Legal Services Act 2007 ss 91 and 92), possibly too wide as it requires a report of all failures to comply. In practice, the duty of all (including ABS) has been taken to be to report that defined by the regulations, which is currently serious breaches.

There was, prior to 2011, a requirement to report to the regulator in the event of a serious matter occurring, so this part of the regulations is not new. It is new within the legislation, and the definitions of the HOLP and HOFA are unique within the 'four Acts'; they are not mirrored elsewhere. However, there are implicit reporting requirements for some serious breaches outlined later in this section.

Individuals who are not COLPs and COFAs within regulated firms can also be held responsible for a failure to report to a regulator. The SRA has prosecuted individuals before and, in 2018, advised the Legal Services Board that individuals could be held responsible for failure to report breaches. The power available to the SRA in respect of unadmitted individuals is the Solicitors Act 1974, s 43, which has the effect of preventing that individual from working for a solicitor. For many people, this would be the end of their career in law.

Not only is the individual solicitor required to report matters which are serious breaches, they are also required to report matters which the regulator may want to investigate. The solicitor or firm must investigate the circumstances and provide any evidence or documentation to the SRA as required.

The solicitor, their staff, and their firms are in an unenviable position by virtue of their constitutional role. They protect the rights of individual subjects from the power of the state but, in so doing, must theoretically:

- be pillars of society and the community;
- report themselves for wrongdoing;
- report themselves if they are investigating wrongdoing internally if they think the regulator should know; and
- put aside their own personal and commercial interests, including their roles running companies.

These are heavy responsibilities to place on individuals, and there can be a lot of sympathy towards an individual solicitor who, by mistake or as a result of the actions of another, has found themselves in a situation which impacts their future career.

Accordingly, individual solicitors and firms affected by the reporting provisions are advised to take independent legal advice about their position, the investigation, and how to proceed. Those working in a solicitor firm who may be subject to an investigation where the firm has a different interest may be advised to take their own individual advice, particularly if the matter to be reported is career threatening. There is a further section on seeking advice later in this Part of the book.

The writer has run a course on the requirements to self-report for many years, and from that course many individual solicitors and firms agree with the reporting requirements as a means to promote and uphold standards. However, the question of what to report is less clear cut, and individual ethical views differ on what may or may not be acceptable.

Definitions of 'serious'

We discuss material breaches later in this section and, between 2011 and 2019, solicitors, their staff, and firms were required to report material breaches to the regulator. There was a definition of 'material' as discussed and provided in Rules 8.5, 8.7(a), and guidance note (xi) to Rule 8 of the Authorisation Rules 2011.

The position changed in 2019; with the introduction of the new Standards and Regulations 2019, the SRA moved to a requirement to report 'serious breaches'. The SRA's enforcement policy is the closest explanation of serious breach available, although there are further examples on its website of how it will enforce different types of serious breach in different circumstances.

The enforcement policy sets out some examples of situations which may in themselves be serious, or where if breaches occur or have a particular result, they may be serious. These situations include (amongst a much longer list):

- criminal convictions;
- vulnerability of any party;
- harm; and
- intent.

However, these are examples of circumstances where a serious breach might arise. What about actual serious breaches?

Example serious breaches

There are now many published lists citing examples of serious breaches published by the regulator. These lists did not exist when we first started the course back in the early 2010s. Attempting to define then what should be reported was an exercise in professional reflection.

Of course, the writer had been involved in regulatory decision making for some years at the SRA and CLC, and brought her own perspective and experience of prosecution to the ethical examination.

We examined situations and circumstances which, for some reason, might be unacceptable:

- to the public;
- for those in an administration of justice role; and
- for those who have a leadership role in their local community.

The definitions of integrity and dishonesty are discussed further in Section 2. These are important definitions and the regulator has sought to pull from them example issues which, in their view, meet these definitions.

Sometimes, the concept of serious breach is somehow intangible; an ethical standpoint that somehow means a certain action offends the professional position of the solicitor, but the same action with less serious consequences is deemed acceptable or de minimis. The question sometimes is whether it is the action which is causing the problem, or the consequence?

The Impact Argument

If we say the solicitor can only be involved in legal services if they have exemplary behaviour, because their role in justice depends on their professional conduct, we are placing their actions or behaviour at the front of the argument.

If we then say those actions may not be reportable if they result in minor consequences, are we saying that the solicitor can behave as they wish, provided there is no or minimal harm?

Allowing any behaviour, provided there is no or minimal harm, potentially could undermine the justice system.

We can see the SRA has, in its enforcement strategy (along with other matters), confirmed it considers issues of impact, harm, motivation, and intent, when assessing whether a matter is serious, but it does not give concrete examples.

Below is a diagram the writer draws in the course quite frequently to illustrate the difficulty:

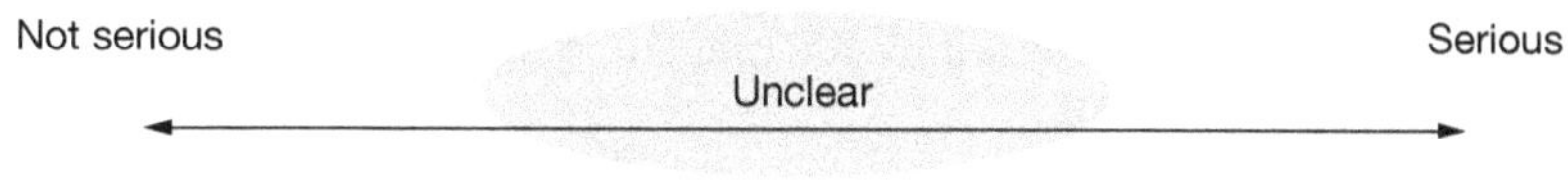

For example, if a solicitor removed £50,000 from a client account which belonged to the client, that would be a breach of the rules, and would be serious. If the solicitor removed 1p from the client account that would be a breach but would not automatically be serious. The regulator does not have a de minimis provision, so it is possible to get lost in the middle section as illustrated. At which point does the removal of client funds become serious?

In this scenario, our own moral compass is relevant to how much money should be missing before it is reported; some feel none at all if taken with intent. Other delegates sometimes say £70.00 or £100.00.. The reasoning for the low amount is the impact on the reputation of the justice system, through the solicitor's dishonesty, or sometimes that the solicitor could have the intent to remove more client monies at a later point. We have to remember at this point that solicitor accounting is complex, mistakes are made, and monies can be removed without intent to steal as they may have been misallocated to the incorrect ledger, for example. Any mistakes, or shortfalls in the client account, should be rectified without delay.

PROPOSED DEFINITION

If we take the position that any behaviour which breaches the rules (or possibly the overarching principles) could potentially undermine the justice system, we could then say the SRA is measuring impact or potential impact as the definition of serious breach.

Therefore, the writer's definition of a serious breach is:

> 'A breach of the overarching principles which has a serious impact on clients, staff, third parties, or the justice system or where it has the potential to do so.'

Of course, this definition is not intended to take away breaches if the firm then mitigates them with monetary or other compensation. For some, there are red line breaches which cannot be resolved with monetary compensation, and the writer's view is these also fall *within* the definition above, in that they already had a serious impact on others, or had the potential to do so, and that is why they are being mitigated. Alternatively, we can argue that most serious matters could have a serious impact on the justice system.

Practical application

The regulator's decision making about serious breach is often informed by their risk management tool, which illustrates: the risk of the situation developing; the intent of the individual; and the overall circumstances, mitigations, and the relevant regulatory history, other intelligence or known information about the firm or solicitors. You will find, if looking on the regulator's website, that their description of possible outcomes is influenced by the mitigating actions of the practitioner or circumstances going forward.

So, with all of that in mind, we must (for now) look at examples of serious breaches in their overall context. Bear in mind the totality of a situation when you consider the list below and, if you are ever concerned by a serious breach yourself, it is an opportunity to also see the picture of the firm and individual in relation to that serious breach:

Example serious breaches:

- criminal convictions;
- misleading the court;
- money laundering;
- Accounts Rules breaches;
- client complaints of circumstances which have resulted in severe loss to the client;
- forgery of documents;
- misleading costs; and
- involvement in scams.

All of these, of course, are clearly serious or potentially serious, with consequences for clients, firms, third parties, or others. In such circumstances, it is important to involve the regulator, and very few solicitors or others involved in professional services would disagree.

Other reporting and regulatory requirements

Solicitors, COLPs, and COFAs have a host of other reporting requirements. Money Laundering Reporting Officers, and Data Protection Officers do too. This is not a book about money laundering as such, but money laundering would of course be a serious breach so it deserves a mention.

The main reporting requirements for an SRA-regulated average high street practice include:

COLP	Reporting serious breaches
	Reporting matters that may require investigation
	Diversity data
	Reporting loss of authorised officer / role / temporary authorisation
COLP / HR / Other authorised officer	Renewal requirements for lawyers or regulated individuals authorised by other regulatory bodies
	Renewal requirements for membership bodies

COFA	Reporting breaches of the Accounts Rules
	Reporting matters that may require investigation
	Accountants reporting; managing the process and sending the report when necessary
MLRO	Reporting money laundering suspicions
MLCO	Reporting to the board / management structure about AML
Data Protection Officer	Reporting breaches of Data Protection obligations
	Communication with ICO
ORC (Organisation Contact) / AUS (Authorised Signatory)	SRA renewal obligations and ensuring MySRA is up to date
Management	Insurance notifications
	Reporting to the Legal Aid Agency
	Authorisation forms, such as change in structure
All staff, including management	Reporting money laundering suspicions to the MLRO Reporting data protection breaches or requests to the Data Protection Officer Reporting serious breaches to the SRA if the COLP or COFA has not agreed to report

There can be other touch points across the business if the firm is, for example, under investigation, is subject to a thematic review by the SRA, or must report a serious breach. The SRA might, in those circumstances, be in regular contact with the COLP, COFA or other nominated contact. Similarly, if the firm has someone with conditions on their Practising Certificate, the regulator may be in regular contact.

Larger firms or those with specialist areas to consider may also be regulated by the FCA or another regulator. Individual lawyers can have their own regulators which may have their own reporting or renewal, which a firm also must consider.

In addition, there can be events which are not serious breaches, but need reporting to the regulator to prevent them happening to others. For example, attempted cybercrime attacks, scams, and fake firms. Some of these matters may be criminal offences perpetrated by non-solicitors against firms.

Aside from reporting under the renewal or for serious breach, a firm may have several other regulatory approvals – codes, memberships, or quality marks to comply with, and oversight bodies it must liaise with. There are potentially several bodies to report to, notification schedules to maintain, and investigatory capacity to evidence. The volume of work can seem overwhelming to small practitioners, or to place on the shoulders of a single individual (often the COLP or COFA) within a regulated firm.

The difficulty may be exacerbated by the varying standards of reporting that exist between regulators; in some cases, a matter may be reported to one regulator, but not to another, and vice versa. In the non-reporting standard, some find justification for not reporting to any regulator, and the same the other way – if I must report it to one, must I report it to both?

The existence of memoranda of understanding between regulators can also make the position even more complex. A report could be made via another channel. The separate positions of the regulators have apparently been arrived at by independent policy work and research, without reference to another regulator or standard. Of course, each regulator should work independently, but often the regulator has a remit to exchange information with other regulators.

Many of the problems the writer has heard in working with law firms relate to the difficulty COLPs and COFAs experience in seeking to manage the commercial expectations and interests of the firm with the need to report breaches. Even when firms have not committed breaches, some worry about the possibility that it will happen, and the consequences.

COLP and COFA

The roles of COLP and COFA are worthy of consideration in their own right. The COLP and the COFA are presented as two sides of the same coin, but the reality is quite different. The COLP role is arguably wider, encompassing all aspects of compliance, the terms of the law firm's authorisation, and all statutory obligations. The COFA role might be small by comparison, only responsible for compliance with the Accounts Rules.

We have defined the COLP and COFA and statutory basis earlier in this Part of the book. The definitions in regulatory and legislative terms provide that the COLP should not only ensure compliance, but also ensure the firm, its interest holders, or employees do not cause or substantially contribute to a breach of the rules. The COFA did not receive the same extension of ensuring compliance. The new 2019 rules also remove the requirement to maintain records.

In the 2019 regulations, a new requirement was introduced for the COLP or COFA to have a reasonable belief before making a report. The 2019 position of the rules is reflected below.

The COLP and COFA roles were worded slightly differently to the statutory roles, but we can draw across a broadly similar meaning. The statute gives us additional context of the parliamentary and legislative intention of the roles.

Both roles have to:

- ensure compliance within their area;
- report serious breaches under the Standards and Regulations 2019; and
- report breaches of the rules under previous Handbooks, dependent on the rules in force at the time (for example, material breaches under the Handbook 2011, if the breach occurred before 26 November 2019).

COLPs and COFAs should note they may be required to keep the records they had of breaches prior to the change of rules in 2019.

Although the regulator may seek to correspond with the COLP or COFA, another person can take on the role of corresponding with the regulator if needed.

The roles of the COLP and COFA should theoretically work together. However, achieving that balance is complex and may rely on the personal ethical judgement of both being aligned with each other, as well as an acceptance of the systems and procedures needed for the implementation of the roles. There are various different ways to implement a management system, and the COLP and COFA should agree to make the system work effectively. That is not forgetting that the COLP or COFA will have their own professional status and judgement about how the work should best be completed.

The regulator recognises the personal influence and leadership of the COLP and COFA in their approach to conditions. As we can see in Part 3 of this book, they commonly impose conditions not to be a COLP or COFA on those who are currently not fulfilling their compliance obligations and are therefore deemed unsuitable to become a COLP or COFA. Those whom the regulator is perhaps not satisfied will ensure the firm is overall compliant may not, in their opinion, be COLPs or COFAs.

The regulator does not prescribe the policies or procedures it requires for the COLP or COFA. However, these are positive obligations and the onus would be upon the COLP or COFA to demonstrate the systems and procedures they had put in place.

Ideas for implementation are shown below, including effective policies and procedures, internal communications; and evidence of systems of management, such as quality marks or audit-based reviews, will all be helpful. COLPs and COFAs should also consider the influence of parent or connected companies, or vice versa (the firm's influence over them), and how those feed into the compliance experience.

Outsourcers and other structural arrangements will also warrant consideration, particularly given the openness or range of business models available to the COLP and COFA within the rules. Loose arrangements with outsourcers, or a lack of leadership within a firm or within these roles, can cause concerns about the organisational culture or attitude towards compliance within a firm. Certainly, those with very strong leadership and a strong and visible grasp of the rules, particularly the Accounts Rules, are often regarded by the regulator as being the most compliant.

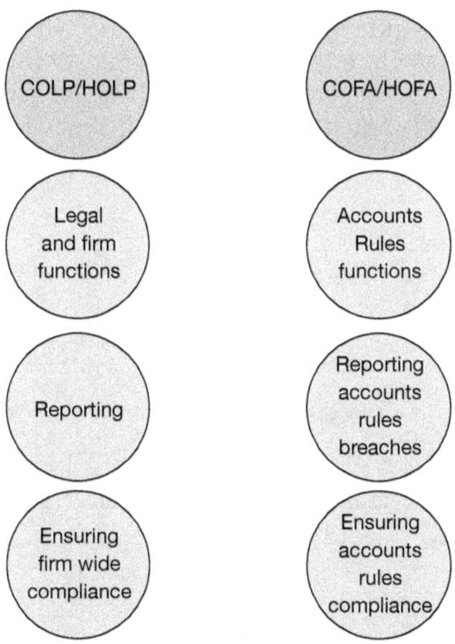

There are further ideas and information regarding the Accounts Rules and COFA compliance within Part 6 of this book, which also covers the annual accountants' reports. But it is clear the COFA needs to have a handle not only on reconciliations, but also on some aspects of day-to-day management of the Accounts Rules, which probably necessitates some form of file review procedure from an accountancy angle. Of course, this is perhaps where the COLP and COFA would need to work together, given the fiduciary duties owed to the client by the solicitor, which are again explored further in Part 6 of this book.

The COLP's role is potentially not over yet; with clear links between the Accounts Rules and office account, the financial management of the firm should be firmly within their grasp. The financial management of the firm also theoretically falls within the remit of the COLP, given reference is made to it within the Codes of Conduct in the Standards and Regulations, and not within the Accounts Rules themselves.

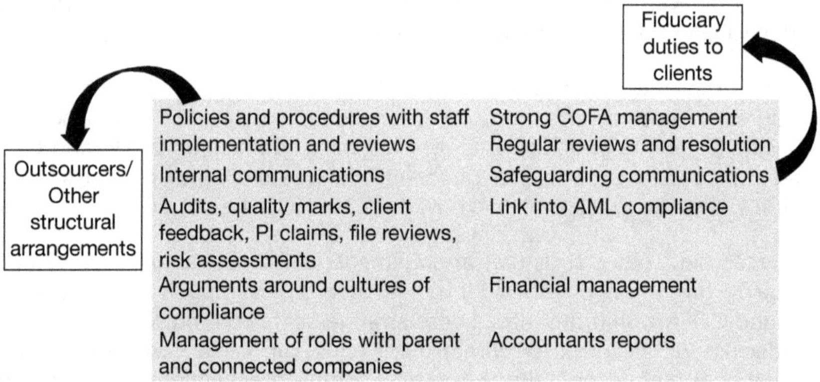

Statutory requirements should not be forgotten, and AML gives us a different example of the types of obligation a firm may have, both within and beyond the regulatory compliance which would be expected by the SRA or within the SRA rules and regulations. Anti-money laundering compliance is expected within the Standards and Regulations, with references to establishing the identity of the client, and is currently a deep focus of the SRA communications, particularly since the establishment of the Office for Professional Body Anti Money Laundering Supervision.

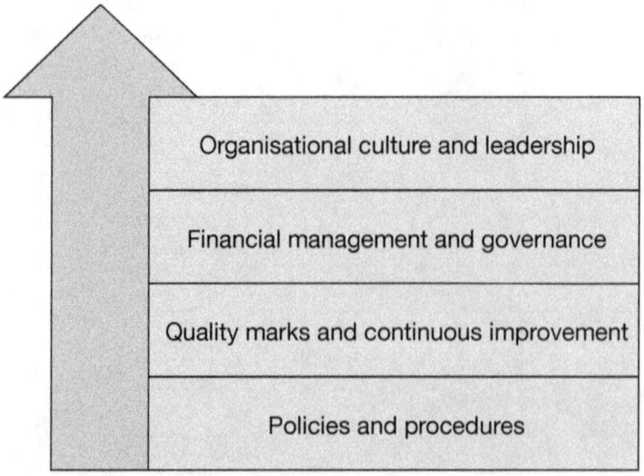

At a baseline, firms might have policies and procedures in place. All firms experience drift from their office manual, and it can be important to develop systems and procedures that reflect the work of the firm, particularly given the importance of these roles. Firms may want to develop specific policies and procedures for reporting, given the statutory basis of the role of COLP and COFA.

Moving on from reliance on policies and procedures, adopting a quality mark or other audit system can also demonstrate your commitment to compliance. These suit some firms more than others. Some can be very prescriptive, and a lot of work. The downside to using the quality mark approach is the loss of control over the content of your policies and procedures. For some small firms or those with a particular expression in their work, there may be other ways to evidence your compliance – for example, through a well thought-out and very tailored office manual, reflecting your approach.

As outlined above, strong financial management and governance can also play a strong part in the approach of COFAs. The writer's experience is this demonstrates very effective leadership to the regulator, and provides comfort that clients are being taken care of financially; a very fundamental concern.

At the top of the table is organisational culture and leadership, with culture being an expression of the firm's approach, both internally and externally, encompassing the written and unwritten rules of behaviour that govern its staff and interest holders. Achieving compliance buy-in at this level is extremely difficult; compliance is a complex subject and individuals have a right to their own view about the interference of the state and its functions in their lives. However, we all may be able to buy in to a view of honesty and integrity, keeping client monies safe, and doing the best for the client and local community. Implementing a culture which reflects these behaviours can be extremely complex, and takes genuine leadership and belief and commitment, as individuals have a right to personal expression of their views, and may not always agree with the regulator's approach. The best advice at this level might be to find something positive you and the firm believe in and adopt this as a cornerstone of your approach.

A further analysis of the position relating to organisational culture is contained in Part 4 of this book.

Reporting relationships to other roles

Of course, the COLP and the COFA sit alongside many other roles, including health and safety, data protection, and IT security. The COLP's role arguably encompasses all of these points, and more, due to the requirements to consider statutory protections. Most prominently, the COLP and COFA have connections to AML and AML compliance, with an overlap in the roles. Some matters of AML are also matters of professional conduct, or would even arguably be covered in the COLP role, again because of the wide coverage of statutory requirements.

The COLP (and potentially the COFA, dependent on the impact on the Accounts Rules) also covers issues such as Practising Certificate renewal, character and suitability of staff, connections with related businesses, and the crossover of professional conduct requirements of those from abroad. Of course, we have not even mentioned the possibility of regulation by another legal regulator, or another regulatory body such as the FCA!

The myriad different requirements can lead to reporting overload. An issue gets reported to a person in charge; decisions have to be made by the firm and within the firm about which responsible person is most appropriate, and which one of the range of bodies the matter needs to be reported to.

There are also a range of different roles that must be fulfilled within the business, that have different training requirements, specialisms, and responsibilities to compliance that a firm must keep up with.

Anti-money laundering can play a role both within the businesses and outside of it that need to be factored into the regulatory response. Of course, COLPs should be aware of reports made under the Proceeds of Crime Act 2002, and may have comments around issues such as legal professional privilege, or whether a matter also needs to be reported to the SRA.

However, there is a clear crossover between the role of the COLP as a safeguard of professional standards and the role of AML within the firm. We often see matters which appear to be (or are prosecuted as) anti money laundering issues at the Tribunal. These are issues which are prosecuted as breaches of the rules of professional conduct. The COLP and COFA (in so far as these are often also financial issues) should then also be considering the conduct issues that arise and whether the firm has breached any of the rules of professional conduct in this respect.

Perhaps the most clear-cut link we can see is the link to integrity. The regulator has done a considerable amount of work in this area, which is explored further later in this Part of the book, and has linked integrity to taking unfair advantage, scams, and links to inappropriate financial schemes. Unwitting involvement in money laundering, or failure to identify the warning signs, may be the same; with deliberate intent possibly falling into the category of dishonesty. At the moment, this is a separate principle in the SRA overarching principles, and involvement in money laundering would be a ground for intervention.

As a matter of integrity, COLPs and COFAs may therefore also want to cast an eye over the AML policies and procedures of the firm, and understand the value in making a report on the grounds of suspicion, even if that suspicion simply ends up as intelligence sharing. The SRA is ever more keen on this area as an area of compliance, with more requirements, compliance materials, and concentration of their resources in AML. OPBAS as the oversight regulator may be an important body to watch in terms of regulatory compliance policy in the future.

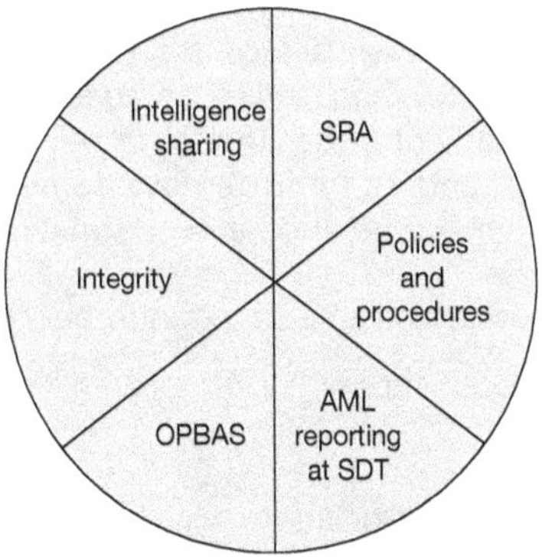

Seeking advice

If faced with a potential breach, firms are often concerned, worried, and unsure how to proceed. Conducting your own investigation may be necessary. This investigation should start from a neutral standpoint, considering whether a breach has genuinely taken place.

A firm may need to take independent legal advice. This can often be beneficial early in the process as it can clarify whether there is any issue, what the component parts of any issue might be, what actions might be necessary immediately, and provide direction and support with any needed investigation. Firms and individuals may also benefit from the advice concerning their own circumstances.

Legal advice can also safeguard or attempt to defend people's and the firm's rights in the face of the required reporting; it can assist with ensuring nothing further occurs that requires reporting, and keep any investigation focused on the issue in question. Sometimes the situation and consequences for the individual or firm are significant.

Therefore, it can be important that firms, COLPs, and COFAs, consider what would happen if they were to uncover a breach, and where they would seek advice. Perhaps having two or three sources of advice and support can also help in case of conflict of interest between different parties. Do you also wish to indemnify your staff; to what extent is this covered by your insurance or do you require a separate policy? The speed at which some situations evolve can mean deciding where to turn in advance can be an excellent decision.

Even obtaining assistance with the investigation can help with independent decision making. A COLP or COFA is in an unenviable position. They have duties to their firm, and individual duties, but also regulatory duties. The decision to report is almost always one which has some form of conflict with a regulated firm. It may also conflict with their own individual duties or their own position personally. At times, the conflict may be overshadowed or taken away by the seriousness of the possible consequences, including the loss of a Practising Certificate due to suspension, or because there are grounds for intervention. In this situation, all parties are likely to need advice.

There is no doubt that reporting another person, yourself, or a firm is a decision most legal professionals do not wish to face. It is emotive, challenging, and places professional responsibility into sharp relief as against what may be a human reaction to forgive, particularly of those close to us. An independent voice, review, or consideration can help, and can also remove some of this burden from the shoulders of COLPs and COFAs who also have personal relationships within firms.

Advice and broader support is available from a number of sources, including:

- the Solicitors Assistance Scheme;
- LawCare; and
- the Solicitors Benevolent Association.

You may also find advice available from legal professionals who specialise within this field. There are a number in law firms across the country.

The regulators may prefer individuals to have and seek legal advice. It can be helpful for the individual or firm in understanding the usual processes of the regulator, what might be required, and in ensuring the regulator has challenge from someone with the requisite experience in their area of administrative law.

Unrepresented parties can, as in all legal situations, face difficulty in having their voice heard or be placed at an unfair disadvantage when dealing with such a large organisation as a regulator. Although solicitors are trained in professional conduct, this is a branch of administrative law, and the legislation, regulations and powers of the regulators are specialist subjects with legislative histories, accepted practices, and caselaw. It is possible to provide advice as to the likely outcome of matters, and for advocacy on the respondent solicitor's behalf to be effective.

Those who are represented are anecdotally more likely to obtain a satisfactory outcome. Sometimes, those who are unrepresented find their advocacy is 'piecemeal effective', meaning the final decision might be correct in some respects but in others can feel that it has not effectively taken account of their individual circumstances and what happened directly to them. Somehow, sometimes a voice feels missing from the case without representation, and the weight of experience of an advocate can assist the practitioner in confident communication.

Those that are unwell, vulnerable, or who are facing a serious sanction can particularly benefit from representation, and it can help to relieve some of the stress or worry of the situation from the shoulders of those being prosecuted.

The writer's experience is that those who are being prosecuted are often remorseful and upset. Sometimes, in addition to legal representation, respondents may need to speak to organisations such as LawCare, who provide pastoral support.

Anecdotally, there are some cases in which respondents do not correspond with the regulator as much; particularly those cases which are extremely serious. These matters include significant breaches of the Solicitors Accounts Rules, significant interventions for dishonesty or fraud and money laundering, or where a criminal conviction has occurred. In these cases, particularly where the evidential test is clearly met, the solicitor may simply be a bystander to an inevitable conclusion.

However, in cases where the evidence is disputed, less clear cut, or where there is complexity to the case, advice and advocacy can work wonders. The process is less emotive, and the respondent may begin to see the process as a process.

Serious breach and material breach

The SRA has moved, under the Standards and Regulations, to a requirement to report 'serious breach'; that is, the breach or potential breach must be serious to be reported. This is a movement from the position of reporting 'material breach'. Many solicitors and accountants have, on the courses, discussed whether the change implies the regulator is now looking for matters which are more likely to be prosecuted, bringing them further along the line than when the definition was 'material breach'.

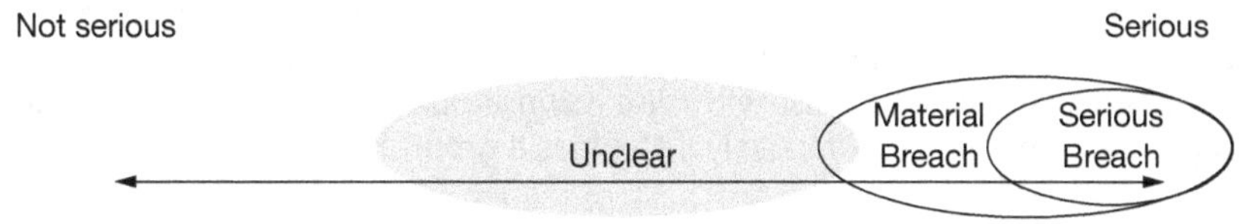

Material breach

The previous definition the regulator used (from 2011–2019) was 'material breach'. The regulator both sought to define it and didn't, all at the same time. The regulator asked solicitors to consider:

(a) whether there was a breach of the rules of professional conduct; and

(b) if there was a breach of the rules of the rules of professional conduct, whether that breach was material.

Within (b), the regulator further defined that a material breach was a breach which had a sizeable impact on clients or others, or impacted the standing or reputation of the legal profession or firm, or placed clients at loss or risk of loss. There were a number of measures which were provided in guidance at the time the regulator published the 2011 rules, even specifying possible numerical measures of material breach.

The writer is not using the actual definition of 'material breach' here, but readers can find it in Rules 8.5, 8.7(a), and guidance note (xi) to Rule 8 of the Authorisation Rules 2011.

Since starting to present the course in 2013, the writer has explored these themes with many hundreds or thousands of solicitors, accountants and their staff. In each case, the participants have been given made-up scenarios to consider, and make decisions about what to do. The writer provided the numerical guidance in a table for delegates to consider. Almost none of them used the table published by the regulator as a basis for the decision. A few used the guidance, but the vast majority used an internal compass or belief that directed them to form a decision. The table is not re-published here for this reason.

That the SRA also did not seek to define 'material breach' any further than the Authorisation Rules and the numerical guidance, is also worthy of discussion. We did not at that point have the backdrop of examples on the regulator's website of what they wanted to be reported. We had the examples of prosecutions from the Solicitors Disciplinary Tribunal, and the matters the SRA publishes, but the introduction of 'material breach' with the definition and examples above was intended as a new style of regulation. Known as Outcomes-Focused Regulation (OFR), the style was intended to be more open, taking account of wider business influences and allowing a freedom in practice to benefit the newly formed Alternative Business Structures.

With this new approach came a focus on law firm financial stability, while allowing the market to develop the variability in the type and nature of work that could be delivered by lawyers. Examples of concerns from the time include: inappropriate investments in law firms; worldwide risks and investments from nations perceived to be high risks; and ensuring the profitability of law as a sector. The position of intervention was a large focus, with discussion around prosecution for failing to manage the firm finances effectively if this was a ground for closure.

The position post-Brexit seems quite different now, particularly as ABS have not made the expected inroads into the sector, and outside investment in law firms has not to date been the transformative force expected. Shortly after the Brexit vote, around 2016, the SRA announced its intent for a new Handbook, commenced writing and consultation, and the debate around 'serious breach' began.

Material breach, as a discussion point with accountants, is discussed in Part 6 of this book.

Serious breach

The actual move to serious breach came in 2019, with the introduction of the new Standards and Regulations. As set out above, the wording suggests the intent is for the breaches being reported to be 'serious'. There may be an expectation that the breaches are 'more serious' than those reported as material breaches. The change in wording coincides with the following changes:

- to the overall look, feel, length and detail of the rules of professional conduct, with the Codes being much shorter than previously;
- a separation of firm and individual Codes of Conduct, despite much of the content being comparable;
- a move to a lower standard of proof at the SDT; and
- ongoing changes to the accountant reports, lessening the number of reports the regulator receives (discussed in Part 6 of this book).

One analysis of the new Codes of Conduct is the brevity is intended to encompass the previous requirements but promote and allow flexibility in the Codes. The writer presented several sessions alongside the SRA during the consultation periods and this was part of the message being communicated.

The intent may be for the regulator to focus more on investigating and prosecuting breaches which clearly require the regulator's attention. At the time of writing, the SRA had also been more willing to incur costs in the prosecution of individual solicitors (*SRA v Beckwith*), which might be seen as a demonstration of strength and determination.

Although the new Standards and Regulations allow the solicitor more freedom in their expression of practice, there may be a greater signal from the regulator that they are intending to take a stronger approach to discipline where matters are serious enough to warrant prosecution. Asking solicitors, their staff, and accountants to make such distinctions, and get them right, is a complex task.

The regulator has more recently published extensive guidance covering the matters it might wish to see reported, and how it may view those matters. Although the Standards and Regulations are open in their interpretation, the guidance in this area is now very extensive and it is often possible to find a specific answer about whether a situation should be reported or not.

The writer has noted the following available sources of information:

- An enforcement strategy, which sets out the matters the SRA regards as serious.
- Subject matter guidance for specific 'serious' concerns.
- Guidance for those practising overseas, which includes matters the SRA regards as serious.
- Guidance on issues of integrity and dishonesty.
- Guidance for reporting accountants, which is also helpful to COFAs.

In all cases, the SRA appears to take the line that there are circumstances in which some matters might be acceptable, and some cases in which they are not, and that the seriousness of the situation depends on a variety of factors.

In the writer's view, this might include:

- intent;
- the reality of a situation, rather than how it has been presented;
- the position of the other parties, both before and after, and any mitigation;
- accepted social standards of behaviour;
- accepted behaviour by firms; and
- the personal position of the individual, including the impact of the position on the individual or whether the behaviour was out of character.

The Standards and Regulations separate the individual and firm responsibilities, but both still face requirements to report matters. The COLP and COFA also have those responsibilities, and individual and/or firm responsibilities may be discharged if the COLP or COFA agrees to report to the regulator. Otherwise, the individual or firm may have to report directly. Obligations to report may extend to investigations for the regulator as well as for the firm.

There may be two points in the process where a report to the regulator is required. We might see a possible serious breach being reported to the COLP or COFA. They (or the firm, or individual) then have to decide whether to report to the regulator, bearing in mind the regulator may be interested in the issue at investigation stage. This is the first possible report. It is often useful to have advice at this point. A report does not always need to be made at this stage if the matter would not be serious, and firms may be able to proceed to their own investigation. The second possible point of report is at the conclusion of the investigation, or when the firm become aware that it is 'serious'. If a report has been made prior to investigation, it can be helpful to consider a further report, or update, later.

With the duties and responsibilities of the individual falling squarely on individual shoulders, it is worth remembering that the regulator has powers to act against both individual solicitors and those working for solicitors. Individuals could find themselves in difficulty if they do not make a report of a serious matter where the COLP or COFA will not be reporting it for any reason. However, the COLP or COFA are usually, if not always, a member of the senior management team and may have access to different information to the employed individual. The COLP / COFA or senior management team could find themselves undermined in a decision-making process by a report from an employee.

We have already within this book discussed the different pulls of COLPs and COFAs and how their role within the business and duties to the business may have an inherent conflict with the statutory framework surrounding their roles. Individual solicitors or unadmitted persons may find themselves in a similar position. They owe duties to their employer, but can simultaneously be subject to requirements to make a report to a regulator. The consequences of reporting can be severe and the individual is required to weigh this up themselves. The regulator has taken action against individuals for failing to report.

The solution for firms may be:

- to provide information about reporting to the regulator;
- to provide information about firm decision-making structures and an explanation that some matters are confidential;
- to provide information about COLPs and COFAs;
- to set out matters within employment contracts (noting that the firm cannot prevent reporting); and
- to provide alternative reporting lines (for example, to a different office), where a question arises as to the requirement to report.

As always, separate legal advice is available from the sources listed above, and firms can also signpost staff as appropriate.

USING YOUR JUDGEMENT

The following excerpt is from the writer's early Material Breach and Practising Certificate courses, but it is included here as it is still relevant to discussions of serious breach reporting. The excerpt covers using risk management or other mathematical scoring techniques to assess the seriousness of breaches:

> 'An important part of material breach is understanding that from the SRA's perspective, your judgement is key. They would like to see that you have thought about the issue yourself and determined whether it is a breach or not and its' relative seriousness. Getting this judgement wrong could be indicative of a failure to appreciate the wider compliance agenda.
>
> Any system is like a risk management system – not an exact science. This is because any system cannot replace your own judgement and it is important to take responsibility for yourself. So, whilst you can use a structure such as this, it is important to note that you will need to exercise judgement as well. Even the SRA has a manual override for [their] risk scoring system, and you should use judgement to determine your breaches and their materiality. A risk management scoring system can only ever be used to help understand and explore the issue; you must make the final decision.
>
> Reporting issues to the SRA is a serious matter and should not be taken lightly. These techniques are presented as ideas for managing your processes and increasing your confidence in identifying problems in your firm, as well as understanding your obligations to your regulator. However most governance systems also have the benefit of legal advice and this should also be a consideration before making your final decisions.'

Freelance solicitors

Freelance solicitors will also be subject to duties to report themselves, and individuals working directly for them could also be subject to 'section 43'. This is a colloquial term for an order made against an individual who is not a solicitor. The order is made pursuant to the Solicitors Act 1974, s 43. It has the effect of preventing them working in a solicitor's office again. It is a very severe sanction and often used in extremely serious cases. The writer has seen it being used against fraudsters and those who have inappropriately taken money from clients or from client account. In all instances, the person concerned was employed at a solicitor's office at the time of the wrongdoing.

Those working with or for solicitors in unregulated businesses will need to be careful about the extent to which the regulators' duties apply to them, and an unregulated business will want to consider whether solicitors should have any reporting lines or supervision within their business as a result.

The regulator has issued guidance for those working in unregulated businesses, and this includes unregulated businesses developing their awareness of SRA rules and regulations.

Part of the point and purpose of legal advisers working together is a shared awareness of the regulations of working in this area, and an awareness of the constitutional functions of solicitors. The rules of professional conduct are familiar to all solicitors, and their staff. However, those working in unregulated businesses are unlikely to have any awareness of the rules and the potential impact on their employees. There is also the question of disparity between an unregulated business and a regulated business, with regulated firms themselves open to prosecution, but unregulated businesses operating without the same requirements. Nonetheless, a section 43 prosecution against an individual within an unregulated business could be a nasty shock, and unregulated firms might wish to make their staff aware of the duties owed by solicitors to clients and others.

Statutory events

Certain events trigger a response in respect of the solicitor's Practising Certificate.

These events include:

- insolvency events relating to a solicitor (including personally and in relation to their legal or outside business interests) – Solicitors Act 1974, s 15;
- indictable offences committed by the solicitor – Solicitors Act 1974, s 13B; and
- offences involving dishonesty committed by the solicitor – Solicitors Act 1974, s 13B.

The above events can suspend the Practising Certificate of the solicitor. It is necessary for the Practising Certificate to be re-instated (if possible) and, in some situations, conditions imposed.

The SRA may not always reinstate the Practising Certificate if the situation is serious (for example, if the solicitor has committed an indictable offence involving dishonesty).

A failure to report in these situations could be very serious. The solicitor technically doesn't have a Practising Certificate, could be practising uncertificated and therefore may not be insured. The regulator would have the right to intervene in some circumstances, including into a sole practice (if the solicitor was a Sole Practitioner), or into the individual practice of a solicitor within a practice. This latter option may, however, depend on the circumstances of the firm or partnership, but the situation may still be very significant.

The grounds for intervention into practices can also give information about the circumstances in which matters should be referred to the regulator. This includes, for example, abandonment of practice, dishonesty, or reason to suspect dishonesty, or incapacity of the solicitor. Understanding the circumstances in which the regulator might take a statutory action can also help us map our decision making about serious breach against that of the legislative framework, and help firms make suitable contingency plans.

The grounds for intervention as a quick reference point can be found in the Solicitors Act 1974, Sch 1. These grounds are mirrored across the 'four Acts' we have seen elsewhere in the book, ensuring all forms of solicitors' practice (as discussed in Part 2 of this book) are covered.

SDT and the standard of proof

The Solicitors Disciplinary Tribunal has now moved to hearing cases at a civil standard of proof, which is a change from the original sliding scale of proof. Their previous sliding scale was the more serious the allegation, the more proof required.

As above, the SRA has moved to asking for more serious matters to be reported. This, coupled with the lower standard of proof, may mean easier prosecutions. It may also be possible for the SRA to devote more resource to the investigation and prosecution in-house if it reduces the volume of matters referred.

In practice, the weight of some allegations gives some pause for thought. Quite often, faced with a serious allegation, the writer has found her own breath taken away. 'Are you sure?' is the natural reaction. Whether or not the Tribunal will be able to move from this standpoint to a lower standard of proof will remain to be seen.

The question also arises as to whether their distinction is due to the possibility of separate police investigations for some matters.

Evidential requirements for reporting

The Standards and Regulations 2019 introduced a test for reporting, that is that the COLP or COFA has a reasonable belief there has been a breach. This is the standard of proof for an Employment Tribunal, and raises the question of whether there could be liability for reporting if there is a concern. The writer is not aware of any Employment Tribunals for incorrect reporting at the time of writing. This possibility may need to be counteracted in the same way bad faith money laundering reporting has been, through legislation, or even through regulatory rules making the position clearer.

Of course, the SRA did make the position clear in early 2018 that non-disclosure agreements could not prevent reporting to the regulator, and that position has not changed.

This is a markedly different approach and position to the decisions of some firms when COLP and COFA responsibilities were first introduced; many firms at that time decided to report all breaches to the regulator, and many still do. The writer spoke to a number of firms at that time, and there have been a number on the courses who decided to take the same approach. The regulator does have fairly robust and strong investigatory procedures in place, which in some ways must be quite fair because of the ability of firms to take this step. However, in so doing, the decision making is taken away from the firm and left to the SRA. Firms may wish to take decisions themselves.

The SRA is asking (in some senses) for the COLP or COFA to conduct an investigation first and make decisions about the position of the individuals and the firm as a whole. This is said in the knowledge that the regulations do say the SRA may want to know about ongoing internal investigations and these should be reported if appropriate; but within that and the rules as a whole, there is an implicit requirement to investigate, consider and decide. This requires a different skill set from the COLP's day-to-day work of overseeing compliance, and in fact the investigation might be a different role altogether. The COLP (or whoever is leading the investigation) must weigh up very carefully the possibility of breaches by persons in the firm, the evidence of that breach, and the evidence against.

There are a few points to note in this respect:

- The regulator does not often take one person's word against another's – they usually look for independent evidence and proof; this can come from a number of sources, including the accounts, telephone records and notes of calls, correspondence, files, internal procedures, internal notes and records, court judgments and agreements, for example.
- People make mistakes – sometimes a wording or turn of phrase has been used incorrectly, and caused offence, or been taken the wrong way in that, when you read it one way, it appears misleading, but read another way, it is not (and let's say in this situation the second interpretation is more likely). Dependent on the nature of the allegation, and what has happened, the regulator may not pursue such cases. We have to view them in the prism of the standard of proof.
- There is a separate route for complainants who were clients of the firm – this route goes through the Legal Ombudsman and, if the client wants to, and the circumstances are appropriate, they can take legal advice and separately pursue the firm for negligence. This may be completely different to professional misconduct, but the two are often confused. The Legal Ombudsman will make a referral to the regulator if necessary and if they think there has been professional misconduct.
- Mitigation is a great starting point and may resolve many issues – can you put any impact right and comply? That can make a breach a delay in compliance which has been resolved by the firm. Examples of this can be breaches of undertaking, where a delay in failure to comply could be a reportable breach, but compliance with the undertaking can (in some circumstances) resolve the issue. We have seen above that some of serious breach reporting is about impact; what can you do to resolve the impact on the situation? This, in some circumstances, may not prevent you from also reporting, but it can sometimes be ethically correct, and make a difference to those impacted. The SRA will likely take it into account.

This is not an exhaustive list of all points to consider when weighing up the evidence, and the approach of the regulator is in some respects an area of law in itself. Taking independent legal advice if you are unsure will assist you in considering the situation and making this complex decision.

Regulatory investigations

The issue of regulatory investigations is a difficult and emotive subject and the writer is aware of her own role as an investigator and decision maker at the SRA for a number of years. It can be difficult to discuss previous investigations and personal experience without breaching confidentiality, and the writer is not doing so here, but the experiences of those investigations and the worry for practitioners associated with them remain with the writer.

The writer can describe in detail the process of the regulatory investigation, and has included an annex to this Part of the book showing that process, in a map. It starts with an assessment of the situation or any report made to the regulator. This is risk assessed and the writer discusses this extensively on her courses. Understanding that the SRA undertake a regulatory risk assessment is helpful, as firms can place themselves against it to work out where they are. The risk assessment is not reproduced here, but is available on the SRA website.

The second stage is what to do next. We can sometimes separate out very serious breaches at this stage; for example, ones which would result in intervention. These are discussed shortly. The ones which would not result in intervention, but would need an investigation, would be referred to ask the solicitor or other regulated party for an explanation. The letters asking for an explanation can be very detailed with a number of warnings, and the practitioner may need legal advice to respond, particularly given the potential sanction. Once the practitioner has had the chance to respond, the matter is referred for a decision. Adjudicators (who are often former solicitors) often make the decisions, although in some cases it can be the caseworkers. A sanction may be an internal fine or regulatory outcome (for example, in relation to a conflict of interest which has moderately impacted clients). In other cases, referral to the Tribunal may be the result of the investigation.

Many of the SRA's internal decisions have the right of appeal internally, to a Panel, which is usually composed of two legally qualified professionals and one lay person (as defined as 'lawyers' and 'non-lawyers' within the Legal Services Act 2007). In some cases, there may be the right of appeal to the High Court. Of course, none of this touches on the right of judicial review, although practitioners are obviously encouraged to use the formal decision and appeal processes which are usually adequate to address their concerns.

If a decision is made to refer to the Tribunal, this is usually an internal decision following receipt of the solicitor's explanation. A decision to refer to the Tribunal can be made by the caseworker, by an Adjudicator or by an Adjudication Panel, and is communicated to the solicitor and firm concerned. The matter is then referred to the Legal department of the SRA, who prepare the case for presentation before the Tribunal. If not already instructed, the defendant solicitor is asked to seek legal representation at this stage.

Some firms will experience 'supervision'. This is a concept introduced in 2011 with outcomes-focused regulation, and is intended to work more closely with the firm than other regulatory interventions. A supervisor will often seek an overall outcome for the firm, working with them. Characteristics of supervision include:

- ongoing discussions;
- thematic visits;
- notice before visits;
- a named supervisor or relationship manager for larger firms;
- larger firms – regular contact, interest in financial matters related to firms;

- greater emphasis on co-operation; and
- can have a serious, investigatory arm.

We need to consider intervention and some serious breaches in a different way, particularly given how serious they may be, and that they may involve the police or other law enforcement. In some respects, we can see the SRA as a quasi-judicial or law enforcement authority, with a number of different powers. We have touched on intervention above, which is one of those powers. We must always be aware that, for some serious breaches, intervention is the end result. For example, reporting significant dishonesty in relation to the client account, or a firm being 'acquired' by fraudsters, will, if true, result in intervention of that firm.

Regulatory interventions may be conducted in a different way to that described above. If there is an immediate risk, there will be an immediate response from the regulator, and sometimes firms can be closed down very quickly, sometimes with the support of law enforcement.

Below are some excerpts from training in SRA Investigation and Enforcement produced in 2014 by the writer:

> 'Since the introduction of the Legal Services Act 2007 (and the repeal of certain sections of the Solicitors Act 1974) SRA created new systems and procedures to modernise regulation and handle the challenges of Alternative Business Structures. This included developing a new risk management structure, to allow for the assessment of the risks these new businesses would bring.
>
> To keep up with the potential changes to the market under the Legal Services Act, the SRA also altered their investigation functions. Instead of investigating every allegation they would now 'supervise' firms; this meant a more co-operative approach where allegations or issues were felt to be resolvable. However the sharp end of investigation and enforcement has not altered much following the Legal Services Act. There are new powers to fine, an alteration of some internal outcomes, and the introduction of regulatory settlement agreements, but the average solicitor will not see much difference in the way the SRA investigates and enforces serious issues such as dishonesty, money laundering, and criminal activity.
>
> It is important to understand why the SRA may be investigating or coming to visit you. The SRA risk profiles all firms, and the reports it receives. You may be receiving a visit because the SRA would just like to catch up with you, it may be because you are a very large firm and therefore pose a risk to the SRA, or it may be because they have intelligence about wrongdoing in your firm.
>
> Supervision is the day to day oversight of firms by the SRA. The equivalent for larger firms is relationship management, which is a regular, possibly intensive review of the business.
>
> Supervisors or relationship managers may visit as part of a wider attempt to tackle a specific problem (thematic review), because of specific intelligence, or because of the profile of the firm. At the moment, there

is no set inspection programme at the SRA (i.e. they are not attempting to visit all of the firms they regulate).

If you are visited by a Forensic Investigator, things will be more serious. More often than not Forensic Investigators arrive following receipt of specific intelligence about the firm. They are often there to look at accounting issues, but can also be called upon to look into serious issues of criminality or dishonesty. Occasionally, a supervisor or relationship manager may attend before a Forensic Investigator. If reasons for an investigation appear vague, this should be enough to raise concern.

If Forensic Investigations do arrive, they may not give notice, or they may give a week to five days. They often do not give reasons for visits. They will usually start with a three way reconciliation before a meeting with the partners. The Forensic Investigators may then undertake further investigation by reviewing accounts, files, procedures, or interviewing staff. Meetings and interviews may be taped. A visit by a Forensic Investigator, (and occasionally by a supervisor), can warrant legal representation during the visit itself, as it is usually connected to an extremely serious allegation or suspicion.

Any visit will usually end with a final meeting to discuss what has been seen at the firm. You may be aware of what the SRA is looking for at this stage, but sometimes, if the allegation is particularly serious or they are concerned with the destruction of evidence, this will not be revealed.

SRA Enforcement

SRA Enforcement approaches differ dependent on the seriousness of the allegation, the evidence available and the response of the firm concerned.

If the investigation finds evidence of a breach, the supervisor may come to an agreement with the firm to correct it. Low level outcomes may also be imposed by supervisors or others with delegated powers, without the issue of a report. However, further action may also be taken – the SRA's official line on this is this will happen if a firm is unable or unwilling to put the matter right. This can mean where the misconduct has been so serious it cannot be 'put right', or where a firm is unwilling to co-operate with the SRA.

Proceeding further usually means an internal report is prepared before being referred to an Adjudicator for a fine or rebuke. If a report is prepared and referred to an Adjudicator, a recommendation will usually be made, but this is not binding upon the Adjudicator. The report is usually sent to the firm / individual concerned, with time to respond before adjudication. It is not usual to attend before the Adjudicator, and most requests to do so are declined unless there are exceptional circumstances. Appeal of the decision of an Adjudicator is made to the Adjudication Panel, a three member panel or lay and professional members. Occasionally the Adjudication Panel may consider first instance decisions, although this is very rare.

In order for the SRA to refer the matter to the SDT, the public interest and evidential tests must be passed. …

A decision to refer to the SDT is not a decision that the case has been proven, rather that it is being referred to a higher authority. The decision to refer is often made by an Adjudicator following a report, but where the tests are clearly passed, the matter may be fast tracked and the decision made by an SRA employee with delegated authority, without reference to the firm or individual concerned. The SRA may publish the decision to prosecute on its website once the SDT has certified there is a case to answer.

Cases may take months, even years, before appearing at the SDT.

…

Some serious types of cases which had been previously decided before the SDT may now be resolved by Regulatory Settlement Agreement (RSA). This could include cases where a strike off would be sought by the SRA, but the individual is willing to concede to not practising again. RSAs can be used in most circumstances, but can be very useful where the alleged misconduct is serious or semi-serious, and the individual accepts the SRA's position. Other, specific issues which are part of a wider investigation may be settled by 'Regulatory Issue Agreements'; these are used to deal with one particular issue within an investigation, upon which agreement can be reached. Both Regulatory Settlement and Regulatory Issue Agreements are usually drafted between the SRA and the legal representatives of the firm / individual, so if you would like further information about this outcome you should contact a qualified legal representative.

Interventions

The SRA has the power to close down any practice it regulates; this is an intervention. When it exercises this power, all practice monies and papers vest in the SRA. This is an extremely draconian power with far reaching consequences for the livelihood of the individual.

…

Interventions can be undertaken by agreement, appointment, with no notice, or anything in between. Usually a member of SRA staff will attend the practice along with an appointed agent (usually from another law firm). The agent will remove live papers and monies and begin actioning immediate issues and re-distributing others according to client instructions.

A decision to intervene can also often have the effect of suspending the Practising Certificates of those involved, and of referring the matter to the SDT. The SRA will also usually look to the individuals or the firm for the costs of the intervention.'

Regulatory reporting

We should also note the range of information the SRA can acquire which can result in a regulatory investigation. This can include reports (for example, letters or emails) from a range of sources, and the SRA receives thousands of reports per month. We cover accountants' reports in Part 6 and the link across to regulatory reporting. Solicitors and accountants are reminded that the annual accountants' report is not the only form of reporting, and reports about breaches of the Accounts Rules can be made at any time.

DISCLOSURE CONSIDERATIONS

The following excerpt appears in the writer's 2021 Serious Breach and Practice Frameworks Course:

> '... This subject should .. note the recent discussions on Non Disclosure Agreements; which are not allowed to prevent reporting to a regulator, and that Legal Professional Privilege cannot apply if the retainer or subject is in furtherance of a crime.
>
> ... If a report is made to [the regulator] which requires disclosure of client confidential information, that consent should be obtained, or if necessary they will obtain a statutory production order to obtain the information.
>
> ...
>
> Firms must obviously consider their position regarding disclosure with reference to the GDPR.
>
> However directly relevant are:
>
> a) the statutory powers of The Law Society to request information, and
>
> b) other statutory provisions relating to reporting crimes.
>
> These may mean there is a legal obligation to process and disclose the personal data.
>
> The Law Society's statutory powers to request information are contained within the Solicitors Act 1974, (as amended by the Legal Services Act 2007), under s44B, which provide that The Law Society can require documents and information from solicitors, on the provision of a notice. The power to obtain information from other persons (non solicitors) is also contained within the Act, but requires the Society to make an application to the High Court. In practice, requests are directed at the solicitor within the practice.
>
> Consequently, for most solicitors reporting a breach, disclosure is obtainable.
>
> The writer's experience in working for the authority is that solicitors can [usually] do one of the following:
>
> a. make a report without breaching client confidentiality;
>
> b. obtain client consent to a report;
>
> c. rely on a statutory provision such as the reporting of a crime, where relevant.

> When there is difficulty obtaining information that the SRA requires, the SRA will produce a statutory order; this is often discussed with a solicitor prior to issue if a solicitor raises the problem of confidentiality or Legal Professional Privilege.
>
> It is important to note the difference; the SRA may require the information and they should make the request, but that is for them to decide. However the practitioner may need to draw the non disclosure to the SRA's attention.
>
> Practices should remember that the SRA has the right to intervene into their practice which confers upon the Society all practice papers and client monies. In effect, the Society has the right to request any file they require in full, which can make objections in this area redundant.'

Regulatory outcomes

The reporting of a serious breach has or could have several consequences:

- SRA investigation;
- SRA internal finding or regulatory outcome;
- SRA prosecution before the Solicitors Disciplinary Tribunal; or
- no further action.

These consequences are not mutually exclusive (for example, an investigation is usually required before an internal finding or sanction).

Internal findings and regulatory outcomes include:

- rebuke;
- fine;
- Practising Certificate conditions or firm conditions; and
- SDT prosecution.

Solicitors Disciplinary Tribunal prosecution outcomes include:

- strike-off;
- suspension;
- section 43 order;
- conditions (and variation of imposed conditions); and
- any other regulatory outcome.

Readers will see that the outcomes before the Solicitors Disciplinary Tribunal are the most serious.

These lists are not full or complete but reflect the main outcomes of reports for serious breach. As above, the outcomes are also not mutually exclusive (for example, a fine might accompany a rebuke).

Other firm and individual implications

As well as the regulatory outcomes listed above, firms and individuals may also want to consider several additional issues. These include the costs of the SRA investigation, the impact on the reputation of the individual and firm, and the stress of the investigation process.

Sources have been provided of further advice and support, including emotional and pastoral support. Some of this support is free of charge, but there are evident charges for accessing legal advice and support, even in the face of a professional investigation.

All solicitors have some form of professional conduct training and understand the role of the regulator and their responsibilities. It can be helpful for firms to develop their own understanding of the investigations process and the role of the regulator in their professional lives.

This is a distinct and separate area of law with a Tribunal, regulatory and procedural rules, and related scope of work in other areas of professional discipline and practice. The role of the COLP has begun to take part of this understanding of regulatory practice and professional discipline as their own, but this does not replace a detailed understanding of the operation of the procedures for investigation in practice.

There may be a limit then to what you can achieve in internal investigatory terms as a COLP or other nominated breach handler, alongside your own professional practice and area of law. Consider whether you have insurance, whether your staff are covered, or whether you know someone who could represent you. You may also consider media training or considering who might represent you if there was media involvement in your case.

It should be noted at this stage that the SRA does claim the costs of its investigation if it goes beyond a certain point. Matters which are prosecuted before the Tribunal can incur costs, not only of representation, but also of the investigation in full.

Section 2: Discursive content

Standards of behaviour for solicitors

Reflecting on the role of the solicitor within the ethical context of professional practice has been part of the courses the writer runs for the last ten years. Exploring that ethical position with reference to various scenarios continues to engage law firms, reporting accountants, and their staff. Readers of this book employed working for law firms directly, or in accountancy practices delivering accountants' reports, are invited to join us in person.

Of course, questions arise as to whether the ethical context is too self-contained; do we in legal services only see our own reflection in the ethical context of what we do? How would other groups of individuals see or understand how solicitors' practices work and understand when a solicitor would or should be disciplined? Sometimes, societal groups become so self-contained they fail to see how others see them, or the reality of the situation.

The SRA's publication 'A Question of Trust' explored the issue of professional conduct with members of the public and found that, amongst other things, the public expected solicitors to be honest with the court and in their dealings with client financial matters. This is perhaps mirrored in the current regulatory approach to prosecution. By far the most investigations and prosecutions centre around breaches of the Accounts Rules.

EXERCISE: COFAS

This exercise is for your COFA and accounts staff. Reporting accountants can also use it.

A set of solicitor accounts can be fantastically well organised, or they can be very awkwardly set up. A healthy client or office account balance can sometimes mask other problems.

Consider which of the below should be reported to the regulator, without reference to the rules of professional conduct, Accounts Rules, or guidance for Reporting Accountants:

1. A pattern of unjustified withdrawals from client account (placed against different client ledgers) for small amounts, mostly pence. The total amount withdrawn adds up to £20.00.
2. A very small firm with a number of aged client balances, mostly small, but a few large, totalling £8,000.
3. A 'miscellaneous' client ledger operated by a firm which is in debit by £20,000.

Also consider:

- What else might be going on 'underneath the waves'?
- If you don't consider the issue in question reportable, what would be?
- What could these scenarios mask, either now or later?

What guidance would you look at to decide whether the above was reportable? Would you check with the COLP in each case to see whether there was an explanation?

Write an explanation of your justification for your decision regarding reporting on each matter, with reference to rules or guidance and your own professional opinion.

The reasonable man

When considering reporting serious breaches, we might take the role of the reasonable man. How much would the reasonable man be prepared to part with before he would report it to a relevant authority? Asking this question can sometimes help us put into perspective managing a client account which, with its list of numbers, can be a dehumanising experience. We do not always recognise the person behind those entries.

Other matters may be an issue for debate. We have seen earlier in the book that there could be debates about different decisions of law firm management and whether they would require regulatory action. Asking the fictional man on the bus, again, helps us to understand that wider society has a view on the professionalism of solicitors, which can sometimes extend into that solicitor's personal life.

The courses take the view of the peers of the solicitor, primarily because these are often potential disciplinary matters and matters of specialist discussion. It might be quite complex to discuss the detail of some breaches with the fictional reasonable man, even though we can bear him in mind. The peers of a solicitor may find the challenge of deciding on the fate of their fictional colleague or professional difficult to do, as it brings the situation home to them. The course sometimes demonstrates, however, that solicitors can make the ethical decisions in a room with other delegates on a training course, but struggle with those same decisions when they know the people in question.

The writer has met people who feel confident about decision making in a neutral context, but have difficulty in their role making similar choices – often because they know the people involved, or are worried about the consequences of the decision, or because the scenario was one that no-one could have foreseen and therefore they were unprepared. We can transfer this experience across to serious breach and COLP and COFA decisions.

In all of this we have to ask, as well, whether the COLP or COFA (or even other staff members who have to report) can be reasonable themselves. The COLP or COFA (and those other staff members) have to report and, if they do not, they can be prosecuted. How does the position of the COLP or COFA affect their reasonableness overall?

To test COLP and COFA reasonableness, we could ask the fictional man on the bus to be in charge of our compliance and then provide him with a difficult scenario in which he has to report his own colleagues. The man on the bus might be quite stressed and concerned. There can be an issue with expecting a great deal from a COLP or COFA in their reporting and line management role. There may be a few people we know who can carry off such a role in all aspects of its expected clout, decisiveness, and oversight, but possibly not one such person in every law firm in the country. There will doubtless be interpretations of the COLP and COFA role, and so there should be to meet the variety of needs the different law firms have, but the weight of expectation on such a person is significant. They are expected to remain calm and make complex and difficult decisions in possibly extreme circumstances. We might say those decisions could be incorrect sometimes, due to the stress and pressure of the situation.

Turning a blind eye/dishonesty

However, in all of our discussions about the reasonable man, we must not forget that individual solicitors (or whole groups of law firm management) must not turn a blind eye, or be dishonest in their approach. We might make the assumption that solicitors and COLPs and COFAs have a good level of awareness of their circumstances, their law firm operation, and some expertise which has led them to their particular appointment. We might go on to assume that it becomes more difficult to unknowingly 'turn a blind eye'.

The writer has seen a number of cases where it was alleged solicitors have turned a blind eye to the activities of their partner(s). In each case, either:

(a) the original breach and the main perpetrator were prosecuted; or

(b) the original breach and the main perpetrator were prosecuted *and* the partner(s) were prosecuted as well, due to turning a blind eye.

The prosecutions were before the Solicitors Disciplinary Tribunal, and almost all were Accounts Rules breaches of significance or potential significance. We might ask why the partners were not prosecuted in some cases, but perhaps another question needs to be asked instead: 'Could the partners have prevented the prosecution at (a) or (b) either completely or in part, had they taken steps to *counteract* the actions of the partner who had gone astray?'.

Sometimes, when discussing whether or not to make a report, and the potential consequences, we can lose sight of the consequences if we do not take action or make a report. You can clearly consider the potential consequences of failing to take any action, or make a report at all, by using the Scenarios in Part 8 of this book. At times, the consequences could be highly damaging for legal services.

We also briefly mention *Twinsectra v Yardley* later in this section which deals with a step further on and third party assistance in breach of trust, where turning a blind eye and dishonesty were also a consideration.

Integrity and dishonesty

Issues of integrity and dishonesty are issues which are measured by the regulator against a legal standard. The approach of the regulator and the SDT might be considered unusual, in that some aspects come from case law, and others come from the regulator's rules. It is a specialist Tribunal, as we have said elsewhere in the book. The SRA will take the same approach to its internal decision making.

We can see the overlap between those regulatory rules and caselaw in the overarching principles. There are separate overarching principles for honesty and for integrity.

The regulator will measure the legal tests for dishonesty in their decision making for:

- intervention; and
- prosecution of breaches of the Codes of Conduct which involve dishonesty; these might include deliberate breaches of the Accounts Rules, for example.

There are a number of other discrete rules within the Codes for Conduct and elsewhere which may be breaches of integrity, where the regulator will also take account of the tests at law. These include rules for:

- taking unfair advantage and misleading (1.2 and 1.4 in the Code of Conduct for Individuals);
- provisions for seeking to influence the content of evidence, other matters in the dispute resolution section which focus on providing proper evidence and information to the court (Part 2 of the Code of Conduct for Individuals); and

- referrals and introductions (Part 5 of the Code of Conduct for Individuals), part of which focuses on providing full information to clients about the structure of your business and how services are provided (including whether regulated or not).

Of course, this is not a full analysis of where integrity spans the rules. There are a number of provisions across the Code of Conduct for Firms and the Code of Conduct for Individuals which have 'integrity' as an implicit focus. Any aspect of the rules which focuses on not providing full information, or in some way manipulating a position to provide incorrect information or taking unfair advantage, can be seen as a lack of integrity. You may also find the regulator is willing to prosecute a lack of integrity on expected standards of behaviour, including those expected by firms and wider society. They have, for example, published guidance on the use of social media.

The SRA's tests for integrity are set out in two cases, which were heard together (*SRA v Wingate* and *SRA v Malin*). In these cases, a number of examples were put forward of cases which the SRA (and previously The Law Society) had prosecuted, which provided examples of breaches of integrity. The judgment describes integrity (to the writer's view) as both a fullness and correctness of approach; upright in its application and adherence to the rules. Whilst the judgment describes a number of applications of the rules, with reference to cases heard before the courts, it must be remembered that these are cases so serious they have reached this stage.

The regulator deals with many more cases (thousands) every year which do not appear before the courts, and which reflect a far broader spectrum of reporting and implementation of compliance. Integrity may be said to span the rules and it is true that most rules can be broken with an element of dishonesty or lack of integrity if you try! However, some of the rules are not to be read in that way; they are to be read as, for example, straightforward requirements to implement business systems to manage risk. Breaching this rule could be done in a serious way without any lack of integrity, it could be a catastrophic error or misjudgement.

We might then say the cases discussed above and in the judgement of *Malin* and *Wingate* are reflective of the *legal professional* element of the rules of professional conduct, rather than the wider professionalism we might expect of business persons, and make a distinction between the two. This can be, returning to the idea discussed in Part 1 of this book, about professionalism and what it means to you.

Dishonesty

This book is not about *the tests for* dishonesty, and readers will no doubt appreciate that an entire book could be dedicated to the subject of the tests and the change from *Ghosh*. However, for the sake of completeness, and to underline the point, the SRA will, in cases of alleged dishonesty, consider the up-to-date test for dishonesty. The writer also acknowledges the two-stage test from *Ivey*.

In this sense, we are applying a test which looks firstly at the subject's (not yet defendant, if they are under a COLP or COFA investigation, for example) knowledge or belief regarding the situation, and secondly, the standards of ordinary people regarding that situation. In both of those cases, we would be considering dishonesty.

However, the SRA does not ask COLPs and COFAs to consider dishonesty in itself as part of the criteria for reporting. COLPs and COFAs can find it helpful to consider, but equally may find it adds to the list of regulatory criteria to manage when dealing with the situation.

Ethical considerations

The requirement to report is also reflective of an ethical position which might be something for the individual solicitor to consider personally. It may be something for a partnership to consider together, or for a firm to take a position in respect of. The issue of integrity is discussed further below, but there are elements of:

- societal expectation of individual behaviour;
- personal ethical standpoints, including personal cultural or religious views;
- maintenance of standards within your own profession;
- maintenance of standards expressed as leadership, collective voice, and collective responsibility;
- maintenance of professional voice and honesty or integrity, either as an individual or collectively. This professional voice may be distinct from a personal voice or used as an expression of many years of professional practice;
- expectations of others (non-professionals or members of other professions) towards professional persons; and
- community or local leadership.

Additionally, some standards of behaviour or personal ethical viewpoints seek to explore what might be the reality of a situation, rather than how it is presented. At its extreme end, this is the exploration of possible fraud (presenting something as that which it is not); but, at a lesser juncture, it may be presenting the position in a way which might be professionally acceptable, but where there is another angle or possible interest which is undisclosed.

EXERCISE: INTEGRITY

This exercise is designed to allow us to think about the concept of integrity and the definition of it.

Step 1

Have a think about your role as a solicitor. Try to draw the component parts on a piece of paper. You could draw a circle and use it as a pie chart to show the different aspects of your role, or represent it in any way you choose.

Step 2

Now look at the list under 'Ethical Considerations', have you encompassed any of that list, such as 'maintaining professional standards', or 'community or local leadership'? Do you think they form part of your role, or should we have a separate circle for expectations of a solicitor? Can you draw that circle and label it with your views?

Step 3

Do you now think we have every aspect of a solicitor role? If there's more you can think of, add it in, with separate circles if you need to. Don't worry if you're not sure, you can keep these diagrams and add to them at any point in the future.

Integrity in one definition means 'completeness'. If you would like, you can compare your drawing to the rules of professional conduct; where does a breach of the rules take away from your role as a solicitor?

EXERCISE: INTEGRITY

Mr Arrow, a fictional solicitor, is working with a local holiday company that operates in England and Wales. The holiday company manages buy-to-let properties by the seaside for their owners, who often own two properties. However, the holiday company is inundated with requests and cannot meet demand. The holiday company comes up with a new plan; it decides to contact all homeowners in the local area and offer them two weeks in a caravan in another part of the country, in return for letting out their property for the same time period.

Many of the local population who live there are elderly.

The holiday company enlists the help of Mr Arrow to write to the residents. It asks Mr Arrow to send a solicitor's letter to all the local residents asking them to vacate their homes for two weeks this year and provide the keys to the holiday company. The residents are to be informed they will be provided with keys to a caravan in another part of the country for this period.

The holiday company offers to pay Mr Arrow a share of the profits in addition to a fee for the letter. Mr Arrow agrees to the scheme.

Mr Arrow writes the letter to the residents. The residents' association is given the letter by a local resident and hears from several other concerned residents. The association complains to the regulator that the letter has worried some of the residents and the local population should be left in peace. The residents are advised by the association not to contact the solicitor or the holiday company and the scheme is abandoned.

Do you think Mr Arrow has breached the rules of professional conduct? If so, which rules, and why? Does Mr Arrow's conduct breach the overarching principle to behave with integrity?

Dishonesty and reporting

It may be fair to say that those who are dishonest, particularly those who are deliberately so, are not likely to report their actions to the regulator. Unfortunately, there are interventions by the SRA into practices that have breached the Accounts Rules, by making unauthorised transfers from the client account to their own personal accounts, or by using the client account inappropriately. In some cases, solicitors have run off with the client account.

Deliberate scams, false accounting practices, fraudulent files or parts of files, and issues such as deliberate tax evasion, are all possible in the hands of a dishonest solicitor. Having access to a client account can also be a major temptation for some practitioners, particularly when it is in one person's hands alone.

There is little motivation for those who are dishonest to come forward. The consequences for a solicitor self-reporting a serious breach involving serious dishonesty involve possible intervention and being struck off the roll, along with the costs consequences of those actions.

For some, the guilt becomes too much, and they do make a self-report. While it can sometimes seem that ethics, compliance and professional practice are too much, and solicitors often complain about the burden, there is an expectation of the profession to behave in an upstanding and honest way. Many solicitors are proud to do so, and value their professionalism highly.

Imagine the situation where you have done something wrong; the guilt for the betrayal of staff and partners can overwhelm some practitioners. Some who have been dishonest do write to the regulator and, for some, the relief of intervention when the burden is too much (whether dishonesty is involved or not) is apparent.

For others, it is too difficult to hide what they have done. Over time, maintaining the appearance of matters remaining the same is too complex; even a small error can lead to discovery, and often does. Regular audits, staff vigilance, and promoting ethical behaviour, can make a difference.

EXERCISE 1

Ethics – Past, Present and Future

You can have a think about this exercise yourself, or with your team.

Have a think about your own professional training. When did you learn about or study solicitor professional conduct or legal ethics? What was the content? Revisit some of the content:

1. Can you remember any points you have taken on board during your career?
2. Can you see the difference in legal ethics and regulation or professional conduct?
3. If you have any background in medical legal ethics, family law, or personal injury, how does the ethical emphasis differ?
4. What is the ethical emphasis in your area of law, and how does this inform your professional conduct or approach to professional ethics?
5. What changes to the rules of professional conduct would you like to see in the future and why?

EXERCISE 2

Dishonesty

You can have a think about this exercise yourself, or with your team.

In each scenario, consider whether the solicitor has:

1. been dishonest; or
2. committed a serious breach.

Scenario 1

Hildred is a solicitor practising on her own account. She writes to a client to inform them she is going to purchase an insurance policy for them. Hildred is unwell shortly after the letter is sent. She is away from work and, when she returns to work, she forgets to purchase the insurance.

Scenario 2

Hildred is a solicitor practising on her own account. She writes to a client to inform them she is going to purchase an insurance policy for them. Hildred is unwell shortly after the letter is sent. She is away from work and, when she returns to work, she forgets to purchase the insurance.

Hildred's secretary charges the client for the policy based on the letter. Hildred is unaware.

Scenario 3

Hildred is a solicitor practising on her own account. She writes to a client to inform them she is going to purchase an insurance policy for them. Hildred is unwell shortly after the letter is sent. She is away from work and, when she returns to work, she forgets to purchase the insurance. Hildred realises she has forgotten to purchase the insurance two weeks later but decides not to purchase it after all. She still bills the client for the cost of the policy, and says nothing further to the client (who still believes she has purchased it). Hildred does not particularly care either way whether the client is out of pocket or disadvantaged by her actions.

Scenario 3

Hildred is a solicitor practising on her own account. She writes to a client to inform them she is going to purchase an insurance policy for them. Hildred is unwell shortly after the letter is sent. She is away from work and, when she returns to work, she deliberately does not purchase the insurance. She informs the client by letter that she has purchased the policy when she has not, and charges the client.

Section 43

The SRA has the power to prevent any non-solicitor from working in the solicitor profession as a result of the Solicitors Act 1974, s 43. The power applies not only to direct employees, and those supervised by the solicitor, but also to consultants.

The power is absolute, and career-ending for paralegals, trainee solicitors or those working in the profession and looking to gain experience prior to qualification. The difficulty in working at this level is, of course, that individuals just starting out in legal services, perhaps straight from school, have no training or education in solicitor professional conduct and are largely reliant on the firm to model behaviours, provide information about the rules of professional conduct, and make clear the potential consequences of breaches.

The power can equally be used against those in senior positions; this might be in ABS investment positions, or positions of in senior management. Now ABS are permitted, there is far greater opportunity for management or senior individuals within firms to be prosecuted under section 43. The result is the same as above, being unable to work for a solicitor or in a solicitor practice. Of course, as we have seen, management within firms are also prosecutable under the Firm code and are jointly and severally liable.

The power is only used in very serious circumstances, such as dishonesty, or criminal convictions, but it remains important to report serious breaches in relation to anyone in the firm, including unadmitted staff.

Of course, the position could apply to unregulated practices and those working for solicitors within them. Those hiring solicitors within unregulated practices are advised to note the position and the position of the staff.

SECTION 43 – INFORMATION FOR STAFF

The consequences of breaching the rules of professional conduct for unadmitted staff are so severe, firms might be well advised to consider some form of training in the rules of conduct for their unadmitted staff.

Formal training might be necessary, or you could make information available to staff on your intranet, in your office manual, or as part of team meetings. Raising awareness of the rules can start staff on a professional career they perhaps didn't know was open to them, or simply encourage compliance. Raising awareness of the rules can also prevent unintentional breaches.

The purpose of this exercise is not to alarm your staff, but instead to place the emphasis on compliance with the rules of professional conduct overall.

Prosecution for failure to report

There have been a few prosecutions for failure to report to the regulator, but this small section covers the writer's experience.

Generally speaking, the regulators perhaps have a stronger belief in the co-working (alongside the regulator) of the businesses they regulate than the businesses themselves do. It can be easy for the regulator to become isolated from the businesses they regulate and fail to understand their motivations, and the difficulties the regulations cause in practice.

Relatively low levels of interaction with the regulator, and low levels of interaction with consultations, can exacerbate that position. It leaves the regulator in a position where they implement rules and regulations without a clear understanding of how these will be implemented in practice. Law firms often have pre-existing practices with policies and procedure developed around previous Codes of Conduct, and do not wish to change those ways of working. Of course, making changes risks serious breaches as staff, practised in the old ways, make mistakes as they learn new ways. Continuous changes are situations many find frustrating, as established businesses have to spend a large amount of money in implementing new requirements.

The writer has seen failure to report prosecuted and not prosecuted, albeit these differences occurred some time apart and under different Codes. The difficulty is, in some situations, the cliff edge faced by the practitioner who will stand to lose so much by reporting themselves. The writer may like to see a safety net for those who report themselves to the regulator and, in some situations – perhaps where dishonest intent and motivation (or lack of integrity) are not present – support for practitioners.

Clear policy on the extent of continuous change to the regulations, and on the support and safety nets available to practitioners, in all circumstances of reporting would be very welcome. It would also support those who, for example, are forced to work into retirement, who are incapacitated during practice, or become otherwise unwell and cannot continue. There are many situations where the regulator is involved, where more formal support systems would assist.

Managing investigations

This book discusses the position relating to managing SRA investigations, which is quite different to other investigations, such as, for example, a criminal investigation or a human resources investigation. There can be an overlap; some serious breaches are so serious as to amount to a criminal offence, and a serious breach within a firm may also amount to a human resources or disciplinary issue for a firm to deal with directly. We focus here on the disciplinary matter, but you may need to report the matter to the police or take action within your own firm.

The COLP and COFA roles are roles which deal with compliance, but there can be an assumption that they would undertake the role of investigation manager, or that they would deal directly with the SRA on behalf of the firm. You may wish to appoint an investigation manager in the event of an SRA investigation or ask another person to communicate with the SRA during the investigation.

Of course, the COLP or COFA may be best placed to deal with such issues, but considering the skills needed in the investigation is important. You may find there is a different skill set needed to run and manage an investigation, which is more robust than the skillset required to understand regulatory compliance, and develop, maintain and communicate policies and procedures.

For an investigation you may need:

- an independent view;
- an understanding of the position of the employee and employer as an issue of employment law or on a contractual basis;
- interviewing skills;

- forensic analysis skills, including potentially forensic accountancy;
- tact, diplomacy, and experience in using these skills in an investigation;
- a calm, methodical, and level-headed approach;
- seniority and credibility with a range of internal and external partners;
- detailed knowledge of the law in anti-money laundering;
- detailed knowledge of the rules of professional conduct and their application; and
- detailed knowledge of the area of law in question.

Alongside all of this you may need a full understanding of the SRA's powers, policies, and procedures, as well as an understanding of the same at the Solicitors Disciplinary Tribunal. You may need to take external legal advice to manage this final step, and we have covered the sources of information and advice available. For some, media advice may be necessary, and there are specialist agencies offering the same.

You may find that the above is not available in one person, but a number of persons need to be involved to make decisions and guide the firm and staff.

Having an independent view might be important, and firms sometimes bring in external partners to assist with the development. However, ensuring control remains with the management structure of the firm is essential. Some of the investigation structure and planning should also be intended to wrest control of firm operations and decision making *with* the firm, *while isolating the incident in question*. There is no substitute for effective leadership and decision making when recovering from an incident, and making a distinction between the incident and the ongoing position of the firm can be helpful. Planning your investigation and response, with reference to the skills of your team and any external partners, can help you take control of any issues immediately, demonstrate effective management and protect the interests of the business and staff.

Investigation Response

You may wish to consider:

- isolating the incident(s);
- how to ensure business as usual;
- planning communications with staff members;
- planning external communications if necessary;
- whether any AML or other investigation would need to be opened and, if so, the resultant impacts (for example, tipping off);
- investigative timeframes;
- internal investigative skills and capacity;
- insurance;
- long-term management of any ongoing issues, such as any longer-term investigation;

- pastoral support for staff affected (see below); and
- retaining records of your processes and decision making, to aid with any queries, questions or support in the future.

External support with any of the issues above can be helpful.

An investigation itself might be composed of:

Stage 1

Understanding the report

We need to understand the report that has been made, any facts, any evidence, and the basis for the concern.

You might ask questions such as: What matter has come to light? What do we know about it? Who has made the report and what can we ascertain from them? Is there any evidence? Why was the alleged action wrong? How certain is the report?

You may be able to obtain some evidence from the person making the report or ascertain where any evidence is.

It is also helpful to maintain written records of your investigations, including discussions with key persons. You may need to explain your investigation, and the consequences, to others.

It can be helpful to have a solicitor or barrister involved at this stage to provide independent advice. This could also be someone from the firm who is not otherwise involved.

The process below assumes the firm does not have insurance which covers a possible breach and consequent representation. If it did, the steps would need to be altered to cover the need to involve the insurer and the impact on decision making accordingly.

Stage 1A

Breach assessment

Consider the position and assess:

- Has there been a breach? If the answer is no, we may not need to take further action, unless it was a disciplinary or other actionable matter for the business.
- Is it a serious breach? Similarly, if the answer is no, we may not need to take further action, unless it was a disciplinary or other actionable matter for the business.

You may be able to close the matter at this stage.

Stage 1B

Evidential assessment

Consider your evidence and the tests for reporting:

- Do you have a reasonable belief?

- What evidence are you holding at this stage?
- Are there any inconsistencies in the evidence? How do you feel about the evidence?
- Consider the SDT standard of the balance of probabilities: 'what is more likely than not'.

Again, following this test you may be able to close the matter if the evidential test is not met, and the issue is not otherwise actionable within the firm.

Do note the evidential test for reporting money laundering is different, and you may need to weigh up whether a different regulatory report is necessary. This is covered below in 'other considerations'.

Do be careful with closure on evidential assessment and note that the SRA may still wish to receive a report of a matter if it should conduct its own investigation, noting that it may be able to obtain evidence from a variety of sources.

Stage 2

Investigating the report

This next stage goes beyond obtaining the initial facts, evidence, and speaking to the person who made the report.

Consider the position carefully before doing so. Do you need to speak to the police, involve HR or involve the SRA? Consider the law on anti-money laundering and tipping off. The firm may need legal advice concerning their position.

You can then formally discuss the matter with the person concerned. You may need to provide warnings concerning the SRA or HR consequences and in relation to the rules of professional conduct. Ensure you keep written records of your meetings.

Your staff member concerned may need to be accompanied by a representative, and do ensure you have considered their position.

This book does not provide advice on the HR or employment law consequences of this investigation process. Ensure you follow your own internal procedures and take advice where necessary.

Stage 3

Consideration

You may need to repeat aspects of the previous stages until you are satisfied you have the right outcome. If you do think it is serious, and you are involved in an investigation at stage 1 or stage 2 that you think the SRA would also wish to investigate or should be aware of, you may also have grounds for reporting to the SRA. Do also note the requirements to report for money laundering if necessary and other regulatory reporting requirements.

At this point, and at every stage of the reporting process, it is important to be pragmatic in your decision making. That is not to encourage turning a blind eye or doing something unethical, but it is about bringing common sense to the process and asking whether it is a matter that needs reporting or requires investigation.

Be careful of taking massive leaps and making assumptions; connecting two dots or considering whether a situation is likely to be something more underhand or sinister is reasonable, but try to keep a level and firm head about this consideration. Very often, reports are made because assumptions have been made by the parties, and the regulator has to take a step back and ask whether a prosecution or even investigation is possible or justifiable due to the lack of evidence. It can help to practise your decision making by asking what evidence you have or would need to form a view, and consider the position carefully before making a report.

You may at this stage also take a moment to pause and consider the situation. Be aware that, as soon as you have reported a matter, the situation flips back the other way, and the firm or individual could be under investigation and could result in prosecution. At this point, and at Stage 4 below, it can be important to take legal advice to safeguard the overall position of the firm and the individuals involved.

There are no provisions within the regulations for reporting another in bad faith, as there are in AML. The writer has seen a few such cases where it has been alleged, and in each case it was fairly evident that is what had occurred. This is another reason the writer advises individuals to obtain legal advice.

Stage 4

Mitigation

Stage 4 may need to be conducted at the same time as some of the other stages. Consider whether, as a firm, you can put the breach right, and whether this is the right outcome rather than a report, or as well as a report. We have used the example of the undertaking elsewhere. If there is alleged to be a serious breach because of a breach of undertaking, can the firm comply and therefore relieve the breach? This may be true if the undertaking was not time-specific and the firm or individual solicitor simply needs to comply. There may be other examples of mitigation which do not resolve or absolve the seriousness of the breach, but can go a long way to rectifying the impact, or even show insight into the situation.

Stage 5

Reporting or other outcome

You may need to make a formal decision regarding the outcome of the matter, including whether to report to the SRA. As matters of SRA professional conduct, the COLP or COFA may have formal authority to make this decision, but the decision-making structure of the firm may be the most appropriate forum, given the serious consequences. You may also need to involve others to take account of any AML or law enforcement, data protection, financial, and HR or management decision making, amongst other considerations.

The firm may need legal advice concerning reporting and, as we have said at Stage 3, decisions should be not only pragmatic but also practical. Legal advice can help you safeguard the position of the firm and the individual (separately if necessary) and assist you forming the right approach to the situation.

Once a decision has been made about reporting, the report should be made to the regulator. It can help to set out the full circumstances of what has happened.

Stage 6

Legal advice or other representation

If a matter has been reported to the regulator, it can be helpful to consider legal advice or other representation, for the firm, and possibly separate advice for the individuals concerned. You may wish to make a contingency plan for such a situation in case it arises, with arrangements with individuals who can support, or telephone numbers of firms who offer such advice. Your insurer may also be able to assist, particularly if your insurance covers any part of the process.

Further information about the SRA investigations process is provided in the 'Regulatory Investigations' section of this Part of the book.

Other considerations

Is a regulatory response the right one?

You may wish to consider whether the matter is actually a police matter, or would be better suited to another regulatory reporting avenue, such as reporting to the Information Commissioner's Office, insurance (in cases of possible negligence), or even the National Crime Agency in cases of suspected money laundering. In some cases, the SRA is not the appropriate authority at all.

An example might be a suspected cyber-attack on a firm, which was unsuccessful. You might decide to report that matter to the police, but decide it was not necessary to report it to the regulator as no information was stolen.

The evidential tests for reporting money laundering are different, and do bear that in mind. Of course, there is a separate reporting process, test, and responsible individuals for that situation.

Employee and Management Response

This analysis deals with the regulatory response of the firm, and how to manage that stage. It does not deal with what can often be a simultaneous HR, employee, and management approach. You may need to consider:

1. The appropriate employee response in respect of anyone involved in a serious breach, including, for example, whether it was a mistake (which does not warrant further action) all the way through to deliberate misappropriation (which does warrant further action).
2. The appropriate internal communications response about any situation and how this should be dealt with by staff. For example, do you expect staff to take any steps? Will another member of staff have to manage anything or step in?
3. The management response, and this can be management steps to deal with any situation as it arises, through, for example, a specially convened management committee, or invoking a contingency plan to deal with the management steps required.

In each of these cases, it can help to have a plan in place to deal with the situation, or an outline of the steps you would take, and who will make decisions.

If you do need to report this matter to the regulator, it can be helpful to include these details in your report, as it shows that the firm is proactively responding and managing the situation.

Learning lessons

If any of these scenarios occur, take the time to learn from them and communicate what you can through the firm. It might be management learning, or it might be something you can share with the firm as a whole. It may even be personal learning for those involved, from an employee who, for example, made a mistake, to the COLP or COFA who resolved the situation. It may be after some time has passed, but take the time to reflect on the situation. Such reflection is, of course, helpful for the regulator to see if you make a report, but is also genuinely helpful for those involved.

Investigation response

The points earlier in this section can also be helpful to consider during the stages of the investigation.

EXERCISE: INCIDENT PLANNING

Consider the following scenario:

You have uncovered an unauthorised transfer from client account to the personal bank account of a mid-level associate solicitor employed in your firm. Your COFA found the transfer on a file review. The file was selected following unusual accounts activity, including unusual transfers from client account.

Plan your investigation response:

- What do you need to investigate? Consider whether to investigate this incident and any others. What are you looking for?
- What policies and procedures would you usually expect to be in place and what would you usually expect to happen?
- Who would investigate in your firm? Consider the experience and skills of your team.
- How would your management team deal with the situation?
- How would you deal with any:
  (a) employee response (including both the individual and wider staff); and
  (b) regulatory response.

You could use the above scenario to develop your response into an incident response plan or policy for your firm.

Pastoral support; thoughts and feelings

Often those involved in investigations, or who are involved in a situation where there may be a serious breach, need pastoral support. This may not just be the persons directly involved in an investigation, but could be others within a firm as well. Even those charged with managing the investigation may need additional emotional support.

The needs of the business, weight of expectation of colleagues, and worry about the consequences for the firm and individuals within it, can be difficult for anyone to manage alone. Pastoral support is available from LawCare, and organisations may consider signposting staff to this and other support services to discuss their worries.

Alternatively, firms can bring in outside counsellors or management coaches to work with them in delivery of their roles. Recognising the stress that making decisions such as this can have on management decision making is important.

If you are in a situation where a member of staff is under investigation for a breach of the rules, but you are defending or assisting that member of staff, do be aware of the stress and personal consequences for them and consider how best the firm can support them in this situation. Again, the solution may be support in the workplace or counselling or coaching.

Improving compliance following a breach – the importance of leadership

The question might be whether to improve compliance or not. From many years of experience, the message might be not to throw the baby out with the bathwater. Even if you have experienced a serious breach, there is likely to be much good in your existing compliance, and plenty to be proud of in your firm. None of us are perfect and mistakes do happen.

We have already discussed how to isolate an incident, take legal advice, and implement investigation and investigation management. It can be useful to reflect on your approach in the area concerned, to demonstrate effective management and leadership in the future.

Leadership can be an important quality in helping the firm and staff recover. If the breach is serious, taking control should be the preserve of the Senior Partner, Chief Executive, or Management Team. The COLP or COFA may also be suitable, provided they are senior enough. The steps taken should be visible, prompt, and direct. For example, if procedures have been circumvented then close the gaps and train the staff. This can also be useful as a direct short-term fix. Decisive, positive, immediate action, confirmation of the firm's position, and the visible backing of the most senior staff can work wonders for the mood of staff and direction of the position thereafter.

Even if the firm is being prosecuted, then again taking a grounded approach, and confidently managing the investigation with external help as necessary, can be the same. Don't be afraid to take decisive action and be visible in your approach.

Actions like this will speak volumes about the importance of compliance in the organisation, particularly when delivered alongside positive ethical messages and the value the organisation places on the compliance efforts of staff who work hard to deliver an effective service for staff.

EXERCISE: LEADERSHIP

This exercise is for management to consider.

Consider leadership following an incident that needed reporting. This might be leadership in the months and even years following a report.

Consider with your management team which senior persons will take charge of the communications, internally and externally? How will you confidently communicate a vision of the outcome of this matter, or inform the staff of what you are doing?

Discuss with your senior management team:

- What is the difference between leadership and management?
- How will the firm reflect that in long term incident responses?

Whistleblowing

Whistleblowing is a complicated area of law. Blowing the whistle means to speak out about issues with or affecting the workplace which could break the law or put other people in danger. When we say 'speaking out', this does not have to involve the press or other public forum; the point is to raise the issue with a suitable authority. In the first instance, this might be internally at your workplace; and secondly, if you are not heard, this might be to a prescribed organisation. There are lists of 'prescribed organisations', which are mostly government departments or government-associated regulators.

The reason for the complexity in whistleblowing is also apparent, whistleblowing *could* provide a defence against many prosecutable actions if the defendant was able to make a whistleblowing disclosure. That was not the point of the legislation; the point was to ensure a means for workers and others to speak out about malpractice in the workplace. Whistleblowers are entitled to some form of workplace protection.

The test for a matter to qualify as whistleblowing is for it to meet a public interest test. Has the matter been disclosed in the public interest (for example, to save lives), and has that disclosure been made in good faith? If the first limb fails, the entire claim fails. The second limb of the test is whether it qualifies as a protected disclosure, and there are categories of protected disclosure covered in the Public Interest Disclosure Act 1998, s 1, and the Employment Rights Act 1996, s 43. Both are amended as a result of the Enterprise and Regulatory Reform Act 2013.

Categories of disclosure which are covered in the second limb include (but are not limited to):

- criminal offences;
- health and safety issues;

- miscarriages of justice; and
- environmental damage.

The relevant legislation is:

- Public Interest Disclosure Act 1998, which lays the foundation for the current whistleblowing structures;
- Enterprise and Regulatory Reform Act 2013, which adds to and amends the Public Interest Disclosure Act 1998; and
- Employment Rights Act 1996 (as amended by the Public Interest Disclosure Act 1998), which provides the right to an employment tribunal claim for those who have blown the whistle – compensation can be reduced if tribunal claims are not made for the right reasons.

Readers may want to refer to the Department for Business, Energy and Industrial Strategy for an interpretation of the legislative position on their website.

How does this all relate to serious breach? The question could be raised whether serious breach could be an issue of whistleblowing. It should be noted that whistleblowing comes within the scope of the Employment Rights Act 1996 (by virtue of the other Acts above), and is an issue of employment law. Whistleblowing should not be confused with a grievance.

If we compare whistleblowing with serious breach reporting, we can see a number of differences. The first is the difference in reporting requirements. We must consider the reporting requirements for whistleblowing separately to those for serious breach. We can see an overlap in a small number of the issues raised by the relevant provisions, including the second limb issues of criminal offences, and miscarriages of justice, which could be serious breaches if involving a solicitor. However, the public interest test must firstly apply before the second limb is considered; is the person reporting the concern in good faith and in the public interest?

The question of whether the report to the COLP or COFA is made in the public interest may come down to the level of concern raised by the report – for example, is the issue very serious, and would other people be affected and is the issue a wider concern rather than a personal one? If so, and a second limb is also met, it could be both whistleblowing and serious breach reporting.

However, and importantly, the vast majority of serious breaches or potentially serious breaches fail to meet the criteria for whistleblowing because:

- The disclosures are not made in the public interest – this can be because the issue is reporting an individual solicitor's actions, rather than reporting concern for others, and the report is not or would not be sufficiently dramatic in its impact. Any report for personal reasons would also not apply.
- The disclosures do not meet the second limb circumstances for protected disclosures – in that they do not fit into the categories provided, and/or they are correctable issues which could be resolved by the firm.

It is important to remember when discussing serious breach that we are discussing the conduct of an individual solicitor, or the overarching conduct of a firm at a snapshot in time. Their individual or corporate conduct, as a matter of the rules of professional conduct, is the matter being reported and discussed, which can be quite different to a public interest disclosure.

In writing the training for whistleblowing, the seriousness of the subjects also stood out with disasters such as Piper Alpha, Clapham Rail, and Zeebrugge, which would have benefited from whistleblowing disclosures.

In 2018, the Solicitors Disciplinary Tribunal considered the case of *De Vita, Platt & Scott*, a prosecution brought for breaches of the Accounts Rules, forging documents, and dishonesty. The allegations related to matters which had occurred over a number of years, and one of the defendant solicitors had, after some time, reported the matter to the SRA. The SDT noted the report, but found they could have reported earlier. The SDT used the phrase 'blowing the whistle', in respect of the report, but did not find this was a whistleblowing disclosure. It is noted that there are specific tests for whistleblowing and the SDT did not consider this case met those tests, but did expect a report from the defendant solicitors to the regulator, thus making the distinction between the two.

The intent of serious breach reporting is *not* to reflect whistleblowing legislation or criteria. As a competent regulatory authority, the SRA has established its own criteria for reporting which should be considered carefully. We can draw a comparison to reporting to the police or, in money laundering, reporting to the NCA, both of which are done separately to making a report to the regulator.

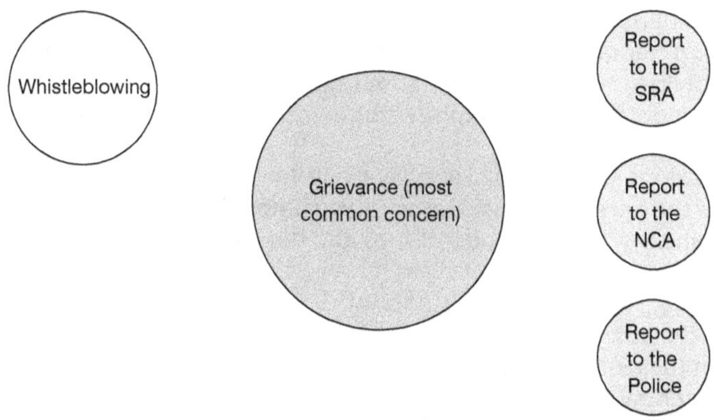

The diagram above shows the relationship of some of the issues. There is and can be a relationship between a grievance and whistleblowing, but the other reporting relationships to the police, NCA, and SRA are also in the picture, but demonstrated separately. There may be different criteria for us to consider for each issue, even if we are doing so subconsciously.

EXERCISE: WHISTLEBLOWING

Have a look at the examples of possible serious breaches in Part 8 of this book. Consider whether the examples you can see would fit into the category of whistleblowing. How many can you find which would *definitely* also be a whistleblowing disclosure, and what were the differences with the ones which were not?

Fiduciary duties

When discussing serious breach, we must consider the fiduciary duties of the solicitor to the client and the potential for privileged legal advice to exist as well. The solicitor, as well as taking instructions from the client, must act according to their relationship and their mutual understanding of the direction of the matter. The client is often not legally qualified, which means they do not understand the matter in the same way as the solicitor, and so there is an element of interpretation on the part of the solicitor when dealing with the client's matter. The solicitor also holds money on trust for the client and their fiduciary relationship dictates how this is directed.

As a result, the solicitor has an important fiduciary relationship with the client, and must take steps to ensure that is not broken. The current Standards and Regulations provide an open-ended means to deliver this solution, but previous Handbooks and particularly the Guides to Professional Conduct were excellent sources of information and advice about proper behaviour including, sometimes, in a fiduciary sense. The old guides still provide these solutions, and can be helpful sources of suggested outcomes.

The fiduciary behaviour may be completely different, however, to professional conduct in other senses. The fiduciary duty may guide the solicitor to act in one particular way and – provided that is within the rules of professional conduct – that is also acceptable. For example, if we changed the rules of professional conduct to require all undertakings to be performed within a set timescale, could protracted conveyancing transactions still go ahead without a serious breach of the rules? The solicitor is obliged to comply with those undertakings to adhere to their fiduciary duties, and might be expected to breach the rules to comply with those duties.

The undertakings in The Law Society's Code for Completion themselves do not form part of the rules of professional conduct, although they were printed alongside them for many years. Those undertakings and the conveyancing system are in their interpretation and, in holding of client monies, fiduciary duties. Some might argue the undertakings (and even the Codes of Conduct) should be formalised within legislation; that they are so central to the conveyancing system they should be protected in their interpretation and be upheld. Whether the conveyancing system, which is so central to the economy and status of individuals within British society, should be defended with more than fiduciary duty and professional conduct breach, and instead with specific sanctions, is a matter for debate.

What we are also missing is a consideration of whether a 'serious breach', as defined by the Standards and Regulations, would always be a breach of trust or breach of fiduciary duty. Readers are invited to consider the scenarios set out in Part 8 of this book. The scenarios are there for discussion and reflection of what constitutes a serious breach; but in this case, look and see whether you would say the circumstances would also constitute a breach of trust or a breach of fiduciary duty. Can we always say in each case that a serious reportable breach would also be a breach of fiduciary duty or a breach of trust? Probably not, but some would be.

A leading case in this matter, for reference, is *Twinsectra v Yardley* which may go some way to defining trusts in solicitor's hands (and the extent of assistance), including those involving third party solicitors. Readers may also be interested to note the recent case of *Dreamvar*.

COLP and COFA

We may be able to go further with the duties owed by the COLP and COFA to link their specific roles within the scope of the trust and fiduciary duties owed to the client. Given their specific role, it may be possible to extend the scope of the trust and fiduciary status to form a specific position within that for the COLP and the COFA. However, as above, we cannot completely say the COLP's and COFA's duties extend across the fiduciary duties of the firm and trust of the client account, as those duties are also held by individual solicitors and the firm as a whole.

We can say that we can gain clues and information about the intended ethical standing of the solicitor and their fiduciary role from publications such as 'A Question of Trust' and also even the Competence Statement. 'A Question of Trust' asked consumers how they felt about the different ethical outcomes with their solicitor, and also what was the most important service to them. Consumers were rightly concerned about their funds. The Competence Statement considered the means by which the individual solicitor met their proficiency, but also provided information about their intended ethical standing.

Management and compliance

The serious breach reporting requirements raise with them the issue of management of a firm and the direction a firm takes. Sometimes, we see firms prosecuted before the Tribunal where all the partners are prosecuted; are we saying in that position that the firms have failed in their management and direction? Indeed, firms can themselves be prosecuted, and even intervened as a result of systemic bad practice and poor professional conduct.

There are steps a firm can take to evidence their strong management and effective decision making. We might talk about what a 'well-run' firm looks like, with the emphasis in that phrase being placed on the management of the firm. There are steps firms can take to ensure they are compliant and are protected from prosecution should any difficulty arise.

Those steps include implementing strong governance. This does not have to place compliance at the centre of all operations, as long as legal and ethical obligations are adhered to. There can be a difficulty with compliance decision making taking over the operation of the firm itself, which, if taken to the extreme, could result in the closure of the firm due to the diversion of resources and failure to concentrate on core business.

However, this is not an excuse or, as said previously in the book, any veiled argument not to comply. Underlying the need for a commercial mindset is sound evidence that compliance, legal, and ethical positions are appropriately considered at the right level. Firms are encouraged to find a balance and a place to allow ethical expression and consideration.

Evidence which gives regulators and others confidence in management does not need to be expensive. Following the rules well, or doing your job well, can be more than sufficient. That might translate into strong financial management, with a good grasp on the finances of the firm and reconciliations. Or it might be strong organisational skills, with sound timekeeping and strong set procedures which minimise the risk in a process. Placing the client at the centre of the experience can also provide a good impression, if those other aforementioned matters are also aligned. Firms might include audit as part of their management and governance, using the feedback to inform their decisions.

However, if a firm is small or cannot afford such a team, consider how to evidence compliance issues in your management or partnership meeting to show they have been considered and acted upon appropriately. Sole Practitioners can achieve a similar effect through their training records – for example, demonstrating you keep up to date through watching webinars from the regulators or other industry bodies, and attending events. This does not have to be expensive, and sometimes this training is free.

Underlying the sound management practices should also be a respect for the statutory and regulatory roles of the COLP and COFA. Whilst not specified by the Legal Services Act 2007, these roles could be seen as forming part of the firm's duties, in that the firm appoints the individual and maintains their status. The firm also has to accept their position, authority, and the way in which they would like matters conducted. Whilst some may see the COLP and COFA roles as having duties, others may also see them as having specific privileges around decision making, oversight, and influence.

The roles can be a lot of additional work, so ensuring time is made for them can be important, particularly in a large firm. Ways for the COLP or COFA to demonstrate they ensure compliance include delivering training or considering other methods to communicate the Standards and Regulations and guidance, reviewing policies and procedures and the legal requirements on the firm, and bringing in outside advice and support where necessary. A wider role may be to consider the effective risk management of the firm and what the firm's overall profile looks like. Whether you take on particularly risky clients or work in particularly risky areas, you can make these considerations, and take appropriate steps to protect the firm and comply with the regulations and requirements.

Regardless of your management style or the size of firm, you will want to ensure you deliver a firm-wide solution to compliance. We often see allegations of failure to supervise before the Tribunal, and all firms have departments that don't always comply or where, for whatever reason (be it political – with a small or large P – or otherwise), they do not accept some or all of the compliance agenda. Negative reaction to compliance is not often discussed. There is always a part of the regulations that requires co-operation, but we can also legitimately express our own opinion.

Reaching out to different departments that do not agree can be complex, but it can help to take compliance out of a regulatory agenda. Implementing a quality mark or standard can help, as all departments have to meet its requirements and there are usually complementary provisions. Alternatively, for larger firms particularly, access to outside legal advice can also provide another voice in the process; while that can provide support and valuable input, the presence of a third party can also add another perspective to a situation.

Using an outside party such as a solicitor or consultant can help you provide a pocket within the business in which to contain issues while you resolve them. In all the reporting scenarios we discuss, involving the wider business is rarely desirable, until perhaps the end of the process when policies or procedures need to be changed or training needs to be implemented. Sometimes we need to recognise that the creation of the COLP and COFA has created an internal client base within the firm. The COLP or COFA perhaps has to be aware that individuals may come to them for advice and guidance, and they may be giving privileged legal advice, within their own firm. As solicitors, as accountants, and as company directors, COLPs and COFAs can find themselves in a conflict of interest position if the situation is serious, so planning and making provision in advance can assist.

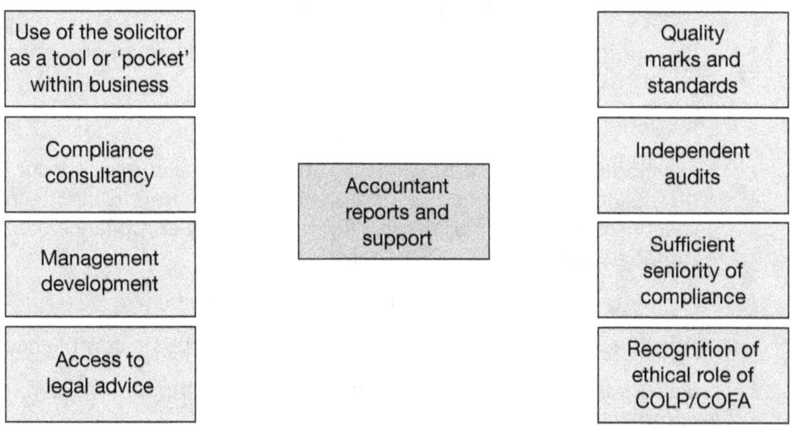

To achieve the firm-wide solution, it is also desirable to ensure the seniority of compliance and the compliance agenda. COLPs and COFAs should be senior within the business, but seniority can take many forms, including experience, age, expertise or leadership. Management development and attending to the leadership needs of the team are also important, as is CPD amongst the senior staff, and will also, as a knock-on effect, help compliance achieve the agenda it needs to. Very often, these key skills can make an enormous difference in demonstrating effective behaviours to staff and providing supportive workplaces.

There are then many opportunities to advance a compliance agenda, including in indirect ways (for example, through management development). This may help you to achieve a common ground, a firm-wide solution, or simply place your staff on similar footings with similar, commonly agreed, goalposts. Development-based solutions can also bring in new ideas, test out new solutions, and leave your staff with a legacy of possible solutions to their end goals. You may come away with your own toolkit you can use on a day-to-day basis.

Below is an excerpt from training on Serious and Material Breaches used by the writer between 2013 and 2021 (inclusive):

> 'We have seen that the SRA are providing a greater focus on governance and business management for law firms. This will only continue; law firms should expect to have to pay greater attention to the management of their business as time continues.
>
> One way to fulfil these obligations would be to use:
>
> Management systems for monitoring and auditing the business. These should also look for breaches. You might consider (amongst other things):
>
> a) Auditing against the risks you identified to the business, this might include:
>
> 1. instituting audits at different stages in the case life-cycle where there may be particular risks (for example at business acceptance, when there is a material change in the case, when large sums of money are withdrawn, on large linked files, or on aged files)
> 2. file audits of high profile work or particular fee earners where problems have been identified;
> 3. random file audits.
>
> b) Developing your compliance culture, for example through discussing compliance successes and improvements in team meetings and in appraisals, and floor walking by compliance team members and COLP / COFA to discuss issues;
>
> c) Ensuring compliance information is readily available;
>
> d) Providing regular training for all staff and new starters in compliance;
>
> e) Developing a process to learn from and improve following complaints, reports and negligence claims;

f) Ensuring your whistleblowing policy is up to date and easily accessible;

g) Ensuring a policy is in place requiring all staff to report material and non material breaches and ensuring they know how to use it;

h) Supporting staff members who raise legitimate compliance issues and reacting quickly and proportionately to those issues;

i) Putting in place an investigation procedure for breaches reported or identified, including specific arrangements for compliance staff and other important post holders;

j) Requiring staff members to take a minimum two weeks' leave every year and having someone else look after their files and conducting a random file audit;

k) Requiring partners and other senior staff to lead by example in their commitment to compliance;

l) Ensuring your compliance staff are appropriately positioned in the organisation, with clear reporting lines to senior management, and that they and the COLPs and COFAs are supported in their jobs. This will link into governance, below.

A well considered governance system for decision making and holding the business to account. Boards and committees are often victim of politics and the advancement of personal interests. Independent input into the governance process may assist, as will strong leadership. You may consider (amongst other things):

a) Using a team of internal auditors, or a member of staff to audit files. If you are a Sole Practitioner (SP) you could use another local SP.

b) Putting in place an audit committee to oversee the work of the auditors and ensure the direction and outputs are correct.

c) Putting in place a compliance committee to discuss compliance issues and to take reports from the auditors and audit committee. The compliance committee could make decisions on the material / non material breaches.

d) Using the governing body of the organisation to ensure the processes for compliance are working effectively and that those involved are held accountable, the correct policies and strategies are developed for regulation and compliance is effectively monitored and supervised.

e) Having independent input into each stage of the process. From independent auditors to non execs, independence can bring an additional check and balance into the business.

f) If you are unable to afford non execs you could use staff who have not been involved in matters previously. Ask them to genuinely challenge your decisions to see if they are robust – this is known as a point / counterpoint scenario. You may also find groups of COLP / COFAs or local law societies willing to assist.

Once you have your systems in place, you should start to identify breaches. Once a breach is reported, or identified, the appropriate officers can investigate to see if it really is a breach.

...

Reporting issues to the SRA is a serious matter and should not be taken lightly. These techniques are presented as ideas for managing your processes and increasing your confidence in identifying problems in your firm, as well as understanding your obligations to your regulator. However most governance systems also have the benefit of legal advice and this should also be a consideration before making your final decisions.'

COLP and COFA: balanced scorecard

EXERCISE: COLP, COFA, AND MLRO – THE BALANCED SCORECARD APPROACH

This exercise or management technique is suitable for COLPs and COFAs in small firms or who would like a different way of implementing their compliance leadership agenda. Try communicating your headlines to management in a balanced scorecard approach.

This example has a particular conveyancing angle, but you can change it to suit you.

Change the colour of the final column to 'red', 'amber' or 'green', dependent on your compliance position. Red signals difficulties, amber signals problems being resolved or where there could be issues, and green signals that everything is going well.

Area of Compliance	Comments	Red/Amber/Green
Management & Continuity		
Turnover		
Liquidity		
Profitability		
Structure		
Other businesses		
Capital adequacy		
Business continuity		
Staff management		
Policies & procedures		
Handling Client Money		
Client reconciliation		
Office reconciliation		
COFA file reviews		

Area of Compliance	Comments	Red/Amber/Green
Client Care		
Client care letter		
Terms of engagement		
Complaint handling		
Fee estimates		
Website / transparency		
Completion statements correct		
Monies returned to client		
Ledger correct		
Statutory & Professional Obligations		
AML risk assessment		
AML training		
Insurance intermediary		
ICO registration		
Acting on both sides		
Referral fees		
Competence statement		
Document storage		

Annex 1 – SRA Regulatory Investigation Process

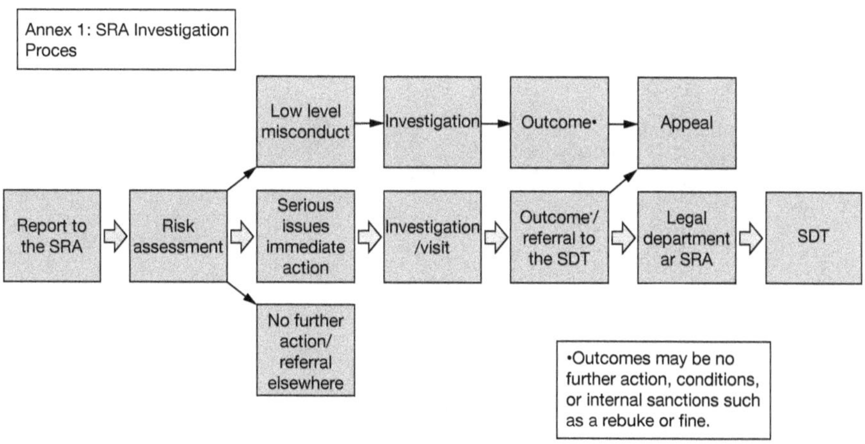

Part 6

Reporting Requirements for Accountants

Contents

Section 1: Technical content
- Statutory reporting basis for accountants
- Annual accountants' report: material breach, serious breach, and weaknesses in the firm's accounts
- Materiality
- Regulatory approach
- The move away from material breach
  - What are the effects of the changes overall?
- Requirement to obtain an accountants' report
- Requirement to send the report to the SRA
- COLP, COFA and the reporting accountant
- Conditions to obtain an accountants' report
- Challenges in the new Accounts Rules

Section 2: Discursive content
- Audits and accountants' reports
- Material breach and serious breach as issues of judgement
- The COLP perspective
  - Exercise: Mansion House
- The COFA perspective
- The management perspective
- Fiduciary duties
- Standard of proof at the Solicitors Disciplinary Tribunal (SDT)
- Internal accountancy conflicts of interest; the third view
- Sectoral accountancy conflicts of interest
- De minimis provisions
- Using an accountants' report for another purpose
- Closing gaps in the new Accounts Rules
- Third party managed accounts
- Holding client money – use of Escrow (or Third Party Managed Accounts)
- 'Client' accounts
- Example breaches register
- Annex 1– Areas of Potential Audit for Law Firms (2016–2021) (Non Accounts)

Section 1: Technical content

The SRA accountants' report is a statutory report which must be delivered by the firm to the SRA. The firm commissions the accountant to write the report, the report is delivered to the firm, and in some instances it must be sent on to the regulator. The report covers the broad basis of the Solicitors Accounts Rules, and currently discusses the firms' accountancy systems and controls and details whether or not the firm has complied. Accountants are currently asked whether there are significant breaches of the Accounts Rules and/or whether there are significant weaknesses in their systems and controls.

This is a form of serious breach reporting, but with an accountancy basis. The accountant is conducting a review of the firm's accounts in order to determine any weaknesses and whether or not the firm needs to take any further steps to comply.

The accountant must also determine whether there are any breaches of the Accounts Rules governing solicitors. The accountant must examine the client and office account and transactions to ensure the client monies have been handled correctly. This often includes examining client files, and examining the firm's case management system or IT position in order to determine the correct position for each file selected and for the firm overall.

We examine the basis of this report in this section of the book, along with the development of the report for Reporting Accountants over the last ten years. What has been a fairly static position of the accountant reporting form has changed dramatically with the introduction of outcomes-focused regulation and the greater use of the firm's professional judgement. The Reporting Accountant's forms have altered from standard tick box forms relating to the accounts, to an open-ended box for reporting with a signature space. The wording has changed and altered over the last few years, asking accountants to report, firstly, material breaches of the rules and, secondly (and currently at the time of writing), significant breaches of the rules, and significant weaknesses in the firm's systems and operations.

These changes have occurred alongside changes to the Accounts Rules themselves, with the changes to the Accounts Rules fundamentally changing the way client monies are held. We look at some of those changes briefly later in this section of the book.

Statutory reporting basis for accountants

The accountants' report is produced pursuant to the Solicitors Act 1974, s 34. The preceding sections of that Act cover the Accounts Rules which should be produced by The Law Society (now the SRA), interest due on the client monies held, and the right of the regulator to inspect the accounts.

The legislation also notes that client monies can be held on trust, which we speak about later in this Part of the book.

The requirements for the accountants' report require the accountant to provide a report to The Law Society (now the SRA), in the terms required by The Law Society, but also to report any instances of fraud to The Law Society as well. This is a specific reporting requirement and requests the accountant to make a direct report to The Law Society. The writer's experience is this does happen; accountants do make such reports.

The various iterations of the accountants' report form (which we cover below) may or may not be sufficient to include the required reporting for theft and fraud and, in the courses the writer has run for accountants, specific attention is drawn to the requirement to report these offences. In saying this, the writer notes theft and fraud are specific offences, and fraud in particular may involve more than the accounts to even form a suspicion.

There is a further requirement to report information acquired to The Law Society about whether the person concerned is suitable to hold client or other monies, and we cover that later in this section. The breadth of reporting required by the accountants' report does cover most circumstances that can come to light as a result of an accountant's usual investigations. This book argues that the circumstances outlined on the AR1 are wider than those specified in the legislation.

However, should there be further cause for concern, about the standing of the person concerned, or their activities, the Reporting Accountant can make:

- A further report to the SRA, separately to the accountants' report. Further information about regulatory investigations and regulatory reporting is contained in Part 5 of this book.
- A report at any time to the SRA; the reporting for the accountant must comply with the requirements in the report. However, is it also open to the accountant to make another report at any time, should that be required or in compliance with their duties.
- Contact with any other agency that is appropriate. This may be law enforcement or any other agency.

Accountants should also be aware that, when dealing with the requirements to report, including the requirements to report fraud, a report to the National Crime Agency may also be appropriate if the accountant has reason to know or suspect money laundering. Accountants can make a report to their money laundering reporting officer if they suspect money laundering. Their money laundering reporting officer can make a report to the National Crime Agency if appropriate. Accountants and their firms may need legal advice in such a situation concerning the relevant provisions of the Proceeds of Crime Act 2002 (notably in Part 7) and, in particular, tipping off (section 333).

Annual accountants' report: material breach, serious breach, and weaknesses in the firm's accounts

The form of the annual accountants' report has changed over the last ten years. The previous prescriptive tick box form was in place for a long time. It provided a large degree of comfort to Reporting Accountants and law firms alike because of its stability and ease of use. It prescribed the specific areas of the accounts to be reviewed and provided the means by which they would be assessed. In essence, the form directed the Reporting Accountants' activity. It allowed the Reporting Accountant to select a sample of files, along with the key documentation from the firm, such as the reconciliation, and report their findings on the same to the regulator.

Both the Accounts Rules and the form for reporting itself were highly prescriptive and detailed. Any deviation in the accounts would be marked accordingly. The Reporting Accountant was using their professional judgement in interpreting the accounts, in selecting the files, in analysing whether there were any breaches or likely to be any breaches, and in dealing professionally with their client.

The changes to the report began following the introduction of outcomes-focused regulation (OFR) in 2011 alongside the new SRA Handbook of that time. The policy intent of outcomes-focused regulation saw the introduction of a new way of working for the regulator. It brought a step change in regulatory intent, moving away from a formal and prescriptive interpretation of the rules based on strict analysis of them, and towards a more fluid operation of the regulator's position. The regulator signalled at the time that it wanted to focus squarely on the serious matters it was seeing, and work towards resolving them at an earlier stage.

This meant a far more interpretive role for the regulated community. Solicitors would be expected to interpret the rules and apply them themselves. The COLP and COFA were appointed, from statutory roles envisaged by the Legal Services Act 2007, and were there to oversee interpretation of the new, much wider Handbook.

In 2011, the SRA moved to a definition of 'material breach', alongside its agenda of OFR. The purpose of OFR was to free the solicitor profession from a prescriptive and very detailed Handbook, which had been in place since the 1970s (and even before), and grew with any instance of a breach of the rules. The Handbook and its various iterations were, are still are, useful resources of guidance for the practitioner operating in an important constitutional role. However, the profession is also a business, and a contributor to the economy of the country. In theory, the profession could not only increase its income through innovation; it could also contribute to the growth in other business areas if legal advice was more accessible.

The Accounts Rules themselves did not change with the new Handbook in 2011, but the signs of change were elsewhere within the rules. The prescriptive guidance concerning the 'professional behaviour and conduct of a solicitor' was replaced with indicative behaviours, but also a more open-ended style where non-compliance could in some limited instances be justified, if the overall outcome of the rules was met. The regulator, of course, was envisaging a more modern profession, with a more up-to-date code of professional behaviour, and the main code and associated rules had begun to reflect that.

The times had changed. The introduction of the new codes in 2011 came alongside Alternative Business Structures and the intent for the professions to move forward, perhaps in a different way. We have seen in Part 4 of this book that the change as a result of the introduction of Alternative Business Structures has not been as dramatic as we expected, and elsewhere in the book that the appetite for change comes from a continuous historical intent to change the legal services sector and that new steps will continue to be taken if change is not effected.

The changes to the Accounts Rules began separately to the changes to the main sets of rules. The SRA started with changes to the format of the accountants' report in 2015. The new form of the report took away the prescriptive list that accountants and law firms were used to and presented the form in a new format. The form had open boxes for the Reporting Accountant to complete, and allowed the accountant to express their own professional judgement about compliance or non-compliance with the rules accordingly. The wording of the form was now for the Reporting Accountant to consider, and the decision about whether to look at certain aspects of the rules was now left solely to the Reporting Accountant and their firm.

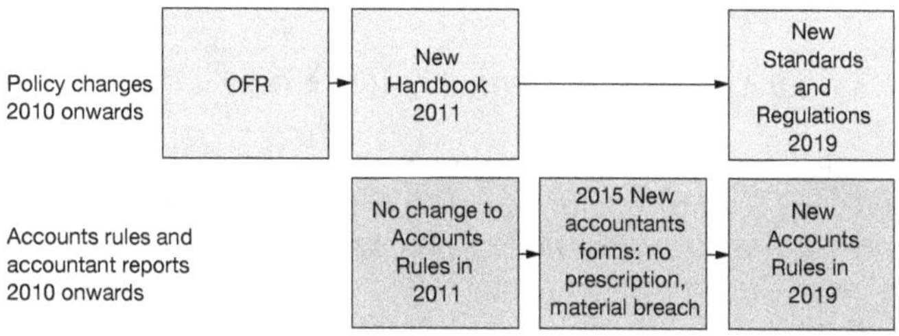

Previously, the accountant would need to consider the long list on the form and the specific rules mentioned, in order to tick off whether or not a rule was complied with. This was a very straightforward means of identifying any breaches, particularly for those at the regulator in receipt of the form.

Now the Reporting Accountant had to plan their own consideration of the position and their own development of the work. The Reporting Accountant might consider a variety of different positions in planning their work, the approach of one firm might be completely different to that of another firm, and the questions being asked were much wider. Some Reporting Accountants on the course for accountants wondered whether the accountants' report was now a general audit of the firm, looking at all of their business functions and financial stability. Others focused primarily on the Accounts Rules themselves. A very wide variety of views was expressed between Reporting Accountants. The general consensus was that different firms of accountants might reach different conclusions. The SRA issued specific guidance, but the actual coverage of the accountants' check and how they might form an overarching view was left up to the firm. Guidance and a variety of views was also expressed by other influential individuals and bodies at the time, including the ICAEW. This guidance is not produced here, but it was clear that the change for Reporting Accountants was significant.

The loss of the prescriptive form and list of rules to tick was, to the Reporting Accountants, posing the question as to whether they were to look at the rules any longer or whether they were now to consider an alternative. The Reporting Accountants on the course frequently expressed that the partners of their firm were specifying their approach to the new form according to the policy of the firm.

When the new form was introduced, a new phrase was introduced to Reporting Accountants: 'material breach'. The Reporting Accountant was being asked by the form to firstly consider the accounts of the firm and the handling of client monies in line with the Solicitors Accounts Rules 2011. Secondly, the Reporting Accountant was being asked to consider whether there were any material breaches of the Accounts Rules. If so, the Reporting Accountant was asked to specify what they were.

As well as changing the format, structure, and wording of the reporting form, the SRA was seeking to receive fewer reports in order to manage the volume of work it was receiving annually. It should be remembered that not all accountants' reports were qualified (reported a breach of note), but the SRA received all of them regardless, due to the perceived risk in holding client monies. This meant the SRA received every accountants' report produced in respect of solicitor practices across the country.

Below is an extract from training produced by the writer in 2015:

> 'The SRA are conducting further reviews and improvements of the Handbook, including a fundamental review of the Accounts Rules. This review is in three parts, with the final and most comprehensive stage due next –a complete re-write of the Accounts Rules into principles-based rules.
>
> As part of the review, a series of changes have already been made to accountants' reports with the aim of providing better value. Previously, all firms would commission accountants' reports. The SRA would receive thousands of reports every year and have to consider each one. Now the SRA have made changes to ensure they are looking at the key areas of risk, and to offer better value for firms.
>
> We can split the changes into three parts; delivery of accountants' reports, format of accountants' reports, and qualified accountants' reports. The final part covers the circumstances in which an accountants' report would be qualified, which has now changed to be similar to the "material breaches" regime.

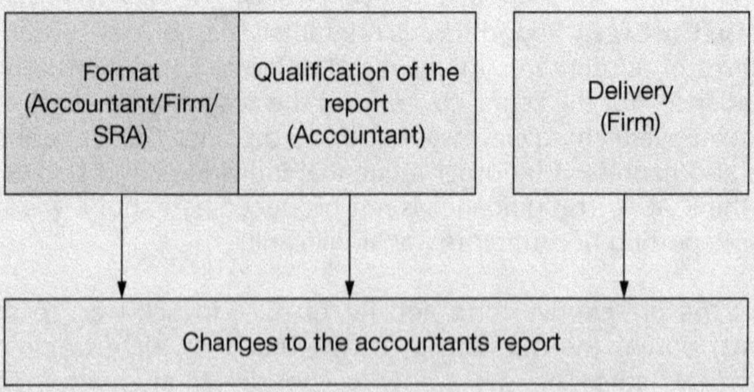

> The changes apply to those whose next accounting period end date is after 1 November 2015. Those with an accounting end date prior to this will need to use the previous system until next year.

Delivery of accountants' report

The changes broadly mean you don't have to obtain an accountants' report if:

- you are doing 100% legal aid work, or
- your average client account balance is low (defined in the rules).

In addition, broadly speaking if you have obtained an accountants' report it does not need to be sent to the SRA unless it is qualified.'

Material breach, its history and definitions are covered in Part 5 of this book, alongside the new term 'serious breach' which was introduced in 2019. The requirements for Reporting Accountants were the same as they were for COLPs and COFAs. Importantly, the definition of 'materiality' the SRA was using was contained within the Authorisation Rules 2011, which is covered in Part 5 of this book. However, for ease, broadly a material breach was felt to be an assessment of the impact of an action which was in breach, this included loss or potential loss for clients (widely defined), and the standing and reputation of the profession or legal services. The SRA did provide a numerical definition, but there were large exclusions from it (including the impact on individuals) and it was rarely used because solicitors used their own ethical compass. Solicitors may also feel differently to a numerical definition because they have and are used to exercising fiduciary duties. We explore the position related to fiduciary duties later in this Part of the book.

There is another mention of material in the legislation. The Solicitors Act 1974, s 34 asks whether the accountant has evidence or information in respect of the ability of the solicitor to hold client (or other) monies, and requires a report in that respect. Material breach of the Accounts Rules was not the same as this materiality referred to in the legislation. A different question was being asked as to whether there has been a material breach of the rules, when 'material' has been defined by the Authorisation Rules 2011.

Material breaches of the rules as defined by those rules are wider and, as discussed in Part 5 of the book, encompassed a range of circumstances which may have an impact on clients or others. This is much wider than asking whether or not the standing of the solicitor in respect of client money is damaged. In effect, the legislation might be asking the accountant whether or not the solicitor should be struck off, whether they require more professional training in respect of client or other money, or whether some other sanction should be imposed to prevent them holding client or other money, such as a condition.

We can all see that 'material' or 'serious' breaches of the rules or qualified accountants' reports can sometimes result in no further action or in SRA internal regulatory outcomes for solicitors and their staff. Not all affect the standing of the solicitor, or result in a referral to the Solicitors Disciplinary Tribunal. Not all result in conditions restricting the holding of client or other monies. We can see from Part 3 of the book that, from the thousands of referrals to the SRA (and hundreds of accountants' reports, after 2015), a small number result in conditions restricting access to client and office accounts, and that condition is also often imposed because of bankruptcy or other insolvency, meaning very few qualified accountant reports result in this restriction.

For example, we could see a situation where there had been a failure in the systems and controls of the firm that resulted in a breach of the Accounts Rules, but that breach was time limited and was rectified by the firm. Due to the potential impact on clients, the firm has to make a report to the SRA under the SRA Authorisation rules as it meets the criteria for serious (or material) breach. However, it does not affect the ability or fitness of the solicitors or firm to continue to hold client monies as it was identified and rectified immediately. Therefore we can see the difference in the two definitions and how they produce different results in what needs self-reporting to the regulator. There are countless more examples, and any shift in the definition produces different results in what should be reported and what should not.

Accordingly, we had seen a movement from a very prescribed way of working with a tick box list, to an open set of rules reliant more on the accountants' professional judgement. The regulator certainly felt the first tick box list was generating too many reports as there was not a measure of judgement against it as to whether or not the accountant felt the matter should be reported. The regulator published information at the time covering the expected reduction in receipt of accountants' reports. We were seeing a movement towards the more serious end of the scale in what the regulator expected to receive from the accountant.

Training produced by the writer is included here, and you will see the regulator specified the types of reports they expected to receive, and gave examples of whether or not a report should be qualified, and when. At around this time, the regulator also provided examples of the types of matters the accountant should look at, including whether or not the accounts were held on an IT system. As matters such as this (failure to hold accounts on an IT system) would not be a breach of the rules, some accountants were left wondering what they were being asked for.

An extract from Training from 2016, written by the Author, and referring to SRA guidance on the accountants' report:

> **'Format of accountants' report**
>
> A new form AR1 has been published by the SRA, replacing the previous AR1 form and accountants' reporting checklist. The new form is intended to be less prescriptive than the previous form and checklist. This form simply provides a space for the accountant to describe the reasons for any qualification placed on the report.
>
> The sections of the Accounts Rules which required a detailed series of checks by the accountant, have been deleted. Rule 43A now requires accountants to use their professional judgement in examining the accounts and deciding whether any report should be qualified. However further information about the standard checks an accountant is expected to do has been published by the SRA in their 'Guidance on Completing the New AR1 Form'.
>
> ...
>
> *Qualified Reports*
>
> Accountants are now being asked to use their judgement when considering whether an accountants' report should be qualified, and

are being referred to the SRA's rules and guidance on material breaches. This will be quite a challenge for Reporting Accountants, who have to decipher what the SRA means by 'material breach', rather than simply filling in a checklist. It remains to be seen whether the SRA will get the kind of responses and information they are looking for.

Guidance for the Reporting Accountant is again contained in the 'Guidance on the New AR1 Form' ... and does provide some useful examples of what is considered material. For example, they suggest serious breaches include significant and unreplaced shortfalls, actual or suspected dishonesty, and significant failure to provide documentation. Potential material breaches include lack of regular three way reconciliations, significant but fully replaced shortfall, and longstanding residual balances due to clients.

It is recommended that you ask your accountant to read the SRA guidance fully before completing your report.'

Materiality

Accountants have a separate definition of materiality and material breach, which may form part of the exercise of their professional judgement. The SRA definition was not and is not the same. The SRA definition required fairly substantial explanation, to an audience who are not themselves specialists in the rest of the SRA Code of Conduct, and may not deal with accountants' reports for solicitors on a day-to-day basis.

The writer's master's degree covered some accounting and particularly using, compiling, and analysing financial statements. The accountancy definition of materiality refers to the potential impact of a misstatement in the accounts. (Sarbanes-Oxley (2002), the American Act, is noted.) The judgement of that misstatement is a professional issue for accountants and can vary, but is often an issue of proportionality. For example, a mistake by a large company might not count as material because the accounts are correspondingly large and it has a small impact. The same mistake by a small company might count as material because the accounts are correspondingly small and therefore the mistake might have a large impact.

There is no concept of accountants' materiality within the Solicitors Accounts Rules, as solicitors are dealing with client (or others') money. The solicitor owes fiduciary duties to their client and others, and the money may be held on trust. This applies to all clients and all monies.

Solicitors are obliged to account to the client at the end of the transaction, down to the last penny. The writer might be considered very strict; she has been to practices where they send stamps to the client at the conclusion of the transaction to cover the remaining pence. The writer advocates this approach.

Reporting Accountants will also note the grounds for intervention (closure of the solicitors' practice by the regulator), which include breaches of the Accounts Rules and dishonesty. These rules are in place to protect client monies, the rule of law, and the operation of the justice system. They are not to be taken lightly. Practices have been closed, and solicitors struck off the roll, for dishonesty in respect of client monies.

In dealing with material breach, the accountant may rightly become confused. They have been asked to consider the position regarding a material breach of the rules, and there is an accountancy definition of materiality. If the regulator does not want them to apply that definition, then why have they been asked to use their professional judgement?

The professional judgement the accountant has been asked to use is their assessment of the accounts overall, their judgement in what to consider and how to prepare the report, and whether there is any:

- material breach (as previously, but defined by the Authorisation Rules 2011);
- significant breach (as currently); and
- significant weakness in a firm's systems and controls (as currently).

The Reporting Accountant may also wish to consider whether there is any serious breach (as currently), and as required to be considered by the COLP and COFA.

We consider the current position, including serious breach and significant weaknesses, later in this Part of the book.

It is very important to remember that, regardless of any report to the regulator, any breach of the Solicitors Accounts Rules should almost always result in rectification of the sum and full payment to the client (or other party) if it has resulted in a loss.

In Part 5 of the book, we considered the question whether there was a de minimis provision for material or serious breach, up to which we considered reporting to be inappropriate. The same debate exists for COFAs and accountants as it does for COLPs. However, with the Accounts Rules, the amounts that might fall within this 'de minimis' approach are very small, regardless of the size of the practice.

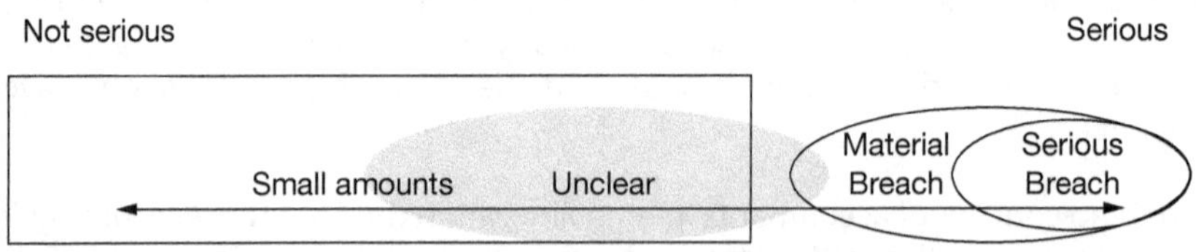

This is where the definition of material breach and serious breach for solicitors differs from the definition of materiality for accountants. For solicitors, there may be a defined level or amount of mistake or missing monies, which is possible to quantify, which is acceptable, and does not amount to a reportable breach. That amount might be very small and should be rectified. Beyond that, it may be reportable. The solicitor definition would apply regardless of the size of practice, because the solicitor held the monies on trust and with a fiduciary duty.

We could use the definition of 'aged balances' as the acceptable starting point for de minimis breaches. However in doing so, we should note that we are just discussing whether an amount *could be a reportable breach*. If it was not a reportable breach, the solicitor would not 'get away with it', even for that small amount, because they would still have to replace the sum according to their fiduciary or trust duty, and/or comply with the aged balances guidance.

If we take an example, the Accounts Rules allow for small sums to be transferred to charity or the firm in limited circumstances. Larger sums can only be transferred with the permission of the SRA. This indicates the continued strict interpretation of the rules which is provided to the accountant.

Regulatory approach

Upon receipt of the accountants' report, the regulator considers whether or not to take regulatory action, commence an investigation, or add to an existing investigation.

We have covered regulatory investigations in Part 5 of this book. Sometimes, receipt of a qualified accountants' report can be serious, and the SRA can take action such as intervention. At other times, a regulatory investigation may result in the matter becoming an on-site investigation with a full inspection of the books of account. Again, such matters can result in interventions or other serious consequences for solicitors.

We can all look for information about the latest regulatory approach to the rules within the SRA's:

- regulatory rules;
- regulatory documents and policy documents; and
- internal decisions.

It can also be useful to review the decisions at the Solicitors Disciplinary Tribunal, which give a useful perspective on the role of the solicitor, their fiduciary duties, and disciplinary consequences of breaches of the rules.

The SRA does not apply a different standard to Reporting Accountants or the accountants' report. The regulator considers the accountants' report as a form of reporting. It does not consider the accountants' report differently to other intelligence, reports, or regulatory information it receives. We must also remember that the accountants' report continues to reflect and measure the Solicitors Accounts Rules and the compliance position in respect of that. It is clear there is not a different standard the SRA applies to the Accounts Rules to that of the rest of the Handbook as it was, or Standards and Regulations as it is now. We must take the position of the Solicitors Accounts Rules and the form for Reporting Accountants as within the set of rules as they have been defined.

The move away from material breach

Almost as soon as the new AR1 form had been introduced asking for an assessment of material breach, the SRA made further changes. The new style of AR1 was introduced in 2015, and the SRA started consulting on further changes to the wider Accounts Rules under 'Looking to the Future' in 2016. 'Looking to the Future' became the new Standards and Regulations.

The SRA, in consultation for the new Standards and Regulations 2019, consulted on changing the definition of 'material breach' in the Authorisation Rules 2011 (as discussed above) to 'serious breach'. We have discussed this further in Part 5 of this book. The change has taken effect in the Standards and Regulations 2019. This change is significant and implies that the regulator is now more interested in serious situations than they were previously. The regulator had looked at implementing this change across the board, including with the accountants' report.

Readers will see that COLPs, COFAs, and staff within law firms are now required to report to the standard of serious breach, and that this is specifically mentioned within the SRA's Codes of Conduct.

The SRA proposed to change the standard for Reporting Accountants in the AR1 to serious breach in the new 2019 Standards and Regulations, but the change did not go ahead. At the eleventh hour, in July 2019, the regulator changed its mind, and implemented a change to the forms instead requiring the Reporting Accountant to consider whether there were:

- significant breaches of the Accounts Rules; and
- significant weaknesses with the systems and procedures the firms have in place, such that there is a risk to client monies.

This is the current position. This situation points to the professional judgement of the accountant in determining whether or not the rules have been complied with but also whether the policies, procedures, and controls in place in the firm are adequate and whether they are working effectively to ensure the safekeeping of client money.

This is a different question to asking about serious breach or material breach; however, the Reporting Accountant will still, in their review of the firm's systems, controls and procedures, see and review the content of the firm's reports to the regulator. We discuss below in the section on 'COLP, COFA, and the Reporting Accountant' that the Reporting Accountant may in effect be performing an additional check on the material (pre November 2019) and serious (post November 2019) breach reporting of the firm overall.

At the same time as introducing the new AR1 forms in 2015, the SRA reduced the volume of accountants' reports that needed to be sent to them, and this has remained the same since 2015. Their policy position since has been the forms did not need to be sent to them if the report was not qualified. The SRA monitored the position in light of what they were receiving. The SRA has clearly sought to focus the Reporting Accountant on the more serious situations.

In all of this change away from material breach, of course, nothing took away the Reporting Accountants' continuing and statutory obligations to:

- report fraud and theft under the Solicitors Act 1974, s 34, or fulfil the other statutory duty to report a solicitor if they are concerned about their standing or fitness to hold client monies; and
- report money laundering under the Proceeds of Crime Act 2002, and take any other required steps as required by money laundering legislation.

The SRA's current reporting form and guidance are not intended to prevent reporting of these obligations in any way, and sit alongside them.

The writer has seen these sets of obligations separately given the wording in the AR1 and the wide guidance which supports it, which goes beyond the statutory obligations, and sits within the regulatory rules made by the regulator. The ability of the SRA to make these rules and their statutory basis is explored further in Part 1 of this book.

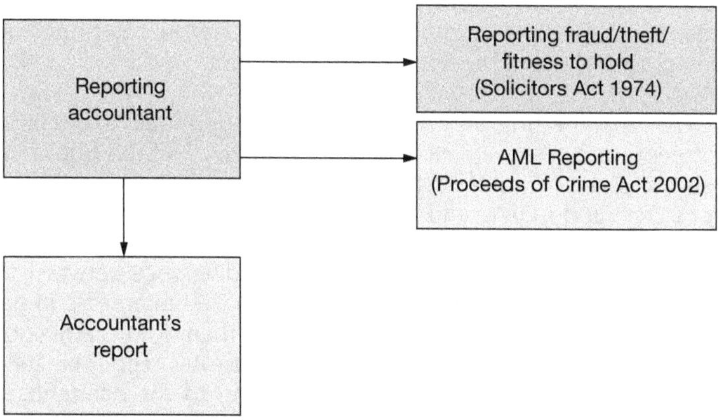

Reporting Accountants may of course have their own professional obligations as well and those obligations should be adhered to. Reporting Accountants may also take independent legal advice if they so require.

Reporting Accountants may have to advise their clients to obtain legal advice in the face of a qualified report or a potentially qualified report, given the consequences.

What are the effects of the changes overall?

Reporting Accountants have been given changing objectives: firstly, the long-standing tick box approach, which followed the specific rules; secondly, the more open and interpretive form, with the concept of material breach; and, thirdly, a retreat from material or serious breach and a re-focus of the accountant on significant breaches and significant weaknesses in a firm's systems and controls, alongside reporting for the firm of serious breach.

The last two sets of changes have occurred within five years, and were accompanied with debates about the extent of the checks the accountant should undertake.

The accountant may be being asked to answer the same question, but in different ways; that being whether the firm itself poses a risk to client monies. However, this may be a baseline question; in those circumstances, you must make a report. The reporting guidance and questions from the SRA lend themselves to reports being made in much wider circumstances, as sometimes the SRA may want to conduct its own investigation.

The latest iteration of the form, with its additional focus on systems and controls, risks unintended effects. A firm with a strong understanding of the previous

Accounts Rules (2011 and previously) but whose understanding is embodied within a very strong COFA or finance manager, or a Sole Practitioner who is excellent with client monies, risks falling foul of the new requirements because they don't have a written finance manual. Far and away the clearest message from 2011's Outcomes-focused regulation was that firms could design their systems and procedures in the way they wanted, in order to deliver the outcomes best for the client. We can only hope that common sense prevails and small firms with strong individuals who run their practices meticulously and who understand the Accounts Rules as a result of being trained by their supervising partner or in another legal capacity (rather than as accountants) are not left crying 'but I've always done it this way', when faced with questions about their 'control systems'. After all, accountants hopefully want this iteration of the rules and the latest questions to last.

COLPs, COFAs, and the firm as a whole, are currently required to consider the concept of serious breach in reporting, as set out in Part 5 of this book. Reporting Accountants are asked to note carefully the difference in the reporting standard required for COLPs and COFAs, and those for the accountants' reports.

There have been many arguments concerning the difference between the two, and accountants are asked to consider the reporting requirements imposed on the COLP and COFA at the time, if their checks take them into examining serious and material breach records. The answer as to whether it is reportable for a COLP or COFA, or for an accountant, may differ according to the different reporting standards and their interpretation.

Requirement to obtain an accountants' report

As we set out briefly above, requirements for accountants' reports changed in 2015. One of the other changes was the requirement to obtain an accountants' report. The SRA introduced exemptions to obtaining the report on a compulsory basis for those holding small amounts of client monies and for those purely delivering legal aid.

The reason for not obtaining reports for those in these circumstances is straightforward; those with small amounts in their client account are generally determined to pose less of a risk to the public. Those delivering legal aid contracts will have their legal aid payments paid directly by the Legal Aid Agency (LAA) and those payments are managed and reconciled directly by the LAA. The LAA also audits the claims legal aid firms make to ensure they are genuine and within permitted boundaries. Legal Aid firms therefore have their financial checks and balances built in.

Accountants' reports can still be obtained by exempt law firms if they want to. This might be for peace of mind, as part of their COFA duties, to obtain a second opinion on Accounts Rules matters, or for any other reason. The regulator has set a minimum threshold of the amount of independently held client monies, above which the firm must obtain a report; however, those below that threshold still have to comply with the current rules in place. At the time of writing, these are the Solicitors Accounts Rules 2019 and the SRA Standards and Regulations 2019. Although no accountants' report is due, firms below the threshold must still comply and make a serious breach report if necessary.

But can we be so sure about those who hold client monies in small amounts? For example, imagine a practitioner running a small firm with a very small client account (below the threshold). They have limited time and limited experience holding client monies, so they make mistakes without practice. However, if those mistakes amount to small amounts of client or other monies missing, we also have to question whether they warrant the regulator's attention. The SRA has chosen to provide a cut-off point for accountant reporting, perhaps because of the cost of the accountants' report, not because they are saying the solicitor is free to behave as they wish with client or other monies as long as it does not go beyond a set amount.

We should also remember that the SRA has Practising Certificate conditions and firm conditions available to them to restrict holding of client monies, or it can put in place requirements for systems and procedures, should the risk be sufficient. The SRA does impose Practising Certificate conditions on those who pose risks, and those conditions are discussed in other chapters and later in this Part of the book.

We may also question whether or not unscrupulous law firms would use the small size of client account exemption to either:

(a) hide larger holdings of client monies (by under-declaring); or

(b) deliberately set themselves up to take monies under the threshold for reporting in order to commit breaches.

There are a number of checks and balances the regulator has in place to ensure such behaviour does not go unnoticed and the regulator takes information from a variety of sources.

On the course, we also cover another means to 'cheat' the rules in this respect. The writer calls it 'The Backdoor Exemption', as it is a means to circumvent this set of Solicitors Accounts Rules. This is contained later in this Part of the book within the sections entitled 'Challenges in the Accounts Rules' and 'Closing gaps in the new Accounts Rules'.

Firms with more than one office can have different accounting periods for each office and obtain separate reports.

Requirement to send the report to the SRA

It was not only the need to obtain an accountants' report that changed in 2015, it was also whether or not it needed to be sent to the SRA.

The SRA now only wishes to see accountants' reports which are qualified. This currently means the report is noted as demonstrating a significant breach of the Accounts Rules or a significant weakness in the firm's systems or procedures. On receipt of the qualified report, the solicitor has six months to send the report to the SRA.

Do bear in mind that, in qualifying the report, the Reporting Accountant is asking the firm to make a form of self-report to their regulator. This can have consequences for the law firm, the individual solicitors, their staff, and those they do business with. In some situations, breaches of the rules can result in prosecution of solicitors and their staff. The SRA has regulatory outcomes ranging from the low to mid-level through to full prosecution before the Solicitors Disciplinary Tribunal for the most serious Accounts Rules matters.

The firm sending the report to the SRA can assist their position by explaining the breach or weaknesses, in a letter accompanying the report. The firm may need to take legal advice concerning this position. However, in cases where the breach is explainable, or there is a disagreement as to whether there is a breach, the balance of the firm's voice can assist the situation by putting across their perspective.

Particular points a firm may try include:

- Mitigation – explaining any attempts they have made to put the situation right.
- Explanation – explaining what happened and why – if it feels to you like it would assist. For example, 'we did not consider this was a breach because …', or 'these were the unusual events which led to this breach …'.
- Forward focus – explaining how the firm has reacted to prevent the breach occurring again or in what other ways you have taken steps to do things differently.

A firm may need legal advice prior to sending the report, particularly if admitting any breaches.

Dependent on the report the SRA receives, it may ask the Reporting Accountant or firm for further information.

Demonstrating management of the situation and leadership in dealing with the issue can provide confidence to the regulator of the intent to comply with the rules and a strong indication that this is a well-run firm. Detailed knowledge of your own procedures and how you can adapt also provides the same perspective.

Sometimes, disagreements do arise between parties when completing the accountants' report and it can be helpful to have another opinion. If you are a firm, do not be afraid to consider a second Reporting Accountant firm if the matter has caused serious debate. A qualified report can be a cause of prosecution, conditions, or other regulatory action and it is worth taking all the steps you can to resolve the position.

If you are a firm or individual who has become aware of breaches in the Accounts Rules as a result of an accountants' report, also consider whether or not you need to make a report to anywhere else as a result. This can include:

- the SRA (as a serious breach report, noting the difference between the two);
- your MLRO and, for them, the NCA, if you know or suspect money laundering; and
- the police, if you are concerned criminal offences have been committed.

COLP, COFA and the reporting accountant

A version of the serious/material breach course operated for accountants for a number of years, with a discussion of the requirements placed on Reporting Accountants, and how their decision making may differ from that of the firm. In some cases, accountants and COFAs reported significant differences of opinion in whether a breach was material.

From 2011, accountants were being asked to make judgements about matters that required a greater discussion of compliance and, for some, began to involve the full audit functions of accountancy practices.

Until the introduction of the Standards and Regulations 2019, Reporting Accountants were required to consider the same standard as the COLP and COFA, that being whether there were any material breaches of the Accounts Rules to report. There was frequent disagreement between Reporting Accountant and COFAs due to the:

1. Alternative definition of material breach in accountancy terms.
2. Existence of additional information within a firm which may not form part of an accountant report or any accountant remit, including matters which fall under the remit of the COLP, such as legal advice to the client which might demonstrate why certain actions had been undertaken in the accounts.
3. Extent of the accountant report, which, following the introduction of outcomes-focused regulation, became much more open to interpretation. Some firms did not agree that the report was akin to an audit, or that this was the function of the report.

Accountants were placed in a difficult position by the shift in 2011. We can demonstrate the position with reference to the Legal Services Act 2007. Under this Act, the roles of the HOLP (Head of Legal Practice) and HOFA (Head of Finance and Administration) are separate. The HOLP has responsibility for legal aspects of the practice and ensuring the rules of professional conduct are complied with. The HOFA has responsibility for ensuring the Accounts Rules are complied with. The SRA has its own versions or interpretations of these roles – called COLPs and COFAs. The roles are quite distinct from each other, and it is often said that the COLP role is wider than that of the COFA as it encompasses all of the work of the firm and the legal functions, whereas the COFA role purely looks at the Accounts Rules.

Of course, accountants are not commonly fully legally qualified. Some accountants have started to undertake probate work, but this remains rare. An accountant would not be qualified to review or comment on the legal work of the firm, and the accountants' report arguably does not encompass a review of all aspects of the firm's work.

The accountant should, for the most part, be liaising with the COFA in the discussion of compliance with the Accounts Rules. However, the COLP, or the department concerned, may have far more information about a particular situation which might then reveal whether it is a breach or not. The COLP is almost always a solicitor, or someone with the requisite legal experience. An accountant may not have the professional qualifications or judgement to make the same decisions as the COLP, or the standing to do so.

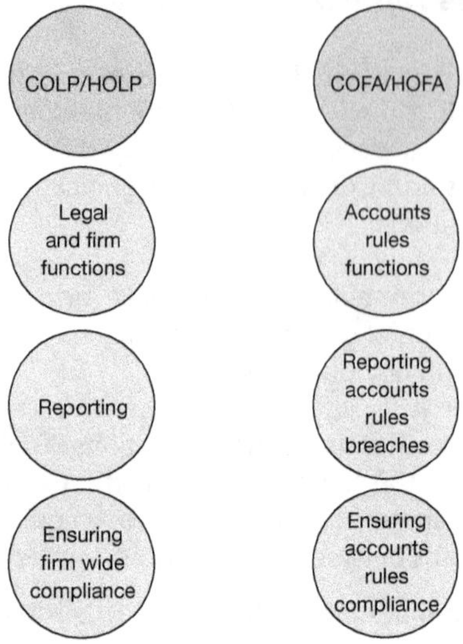

The accountant then, between 2015 and 2019, was being asked to review the decision of the COFA in deciding whether to report issues of material breach. The definition of material breach may not simply be a question of accountancy, it may also be a question of the legal position of the practice and client, which must be considered with reference to the COLP. The question may be impossible for the accountant to resolve or complete the answer to fully, as they may not be appropriately qualified to answer it.

This position also neatly demonstrates the role of the trust and fiduciary duties in holding client monies; that we have to refer to the COLP in this situation shows the operation of the trust and the client (or other) requirements.

If a firm had not reported a material breach between 2015 and 2019, and the accountant conducting a review found it, and considered it was material, the accountant would be obliged to report it. The accountant may have to discuss the position with the firm first as part of the discussion about their draft report. The potential consequences for the firm or COFA are evident; they could be prosecuted if the SRA shared the view of the accountant and not the firm. However, sometimes, the firm will be taking into account more information.

Anecdotally, there have been a number of disagreements in the interpretation of the Accounts Rules alongside the remainder of the Code of Conduct, particularly when involving the COLP. It is important to remember that the law firm is a separate business. The COLP and COFA occupy a statutory role and are appointed by the firm as employees of senior authority and decision making. The accountant in that situation can only use their professional judgement in assessing their view of the Accounts Rules.

The accountant has a statutory role, and is appointed as an external agent by the firm for their professional judgement and skill. The accountant must make a report in some circumstances (for example, if they suspect fraud or money laundering); they also have to sign the accountants' report. If the accountant is unable to sign the report due to a disagreement with the COLP or COFA, the firm may consider appointing new accountants. Sometimes, this does not have to be a problem of professional judgement, but can also be a personality clash or a difference in approach.

Furthermore, accountants are regulated as legal services providers in direct competition with law firms. There may be an inherent conflict of interest between accountants as a profession and solicitors or law firms as a professional group in conducting the review. The basis for the statutory requirement was established in the 1970s with a consideration of the client account. Given the competition in the sector, there may be a need for an independent means of reviewing the monies held for clients.

In 2019, the SRA made substantial changes to the long-standing Accounts Rules, and alongside this backed down from a position of accountants considering material breach in the same terms as the firms. The SRA has not asked accountants to consider serious breach in the same terms. The new forms require the accountant to consider whether there is significant breach of the Accounts Rules or a significant weakness in the policies and procedures (systems and controls) of the firm, alongside considering compliance with the Accounts Rules.

The new position allows the accountant to express a more independent view of the operation of the accounts, as they are not focused on the same terms as the firm. However, the different standard may still cause a problem. They are being asked to express whether the operation of the firm is likely to put client monies at risk. By focusing on the policies and procedures and their operation, there is a greater focus on the part of the firm the accountant would naturally be concerned with.

Conditions to obtain an accountants' report

We have seen in Parts 3 and 4 of this book that conditions can be imposed on Practising Certificates and firm authorisation. Sometimes, the conditions include:

- more frequent accountants' reports, sometimes one every three or six months;
- obtaining an accountants' report, in circumstances where a firm would not be required to obtain a report;
- sending a report to the SRA, in circumstances where a report might not always be sent (for example, if the report was not qualified); and
- other relevant conditions, including conditions on the holding of client monies, or the prevention of access to the financial functions of the firm.

If faced with a firm or individual within a firm with conditions, Reporting Accountants should take care in this situation. The regulator is asking for a report on a situation which has been identified as posing a risk. It may be a piece of work that needs careful planning and a report that needs careful thought. Senior staff within the accountancy practice may need to direct the work planning and investigation and carefully supervise those involved.

The Reporting Accountant may want to know:

- What the condition is, and whether there are any dates attached to it which vary beyond the usual reporting dates for the accountants' reports.

- Whether any other accountants have been involved in producing reports and the outcomes of those reports.
- Whether the regulator has visited the practice, and the circumstances and outcomes of those visits.
- Why the condition has been imposed, in what circumstances, and what the regulator is seeking to achieve or the risk it is seeking to manage by imposing the condition.

There could be a question mark as to whether the firm or individual is obliged to provide that information to the Reporting Accountant, and whether it could influence the outcome of the report. However, conditions are usually published and accountants will want to consider risk planning in their approach.

The last point above is particularly helpful when dealing with firms with conditions. Understanding the condition as a response to a risk can help the accountant pinpoint any areas for risk management and issues that need to be investigated. There may be specific breaches that have been identified by the SRA already, or circumstances that may lead to a serious breach. If so, the Reporting Accountant can take a view on this and build it into their work and report.

From speaking to Reporting Accountants and their staff on the courses, it is apparent that very few of them are aware of conditions being imposed, or the circumstances in which they would be imposed. Even being aware that there is not a condition or has not previously been a condition can be helpful, and practices who have attended the course may feel they should ask about regulatory history going forward, perhaps in the knowledge it may not always be forthcoming, but it can help with planning.

On the courses, the writer often discussed using Regulation 3 of the Practising Regulations 2011 as a risk management tool, starting this approach with Reporting Accountants in 2016. Regulation 3 is a useful set of indicators which allows the person reviewing the firm to determine high-level risks which have in the past attracted regulatory attention. Reporting Accountants faced with conditions might find looking back at the previous SRA Handbook at this set of regulations helpful in understanding the types of situations which have historically resulted in conditions and one possible interpretation of risk within the sector, albeit this approach is intended to pass with the changing sector.

If the Reporting Accountant returns the following year or even within three or six months, it can also be helpful to see whether the situation has changed or evolved, and whether the risk has been managed by the practice themselves. Sometimes, a condition is imposed to obtain an accountants' report and send it to the SRA, with the threat of the accountant, consequent reporting, and possible prosecution all motivations to making changes and a means to control the situation. However, these measures do not solve the problem itself. The regulator cannot take on the role of managing the practice and the condition is intended in two parts to both motivate changes and provide a risk management-based oversight of the position. The alternative for the SRA would be to impose a condition to, for example, recruit a new cashier, or specify procedures to improve. At the moment, conditions are being imposed at a much higher level, but the regulator does have the opportunity to consider again how they deliver their regulatory involvement with a law firm and this could be an idea for the future.

Challenges in the new Accounts Rules

The new Accounts Rules themselves may provide some significant challenges for some law firms. The previous Solicitors Accounts Rules 2011 (and their versions) were successful in providing a clear basis for the firm to hold client monies. There have been a significant number of prosecutions, but the prosecutions are often the result, unfortunately, of dishonesty rather than the rules themselves. The writer has seen countless examples of firms who have adhered to the rules and whose accounts are well organised, clear and explainable, and whose liability to clients and others is clear.

For those firms who are managing the situation well, and for whom the previous consistency of the Accounts Rules provided a system of managing client monies, there is theoretically no need to change the way they have run their systems. Keeping a copy of the Solicitors Accounts Rules 2011 and adhering to that set of rules is acceptable from a compliance perspective; there is nothing within the Standards and Regulations 2019 that would prevent that. For firms who are comfortable and for whom the system works well, there seems little point in jeopardising client monies or the firm's well-run financial systems to move to new sets of rules which may change again in the future. Law firms and their accountants are reminded of the focus of outcomes-focused regulation which allowed firms to develop their own approach within a freer set of rules. This is no different; the SRA took OFR further in some ways by pulling back the rules even further, and firms should not feel obligated to make changes if they do not wish to.

The new rules bring a new definition of client money. The rules allow some monies which would previously have been held as client monies to be held as office monies. Firms and their accountants are advised to be cautious about these new definitions and ensure both they and the law firm understand when monies clearly fall within the definition intended.

In particular, firms can now hold monies for their fees as office monies in some circumstances (as defined by the rules). Accountants are advised to consider the extent of the solicitor's fees, whether they are reasonable, and whether or not they have been agreed with the client. There is legislation dealing with fees in some areas of law, and costs lawyers are often employed in these and other areas to assess costs. Accountants are not expected to be specialists in this area of law, or use their 'professional judgement' in making a decision; arguably, it would be better if they didn't. It may simply be a case of raising the issue if fees seem out of keeping with the situation, if fees are being kept in the office account that are not genuinely fees, or if the amount of monies kept in the office account has not been agreed with the client. Accountants may also look out for a dispute between the client and the firm.

Note that clients have two forms of redress in dealing with a solicitor whose fees are unreasonably large:

1. Complaint to the Legal Ombudsman (the Legal Ombudsman can make a referral to the SRA if necessary), but the Legal Ombudsman provides a range of customer-focused solutions and may give a view on charges, mediate disputes, and award compensation for poor service.
2. Assessment of the solicitor's bill by the court; this is a separate area of law, with specifically qualified sets of lawyers.

The matter could be a matter of misconduct if there was a significant overcharging issue, hence the possible referral to the SRA by the Legal Ombudsman. The SRA could, of course, prosecute if the matters were considered very serious.

Holding client monies and ring-fencing monies for fees within the office account is controversial, particularly given the history of complaints and scandals in this area. We have seen in the first two Parts of this book that The Law Society and the SRA were separated. This was due in part to concerns about solicitor charging practices, and major changes have been made to the sector as a result of ongoing issues in this area. The writer has herself seen a number of solicitor overcharging cases in her career which were prosecuted. All firms and Reporting Accountants should be aware of this as a potential issue and decide on a course of action or approach in dealing with this particular issue; noting, of course, that this is a specific area of law.

The consequences of holding client monies incorrectly could be prosecution by the SRA. We have yet to see the volume of prosecutions under the new rules. A large number of prosecutions or problems could result in a reversal of approach. We wait to see the prosecutorial approach the SRA is going to take to the interpretation of this definition of client monies. However, getting it wrong in the meantime could result in a liability to clients which has not been foreseen.

The timing of the introduction of the new rules in 2019 has been impacted by coronavirus and many firms are likely to see a decline in instructions in some way. Reporting Accountants and law firms will want to consider the financial position of the firm. An unforeseen liability to clients as a result of an incorrect interpretation of the new Accounts Rules could cause significant liquidity problems for firms.

For example, a firm determines they will hold all client monies due for fees in their office account but sets a definition of 'fees' that is over-optimistic about what they can charge or is not being agreed with the client. They decided to keep 10% of all client monies held in their office account to cover fees, but this was not agreed with the clients and did not reflect the firm's actual fees, which were closer to an average of 5% of client monies held. The firm has both broken the Accounts Rules by holding the additional 5% in office account, and may have also placed reliance on the additional monies in the firm, by including it in their financial management calculations. This firm may also find themselves in financial difficulty, in breach of the Code of Conduct for Firms, as well as being in breach of the Accounts Rules. Accountants should, of course, be aware that insolvency can be a ground for intervention (closure) of the law firm, and that overcharging of a sizeable amount can be a disciplinary matter. In addition, the office account is not labelled as a client account so this could also cause a problem in the depositing of what are client monies.

The new definition of client monies is likely to be a strong focus for the SRA to ensure the position is adhered to, and accountants working with or supporting firms under SRA investigation will want to ensure those who have moved to using the new rules have strong systems in place to adhere to the new definitions.

The Reporting Accountant may themselves face challenges in producing the accountants' report. The change to the new definition of client monies puts the accountant in the position of investigating a mixed monies office account and attempting to assure that the monies within the account fall within the definition of client monies. Firms are in a similar position. They also have to keep a track of the monies received from clients which have fallen within the definition of office monies and not client monies, and the point at which they did. As a result, firms are likely to need quite strong policies and procedures in place to help manage the situation.

Firms and Reporting Accountants may want to remember that law firms owe a variety of duties to clients concerning the monies they hold. Complaints could also be made by the client to both the Legal Ombudsman (who handles consumer complaints about law firms), and the regulator themselves if the client or third party found any irregularity with the application of the new definitions, and in some circumstances this may not need reference to the firm themselves.

Other features of the Accounts Rules under the Standards and Regulations 2019 included:

- Simplified rules – the rules were intended to be simplified to improve compliance.
- Changes to definition of client money to include disbursements for which the firm is liable (not the client).
- Allowing the use of third party managed accounts (TPMAs), in circumstances where the TPMA provider is regulated by the FCA. Monies held within TPMAs do not currently count as client monies (for the purposes of the Solicitors Accounts Rules only), but the writer wonders whether this will change in future.
- Clarity on banking facilities – use of the client account must be supported by an underlying legal transaction.
- Client monies can be held outside the client account if the client permits – this is covered later in this Part of the book in 'Closing gaps in the new Accounts Rules'.
- Confirmation of the simplification of the circumstances for obtaining accountants' reports, introduced in 2015, and covered earlier in this Part of the book.

In the new structures we have seen available to solicitors and firms in Parts 1 and 2 of this book, solicitors working in unregulated firms are not permitted to hold client money if they conduct reserved work. This includes freelancers. However, solicitors who are freelancers can use TPMAs, meaning they can undertake reserved work for clients which involves handling client monies.

Given the openness of the new rules, there are a number of new structures possible. We have to ask how the Accounts Rules are intended to operate. If a solicitor is working in a parent company structure, and the child company is regulated, could the solicitor argue they were the 'you' in the Accounts Rules, particularly if they held a role in both companies? If this were the case, they could seek to breach the rules or bend them and retreat to an unregulated position. Firms, solicitors, COLPs, COFAs, and Reporting Accountants are advised that the rules form part of the terms of authorisation of authorised practices and are not intended to extend beyond that. If you find such a situation occurring, this may be an attempt to breach the rules, unless the regulator has been made explicitly aware, and solicitors in associated structures can be prevented from crossing such lines through internal policies, terms, conditions, and procedures.

There is the possibility that the new rules could open the door to law firms conducting scams, mishandling client monies, and even becoming involved in money laundering, all while apparently in compliance with the new rules. There are, from this angle, very significant challenges in dealing with the new rules. We have to make the basic assumption that the majority of firms will behave honestly when dealing with client funds, but the section later in this Part of the book about 'Closing gaps in the new accounts rules' deals with some scenarios that could develop as a result of gaps in the new rules, and ideas of how to tackle them.

Section 2: Discursive content

Audits and accountants' reports

The SRA's research publication 'A Question of Trust' focused on views of the public concerning the behaviour of solicitors. One of the key findings was around the handling of client monies. The public were understandably concerned to ensure the solicitor was handling their monies appropriately and this was a key area for regulatory focus.

If we draw a map of the areas of the firm, and consider how firms should audit or assure the firm's operations, we can see that some areas already have built-in assurance, through the COLP or COFA. The COLP or COFA's role may be larger than set out below, dependent on the regulatory requirements in force and the supporting guidance, but they certainly have strongholds in these areas. The accountants' report provides the additional check and balance for the regulator in the risky area of holding client monies. It is a double assurance mechanism.

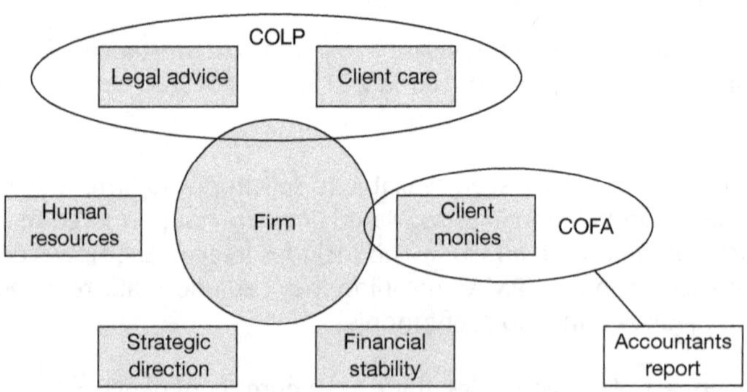

The question could be asked whether the accountants' report is now considering the operation of the role of the COFA, given the focus on systems and controls. An accountant should be careful here, as the COFA role is a statutory one with significant responsibility; the relevant provision is set out at the Legal Services Act 2007, s 92 and note that the COFA is the regulator's name for the HOFA (but also operating in non-ABS authorised bodies – see Part 2 of this book for a detailed explanation). COFAs (or HOFAs) in some cases also have significant potential liabilities; a HOFA in an ABS could be fined up to £50 million. The penalties for making the wrong decision are incredible, and the Reporting Accountant could also be made liable.

There were significant debates in the accountancy community and with their supporting organisations about whether their role was becoming more like the role of an auditor after the 2015 changes. Some accountants started to develop their role as an overview of the firm more generally. However, the regulator's focus for the accountants' report remains the solicitors' Accounts Rules and their operation within the firm.

There are a number of other tools the regulator and others can use to give an overview of the firm including:

- the annual information return on the renewal;
- the audit within the money laundering regulations (if applicable);
- company accounts audits required under the Companies Act 2006 (as applicable);
- complaint-handling information and data from the Legal Ombudsman;
- interactions with the regulator by the firm, including regulatory information provided on applications and any investigations;
- intelligence from Memoranda of Understanding with a range of external agencies, including the police, national crime agency and others; and
- information from the court, not forgetting that solicitors are officers of the court.

All of this means the regulator gathers, analyses, and uses information from a variety of sources to form regulatory opinions on the law firms it authorises. Some of this analysis can be quite complex, including risk-based algorithms for measuring the information received.

Consequently, the regulator is not asking the Reporting Accountant for an overarching audit. They are asking for a second-level assurance of the holding of client monies. This is a third or fourth 'line of defence'. The lines of defence the firm has in dealing with client monies are:

- the solicitor in charge of the case;
- the firm itself, with their policies and procedures;
- the COFA, with their overview of the accounts;
- the Reporting Accountant, with their annual review;
- the firm management, including the MLRO and their decision-making and governance structures;
- the management of the TPMA (if used); and
- the FCA as regulator of the TPMA (if used).

The use of the accountants' report in considering the position of client monies cannot be underestimated. Both the firm and, if necessary, the regulator can use the report as an independent review of the position of the client vis-à-vis the firm, and with the specific Accounts Rules in mind. The Reporting Accountant's role is as a second double-check on the position to verify the firm's declarations, safeguard client positions, and report their findings as appropriate.

On occasion, the accountant may report that they could not form a firm conclusion on a matter. This in itself is valuable information and may lead the regulator to its own investigation. Of course, there are times when the accountant will report specific issues that are being handled incorrectly, and again the regulator will either prosecute, where necessary, or commence their own investigation if appropriate. In some cases, the regulator does not take any action, but the Reporting Accountant should be satisfied that the regulator's decision often reflects a range of information about the regulated firm, their analysis of risk, and their own policy-driven analysis of the situation.

One area where the regulator recently (approximately 2016 onwards) decided to ask Reporting Accountants to go beyond a pure analysis of the Solicitors Accounts Rules was whether the firm had implemented sufficient information technology. From the policy documents, this answer was supposed to be in the affirmative. The adoption of case management technology, IT solutions and other accountancy software is controversial in light of the decisions in the *Horizon* cases. So often in dealing with the Accounts Rules, we hear about liabilities to clients that cannot be repaid, or sets of accounts that, for whatever reason, cannot be reconciled. Imagine if that was the fault of the software.

The writer has herself seen a number of instances where accounts software has malfunctioned, where case management systems have lost data, and where integrated systems have generated random entries which cannot be undone or removed. In some instances, a sales person has been sent back to the practice to attempt to restart the system and clear any erroneous entries, but the position has got worse, or the solution has to be abandoned. The results can be devastating for practices who have invested significant sums in technology. Paper solutions cannot be underestimated, and the relief of practices when they have maintained paper systems, and the IT has malfunctioned, is evident. For those that are too large to maintain paper systems, daily reconciliations, knowing your accounts, and individual fee earners knowing their transactions, are also an excellent defence. Maintain clear records of any issues and record your attempts to resolve them.

In working with firms from across the country, it is clear that there are few IT systems which are completely faultless. Thankfully, the regulators are aware of the issues and accept there can be anomalies.

EXERCISES: AUDIT APPROACHES

Exercise 1: Audit or assurance of client monies?

This exercise is for COLPs, COFAs, and finance and compliance staff in law firms, as well as Reporting Accountants.

Discuss the following issue with your team.

What do you think is the difference between these two?

1. An audit of a law firm
2. Providing assurance of client monies

If you are a law firm, discuss the accountants' approach with them and understand what they are expecting from your firm. If you are an accountant, work with the law firm to develop their appreciation of your intended approach to their holding of client monies.

Exercise 2: Problem resolving

Have you experienced a problem with your accounts? Sometimes small niggly problems exist and we have to resolve them. These might be IT issues, new procedures that need writing or researching, or even aged balances that need sorting out.

Try:

1. Take some time to see if you can solve the problem, but this time have a think about what procedure you can put in place to resolve these issues earlier, next time.
2. If it is an IT issue, maintain a paper system alongside your IT, even for a day or two. Can you see any difference?
3. Are you a firm without IT? Listen to an IT presentation for your CPD.

Material breach and serious breach as issues of judgement

On many of the courses, we discuss whether different issues are material or serious breaches or not, and the accountants' course between 2016 and 2019 was no exception. What is clear from many years of running those courses is that accountants, solicitors, and others, draw from their gut instinct in dealing with the issues. Accountants, like solicitors, often disregarded the advice and guidance from the SRA about what would or would not be material or serious, including indicators, or possible measures, and instead continued to develop their own approaches to the situation. Personal viewpoints, ethical discussions, and comparative professional standards have all been used when discussing the approach to take. It should be made clear here that the writer encourages this approach on her courses, as personal and professional ethical decision making is a good skill to practise.

Individuals and groups have tried to solve the problems in different ways, including:

- Deciding to start an investigation. Sometimes, groups start to form their own approaches to investigation, citing what they would look for, who they would speak to, and what factors they should consider.
- Deciding to telephone the SRA for Ethics Guidance advice and discussion.
- Deciding simply to report every issue.
- When in groups, taking a vote, as they might in a partnership or other democratic institution.
- Allowing the ethical conscience of each individual to guide their own actions.

Delegates are asked to work in groups on the courses. Sometimes, group participation changes the perspective of the individual. Often, individuals are more ethically led than groups (deciding to report more matters to the regulator), but groups are often more certain of their actions, having discussed, heard all the arguments and formulated a final viewpoint. Sometimes, an individual can be swayed from their decision (which does not have to be for or against reporting, it can be a decision to take an investigation in a particular direction), after hearing the argument put across from another person or group in the room.

Does this mean we are affected by group think or confirmation bias? We might be. However, making decisions in groups is the norm within business, within law firms, and accountancy firms. Understanding your own personal ethical perspective is helpful in evaluating whether we have gone too far in our group approach.

EXERCISING YOUR JUDGEMENT

The below exercises are suitable for anyone within law firms or accountancy firms. The final exercise is targeted at accountants.

Exercise 1: Group influence

Have a look in your newspaper. Find an example of behaviour that you think could be offensive to someone else.

Consider who the behaviour could be offensive to.

- Do you personally find it offensive?
- Who might and why might they?
- Could you be influenced by the opinion of the person who found it offensive and if so how and why?
- Would the behaviour be suitable for a solicitor or another professional?
- If not, why not?

Consider your ethical perspective, and also the perspective of wider society or a professional firm – imagine if that person was employed at a professional services firm? Is there a difference in perspective?

Exercise 2:

Find an example of a scam in your newspaper.

Consider if this was a solicitor or accountant who had perpetrated the scam. Do you think it should be reported to their regulator? What is your main reason for reporting or not reporting? Do you have supplemental reasons?

Write down your reasons (main and supplemental, in order).

You can ask a colleague to do the same with the same news story and compare your individual responses.

Do you agree or disagree with what your colleague wrote? Did you colleague have the same reasons in the same order?

Exercise 3: Accountants

The SRA does not ask you to use the accountancy definition of material breach as Reporting Accountants, but it can be helpful to understand the different outcomes a different definition can produce.

With this in mind:

1. Look up the accountancy definition of material breach
2. Consider the problems in Part 8 of this book related to the accounts
3. Would your view change about whether the issues were material breaches if the SRA used the accountancy definition? In answering this question, imagine in each case it was a very large firm with a client account value in the millions.
4. What are the benefits or drawbacks of the different definitions?

Note: This exercise is for discussion of breaches and different ethical viewpoints only. Note that the SRA are no longer using the definition of material breach, and this does not currently form part of the Reporting Accountants' form.

The COLP perspective

When giving legal advice to the client, the duty of the adviser is to act in their clients' best interests. There might be a number of different solutions to any problem, a number of different interpretations of the information provided, and a number of different provisions within the law to consider. Indeed, in some instances the law in a particular area can be complex, and apparently contradictory or finely balanced in its distinctions. As a result, the advice given to the client and the use of the client account or finances of the client can all provide information about the nature of the transaction, the intent of the parties, and the way in which they have been advised.

Different approaches could theoretically be taken to different client problems, including the handling of client monies, reflecting the nature of the advice. Advice may be expressed within the handling of client monies, and the way in which the solicitor deals with them.

Clients are sometimes entitled to legal professional privilege, or are given advice in 'privileged circumstances'. These are situations of professional secrecy, which do not have to be disclosed, even in court. The idea is that clients are entitled to legal advice, which is not to be disclosed to the state, provided it is not in furtherance of a crime.

The COLP or legal adviser to the client can face questions about their handling of client monies during an accountants' report which may be the result of legitimate advice to the client, and/or which is subject to legal professional privilege. The legal advice to the client, or the occasion of legal professional privilege, is not an excuse to breach the rules but, if the full legal advice or reasons for it were known, would they explain what appears to be a breach? Sometimes, this happens and the solicitor, COLP, or firm, cannot explain why they have taken the action they have because it is privileged advice.

A firm could be in the unenviable position of being on the receiving end of a qualified report for a breach which would be explainable but for legal professional privilege. The firm then has to attempt to explain that to the regulator. The regulator has specific powers to deal with the issue but this is a situation that should be avoided at all costs.

Of course, not all advice is privileged, and some areas of law may be considered fairly transactional and straightforward. A client or firm may struggle to argue legal professional privilege or privileged circumstances in some areas. That said, an accountant should respect that a law firm's files and other documents are confidential and have to be maintained as such.

On other occasions, a COLP may be able to look into the situation and revert to the COFA and Reporting Accountant in respect of any alleged or perceived breach, in order to explain the position to the Reporting Accountant. Do not underestimate the importance of asking the legal advisors in this situation for their opinion and input into the process, as they can explain the transaction in ways books of account may not be able to.

EXERCISE: MANSION HOUSE

This exercise is designed for Reporting Accountants, COLPs and COFAs. Imagine you have been instructed by a firm as a Reporting Accountant. Consider the scenario below and decide:

a. Are there any indicators here of a problem? If so, what are they?

b. Would you investigate?

c. If you would, what could you look at and why?

Problem to solve: Your client is instructed in the house purchase of 2 Mansion House, Castle Lane. You can see they received monies on account of costs and disbursements totalling £700, which are largely accounted for in searches. The next receipt into the client ledger is the purchase monies of £525,000 received in three tranches. The ledger shows the monies leave the account in full on 15 July, but the bank does not match, unless it went as part of a larger sum. The reconciliation balances. Would you look further, and if so, what at?

Answer: There is a sample answer to this problem at end of Part 7 of this book. Do not look until you have written out your answer.

The COFA perspective

A COFA has a complex task with a heavy liability. COFAs are expected to be senior members of staff within law firms, but do not have to be part of the equity partnership; they may be salaried, and sometimes may not be a partner. The consequences of failure to meet the obligations on them are extremely serious; we have discussed the fining powers earlier in this Part of the book.

We have to wonder whether Parliament realised when they made the fining powers that the accounts leave very little room for manoeuvre, and not nearly as much as there might be in the COLP role. Breaches are often clearly breaches, but the COLP can sometimes explain them.

Sometimes, breaches of the rules can take place because of the activities of other parts of the partnership or one solitary fee earner. On occasion, the breach might be accidental, or perhaps part of a wider problem with an individual that also includes other performance issues. In other circumstances, it can be a problem of interpretation by a particular fee earner. That fee earner might make a lot of money, and the partnership may want to retain them. The COFA has to try to marry that situation; convincing the fee earner to take a different path, or considering how else they might comply that would assist this fee earner. Taking responsibility for someone else's compliance is an incredibly difficult job and can also be about the ability to manage people, coach them, and even teach them accountancy! We have to remember that most solicitors only learn academically about the Solicitors Accounts Rules briefly during the second stage of their qualification (previously called the LPC, and now part of the SQE).

The COFA role is a job made even more complex by the management and governance arrangements of any firm. The COFA may owe employment duties, and is expected to be a figurehead for Accounts Rules compliance, but the management may decide to go in a different direction to that preferred by the COFA. The COFA's professional integrity can be called into question by this position.

The task of the COFA is to ensure compliance with the Accounts Rules. Other tasks or interpretations of this may be written into a job description or Employment Contract. If dealing with a COFA in a law firm, it can be worthwhile asking what they are expected to do by the firm as the COFA. Similarly, it can be helpful for a law firm to set out their expectation of a COFA vis-à-vis the management structure, and where the lines of responsibility lie.

A COFA might be expected to:

- Put in place policies and procedures for dealing with compliance, and maintain those policies and procedures.
- Be a figurehead for accounts compliance, understanding the Solicitors Accounts Rules, and directing compliance with them.
- Solve problems related to the Solicitors Accounts Rules, and give advice across the firm.
- Promote compliance throughout the firm (for example, by modelling compliance, offering training, supporting queries, and providing information).
- Ensuring the firm has sufficient policies and procedures to deliver compliance with the Accounts Rules, and ensuring those policies and procedures work in practice. This might include:
    - designating responsibilities in job descriptions;
    - requiring those responsibilities to be reviewed on appraisal;
    - conducting their own in-house audits of the accounts; and
    - conducting file reviews of individual files to ensure the Accounts Rules and firm policies and procedures are complied with.
- Act as the liaison point with the Reporting Accountant.

During the writer's courses with Reporting Accountants and COFAs, a system was proposed covering the work of the COFA which included maintaining and overseeing compliance with financial / risk management systems within the firm. Specific duties included:

- Obtaining and maintaining access to all accounting records; this is particularly important, given the firm could under the new rules hold monies outside the client account for the client.
- Controlling the circumstances in which monies are held outside the client account and why.
- Developing effective policies and procedures for financial management and financial risk.
- Providing access to the accounts to the Reporting Accountant.
- Promptly remedying breaches of the Accounts Rules.
- Performing a reconciliation check on a daily, weekly, or monthly basis, dependent on the size of the firm.
- Maintaining a breaches register.
- Undertaking a regular accounts review to conduct an overarching review of the accounts for compliance with the Accounts Rules.
- Undertaking COFA file reviews, and particularly looking at compliance within each file and across related files where appropriate.
- Undertaking specific ledger reviews.

This system was to be part of larger system of compliance with COLP file reviews and Money Laundering Reporting Officer or Money Laundering Compliance Officer activity and information-sharing between the three roles and management as appropriate. The links between COLP and COFA are particularly important, and using the knowledge of the COLP to assist the COFA can also be critical. The COLP may have a system of file review in place; if this links to the COFA, the COFA can also examine the same files for breaches of the Accounts Rules at the same time, and with the benefit of the COLP review.

Understanding the role of the COFA, as interpreted within the firm you are working with, can be important to developing your understanding of the way the firm works and directs financial management.

Do also consider the position of the COFA. Have they been in post a long time or are they new? Taking over another person's compliance regime might be difficult. If the previous post holder has left a difficult situation, there may be an enormous amount to do to put things right, and this can take time to implement.

With the new focus in the AR1 on the systems and procedures within firms, do also consider the expectation of the Reporting Accountant. Do they expect the firm to have certain policies and procedures in place? If so, it is helpful to specify, bearing in mind the regulator has not published extensive guidance in this area.

EXERCISE: THE NEW COFA

This exercise is suitable for COLPs, COFAs, Reporting Accountants and anyone who would like to consider how to approach this complex role.

You are a new COFA and Finance Manager just appointed by the (fictional) ABS, Hutchinson & Rath LLP. You arrive on your first day to find the accounts have largely been ignored since your predecessor's departure, and the Reporting Accountant is about to arrive for the annual accountants' report. The reconciliations have not been done for 4 months, there are large amounts of uncleared transactions, incoming client monies have not been matched to the appropriate accounts, and fee earners have been directing the two remaining and very hard-working accounts staff to send monies to different places without the appropriate partner level sign off. It has been all hands on deck just to maintain this level of compliance since the last COFA left.

Consider:

1. What you could do to assist with the situation.
2. What the firm could do to assist with the situation, including assisting you.
3. What the Reporting Accountant is obliged to do, and whether there are any steps they could take to assist.

Consider the position in the widest possible terms, and your own position as an employee as well as a COFA.

The management perspective

The management perspective of the situation with the accountants' report is equally complex. Law firm structures can be tight knit, with founders working together, equity partners forming another group, and salaried or named partners, again, working separately. There may be factions within fee earner groups considering who is a partner and who has been overlooked for, or declined, partnership. In some cases, law firms can be family units. The health or otherwise of the partnership can also come into play, with the financial wellbeing of the business a key issue. Negligence claims, overheads, and risky client bases, can all cause tension in a situation.

Working with a regulator can also form a backdrop to these issues. The regulator can be involved for a number of different reasons, from investigating specific issues to reviewing the work and profile of the firm. But even if they are not, the increasing demands on law firms from a compliance perspective find their way onto the agendas of the management table. We now have not only COLPs and COFAs, with annual Reporting Accountants, we also have Money Laundering Reporting Officers, Money Laundering Compliance Officers, and independent Anti-Money Laundering auditors.

In a small firm, most individuals around a management table would have a compliance role. In a medium-sized firm a number of individuals, particularly those with the expected sufficient seniority, may carry a role or have carried such a role in recent times. Sometimes, these roles can involve a lot of keeping up to date with the latest developments, implementing the required standards, and monitoring the effectiveness of compliance. This in itself can be a full-time job. If so much time is dedicated to managing compliance, and many of the standards are the same or require the standardisation of business, how can we then say that the management of the firm is acting in the best interests of that specific firm?

Completely outside the perspective of the accountants' report is the Transparency Rules, a set of SRA rules that require standard information to be presented about price. The regulator has provided templates for use on websites. This is a key example of regulatory standards effectively providing for the same service to be provided to clients, regardless of the differences between the businesses. Clients shopping around may find the same wording on the websites, as a result of the regulator's guidance.

Partners and partnerships are in a difficult situation; having invested significant sums of their own monies, they may find themselves with complicated businesses, in tense situations, and facing more compliance requirements and roles in their management, making it more difficult to distinguish themselves.

EXERCISES: THE ACCOUNTANTS' REPORT HAS ARRIVED

You can try these exercises yourself or with your team. The exercises are designed to consider the management perspective of receipt of the accountants' report, but can help you formulate a view of management tables and discussions anywhere.

You are the COFA of Hutchinson & Rath LLP, in the circumstances set out above. The accountants have been in to visit the firm and have noted that:

1. The reconciliations have been completed late in breach of the rules.
2. There is an operating 'miscellaneous' client account ledger, in breach of the rules.
3. There are two queries relating to two transactions where monies have been paid out of the client account in breach of the rules, as it was not in relation to that client's matter, in breach of the rules.
4. Point 3 was caused by the failure to maintain client account ledgers in breach of the rules. This led fee earners to believe monies were available on client matters when they were not.

All 4 points have now been rectified, and the monies replaced.

The accountants have drafted a report for the firm, and have qualified the report on the basis of points 1–4. The accountants have asked for any further evidence to demonstrate compliance before the report is issued.

There is no further evidence within the accounts or files. Consider:

1. What could you do to explain the situation to the accountant and / or regulator?

Now imagine this matter is on the agenda for the next management meeting. Consider the meeting itself. You have to present the issues and situation as the COFA, in a salaried position. Consider how the management team might react. Specifically:

2. What kinds of opinions might you hear around the table?
3. Whether there would be disagreements? What would the disagreements be motivated by?
4. How you think the different compliance roles within the management structure would react and what their overall view of the situation would be?

If you wanted to, you could role play this scenario with your team members, with each team member being given a different role to play. Try the following:

- The senior partner, a founding member, the largest investor in the firm and a quiet force behind the success of the firm. Not fulfilling any compliance roles, and believes compliance is a significant challenge.
- The COLP, a salaried partner but chosen because a very motivated individual, who passionately believes in great client service, often at the expense of all else. Often credited with great feedback and reviews for the firm.
- You, the COFA, new to the firm, and exhausted from the work to get everything back on track. Looking for support from the firm.
- The wills and probate partner, an equity partner, and MLRO. A strange person, who often does the opposite of what you might expect.
- The shipping partner, an equity partner, and real specialist in maritime law. Joined the firm due to long-standing family friendship with the senior partner and will support anything the senior partner says.
- The conveyancing partner, a salaried partner. Often stressed, and sometimes cross. They always support the COLP as the COLP resolves all of their client concerns so easily.

Alternatively, instead of a role play you can imagine the different reactions and how you might put forward your perspective and agree a course of action. Faced with these individuals, how could you manage this situation and decide on a plan of action?

Fiduciary duties

We have seen that the legal aspect of any transaction can influence the way in which monies are handled. Solicitors do have to follow the instructions from their clients, but there can also be interpretation in the way those monies are dealt with. As well as having a legal interpretation, this can also be a 'fiduciary duty', meaning that the solicitor and the solicitor's firm have to act in the best interests of the client overall, including in financial matters.

This is very similar to the COLP perspective section above, but not quite the same thing. A fiduciary and a lawyer can be different, but the lawyer owes fiduciary duties alongside the confidentiality, professional secrecy, and other aspects of their role.

A fiduciary is sometimes in charge of a situation; in the case of lawyers, because of their knowledge, and professional skill. They know more than the client in the vast majority of cases, and are appointed for that reason. The fiduciary duty is to consider the situation and act, using that professional skill in the way that is correct for the client and considers their situation overall. The position is one of trust (with a small 't') and cannot and should not be abused. We have discussed professionalism in Part 1 of this book, and the position of the solicitor in the interactions with the justice system and the state is relevant to the consideration of the fiduciary duty and expectations of the client.

The solicitor as fiduciary acts on behalf of the client, meaning that their interpretation of the situation, including the legal interpretation and the financial interpretation of the situation, is important. The fiduciary (solicitor) could take certain steps, without formally documenting them, and these steps might be indicative of an overall action intended to assist the client. That overall action could be an interpretation of the law. For example, the movement of monies within a transaction might indicate a legal interpretation of a situation rather than a transactional one.

The Reporting Accountant has to be careful in this situation; they may not understand some transactions sufficiently to understand why or how certain points have occurred. The COLP or COFA may understand, but sometimes the best interpretation comes from an experienced lawyer in the same field.

Fiduciary duties are also covered in Part 5 of this book.

In saying all of this, it is also often true that those auditing a firm in any capacity should 'say what they see'. Fiduciary duties could be an explanation in some cases but, faced with Accounts Rules breaches, the Reporting Accountant should also remember they are being asked to report according to their professional judgement.

Standard of Proof at the Solicitors Disciplinary Tribunal (SDT)

At the same time as the SRA's consultations on the new Standards and Regulations, the SDT consulted on changes to their operating procedures, to allow for a new standard of proof.

A standard of proof is how much evidence is required before a matter can be proved. Standards of proof vary between criminal matters (beyond reasonable doubt) and civil matters (balance of probabilities).

Previously, the standard of proof at the SDT was a sliding scale, with the most serious allegations having to be proved beyond reasonable doubt. The least serious allegations had to be proved on the balance of probabilities. The balance of probabilities is what is more likely than not; it requires some degree of evidential capability to prove it, but the evidence does not have to be complete, as it would in the case of beyond reasonable doubt.

To assist, you might imagine the scales of justice.

Firstly: What tips the balance? That is the balance of probabilities.

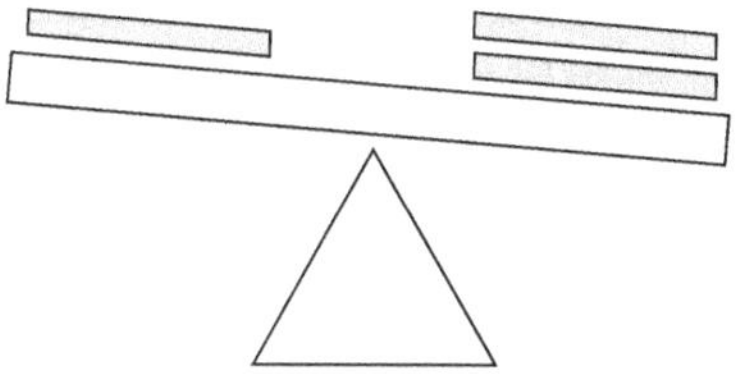

Secondly: What completely weights the scales? That is beyond reasonable doubt.

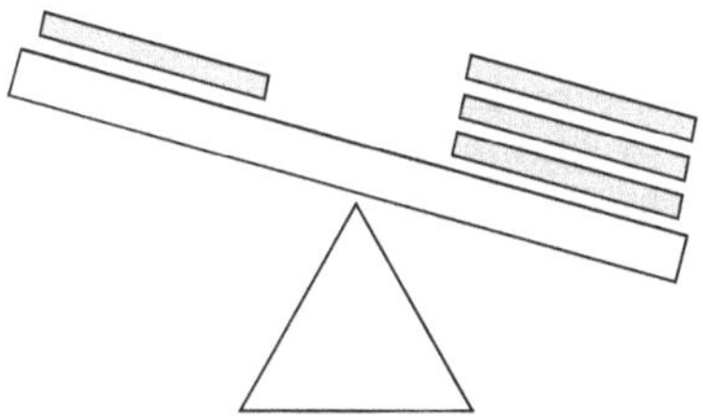

The sliding scale meant that the SRA and SDT would look for the allegation to require more proof, the more serious it was. The most serious allegations required the most amount of proof, including cases of alleged dishonesty.

The writer has included the position on the standard of proof in her courses due to the perceived need for accountants to understand the evidential tests for proving allegations at the SDT. Evidence is, of course, needed to demonstrate any allegation; without evidence against an individual, any prosecution would fail.

Criminal cases need to be proved to the criminal standard (beyond reasonable doubt), whereas civil cases need to be proved to the lesser standard, on the balance of probabilities.

The movement at the SDT causes some concern, in that it now becomes easier for the SRA to prosecute the most serious cases. The SRA will have to provide less evidence in respect of the most serious allegations for a prosecution to be successful. In some cases, we could be discussing simultaneous criminal allegations. Reporting Accountants, as we have discussed, are required to report fraud to the regulator and money laundering to the NCA; but these are reports of possible or suspected criminal activity. The SRA is adopting an approach of a separate report of these allegations, and a separate professional prosecution, albeit at a lower end of the scale of proof.

This could cause a problem. If a criminal court found the solicitor had not committed a fraud, but the SDT found they had acted in such a situation or way, where does this leave the individual solicitor's career? Whether or not the SRA would in that situation be able to prove the allegation against the solicitor is questionable. The SRA may choose to leave the prosecution of the solicitor to the criminal courts. If the prosecution against the solicitor failed, the SRA may consider whether it had sufficient evidence and information, or grounds of a breach of the rules of professional conduct, to mount its own prosecution of the breach of the rules as a lesser matter.

The SRA already defers to the court in some circumstances, where the court has jurisdiction over a discrete area of law which can cross into professional conduct. This includes in some matters of employment law, for example, where the issue of professional conduct crosses over into the matter of another area of law. The SRA does not usually go beyond another court's jurisdiction, or behind their decision making on the same facts. Often, the SRA will ask for a report on a matter after the court has decided it, and will decide at that point whether issues of professional misconduct occur or otherwise. What we may then see is the SRA or SDT stepping back where issues of criminality present themselves, and the criminal courts taking on the prosecution. The SDT may be taking a line where they will consider lesser matters.

For a criminal offence to be prosecuted, a breach of the Accounts Rules would need to be so serious as to amount to an offence, and capable of proof beyond reasonable doubt (taking into account legitimate explanations of fiduciary or legal duty). On occasion, such matters are prosecuted by the police, and sometimes solicitors are convicted of matters such as money laundering or fraud, due to movements through their client accounts.

At the same time as the movement at the SDT, the SRA has asked Reporting Accountants to provide reports to it which represent the most serious breaches, and has undertaken work to improve the quality and consistency of accountants' reports. The overall effect of this action is to squeeze the reporting in the middle, meaning the SRA is asking for sharper reports from the accountant, and prosecuting matters before the Tribunal at a lower standard of proof. The SRA is asking the Reporting Accountant to weed out some of the reporting that they were doing previously, and to focus on the most serious matters to report.

The net effect may be to cut off the flow of information to the SRA, meaning it needs less staff to undertake the work, but the matters it receives are more likely to be prosecuted. At the moment, and previously, the SRA has taken on large volumes of work in sifting through intelligence and information from a variety of sources. In asking the Reporting Accountant to send less in, the accountant might perceive (rightly) that a qualified report is now more likely to lead to investigation and prosecution than it was before.

The SRA does not ask the Reporting Accountant to consider the reporting evidence it sends in. This is a legal task. It is for the SRA to determine whether the evidence meets the test for prosecution and for the SDT to determine whether the SRA has made its case with regard to both the allegation of a breach of the rules, and whether there is sufficient evidence. Nonetheless, it can be worthwhile for an accountant to ask whether or not they have the evidence to substantiate the report they are making or whether what they are sending to the regulator is, for example, suspicion. That is not to say that suspicion should not be reported, in any way, and Reporting Accountants will be familiar with the test for reporting suspicions in cases of suspected money laundering.

The test for reporting for money laundering does not require any evidence at all; you are asked to report suspicions, which are sometimes formulated prior to gathering evidence. The difference with the accountants' report is the regulator is asking for a professional's view on the position of the accounts and in particular the client account, with reference to the regulator's standards. It is for the regulator to assess whether to prosecute, with reference to the relevant professional and evidential standards. However, it can be helpful for the accountant or COFA to practise his or her judgement in assessing evidence or proof, and sometimes this is also a helpful exercise in practising reasoning skills.

EXERCISE: EVIDENTIAL TESTS

Before you begin this exercise, a reminder:

1. The SRA does not require the Reporting Accountant to assess the evidence before the report is sent to them. It is the SRA's role to assess the evidence if they wish to take the matter further.
2. The NCA (and other law enforcement agencies) do not require evidence of money laundering to report suspected money laundering.

This is simply an exercise in understanding the evidence required to begin a prosecution.

You are a Reporting Accountant and you have heard about a case with another accountancy firm where a law firm has been making inappropriate client account transfers to the personal accounts of the partners. The accountancy firm found it happening and reported the matter to the SRA. The SRA intervened into the firm.

Consider the following questions:

1. What standard of evidence does the SRA currently need to bring a prosecution at the SDT against the law firm?
2. What evidence could you think of that they might be able to gather?

Now contrast the position with a law firm who were accused of money laundering. This is a criminal offence and would need to be proved accordingly. Imagine the scenario is that the partners of a law firm, clients of another accountancy firm, were arrested on suspicion of money laundering. The allegation was that they were laundering the proceeds of crime through their law firm client account.

Consider the following:

1. What standard of evidence does the police need to bring a prosecution against the law firm?
2. What evidence could you think of that they might be able to gather?
3. What is the difference between this scenario and the first scenario in evidential terms? Have you taken that into account?

Hopefully this exercise allows you the opportunity to reflect on the different standards of evidence required by prosecuting authorities before action can be taken.

Internal accountancy conflicts of interest; the third view

A question that has often been asked on the courses is whether there is a conflict of interest between the Reporting Accountant and the firm if the firm has employed the Reporting Accountant to undertake accountancy work for them in the past. The question arises because accountancy firms are being asked to provide an independent view of the accounts, but in some cases have undertaken extensive work for the firm.

This is a matter for the relevant accountancy professional body, but the SRA is asking for an independent view. As discussed on the courses, the accountant must be independent of the firm – for example, the accountant cannot also prepare the firm's accounts and then prepare the accountants' report, or be an employee of the firm.

If you have concerns about the ability of the staff to remove themselves sufficiently from the client situation to provide an independent view, you could ask the law firm to bring in another accountancy practice.

To establish whether there is a conflict or not, the writer uses a 'third view' technique herself with law firms to ensure there are no potential or perceived conflicts of interest. If a party within the firm perceives a potential conflict, the 'third view' requires the firm to involve a senior independent third party within the firm to assess the risk. The third view has to ask at this stage, 'why do you perceive a conflict, do we need to stop acting, and what is the best course of action?'.

This is where the third view steps in and gives a second opinion on any point of contention, to ensure a minor issue, which is not in fact a conflict, does not derail the entire transaction or cause difficulty with established and valued clients. The third view should ideally fall to *very senior and experienced management level individuals* with a solid understanding of the rules of professional conduct and control of the operation of the firm. The third view can veto the transaction if there is a conflict of interest and, of course, should act appropriately.

The third view is *not* an excuse not to comply with the rules of professional conduct or company law, or any veiled attempt at non-compliance. It is also not an excuse to act in conflict of interest situations.

Rather, it is an acknowledgement that often the decision to act or not to act and the investigation into the same can disrupt working for valued clients and cause upset to all parties. Creating a scenario where questions can be asked neutrally, but clearly within the procedural bounds of the firm, allows for the exploration of the issues under the oversight and decision making of a very senior individual. This allows steps in exploration to be taken which do not derail any relationships and allows client care needs to be met at all times. The person with the third view has to ensure the firm's interests are protected, *and* the client's interests are protected, while taking a step back from the actual transaction. The person with the third view must have the authority to say the firm must cease to act for the client if necessary. It allows a balance in the transaction, and a view of the strengths and weaknesses of the firm. It allows the transaction to be managed effectively, including ceasing to act, or not taking instructions, and any potential complaints to be dealt with.

This is a technique that needs planning in advance, adopting by the firm, and an understanding by all parties involved. It should not be attempted without sufficient planning, procedural implementation, and buy-in from all staff members and management. However, once introduced and tried a few times, it allows professional services firms go forward slowly, safely and in a timely manner, whilst still allowing them to stop if needed and before any damage is done, because they are doing so both step by step and under the watching eye of an experienced, suitably senior individual within the firm, with the authority of the firm to act as needed.

There is no exercise at the conclusion of this section because the third view needs the procedures, support, and buy-in of the firm. Consider whether it is suitable for your firm and whether you have the need for such a system, the personal skill sets and interpersonal dynamics suitable for such a scenario, and the availability of the senior individuals needed to give the 'third view'.

Sectoral accountancy conflicts of interest

Of course, accountants regulated by the ICAEW may have a separate conflict of interest. The ICAEW has recently become authorised to regulate probate, allowing accountants regulated by them their first opportunity to deliver legal services.

The ICAEW is regulated and overseen itself by the Legal Services Board (LSB), which is the oversight regulator for the SRA and other regulatory bodies who themselves regulate reserved legal work. The position of the LSB and legal services regulation is discussed in Part 1 of this book.

The potential conflict arises as accountants are now potentially in competition with law firms for the same customers and the same work. The use of accountants to complete independent reports in this scenario is questionable.

In particular, you might ask:

- Does the accountant have a vested interest in the outcome of the accountants' report?
- In completing the report, does the accountant have access to information about clients and law firm financial matters that may be of commercial use to the accountant?
- Could staff leave the accountant and go to work elsewhere, where the knowledge of the law firms they have worked with would be commercially useful, to the detriment of the law firm?
- Could regulated accountants as a whole use the position within the sector (outlined in Part 1 of this book) to their advantage as a regulated community?
- Could either party undertake actions in this situation that are anti-competitive?

There may be solutions available to some or all of these situations.

Both the SRA and ICAEW are regulated by the same oversight regulator. The LSB does not regard the ICAEW as being superior in the delivery of probate or handling of client monies to the SRA.

Depending on how the situation develops within the sector, in the medium to long term, the accountants' report may have to cease due to conflict of interest between the two styles of professional practice. We have seen that the accountants are offering independent reviews of SRA-regulated firms at present. It appears there are sufficient accountancy practices currently offering this service and relatively few offering the probate service. Should those numbers change dramatically, there may need to be an alternative to the current independent view of client account.

Of course, Alternative Business Structures are also a possibility and, despite their failure to yet take hold within legal services, we could still see the greater merger of professional services firms in the future.

De minimis provisions

The Solicitors Accounts Rules have very limited de minimis provisions. We can include:

- The requirement not to obtain an accountants' report if the amount of client monies held is small.
- Aged balances, which can, in some circumstances and for very small amounts, be given away to charity or to the law firm, provided the law firm underwrites the transfer if a client ever reclaimed the monies (another example of fiduciary duty).
- Exemptions from specific Accounts Rules, which are sometimes granted if the firm can demonstrate that to comply would be a burden and the risk posed by their non-compliance is small.

The compliance burden could therefore be considered to be quite heavy, particularly for small law firms who have to comply with the same standard as larger law firms. Conversely, large law firms are likely to find themselves in difficulty due to the sheer volume of work they undertake, and the difficulty with keeping track of all of the transactions.

The writer's experience is that it is possible for large and small law firms to maintain an excellent standard of compliance with the Solicitors Accounts Rules, but that it can be hard work to do so. Difficulties with previous breaches or prior management of the accounts can also make working with ongoing accounts complex, and a source of continuing breaches.

In the management of these complex issues and continuing breaches, it can be tempting to suggest minor issues are de minimis while we sort out larger issues. Take care with this approach, as the Accounts Rules only allow for a limited number of issues (those identified above) to be treated this way. They are a strict set of rules, and the SRA is clear in its approach; that they should be adopted to the letter. Doing so often creates a workable and clear set of accounts, which to those reviewing them look like a work of art.

Using an accountants' report for another purpose

We have discussed above what the purpose of the accountants' report is. As we have already seen, the changes implemented by the SRA in 2015 allowed the debate to flourish amongst accountants concerning the changes and whether or not the accountant has to undertake a full audit of the firm, and what should be included.

We debated on the course the breadth of the possible audit approach, and what the SRA was actually asking for. The difficulty may be the potential for the firm to use the report in other ways. For example, if a potential firm investor or purchaser required some form of assurance of compliance or an opinion on what was being purchased, how would that be reflected in the accountants' report?

The important answer to this question is that it is not. The accountants' report is subject to a statutory function and a regulatory interpretation and has been produced pursuant to that. The report has not been produced for another or wider audience and may not be suitable for that purpose. To produce the report for a different purpose may place the accountant in a conflict of interest position overall.

The accountants' report is a snapshot in time; policies and procedures may change, and in particular the Accounts Rules changed significantly in 2019. The accountant may feel the Accounts Rules have or have not been complied with, but the COLP, firm or SRA may feel differently according to fiduciary duties, legal arguments or issues of holding monies on trust, which would all be considered in any subsequent investigation. An accountant may also be required to report their suspicion (for example, of money laundering), which again could impact the outcome of their report, but that suspicion may or may not be well founded.

Because of the fiduciary duties of the solicitor and holding monies on trust, the accountant cannot provide a full view of the situation in every case; they are not qualified solicitors. The same may be true of the assessment of mixed monies in the office account under the new rules; the accountant is not a costs lawyer.

Even considering this in the future is not an option. SRA policy and focus change as new attempts are made to open up the legal sector. Changes to the Accounts Rules are no exception, and we may see further amendments to the rules. That focus may not provide the information an investor is looking for, and making client account an investment subject could in itself cause difficulty.

Even though we have seen in the first two Parts of the book that there is an intent to attract investment into the sector, the accountants' report is not defined as being for that purpose and the link has not been established between the two. The accountants' report is, under the direction of, and for the purposes of, the regulator, serving a quasi-regulatory perspective.

We have seen that the accountancy definition of materiality was not to be applied to the client account (and arguably is not now to the office account, if there could be monies for 'fees' in there, which could be disputed), which means there is equally a different consideration to be given to the statutory reports to be produced under the Companies Act 2006 (as appropriate).

As a result, firms, accountants, COFAs, and others reading or using the accountants' report produced for the SRA should be aware that accountants are being asked specific questions. They are used to dealing with accounts and the SRA is asking them to investigate and determine, in their professional view, what the answer to the question on the form is, with reference to information provided by the SRA.

Closing gaps in the new Accounts Rules

We have discussed some of the possible gaps in the new Accounts Rules earlier in this Part of the book. On the course, we had begun to discuss how to close those gaps in implementing the new rules.

There are a number of potential problems with the new Accounts Rules introduced in the Standards and Regulations 2019. The rules effectively allow solicitors the ability to hold client monies outside of the firm but with client consent. This can mean the firm does not need to declare some client monies it holds, and may not need to declare them to a Reporting Accountant. It could also mean a firm could do away with the accountants' report altogether, despite holding sufficient client monies.

The rules permitting monies to be held outside client account in some circumstances mean it is questionable whether a third party could hold monies on behalf of the firm or individual solicitor. What if the solicitor was a signatory to a parent company? Would they owe two separate duties to the client and parent company – could the parent company hold the money on behalf of the client? The SRA hasn't answered this question directly; however, with the potential for more complex structures, it will probably be tested.

The rules imply the monies should be held by the structure regulated by the SRA, but there is not a specific definition; it simply says it should be read accordingly. With the potential for different structures, including those with parent companies overseas, this is an interesting development. Would it be possible to circumvent the compensation fund and complaint handling arrangements? Would it be possible to, in effect, 'hide' client monies whilst being held by a UK regulated structure? These questions remain unanswered.

An accountant would need to be careful in these situations. They may realise monies are held elsewhere (for example, through transactions on a bank statement), but they may not have full knowledge of the situation or what they are involved with. A previously straightforward report to the firm, and potentially the regulator, now becomes a much more opaque situation.

As we have seen earlier in this Part of the book, the accountant also faces potential problems in dealing with a mixed monies account if a firm has not been sufficiently clear in its division concerning when monies are owed to the firm.

Accountants may find difficulty arising from the changes if the monies are being held outside of client account. They might find they are looking in a variety of places. Adding complexity in this way is reminiscent of other anti-money laundering situations where layers are added to disguise the origin or travel of funds. From experience, these can take extremely detailed analysis or may not be able to be unravelled at all. Complex company structures, additional layers in accounting processes, and variation in who holds the purse strings may be used to disguise illicitly held or obtained funds. Accountants may be chasing their tails.

In some circumstances, there may not be an accountant or an accountants' report. This is what is known as the 'backdoor exemption'. As we have seen, client money can be placed outside of the client account, provided it is agreed by the firm and both the client and the firm have access to and a view of it. The requirement of obtaining an accountants' report is based on the value of the sums *within* the client account and the balances of the client account. Therefore, if monies are held outside the client account, there is no need to obtain an accountants' report.

This backdoor exemption creates an enormous problem. Firms can easily obtain client monies, convince clients to place them outside the client account, and have no check and balance on the funds at all. The client monies can then apparently be taken from the client with limited recourse to the authorities. We must remember that one of the bases of law firm intervention is the monies held on behalf of clients. This situation potentially leaves the door wide open for fraud, and misuse of client monies, with no view of the position at all.

Specific problems the accountant or firm may encounter are:

- Individuals holding monies outside of client account with client consent, but without firm consent or knowledge, but claiming to be in compliance with the rules.
- Members of the firm or partners within the partnership creating a situation where declared client monies held are within the exemption from obtaining an accountants' report, while other undeclared monies are held with client consent outside of the client account.
- Firms adopting a 'generous' definition of the monies due to the firm, which are able to be held in office account, but later leading to disputes and liabilities or indebtedness to the client from the firm.
- Investigating mixed monies accounts (client and office).
- Insolvency issues arising for firms due to the client liabilities presented above.
- Money laundering being conducted by the law firm, or in the name of the law firm, with monies being hidden in another location or another account.
- Monies being stored in third party accounts and being used for fraudulent purposes.
- Failure to present all monies for inspection by the accountant.

Key tools in dealing with the openness of the new Solicitors Accounts Rules are:

(1) A commitment not to hold client monies outside of client account from the firm, staff, and associated parties.

(2) Clear and established reasoning for believing monies are due to the firm.

The ways in which the firm can implement these pointers are:

(a) the employment contract of the individual solicitor, member of finance staff, or other staff member within the firm, including partners;

(b) the procedures and definitions in place within the law firm, particularly if the law firm has adopted changes to the holding of client monies under the Standards and Regulations 2019;

(c) the activities of the COFA and compliance team in checking how monies have been dealt with and the activities of the firm overall; and

(d) training for all staff on the Accounts Rules as a whole, including the firm's approach, a detailed understanding of monies being properly due from the client, and clarity as to how monies will be held.

Each of these points can be tailored to the firm approach, which can be made explicitly clear and written or implemented in such a way as to prevent the problems outlined above. For example, the employment contract may specify when monies can be held for the client outside the client account, and when monies will be held as client monies and office monies. That may be never for some firms, or with COFA authority for other firms. The procedures in place may also reflect the position of when the firm regards monies as being properly due from the client, and whose authority is required to hold monies, previously regarded as client monies under the 2011 rules, in the office account.

The COFA and compliance team can make part of their focus the checking of the implementation of these rules, including how and when monies are held in client account and in office accounts, and whether there is any agreement within the file with the client to hold monies outside of the firm accounts.

The rules prevent SRA-regulated firms from providing a banking facility to clients and, to ensure this meaning is understood, the SRA has provided a warning card which sets out how it should be interpreted. Arguably, all firms provide a banking facility in a way, by holding client money. The SRA's meaning is more discerning than this, excluding any transaction which forms a usual part of the legal transaction and advice being given. Should the client, for example, ask that monies be diverted to pay debts to third parties, or their usual outgoings, this should be resisted. Anything unusual or not part of the legal transaction should be avoided completely. In the same way as GDPR allows the client to access all their data and port it, the client has a right to their monies, but the rules preclude the regulated firm becoming involved in anything beyond the legal transaction. The note also provides instruction on how such transactions may be money laundering and may attempt to avoid detection.

Those holding client monies (including in escrow situations) may also find this needs a tighter definition of who must comply with the rules, and whether a third party holding monies on the client's behalf is also caught by them. Of course, we could see the situation where the third party is holding monies on the client's and firm's behalf, and is providing a banking facility to the clients, with the transaction being conducted under the name of the law firm. This poses a high risk for money laundering and using the good name of the solicitor inappropriately.

Of course, a neat solution to all the problems outlined may be to continue to adopt the previous set of Accounts Rules from 2011. There is no bar within the 2019 Solicitors Accounts Rules to doing so, and firms with well-designed systems and procedures may prefer to continue to do so.

Third party managed accounts

Third party managed accounts (TPMAs) are client accounts which are managed by another provider. The provider must be approved by the Financial Conduct Authority.

It has long been debated whether lawyers should hold monies in the client account directly or not. When working for the SRA many years ago, it was a subject of debate. So many of the SRA's prosecutions arise from breaches of the Accounts Rules, and ordinary practices have to spend large sums in maintaining compliance. Law firms are not banks; they are legal advisers and actors. They have to keep the clients' money safe and return the money to the client at the close of the transaction. Maintaining the client account is hard work. With any number of transactions happening at one time, the client account is a busy place, with lots of monies incoming and outgoing at any one time, meaning effective accounting records are essential.

It is now possible to hold monies through a third party, known as a TPMA. For transactional work which is not complex, fairly easy to predict, and where there will not be issues of confidentiality or legal professional privilege to contend with, a TPMA offers an excellent solution. The TPMA solution comes with a price; usually a management fee and fee per transaction, based on, or as a percentage of, the amount of monies passing through the account.

The writer produced a training course for Datalaw in approximately 2016 covering the Solicitors Accounts Rules. The course included looking at the position then of TPMAs. At the time, the idea was in its relative infancy, with the Bar operating a TPMA through the company BarCo. This was on offer to a range of legal businesses, not just barristers. The Bar set up BarCo as barristers were starting direct access offering of advocacy and barristers do not hold client monies directly. BarCo has since ceased operating, but the number of commercial TPMA services in the market has increased.

TPMAs might be an example of problem solving within the market, which is now offering real commercial opportunity. We wonder why Alternative Business Structures have not found their place in the market, of caused a 'big bang', but we already have provision for legal advice that consumers know and trust. At the moment, there are no effective facilities for solicitors and other lawyers to hold and account for client monies without a compliance investment and support. There is a heavy burden of compliance on the solicitor, and this might solve a problem in a valuable way for the less complex transaction. Using the TPMA allows the solicitor to remove transactions which are transactional and straightforward to another account, and frees the client account for those transactions which are more complex. Because a TPMA can be used per transaction, there is no obligation on a law firm to use the TPMA for all of its work; they can choose to use it as little or as much as they please.

Those law firms exclusively using TPMAs do not need to provide an accountants' report. If you are partly using a TPMA, you may still need to obtain an accountants' report, dependent on the amount in the law firm's own client account.

There could be long-term consequences for regulation of using the TPMA. We may find that:

- Fraud and Accounts Rules breaches are still possible through a TPMA, and that new frauds emerge to take advantage of any perceived weaknesses in the system. This could simply transfer regulation and compliance burden to a TPMA rather than impose it on a law firm.

- The TPMA results in less self-reporting to the legal regulator, and less serious breaches by law firms. Where there are serious breaches, they may be in relation to the complexity of a legal transaction rather than complete accounting failure, as is sometimes seen in the prosecutions of some solicitor firms.
- A change in the use of the accountants' report. The accountant may be looking at smaller numbers of transactions in firms that also use TPMAs, allowing the accountant to focus on the transactions in the client account in more detail. The accountant also has a greater confidence interval in respect of the matters that make it into the accountants' report, given the greater percentage of files sampled.
- There is an increase in costs passed to the end client, due to the cost of maintaining the TPMA.

It seems unlikely the TPMA would remove the need for the accountants' report altogether. Issues of fiduciary duties, confidentiality, and legal professional privilege are not resolved by a TPMA. The overheads are also potentially high for using a TPMA exclusively. However, we might see changes in the use of the client account, client account procedure and costs in different types of transactions, and the focus of the accountants' report on different types of matters. Whether or not the use of the accountants' report, in circumstances where legal professional privilege is more likely to occur, is suitable is an issue for debate.

EXERCISE: TPMAs

This exercise is for you to consider on your own or with your management team.

If you work in a law firm:

- Does the above debate give you pause for thought about the use of your client account or the transactions processed through it?
- Do you think your firm or other firms will use TPMAs in the future?
- What are the major stumbling blocks to implementation?
- Where does the TPMA leave issues of self-reporting and risk management within law firms?

If you are a Reporting Accountant:

- Can you see the benefits for some law firms?
- Where do you see the future of the accountants' report for law firms?
- What does the TPMA do to the accountants' report? Does it change the nature of the work to be completed, reporting to the regulator, and possible response?

HOLDING CLIENT MONEY – USE OF ESCROW (OR THIRD PARTY MANAGED ACCOUNTS)

Below is an extract from training produced by the writer in March 2016:

> 'The SRA is open to discussions with firms wanting to use escrow accounts to manage client money - also known as Third Party Managed

Accounts (TPMA). The idea is a third party holds the money rather than the solicitor holding it in client account; the money is paid to the TPMA directly by the client. Money can be held in pooled, segregated accounts. One prominent example of this in the sector is BARCO, a third party company operated by the Bar Council, who hold client money on behalf of barristers. BARCO also offer the service to solicitors. All TPMAs are regulated by the FCA.

Why TPMA?

There are serious risks to holding client money. From internal fraud to email and telephone scams, firms must be constantly vigilant.

...

If you undertake conveyancing or probate work, for example, you may need to carefully consider whether there would be enough speed and flexibility for you. However those undertaking the odd transaction may find the system less burdensome than operating a client account.

SRA Policy Position

The SRA has long wanted alternatives to client account due to the regulatory risk it poses. The idea was also advocated by the Legal Services Board in their 2012 Conveyancing Thematic Review, which identified misuse of client account as a major risk to consumers.

Exploring escrow accounts has been seen by some as the first step to removing client account altogether, however the situation is probably more nuanced than that. The SRA have accepted that those making regular use of client account may not find TPMA as efficient as client account, but they have suggested other suitable alternatives may be available in future. This means client account is safe for now, for those that want it, but choice is also available for those that would like to structure their business in a different way.

The Rules

The SRA do not need to make any changes to the Accounts Rules or handbook, as there is nothing within them prohibiting the use of TPMAs.

...

The final decision on the use of escrow accounts and how they will be approved will be taken during review of Accounts Rules coming later in 2016. However the SRA are currently open to discussions with firms who would like to use a TPMA. Firms exploring the issue with the SRA should note conditions may be imposed on doing so.

For those keeping their client account, or those considering a TPMA in the longer term, the SRA are looking at making further improvements to the Accounts Rules in 2016, with phase three of their review of the rules due for consultation. This is expected to be a more fundamental review of the Accounts Rules, intended to simplify the rules down to a principles-based system. Whether it is possible to simplify the system, while maintaining the same level of protection, remains to be seen.

> *Costs*
>
> There are a number of TPMA providers available, all with varying costs. By way of example however, BARCO, the escrow provider set up by the Bar Council, provided us with some information about their charges. They told us their fees are charged on a case by case basis and are only chargeable on the lawyer's fee. They take fees from the account, usually at the end of the case and do not make any charge for handling or paying out other funds. Their costs vary according to the type of work. They said:
>
> > "For example, for domestic litigation and commercial conveyancing we operate a sliding scale starting at 2% on fees up to £50,000, reducing in stages to 0.75% for higher amounts. For international litigation and commercial conveyancing the tariff is the same but with a minimum charge of £50. For personal injury, the same applies but with a minimum charge of £125. And finally, for residential conveyancing it is simply a flat fee of £125. (February 2016)".'

Readers are asked to note that BARCO is no longer in operation.

'Client' accounts

Solicitors' client accounts have always had to be held under the name 'client'. This has been part of the rules for many years and continues under the latest set of rules.

This provides important protection for the client in the event of law firm insolvency. The client account monies are said not to belong to the law firm, but to the client themselves. If the regulator intervenes into a law firm due to insolvency, the client account belongs to the clients themselves, subject to the regulator's (or appointed firm's) reconciliation of the client account with the client files. If there is a shortfall, a claim can often be made on the Compensation Fund.

However, monies are also guaranteed by the compensation scheme in operation in financial services following Northern Rock.

Changes under the new rules include changes to the definition of client monies, meaning that, in some cases, what has previously been defined as client monies can now been defined as office monies. There is a change, or shift in expectation, about billing. The firm can now earmark costs owed to them in advance, and move those monies to the client account.

As we have seen, this can cause problems. All it takes is a difference in opinion about whether the monies are due, an argument over costs or billing from the client, or a definition or interpretation from the firm or solicitor which is too wide, and the firm has a liability to one or more clients.

However, on the other side of the argument, the firm has undertaken work for the client before billing takes place. This can include:

At the outset of the transaction:

- initial advice, in person, over the phone, or in writing;
- a consideration of the matter and any risks;
- investigations of the proposed transaction; or
- compliance-related issues such as checking client identity and ownership of relevant assets.

During the transaction:

- ongoing advice, support and guidance;
- liaison with other parties to the transaction; or
- movement of the transaction to the conclusion.

At the conclusion of the transaction:

- final advice and future pointers;
- closure of the matter and closure formalities; or
- ensuring all other parties (as required) have been notified of all formalities.

This is a broad summary of the types of advice that can be given during a transaction, but the billing only occurs at the end of the matter, or at key stages. Accordingly, it is likely that, prior to the end of the matter, or the next key stage, a large amount of the monies on client account earmarked for fees will belong to the firm, provided those have been agreed with the client and there is no dispute.

We could then say some monies within the client account are, in fact, office monies, and a generous interpretation of the rules has allowed it to be shown as belonging to the client. Indeed, if the monies were not due on account of costs, why have they been paid to the firm already?

Even if a client's matter does not reach a conclusion, the client has still received advice and support from the firm and should be charged. The client may have been agreeing to this position by providing the funds to the law firm in the first place.

So where does this leave the name of the account? Going forward, client monies in the client account will continue to receive protection. Client monies in the office account (for example, monies which are due to the firm as a result of work done for the client or anticipated to be done) will not receive the same protection in the event of insolvency, but the office account may need to be considered by the regulator in the case of insolvency, due to the potential for the existence of client monies within the account, for the reasons given earlier. The policies and procedures of the firm may be relevant.

We may see changes to reporting for insolvency and the imposition of Practising Certificate conditions because of this change. Reporting for insolvency could reduce (unless firms are in the position of misinterpreting the monies due to the firm), and the nature and type of Practising Certificate conditions may also change. We could, for example, see fewer conditions imposed restricting access to client account, and more restricting access to the financial functions of the firm, to prevent access to the billing arrangements and policies and procedures of the firm, or the arrangements for the transfers specifically. That type of condition, and the ability to pinpoint the issue within the firm (or manage a risk connected to it), is very valuable for a regulator. However, the wide scope of such a condition may also cause problems for a firm in managing their compliance.

EXERCISE: WHAT'S IN A NAME?

Can we call the office account the office account anymore?

Debate these ideas with finance staff, your COLP, or with your accountancy firm.

Could the regulators do any of the following and what would the impacts be?

a. Change the name of the office account to something else. What would the name be?

b. Introduce capital adequacy requirements for law firms.

c. Require compliance with a stricter set of Accounts Rules for firms who are carrying too many liabilities or too much debt.

   In particular, consider whether those with larger amounts of liabilities should be subject to stricter rules around what constitutes client monies and what constitutes office monies, to prevent advance billing (and potential overbilling) propping up the firm.

d. Impose stricter sets of Accounts Rules as part of risk management, preventing risky practices holding monies for fees in the office account?

e. Impose conditions for compliance with previous sets of Accounts Rules for non-compliance?

f. Require law firms to provide a deposit scheme for fees taken in advance, in case of dispute.

Example breaches register

The following breaches register can be used in any SRA-regulated firm to record breaches. It is not a requirement to keep a central breaches register any longer. However, doing so can help in the following scenarios:

- Keeping a record of mistakes in reconciliations which have been corrected.
- Keeping a record of general accounting errors which have been corrected.
- Remembering what happened – maintaining a breaches register can help you recall the situation accurately without a lot of paper.
- When working with an external accountant who produces your annual accountants' report, it can help to demonstrate the steps you have taken to achieve compliance.

This breaches register should be maintained by the COFA within the firm who can record the breaches, ensure the correct remedial action has been taken, and make decisions to report if necessary. The breaches register below can be signed off to demonstrate this ongoing compliance to the satisfaction of the practice.

COLPs may also find this breaches register useful for dealing with breaches which occur in the legal or practice management areas of the business.

Breach circumstances, team and fee earner	Regulations in question	Minor or Serious?	Reported to the SRA? Provide explanation of decision	Final outcome	Signed by (COFA / another partner)

Annex 1 – Areas of Potential Audit for Law Firms (2016–2021) (Non Accounts)

This annex provides a list of the possible areas of audit within a law firm, which are not contained within an accountants' report. It was produced in 2016, and the writer has updated it very slightly in 2021. It is not exhaustive, but it gives an excellent indication of the breadth and depth of compliance and the work required of a COLP and COFA, even in very small firms.

AREA OF COMPLIANCE

Management & Continuity

Strategy & planning

Turnover

Liquidity

Profitability

Business model

Debt

Assets

Structure – within regulatory requirements; group profitability & risk of contagion

Other businesses / equity risk

Capital adequacy

Business continuity

Staff management

File supervision

IT support

Outsourcing adequacy

Cybercrime

Employee checks

Single client reliance

Outside influence

Document storage and confidentiality

Training and development

Whistleblowing

Governance and decision making

Firm security

Marketing and reputational risk

Continuous improvement (linked to complaints strategy)

Risk management

Client Care

Client care letter

Terms of engagement

Complaint handling

Complaints strategy

Fee estimates

Completion statements / bills correct

Monies returned to client

Ledger correct

Claims management / handling

Advice quality

Vulnerability of clients

Statutory & Professional Obligations

AML policy

AML awareness

AML risk assessment

AML annual report

AML ID and reliance policy

AML training

AML information for clients

NCA reports

MLRO

Deputy MLRO

MLCO

COLP

COFA

Insurance intermediary

Data protection

Data controller

Acting on both sides

Conflict of interest

Confidentiality

File reviews

Document storage

Referral fees

Separate businesses

Competence statement

Practising Certificates and registrations

Acting in the best interest of the client (particularly charging policy, fee policy)

Treatment of third parties

Equality and diversity

Health and safety

HMRC

HMLR

SRA reports (received and made)

SRA inspections

Quality marks (Lexcel, IIP, etc)

STEP registrations

BSB, CILEx, CLC, FCA, and other regulators

Regulatory liaison

Insurer reports (linked to complaints handling)

External compliance publicity

Risk register

Ensuring up-to-date advice and guidance on compliance and risk management available across the firm

Part 7

Conclusions and Future Developments

Contents

Conclusions
- Defining serious breach
- Reframing conditions positively
- Complying with the spirit of the Accounts Rules
- Regulatory focus

Future developments
- Re-Interpretation of the Legal Services Act 2007
- The Future of Legal Services Regulation and the Single Legal Regulator
- Harmonisation of regulatory standards
- Ten-year revalidation
- Citizen rights of audience and education

Exercises:
- Mansion House: the suggested answer
- The reflective exercise: what did you learn?

This Part of the book is not written in two halves, as the previous Parts are. In this Part, we think purely in terms of bringing the book to a close, and what the future may hold for the different subjects we have covered.

At the end of this Part, you will find an exercise which hopefully helps you to reflect on what you have learned in the course of reading this book and completing the other exercises along the way. You may want to complete this reflective exercise after you have completed the other exercises in the book, including the example exercises from previous courses in Part 8.

Conclusions

We can see from the first Part of this book that the debates and options for practice we were covering in 2013 are still relevant now, albeit being approached in new ways through freelance solicitors and unregulated practices. That change has not come quickly, perhaps due to the number of solicitors who work and train in similar ways and the culture that exists around that training and learning.

We are still in an age of challenge to an accepted version of a solicitor model. It is questionable whether, moving further through the book, innovations such as

Third Party Managed Accounts will disrupt the fiduciary duties owed by solicitors to clients and involve solicitors in a purely transactional role, rather than an advisory one.

Of course, there have been major changes to the policy of the SRA, and intent to open up the legal services market. The SRA model, the solicitor blueprint, and the current Standards and Regulations continue at the moment. Whether the weight of current solicitor practices will be sufficient to hold up the progress or attempts at change in the sector is open to question.

Looking back to 2016, the writer delivered a presentation covering the ongoing changes at that moment in time. The list of areas covered is below. We can see now dramatic progress in all of the areas concerned, with a complete re-write of the rules or attempts at changing the market in most areas covered below:

- *Competence Statement & CPD* – this changed in 2014, with the removal of requirements to record 12 hours' CPD, and the implementation of personal reflection. As we will see later in this Part, it may change again.
- *Accountants' Reports – No need to submit unless accountant qualified report* – and other changes from 2015 which we covered in Part 6.
- *A Question of Trust* – looking at the views of the public and how these should be reflected in the rules; one of the developments that led to the Standards and Regulations 2019.
- *Separate business rule* – implementation of changes allowing solicitors to work more closely with those running other businesses, provided clients were appropriately informed. This led to the changes in the Standards and Regulations 2019 allowing solicitors to work freelance and with unregulated businesses.
- *Holding client money (escrow)* – now permitted with certain providers; this is also covered in Part 6.
- *Solicitor qualifying exam consultation* – another attempt at changing the barriers to entry and exit within the market, which has, at the time of writing, just been launched.
- *Deregulation Act* – which resulted in further powers being created for CLC practices, beyond the 'four Acts'.
- *Coming up – major re-write of Accounts Rules.*
- *Re-write of Handbook?*

These last two points became the Standards and Regulations 2019, just three years later.

On a micro level the changes are taking effect, and firms are likely to see this in the way they do business. However on a macro, or market-wide level, we are still having the debates we saw in 2013, about whether outside businesses will more closely integrate themselves with the solicitor market and how those businesses will operate offering legal services.

The issues that drove the changes to the SRA Handbook in 2011 remain strategically important right now, albeit with more impetus behind the change or potential change and far greater freedom in practice. We have seen, in some places in this book, the writer describe the market as being taken out from underneath solicitors and their traditional modes of practice. The ability to exit their existing structures is limited by their:

- investments in the practice;
- ongoing work and insurance requirements;
- qualifications and the ability to transfer to new areas of work; and
- cultural factors, such as expectation of solicitors in similar positions.

Asking whether the market could collapse seems dramatic, but the potential rush of new business models will draw legal services business from somewhere and, although it is perceived as a growth market, some of that business will come from solicitors and their existing client base. Thus disrupting, and even closing, existing solicitor firms.

What can you consider if you are reading this? Have a think about:

- Client base – how secure is that and can you guarantee your income? What can you do to generate client loyalty?
- Structure – what can you do to work either more flexibly or review the structure of your operations? Not all work needs to be regulated but you may find benefits in continuing with regulation.
- Your competition and the potential competition – consider your competitors at the moment, but also the competitors that could start up against you as a result of the new structures. Have a think how you do business and where that might take you.
- Your expenditure – ensure your expenditure remains within reasonable bounds, given the potential changes in the market; strong management and a focus on liquidity are important.

In all of this and if you consider making changes particularly to your structure, ensure you consider the relevant requirements of separate business, outside influence, referral fees, conflict of interest and confidentiality.

While the new structures are attractive, they could also have some risky elements. Solicitors will be working alone in some of the new structures without the support of their fellow professionals, possibly leaving them more exposed to outside influences that may not feel the same way they do about their professional status. The trust that has been built in the solicitor model may easily be eroded.

Do ensure your own compliance continues, and that you support others in this position to achieve the requirements expected of them. We have seen the higher standards expected of solicitors and their staff, and continuing to maintain them may be a source of competitive advantage for you, and appreciated by your clients.

The reputational impact of breaches can be significant, as can prosecution for failure to report. We have discussed various models of COLP and COFA compliance within this book, and there are more available out there. Each business will have their own mechanisms of ensuring compliance and supporting their staff to achieve the correct outcomes.

The weight of compliance and expectation can be significant for some, and the implications of the amount of work involved can be significant. However, at the other end of the spectrum, the professionalism of the individual solicitor, their means of carrying on their own business, and their own ethical standpoint may be sufficient in some cases to see the solicitor through most compliance situations; provided they keep themselves up to date with the latest requirements.

Our examination of serious breach allows us to see the importance, within democratic society, of the role of the lawyer, and their ethical standard. Solicitors, barristers, and other lawyers are somewhat isolated within society as a result of their qualification, being placed in the unique position of having access to justice. Standards of education in modern society have, however, increased over time and the idea that a solicitor might speak for another if they could not might be redundant in some cases. There is an argument for legal and citizenship education alongside general education in schools, and this may allow us to re-examine the need to report solicitors, the need for solicitors to report themselves, and the necessity of solicitor professional conduct. Holding solicitors to 'higher standards' than the rest of society is stressful for the solicitor and possibly unnecessary, as we see other institutions fulfilling some roles, such as third party managed account (TPMA) providers assisting with client money management.

Innovations such as TPMAs may go a long way to providing a solution to the problem of holding client monies, even if they do not go the full way. These are issues which are responsible for the majority of serious breaches prosecuted against solicitors at the Tribunal. Difficulties in holding client monies or in managing accounts are also responsible for a number of Practising Certificate Conditions. The problems with solicitors holding client monies are issues long debated by the regulators; with solutions often being sought, and the end of client monies often on the table. The fiduciary duties owed by the solicitor to the client, and the legal professional privilege which attaches to the advice sought from the solicitor by the client, prevent all this from happening. The same issues pose the problem of using a TPMA; it theoretically breaches client confidentiality and could even breach privilege if the TPMA provider or another could work out what the solicitor was doing. This is why they might not go the full way, and why some solicitors may still need their client account for work which is not transactional, or for a mix of work, to provide sufficient coverage of non-transactional work for the same reasons.

Defining serious breach

When we discuss serious breaches, it is important to note there are often examples of serious breaches which are also anti-money laundering concerns, or might be indicators of the same. The examples at the end of this book feature a number which might cross that line and in respect of which a report to the authorities might be required in any event. While there are examples at the end of this book, but readers are also reminded, if they are faced with any situations where they know or suspect money laundering, of the need to make a report to their Money Laundering Reporting Officer and for them to make a report to the National Crime Agency as appropriate.

There are many other examples which are not money laundering concerns, and the purpose of the discussion is to ensure firms and individual solicitors:

- get to grips with their ethical standpoint;
- have confidence in that standpoint and feel able to discuss their position;
- don't shy away from the issues, or bury their heads in the sand;
- develop action or contingency plans for the events that can unfold in the event of a serious breach;
- develop the roles of the COLP and COFA respectively; and
- continue to be respected in the face of significant change in the sector, which could threaten the reputation of legal services as a whole.

The writer is acutely aware of the consequences of self-reporting, and has seen the outcomes first hand. However, practitioners should remember the breaches that are reportable are serious ones; ones which might result in the closure of the firm (for example, the misappropriation of client monies), which have resulted in convictions, or demonstrate, for example, violent behaviour. These are all examples of issues the SRA would expect to be reported, and it should be remembered that the vast majority of firms would also wish to report them as well.

The first and most important thing to say in respect of prosecution, possible prosecution, or possibly having to report yourself, is to take legal advice. In the best case scenario, it might be you do not have to report yourself after all and, in the worst, you are fully armed defensively. Having advice from someone experienced in these matters can make a real difference to you and your firm. The staff at the SRA might also be more sympathetic than you think; the subjects are so affecting and the stories behind them so human, staff at the SRA also sometimes want to do their best for the firm and the solicitor as well.

No-one wants to have to report themselves, and the consequences of doing so can be catastrophic for the solicitor and the firm. We have seen the arguments for protecting the public, upholding the criminal justice system, and maintaining the trust in the rule of law. We know that solicitors have a constitutional role, and professional standards to adhere to, but the concept of reporting yourself to an uncertain career future possibly goes beyond human behaviour.

It is not only the self-reporting that is at issue. We also have a situation where the regulator would need to be notified of any relevant investigation. We might have been able to say, 'it's ok, you have the opportunity to fully investigate before coming to a pragmatic conclusion that the matter is so serious as to amount to a serious issue of professional misconduct'. However the regulator would like to know about the investigation as well.

The solicitor has to make a quick decision; to report or not report. Matters of criminality would need to be reported, as would unauthorised and inappropriate transfers of client monies, as may taking unfair advantage of vulnerable people. Small errors and minor mistakes do not need to be reported to the regulator, but the area in the middle where the mistake is a bit more than minor and could have serious consequences, or where something has been done recklessly, causes considerable debate and concern.

There is now more guidance than ever before on self-reporting and the accepted standards of serious breach. This is a very welcome step forward for the regulator and helpful for the regulated community. What might be more helpful in time is a mechanism for safe harbours; the idea that a regulator could give people assurance in different circumstances that they would not be prosecuted, and save that prosecution for circumstances which truly deserve it.

To reach this understanding, new lines of enquiry may need to be developed, and work in different areas other than law may need to be undertaken. If the regulator had a greater breadth of experience or could draw on a greater knowledge from other areas, would that assist in articulating the level of seriousness they are seeking to be reported? Material breach had a definition, and a set of clarifying, fairly specific examples to support that definition. As we have seen, most people disregarded that definition and leapt into the ethical debate of whether professional reporting and prosecution or some form of outcome was required.

Perhaps we can use this debate to inform the definition of serious breach. We have already considered a definition of serious breach in Part 5 of this book. Asking the regulated community and other interested parties what they regard as a serious breach might also lead us to some form of definition.

Within our definition in Part 5, we could add 'misconduct involving the client account' as an aggravating factor related to that definition, given both the public disapproval of that position, and the continued prosecution of such cases before the Solicitors Disciplinary Tribunal.

When we discuss issues of integrity, we are often discussing the solicitor's standing in their own community as part of the reputation of legal services or justice. Defining the community the solicitor is in may be a complex task but, during the writer's own master's degree thesis, she mapped the locations of law firms against geographical population statistics of England and Wales. There is a close match, with greater concentrations of law firms in populous locations. We are also likely to see law firms in local towns and village locations. The match of law firms to areas of population was striking. The local solicitor has standing in his or her area, and local attitudes to their behaviour and acceptability of the behaviour of such a person in the community are important. This can be a local person who holds client monies, may defend local persons from the police, and may provide legal advice on a range of matters across the community. The standing in the local area can be similar to that of a local MP; certainly, they are a point of contact if needed by the community.

If a solicitor works in the city, the position may be the same with the businesses and other financial interests they represent. Their standing with their clients, their firm, and the firms around them may be damaged by some types of behaviour. However the perceptions and definitions of serious breach for a high street firm may be different due to the local importance of the individual and interaction with consumers.

We have seen that integrity can be expressed as completeness; perhaps a unique completeness that provides a place for the expression of positive human qualities. Qualities such as fairness, open-mindedness, care for others, independence, and probity. All of the things that make us human, in a good way. Striving to embody these qualities, and not allowing the negative aspects of human nature to gain control. There can also be a consistency, or steadiness to the individual which allows the continued trust in their practice and personal position.

Breach of integrity may be a shorthand for a form of serious breach. Many breaches of the rules may be serious; when does the point arise at which we can no longer say it is suitable for the individual to be a solicitor? Perhaps when that completeness has been damaged? It could be damaged by conflict of interest or hidden financial motive; it could be damaged by behaving unfairly or taking unfair advantage; it could be damaged by financial problems or inappropriate dealings with the client account.

One of the exercises in the book asked about offensive or potentially offensive behaviour; if we link a solicitor to his or her local community, or England and Wales as a whole, we might start to see how views of a solicitor's behaviour can shape their career or standing, and how damage can be done to the provision of legal services in England and Wales by their behaviour. However, we also see the stress of expectation this can cause to the individual, and that solicitors are the same as other people.

This is not, however, a manifesto for representation of local interests. The solicitor, although occupying a constitutional role, and exercising powers of law on behalf of clients, does not have a basis to represent their interests otherwise. Some feel they are there to challenge the system, and safeguard rights, whereas others see their role as more commercially focused. Whichever route you take with a legal qualification, there is no specific role or basis for representing individuals in the same way as an MP might.

The basis of self-reporting allows the solicitor, by not reporting any matters, to declare that his or her standing remains intact. They are declaring to the regulator that there are no serious breaches that the regulator needs to be aware of. The annual renewal also allows a declaration to be made annually that demonstrates again that there are no matters the SRA needs to be aware of. Of course, we are assuming the solicitor and the firm are being truthful.

When needing to make a report, there are:

- safeguards of legal advice;
- rights to make representations to the regulator;
- a range of regulatory outcomes including:
  - minor letters of advice,
  - rebukes,
  - small fines,
  - and internal regulatory settlement agreements;
- rights of appeal both internally and externally; and
- an oversight regulator.

There are also, as we have seen, a range of more serious regulatory outcomes involving the Solicitors Disciplinary Tribunal, including striking off and suspension.

We have also seen the range of checks and balances on the regulators from the other bodies in the sector.

A key check and balance in this process is the accountants' report. The report acts as an oversight of the client account and the systems the law firm has in place. The accountant is there to both sense-check the operation of the client account, but also provide an independent view of the law firm, from outside the firm. The accountants' report is a form of serious breach reporting, allowing and requiring the accountant to make a report in certain statutory situations, and allowing the exercise of the accountants' professional judgement in other situations.

We have seen that the COLP occupies an important role in these situations, particularly given the fiduciary duties of the solicitors within a law firm. The accountants' report provides the check and balance, but the COLP must check the role and power of the accountant as well. The cliff edge of serious breach reporting, and the consequences for firms and individuals of getting it wrong, are so serious as to warrant a significant amount of time and effort by firms in getting it right.

This system of checks and double checks provides so much complexity within law firms, it is a wonder anything gets reported at all. In fact, it does, but often by outside sources. Clients, third parties, the other side, interested bystanders, and the court, all have roles to play, as do outside agencies. The regulator is increasingly asking for only the most serious issues to be reported, by law firms and accountants. This will doubtless help their workload, and concentrate their work on prosecutions rather than lower-level regulatory outcomes. However, it may also be a response to criticism of the self-reporting regime, which of course can spell the end for careers, law firms, and personal finances of individuals.

By focusing on the most serious reports, the regulator is focused on responding to issues of:

- financial impropriety or dishonesty involving client monies;
- the involvement of solicitors in scams; and
- the prevention of legal services being run and administered by criminals.

These are the kinds and sorts of issues the legal regulators should be interested in. These are the types of issues where, for the regulator and for others, the individual involved becomes unsuitable to run a law firm and the individual career or the law firm operation would come to an end.

While we see law firms as commercial enterprises, and increasingly this becomes the case, they still occupy an important position within communities and in the public mind. They are also in a privileged position, having rights to undertake legal work which others do not, and dominating other types of legal work in a way which is unrivalled. Solicitors, and other legal professionals, have placed themselves in a dominating position over access to the courts and other forms of justice, that the regulator must provide a check and balance to their power. We have certainly started to see this in the implementation of rules requiring solicitors publish their prices online.

The regulator's response to different issues is important. The worry about serious breach can be about whether to report or not and, in an emotive situation, this is complex for the individual or firm who has to make the decision. What is important is the reaction of the regulator who has to make decisions about the consequences for the individuals, and the firms, who are perhaps not in the situations which are the most serious. While the regulator does not provide safe harbours, there might be a case for doing so sometimes, or offering greater clarity in the position of the solicitor and the costs consequences of prosecution.

At the moment, aside from further prosecution for failure to report, there is little incentive to confess to the regulator; whilst it is part of the rules, there are no lower sanctions or lesser costs for doing so. The regulator takes the same line with solicitors discovered breaching the rules as they do with those who have reported themselves.

There is little leeway in some of their statutory provisions – for example, intervention is the solution to the existence of firms who pose a serious risk to the public. However, a solicitor not in this situation, and not in a situation which would warrant strike-off or suspension, would appreciate clarity as to the likely outcomes and costs consequences of their actions. This, in turn, could assist with decision making in firms and by reporting accountants about:

- whether firms are required to report;
- whether accountants are required to report;
- whether the regulator would wish to investigate or not, and whether the investigation of the issue needs to be reported to the regulator; and
- the support the firm or the individual requires, and whether to invoke any form of contingency planning.

At the moment, decisions by the SDT are published in full, including the circumstances. The SRA publishes information which concerns the outcome of the decision, but not the circumstances. It might assist firms to have the information about the decision, the circumstances, and the reasons, for the internal decision, or for the SRA to regularly publish decisions which represent average circumstances of individuals and firms who have come before the regulator.

In law, there is a tradition of publishing and focusing on the unusual, to develop a body of legal reference and case law. However, in some circumstances it can be right to recognise the force and power of the institutions of the state and their decision making.

For the SRA, publishing its average casework would provide an insight into not only the legislative basis of its power, but the effect this legislation is having and the way this power is being exercised. Solicitors would also gain some of the insight argued for above. The interpretation of the legislation, the use of the regulatory rules, and the extent of the use of powers a body is afforded are arguably just as important as the unusual or leading cases it reports.

Those who observe the SRA may be aware that not all serious cases reach the Tribunal. Interventions sometimes do not and, in other cases, the evidence required for prosecution may not have met the required standard, or the solicitor has explained or mitigated their actions. In other cases, a decision may not have been reported as it was not in the public interest to do so. We cannot change these cases and this is not an argument to do so; however, the more information we have, the better the information is likely to be that the regulator will receive, and the better supported and informed the solicitors and firms are likely to be.

This might be an example of a virtuous circle, where the more information the sector receives about regulatory prosecutions and outcomes of serious breach reports, the better the decisions to report and consideration of the circumstances, the better the support for the law firm, and the better informed the arguments are on both sides about the circumstances. The position is also likely to improve the compliance of law firms, as firms are better able to understand their obligations without fear, and it may also improve the support available for law firms, provided in a more measured way, with a realistic expectation of the outcomes likely from reporting serious breach.

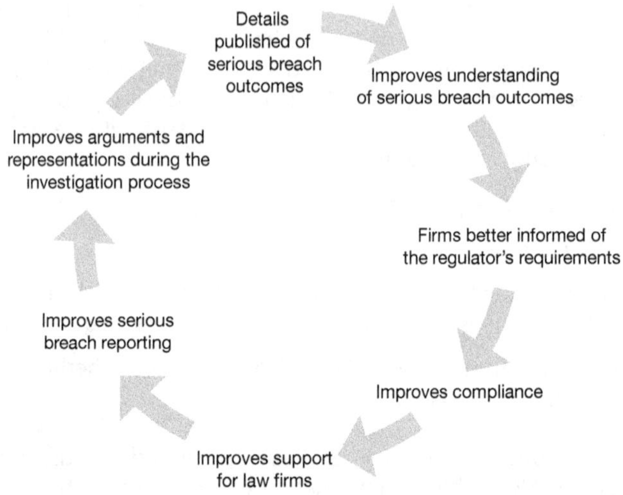

All of this is only possible with a sensible approach from the regulator to decisions and processes; with the same being true of approaches to costs.

The question we might ask is whether the regulator has fully utilised their regulatory tools in dealing with the reports they receive about serious breach. The writer has been exploring serious breach and Practising Certificate Conditions for a long time now with law firms and accountants. Practising Certificate conditions and firm conditions have the ability to manage or deal with the risk the law firm or individual poses to the public. We can make the link between Practising Certificate conditions and serious breach under the scenario of insolvency, when Practising Certificate conditions are the likely outcome, and the insolvency event is the serious or reportable breach.

If we recognise that law firms should report their own serious breaches, and we recognise that the regulator must also take steps to manage risk , Practising Certificate conditions become a possible contender in the outcomes for firms and individuals. We have seen earlier in the book that the regulator uses Practising Certificate conditions to deal with some issues, but not all of them. They also use:

- rebukes;
- fines;
- interventions; and
- a range of regulatory tools including:

- ongoing monitoring,
- consultation,
- education, and
- compliance support.

to achieve their end goal. The question is whether some of these regulatory outcomes are effective in achieving the regulator's aims, whether they deliver value for money, and whether the practice or practices at issue (or the individual solicitors) continue to cause concern that could pose a risk to the public.

If that is the case, the regulator could easily and more readily use a condition, even a small one, to manage that risk. A greater use of conditions on individuals and firms might develop a situation where conditions become commonplace within the solicitor market, and it becomes the norm to find firms and individuals with some form of restriction on the activities they undertake.

Re-framing conditions positively

The terms of the condition, being framed as 'some form of restriction' sounds negative, and the reaction from firms and individuals to this idea might be that conditions on their practice are unwelcome. But what if we could frame the condition in the positive? Is there a manner of writing a condition that allows the individual or firm to have their achievements or experience recognised, or focuses on the positive within the practice, that might be acceptable to the individual or firm?

For example, if we said Law Firm A has a problem department. The department does not fit very well with the rest of the practice and seems somewhat out of place. The other partners and departments in the law firm are not very good at providing oversight of that department, and the other departments work closer together as there are more referral opportunities. Eventually, the partner in charge of the problem department (partner Z) leaves, but when they do the remaining partners uncover a host of serious breaches and possible negligence claims. The firm cannot completely blame partner Z as the firm had some management failings as well. As a result of the situation, the SRA imposes a condition requiring the law firm to focus on their most successful departments (the remaining departments) for the following years.

In this sense, the condition is positively framed, but also takes Law Firm A away from the problem area, thus hopefully managing a situation and preventing any further breaches. Law Firm A is highly likely to have to put in place referrals to other law firms to deal with the problem department, as they are not taking on any more of this work, again taking them away from the particular area that has caused an issue. We will leave the debate about whether to impose individual conditions on partner Z up to the SRA, as partner Z moved on to another firm.

A law firm authorisation allows a firm to work across a range of legal disciplines. You might be a specialist in construction law, for example, but, if authorised by the SRA, your law firm might be able to undertake any legal work at all, within the bounds of rights of audience and your insurance. There is an argument to make for imposing conditions on firms binding them to stick to the area of law they work in and undertake nothing further.

This could solve a problem, seen fairly regularly, of firms moving into areas in which they are not specialists, but where there is a perceived need for the service or a profit to be made. Providing advice in non-specialist areas of law is not advised; unfortunately, the SRA frequently sees solicitors who have taken this step get into trouble as they have failed to precisely understand a situation or, worse, fallen for a scam. Believe it or not, that does happen when solicitors operate in areas of law they are unfamiliar with.

Other risks the SRA may be able to manage include risks poses by groups of law firms. We have seen the market in personal injury law curtailed in recent years, and referrals in personal injury banned. The SRA said, at the time of the ban, that it would struggle to enforce such a ban, despite being responsible for doing so. We could suggest the use of conditions in this situation, whereby all personal injury firms are required, by way of condition, not to accept referral fees. A breach of the condition clearly affects the law firms' authorisation and becomes a matter of professional conduct for the regulator to deal with. In addition, the condition is published and available for all to see on the regulator's website. If the condition was imposed across the board, the regulator would again be advertising that referral fees were not allowed, to anyone who looked up a personal injury firm.

This position need not just apply to personal injury lawyers, it might apply to any type of firm where there was a significant risk of an issue occurring and a condition would manage that risk, or a published condition would manage that risk. All conveyancing firms, for example, could be subject to a condition to comply with the Code for Completion by Post, and this becomes part of their authorisation. There is power in applying the condition to authorisations or individual practice, and even greater power in publicly stating the condition on a webpage for everyone to see.

The range of circumstances the regulator could use conditions for is vast. At the moment, we see a regulator whose work is focused on and responds to the receipt of large numbers of individual reports from a variety of sources. The number of firms it regulates is huge, making in-depth involvement difficult. We could see that process reimagined to focus more broadly on different types of regulatory issue, as was the original intention for thematic review, when it was first introduced in 2011.

Even taking a step back as a regulator and starting to work with the regulated community, or different groups within the regulated community, might generate a different regulatory outcome to the one we have seen so far. For example, working with personal injury lawyers and their groups might help to identify common risks to their groups and help to formulate a regulatory response. This response might include proportionate conditions to manage a risk. The same might occur, for example, with city firms or Sole Practitioners. Any group at financial risk or posing a financial risk could, for example, see a group-wide requirement for capital adequacy.

There is, of course, the need for conditions to be proportionate, and manage a specific risk, but we are discussing a development in regulatory style and complete departure from the current regulatory interpretation of the statute and SRA internal rules.

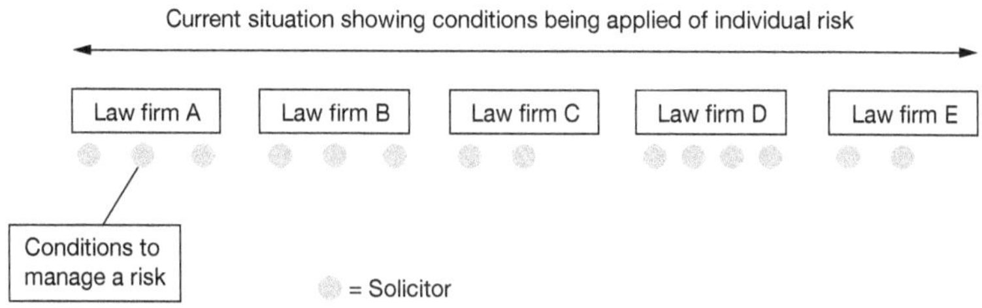

The diagram above shows the current situation, with conditions being applied to the individual solicitor to manage a risk, but impacting the firm. The SRA, of course, has the option of placing conditions on the entire firm. A possible use of conditions is shown below, with a group of firms having a condition applied. Of course, given the size of the regulated community, the reach of the condition would be much wider than five firms, but the diagram hopefully makes the point.

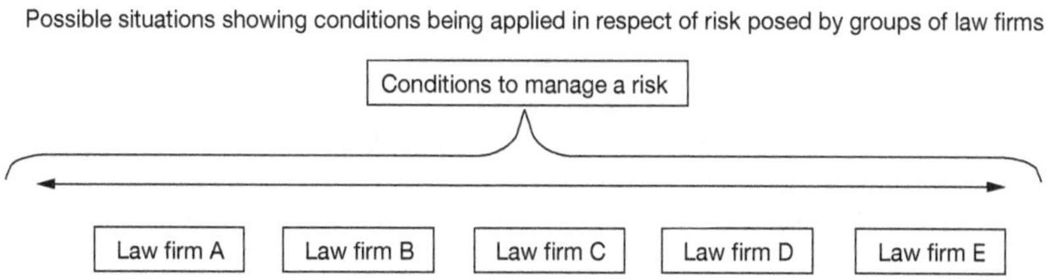

Similarly, we could also see blanket conditions imposed against groups of individual solicitors – for example, in-house solicitors, freelance solicitors, or solicitors returning to practice after some time away. Equally, the condition could be imposed on those in certain areas of law, or undertaking certain types of work. Sometimes, the regulator undertakes work in different areas as the rules and legal position of regulation change around the solicitor and solicitor's firm. 'Are firms undertaking this work?' is a fairly common question; 'If so, you must now do this'. Again, standard conditions dependent on the area of work, and renewable (or otherwise) every September, would be a straightforward mechanism to manage this type of work and an easy way to communicate with the regulated community.

If large numbers of the regulated community were subject to conditions, of different types, there would not be the stigma attached to them there is now. After all, all lawyers are risky in different ways, as are all law firms.

Maintaining the condition and complying with it might be part of the professionalism of the solicitor and his or her firm, and could become part of a shared view of the regulator and regulated firm about their competence, specialism, and how they should practise.

There are a variety of ways in which we can see individual and firm conditions being used, perhaps more creatively than they are at the moment. Earlier intervention into problems (when they are first perceived as an issue), and combatting that problem with a condition, could help firms manage the situation and develop their position accordingly. For example, an ABS with external investment could operate subject to conditions guaranteeing the financial stability of the ABS; the perceived risk being liquidity perhaps in the current economic climate of Brexit and coronavirus. This type of condition may prevent the collapse of a firm as a result of the economic climate, and could be imposed as soon as a problem was perceived.

Similarly, the risk of a Sole Practitioner operating across a range of legal disciplines, or switching their practice to another type of practice, could be managed by a condition relating to their legal education and continuous development. This condition could be imposed if the regulator were more proactive in their analysis of situations relating to individual practice, competence, and practice management.

Another example might be oversight; if we see an individual operating in a situation where they are not coping, perhaps they need more close monitoring. Perhaps in this situation a condition might be imposed to contact or check in with the regulator more frequently.

At the moment, the regulatory position remains fairly reactive; responding to the concerns of reports that are sent to the regulator, rather than proactively working with the regulated community to identify issues and act upon them.

The difficulty of taking this approach is the number of individuals and practices regulated by the SRA. The size of the regulated community means proactively working with all of these practices and individuals would be a significant challenge. However, instead of responding to every single concern that was raised, an alternative approach might be to attempt to develop a picture of a practice and address specific concerns with them. Of course, this may only work if the concern raised was not significant or required prosecution.

In any event, the more proactive use of conditions may result in fewer prosecutions, and serious outcomes for solicitors by addressing issues before they resulted in significant harm or required regulatory outcomes. There are certainly units within the regulator that work with law firms with a number of concerns raised against them and, if conditions were accepted not as a regulatory prosecution, but as a standard approach for many solicitors, or across many firms (or groups of firms), there could be means to avoid some of the risk and levels of prosecution we see currently.

If we then used the simultaneous path of self-reporting for serious breach, could we avoid much of the lower-level regulatory outcomes we see at the moment? This system would see the regulator concentrate far more on management within firms whereby conditions would become more commonplace. Self-reporting (or reporting amongst the community, or by other parties) would then tackle issues which need to be prosecuted. This could work if the regulated community and other parties were told which issues the regulator would individually investigate and consider prosecuting, and that the rest would be fed into a management consideration for the firm or individual.

The current position looks like this:

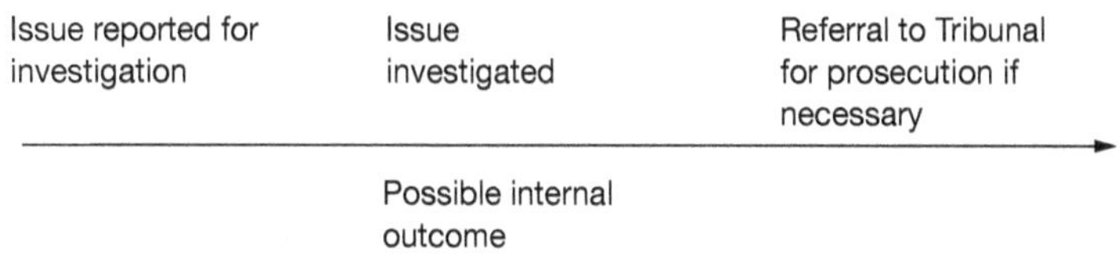

The alternative position might look more like this:

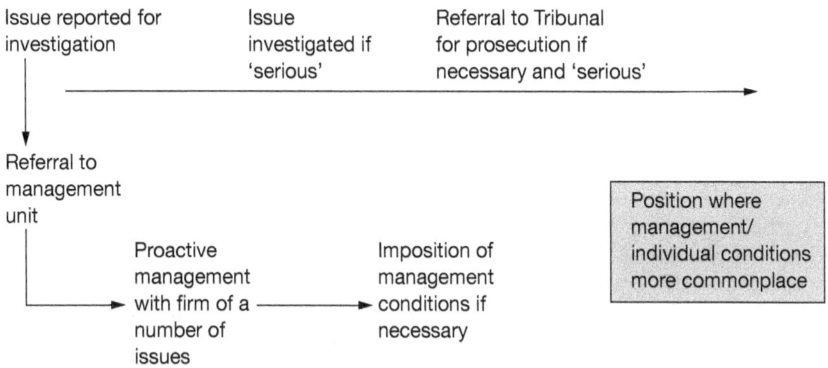

This divide in the two outcomes might also lend itself to the regulator's current resourcing levels; diverting the resources away from dealing with low-level regulatory investigations and more towards management considerations. Of course, staff would need to be adequately educated in management, and associated disciplines, in order to deal with these types of issues.

Of course, the use of serious breach and conditions might be the writer's vision of the future for the regulator, rather than the regulator's. Doing away with low-level or minor misconduct outcomes in the process, and re-envisioning the approach of the regulator, might not be on the agenda, but these can be helpful discussions to have to inform ourselves about regulation and its scope.

The question is whether this approach would disrupt the idea of solicitor professionalism, or in some way lower the standards clients or others expect from the solicitor. At the moment, those who complain do receive correspondence from the regulator, even if just to refer the matter to the Ombudsman. In some cases, the correspondence can be quite extensive. Whether we require that level of correspondence in respect of solicitor conduct is questionable. The current visions for greater access to legal services for consumers and others may level the playing field between solicitor and client, doing away with this level of correspondence as a means of making the position between the two more equal.

We have explored professionalism within this book, including the history of professional practice and the development and position of legal regulation at the current time. There is a large amount of pressure for change within the sector, and the status of solicitors is being called into question. We have seen other professionals given the opportunity to become partners in law firms, and a number of promotions as a result. But the questions remain whether work should be reserved to solicitors at all, and whether other types of legal advice or alternative legal solutions would be more effective than the current delivery.

Legal services are still perceived as being expensive. Solicitor costs and legal fees can be very expensive indeed, and the lack of clarity for non-lawyers about the legal options available to them is causing problems for small businesses and individuals. There is significant challenge to the solicitor model; reserved work has never been more open – there are now a number of approved legal regulators providing competition, and threatening established ways of providing legal services.

Solicitors may also see the new Standards and Regulations 2019 as a challenge to their professional position. The removal of large amounts of the previous handbooks, the loss of the indicative behaviours, alongside the alarming changes to the Accounts Rules, provide much less of a professional guide than was previously available.

Of course, there is a large amount of guidance, and some professions only have a very small amount of rules available, against which all behaviour is categorised and judged. However, solicitors do occupy important and essential positions in the legal framework of the country, provide local community support, keep confidences, and maintain a client account. Major changes to these rules may undermine their local standing, their professional status, and allow those with unethical motives to attempt to use gaps in the rules to undermine the rule of law.

Complying with the spirit of the Accounts Rules

We might see a similar situation with the changes to the Accounts Rules where we have a number of new gaps which could lead to confusion, mistakes, and mixed monies accounts. The potential difficulties of ensuring the monies in office account due for 'fees' are genuinely so, or the clients who 'agree' to monies being stored 'elsewhere, but with their agreement', are both issues where clients could be taken advantage of without truly understanding the situation. Whether the gaps are intended to undermine confidence in the solicitor profession, given the previous complaint handling and overcharging scandals of the past, is possible. Accountants, Reporting Accountants, COFAs and others in the accounting side of the profession are warned to be careful and take steps to protect their position and those of the accounts against wilful misuse. We have, of course, set out possible steps to close some of the gaps within the rules in Part 6 of the book, but there will clearly be more ways to apparently act in compliance whilst not acting in the spirit of the rules or, in fact, in accordance with the law.

It is important for COFAs and Reporting Accountants to remember that the accountants' report is not measured in accountancy terms of materiality, and that questions of fiduciary duty and holding monies on trust arise, and so should be considered. Reporting Accountants would want to look at the files and understand the legal explanation for any anomalies, or seek the same. Of course, some situations are subject to legal professional privilege.

The changes to the format and style of the accountants' report, combined with possible turbulence in the market and the changes to the Accounts Rules, create a situation which we have not seen previously. Accountants' reports and the Accounts Rules had largely escaped untouched from changes in previous sets of the rules, but the situation has been different since 2015, coinciding with the decision to leave the European Union. This might be a coincidence, but it is a marked change in policy from the SRA of a system which was comprehensive in its breadth, and allowed few if any opportunities to get around the rules. We may be seeing a system which can work to prevent the exercise of absolute power by the state, given the loss of a layer of democracy and oversight. However, if this is the case, practitioners should be cautious about using it, and Reporting Accountants should equally be cautious about firms who would seek to utilise this function, particularly if done extensively, and of course the writer is in favour of firms working to close those gaps. This is for fear that few individual or firm aspirations are so lofty as to safeguard democracy, and the opportunity for abuse of the client account is very real and without a check and balance in place.

The changes also bring the threat of prosecution of the Reporting Accountant and, possibly more frequently, of COFAs working in firms. Such a shift of emphasis from the SRA, and the combination of new rules for both firms and accountants, alongside a change in accountants' report, will catch people out. Accountants and COFAs who have been working to long-established procedures, methods of investigating client account and holding client monies, will have to re-think their procedures. For Reporting Accountants, the Standards and Regulations were the second major change in four years. There are reasons why mistakes can be made. However, prosecution for failure to report issues such as fraud in client accounts might take a greater role in future, as the Accounts Rules are now (rightly) some of the most detailed provisions in the otherwise much more open regulations; perhaps signalling an intent from the SRA to focus more resource in proactively checking this area in future.

Regulatory focus

At the moment, the SRA's focus in investigatory terms is on breaches of the rules, to which it responds to many complaints from a range of complainants, including a large number of third parties. This focus, with a widened and more open Standards and Regulations, *could* change towards more proactive visits to firms to consider their accounts, client monies and bookkeeping. There is some reticence about confidently predicting a change in approach here due to the difficulty of organisational change and shifting attitudes towards new ways of working. Of course, the new Standards and Regulations are not meant to be read as a lessening of standards at all, and encompass many broadly similar standards, just in fewer words. Theoretically, though, there could be fewer technical or lower-level breaches of the rules as a result, freeing up resources to focus on accounts and client money provision.

If this happens simultaneously to the growth in TPMAs, the collision of the two may result in much greater attention on client accounts not held in TPMA. TPMA providers are, of course, FCA regulated, and under a separate system of oversight. This effect might be in the much longer term as it would theoretically take many, many years before we saw the reduction in the volume of client accounts. However, we are also seeing an attempt to hasten the speed of change in the legal services market through opening provision to new types of services.

What we may see, which had not been seen before, is a new focus from the SRA on those freelance solicitors and individuals working in unregulated practices, with new forms of information for those in these situations and a change in emphasis to take forward their issues and problems. This could include exploring the different influences on those solicitors, including commercial influences and whether independence of advice or access to justice will be under threat. We may also see the involvement of HMRC in the permissive 'freelance' solicitor model, which may need to be considered further.

All of the individual focus is reminiscent of the continuing focus by the regulator on Practising Certificates rather than firms; on individual prosecutions rather than firm prosecutions. Comparatively, other regulators do have the focus on firms and businesses, rather than on individuals, but we are dealing with professional services regulation, which naturally has a reflection on the firm and individual behaviour.

With all the changes, we have not seen a disruption or dismantling of the Practising Certificate process or any suggestion that this would be done away with. In fact, as we can see in the 'Future developments' section below, at the time of writing, the LSB were proposing a new revalidation process. This would theoretically increase requirements on the individual practitioner for Practising Certificate requirements. We may therefore see a regulatory shift in the much longer term away from firm regulation and towards individual regulation.

We might ask how this would work with holding client monies and legal professional privilege. The model here might be a barrister model of practice. Barristers traditionally do not hold client monies, but do offer privileged legal advice. With the advent of TPMAs, the focus in traditional law firms could move away from holding client monies and, with new forms of practice available, individual practice or practice 'in chambers' may become more common.

We have not seen the major changes we expected from the introduction of Alternative Business Structures, and these new forms of practice could yet take the same turn. There is, the writer theorises, a legal services culture, which we have commented briefly on in Part 4 of this book, which prevents the implementation of change and the movement of established businesses and institutions. The concern perhaps is that young solicitors who might be more open to commercial influence or lack of independence will be the ones caught out by the changes.

Future developments

There are a number of potential future developments to be aware of which may affect regulatory reporting, the breadth of regulation, and the development of the law relating to solicitors. We explore some of these potential developments below.

Re-interpretation of the Legal Services Act 2007

The Legal Services Act 2007 was reconsidered and re-interpreted for the new Standards and Regulations 2019. The new forms of practice (unregulated practices and freelance solicitors) come from a discussion of the statutory basis for regulation. There is nothing within this or any of the other three Acts discussed earlier that prevents a solicitor working outside an authorised law firm (defined in Part 2 of this book) or recognised sole practice. But, up until recently, the SRA was regulating on the basis that these were the only forms of practice permitted, and solicitors had to practise in one of these ways.

The new forms of practice will provide a challenge to the accepted delivery of legal services, and we have seen that the apparatus around the regulation of legal services has changed since 2007.

Could the Acts be re-interpreted again? They could be. If we look at the Acts there are:

- regulatory objectives for the regulators;
- specific requirements in the building blocks of professional practice;
- specific regulatory outcomes;
- regulatory tools and oversight requirements; and
- regulatory and disciplinary outcomes.

Some of these points have been loosely relied on in comparison to the other sections which have been given more weight. Acts and legislation are not weighted when they are implemented; we might ask why HOLPs and HOFAs (intended for ABS) have been implemented across the board in all forms of practice, when they were intended only for Alternative Business Structures. The same level of implementation has not been expected or delivered in other sections of the Legal Services Act 2007.

At any point, the Acts could be re-interpreted again beyond their current use, or a new emphasis could be placed on existing provisions. However, the new position under the Standards and Regulations has gone quite far. If we look back to the implementation of the legislation, vast focus was on ABS, and their potential to change the market through investment. The same emphasis was not placed on different provisions under the Acts, meaning the levels of consultation expected may not be there. If the re-interpretation of existing statute goes beyond the current use, there may be an argument for fresh legislation and further debates by Parliament on the operation of the legislation, and the current institutions as they stand. Of course, we have recently seen the suggestion of the single legal regulator being proposed, and this would require a fresh legislative approach to drive it into being.

In 2016, the writer invited the SRA to discuss the proposed changes to the Handbook with a group of lawyers in London. The session took place one evening and contained one presentation from the writer and one from the SRA on their new proposals. Those proposals later became the Standards and Regulations. The writer prepared questions for the session and provided them to the SRA in advance. The questions posed included a number of issues that have still not yet been resolved. Those questions are provided here:

'1. How will the changes (freelance solicitors, working in unregulated practices) impact solicitors?

2. The continuing distinction between reserved and unreserved activity. Will this disappear in 5-10 years? Will we see a complete re-structure of the legal services market?
3. Whether the regulator could clarify the position on legal professional privilege and how it would operate in an unregulated practice?
4. Whether we will see a single legal regulator (and whether the changes are bringing SRA into line with other [legal] regulators with that aim in mind)?
5. Whether the new system will create two tier regulation (in that solicitors working in firms will be fully regulated, including the firm, and those not working in firms will not be)?
6. What the changes (working in unregulated practices and freelance solicitors) mean for in house lawyers and their specific status?
7. What the changes mean for special bodies?*
8. Will there be difficulties for lawyers not in regulated practices with conflict and confidentiality?'

Not all of those questions were posed, directly during the session, as the lawyers in attendance had their own. However, the questions were posed to the SRA, and continued to be as the writer liaised with them during the year following that meeting. In some cases, we can see there are answers on the horizon, including with the single legal regulator. In other cases, we continue in a compliance, regulatory and legal system which has a number of questions about the future.

These questions may always exist; for example, we may always have questions about reserved and non-reserved activity, but they may also be indicative of the broader policy changes the SRA and other regulators are working on at the moment. With potential changes, including the possible introduction of the single legal regulator (examined later), more of the above issues may be resolved. However, law firms working in regulation may want to consider the issues presented in this book and the potential impacts on them and their firm.

* Special bodies are bodies not currently licensed under the Legal Services Act 2007, but which may be delivering legal services. These may include charitable bodies. The Legal Services Act 2007, ss 105–107 apply but, when the Act was introduced, these were subject to transitional provisions which have not come to an end or been implemented. It was felt at some time that special bodies would be regulated by the SRA (and the writer remembers this herself from her time of employment with the SRA), but the date for that regulation has not arrived.

Special bodies remain something of an anomaly in that solicitors could work in these unregulated bodies giving advice to the public, long before the Standards and Regulations 2019 were introduced. Of course, that freedom in practice now exists for more types of business. The question is whether the special body has been given a strategic advantage by its position.

The future of legal services regulation and the single legal regulator

The future of legal services regulation hangs in the balance. At the time of writing, we have just seen the outcome of a review of legal services led by Professor Stephen Mayson. This recommended the abolition of the different legal regulators (including the SRA), and the introduction of a single legal regulator.

Whether we will see a single legal services regulator remains to be seen. Coronavirus, and the economic and social recovery of the country from lockdowns, means the priorities for the government will have changed dramatically since the report was commissioned. We might instead see this issue become less of a priority for now, and the oversight of one of the legal services regulators extended instead.

Following this report, it is important to remember that the approved legal services regulators may be obliged by statute to recognise anyone who has met the standard of qualification; meaning other lawyers may meet the standard and could be recognised. This could mean, in time, one regulator could become the single legal regulator by default.

A single legal regulator could be one of the most important future developments for legal services, and that legal services in England and Wales (and possibly even into Scotland and Northern Ireland) has ever seen.

One legal regulator would potentially:

- remove the differentiation between solicitors and barristers;
- recognise many different types of qualified lawyer, including ones who hold legal qualifications but are not formally regulated;
- provide a level position for reserved and non-reserved work, and for those whose professional status is not widely recognised or is (often unfairly) considered to be lower;
- provide wider access to justice through more open rights of audience; and
- break the long-term link between regulatory organisations and representative bodies.

The change of regulation could transform legal services delivery and standards of legal services within England and Wales. Our unwritten constitution provides a barrier; does Parliament have the right to take this step and legislate for legal services regulation in these circumstances? This is a question that cannot perhaps be answered, but the current system is historic, and we are moving into a new constitutional position, beyond the European Union. A layer of democracy has been removed by a close referendum, and political parties are often in power for many years at a time. It might be time for a change, and democratically that change might be needed.

Those watching and planning for change in legal services are forewarned; this is a big one.

Below are excerpts from training the writer produced in 2016, covering the developments after the Legal Services Act 2007:

> **'Introduction**
>
> Quietly, behind the scenes, a number of moves have been made to consider what next after the Legal Services Act 2007 (LSA). Our government is committed to deregulation and promoting growth, and the current settlement sees a number of legal regulators in competition with each other, offering similar services, and potentially duplicating regulation. In addition, concerns about representative and regulatory ties, and the situation with reserved and unreserved activities, mean regulators, consumers and firms are not always completely satisfied with the current system.
>
> …
>
> In the summer of 2013, the government called for evidence on changes and improvement to the regulatory structure of legal services. It asked for evidence on concerns with the legal regulatory framework, how regulatory burdens could be reduced, and how the whole regulatory structure could be simplified.'

The responses and the consideration of the options were, in some cases, disappointing and, in other cases, dramatic. On one hand, some of the options were small, such as removing HOLPs and HOFAs to reduce the anomaly with ABS; on the other hand, the removal and restructure of all legal regulators was also proposed, with consideration given to a single legal regulator.

A commitment was given to change within the Parliament. Given the implementation of the Legal Services Act 2007 was barely two years old (there was a lead-in time for implementation), the time frame for further change was alarming. Following these developments, further options were explored by the regulators. As we have now seen, a single legal regulator has been proposed.

> 'We have already seen significant change at the SRA since the introduction of OFR, and despite it only being five years since the OFR Handbook went live, we seem now to be in a post-OFR era. Since 2014, the SRA appears to have a different strategic direction. The changes include:
>
> - Appointment of a new senior leadership team
> - SRA Corporate Strategy focused less on OFR; more on reducing burden and operational strategy;
> - A new regulatory reform programme – seeking to reduce regulatory burden – changes to accountants' reports, separate business rule, small firms initiative, consultation on changes to compensation fund and insurance, and planned further consultation on a re-written set of Accounts Rules;
> - The suggestion that the SRA Handbook could be re-written, drastically reduced and simplified.

> The SRA are trying to demonstrate their commitment to deregulation; to reducing the burden they are placing on law firms. They may also be concerned for their own survival; as may the other regulators.
>
> The mix of regulators offering similar services now raises the prospect of further confusion and complexity in legal services regulation. A law firm could now be regulated by the SRA, CILEx, the CLC, or the BSB, for example. If they are not conducting reserved work, they may choose not to be regulated. If there were practising solicitors in the firm, they would still have to comply with the SRA Code of Conduct, in addition to the Code of whoever was regulating the firm. The choice of regulators for firms may be a good thing, in that competition could promote better working practices, but it may also lead to a confusing mix of competing regulations, or a race to the bottom. It seem unsustainable to have this many legal services regulators offering the same product, and given the government seems set on deregulation to promote growth, a single legal regulator is a distinct possibility.
>
> One of the conclusions drawn in the call for evidence was that the government would seek to end two-tier regulation in the current parliament. It was not clear whether they meant the abolition of the Legal Services Board; the difficulties between reserved and unreserved legal activity; or the separation of representative and regulatory functions.
>
> The separation of representative and regulatory functions seems likely; the SRA appear to have set their stall out in favour of this, funding a recent piece of research showing consumers would be in favour. In addition, this year the amount of money being used for the Practising Certificate fee will for the first time show how much is taken by the Law Society. Similarly, the abolition of the Legal Services Board may not be out of place, depending on the changes the government decides to make. The challenge of policing the legal regulators to achieve the LSA settlement may now be complete, after ten years, and it may be time to move on to a new regulatory landscape.
>
> It is clear that the government are planning some change in this parliament. What change will come, is not yet clear, but the options are on the table. If we do not see a single legal regulator in this parliament, it may come later. With so many legal regulators now offering a similar product, and potentially increasing the regulatory burden on firms by doing so, it is unlikely the question will go away anytime soon.'

Harmonisation of regulatory standards

The intent for a single legal regulator has been outlined from some quarters. We are now seeing some regulation and regulatory standards occurring in common between the regulators.

The recent transparency rules are an excellent example of these standards; they have been introduced across the board between the legal regulators. Observers might also say that the influence and oversight of the Legal Services Board has created a similar standard and outcome of regulation between the approved regulators.

We might be seeing both the intentional and unintentional harmonisation of standards between the regulators, with comfort being sought between the regulators that their approach is justifiable. There is also a sense that the regulated community have accepted the position of a certain standard of regulation – a risk-based, outcomes-focused standard, which has a deregulatory agenda. Adopting a common approach allows firms and individuals to transition between legal services regulators, and hopefully comply across the board.

This may then lead in practical terms to the single legal regulator; whether we like it or not, the inevitable conclusion of the standardisation of legal services regulation is the development or option of the development of the single legal regulator, perhaps condensed into one currently operating regulatory body. This is likely to be very unpopular amongst other regulators if it occurs.

Convenience should not be the buzz word for the regulators, however, and the proper application of regulatory standards is important for the pride and motivation of the regulated community, as well as protection of the public. It would be useful to see, even if the single legal regulator was considered likely, ongoing separation between the regulatory bodies in their current form. After all, different representations, voices and perspectives within the legal community are also important as a check and balance on the power of one organisation, and for the development of new ideas.

Another force may overtake us, however, and may mean we need the debate and brilliance of competitive forces. Brexit may force our hands in a number of ways. To compete as a much smaller country, we need all of our best ideas, our best people and we need to stand out. This goes for legal services (which we export), as much as it does for compliance.

If we think of the array of compliance requirements a law firm is subject to, we could see some of those being harmonised. Whether it be a single body for AML regulation, or GDPR being taken under the control of professional bodies; the different requirements and reporting bodies could be reimagined now under British direction and control, but with the requirement to achieve equivalent outcomes. This is likely to mean the maintenance of standards, but with the option to set higher standards or design our own outcomes.

Brexit, and the loss of both:

- a layer of democracy, and
- interlinking standards, bodies, or best practice in some areas,

may also be a trigger for greater examination of standards in a variety of areas in England and Wales, and Britain as a whole. We may need to more carefully consider the access to justice of individuals, the democratic and constitutional rights of citizens, and the regulatory intent and application of regulatory standards. The loss of the EU as a directional force, a democratic voice, and a source of rights requires a replacement. The current operation of our state institutions, including regulatory bodies, may need reconsidering in order to provide citizens with a continuation of rights in a post-Brexit country. Fairness, seen and perceived; tackling issues of corruption; and equality of access – these may all be important to maintain living standards following the departure from the EU.

This blog was written by the writer in 2019 following a presentation with Brunel Professions and Legal Eye concerning developments in the legal services market:

> **'Brexit, Regulation and the SRA Handbook**
>
> The new SRA Standards and Regulations will allow solicitors to work in non-regulated practices, carrying the title "solicitor". The handbook has been extensively re-written to provide a shorter set of rules, with less guidance and indicative behaviours. More will be left to the individual judgement of the solicitor, particularly those working alone in non-regulated practices.
>
> It's no coincidence we are discussing this at the same time as Brexit. The SRA's justification for bringing in the new rules is based on the premise that the legal services market needed to do more to serve consumers and small business. Market perceptions are that legal services are too expensive… The point perhaps being that better advised consumers and businesses would make better economic decisions.
>
> Brexit, particularly no deal Brexit, brings fears of recession. The launch of the new SRA rules and their revolution in the way solicitors can practice could be seen as an attempt to stimulate the legal services market (and consequently other markets) post Brexit. The question is whether firms and other businesses will take the opportunities presented or whether the potential change is too great; whether cultural factors within the legal services market will constrain what roles solicitors are willing to take on; and whether the uncertainty and risk created by Brexit, and the need for comfort in the status quo, will keep us all working in the same way.
>
> There is also a question whether the SRA have the power to re-write the Handbook in this way; the last few attempts to open the market have taken parliamentary approval. ...
>
> More immediately, Brexit, and particularly no deal Brexit, has created question marks around a number of regulatory points. Adequacy, passporting and equivalence agreements all take time to implement and to agree.
>
> Here's our pass notes:
>
> Understand the regulatory and legal basis for your current work in the EEA, including data transfer – the ICO say the GDPR remains the same, and there should be no issue sending data to the EEA, there may be an issue receiving it. Understand your position, and the position of any parent companies. The FCA have provided detailed guidance for those under their regulatory regime, particularly for those impacted by the passporting requirements.
>
> Financial implications – understand your financial position and the current trends for your work. Brexit could create an economic downturn.

The new Standards and Regulations do not have the same emphasis on risk management, but they do require you to report to the SRA should there be any risk of insolvency.

Registered European Lawyers and Registered Foreign Lawyers (RELs and RFLs) – there are 700 RELs in England and Wales; the SRA have suggested they are likely to be able to continue to practice as RELs with their European Qualification until 2020. During this period there is an "integration route" (although we push back on that phrase) being offered to qualify as a solicitor. This is comprised of the QLTS, or it's broader replacement, the SQE. The SRA have confirmed there will be exemptions to parts of the qualifications based on a lawyer's prior experience and learning, considered on an individual basis. It appears those not wishing to qualify as a solicitor will become RFLs post 2020. Under the current rules REL status confers more practice rights than RFL status. The SRA (or parliament) have not confirmed whether RFL status will continue long term in its current form. There are mixed feelings about Brexit; ensure your staff are well supported, feel welcome, and clients are not left without representation.

Likely continuation of standards in different ways – if we want adequacy, passporting and equivalence arrangements post-Brexit, we need to ensure our standards are set and maintained appropriately. There will not necessarily be a relaxation of regulatory standards post-Brexit. The removal of some requirements in the SRA rules, sees them replaced elsewhere (in the latest changes to the CQS, for example). The Law Commission are reviewing the AML framework with the intention of strengthening it. The latest guidance on developing your risk assessment in AML may be coming internationally from the Financial Action Task Force, with contributions from the ICAEW and Bar Standards Board, among others.

This is undoubtedly a time of change. Ensure your staff know what to expect both from Brexit and your firm's approach to dealing with the new Standards and Regulations. Now might be also be a time to express you firm's unique selling points to clients more than ever.'

Written by Katie Jackson, Director at Honne Limited and Consultant at Legal Eye, following a Compliance Update hosted by Brunel Professions and Legal Eye Limited.

CHANGES TO THE RENEWAL UNDER BREXIT

The following excerpt is from the writer's Serious Breach and Practising Certificate Renewals Course in 2020; the position reflects the change under Brexit as it happened:

'[At the moment] the deadline for RELs to apply to become a solicitor is December 2021. Whilst the details of the exit agreement are not yet known, they will almost certainly involve a reassessment of the REL status, its relationship to solicitor status, and the associated Registered Foreign Lawyer (RFL) status.

The SRA had originally said that RELs would need to become solicitors by December 2020. Their updated guidance confirms this and states that RELs who are not solicitors, will be transitioned to RFL status in January 2021. It should be borne in mind that we do not know the final outcome of the exit agreement from the EU. RELs still practising as such by 2021 may need to make changes, particularly if they are Sole Practitioners, as RFLs have restricted practising and partnership rights. In time there might be an argument to change this status due to the new forms of practice available and the intent to open the legal services market.

The further option is for RELs to advise the SRA they intend to continue practising under their home title; but conducting non reserved work. If you would like to take this route, you must advise the SRA using a specific form. A link is provided at the end of the notes. This would mean loss of registration with the SRA. Consequently, the SRA are not asking for a renewal fee from those who take this route. RELs in this position can fill in the form prior to the renewal, continue to practice as RELs for the two months until RFL status goes live, and not be charged. After January 2021, and subject to the SRA's approval, they will not be registered with the SRA. Note that although the form is straightforward, and does not ask questions, those who are conducting reserved work in the law of England and Wales will require appropriate authorisation.

The timing (December 2020) almost coincides with the renewal (and the closure of the renewal window, and commencement of revocation – see below). It is not clear whether the actual deadline will occur alongside the revocation of the Practising Certificates of those RELs who have not either applied or become solicitors. The SRA appear to have a choice, to potentially approve any application to become an REL beyond this point as an application to become an RFL. However, the EU have suggested member states (and the UK) may wish to continue to recognise qualifications which were obtained when the UK was a member, and the associated practising rights. All applications should be made properly. Whether the SRA's position is challengeable, given it appears to remove practising rights from those who would previously have been regarded as competent, remains to be seen.

Registered Foreign Lawyers have restricted practising rights (in contrast to RELs). They cannot be a sole partner in a practice and cannot undertake unsupervised reserved work. It is unclear whether this will change in time to give RFLs the same rights as currently afforded to RELs, or whether there will be a shift in the practising qualifications to give greater balance across the board.'

Ten-year revalidation

The writer has been speaking about five- and ten-year revalidation on the courses since they started in 2013. It is an idea from other regulators who provide Practising Certificates or licences for multi-year periods. Revalidation or re-testing is common in other fields, including medicine, and the writer remembers discussions of such from her time working at the regulators.

At the time of writing, the Legal Services Board was consulting on introducing ten-year revalidation, and the SRA had just introduced the Solicitors Qualification Exam; an examination process to qualify as a solicitor. The debate now continues about whether to introduce periodic re-testing in order to validate those qualifications and consider solicitors' continuing ability to practise. Of course, there are a number of points arising from this position:

- Solicitor competence has been, and still will be, assessed during a lengthy initial qualification. The decision about whether they are competent or not is taken by a number of different bodies and individuals as they sit a variety of examinations, complete work experience, and take on board direction. The SQE may be in place, but degrees in law still exist, and prospective solicitors will still have to undertake work experience. Any form of revalidation will not be able to measure solicitor competence in the same way and at the same level as the initial qualification; only a small measure of solicitor competence could be undertaken.
- A difficulty exists when we ask for revalidation on a large scale. The annual Practising Certificate process is a major undertaking for the SRA, and any revalidation would need to be managed alongside that process. Of course, solicitors would not need to be revalidated every year, but undergo an assessment periodically. Even so, maintaining registers and ensuring compliance with those requirements is important, and could be very complex and time-consuming to manage.
- What would the outcome be for solicitors who do not meet the requirements? Would they lose the ability to practise or would they be subject to restrictions? The proposal may be one to extend the use and extent of Practising Certificate conditions in order to restrict the practice of the solicitor until such time as they are successfully revalidated. If this is the case, would there be certain subjects which are considered more important or central to the solicitor qualification than others? We could see then part of the qualification become 'core', and another part become 'optional', with different revalidation requirements for sections, and possible exemptions for other parts.
- The writer envisages exemptions from some requirements as it is not currently possible to close a solicitor's practice without grounds to do so (such as intervention). We might be able to foresee a situation in which a solicitor's practice is closed as a result of failing revalidation.
- If we take this to the nth degree, and perhaps if there are not exemptions, and practices can be closed, this could be used as a means to disrupt democratic participation in society. If solicitor's practices are closed as a result of failing revalidation, and that examination or testing process was abused, practices could be closed for a variety of different political reasons. This could extend across all lawyers (as a result of the single legal regulator).
- Taking a different approach and angle to the proposal, we may consider the content of a solicitor qualification and the role of the solicitor in a different way. Dealing with legal services in the future could be very different indeed for democratic society. Alternative Business Structures, and now the prospect of working in unregulated practices, will expose solicitors to very different working environments than are currently in place for many solicitors. The concept of a solicitor is to speak for another as if they could not speak for themselves, a historical idea which arose before current standards of education. Currently, many people are very highly qualified, beyond the

> levels achieved by solicitors and others. There should theoretically be no reason why citizens should not be able to speak for themselves. Perhaps we simply all need a wider legal education?

Certainly, it appears to the writer that solicitor education in business could be extended dramatically. There is lacking in the sector an appreciation of business literature and empirical business research. Given the difficulty with client accounts, and the volume of prosecutions in this area, solicitors may also need further and more extensive education in accounting to successfully run a client account. Solicitor and other legal services education is based in the law, but that excludes education in a variety of other disciplines which might be essential to the interpretation of those legal positions in real terms.

The writer regards her own business education as essential to operation, and would be in her chosen area of practice. Having an understanding of the theory and operation of different areas of a business, and the key research in each area is, in the writer's view, essential to providing services to those areas of a business. We often see solicitor practices prosecuted before the Solicitors Disciplinary Tribunal and the writer believes a keener understanding of how those practices should in theory operate (according to business and management theory), combined with a discussion of how they intend to operate in future, would assist practitioners in making more informed business decisions and result in fewer breaches.

> Below is an excerpt from the conclusion to the writer's Material Breach and Practising Certificates Course from 2014 (LETR stands for Legal Education and Training Review):
>
> > **'Long term**
> >
> > The SRA is placing a greater emphasis on business management and governance in law firms. The renewals process is increasingly likely to reflect this with traditional Practising Certificate controls moving to become the firms' responsibility where they relate to matters of firm administration.
> >
> > At the same time, movements in Practising Certificate renewals seem likely to concentrate on competence. The LETR mooted a move to a less frequent (perhaps five-yearly) system of re-accreditation, as adopted by the GMC. This system of competence would place greater onus on a firm to ensure the competence of their fee earners and ensure the training and feedback they received kept them at the required standard.
> >
> > However these changes are some way off; OFR has not yet truly been embedded. In the meantime, Alternative Business Structures and the existence of the Legal Services Board mean the SRA could well be merged with the other legal regulators, before the long term changes highlighted here can be implemented.'

Citizen rights of audience and education

Further to the discussion in the section on revalidation, there is an argument that the high level of education in the general population should allow the population to speak for themselves, including before the court. The lack of formal legal education may be all that prevents some from undertaking this task. The solution might not be to extend the education of solicitors; it might be to extend the education of the general population concerning the law and legal services. These points are not often taught in schools but, to achieve the forward-thinking and prosperous society we wish to achieve, greater education of our children, and even adults, might be important.

Indeed, the alternative to reserved work and legal presence is greater rights of audience for citizens and legal training in schools for citizens. This might be a viable alternative to the costs of lawyers and insurance costs of exercising individual or personal rights. This may also be a very positive way of demonstrating individual democratic and personal rights, and building a well-informed and co-operative society for future generations.

In practical terms, there are also reasons for the introduction of legal education in schools, and across a number of adult settings. The significant reduction in legal aid available to individuals, and the financial difficulty many criminal law firms find themselves in, mean representation for individuals is difficult to obtain and fund. As a result, individual human rights are at risk, with judges and juries bearing the responsibility for resolving the situation of an individual defending themselves against the state, without legal representation.

The introduction of formal citizen rights of audience and legal education may help alleviate some of this burden. The alternative may be:

- a publicly funded and managed legal defence service; and
- compulsory legal aid for all law firms, or for all individual solicitors, as was previously the case.

Greater rights of audience for citizens, and the ability to speak for themselves before courts, may come with the involvement in education. Education is very famously a political arena and, of course, we revert to concerns regarding the constitution. However, the extension of legal education into citizenship classes might assist in democratic participation by individual citizens. This will help society place less reliance on the solicitor, which in turn should free the solicitor from some of the expectations placed upon them by society as a result of the position where they have been allowed the privilege of access to the law. If we adopt this approach, it may see the end of serious breach reporting.

Exercises

Mansion House: the suggested answer

POSSIBLE ANSWER TO MANSION HOUSE

There are indicators of a possible problem. The monies for the purchase are sent as part of a larger sum, and it appears there is nothing else on the ledger aside from searches. Given those factors, the monies received in three tranches may also catch your attention.

As the Reporting Accountant you might look at the cashbook, office to client transfers (and vice versa), client to client transfers, who signed off the transactions, and the batch reports. It is possible to look at the solicitor's explanation, but you must be careful in this situation due to the possible risk of money laundering dependent on what you find.

Dependent on the file accounts, it is possible layering of monies from laundered funds. It could be mortgage fraud, or there could be a wider problem with other transactions.

Accountants would not necessarily check the rest of the file. They can, of course, ask for the file.

However, a regulator or another legal services professional, such as a COLP or COFA who was investigating internally, may also look at:

- who introduced the client;
- identification documents;
- whether instructions are given in person or not;
- estate agency documentation and particulars of sale;
- communications with the mortgage company;
- source of funds;
- Zoopla or Rightmove (Zoopla is often more useful, as it shows public information about movements of property);
- survey and searches;
- land registration;
- replies to enquiries;
- relationship with firm on the other side;
- replies to requisitions on title;
- post purchase formalities – charges discharged, property registered, and stamp duty paid; and
- monies accounted to client.

The person investigating would be looking to establish where the money was from, and where it went. Which other transactions were involved in this batch, and which other monies were received and sent to the same places (estate agents and firms on the other side)? The files should be examined as above, to detect any anomalies and similarities.

Dependent on the outcome of the above, or the profile of the firm, there could be a reason to suspect fraud. As a result, the matter may result in not only a report to the SRA, but also a report to the National Crime Agency. Dependent on how the matter proceeds, the reporting accountants may need legal advice about tipping off the firm and others.

The reflective exercise: what did you learn?

This is a personal exercise. You can do this exercise at any time.

EXERCISE: REFLECTING ON YOUR LEARNING

When we discuss learning, what are we speaking about?

Are we discussing:

- Knowledge obtained?
- Skills developed?
- Forming personal awareness and views?
- Broadening our mindset?
- Hearing or feeling something new?

Do we have to have retained knowledge over a set period of time to have learned something? Can we learn things without being aware we have?

We need not think about learning simply as knowledge obtained. Of course, our formal exams and tests measure the knowledge we take in. However, if you think back to the exams you took, did they measure everything you knew? It is doubtful. We all learn so much, how is it possible to measure all the things we learn at school or in one subject? The knowledge we obtain formally is often vast; the knowledge we obtain personally is also very valuable in our emotional and personal development. The variety of what we learn, the people we meet, the skills we learn each day, might impact our views, mindsets and personal perspectives in ways that might not be immediately obvious.

If you attend a training course, you might think, 'did I learn something new? Did I enjoy the course?'. Or you might think more broadly and say 'what did I gain from this course?'. It might be something that cannot be measured. You might reflect on the course in the future and realise you have gained something from it you were unaware of at the time, or you might have obtained a small piece of knowledge that helps you with what you were doing.

We can consider learning as a variety of outcomes which might assist us formally or informally throughout our lives. Small pieces of information, or large ones; personal knowledge or professional development. Take the time to embrace learning in both formal and informal ways, including traditional chalk and talk learning, but also on-the-job learning, peer-to-peer learning, and the learning we do while we are sitting at our desks doing our jobs. Experience is often highly prized and essential for many jobs, precisely because we have learnt while we were doing the job.

Take the time to consider what you have learnt from this book. Perhaps you have read the whole book, and completed all the exercises, including the sample exercises in the next section. Perhaps you have read Parts of the book, or perhaps you were most interested in the exercises, and you have completed a few of those.

Try to have a think about what you have learned in the widest possible terms. Have a think about whether you have:

- Obtained new knowledge or a different perspective.
- Tried something new. What did you gain from the experience?
- Developed a different skill, perhaps by working with your team in a different way (for example, by leading a discussion).

Perhaps you have not fully formed those new skills, digested those pieces of information, or fully considered different ways of working, yet. However, if there are any small things you have taken away, or parts of development you have started, then also consider this as learning.

You might also consider reflecting on your learning from this or any other learning activity, in the future. What did you learn some time ago that stays with you today? What do you find useful and what have you gained from your experiences that perhaps you did not take account of before?

Part 8

Previous Problems

Contents

Introduction
Law firm management and legal system problems
Conflict of interest problems
Equality and diversity
Competence statement or general CPD exercises
Practising conditions problems
Complaint handling problems
Legal market analysis
Serious breaches
Qualified reports and serious/material breach problems
More accounts problems
Anti-money laundering problems
Accounts/reconciliation exercise possible answers
The note at the end

Introduction

This section includes many of the problems the writer has set over the years for solicitors, accountants, and other legal services and accountancy professionals. Some problems did have suggested answers at the time, but those answers were also debated amongst the delegates on the courses. Some of the problems here are problems from the 'Serious/Material Breach' courses; some are from the other courses the writer has produced over the last eight years. Hopefully, they are helpful for solicitors, COLPs and COFAs, the staff in different departments in your law firm, and for Reporting Accountants, and it is this audience they are primarily designed for.

As the introduction to this book explains, the writer presents the serious breach scenarios in a particular way, and those ones are not recommended for group use outside of that context. They are provided here for your use personally; other sets of problems which could be used within groups are noted as such.

The problems are included here as they are an opportunity for CPD, and for discussion of some of the issues we have raised in the book. There is now lots of information available on the SRA website to help you solve these issues, particularly the serious breach issues, and understanding both regulatory expectation and your own ethical perspective is encouraged as ongoing learning, but also could provide the opportunity to contribute to regulatory policy and firm decision-making in future. In the writer's experience, well-considered contributions are always welcome at the regulators, and you may find your own contingency planning informed by your responses. The experience of reflecting on your own ethical standpoint can also help with your career, direction, and in understanding your own motivations.

The problems are categorised into different types, with a short introduction explaining what you can find in that section and how you might use those problems. Although there are separate sections for Accounts Rules problems, you will find a mix of problems which are suitable for COFAs and Reporting Accountants in different sections and, vice versa, that COLPs may also find the Accounts Rules problems helpful. Please do use all of them.

In each case, unless otherwise specified, you have to assume this is all we know. You might be a senior person tasked with making a quick decision on the basis of short facts that you or someone else has been able to establish. Sometimes, scenarios have to be acted upon quickly. In other cases, we have more information and can take more time to make a decision about what to do, or develop a more considered approach. Try to consider your course of action in each case and whether, on the face of it, you think it is a serious breach. If you want to, or if it makes it easier, you can add an 'if this, then that' approach; considering what you would do if certain additional facts you have added in were true. This also helps determining your ethical perspective.

The line the writer presents on her courses can also be used to help you pinpoint your response to the problems. You might use this to help you determine your response level in your firm to various different sets of problems, or to help you find an ethical answer to how seriously you determine different problems to be. For example, you might plot your answer to each problem on the line showing its perceived seriousness, giving you an indicator of your ethical response. Then and secondly, you could look up the suggested response on the SRA website, giving you an indicator of their suggested response, and plot the same on a different line. What you could end up with is a line showing your ethical or suggested response, and one showing the SRA's suggested response from a regulatory perspective.

For example, your line might look like this:

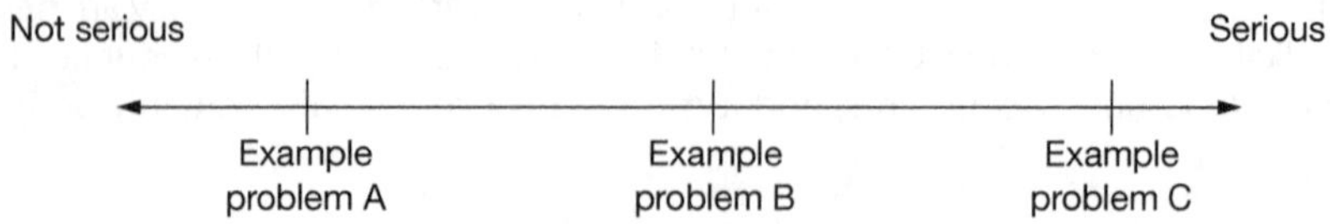

You would then have a second line showing the SRA's suggested response, which you could use to guide your decision making. However, you have also explored your ethical response to different situations, which can be different to the regulators' view.

We might then ask, 'how does your line compare to others?'. If you are brave, you can have this discussion with someone else who is reading the book, but you might also like to keep your ethical perspective to yourself. Ethical discussion can be a difficult and personal subject, guided by different life callings and events. Sometimes, other people don't want to share their personal views, and that is fine. It is not obligatory.

We also have to note that circumstances do affect the decision making in relation to serious breach, sometimes substantially, and your line might change, dependent on situations. If you do make such a line, try to think about what might change your mind about that situation.

In some ways, the writer prefers this level of reflection to be personal amongst those who participate, so as not to disrupt the courses but, as with all things in life, they take their own turn. Once you have started to participate, the writer's viewpoint simply becomes her own ethical perspective and not yours, so in some ways that viewpoint is immaterial.

Where the questions ask if the breaches were serious breaches, you can also look back and ask yourself if they were material breaches. The SRA no longer uses this definition, but it can be useful practice if you deal with any historical breaches in your firm (pre November 2019), when the old SRA Handbook 2011 was in force. It can also be helpful to consider another angle, and if you do not agree that something is a breach or should be reportable, but other people do– understand that rules do change over time.

Where the breaches ask you to consider another element of the rules (for example, conflict of interest), again consider the breach itself, you can also ask yourself, 'does it amount to being a serious breach?'. Another perspective is to take the 'serious breach' scenarios you do not think are serious enough to be reported, and use them to help you understand the Codes of Conduct or Standards and Regulations. Do you think there was a breach at all? If so, where do you think that breach occurred and of which rule? Codes of Conduct come and go but hopefully these scenarios will be helpful for many years, and you can use them in various ways to see where changes to the rules take you with exploring the regulatory requirements in force or proposed, and the requirements for reporting.

You can also use the scenarios to explore the evidential tests required. This might be, for example, using a serious breach scenario where, on the bare facts, you would make a report. The next step is to consider what evidence you would need actually to make the decision to report, if you were in charge of the investigation. This can be a useful exercise to help you prepare if you are ever faced with a reporting scenario. You may even use the questions to help your contingency or scenario planning.

In the courses, these scenarios are often used quite loosely, and the decision making sometimes focuses on the ethical perspective of the individual or group they are working with. They are intended to have that looseness to them, and the writer designs them that way, to enable effective communication, a range of responses, and to ensure delegates are not placed under pressure. If you don't feel one scenario gives you the planning capability you are looking for, try another one. There is further information about conducting your own investigation in Part 5 of this book.

In the book, we have explored the relationship between AML and serious breach, and the role of the COFA in ensuring compliance with all the statutory obligations of the firm. This obviously includes anti-money laundering, the Money Laundering Regulations, and the Proceeds of Crime Act 2002. We have seen, in Part 5 of the book, the overlap between money laundering and the rules of professional conduct, with cases featuring money laundering being prosecuted before the Solicitors Disciplinary Tribunal under the rules of professional conduct. The writer makes the link to issues of integrity and dishonesty. As a result, there are problems within these lists of scenarios that are issues of AML which, again, the writer has been using as example scenarios in AML and serious breach training sessions for many years. Try to have a think about whether or not you also see them as issues of professional conduct, and have a look at the overarching principles or the rules to identify where you would think there was a breach, if at all.

At the end, there is also an AML Quiz which, again, has been in use for many years. Have a think about whether or not you see different perspectives and terminology in the AML Quiz to the rest of the scenarios. What type of problems do you generally see which categorise AML, and what do you see that categorise professional conduct? Can you divide them and find overlaps or differences?

There may be problems in the general exercises that are also AML issues. Can you find them?

Of course, if you see any issues of AML in real life, make a report to your Money Laundering Reporting Officer. Your Money Laundering Reporting Officer should also make a report to the National Crime Agency.

The scenarios, quizzes, and general problems are provided for your individual use or within your firm. The writer has used the majority of the problems at some point over the last ten years; dates of use are not provided. The writer continues to use some if not all of the scenarios, quizzes, and other materials in this book, and the courses continue to run. Therefore the materials here should not be used for commercial purposes or in competition with the writer in any way.

If you are considering using these exercises with your firm (where they are noted as suitable), have a think about your own experience of facilitation before doing so. Facilitation and coaching are separate disciplines, and the writer was trained at masters' degree level as a management consultant by qualified psychologists and scientists who worked as management consultants. This training included workplace facilitation, in which the writer also had some previous experience. Do consider what you can draw on, and do some research if necessary before considering your next steps.

Importantly, the answers are not provided. The exercises are a chance to consider your own ethical view, and to help you develop an ethical perspective on the legal services sector and problems which unfortunately do occur. For other problems, you have the chance to either find the answer within the book, look it up, or attend one of the courses! Whatever you choose to do, this is good CPD, and gives you a chance to interact with regulations, legislation, and concepts in different ways.

Perhaps most importantly, have a read and join in from your sofa or desk.

P.S. there's a note at the end.

Law firm management and legal system problems

The following problems, questions, reflective exercises, are designed to consider the different forms of management within law firms, and also look at the legal services market as a whole. You can complete the questions and exercises individually or with your team. There are some exercises here for new starters.

This mini quiz covers some of the ground concerning the extent of solicitor practices and their separate businesses. Do your own research to find the answer; some information is provided within the book.

Can a solicitor run a separate business providing will-writing services?

Give two examples of potential issues/safeguards that should be considered before referring a client to a separate business? Where can you find more information on these safeguards?

Name two services other than reserved legal services a solicitor's firm can provide?

This is a question requiring some written work from you. You can complete this over a period of time if you would like, and it might count for quite a bit of CPD, with the research included.

You are joining another law firm. They would like to understand the new Standards and Regulations. Draft a summary on the history and development of the Standards and Regulations, its aims, and what the SRA has done and why. You can go back to the Handbook 2011 and OFR (outcomes-focused regulation) if you want to.

Use these questions to help you consider the changes to the SRA regulatory arrangements under the Standards and Regulations 2019.

Is it a good or a bad thing?

What did the SRA set out to achieve?

Will they achieve what they set out to do?

Will it result in growth for the market or not?

What do you think needs to change to make it work?

The following discussion was part of the Material Breaches course for many years, as that course also covered risk management. It has been updated as a research question.

Do you use a risk management system; if so, which one?

Can you find out either about risk management or about different forms of risk management?

Write down the pros and cons of using risk management in your practice, using the information you have obtained.

What are some of the limitations of risk management?

The writer has used the following questions in discussion with junior staff, new starters, trainees, or aspiring lawyers. You may of course wish to omit Group 2 if you use them within your firm. In Group 1, question 4 provides the opportunity for a strategic-level discussion, and you may also be able to make the questions in this group suitable for more senior staff.

Group 1:

- How can solicitors practise?
- Who do they work with?
- Do you know why?
- What is changing?

Group 2:

- What is a market?
- Which market do we operate in?
- Could you start your own business?
- What would you need?
- What would stop you?
- Could you start your own solicitor firm?

The following discussion questions and exercises appeared in the Practice Skills Course in approximately 2017. They have been updated. You can use some of them with new starters or junior staff. Others you can use with any members of your team.

SRA Handbook

What are the SRA Standards and Regulations?

Why do they matter to me?

Facilitate a discussion of the SRA Standards and Regulations, then pose the following question:

What do you think about the changes in the SRA regulatory style towards a shorter handbook with the intention of more freedom in practice?

Compliance changes – ongoing

Have a think about compliance developments for this year – what can you name?

What will have the largest impact on you?

These questions have been used as discussion questions on various CPD courses by the writer over many years. You can use them with your team and they might be useful for solicitors who would like to develop their compliance viewpoints. Some questions might require some research on the part of you as a facilitator or on the part of your team, to complete and debate successfully.

Should there be a single legal regulator? What are the pros and cons?

What changes would you make to the Accounts Rules?

How do you feel about the system for solicitor competence? (For all staff?)

Do you think the current focus on deregulation is the right thing to do? Can you make any suggestions for the SRA about how to make its regulatory system more effective?

What do you know about the future direction of travel for the SRA?

What are the main policy drivers at the moment?

This has been a regular problem on the Material / Serious Breach course for many years, as that course also covers the renewal. Have a look on the SRA website and consider your own firm's approach to solve this problem. Providing an answer to this can help your firm plan and get all the information ready that you need.

The COLP from another firm is on the phone, she is an old friend. They are a large firm with 200 fee earners, including an RFL. The previous COLP left the firm at Christmas, as did all of those who worked on the renewal last year.

What does she need to do to prepare for the renewal?

The following questions were used as part of the Serious Breach courses, around the time of the movement to the Standards and Regulations and the separation of the principles of honesty and integrity. Questions asking what individuals consider to be the difference between honesty and integrity may be personal questions, and you may consider just using these questions yourself, or missing out question 3. You may also need to do some research to facilitate these questions.

Have a look at the Standards and Regulations. What do the principles say about honesty and integrity?

Can you find the latest SRA guidance on the Standards and Regulations?

What do you think about the difference between honesty and integrity?

Is the SRA only seeking to receive reports about honesty and integrity?

These questions were used during training sessions on the new Standards and Regulations in the run-up to their introduction. You could use them with a variety of staff, but the last five may be particularly suitable for facilitation and discussion with your management team.

Where has the SRA changed the regulations (new code) so they are arguably more reliant on statutory provisions?

What are the changes to the Accounts Rules?

Do non-lawyer managers and employees have the same reporting requirements as solicitors?

Could the SRA prosecute a non-lawyer manager or employee for allegations concerning their private life?

Which of your activities are reserved legal work?

Can you foresee any of your competitors being freelance solicitors?

With reference to the previous two questions, what are the difficulties for potential new competitors, and how can you differentiate yourselves?

This exercise is sometimes used when the writer is discussing the renewal, and discussing an outside view of risk in a law firm. Try these questions with the full range of staff members; from junior (but keen) staff, to management. These are fairly democratic questions. The second question is more technical and may not be suitable for facilitation; you could, however, set it as a research question!

What information would you ask for if you were in charge of the annual renewal?

Do non-lawyers have to provide information to the SRA in the renewal?

You are risk assessing a law firm as a whole. What information would you ask for?

These are technical questions the writer poses on several of her courses. They can be used personally, or with compliance, HR, or any other group that would like to understand more of the terminology around the nuts and bolts of practice. The group undertaking this task may need to do some research.

What is an REL?

What is an RFL?

What is a Licensed Body?

What is a Sole Practitioner?

The following are questions concerning vulnerable clients, the writer first used in approximately 2016, but they have been updated. They require research, so you can use them personally, or with your team, if you give them the task of completing the research.

Can you find a definition of a vulnerable client?

Name three circumstances that might mean you have a vulnerable client?

Which provision in the Standards and Regulations requires you to treat vulnerable clients fairly?

What examples of vulnerability have you seen? What did you do? Did you feel you could do anything differently?

Are there any issues of vulnerability which come up regularly in your work? Do you know of any local groups that could support your clients?

Do you think large companies or small businesses can experience vulnerability? If so, how could your service take account of that?

The following questions can be useful to understand the answer when looking at your complaints handling and with departments who might experience a lot of contact from disgruntled third parties.

What is a third party complaint?

What are your obligations to third parties?

Conflict of interest problems

Conflict of interest is one of the writer's favourite compliance subjects. The following group of problems are all conflict of interest themed problems. You can take them at face value and solve them using the Standards and Regulations (or, if you are reading this in the future, any other set of regulations). Or you can consider them as serious breach problems and ask whether they could amount to a serious breach if you were in conflict (for example, if it asks you whether you could act, imagine you already are acting, and therefore whether there is a serious breach).

Don't forget there is a separate position at law to that set out by the Standards and Regulations (and previous SRA Handbooks). The SRA's position traditionally mirrors the law, but sets separate standards, which are tailored to solicitor practice and, in that way, diverge slightly. There are, of course, separate complaint and potentially serious professional conduct consequences that flow from the expectations of the SRA. The writer is only asking you to consider the position in professional conduct terms and not at law.

Quick conflict – these questions have been posed by the writer on various courses during the last eight years.

1. Your long standing client instructs you to write his will and says he would like to leave you some money to thank you. Can you act for him?
2. You are instructed by a client to take legal action against his bank. You know that the firm already acts for the bank on other matters. Can you accept his instructions?
3. The firm has acted for Mr & Mrs Smith over the years when they bought their house and wrote their wills. Now they are getting divorced and Mr Smith wants you to act for him. Can you act for him?

This is a point of personal reflection for you or your team. There have been four different versions of the conflict of interest requirements since 1999, with major changes in the 2007 Handbook. Now it's time to try it in your own words! If you were at the SRA, what would you say the rules should be?

Consider your understanding of the term 'conflict of interest'. Try to write out a definition.

THE 'SOLICITORS AND THEIR CLIENTS' PROBLEM – VERSION 1

This problem is a permanent fixture in the writer's career. Try to solve the problem.

A, B, C and D all own plots of land. E is a commercial developer and acquires adjacent land for housebuilding.

E approaches A, B, C and D to sell their land as well, also for house building, and offers individual terms.

A, B, C and D all have a meeting, believing the terms are the same for each of them as they all have the same sized plots of land. They decide to ask you, a solicitor, for advice on the terms.

A, B, C and D all come in to see you, and tell you about the proposal. They ask you for advice. They do not give you the terms of their offers, as you would like to do some research first, before any advice can take place.

Your Land Registry search allows you to piece together the map below, showing the plots of land owned by A, B, C and D, as well as the land owned by E.

Artwork part8-02

Section 1 – Answer these questions first in writing, before reading Section 2

Do you think any information is missing?

Do you think there is a conflict of interest at this stage? Have a look at the rules of professional conduct and work through whether you think you could act for A, B, C and D all together. If you think any information is missing, consider whether it is important in establishing whether there is a conflict.

Section 2

Now let's imagine the initial meeting again, and A, B, C and D, do provide the terms to you. Consider the position of conflict of interest in these two different scenarios:

1. All the terms are the same.
2. The terms are different. Both C and D have different terms to A and B, in that they have been offered lesser sums of money. None of them are aware of the differences in price.

Consider what you would do next.

THE 'SOLICITORS AND THEIR CLIENTS' PROBLEM – VERSION 2

This version is another variation of the problem at version 1, as of course there are a great many. Try to do the first one first.

Once you have attempted the first one, try to solve this problem.

A, B, C and D all own plots of land. E is a commercial developer and acquires adjacent land for house building.

E approaches A, B, C and D to sell their land as well, also for house building, and offers individual terms.

A accepts the terms, but the others reject the terms and the offer. E does not pursue the deal with B, C or D.

You are a local solicitor.

E asks you to act in both of these transactions:

1. for E in the purchase of A's land; and
2. for A in the sale of A's land,

and provides the terms of agreed sale. The map of the land is shown below.

Can you, or your firm, act for both parties? Is there a conflict of interest?

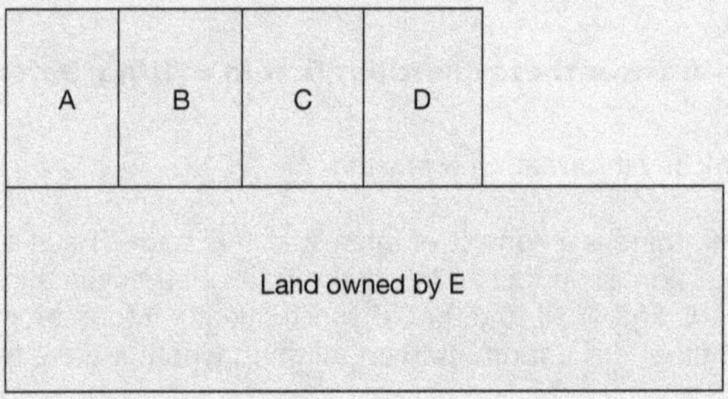

The following problems are all issues the writer has posed before to help with an understanding of the rules or as practice. You can complete the problems separately, or as a group in sequence. If you complete them in sequence, does your reflection on one impact your reflection on another? In each case, try to solve the problem and consider whether you or your firm could act or continue to act. How would you resolve the situation? If there are other factors complicating the situation, also take these into consideration in your answer.

You take instructions from clients X and Y, a married couple, who wish to sell their house to their children at undervalue.

Consider, at this stage, is there a conflict of interest? Can you or your firm act?

You take further instructions and establish that clients X and Y are divorcing.

Consider the situation now, is there a conflict of interest? Can you or your firm act?

Client A asks you to recover a debt from a director of a company; the debt is owed personally by the director. You have acted for the company before.

Can you or your firm act for both parties?

Tania is selling her flat. Her son would like to buy it, but has made her a below market price offer. Tania accepted because he is her son, and is very overbearing. She feels under pressure. The son has asked your firm to act on behalf of both parties in the transaction, and a fee earner has agreed because they are mother and son.

Can you act?

Kam is selling her house to Ram. They are not connected to each other. Both instructed you independently, and the sale and purchase appear straightforward on first review. Houses in the same street have sold for much higher prices but, given the condition of the property, it might be a fair price.

Can you act?

Pad is buying his house from his neighbour. There is structural damage to the house but he does not want to tell the mortgage company. So far, he has said nothing to the lender, and proposes to carry on this way. As far as you can see, the price reflects what the property would be worth if it was not damaged.

Can you act? What should you do next?

Your long-standing client and good friend is tendering for a contract. You are a solicitor specialising in commercial matters. The client asks you to look over the terms of contract offered with the tender.

Simultaneously, another client, who is a competitor of your client, also asks you to look over the terms of the same contract. You realise the competitor client is tendering for the same contract.

You wonder about sending the competitor to another person in your firm.

Can you or your firm act for both parties? Is it a conflict of interest?

Existing client (client A), a large plc, wishes to buy land adjacent to their current factory, which they have become aware is coming up for sale. You are asked to act for client B (a new client) in obtaining the same land. There is a third interested party represented elsewhere.

Can you or your firm act for clients A and B? Is it a conflict of interest?

Client A and client B are executors and sole beneficiaries of an estate which includes is a large and complex family trust; they are also trustees. Client A is the mother of client B. Client A is elderly and unwell. A fee earner in your firm has been looking after the trust and has also made client A's will. The fee earner feels the content of client A's will determines the best way to treat the assets in the estate.

The will has not been disclosed to client B.

No-one else in the firm is aware of the fee earner's position, and the file has not been looked at or reviewed by anyone else.

Client A discloses her will to client B.

Your firm receives a complaint from client B that it should have been disclosed before it was.

Do you think there is a conflict of interest?

Do you think this is a breach of the rules of professional conduct? Who has breached the rules?

Is it a serious breach?

Equality and diversity

The following problems and quiz have featured in the writer's equality and diversity courses. In each case, including with the quiz, consider which parts of the Code of Conduct for both firms and individuals are relevant.

SCENARIOS

You receive an approach from a client who suffers from agoraphobia and cannot leave her house. How can you proceed?

Your complaints procedure requires all complaints to be put in writing, but you have a client who cannot read or write. How can you proceed?

What current events can you think of which pose E&D issues? If a solicitor was involved in any of these events, would it cause a serious breach?

EQUALITY AND DIVERSITY QUIZ

What is a protected characteristic under the Equality Act 2010?

What is harassment?

Which part of the Code of Conduct deals with E&D?

Competence statement or general CPD exercises

The following exercises are themed around the use of CPD and the Competence Statement. As we have seen in Part 7 of the book, the CPD scheme may change as revalidation is introduced, or there may be a ten-yearly revalidation exercise.

The viewpoint below may be best used with your senior staff. The suggestions for personal development can be used personally, or you can suggest staff incorporate them in their personal development plans alongside the requirements for competence in their area of law.

Discuss the following viewpoint:

The Competence Statement or CPD planning provides an opportunity to stretch and challenge your staff in their development

Review your own personal development plan and consider whether to incorporate any of the following:

- strategic goals;
- communication with clients;
- bringing in new clients;
- completing tasks in a timely manner; and
- meeting billing targets.

Give three examples of activities you might use to assess and demonstrate your competence:

Practising conditions problems

The following problems are all Practising Certificate problems. Consider how you would answer the problems using Practising Certificate conditions as a starting point. You could also consider what other risk-based problem solving you could undertake. Would firm conditions be appropriate or would you advocate another course of action? You have to put yourself in the shoes of the regulator.

THE 'BACKWARDS EXERCISE'

This exercise is the wrong way round. We are imagining the condition first, then the imposition afterwards. We discussed in Part 3 of the book that the public interest test had moved from the imposition of a particular condition to more generally 'imposing conditions'. Rather than considering the circumstances, we can consider the conditions themselves. This exercise is not

reality, but is intended to try to challenge your assumptions about conditions.

In what circumstances would the following conditions be appropriate:

- Not to take trainees on.
- Restrict access to financial functions of the firm.
- Approved employment.
- Attend training course.

The remainder of the exercises in this section are all conditions-based scenarios for you to consider, unless otherwise indicated.

You apply for a Practising Certificate. You have recently returned to practice after a period of 20 years as a schoolteacher, when your name was not on the roll. You previously did wills and probate for 10 years, and you would like to return to working in wills.

What do you need to consider? Do you think the SRA would apply conditions?

You have applied for a Practising Certificate, and you are subject to an IVA.

What do you need to consider? What could the SRA do next?

You have been informed by the SRA that you could have conditions applied to your Practising Certificate because you failed to respond to the SRA.

It wrote to you about your conduct in failing to discharge an undertaking, for which you later received a written rebuke. You did not respond to its correspondence, and there was no excuse or mitigation for your behaviour.

What conditions could the SRA apply to your Practising Certificate?

The SRA has made a regulatory decision against you for breaches of the Accounts Rules. Your accounts are not in order and transfers have been made out to third parties in error. You have had to replace the funds immediately. The SRA was not convinced at its last visit that your books were up to date or accurate.

What conditions could it impose? Do you think the SRA would take any other regulatory action?

Ms Bonner, a solicitor and COLP, is in partnership with Mr Well, a solicitor, at Well & Co.

A company in which Mr Well was a director, Well's Football Shirts (a football shirt-manufacturing company), entered into a voluntary arrangement.

Mr Well's company was the subject of an exposé by a national newspaper, saying that the shirts were prone to spontaneously catching fire. Slow sales lead to the downturn in fortune. Mr Well denies the fire allegations and is looking at his legal options.

The COFA at Well & Co, Mr Ahmed, is an accountant, and is truly outstanding. He can demonstrate the firm is financially viable and the accounts are well in order. He and Ms Bonner have put in place carefully thought-out contingency arrangements in case of financial or personal difficulties.

Is there a risk at Well & Co?

What things have you taken into account?

Is there anything else Mr Ahmed and Ms Bonner could do?

Do you think Practising Certificate conditions or firm conditions would be imposed?

Mr Well from the previous scenario has moved to a new firm, as Mr Ahmed and Ms Bonner were very cross with him.

Would Practising Certificate or firm conditions be imposed at the new firm? If so, when?

Is there a risk?

What information would you take into account or would you need to make a decision about the level of risk?

Mr Johnson has just joined your firm. He had conditions on his Practising Certificate last year because he was un co-operative with the SRA during an investigation. He explains to you that he was unwell during the investigation and produces a doctor's note explaining as much. He didn't have a chance to challenge the Practising Certificate conditions because he was still unwell so he has accepted the conditions. You accept the explanation and Mr Johnson settles into his new job.

You review his disciplinary record at the SRA. The conditions require him to attend a training course about the SRA Standards and Regulations 2019 and to inform his employer of the reasons for the condition.

During the year, Mr Johnson refuses to attend the training course. When you raise the matter with Mr Johnson, he says that, because he was unwell and didn't have a chance to respond, he does not have to attend the course. When he told you he was 'accepting the conditions', Mr Johnson actually meant he did not challenge them. He was simply not going to go.

What would you do?

Do you think conditions would be imposed the following year if Mr Johnson refused to attend this year?

This exercise is helpful to consider with your Human Resources department. The list of situations in the (previous) Regulation 3 of the Practising Regulations 2011 is helpful as a list of circumstances where the SRA may consider Practising Certificate conditions, or where in the past a risk has been identified by the regulator.

You have decided to hire a new person to join you at your firm. What information will you look for in advance, to help you evaluate that person?

Would the information change if that person was more senior? Would you ask for anything else?

Would you ask about disciplinary history or conditions?

Would you ask about regulation 3 circumstances from the SRA Handbook 2011?

Ms Ricks, Mr Fox, and Mr Sim are all partners at a medium-sized law firm. They were all fined individually at the SDT one year ago due to breaches in respect of referrals. The investigation was commenced about two years ago and, before the Tribunal took place, the partners told the SRA they had ceased accepting referrals. You work for the regulator and have received a complaint about the referral arrangements again recently.

The Tribunal found the partners had entered into referrals arrangements which took unfair advantage of clients.

What further investigation would you undertake to find information to help you make a decision about what to do?

What information are you looking for to make your decision?

Imagine the allegation was true, and they had re-started accepting referrals in breach of the rules:

a. Could this be a case where conditions could be imposed? Do you think another outcome is suitable?

b. If you think conditions are suitable, should they be imposed on the firm or the individual(s)?

c. If you think conditions are suitable, what conditions do you think should be imposed?

Don't forget that the information you submit on the annual renewal can be used to make a decision about anyone in the firm who could be subject to conditions. Try this exercise to help you understand the type of information you submit. How would you use it?

Consider the information you submit on the annual renewal.

What information do you think is necessary for the regulator to make a decision about risk and how to manage it?

Which information from the renewal could they use when making decisions about conditions?

Complaint Handling Problems

These exercises featured on a Practice Skills Course in 2017. They are role-play exercises and require at least two people to make them work. The exercises work best if each person has not seen the other's instructions. Therefore you, as the reader of the book, should probably set up the exercise to make it work for other people. You can, of course, try it out yourself.

This exercise is also helpful for those who would like to practise complaint handling. Ensure you discuss the idea of the exercise with the staff members first, explaining that they will be role-playing complaint handling.

Will Complaint Files – Exercise 1

Print out a template will.

This exercise is for two members of staff. Provide the following instructions to them. Each person should not see the other's instructions.

Person 2 can have the template Will to use as a prop or for the purposes of the role play.

Person 1 instructions

You are a customer. You are angry with a law firm as they have not written your will. You came in seven weeks ago and paid £150 in cash for a will. You gave some brief instructions. You are very angry. You would like your money back in cash today. You will only calm down if the solicitor / paralegal either gives you the cash or produces a will immediately.

You speak first.

Person 2 instructions

You are a solicitor or paralegal. You are faced with a furious customer who has not received any correspondence for seven weeks. She came in to see someone about making a will and she hasn't had anything back. She paid £150 and feels she has been ripped off. Respond to her complaint and try to defuse the situation.

Let the customer speak first.

Will Complaint Files – Exercise 2

This exercise is for two members of staff. Provide the following instructions to them. Each person should not see the other's instructions.

Person 1 instructions

You are a customer. You are unhappy that your solicitor/paralegal has given you incorrect advice about a will which resulted in you selling a property that was not yours to sell. You are visiting them in their office to ask what they intend to do about the situation. You are to be cross but not unreasonable.

The will said that all assets were left to Barbara, including all property. The will went on to say that £500 was left to Mara and £1,000 to Michael. Small items of jewellery and other similar items were left to Sara and Sheena.

You are Barbara. The will was made by your grandfather but you have been told since the will intended to leave the property to a family member you usually call Barbie (but who is also called Barbra).

You have sold the house since inheriting it.

You speak first.

Person 2 instructions

You are a solicitor or paralegal. Your client complains that they have been given incorrect advice about a will. You are seeing them in your office and they are very unhappy, saying they have sold a property following your interpretation of the will, but it was not theirs to sell.

The will said that all assets were left to Barbara, including all property. The will went on to say that £500 was left to Mara and £1,000 to Michael. Small items of jewellery and other similar items were left to Sara and Sheena.

The client is called Barbara. The will was made by her grandfather but she has been told since the will intended to leave the property to a family member she usually calls Barbie (but who is also called Barbra).

Barbara has sold the house since inheriting it.

Decide what you can do and how to manage the situation.

Let the customer speak first.

Legal Market Analysis

The following three case studies were used by the writer on a Practice Skills Course in 2017. In each case, delegates had to review the profile of the firm and come up with a strategy for the firm; the full situations and analysis from the course are not provided here, but the scenarios are helpful in asking how changes in the legal services market could impact firms, and what steps they can take to sustain their businesses for the future.

Have a look at each case study below. Do you think any of these firms would benefit from changing their structure as a result of the regulatory changes which have occurred over the last ten years? Would any firm benefit from:

- Outside investment – becoming an ABS?
- Hiving off part of their firm to an unregulated structure?
- Moving to another regulator?
- Adopting a new form of practice (for example, utilising freelancers or working flexibly on contracts with other firms)?

Your task is to write a strategy for each firm based (primarily) on the regulatory changes, and where you can see benefits to the firm. You might decide the firm should not make changes in light of regulatory change, and you can provide this answer and reasoning if you decide as much. You might decide the firm should make changes not to their structure, but to their service offering, and ideas are provided in each scenario.

In reality, what do you think the costs will be to each firm of making such changes? What would the projected benefits be? It is difficult to make projections without full costings but stopping to consider the costs of making changes and the benefits of doing so is important in the long term, as is considering the basis of those decisions.

In each case, also consider the competence of the individuals or the firm overall in light of the regulatory discussions in this book. Ask the following questions:

- What does it take to achieve competence in a new area of law?
- How could you achieve competence if you already worked in a firm and you had to move into a new area of law? How long would it take you?
- What are the risks of taking on work in another area of law?

Could a firm instead use a freelancer who was experienced and competent in a particular area of law to test entry to the market? What are the risks in working with a freelancer and outsourcing work to them if you don't understand what they are doing?

Hopefully all of these ideas give you plenty of material for considering the strategy of the firms below.

CASE STUDY 1

This is a large local law firm in a county town covering a wide range of legal areas, including:

- Conveyancing (50% of turnover, 30% of profit, but a growing area);
- Family (10% of turnover, 20% of profit and stable);
- Litigation (15% of turnover, 20% of profit and stable);
- Crime (5% of turnover, 1% of profit and stable);
- Personal Injury (19% of turnover, 28% of profit and declining rapidly); and
- Education (1% of turnover and 1% of profit).

The firm is uncertain about future strategic direction. PI reforms have hit the firm hard and the work is declining in profit dramatically. Its next most profitable areas are in family and litigation; however, it wonders about using conveyancing as a loss leader for referrals and reputation, and expanding geographically by buying up other conveyancing firms to obtain further work in litigation and family.

The firm has historically focused on being known as a 'local', personable firm with strong customer service and has a strong reputation associated with this strategy. The firm's prices are on the high side because of this market positioning.

There are a number of local competitors in the area in conveyancing and, nationally, there are a considerable number of very large firms who conduct conveyancing for very low fees as a loss leader for estate agents. However, the firm has benefited from a major investment program in the local area, which has driven desirability for houses nearby. This, coupled with a major house building program nearby, has helped drive business to the firm.

In family and litigation, fees are high, but there are a few local competitors. The firm hold the largest market share. It is questionable whether they have reached saturation point in both of these areas. The firm have considered moving into new nearby localities where there are opportunities for growth due to a fairly segmented market. In the next county, there is a very large family provider who is very popular due to their senior partner's reputation, but there is little or no provision in litigation.

In the long term, the firm wonders about the threat of change in the legal services market from low-cost providers and supermarkets taking on unreserved work. They wonder about whether reserved work will disappear and whether the professions will come to an end.

CASE STUDY 2

National law firm:

- Debt recovery (50% of turnover, 30% of profit, and decreasing);
- Conveyancing (25% of turnover and 25% of profit and decreasing); and
- Employment (25% of turnover and 45% of profit and increasing).

This is a national firm that was known for debt recovery but has in more recent years developed its offering in employment which has been very successful. It has been struggling with compliance requirements and has been in trouble with the SRA.

Debt recovery does not make much money due to the price pressure; a large number of staff are needed as it is volume work, and margins have dramatically decreased. The same pressures apply in conveyancing.

The firm wonders whether to continue with offering the debt recovery service, and instead focus on a new area of law.

There are four partners, two in debt management, one in employment, and one in conveyancing. The employment partner is happy and does not want to change their workload. One debt management partner has previous experience in personal injury. The conveyancing partner has some experience in crime and mental health, due to previously working for a legal aid firm at a time when many firms still had legal aid contracts.

There are strong local competitors in crime, but many PI operators are closing. The partner with experience in mental health has not worked in this area for some time.

CASE STUDY 3

This is a large criminal firm which has just been successful in the latest round of legal aid contracts. However, the profits from running the criminal contract are very small. The firm has wondered about diversification into a number of other areas, including:

- privately funded criminal work (for which there is limited demand in the immediate locality which is very poor, but there could be in the wider county which is richer);
- very high-cost cases (for which they would need specialism such as fraud and a good track record, as contracts are competitive);
- personal injury work;
- family work, which would require recruitment of new staff or the purchase of a pre-existing firm, but there is limited competition in the local area;
- conveyancing, which is highly competitive with a number of local firms, and large national competitors;
- increasing overall profits by increasing volume by a move into nearby counties; and
- another move into another area of law, such as business and contract law, housing, or immigration.

Serious Breaches

The following problems have all featured on the Serious Breach or Material Breach courses over the last eight years. The premise of these exercises is simple; to consider whether you think the matter needs reporting to the SRA under its current rules for reporting, but also to consider what you might do next.

The majority of the matters below are issues related to self-reporting, which is what we have covered in the main in this book. However, some of the matters also relate to breaches in other firms, or even different industries. Again the question remains the same. What would you do?

You can also consider whether the matter would also/or in the alternative be reportable:

- for another reason and, if so, who to; or
- as an issue of suspected money laundering. In saying this, we remember, of course, the requirement to report to your MLRO and to the NCA if necessary.

In other Parts of this book, the writer has suggested you can also use these scenarios to test out different viewpoints, outcomes, or regulatory situations. Please feel free to do so.

A COLP from another firm is on the phone. It is the same COLP who calls you sometimes. She is an old friend.

She is worried about possible breaches. In conducting file reviews, she has noticed one department not using the standard client care letters. The effect of this is that clients were not told of the right to complain to the Legal Ombudsman. You both agree it is a breach. The COLP says she thinks three clients were affected, which is small compared to their thousands of clients. She does not think there are any financial consequences for the clients, but she is concerned because she thinks one of the clients is vulnerable. You agree to give the COLP your opinion, but recommend she put in place some new procedures to help her in future.

Do you think this is a serious breach?

What did you take into account?

What ideas for procedures do you have for the COLP?

Now add in these three additional scenarios. The position in each scenario below occurs after the situation above. **Each scenario below stands alone and does not impact the other scenarios, but they all affect the position above.**

Scenario 1

The COLP goes away and finds the client is vulnerable. The other two clients have not been affected. The vulnerable client has suffered severe distress and inconvenience.

Scenario 2

The impact on the vulnerable client is very small. In fact, the fee earner has done an outstanding job working with all of the clients. All clients are very happy.

Scenario 3

The COLP decides to investigate this department some more. She finds a pattern of cases in this department with very poor client care, including unanswered complaints and client monies left undistributed on client account.

You are approached by potential clients in the following scenarios:

- A client who is unhappy at work as she has concerns that may amount to whistleblowing. The client does not work in legal services. You do not do this type of work, but think the client could approach another organisation. Could this matter be reported to the SRA? If not, where should the client go?
- An individual client (who does not work in legal services), who has been scammed by a fraudster and came in to enquire if you could help. You are a commercial solicitor and do not handle this type of work on behalf of individuals. Where would you direct the client? Would it be a matter for the SRA?
- A married couple who have sold their house, but believe the solicitor previously representing them has taken the monies from the sale. Could this matter be reported to the SRA? Where else might you refer the matter, and why?
- A client has come in from another firm with a complaint about another solicitor, who has written a will for them, but has not honoured all of their wishes. The client cannot understand why, and only realised when they received the draft will. He asks you to put it right. Could this matter be referred to the SRA? Where else might you refer the matter, and why? Do you need to ask any more questions?
- A client (Mr Barn) comes in to see you to explain he has conducted his divorce through another solicitor, but the other solicitor has sent him divorce paperwork for a different client (Mr Ali). Mr Barn is very concerned. What steps would you take next? Does the matter need referring to the SRA or anywhere else?
- You are contacted by a former client who moved away some time ago. He moved solicitors as a result of his house move. He is concerned by the behaviour of his new solicitor, who has been behaving erratically. Does this matter need referring to the SRA? Does it need referring anywhere else?

You are reviewing a file as part of your usual file review procedures, when you come across a conveyancing file. It is a sale file.

It has estate agent particulars showing a photo which looks like this:

You understand the property for sale is the one in the middle and is known as 26 Peak Close. The properties either side are, you understand, 24 Peak Close and 28 Peak Close.

You review the Land Registry entries and find the map of the plot, which shows 26 Peak Close as below:

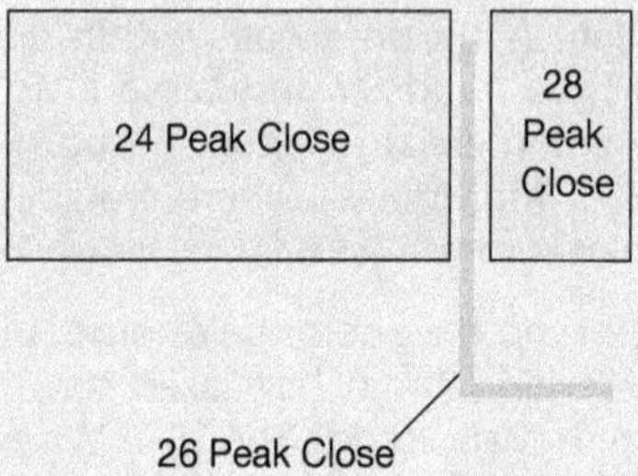

What will you do next?

You have a long-standing client who has been your client for 30 years. You have not seen her for perhaps five years because she has become quite old and stopped going out as much, but you still see the family in town.

One day, you hear from a member of the family (D) asking if you are holding a will because your client has died. You do have a will, and you ask your staff to find it from storage.

D calls you back distraught because there is apparently a later will made by another solicitor in favour of a person unconnected to the family. D is convinced the will is not real.

Is this a serious breach? Does it need reporting? What steps might you take next?

You are a junior fee earner. You are being pressured to take action in a particular direction that you do not ethically agree with because a client has asked you to do so. The firm management appear to support the client, and you suspect it is because they bring in a lot of fees.

What could you consider? What do the rules require you to consider?

You are a COFA, and a staff member reports to you that another staff member has repeatedly overcharged clients £50.00 for insurance policies that have not been taken out on matters. The matter has come to light when the fee earner was unwell, and his files have been looked at by another person.

What can you consider next?

Items of value were left with your firm for safekeeping. They form part of an estate not yet distributed. A new and very junior member of staff mistakes them for having little value and, when you move offices, she places them in a cardboard box for disposal.

You later find that, in the confusion of the move, they have been disposed of.

Does this matter need reporting?

Mr Cox is a solicitor.

He receives a passport and driving licence in the post from a client. The photo on the passport looks sellotaped on and different to the driving licence.

The electronic search shows the client is an Ambassador and a PEP.

The transaction is very large – in the millions – with no related purchase.

The client is keen to progress quickly.

Is this a serious breach? What would you do next?

You are a COFA and you have taken over at a firm. You discover to your horror that the books of account are not up to date, and fee earners are not identifying the client on every transaction.

Is this a serious breach?

You are a fee earner in a firm who has pursued a case for a client as per their instructions. However, the matter has not gone their way in court. This was not the anticipated result, and is going to cost the client an unaffordable amount as a result. The client was aware of the possible outcome, but it could mean bankruptcy for them.

Have you breached the rules?

Is this a serious breach?

You are a COLP, and the MLRO receives a report concerning a transaction from within your firm. The firm has a new commercial client who is headquartered in the Cayman Islands, and is reluctant to disclose beneficial ownership. This is not the firm's usual client base.

What steps would you take next?

You are a non-lawyer manager and MLRO, and a file comes to your attention that bears the warning signs of fraud in the handling of client monies. You report it to the NCA and to the COLP. You later find out the COLP has not taken any action.

Why might that be?

What can you do next?

Your friend, the COLP from another firm, is on the phone. This time, the computer system has gone down and she is worried about postings and reconciliations getting behind on client account. She thinks they can manage with existing paper-based systems. She asks your advice on whether and when to notify the SRA.

What do you think? Write some advice.

Re-visit your advice and re-word it to suit a scenario where it is a few months down the line and they were substantially behind with reconciliations and postings.

The COLP from the other firm then decides to invest in a new accounts package, but it automatically calculates monies due from client to office. She finds it is calculating the wrong amount and the firm has taken £20,000 too much. She estimates five clients have been affected; the largest loss was £10,000 for five days. The firm have replaced the money and there was no impact on any transaction.

Is this a serious breach?

Would your answer change if there was a longer pattern of taking too much from client account due to incorrect calculations?

Twenty clients complain to your firm about overcharging. They all allege one of your fee earners has charged them £300.00 more than quoted. You look into this and find the fee earner has been struggling to meet billing targets. They admit to over-billing on some matters. You resolve the issue by compensating the clients accordingly and by disciplining your fee earner. By the end of your work to compensate the clients, no client has suffered any financial loss.

Is this a serious breach?

Would your answer change if the clients were vulnerable?

Would your answer change if you had not found out about it for two years, by which time more than 300 clients had suffered loss?

A very vulnerable client complains about the attitude shown towards her by a member of your staff. You are concerned the complaint is justified and it may be discrimination. You decide to discipline the member of staff and offer compensation to the client.

Is this a serious breach?

The COLP and COFA in a small firm do not get along and do not speak to each other. The COLP identifies a possible billing issue. The COLP believes the COFA is inappropriately dealing with aged balances, but cannot be certain without asking for an explanation. The COLP decides not to raise it with the COFA because they don't speak to each other. The COLP decides not to do anything.

Could it be a serious breach?

For the example in this box, consider two distinct possibilities:

1. **You or the subject have evidence of the alleged wrongdoing.**
2. **You or the subject have no evidence of the alleged wrongdoing.**

Does your position differ? What if you had reasonable belief?

A fee earner in your firm is questioned by police about money laundering on one of his files. The police decide to take no further action.

Is this a serious breach, or reportable anyway?

How would you feel if the fee earner was arrested and charged?

What are the challenges in dealing with this situation?

The writer used these scenarios in approximately 2014 with some of the very first Material Breach courses. Do you think these are serious breaches?

Scenario 1

The head of conveyancing is concerned about a conveyance in her department. She finds a file where a charge has not been discharged on a property, which is a breach of the undertakings in the replies to requisitions on title and means the other side cannot register their charge.

Consider this scenario on its own. Is this a serious breach?

Scenario 2

In a different ending to scenario 1, the head of conveyancing gets straight to work and discharges the charge – it turns out the money was on client account, the fee earner just made a mistake. The delay was four days and the firm made up the interest on the redemption fee from office account. No-one suffered any loss.

What is your view now?

Scenario 3

This is a separate situation to the other two scenarios, above.

Your old friend the COLP from another firm is on the phone again, and their reconciliations have not balanced for some time. She thought she could find the problem and resolve it, but she can't. You tell her to put any missing money back into client account, and she informs you £10,000 is missing which will be hard for her to replace.

What is your view? Is this a serious breach?

Daniel, a solicitor, receives a suspicious phone call and email. The caller and emailer informs Daniel they are the former Chief Executive of his firm, who left recently. Daniel thinks they are part of a scam, and the scammers are trying to extract monies from his firm. Daniel is worried about cybercrime.

Do these matters need to be reported?

Are they serious breaches or should they be reported for another reason?

In a variation of the above scenario, the scammers are successful in pretending to be the former Chief Executive and convince Daniel to send them money.

Does this matter need to be reported?

Is it a serious breach or does it need to be reported for another reason?

Jarrett is a new compliance manager in a conveyancing firm. He finds out a fee earner has failed to discharge a mortgage on a property. The breach lasted six months, but has been rectified now. No-one has been impacted in the long term.

Would you report this as a serious breach to the SRA? What does Jarrett need to consider?

Sarah is a Sole Practitioner and COLP / COFA.

She realises a member of her accounts team has been removing client funds from the client account – luckily, she reviews the accounts regularly and caught it. She estimates £10,000 has been removed from client account over a couple of days. Sarah makes the loss good from the office account and decides to call the police.

Would you report this to the SRA as a serious breach? What does Sarah need to consider?

When completing her day's work, and conducting the reconciliation for that day, a COFA notices a member of her team has made an accounting error of £1,500 on client account. The team member sent it to a financial advisor by accident. The COFA telephones the advisor who agrees to send it back immediately but, because it is the end of the day, it will not get there until the next day. The COFA corrects the error by transferring £1,500 from office account. The money is returned from the advisor the next day, and £1,500 is returned to office.

Would you report this as a serious breach, and what does the COFA need to consider?

Jarrett, the Compliance Manager, has been struggling to get anyone in his office to listen to him about implementing a system for CPD under the Competence Statement for years. As a result, staff are not currently undertaking training; and the position has got worse over the last year. CPD has been completely dismissed, and he has been isolated in his position. He has been concentrating so hard on trying to resolve this directly with the staff and make them see his perspective, he has not been updating his manager and the senior management team. The management team have noticed that some of the staff are not up to date with the latest developments, and in some areas of law there have been major changes. The management are now complaining about everyone's competence and are worried about potential claims.

Is this a serious breach? How would you feel if the annual renewal had been signed off to say competence had been considered?

Charles is approached to act for Stefan and Stefan's brother-in-law, Phil, in the purchase of a flat in London worth £700,000. Midway through the transaction, Charles finds out that the majority of the funds being used are Stefan's, even though they intend to own the property as joint tenants. Charles meets with the clients and feels Phil may be unduly influencing Stefan, who is meek and mild. However, Charles accepts their explanation that the property will be used by the whole family, including both Stefan and his wife. Later, after the purchase has completed, Stefan complains he was not advised properly and there was a conflict of interest.

Is this a serious breach?

Manjinder decides to review the accounts; when looking at her partner's work, she finds some bills to clients some time after the conclusion of the transaction – for the same amount as left on client account. She reviews a few files and finds no evidence of the costs being incurred.

Is this a serious breach?

How would you feel if there were three clients affected and the sums could have been transferred under the aged balances guidance?

How would you feel if there were at least 100 clients affected and some of the sums were very significant (into the thousands – for example, old retentions)?

Manjinder goes on to conduct further investigations into the accounts. She finds several round sum transfers from client to office which do not add up to bills and disbursements.

Is this a serious breach?

Kristin is reviewing the work of her new recruit, Kit. She comes across a will he drew up for a client where he appears to benefit.

Is this a serious breach?

Mr Good is a solicitor who has to travel a long way by various forms of transport. He loses a client file somewhere and he is not sure where. The client is severely ill.

Is this a serious breach?

You are a solicitor acting for Ms Mumble in the purchase of a house. The accounts department approaches you about a payment received into the client bank account from Ms Mumble. It is very early in the transaction. The payment is for £10,000.

You telephone Ms Mumble to query the payment. She asks you to send it on to a limited company you have never heard of, as she owes them some money for some work they did for her.

Is this a serious breach?

You are working for a law firm handling complaints. You receive a complaint that the firm have been pursuing the wrong man for a debt. It is alleged the firm have known it was the wrong man for some time. The court has just entered judgment.

Is this a serious breach?

Jane, a solicitor, is approached by a potential client that she knows. She knows their mum as a result of previous instructions and knows what is in the mum's Will (and, as a result, her long-term financial planning). The potential client would like to instruct Jane in the purchase of property. However, in the initial conversation, Jane realises the purchase has factored in income from the mum that Jane doesn't think is possible.

What can Jane do now?

Is this a serious breach?

Landon, a partner in an ABS, pays for referrals from a local business network. He also refers his clients on to other people within the network (for example, financial advisors). The group decides to do some marketing together to gain new business. One of the group becomes involved with business Landon doesn't like as he thinks it's a scam. Landon tries to leave, but is intrinsically linked to the group through marketing. Landon thinks several of the others feel the same way.

Is this a serious breach?

Mr Green, a solicitor, receives a new instruction from a client wanting to write a will. The client produces some identification documents, but wishes to write the will in a different name.

Is this a serious breach? What can Mr Green do next?

You have three different members of staff. You have concerns about their ongoing development.

Staff member A is very good, but not as good as he thinks he is.

Staff member B needs improvement in her technical skills, and you have concerns about whether or not she is competent and whether she is making some large mistakes.

Staff member C needs to improve his communication with other members of staff.

Could any of these be serious breaches? What if the annual declaration has been signed?

You are a COLP, and a fee earner comes to you very upset. He has heard another staff member has been cautioned for assault.

What should you consider next? Is this a serious breach?

You are faced with an irate customer; no-one has returned her calls or corresponded with her. She paid £250 on account five weeks ago. She would like you to refund her as no-one has dealt with her case. She wants the refund in cash right now, and is very angry.

Is this a serious breach? What should you consider?

Your old friend, the COLP at another firm, has been arrested over concerns about money laundering.

Is this a serious breach? Would you need to report it?

Does this change any of the advice you have given them previously? Do any of those situations need reporting now?

A large solicitors' firm hires in external experts to undertake 'business process re-engineering' in the hope of saving money through improved processes. Some of the changes lead them into conflict of interest situations.

Is this a serious breach? What would you need to take into account?

A solicitor repeatedly makes mistakes on her reconciliation due to accounting software. Some of the mistakes are large; up to £50,000.

Is this a serious breach?

A firm is considering a merger with another firm. It decides to carry out due diligence and cannot find AML policies and procedures.

Is this a serious breach?

A firm is struggling to cope financially after coronavirus. Debts are mounting. Staff have been made redundant as the firm cannot afford to pay them. The COFA, COLP, and partners have declined to report the matter to the SRA as they believe they will be intervened. Some of the assistants still with the firm become aware of the situation.

Is this a serious breach? Does it need reporting for any other reason?

What would you do?

The following quiz has accompanied the Material/Serious Breach courses for many years. There are some slight changes to make it suitable for this book and the content we cover here.

QUIZ

Provide three facts about the renewal:

Can individuals with Practising Certificate conditions renew in the bulk application?

Material breach has changed to what under the new Standards and Regulations?

Can solicitors work in unregulated firms?

When does the renewal process start and end?

When can a firm be subject to conditions on recognition / authorisation?

Name the regulation:

The Solicitors Disciplinary Tribunal has changed to which standard of proof?

Which regulation in the Code of Conduct for firms governs reporting to the SRA?

What happens if you do not think the COLP or COFA has reported the matter to the SRA?

Qualified Reports and Serious/Material Breach Problems

The following problems appeared in some form or another on the version of the Serious/Material Breach course for COFAs and accountants, known as 'Qualified Reports and Material Breach' which ran between 2016 and 2019. COLPs and other fee earners may also find these scenarios helpful.

In each case, consider whether a report needs to be made to the SRA:

1. either under the requirements for serious breach reporting for firms,
2. or under the requirements for Reporting Accountants, either in the legislation or on the latest AR1 form, which are different to point 1.

The questions have been worded to ask whether there is a serious breach, or whether the matter needs to be reported for any other reason.

The point of the exercises is to both explore your ethical perspective, and understand the difference between points 1 and 2. Sometimes the answer to points 1 and 2 is the same, and there can be a large overlap between the two.

As with the previous set of scenarios, you may also need to consider AML and whether you need to make a report to your MLRO and whether they need to make a report to the National Crime Agency in addition to the reporting position above.

You are a reporting accountant and, during the accountants' report, you meet the COFA, Mrs Marta. Mrs Marta has been with the firm for two years but she feels depressed. She does not feel she makes any headway in implementing systems in the firm; she believes, for example, that the law firm partners should sign off every transaction in their department, meet the staff on morning rounds to tidy up any issues for the day ahead (including finance issues), and lead by example in exemplary behaviour. She believes in a proper way of doing things, but the management team seem to ignore her ideas of decorum. She finds the office too loud; the staff are very headstrong and think they know best. The firm has a lot of work and social events with clients that do not fit Mrs Marta's idea of professional practice, as Mrs Marta thinks they should give wholly independent advice to clients, which is compromised by the firm's social activities.

Mrs Marta sits down to tell you all of this during the accountants' report. The accounts seem fine.

Are there any systems and controls you can suggest to Mrs Marta? How might you react to this scenario?

Will systems and controls work to help Mrs Marta's view of the situation or does Mrs Marta need to do more to either establish her view of management within the firm, or help herself personally?

Is this a serious breach? Does it need reporting for any other reason?

You are a new COFA of a firm and feel there are a number of unresolved issues in the accounts of the firm. They use suspense ledgers very extensively, have made some investments which put them in conflict of interest positions and, despite extensive investment in accounts staff, the cashbook is poorly maintained and you are constantly having to correct problems. You feel the accounts staff should be more capable.

The accountants' report is due shortly. You are concerned for your position as the firm did not disclose this to you on interview and you are worried they have been hiding compliance issues.

What would you do?

Is this a serious breach? Does it need reporting for any other reason?

This problem is not a scenario, but formed part of the course for COFAs and accountants. Test your knowledge of who requires an accountants' report.

Consider the following scenarios and whether or not the firms require an accountants' report:

- A firm doing exclusively legal aid work.
- A firm with an average passbook balance of £9,000 and a maximum of £200,000.
- A firm with an average passbook balance of £12,000 and a maximum of £240,000.

Do you think firms who do not need accountants' reports are under more pressure to consider their own breaches?

The following problems are all scenarios to consider in the terms set out at the beginning of this section:

A COFA maintains suspense ledgers on behalf of several partners who are 'extremely busy' and don't have time to keep up to date with their accounts.

Is this a serious breach? Does this need reporting for any other reason?

A firm finds they are mistakenly transferring money from client account instead of office account. There are 12 transactions over six months, all for sums less than £20.

Is this a serious breach? Does this need reporting for any other reason?

You find one department is transferring money for costs some significant time after the bill is sent. An initial review of files finds it limited to one particular fee earner. You find three instances in a review of transfers which occurred during the last two months. The files were supposed to have concluded some years previously, but there are some monies left on account. The sums are small – an average of £14.00. You speak to the COLP and COFA and find the sums are apparently due to the firm for costs, but monies were being transferred late to cover 'anything unexpected' which came up later.

Is this a serious breach? Does this need reporting for any other reason?

What would be your view if this was found to be more widespread (15 instances within three months) throughout one department and started because of advice to do so given by a partner?

Is this a serious breach? Does this need reporting for any other reason?

A firm is charging for a 'same-day bank transfer fee', but transfers are not being made the same day. This has affected 500 files over two years. The charge is £40.

Is this a serious breach? Does this need reporting for any other reason?

How would you feel if 20 files were affected? What if one file was affected?

A bank reconciliation has not been performed properly in a firm for a year; attempts at reconstructing the accounts are underway, but are proving very difficult.

Is this a serious breach? Does this need reporting for any other reason?

How would you feel if they were making good headway with the accounts?

A solicitor has a debit balance existing in his account for 97 days:

a. The balance is £1.52.

b. The balance is £2,000.

c. The balance is £20,000.

Is this a serious breach? Does this need reporting for any other reason?

£500,000 has been mistakenly taken from client account to office account at the very end of the day, and is unable to be replaced that day because of banking cut-off. It is replaced immediately the next day.

Is this a serious breach? Does this need reporting for any other reason?

A firm is not reconciling cashbook and bank statement to the same date.

Is this a serious breach? Does this need reporting for any other reason?

A firm acts in low-value matters (on a volume basis), and does not hold client funds for any length of time. They do not have an interest policy. You cannot find any situation when they would clearly have needed to pay interest.

Is this a serious breach? Does this need reporting for any other reason?

Would your view change if there were circumstances where they needed to pay interest?

Bills from one fee earner do not contain details of the work completed. You have identified 23 bills in one month, and indications show this has been occurring for years.

Would you feel differently if this had occurred on three files and was explained as a secretarial error?

Is this a serious breach? Does this need reporting for any other reason?

A review of files in the Personal Injury Department shows monies being held for counsel's fees. You find three instances of sums between £700 and £1,500; each has been held for a minimum of six months. In each case, the matter is ongoing, but on hold for some reason, and counsel was never instructed.

Is this a serious breach? Does this need reporting for any other reason?

What should the firm do?

Mr H, a solicitor, has prepared false invoices to pay a wasted cost order.

He was acting for Mr D and received monies on account from Mr D to pay his fees. He had over-estimated his fees and Mr D had paid too much. You can see the over-estimation of fees very clearly from the firm's charging structure.

Mr H used monies from Mr D's overpayment of fees to pay a wasted costs order, and created invoices to cover what he had done. You can see the false invoices do not match the work done, and they are all created on the same date. The monies have been sent to pay the costs order.

Is this a serious breach? Does this need reporting for any other reason?

Would you take any other information into account? What does the firm need to do next?

A solicitor told you he did not have time to learn the SRA Accounts Rules. You find he has failed to keep proper books of accounts and failed to remedy breaches.

The failures also include: a failure to carry out reconciliations every five weeks; improper use of a suspense ledger account; failure to maintain separate books of accounts; and use of client account as a banking facility.

Is this a serious breach? Would it need reporting for any other reason?

A firm failed to inform the SRA that they were in financial difficulty and unable to pay various taxes to the HMRC between 2012 and 2014 totalling £380,778.99.

The firm also had unauthorised withdrawals from a client account, as well as transferring money from the client account to the office account in excess of money held in the client account.

Is this a serious breach? Would it need reporting for any other reason?

There is concern at a firm about postings on client account cashbook not accurately reflecting the activity on the client bank account.

An accounts review by the new COFA reveals a number of client account cashbook entries being posted under 'unknown'; the individual sums are all different to the entries in the bank account, but the totals in and out match, so the reconciliation balances.

The COFA has so far only done a one-month review.

Is this a serious breach? Would it need reporting for any other reason?

The following quiz has accompanied the Material / Serious Breach courses for many years. There are some slight changes to make it suitable for this book and the content we cover here. You may need to do some research to answer the questions.

QUIZ

In what timeframe do you need to report a serious breach?

What makes a breach serious?

Do you need to obtain an accountants' report if you only do legal aid work?

How long do you have to deliver a qualified accountants' report to the SRA?

Does the SRA have the power to fine a COLP/COFA for failure to comply with their duties?

Which rule / regulation governs the appointment of a Reporting Accountant?

Can a reporting accountant work for the firm?

The responsibilities of a COFA to report breaches are set out in which rule in the Standards and Regulations?

Name one exemption from obtaining an accountants' report.

Where can you find more information on whether the accountants' report should be qualified?

If your accounting period end date is 31 December, when do you need to send the report to the SRA (if it is qualified)?

What previously made a breach material?

The SRA changed material breach to what?

What is the authority for reporting accountants to report fraud to the SRA?

Holding client money – Escrow accounts

What do the initials 'TPMA' stand for?

Name one reason for, and one reason against, using a TPMA?

What should you do if you would like to use a TPMA instead of a client account?

More accounts problems

The following problems are more general and are suitable for in-house COLPs, COFAs, accounts staff, and cashiers. Reporting Accountants may also find them helpful for junior staff, or for practice.

Auditing and reviewing

If you would like to audit and review your own accounts, you can start with the reconciliation. Is it completed correctly, and are there any errors? What does the unpresented look like – are there old items? You can look at the bank statement – is it named correctly?

You could move on to:

- Client matters – are there suspense accounts and what are they being used for? Are there any miscellaneous, old or unnamed accounts? Are there any large balances in office or client?
- Look at transfers from client to office – do they match bills rendered, are the bills properly due, and do they appear on the bank statement?
- Client-to-client transfers – are they all legitimate?
- Client-to-office transfers – why have these occurred?
- Accounting records – are these written up properly and in a timely manner? Records written up after month end and reconciliation are unlikely to be appropriate.

Reconciliation

Exercise 1

Your former colleagues Lucas and Ricardo started a new firm, 'Property People', on 1 June 2015. They are doing their first reconciliation but it has confused them. They asked you to help. They have given you a bank statement, a computerised reconciliation, and a client matter listing (showing the totals on the client ledgers). Can you spot the problem? What other information would you ask for? What do they need to do?

Bank Statement – Property People Client Account 1 June 2015 – 1 July 2015				
Date	**Item**	**Paid in**	**Paid out**	**Total**
1 June 2015	**Mr M Wool**	200.00	0.00	200.00
	Searches and fees			
3 June 2015	**Mrs A Timms**	200.00	0.00	400.00
	Searches and fees			
10 June 2015	**Searches UK**	0.00	100.00	300.00
30 June 2015	**A Bank Plc**	**100,000.00**	0.00	**100,300.00**
	Mortgage advance Timms			
1 July 2015	**A Bank Plc**	**50,000.00**	0.00	**150,300.00**
	Mortgage advance Wool			

Computerised Reconciliation – Property People
30 June 2015 – Cashbook total: 100,400.00
Client ledger balances: 100,400.00
Uncleared: 0.00
Money at bank: 100,300.00
Difference: 100.00

Client matter listing Property People– 1 July 2015		
Name	**Property**	**Total on ledger**
Wool	47 Beech Avenue Purchase	100,200.00
Timms	55 Leeway Road Purchase	50,200.00

Your answer:

Exercise 2

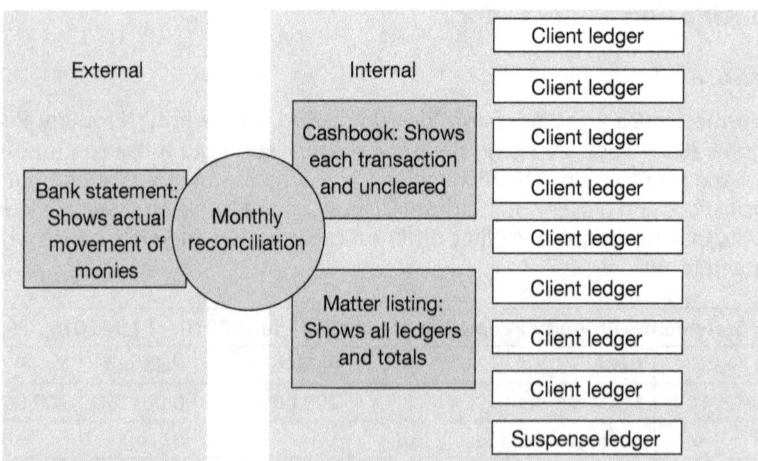

The diagram above is a visual representation of a set of solicitor accounts, with a focus on the client account and the reconciliation process.

Answer the following:

1. Explain a reconciliation in writing.
2. Explain the diagram in writing or to another person.

3. Explain:
   a. where there might be problems in a set of accounts with reference to the diagram showing the reconciliation; and
   b. what problem(s) you can see in the diagram above, or where you would investigate this set of accounts further.

Some of the answers to (3)(a) and (b) are shown at the end of this Part of the book, but you may be able to find more areas for investigation or problems. Try to write out your answer before you refer to the answer.

Exercise 3

Mr and Mrs Walker – Abortive Purchase 3 Net Road							
Date	Description	Client Credit	Client debit	Total	Office Credit	Office Debit	Total
04.04.17	Money on account	300.00	0.00	300.00	0.00	0.00	0.00
05.04.17	Local Search fee	0.00	0.00	300.00	0.00	10.00	–10.00
06.04.17	Enviro search	0.00	0.00	300.00	0.00	150.00	–160.00
10.04.17	Bill for searches	0.00	160.00	140.00	160.00	0.00	0.00
10.04.17	Refund to client	0.00	140.00	0.00	0.00	0.00	0.00

Review the example client ledger above.

Have a look at this example of a client ledger, showing the interaction with the client account and office account. We are going to assume you have checked the corresponding file and it is an abortive purchase of a genuine property at 3 Net Road, by Mr and Mrs Walker, who have been appropriately identified.

Answer the following questions in writing:

1. What can you see in compliance with the Accounts Rules?
2. How would you feel if you checked the file and this was not an abortive purchase of 3 Net Road? What would you do next?

There is a suggested answer to (1) at the end of this Part of the book, but attempt your answer first.

Exercise 4

Matter Number: 08000999555 – A Solicitor– Suspense Ledger							
Date	**Description**	**Client Credit**	**Client debit**	**Total**	**Office Credit**	**Office Debit**	**Total**
01.01.21	Monies in from Mr and Mrs Smith re litigation	1,500.00	0.00	1,500.00	0.00	0.00	0.00
02.02.21	Monies in from Dad's family for car purchase	2,500.00	0.00	4,000.00	0.00	0.00	0.00
02.02.21	Court fee for Mr and Mrs Smith litigation	0.00	0.00	4,000.00	0.00	480.00	–480.00
06.04.21	Transfer to matter Mr B bank facility	0.00	1,200.00	2,800.00	0.00	0.00	–480.00
10.04.21	Court fee Mr and Mrs Smith Litigation billed	0.00	480.00	2,320.00	480.00	0.00	0.00
10.04.21	Money to Dad's family for patio	0.00	2,000.00	320.00	0.00	0.00	0.00
11.04.21	Court fee Mrs and Mrs Smith Litigation	0.00	0.00	320.00	0.00	480.00	–480.00

Have a look at the ledger above and identify what is wrong with it.

Your answer:

Accounts Rules Quick Quiz

What is a reconciliation and how often should it be done?

What should you do with aged balances?

Which rule covers payment out of client money?

Anti-Money Laundering Problems

In this section you will find a series of exercises to consider related to AML.

It is helpful to understand the context of any form of reporting, and the differences between the different types of reporting.

If you are a COLP or COFA (or, in fact, any other member of staff), have a look at the exercises below and try to answer them. Can you see the differences in the types of scenarios, language, and requirements in reporting? Can you see crossovers with the earlier exercises?

If you are the MLRO (or, again, any other member of staff), how do you feel about the reporting arrangements for serious breach and those for reporting AML? Can you see a distinction between the two?

The following quiz appeared as part of the writer's AML courses for many years. We have explored in this book the overlap between AML and serious breach reporting.

You may need to do some research to answer the questions.

Starter questions AML

What is Money Laundering?

What is a PEP?

Name two changes occurring as a result of the ML Regulations 2017 (from the previous ML Regulations)?

What does reliance mean in the Money Laundering Regulations?

What is an MLRO?

Can you be prosecuted for failing to report money laundering suspicions to the MLRO?

What is enhanced due diligence?

Explain the importance of 'know your client'?

What is Hawala?

What is the PSC register? Why might you find it useful from an AML perspective?

Use these questions to prompt discussion about AML with your team members.

What do you think will happen to financial crime legislation post-Brexit?

Can the firm take any additional steps to improve AML procedures?

Can you describe the risk profile of the firm for AML?

Consider the following scenarios. What would you do? You can use these scenarios with your team members to discuss fraud and AML.

You are a solicitor. You are acting in a straightforward purchase when, right before exchange and completion (scheduled simultaneously), you receive a letter advising the other side's representatives have changed. It is on headed paper, enclosing new replies to requisitions with new client account details. You have not heard of the firm before so you look into them. Their name is genuine and the headed paper matches the logo. However, you notice the landline is not the same – in fact, they have an 07 number, there is a Googlemail email address on the headed paper, and there are numerous spelling mistakes in the letter.

You are acting in the purchase of a property which was last sold four months' previously. Looking at the history, the property has been sold five times in the last two years, and the value has increased substantially in that time. This is a privately agreed sale, with a large mortgage. There are no agent particulars on file, no photos, and both the client and property in question are more than 300 miles from you.

Accounts/reconciliation exercise possible answers

Exercise 1

We have to reconcile the books to the same date. The computer has done this to 30 June 2015.

There is a £100 difference. It appears the £100 difference is £100 paid to Searches UK.

Have a look on the client ledgers and cashbook to check the £100 is not there*. Have a look on the file to find the searches the £100 has paid for.

Assuming we are correct, correct the £100, and note the correction with a new printout of the reconciliation, to accompany the previous reconciliation.

The client matter listing is showing the incorrect date. The firm should print the correct client matter listing to the correct date for the purposes of the reconciliation.

Overall answer:

- Correct the errors.
- Keep both reconciliations and show the correction workings.
- Keep the cashbooks and ledgers up to date in future.

* It could also be a different £100 … but we will assume, for the purposes of this exercise, we have found the correct £100.

Exercise 2

There are some possible answers to the problem shown below, highlighting some of the issues we can find and where we could investigate further. Of course, the problem is the suspense ledger. Using a suspense ledger can lead us into further breaches of the Accounts Rules, as shown below. The writer would commonly associate such a breach with the additional breaches listed.

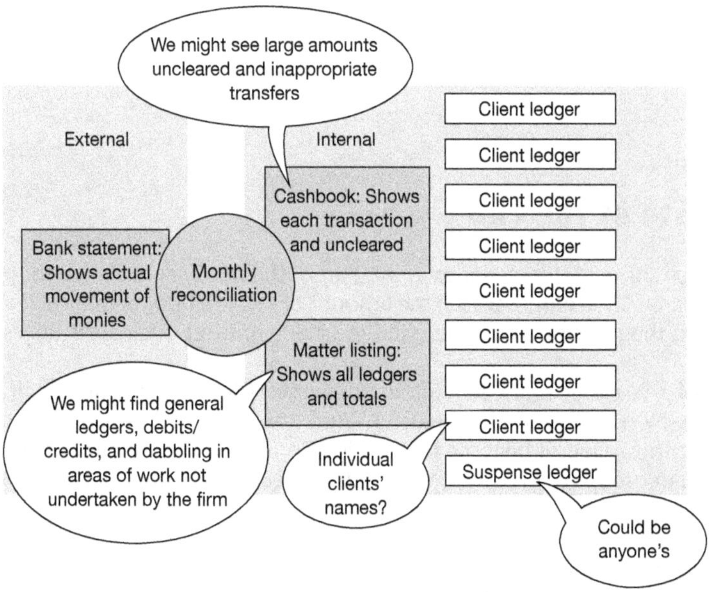

Of course, there may also be problems with the reconciliation itself (for example, conducted incorrectly, backdated, or not signed off). There may also be problems with the office account; with transfers between clients; and with individual ledgers not matching actual client matters. You may also have said using client account as a banking facility.

There are many more possible answers, but you could use this exercise and your answer as an idea of what you can do internally within a law firm to review your accounts and keep on top of your compliance.

Exercise 3

A possible answer to this exercise is below. You may have found more in compliance with the rules than identified below.

Mr and Mrs Walker – Abortive Purchase 3 Net Road							
Date	Description	Client Credit	Client debit	Total	Office Credit	Office Debit	Total
04.04.17	Money on account	300.00	0.00	300.00	0.00	0.00	0.00
05.04.17	Local Search fee	0.00	0.00	300.00	0.00	10.00	–10.00
06.04.17	Enviro search	0.00	0.00	300.00	0.00	150.00	–160.00
10.04.17	Bill for searches	0.00	160.00	140.00	[illegible]	[illegible]	0.00
10.04.17	Refund to client	0.00	140.00	0.00	[illegible]	[illegible]	0.00

The Note at the End

You will see some of the scenarios in this Part of the book seem similar to the others, but there are subtle differences in the amount of information, details such as names, or framing the position in a wider picture or different set of circumstances.

Several of the circumstances refer to suspense ledgers, for example. If we take this on its own, is it a serious breach? What about if it is in a larger picture with other breaches? Does it become forgivable? Do we consider solitary breaches more harshly than groups of breaches, to have the effect of minimising these same single breaches if they are in a group?

There is a concern sometimes that we favour people we know more about; if we take the names out of the scenarios, would you consider them more serious? The same may be true of understanding risk; once we have seen a lot of risk, or very serious matters, we become less shocked by matters that would previously have caused alarm. The writer is guilty of this, having come from a background of dealing with very serious matters at a number of regulatory bodies.

Enforcement, and a fair approach to the prosecution of individuals, along with the proportionate and consistent use of regulatory authority, is important. However, completely following the same approach for every matter, regardless of the objections of those around you, can also be a problem. We have to find a balance.

Bibliography and references

Every effort has been made to include all relevant sections of the legislation and regulations mentioned in this book, however the writer knows some of it so well, procedurally and from her own experience, she does not always need to look up the statutory provision (which of course can sometimes also differ to the practice). The Acts and regulatory requirements referred to below should be read to encompass all parts in their totality, as well as the specific provisions mentioned.

For example, in solving the problems in Part 8 of this book, you may need to refer to the totality of the Standards and Regulations, or individual sections. The writer has not listed each section of the Standards and Regulations here, as it is sufficient simply to reference them as a whole.

The references related to the writer's thesis are included for completeness, but they do not represent the totality of research undertaken in that project. They are however relevant to material in the book, but it should be noted that the content in the book represents the writer's own work.

In compiling the bibliography the writer has also had regard to the sum of her own experience. The writer has spent nearly 20 years working in legal services, and did an LLB before that. The writer first understood the proposed changes at The Law Society and 'Competition in the Professions' when she was in her third year at University. The writer's own interview for the caseworking job at The Law Society in 2005 was based around the Clementi Review, the Office of Fair Trading, and the history of the Society. In 2013, the writer interviewed at the Council for Licensed Conveyancers, and the subject was competition in legal services and the introduction of the CLC in the 1980s.

The writer has lived the changes, debated them, learnt about them, and been impacted by them personally as job moves and career moves change, and as legal services structures do. As a Caseworker, Consultant Caseworker, and Technical Adviser at the SRA, an in depth knowledge of every set of rules (past and current) was essential, and as a Strategy Manager understanding the introduction of ABS, the history and the intent, was what the job was about.

The bibliography is provided as an acknowledgement of all of the different material that makes this current situation what it is, but mostly it is provided so the reader can find their way through some of the same material should they wish to do so.

The writer's own publications or previous works show many training courses written and designed over the last seven years. These are the writer's own works. Acknowledgements are also offered to those who published the works (sometimes under their branding), who may have organised a session, or who have otherwise assisted in a practical way.

Legislation

Treaty on the European Union 1957

Trustee Act 1925, s 61

Solicitors Act 1957

Solicitors Act 1965

European Communities Act 1972

Consumer Credit Act 1974

Solicitors Act 1974 (as amended), ss 1–3, 10, 12 (repealed), 13 A, 13B, 15, 16, 28, 31, 32, Section 33, 34, 40 (repealed), 43, 44B, 46–49, Schedule 1

Administration of Justice Act 1985, ss 9, 9A, 16, 85, Schedule 2

Insolvency Act 1986, s 283

Courts and Legal Services Act 1990, ss 29 (repealed), 66, 89, Schs 8 and 14

Employment Rights Act 1996, s 43

Public Interest Disclosure Act 1998, s 1

Financial Services and Markets Act 2000, Part 20

The European Communities (Lawyer's Practice) Regulations 2000, regs 17, 19

Proceeds of Crime Act 2002, ss 328, 329, 330–333, s 338

Companies Act 2006, s 1239

Fraud Act 2006

Legal Services Act 2007, ss 3, 2, 12, 27, 85, 91, 92, 98, 105, 106, 107, 111, 157, Schs 4, 5, 13, 14, 16 (paras 30 and 9)

Money Laundering Regulations 2007

Equality Act 2010

Bribery Act 2010

Enterprise and Regulatory Reform Act 2013, s 1

Consumer Rights Act 2015

Deregulation Act 2015

Money Laundering Regulations 2017

Data Protection Act 2018

General Data Protection Regulation (EU) 2016/679 (GDPR)

European Union (Withdrawal Agreement) Act 2018

European Union (Withdrawal Agreement) Act 2019

Finance Act 2020

European Union (Withdrawal Agreement) Act 2020

Internal Markets Act 2021

Sarbanes -Oxley Act (2002) (United States of America)

Hansard

Solicitors Bill Lords Volume 374: debated 11 September 1941

Attorneys and Solicitors' Bill Volume 66: debated 13 February 1843

Solicitors Bill Volume 112: debated 4 May 1939

Solicitors Bill Volume 372: debated 3 July 1941

Solicitors (Amendment) Bill Hl Volume 328: debated 2 March 1972

Solicitors (Complaints) Volume 73 debated 12 March 1984

Cases

R v Ghosh [1982] QB 1053

Caparo v Dickman [1990] 2 AC 605

Law Society v Bolton [1993] EWCA Civ 32

Twinsectra v Yardley [2002] (2 All ER 37)

SRA v Wood and Burdett (2004) Solicitors Disciplinary Tribunal, Case Number 8669/2002

Marks and Spencer Group Plc v Freshfields Bruckhaus Deringer [2004] EWCA Civ 741

Three Rivers District Council and Others v Governor and Company of the Bank of England [2001] UKHL 16

R v Da Silva [2006] EWCA Crim 1654

Razeen [2008] EWCA Civ 1220

Lebow (No 13 of 2007) [2008] EWCA CIV 411

Ivey v Genting Casinos (UK) (trading as Cockfords Club) [2017] UKSC 67 [2018]

SRA v De Vita, Platt and Scott (2018) Solicitors Disciplinary Tribunal, Case Number 11696/2017

Wingate v SRA [2018] EWCA Civ 366

SRA v Malins [2018] EWCA Civ 366

Bawa Garba v General Medical Council [2018] EWCA Civ 1879

Uber BV v Aslam [2018] EWCA Civ 2748

Bates and Others v Post Office [2019] EWHC 3408 (QB)

Beckwith v Solicitors Regulation Authority [2020] EWHC 3231 (Admin)

Booth & Anor v R [2020] EWCA Crim 57

Uber BV v Aslam [2021] UKSC 5

Harcus Sinclair v Your Lawyers [2021] UKSC 32

Arthur Andersen LLP v United States 544 U.S. 696 (2005)

Solicitors Regulation Authority Rules and Regulations

SRA Handbook 2011

Glossary

SRA Code of Conduct 2011, Chapter 10

Solicitors Accounts Rules 2011, Rules 12, 14, 19, 29, 32A, 33, 34, 35, 38, 43, 44, 46

Authorisation Rules 2011, Rules 2, 7, 8, 8.5, 8.7(a) (and guidance note (xi) to Rule 8), 9, 10, 21, 22,

Practising Certificate Regulations 2011, Regulations 1, 3, 4, 7, 8, 10,

Other Law Society Guides and Codes

The Guide to the Professional Conduct of Solicitors 1993 – 6th Edition

The Guide to the Professional Conduct of Solicitors 1999 (and in particular Practice Rule 13)

The Guide to the Professional Conduct of Solicitors 2007 (and in Particular, provisions on conflict of interest)

Law Society Anti Money Laundering Practice note 2016

'Money Laundering Warning Signs' 2016

The Law Society Code for Completion by Post

The Law Society Guidance on Freelance Solicitors (2019) https://www.lawsociety.org.uk/support-services/advice/practice-notes/freelance-solicitors/

SRA Standards and Regulations 2019

(see also page xix for detailed references)

Glossary, definition of 'Third Party Managed Accounts', 'Separate business', and 'You'

SRA Principles 2019, Principles 4 and 5

Solicitors Accounts Rules 2019, Rule 1, Rule 2, Rule 3, Rule 4, Rule 5, Rule 6, Rule 8, Rule 9, Rule 10, Rule 11, Rule 12, Rule 13

Authorisation of Individuals Regulations 2019, Regulation 7, Regulation 8, Regulation 10.2

Authorisation of Firms Rules 2019, Rule 3, Rule 4, Rule 6, Rule 8

SRA Code of Conduct for Firms 2019, Regulation 2, Regulation 9

SRA Code of Conduct for Individuals 2019, Regulation 7

SRA Regulatory and Disciplinary Procedure Rules 2019, Regulation 3

Applications, Notice, Appeal, and Review Rules, Regulation 1.2

SRA Overseas and Cross Border Rules, Rule 4.3

Roll, Registers and Publication Regulations 2019

SRA Compensation Fund Regulations 2019 and 2021

SRA Statutory Trust Rules 2019

Other SRA Publications

MySRA Updates – Bulk Renewal (annual)

MySRA Updates – Annual Renewal (annual)

MySRA Renewal (annual)

MySRA FAQ (annual)

SRA published decisions page (ongoing) https://www.sra.org.uk/consumers/solicitor-check/recent-decisions/

SRA AR1 form, versions 1, 2 and 3

SRA Delivering Outcomes Focused Regulation, 2010 (Katie Jackson, co-author)

SRA Risk Scores 2013

SRA Red Tape Initiative (2013)

Training for Tomorrow (2014)

SRA Competence Statement (2015)

SRA's Guidance to Reporting Accountants and firms on planning and completion of the annual Accountant's Reports, under Rule 32 of the SRA Accounts Rules 2011 (2015)

SRA Guidance on Completing the New AR1 Form December 2015

SRA Ethics Guidance – Separate Business Rule 2015

SRA presentation at COLP and COFA Conference 2015 (slides breakout room 2)

SRA Consultation on Regulatory Reform April 2015

SRA Separate Business Rule Consultation and Post-Consultation Documentation, 2015

SRA Board Paper on Regulatory Reform Consultation September 2015

SRA Separate Business Rule Consultation and Post-Consultation Documentation, 2015

SRA – 'Guidance notes to Rule 32A Solicitors Accounts Rules' (2015)

SRA – 'Desirable features of third party managed accounts' (April 2015)

A Question of Trust (2015)

Separate Business Rule Consultation Paper (2015)

SRA Regulatory Reform Programme, 2015

SRA Regulatory Reform Programme – Improving Regulation: proportionate and targeted measures (April 2015)

Looking to the Future (2016 – 2019)

SRA – Providing Services to Vulnerable Clients (2016) https://www.sra.org.uk/globalassets/documents/solicitors/freedom-in-practice/vulnerable-people.pdf?version=4a1ab1

SRA Post Evaluation (Year unknown – approximately 2017)

SRA Enforcement Strategy (2019)

SRA Guidance on Sanctions (2019) https://www.sra.org.uk/consumers/solicitor-check/sanctions/

Overseas Reporting Requirements case studies (2019) https://www.sra.org.uk/solicitors/guidance/overseas-rules-case-studies/

Reporting and notification obligations (2019) https://www.sra.org.uk/solicitors/guidance/reporting-notification-obligations/

Guidance on dishonesty (2019) https://www.sra.org.uk/solicitors/guidance/general-dishonesty/

Guidance on acting with integrity (2019) https://www.sra.org.uk/solicitors/guidance/acting-with-integrity/

SRA Enforcement Strategy (2019) https://www.sra.org.uk/sra/corporate-strategy/sub-strategies/sra-enforcement-strategy/

Individual topic guidance for enforcement (2020) https://www.sra.org.uk/sra/corporate-strategy/sub-strategies/enforcement-practice/

Legal Services Board decision notice relating to matters to report (2019) https://www.legalservicesboard.org.uk/what_we_do/regulation/pdf/2019/SRA_Decision_notice.pdf

Enforcement action for non regulated persons (including those in unregulated businesses) (2019) https://www.sra.org.uk/solicitors/guidance/general-regulation-non-authorised-persons/

Guidance for unregulated organisations employing solicitors (2019) https://www.sra.org.uk/solicitors/guidance/unregulated-organisations-employers-sra-regulated-lawyers/

SRA Standards and Regulations 'Hub', including information about new forms of practice (2019) https://www.sra.org.uk/newregs/

Guidance on regulatory settlement agreements (2019) https://www.sra.org.uk/sra/decision-making/guidance/disciplinary-regulatory-settlement-agreements/

SRA discussion of issuing proceedings before the SDT (2019) https://www.sra.org.uk/sra/decision-making/guidance/disciplinary-issuing-solicitors-disciplinary-tribunal-proceedings/

Other publications

Structure Conduct Performance Framework (Chamberlain and Robinson 1933)

Solicitors Journal, November 18, 1950

Culture Web (1989) Johnson and Scholes, available from Business Balls (online)

The Regulatory Craft (2000) Malcolm K Sparrow, Brookings.

MSc Management Consultancy and Organisational Change (2011), Birkbeck, University of London

Legal Services Board Conveyancing Thematic Review – Regulatory Risks Arising in Conveyancing (2012)

SRA Corporate Strategy 2014

Legal Services Consumer Panel – Guide to Consumer Vulnerability (2014) https://www.legalservicesconsumerpanel.org.uk/ourwork/vulnerableconsumers/Guide%20to%20consumer%20vulnerability%202014%20final.pdf

Rosenthal *Consumer Credit Law and Practice: A Guide* (4th Edition), Bloomsbury Professional

Call for Evidence on the Legal Services Regulatory Framework, Ministry of Justice, May 2014

Barco Website (2015)

SRA Small Firms Initiative (2015)

Legal Services Board 'Alternatives to Client Money' Briefing Paper (2015)

Letter from Michael Gove MP to Chair of the Justice Committee of the House of Commons, 15 September 2015

Professor Stephen Mayson and the Legal Services Regulators (2016) 'Legislative Options following the Legal Services Act'

UK Corporate Governance Code (2018) Financial Reporting Council

ICAEW Technical Release (2018) (TECH 16/15AAF) Solicitors Regulation Authority Accounts Rules: Interim Guidance for Reporting Accountants Following Changes to the Accountants' Report Requirements

Guidance on a Risk Based Approach for Accountants (2019) Financial Action Task Force

Guidance on a Risk Based Approach for Legal Professionals (2019) Financial Action Task Force

Solicitors Disciplinary Tribunal – moving to a Civil Standard of Proof (2019)

Solicitor's Disciplinary Proceedings Rules (2019)

European Commission Slides from the Brexit preparedness webinar inc professional qualifications

The Law Society of Scotland – Conflict of Interest Guidance (2021)

Paris Bar – Code de Deontologie (in force in 2020)

Crown Prosecution Service website 'Update: CPS case redefines the legal test for 'dishonesty' in criminal law' (2020)

Professor Stephen Mayson 'An Independent Review of Legal Regulation' (2020) UCL

Department for Business, Industry, and Skills Website (Whistleblowing guidance – 2018–2021)

Legal Sector Affinity Group Guidance for Anti Money Laundering years 2018 – 2021

Financial Conduct Authority Handbook, CASS 7.13 Segregation of Client Money (as at August 2021)

Author's own publications or previous works

Macro Culture in Legal Services Post Clementi (2011), Master's degree dissertation, unpublished*, Katie Jackson

The contribution of consultants to professional management (2011), Master's degree submission, unpublished, Katie Jackson

The success of a consultancy engagement (2011) Master's degree submission, unpublished, Katie Jackson

ABS Presentation (Anonymised) (2013) Honne Limited/Katie Jackson

The Changing Legal Landscape – Presentation (2013) Bold Legal/Rob Hailstone, Honne Limited/Katie Jackson

Consumer Credit Activities – New FCA regulation for law firms (2013) (Training Course), MBL Seminars, Honne Limited/Katie Jackson

SRA Renewal: Practising Certificate Conditions and Material Breach: years 2013 – 2019 (Training course and notes), MBL Seminars, Honne Limited/Katie Jackson

Standard and Advanced AML Training (years 2014 – 2021) Honne Limited/Katie Jackson

SRA Renewal: Practising Certificate Conditions and Serious Breach: years 2019 – 2021 (Training course and notes), MBL Seminars, Honne Limited/Katie Jackson

Solicitors Accounts Rules: Qualified Reports and Serious Breach years 2016-2019 (Training course and notes), MBL Seminars, Honne Limited/Katie Jackson

Risk Management – (2014), Datalaw, Honne Limited/Katie Jackson

SRA Entry, Exit & Renewal – (2014), Datalaw, Honne Limited/Katie Jackson

CLC Regulation – (2015), Datalaw, Honne Limited/Katie Jackson

Bitesize Compliance – (2015), Datalaw, Honne Limited/Katie Jackson

Everyday COLP and COFA – (2015), Datalaw, Honne Limited/Katie Jackson

Competence Statement Training – Fee Earners and Supervisors (2015) Legal Compliance Services, Honne Limited/Katie Jackson

Training for tomorrow/Confident Competence – (2015), Datalaw, Honne Limited/ Katie Jackson

AML Policy and Practice – (2016), Datalaw, Honne Limited/Katie Jackson

AML: The Crucial Points – (2016), Datalaw, Honne Limited/Katie Jackson

Everyday COLP and COFA – (2016), Datalaw, Honne Limited/Katie Jackson

SRA Accounts Rules – (2016), Datalaw, Honne Limited/Katie Jackson

Anti-Money Laundering – (2016), Datalaw, Honne Limited/Katie Jackson

Professional Skills Course – Anti Money Laundering – (2016), Datalaw, Honne Limited/Katie Jackson

Induction Training (2016–2017), Brethertons LLP, Honne Limited/Katie Jackson

Scripts for Firm Academy (2016) Firm Academy/Phil Gott, Wise Guys/Sam Gott, Honne Limited/Katie Jackson

Handbook Changes: A Discussion with the SRA - Presentation (2016) Honne Limited/Katie Jackson

Handbook Changes: A Discussion with the SRA 'Questions' (2016) Honne Limited/ Katie Jackson

SRA Looking to the Future: Discussion note on hiving off your firm (2016) Honne Limited/Katie Jackson

SRA Policy and Practice (2017/8) Datalaw, Honne Limited/Katie Jackson

Third Party Complaints – (2017), Datalaw, Brethertons LLP, Honne Limited/Katie Jackson

Reporting to the NCA – (2017), Datalaw, Honne Limited/Katie Jackson

SRA Handbook Training (Accounts) (2017), Brethertons LLP, Honne Limited/Katie Jackson

Professional Skills Course– Solicitor Client Care, Strategy, SRA Policy and Practice – (2017), Datalaw, Honne Limited/Katie Jackson

The SRA's Looking to the Future: Song of Ice and Fire (2017/2018) Published by Legal Eye and Legal Futures (2018) and in Practising Certificates and Serious Breaches (2018 – 2021) – Author Katie Jackson/Honne Limited

New SRA Handbook – Strategic Implications of Looking to the Future– Presentation (2017/2018) (Datalaw 2018) Honne Limited/Katie Jackson (including activities for accountants)

Anti Money Laundering at the SRA and CLC – (2018), Datalaw, Honne Limited/ Katie Jackson

Introduction to Anti Money Laundering – (2018), Datalaw, Honne Limited/Katie Jackson

Whistleblowing – (2018), Datalaw, Honne Limited/Katie Jackson

Whistleblowing (2018) Legal Eye, Honne Limited/Katie Jackson

New SRA Handbook – (2018), Datalaw, Honne Limited/Katie Jackson

Complaint Handling – (2018 and updated 2019), Datalaw, Honne Limited/Katie Jackson

Compliance is essential but so is Practical Business Performance (2018), Presentation, Legal Eye, The Cashroom/Alex Holt (Title Alex Holt), Honne Limited/Katie Jackson

GDPR (2019) Datalaw, Honne Limited/Katie Jackson

SRA Standards and Regulations Training (2019) Legal Eye, Honne Limited/Katie Jackson

Legal Services Market Case Study 2019, Big Voice Conference, Honne Limited/ Katie Jackson

Digital Legal Services (2019), Legal Eye/Paul Saunders, Honne Limited/Katie Jackson

Equality and Diversity – (2019), Datalaw, Honne Limited/Katie Jackson

Vulnerable Client – (2019), Datalaw, Honne Limited/Katie Jackson

Risk Management – (2019) (covering anti-money laundering risk assessments), Datalaw, Honne Limited/Katie Jackson

Legal Ethics – (2019), Datalaw, Honne Limited/Katie Jackson

SRA Authorisations – (2019), Datalaw, Honne Limited/Katie Jackson

File Reviews – (2019), Datalaw, Honne Limited/Katie Jackson

SRA Standards and Regulations (2019) Legal Eye/Norman Denton, Honne Limited/ Katie Jackson

Advanced Anti-Money Laundering – (2019), Datalaw, Honne Limited/Katie Jackson

Brexit and Regulation (2019) Legal Eye, Brunel Professions, Honne Limited/Katie Jackson, followed by a Brexit Blog, published by Legal Eye.

SRA Separate Business Rule - 2020, Datalaw, Honne Limited/Katie Jackson

SRA Investigation and Enforcement – (2020), Datalaw, Honne Limited/Katie Jackson

Multone Law – AML Training (2020), Legal Eye, Honne Limited/Katie Jackson

How to build a culture of compliance (2019) MBL Seminar, Honne Limited/Katie Jackson

Macro Culture in Legal Services Post-Clementi

References

Brown C (2011) Future of Legal Services: Or Future Is Now Legal Information Management (11) 2 101–104

Burns T and Stalker G M (1961) The Management of Innovation, Tavistock, London

Clementi, D (2004) 'Review of the Regulatory Framework for Legal Services in England and Wales'.

Council for Licenced Conveyancers (2012) CLC issues licence to Kings Court Trust.

Courts and Legal Services Act 1990.

Director General of Office of Fair Trading (2001) 'Competition in Professions'.

Ernst & Young (2004) 'Report of the Review of the Regulatory Framework for Legal Services in England and Wales'.

Flood, John (2012) Will There Be Fallout from Clementi? The Global Repercussions for the Legal Profession after the UK Legal Services Act 2007.

Flood, John (2012, 1) Demands of a New Legal Services Market – A blog.

Friedman L M (1988) Lawyers in a Cross Cultural Perspective and Comparative Sociology of Legal Professions in Abel R L and Lewis, P C (1988) Lawyers in Society (three volumes) The Common Law World, The Civil Law World, and Comparative Theories University of California Press, London.

Goldstein, J, Kantowitz, M, Mittal, V, Carbonell, J (1999) Summarizing Text Documents: Sentence Selection and Evaluation Metrics Computer Science Department. Paper 347.

Gosling S D and Johnson, J A (Ed) (2010) Conducting online behavioural research, Washington, American Psychological Association

Hadfield, G K (2008) The Legal Barriers to Innovation: The Growing Economic Cost of Professional Control over Corporate Legal markets

Hoftstede, G (1984) Culture's Consequences: International Differences in Work Related Values Abridged Edition, Sage Publications, London

Hoftstede, G (2000) Culture's Consequences: International Differences in Work Related Values 2nd Edition, Sage Publications, London

HM Treasury (2000) Budget 2000 Report.

Jarrett-Kerr N (2011) Alternative business structures: the long pregnancy Legal Information Management (11) 2 82–85

Kerridge, R and Davis, G (1999) Reform of the Legal Profession: An Alternative 'Way Ahead' The Modern Law Review , Vol. 62, No. 6, pp. 807–823

Krejcie, R and Morgan, D (1970) Determining Sample Size for Research Activities Educational and Psychological Measurement Issue 30, Page 607–610

Krippendorff, K (2004) An Introduction to Content Analysis and its Methodology (2nd) Sage Publications Inc, California

The Lawyer (1995) Surveyors to put pressure on OFT over Law Society ruling on MDPs.

The Lawyer (2000) Law Society Licence threatened by OFT.

The Law Society (2011) Annual Statistics Report.

Law Society of Scotland (2009) The Registered Paralegal.

Law Society of Scotland (2011) Annual Report.

Lee R G(2010), Liberalisation of legal services in Europe: progress and prospects. Legal Studies, 30: 186–207.

Legal Services Act 2007.

Legal Services Board (2011) Research Note: The Legal Services Market.

Maute, J (2011) Global continental shifts to a new governance paradigm in lawyer regulation and consumer protection: riding the wave, in Bartlett F, Mortensen R and Tranter K (Ed) (2011), Alternative Perspectives on Lawyers and Legal Ethics – Reimagining the Profession Routledge, London and New York.

Mazur, E (2010) Collecting data from social networking websites and blogs in Gosling S D and Johnson, J A (Ed) (2010) Conducting online behavioural research, Washington, American Psychological Association

McKenzie, A (2010) Legal Services Act: what it means for legal and information professionals Legal Information Management (10) 4 283–286

Ministry of Justice (2006) – Legal Services Bill Full Regulatory Impact Assessment.

Ministry of Justice (2007) Legal Services Bill Supplementary Regulatory Impact Assessment.

Office for National Statistics (2012) JOBS:03 Employee Jobs by Industry.

Office for National Statistics (2012) Labour Force Survey Quality and Monitoring Report January – March 2012.

Office for National Statistics (2011).

Ogbonna E and Harris L C (2002) Organizational Culture: A ten Year, Two-phase Study of Change in the UK Food Retailing Sector Journal of Management Studies, Volume 39, Issue 5, pp 673–706

Oxera (2011) A framework to monitor the legal services sector Published by the Legal Services Board.

Schein, E H (2010) Organizational culture and leadership 4th edition John Wiley & Son San Franscisco.

Silver C (2010) What We Don't Know Can Hurt Us: The Need for Empirical Research in Regulating Lawyers and Legal Services in the Global Economy. 43 Akron Law Rev. 1009–1080.

Solicitors Regulation Authority (2012) SRA licences 15th ABS

Spender, J C (1989) Industry Recipes – An enquiry into the Nature and Sources of Managerial Judgement Basil Blackwell, London.

Stemler, S (2001). An overview of content analysis. Practical Assessment, Research & Evaluation, 7(17).

Terry L S The European Commission Project Regarding Competition in Professional Services (April 8, 2009). Northwestern Journal of International Law and Business, Vol. 29, No. 1, 2009;

Tuft M L (2010) Supervising offshore outsourcing of legal services in a global environment: re-examining current ethical standards 43 Akron Law Review 825

Twitter (2012) Developer Rules of the Road available at https://dev.Twitter.com/terms/api-terms (accessed 13 August 2012)

Webb, J (2004) Turf Wars and Market Control: competition and complexity in the market for legal services International Journal of the Legal Profession Vol 11 No. 1 and 2

Index

[*All references are to page numbers.*]

A

Accountants' report
- annual (material breach, serious breach, weaknesses in firm's accounts)
  - generally 291–297
  - materiality 297–299
- audits, and
  - areas of potential audit for law firms (2016–2021) (non accounts) 341–343
  - generally 312–315
- challenges in new accounts rules 309–312
- conditions to obtain 307–308
- delivery 295
- discursive content
  - audits 312–315
  - 'client' accounts 338–340
  - closing gaps in new accounts rules 332–334
  - COFA perspective 318–321
  - COLP perspective 317–318
  - conflicts of interest
    - internal accountancy 328–329
    - sectoral accountancy 329–330
  - de minimis provisions 330
  - example breaches register 340–341
  - fiduciary duties 323–324
  - management perspective 321–323
  - material breach and serious breach as issues of judgement 315–317
  - standard of proof at SDT 324–327
  - third party managed accounts (TPMAs) 334–338
  - using report for another purpose 330–331
- format 296–297
- move away from material breach
  - effects of changes overall 301–302
  - generally 299–301
- new accounts rules
  - challenges 309–312
  - closing gaps 332–334

Accountants' report – *contd*
- obtaining
  - conditions 307–308
  - requirement 302–303
- practising year and timelines for management 91
- requirement to obtain 302–303
- requirement to send to SRA 303–304
- technical content
  - annual report (material breach, serious breach, weaknesses in firm's accounts)
    - generally 291–297
    - materiality 297–299
  - challenges in new accounts rules 309–312
  - COLP, COFA and the Reporting Accountant 305–307
  - conditions to obtain report 307–308
  - generally 290
  - move away from material breach
    - effects of changes overall 301–302
    - generally 299–301
  - obtaining report
    - conditions 307–308
    - requirement 302–303
  - regulatory approach 299
  - requirement to obtain report 302–303
  - requirement to send report to SRA 303–304
  - statutory reporting basis for accountants 290–291
- third party managed accounts (TPMAs)
  - challenges in new account rules, and 311
  - generally 334–338
- using for another purpose 330–331

Accounts problems
- auditing and reviewing 419
- reconciliation
  - exercises and possible answers 424–425
  - generally 419–422

Accounts rules
  complying with spirit of 360–361
  new
    challenges 309–312
    closing gaps 332–334
  quick quiz 422
Administration of Justice Act 1985
  imposition of practising certificate conditions, and 130, 132
Alternative business structures (ABS)
  benefits and drawbacks of entering legal market 16–17
  establishment 15
  future for legal services in advent of 17–19
  HOLPs (Head of Legal Practice) and HOFAs (Head of Finance and Administration)
    compliance leadership 204
    re-interpretation of Legal Services Act 2007, and 363
    serious breaches, and *see* Serious breach
    standard conditions of recognition, and 185–186
    statutory requirement to make report 29
  imposition of firm conditions *see* Firm conditions
  introduction of 16
  legal services regulation, and
    historical development 15–19
    introduction to 9
  powers in respect of 5
  practising arrangements, and
    generally 69
    law firm strategic direction and qualifications 107–108
    regulatory outcomes
      generally 99
      viewpoint exercise 100
  re-interpretation of Legal Services Act 2007, and 363
  'the reasonable man' in professional regulation, and 34
Alternative employment
  practising certificate conditions, and 173
Annual practising year *see* Practising year
Anti-money laundering (AML) *see also* Serous breaches
  developing culture of compliance, and 207–208
  oversight regulator *see* Office for Professional Body AML Supervision (OPBAS)
  problems 423–424
Anti-money laundering (AML) – *contd*
  reporting relationships to other COLP and COFA roles 241–243
  reserved work, and 85
Audits
  accountants' reports, and
    areas of potential audit for law firms (2016–2021) (non accounts) 341–343
    generally 312–315
  problems 419

B

Bar Council
  checks and balances in regulatory functions 41–43
Bar Standards Board
  introduction to legal services regulation 9
  powers, statutory basis 5

C

Checks and balances in legal regulation
  exercise for use 42–43
  generally 41
Citizen rights
  audience and legal education 373–374
'Client' accounts
  generally 338–340
Client care
  management consultant, exercise 54
Code of Conduct
  historical development of professional practice 4, 15
  Standards and Regulations 2019, and 87–89
Compensation Fund
  protections 72–73
Competence
  imposition of practising certificate conditions, and 165–167
Competence Statement
  exercises 393
Complaint handling
  generally 30–33
  problems 397–398
Compliance
  conclusions 347–348
  leadership
    firm conditions, and 204
    serious breach, and 276–277
  management
    firm conditions, and
      generally 205–207
      Honne AML culture table 207–208
    serious breach, and 281–286

Compliance Officer for Finance and Administration (COFA)
  accountants' report
    annual (material breach, serious breach, weaknesses in firm's accounts) 292, 295, 298
    audits, and 312–315
    closing gaps in new accounts rules 332–334
    COFA perspective 318–321
    example breaches register 340–341
    move away from material breach
      effects of changes overall 301–302
      generally 299–301
    Reporting Accountant 305–307
    requirement to obtain 302–303
  complying with spirit of accounts rules 360–361
  firm conditions, and
    compliance leadership 204
    improving compliance through management 205–208
    representations for conditions and risk management 199
    responsibility within firms 200–201
    standard conditions of recognition 185–186
  governance and decision-making 36–40
  managing others with practising certificate conditions, and 167–169
  problems generally *see* Problems
  regulatory outcomes
    generally 98–99
    viewpoint exercise 100
  serious breach, and *see* Serious breach
Compliance Officer for Legal Practice (COLP)
  accountants' report
    annual (material breach, serious breach, weaknesses in firm's accounts) 292, 295, 298
    audits, and 312–315
    COLP perspective 317–318
    example breaches register 340–341
    move away from material breach
      effects of changes overall 301–302
      generally 299–301
    Reporting Accountant 305–307
  firm conditions, and
    compliance leadership 204
    improving compliance through management 205–208
    representations for conditions and risk management 199
Compliance Officer for Legal Practice (COLP) – *contd*
  firm conditions, and – *contd*
    responsibility within firms 200–201
    standard conditions of recognition 185–186
  governance and decision-making 36–40
  managing others with practising certificate conditions, and 167–169
  problems generally *see* Problems
  regulatory outcomes
    generally 98–99
    viewpoint exercise 100
  serious breach, and *see* Serious breach
Conclusions
  complying with spirit of accounts rules 360–361
  defining serious breach 348–355
  generally 345–348
  re-framing conditions positively 355–360
  regulatory focus 361–362
Conflicts of interest
  accountants' report, and
    internal accountancy 328–329
    sectoral accountancy 329–330
  problems 388–392
Consumer credit work
  reserved work, and 85
Consumer protections
  practising arrangements, and 72–73
Continuous professional development (CPD)
  advice and guidance 45–46
  exercises 393
  generally 43–45
  qualification, and
    exercise 48–49
    generally 47–48
  reflection and planning
    exercise 46
    table 47
Council for Licensed Conveyancers (CLC)
  alternative regulator 95–96
  introduction to legal services regulation, and 9–10
  powers
    imposition of practising certificate conditions 154–155
    statutory basis 5
  regulatory reach 20
Criminal charges
  dishonesty, suspension of practising certificate 138

Customer service
- generally 30–32

D

Decision-making
- annual renewal and information, and 174–176
- exercises for discussion 38–40, 161, 175–176
- freelance solicitors and unregulated practices 40–41
- generally 36–40
- regulatory
  - generally 156–160
  - regulators, and 202–203
- risk management *see* Risk management

De minimis provisions
- accountants' report, and 330

Digital legal services
- cyber-attack 56–57
- generally 55–56

Discursive content
- accountants' report
  - audits 312–315
  - 'client' accounts 338–340
  - closing gaps in new accounts rules 332–334
  - COFA perspective 318–321
  - COLP perspective 317–318
  - conflicts of interest
    - internal accountancy 328–329
    - sectoral accountancy 329–330
  - de minimis provisions 330
  - example breaches register 340–341
  - fiduciary duties 323–324
  - management perspective 321–323
  - material breach and serious breach as issues of judgement 315–317
  - standard of proof at SDT 324–327
  - third party managed accounts (TPMAs) 334–338
  - using report for another purpose 330–331
- firm conditions
  - additional standard conditions 190–193
  - compliance
    - Honne AML culture table 207–208
    - improving through management 205–207
    - leadership 204
  - conditions and relationship to intervention 202
  - effectiveness of conditions 196–199
  - firm vs practising certificate 187–189

Discursive content – *contd*
- firm conditions – *contd*
  - regulators and regulatory decision-making 202–203
  - responsibility within firms 200–201
  - risk management
    - achieving a balance 189–190
    - representations for conditions 199
  - unregulated firms and freelance solicitors 194–196
- practising arrangements
  - differences in regulatory outcomes for different forms of practice
    - alternative business structures (ABS) 99, 100
    - COLPs and COFAs 98–99, 100
    - generally 98
    - unregistered firms 99, 100
  - freelancers and self-employment 121–122
  - generally 89
  - law firm strategic direction and qualifications 107–108
  - management metrics and investigation tools 108–109
  - national and international implications of practising arrangements 97–98
  - options outside scope of regulation or with alternative regulators 95–97
  - organisational lifetime events and closure 109–112
  - organisational structure (freelancers, non-reserved work, unregulated practices) 100–105
  - practising year
    - generally 89
    - reflective exercises 94–95
    - renewal
      - symbolism 94–95
      - timelines for management 89–90
    - timelines for management
      - accountants' report 91
      - annual compliance timetable 91–94
      - diversity data 90
      - practising certificate conditions 90–91
      - renewal 89–90
  - separate business rule 105–107
  - Standards and Regulations 2019 112–121
- practising certificate conditions
  - addressing personal development needs 171–172

Discursive content – *contd*
practising certificate conditions – *contd*
alternative employment 173
annual renewal and information for decision-making 174–176
effectiveness of conditions 169–171
generally 154
imposing stricter set of rules as conditions 173–174
legal advice and conditions 176–177
managing others with conditions (COLP, COFA or HR) 167–169
publication of decisions 172–173
regulatory decision-making 156–160
regulatory outcome, Council for Licensed Conveyancers (CLC) example 154–156
restrictions or more practice 165–167
risk management
achieving a balance, in 160–161
representations for conditions, and 162–164
SDT and SRA outcomes 164–165
unregulated firms and freelance solicitors 161–161
professional practice
checks and balances in legal regulation 41–43
comparative professional practice, management consultants 51–54
comparative standards of regulation
qualification and CPD 47–49
regulation by Code 49–51
complaint handling 30–33
continuous professional development (CPD)
generally 43–47
qualification, and 47–49
customer service 30–31
ethics and reporting 29–30
freelance solicitors 40–41
generally 26
governance and decision-making 36–40
human touch 54–57
individual expression and professionalism as form of practice 26–29
'the reasonable man' in professional regulation 33–36
unregulated practices 40–41

Discursive content – *contd*
serious breach
COLP and COFA
compliance and balanced scoreboard approach 286–287
fiduciary duties 281
compliance
COLP and COFA, balanced scoreboard approach 286–287
improving following breach, and importance of leadership 276–277
management, and 281–286
fiduciary duties
COLP and COFA 281
generally 280
integrity and dishonesty
dishonesty
exercise 267
generally 263–264
reporting 265–267
ethical considerations
exercise 266
generally 264
generally 262–263
integrity exercises 264–265
managing investigations
generally 269–270
incident planning exercise 275
investigation response 270–271
stages of 271–275
pastoral support, thoughts and feelings 276
prosecution for failure to report 268–269
reporting dishonesty 265–267
Solicitors Act 1974, s 43 267–268
standards of behaviour 259–260
'the reasonable man'
generally 260–261
turning a blind eye/dishonesty 261–262
whistleblowing 277–279
Dishonesty *see also* Serious breach
suspension of practising certificate 138
Diversity data
practising year and timelines for management 90

E

Equality and diversity
data *see* Diversity data
problems 392
Ethics
reporting, and
exercises for discussion 32–33

Ethics – *contd*
reporting, and – *contd*
generally 29–30
list of common reported matters 29
Exercises *see also* Problems
accountants' reports
audit approaches 314–315
'client' accounts (what's in a name?) 340
COFA perspective (new COFA) 321
COLP perspective (mansion house) 318
evidential tests 327
exercising your judgement 316–317
management perspective (accountants' report has arrived) 322–323
third party managed accounts (TPMAs) 336
benefits of regulation (the Michelin effect) 96–97
career geography 171–172
checks and balances in legal regulation 42–43
COFAs
accountants' reports (new COFA) 321
compliance and balanced scoreboard approach 286–287
standards of behaviour 260
COLPs
accountants' reports (mansion house) 318
compliance and balanced scoreboard approach 286–287
CPD reflection and planning 46
cross border regulation 98
decision-making
generally 38–40
information, and 175–176
practising certificate conditions 161
differences in regulatory outcomes viewpoint 100
dishonesty 267
ethics past, present and future 266
firm conditions
ABS, independence of advice, and the state 191–192
bridge construction 189–190, 198–199
unregulated firms 195–196
governance 38–40
incident planning 275
integrity 264–265
job roles 159–160
law firm direction and qualifications 107–108

Exercises – *contd*
leadership 276–277
management consultant client care 54
mansion house
generally 318
suggested answer 374–375
preference in regulatory style 155–156
qualifications 48–49
reflective
generally 94–95
what you learned 376–377
reporting 32–33
representations and contingency planning 163–164
whistleblowing 279

F

Fiduciary duties
accountants' report, and 323–324
serious breach, and
COLP and COFA 281
generally 280
Firm conditions
alternative business structures (ABS)
development 222–224
generally 186–187
Macro Culture Post Clementi 208–221
discursive content
additional standard conditions 190–193
compliance
Honne AML culture table 207–208
improving through management 205–207
leadership 204
conditions and relationship to intervention 202
effectiveness of conditions 196–199
firm vs practising certificate 187–189
regulators and regulatory decision-making 202–203
responsibility within firms 200–201
risk management
achieving a balance 189–190
representations for conditions 199
unregulated firms and freelance solicitors 194–196
imposition
current 183–185
effectiveness of conditions 196–199
generally 179–183
SRA and at SDT 187

Firm conditions – *contd*
technical content
alternative business structures (ABS) 186–187
imposition of conditions
current 183–185
generally 179–183
SRA and at SDT 187
standard conditions of recognition 185–186
Firm recognition
practising arrangements, and 81–83
Foreign lawyers *see* Registered European Lawyers (RELs); Registered Foreign Lawyers (RFLs)
Freelance solicitors
firm conditions 194–196
generally 40–41
organisational structure, and 100–105
practising certificate conditions 161–162
self-employment, and 121–122
serious breach 249–250
Future developments
citizen rights of audience and education 373–374
future of legal services regulation 365–367
generally 362
harmonisation of regulatory standards 367–371
possible introduction of single legal regulator 365–367
re-interpretation of Legal Services Act 2007 362–364
ten-year revalidation 371–373

G

Governance
exercises for discussion 38–40
freelance solicitors and unregulated practices 40–41
generally 36–40

H

Human Resources (HR)
managing others with practising certificate conditions, and 167–169
Human touch and experiences
generally 54–57

I

Immigration practitioners
reserved work, and 84
Individual expression
form of practice 26–29
Individual practice
imposition of firm conditions *see* Firm conditions
practising arrangements, and 62–64, 80
In-house solicitors
practising arrangements, and 71–72
Insolvency
suspension of practising certificate 137–138
Institute for Chartered Accountants for England and Wales (ICAEW)
sectoral accountancy conflicts of interest, and 329
Institute for Chartered Accountants for Scotland (ICAS)
introduction to legal services regulation 9
Institute of Paralegals
introduction to legal services regulation 11
Integrity
serious breach, and 262–265
Intervention
current regulatory position 21–22
firm conditions and relationship to 202
Investigations *see* Serious breach

L

Law Society
accountants' report, and 291
checks and balances in regulatory functions 41–43
generally 2
historical development of professional practice 4
introduction to legal services regulation 9, 11, 13
'the reasonable man' in professional regulation, and 35
Legal advice
imposition of practising certificate conditions 176–177
Legal Aid Agency (LAA)
accountants' reports, and 302
Legal education
citizen rights 373–374
Legal Ombudsman (LeO)
generally 2
introduction to legal services regulation 12–13
redress, and 309–310
Legal professional privilege
self-reporting serious breaches, and 228
Legal Services Act 2007
imposition of practising certificate conditions, and 128–130

Legal Services Act 2007 – *contd*
legal services regulation, and
historical development 15
introduction to 9–13
re-interpretation 362–364
Legal Services Board (LSB)
legal services regulation
checks and balances in functions 41–43
impact of regulator 13–14
introduction to 9–11
role 11, 20, 41, 227
ten-year revalidation consultation 372
Legal services market
alternative business structures *see* Alternative business structures (ABS)
analysis 398–401
management and legal system problems 383–387
Legal services regulation
current position
entry and exit requirements 21
generally 21
intervention 21–22
regulatory objectives 23–24
setting standards 21
SRA Standards and Regulations 24–26
taking enforcement action 21
entry and exit requirements
current regulatory position 21
generally 19–20
future of 365–367
historical development 14–19
impact of regulator 13–14
introduction to 9–13
list of approved regulators 9
Limited companies
imposition of firm conditions *see* Firm conditions
Limited liability partnerships (LLPs)
imposition of firm conditions *see* Firm conditions

M

Management
accountants' report, and 321–323
compliance
firm conditions, and
generally 205–207
Honne AML culture table 207–208
serious breach, and 281–286
legal system problems, questions and reflective exercises 383–387
Management – *contd*
practising arrangements, and 83
management metrics and investigation tools 108–109
practising year and timelines
accountants' report 91
annual compliance timetable 91–94
diversity data 90
practising certificate conditions 90–91
renewal 89–90
Management consultants
comparative professional practice
client care exercise 54
generally 51–54
Master of the Faculties
powers, statutory basis 5
Material breach
accountants' report
annual
generally 291–297
materiality 297–299
judgement 315–317
move away from material breach
effects of changes overall 301–302
generally 299–301
generally 245–246
problems
generally 401–413
qualified reports 413–418
Ministry of Justice (MOJ)
impact of regulator, and 13
Money Laundering Reporting Officer (MLRO)
compliance and balanced scoreboard approach 286–287
governance and decision-making, and 36–40
Money Laundering Compliance Officer (MLCO)
governance and decision-making, and 36–40

N

National Association of Licensed Paralegals
introduction to legal services regulation 11
Non-reserved work
practising arrangements, and
generally 85
organisational structure, and 100–105
Non-solicitors
practising arrangements, and 83

O

Office for Legal Complaints *see* Legal Ombudsman (LeO)
Office for Professional Body AML Supervision (OPBAS)
  future regulatory compliance policy 243
  legal services regulation
    impact of regulator 13
    introduction to 11
Office of Qualifications and Examinations Regulation (Ofqual)
  introduction to legal services regulation 11
Organisational lifetime
  stages of (development to closure) 109–112
Organisational structure
  freelancers, non-reserved work and unregulated practices 100–105

P

Partnerships
  imposition of firm conditions *see* Firm conditions
Personal development
  addressing needs and practicing certificate conditions 171–172
Practice events
  practising arrangements, and 78
Practising arrangements
  discursive content
    differences in regulatory outcomes for different forms of practice
      alternative business structures (ABS) 99, 100
      COLPs and COFAs 98–99, 100
      generally 98
      unregistered firms 99, 100
    freelancers and self-employment 121–122
    generally 89
    law firm strategic direction and qualifications 107–108
    management metrics and investigation tools 108–109
    national and international implications of practising arrangements 97–98
    options outside scope of regulation or with alternative regulators 95–97
    organisational lifetime events and closure 109–112
    organisational structure (freelancers, non-reserved work, unregulated practices) 100–105

Practising arrangements – *contd*
  discursive content – *contd*
    practising year
      generally 89
      reflective exercises 94–95
      renewal
        symbolism 94–95
        timelines for management 89–90
      timelines for management
        accountants' report 91
        annual compliance timetable 91–94
        diversity data 90
        practising certificate conditions 90–91
        renewal 89–90
    separate business rule 105–107
    Standards and Regulations 2019 112–121
  generally 61–62
  national and international implications 97–98
  'practice' 66–69
  practice as a solicitor 60–61
  practising statements 62–66
  Standards and Regulations 2019
    development, history and change 112–121
    generally 86–89
  technical content
    alternative business structures (ABS) 69
    available practising arrangements
      'practice' 66–69
      practice as a solicitor 60–61
      practising arrangements 61–62
      practising statements 62–66
    consumer protections 72–73
    firm recognition 81–83
    foreign lawyers 69–71
    generally 60
    individual practice 80
    in-house solicitors 71–72
    management 83
    non-reserved work 85
    non-solicitors 83
    practice events 78
    practising certificate events 80–81
    practising options, summary 73
    practising year 73–78
    reserved work and relationship to other forms of regulation 84–85
    Standards and Regulations 2019 86–89
Practising certificate
  annual practising year, and 6–8

Practising certificate – *contd*
  conditions *see* Practising certificate conditions
  embodiment of professionalism 6–8
  events
    first issue 80–81
    generally 80
    holding over 81
    renewal 81
    revocation 81
    statutory 250–251
    suspension 81
Practising certificate conditions
  discursive content
    addressing personal development needs 171–172
    alternative employment 173
    annual renewal and information for decision-making 174–176
    effectiveness of conditions 169–171
    generally 154
    imposing stricter set of rules as conditions 173–174
    legal advice and conditions 176–177
    managing others with conditions (COLP, COFA or HR) 167–169
    publication of decisions 172–173
    regulatory decision-making 156–160
    regulatory outcome, Council for Licensed Conveyancers (CLC) example 154–156
    restrictions or more practice 165–167
    risk management
      achieving a balance, in 160–161
      representations for conditions, and 162–164
    SDT and SRA outcomes 164–165
    unregulated firms and freelance solicitors 161–161
  imposition
    circumstances
      generally 126–128
      list
        generally 126–128
        Handbook 2011, reg 3 135–137
    common conditions
      further analysis 153–154
      generally 145–147
      notes from samples 152–153
      sample set A and B 147–149
      sample set C
        generally 149–150
        graph 3 150–151
      sample set D 151–152

Practising certificate conditions – *contd*
  imposition – *contd*
    generally 126–132
    powers
      Council for Licensed Conveyancers (CLC) 154–156
      generally 127–132
    process 134–135
    public interest
      generally 132–134, 144–145
      publication of decisions 172–173
  practising arrangements, and 90–91
  problems 393–396
  public interest
    generally 132–134, 144–145
    publication of decisions 172–173
  risk management
    achieving a balance 160–161
    generally 138–145
    representations for conditions 162–164
  suspension of certificate
    criminal charges and dishonesty 138
    generally 137–138
  technical content
    generally 124–126
    historical development and use in other areas of professional practice 126–128
    imposition of conditions
      circumstances
        generally 126–128
        list
          generally 126–128
          Handbook 2011, reg 3 135–137
      common conditions
        further analysis 153–154
        generally 145–147
        notes from samples 152–153
        sample set A and B 147–149
        sample set C
          generally 149–150
          graph 3 150–151
        sample set D 151–152
      generally 126–132
      powers 127–132
      process 134–135
      public interest 132–134, 144–145
    risk management 138–145
    suspension of certificate
      criminal charges and dishonesty 138
      generally 137–138

Practising year
  generally 89
  practising arrangements, and 73–78, 89–95
  practising certificate
    conditions
      annual renewal and information for decision-making 174–176
      generally 90–91
    generally 6–8
  reflective exercises 94–95
  renewal
    symbolism 94–95
    timelines for management 89–90
  timelines for management
    accountants' report 91
    annual compliance timetable 91–94
    diversity data 90
    practising certificate conditions 90–91
    renewal 89–90
Problems
  accounts in general
    accounts rules quick quiz 422
    auditing and reviewing 419
    reconciliation
      exercises and possible answers 424–425
      generally 419–422
  anti-money laundering 423–424
  Competence Statement or general CPD exercises 393
  complaint handling 397–398
  conflict of interest 388–392
  end note 426
  equality and diversity 392
  generally 379–382
  legal market analysis 398–401
  management and legal system problems, questions and reflective exercises 383–387
  practising conditions 393–396
  serious/material breaches
    generally 401–413
    qualified reports 413–418
Professional practice
  comparative, management consultants 51–54
  comparative standards of regulation
    qualification and CPD 47–49
    regulation by Code 49–51
  discursive content
    checks and balances in legal regulation 41–43
    comparative professional practice, management consultants 51–54

Professional practice – *contd*
  discursive content – *contd*
    comparative standards of regulation
      qualification and CPD 47–49
      regulation by Code 49–51
    complaint handling 30–33
    continuous professional development (CPD)
      generally 43–47
      qualification, and 47–49
    customer service 30–31
    ethics and reporting 29–30
    freelance solicitors 40–41
    generally 26
    governance and decision-making 36–40
    human touch 54–57
    individual expression and professionalism as form of practice 26–29
    'the reasonable man' in professional regulation 33–36
    unregulated practices 40–41
  historical development 3–6, 14–15
  technical content
    annual practising year and embodiment of professionalism in practising certificate 6–8
    generally 1–3
    historical development of professional practice 3–6, 14–15
    legal services regulation *see* Legal services regulation
Professional regulation
  'the reasonable man' 33–36
Professionalism
  embodiment of, in practising certificate 6–8
  form of practice 26–29
Public interest
  imposition of practising certificate conditions
    generally 132–134, 144–145
    publication of decisions 172–173

Q

Qualifications
  CPD, and 47–48
  exercise 48–49
  law firm strategic direction, and 107–108
  national and international implications of practising arrangements, and 97

R

Reasonable man *see* 'The reasonable man'

Recognised sole practices
  imposition of firm conditions *see* Firm conditions
Registered European Lawyers (RELs)
  historical development of professional practice 4
  practising arrangements, and 69–71
Registered Foreign Lawyers (RFLs)
  historical development of professional practice 4
  powers, statutory basis 4–5
  practising arrangements, and 69–71
Regulatory decision-making
  practising certificate conditions, and 156–160
Regulatory standards *see also* SRA Standards and Regulations
  harmonisation 367–371
Reporting
  accountants *see* Accountants' report
  ethics, and
    exercises for discussion 32–33
    generally 29–30
    list of common reported matters 29
  serious breaches *see* Serious breach
Reserved work
  relationship to other forms of regulation 84–85
Revalidation
  ten-year, introduction 371–373
Rights of audience
  future developments 373–374
  recognised bodies, and 96
Risk management
  firm conditions, and
    achieving a balance 189–190
    representations for conditions 199
  practising certificate conditions, and
    achieving a balance 160–161
    generally 138–145
    representations for conditions 162–164

S

Self-employment
  freelancers, and 121–122
Self-reporting *see* Reporting
Separate business rule
  generally 105–107
Serious breach
  accountants' report
    annual 291–297
    judgement 315–317
  defining
    generally 348–355
    proposed definition 235

Serious breach – *contd*
  discursive content
    COLP and COFA
      compliance and balanced scoreboard approach 286–287
      fiduciary duties 281
    compliance
      COLP and COFA, balanced scoreboard approach 286–287
      improving following breach, and importance of leadership 276–277
      management, and 281–286
    fiduciary duties
      COLP and COFA 281
      generally 280
    integrity and dishonesty
      dishonesty
        exercise 267
        generally 263–264
        reporting 265–267
      ethical considerations
        exercise 266
        generally 264
      generally 262–263
      integrity exercises 264–265
    managing investigations
      generally 269–270
      incident planning exercise 275
      investigation response 270–271
      stages of 271–275
    pastoral support, thoughts and feelings 276
    prosecution for failure to report 268–269
    reporting dishonesty 265–267
    Solicitors Act 1974, s 43 267–268
    standards of behaviour 259–260
    'the reasonable man'
      generally 260–261
      turning a blind eye/ dishonesty 261–262
    whistleblowing 277–279
  example
    generally 234
    impact argument 234–235
    practical application 235–236
  generally 245, 246–249
  problems
    generally 401–413
    qualified reports 413–418
  SRA regulatory investigation process 287
  technical content
    definitions of 'serious' 233–234

Serious breach – *contd*
technical content – *contd*
example serious breaches
generally 234
impact argument 234–235
practical application 235–236
freelance solicitors 249–250
generally 226–230
material breach 245–246
other firm and individual implications 259
regulatory investigations
disclosure considerations 257–258
generally 252–256
regulatory reporting 256–258
regulatory outcomes 258
regulatory requirements 236–238
reporting
evidential requirements 251–252
regulatory 256–258
requirements 230–233, 236–238
roles of COLP and COFA
generally 238–241
reporting relationships to other roles 241–243
SDT and standard of proof 246, 251
seeking advice 243–245
serious breach 245, 246–249
statutory events 250–251
Single legal regulator
possible introduction of 365–367
Sole practices
imposition of firm conditions *see* Firm conditions
Solicitors Act 1974
accountants' report (s 34) 290
imposition of practising certificate conditions, and 128–130, 132
Solicitors Disciplinary Tribunal (SDT)
generally 3
imposition of conditions on firm 187
practising certificate
conditions
outcomes 164–164
varying 134
suspension of 137
serious breaches, and
generally 229
outcomes 258
standard of proof 246, 251
standard of proof
accountants' report, and 324–327
serious breaches 246, 251
Solicitors Regulation Authority (SRA)
accountants' report *see* Accountants' report
current regulatory position
entry and exit requirements 21
generally 21
intervention 21–22
regulatory objectives 23–24
setting standards 21
Standards and Regulations 24–26
taking enforcement action 21
firm recognition, and 81–83
generally 2
Handbooks *see* SRA Standards and Regulations
impact of 13–14
imposition of conditions *see* Firm conditions; Practising certificate conditions
investigation process 287
legal services regulation
current position 21–26
historical development 15
impact of regulator 13–14
introduction to 9–13
options outside scope of regulation or with alternative regulators, and 95–97
powers
current position 21
statutory basis 4–5
regulation by Code or standards 49–51
regulatory investigation process 287
reporting requirements
generally 29–30
serious breach 230–233
Standards and Regulations *see* SRA Standards and Regulations
'the reasonable man' in professional regulation, and 35
SRA Standards and Regulations
accountants' report *see* Accountants' report
conclusions 346–347
development, history and change 112–121
generally 15, 24–26, 86–89
imposition of firm conditions, and
firm vs practising certificate 187–189
standard conditions of recognition 185–186
imposition of practising certificate conditions, and
generally 128–129
public interest 132

SRA Standards and Regulations – *contd*
practising arrangements, and
generally 86–89, 112–121
organisational structure (freelancers, non-reserved work, unregulated practices) 100–105
separate business rule 105–107
re-interpretation of Legal Services Act 2007, and 362–364
serious breach
generally 246–249
reporting
evidential requirements 251
requirements
definitions of 'serious' 233–234
generally 230–233
roles of COLP and COFA 238–240
'the reasonable man' in professional regulation, and 34
Standards of behaviour
generally 259–260
Suspension of practising certificate
criminal charges and dishonesty 138
generally 137–138

T

Technical content
accountants' report
annual (material breach, serious breach, weaknesses in firm's accounts)
generally 291–297
materiality 297–299
challenges in new accounts rules 309–312
COLP, COFA and the Reporting Accountant 305–307
conditions to obtain 307–308
generally 290
move away from material breach
effects of changes overall 301–302
generally 299–301
obtaining
conditions 307–308
requirement 302–303
regulatory approach 299
requirement to obtain 302–303
requirement to send to SRA 303–304
statutory reporting basis for accountants 290–291
firm conditions
alternative business structures (ABS) 186–187

Technical content – *contd*
firm conditions – *contd*
imposition of conditions
current 183–185
generally 179–183
SRA and at SDT 187
standard conditions of recognition 185–186
practising arrangements, and
alternative business structures (ABS) 69
available practising arrangements
'practice' 66–69
practice as a solicitor 60–61
practising arrangements 61–62
practising statements 62–66
consumer protections 72–73
firm recognition 81–83
foreign lawyers 69–71
generally 60
individual practice 80
in-house solicitors 71–72
management 83
non-reserved work 85
non-solicitors 83
practice events 78
practising certificate events 80–81
practising options, summary 73
practising year 73–78
reserved work and relationship to other forms of regulation 84–85
Standards and Regulations 2019 86–89
practising certificate conditions
generally 124–126
historical development and use in other areas of professional practice 126–128
imposition of conditions
circumstances
generally 126–128
list
generally 126–128
Handbook 2011, reg 3 135–137
common conditions
further analysis 153–154
generally 145–147
notes from samples 152–153
sample set A and B 147–149
sample set C
generally 149–150
graph 3 150–151
sample set D 151–152
generally 126–132
powers 127–132
process 134–135

Technical content – *contd*
practising certificate conditions – *contd*
imposition of conditions – *contd*
public interest 132–134, 144–145
risk management 138–145
suspension of certificate
criminal charges and dishonesty 138
generally 137–138
professional practice
annual practising year and embodiment of professionalism in practising certificate 6–8
generally 1–3
historical development 3–6, 14–15
legal services regulation *see* Legal services regulation
serious breach
definitions of 'serious' 233–234
example
generally 234
impact argument 234–235
practical application 235–236
freelance solicitors 249–250
generally 226–230
material breach 245–246
other firm and individual implications 259
regulatory investigations
disclosure considerations 257–258
generally 252–256
regulatory reporting 256–258
regulatory outcomes 258
regulatory requirements 236–238
reporting
evidential requirements 251–252
regulatory 256–258

Technical content – *contd*
serious breach – *contd*
reporting – *contd*
requirements 230–233, 236–238
roles of COLP and COFA
generally 238–241
reporting relationships to other roles 241–243
SDT and standard of proof 246, 251
seeking advice 243–245
serious breach 245, 246–249
statutory events 250–251
'Tesco Law' *see* Alternative business structures (ABS)
'The reasonable man'
professional regulation, in 33–36
serious breach, and
generally 260–261
turning a blind eye/dishonesty 261–262
Third party managed accounts (TPMAs)
challenges in new account rules, and 311
conclusions 346, 348
generally 334–338
regulatory focus, and 361–362

U

Unregulated practices
firm conditions 194–196
generally 40–41
organisational structure, and 100–105
practising certificate conditions 161–162
regulatory outcomes
generally 99
viewpoint exercise 100

www.ingramcontent.com/pod-product-compliance
Lightning Source LLC
LaVergne TN
LVHW082027200926
848481LV00010B/2939